Florida

Chelle Koster Walton
Revised by David Downing and Janine Warner

Photography by Tony Arruza

COMPASS AMERICAN GUIDES
An imprint of Fodor's Travel Publications

Compass American Guides: Florida

Editors: Chris Culwell, David Downing
Compass Editorial Director: Daniel Mangin
Designer: Fabrizio La Rocca
Photo Editor: Jolie Novak; archival research, Melanie Marin
Map Design: Mark Stroud, Moon Street Cartography
Production House: Twin Age Ltd., Hong Kong

Second Edition
Copyright © 2003 Fodors LLC
Maps copyright © 2003 Fodors LLC
Compass American Guides and Colophon are registered trademarks of Random House, Inc.
Fodor's is a registered trademark of Random House, Inc.

ISBN 0-676-90494-7
ISSN 1539-3240

All photographs are by Tony Arruza unless otherwise credited below. Compass American Guides acknowledges the following institutions and individuals for the use of their photographs, illustrations, or both: **Alan McAnulty,** pp. 114, 117; **Amelia Island Museum of History Collection,** p. 195 (courtesy of Helen Litrico); **Busch Entertainment Corporation,** pp. 106–107; **Discovery Cove Orlando,** pp. 186–187, 188; **Florida Historical Society, Alma Clyde Field Library of Florida History,** p. 112; **Florida State Archives,** pp. 25, 26, 36, 38, 40, 59, 73, 75, 87, 101, 204, 220, 239, 267, 304; **Goodwood Museum and Gardens Archive,** p. 54; **Greater Miami Convention & Visitors Bureau,** pp. 261, 268–269, 274; **Harry P. Leu Gardens,** p. 191; **Henry Morrison Flagler Museum Archives,** p. 245; **Jacobs Highwaymen Archive,** p. 236; **John and Mable Ringling Museum of Art,** p. 121; **J.N. "Ding" Darling Foundation,** p. 135; **Kennedy Space Center,** pp. 226, 228; **Library of Congress,** pp. 31, 39, 212–213; **Lee Island Coast Visitor & Convention Bureau,** pp. 136–137, 139; **Ministère de la Défense, Bibliothèque du Service Historique de l'Armée de Terre,** p. 28; **Museum of Florida History,** p. 234; **National Park Service,** pp. 16, 285; **New Smyrna Beach Area Visitors Bureau,** p. 225; **Orlando Museum of Art,** p. 192; **Sam and Robbie Vickers Florida Collection,** pp. 14, 34, 35, 72, 158, 201, 210, 305; **St. Augustine Historical Society,** pp. 20, 21, 29; **Steven Brooke,** p. 67; **Tampa-Hillsborough County Public Library,** p. 83; **Tampa Museum of Art,** p. 109; **University of Florida Special Collections,** p. 151; **University of Southern Florida Library, Special Collections,** pp. 100, 170; **Universal Orlando,** pp. 183, 184; **Visit Florida,** pp. 119, 131, 203; **The Walt Disney Company,** pp. 175, 177, 178, 180.

Compass American Guides, 1745 Broadway, New York, NY 10019
PRINTED IN CHINA
10 9 8 7 6 5 4 3 2 1

To Ann,
still my best travel bud

C O N T E N T S

Sidebars and Topical Essays

Literary Excerpts

Maps

ALABAMA
GEORGIA
HEARTLAND NORTH
Page 147
UPPER ATLANTIC COAST
Page 196
Downtown Tallahassee
Page 50
Jacksonville
St Augustine
Page 211
Atlantic
Ocean
PANHANDLE
Pages 48-49
Greater Orlando
Page 173
CENTRAL GULF COAST
Page 81
Greater Tampa Bay
Page 97
HEARTLAND
SOUTH
Page 157
Gulf
of
Mexico
JUPITER TO
FT LAUDERDALE
Page 242
LOWER GULF COAST
Page 115
N
W
E
S
Greater Miami Page 265
South Beach Page 266
EVERGLADES
Page 287
FT LAUDERDALE
TO KEY LARGO
Page 254
FLORIDA KEYS
Pages 300-301
Downtown Key West
Page 313

FLORIDA MAP INDEX

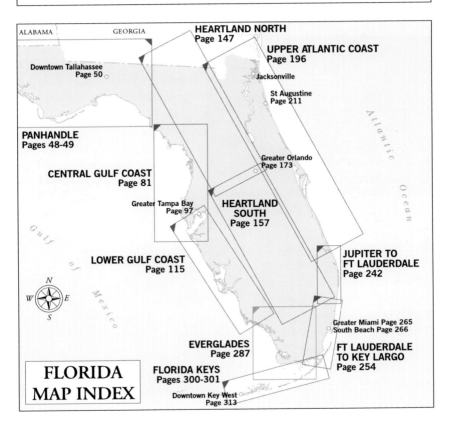

OVERVIEW

❶ The Panhandle
Known for its white-sand beaches and emerald-green waters, the Florida Panhandle belongs culturally to the Old South. The state's capital, Tallahassee, is here, as is beautiful St. Marks Refuge, which is famous for its migrating birds and monarch butterflies.

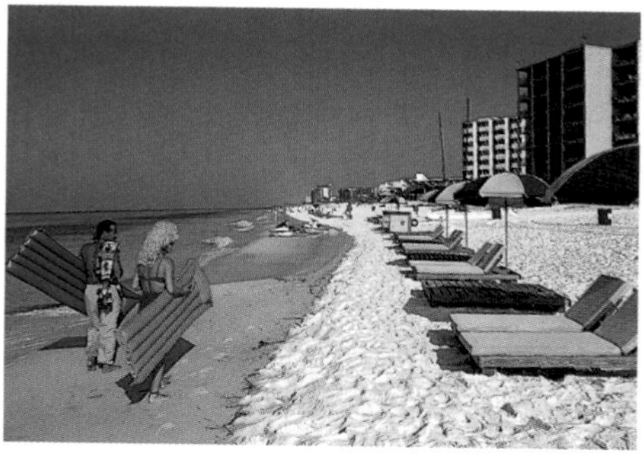

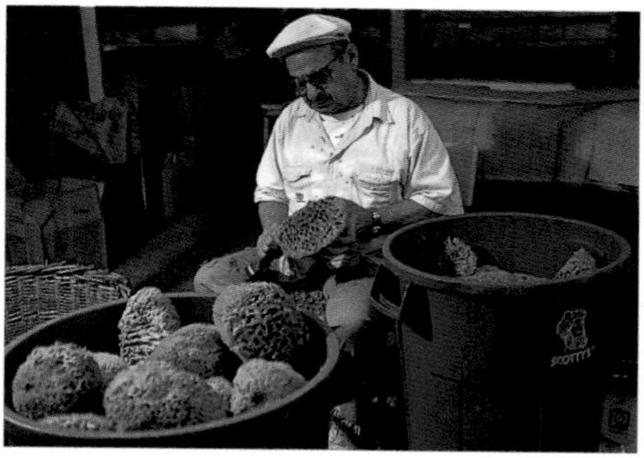

❷ Central Gulf Coast
Fronted by the warm, green waters of the Gulf of Mexico, this is an area of expansive wetlands and rich marine life. Busy beaches, colorful fishing towns, and crystal-clear springs abound here. The region is home to the large, bustling sister cities of Tampa and St. Petersburg.

❸ Lower Gulf Coast
A series of beautiful barrier islands rimmed in white sand and facing warm waters lines this coast. On several islands, notably Sanibel and Captiva, this natural beauty has been preserved. Sarasota is known for its excellent museums and fine climate.

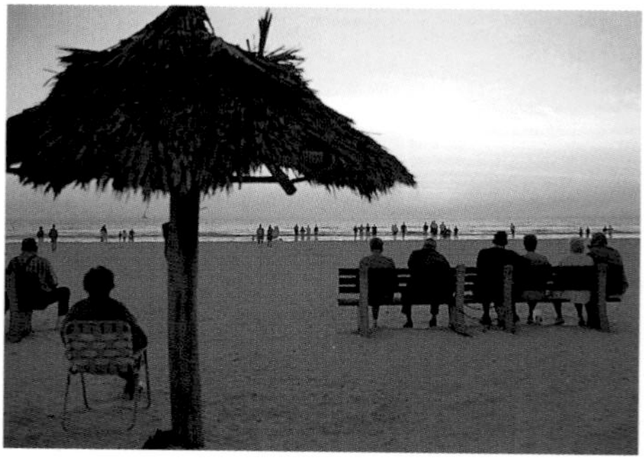

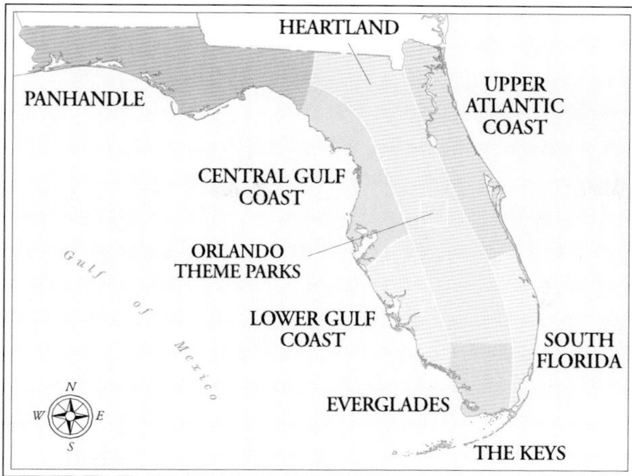
HEARTLAND
PANHANDLE
UPPER ATLANTIC COAST
CENTRAL GULF COAST
ORLANDO THEME PARKS
Gulf of Mexico
LOWER GULF COAST
SOUTH FLORIDA
N
W
E
S
EVERGLADES
THE KEYS

OVERVIEW

1 PANHANDLE
2 CENTRAL GULF COAST
3 LOWER GULF COAST
4 HEARTLAND
5 ORLANDO THEME PARKS
6 UPPER ATLANTIC COAST
7 SOUTH FLORIDA
8 EVERGLADES
9 THE KEYS

4 Heartland and 5 Theme Parks

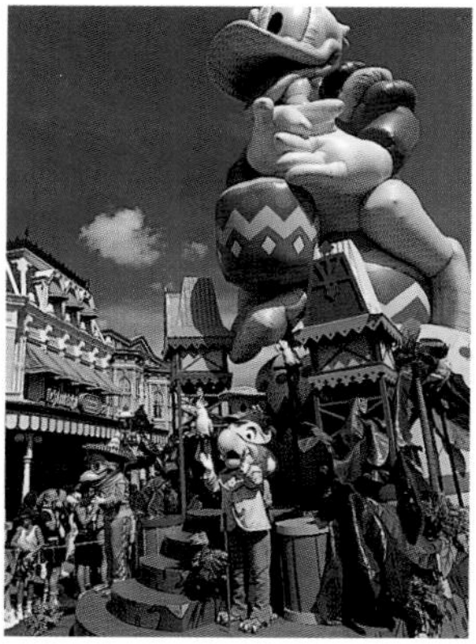

Citrus groves and cattle ranches flourish in central Florida, as well as an old-fashioned "Cracker" way of life. The backroads and old-time resorts recall the era before Walt Disney came to town in 1971. This region is also famous for its springs and lakes, among them Lake Okeechobee, one of the continent's largest, and Silver Springs.

In the Orlando area, Walt Disney World, Sea World, and Universal Studios draw millions of visitors each year to their worlds of fantasy and wonder.

6 Upper Atlantic Coast

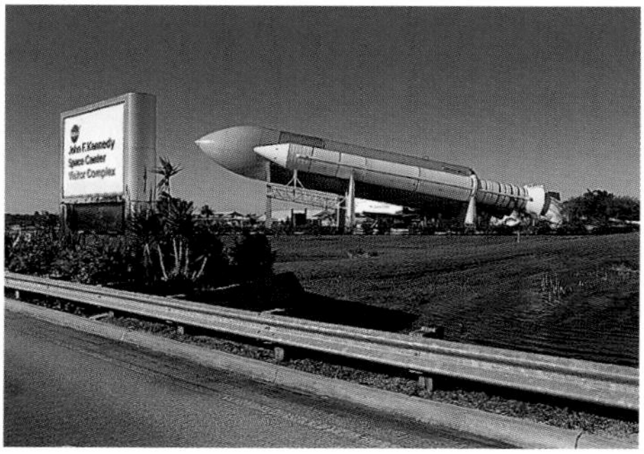

Resorts alternate with natural areas and small towns along the Upper Atlantic Coast. St. Augustine, the country's oldest European city, is of historical interest, as are Cape Canaveral, the launch pad for America's space program, and beautiful Amelia Island.

❼ SOUTH FLORIDA

From posh Palm Beach, with its celebrities and fabulous mansions, to Miami's festive South Beach, with its Art Deco hotels and exciting nightlife, and Cuban and Floridian cuisine, this region is one of America's liveliest and most popular vacation spots.

❽ EVERGLADES

A great river of grass, filled with mangrove islands, cypress swamps, and wetland prairies, the Everglades is famous for its alligators and fabulous birds. Walking and boat tours in the national park introduce you to one of the most unusual and mysterious natural areas in the world.

❾ THE KEYS

A string of narrow tropical islands that curves south and west of the Florida peninsula, the Keys have long been famous for fishing and water sports. Key West, the southernmost of the Keys, is known as an artists' colony and a drifters' paradise.

The reefs around the islands are popular with tourists, divers, and snorkelers. Watch the sun sink below the horizon at Mallory Square, visit the Hemingway House, go for a swim, or just relax and take in the warm sea breezes.

The Gulf Coast of Florida affords the only location in the coterminous United States from which to observe a tropical sunset.

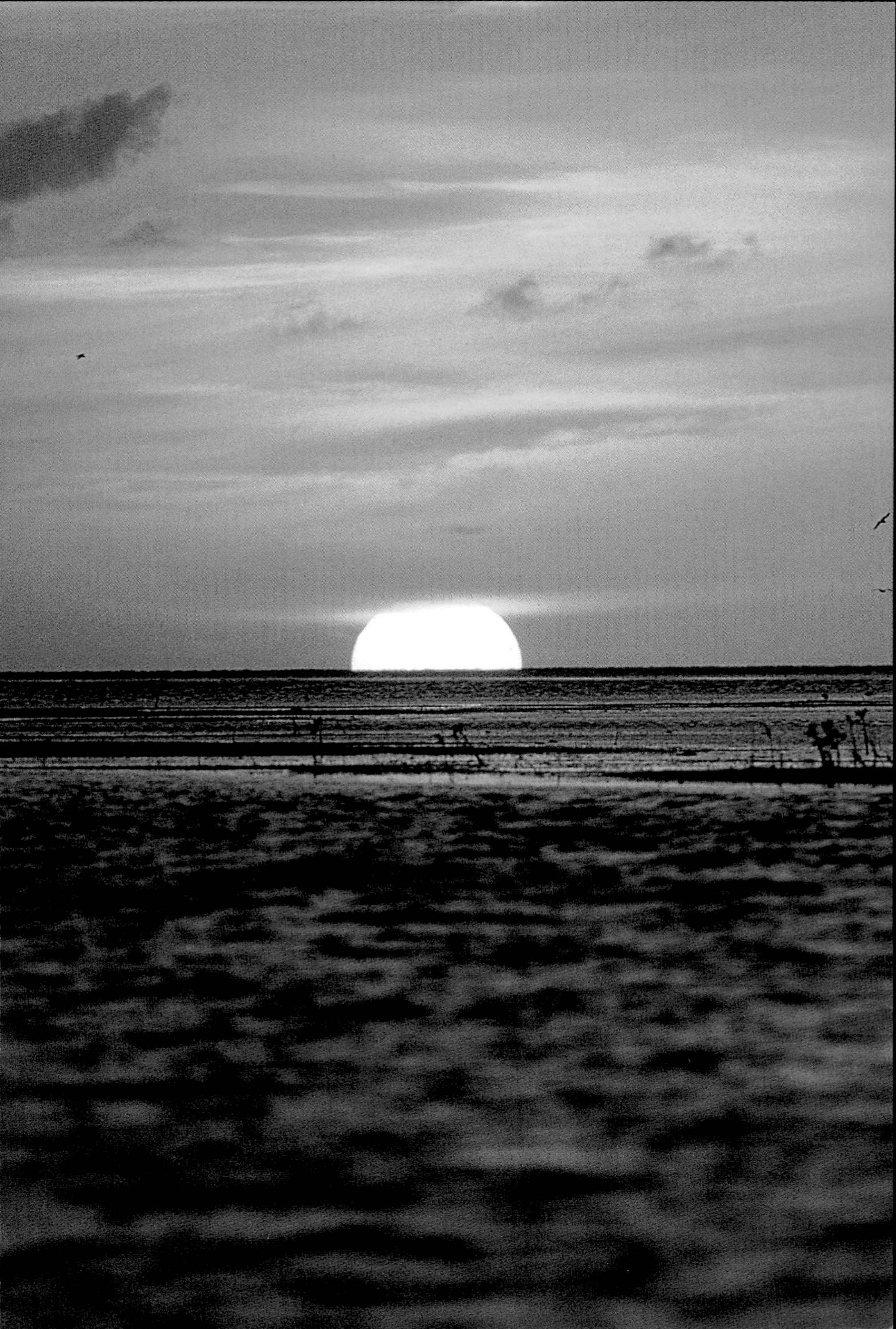

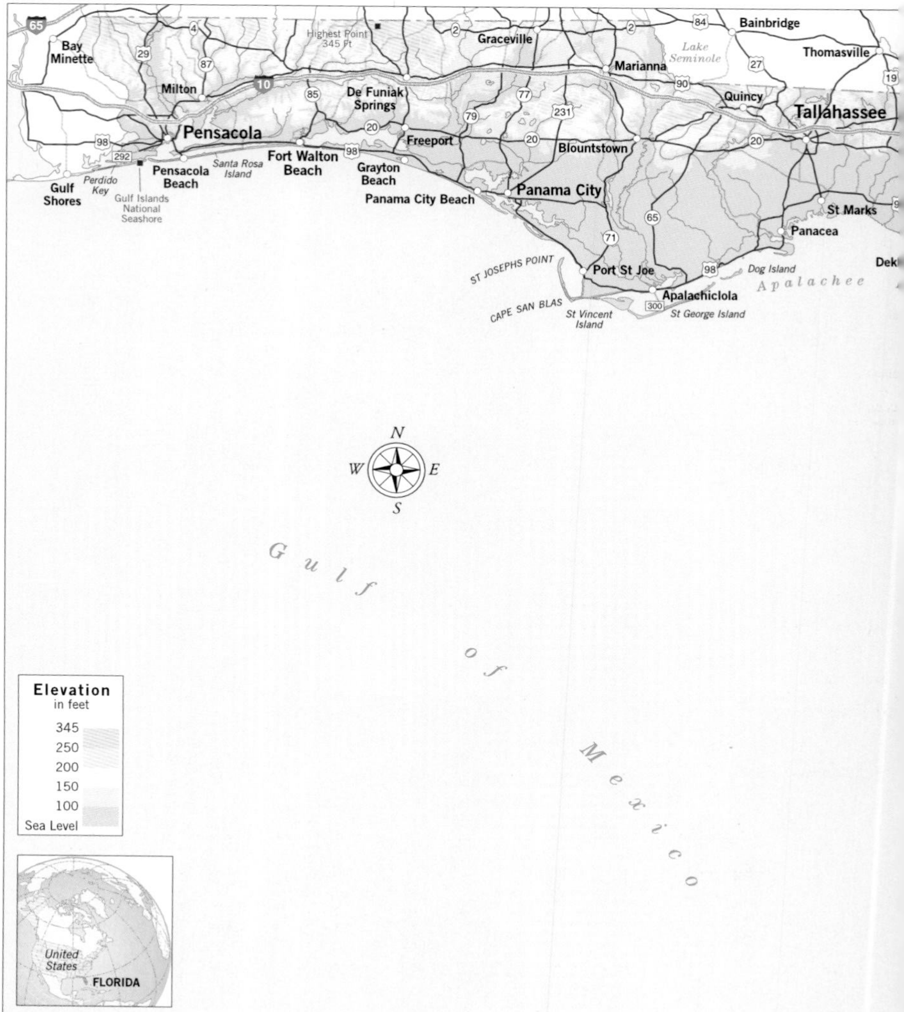

Bay Minette
Milton
Pensacola
Gulf Shores
Perdido Key
Pensacola Beach
Gulf Islands National Seashore
Santa Rosa Island
Fort Walton Beach
Highest Point 345 Ft
De Funiak Springs
Freeport
Grayton Beach
Panama City Beach
Graceville
Marianna
Lake Seminole
Bainbridge
Thomasville
Quincy
Tallahassee
Blountstown
Panama City
St Marks
Panacea
ST JOSEPHS POINT
Port St Joe
CAPE SAN BLAS
St Vincent Island
Apalachicola
St George Island
Dog Island
Apalachee
Dek
N
W
E
S
Gulf of Mexico
Elevation
in feet
345
250
200
150
100
Sea Level
United States
FLORIDA

MILEAGE CHART

	Atlanta, GA	Daytona Beach	Fort Lauderdale	Fort Myers	Gainesville	Jacksonville	Key West	Lakeland	Miami	Orlando	Panama City	Pensacola	St Augustine	Sarasota	Tallahassee	Tampa	West Palm Be
Atlanta, GA	0	439	700	580	230	346	825	358	661	440	480	380	384	507	270	459	
Daytona Beach	439	0	230	263	112	90	419	114	255	57	355	445	57	188	251	140	
Fort Myers	580	263	263	0	260	299	309	154	152	156	468	556	320	73	298	129	
Gainesville	230	112	307	260	0	75	496	128	332	112	243	341	68	178	149	130	
Jacksonville	346	90	318	299	74	0	504	198	341	142	282	359	39	254	163	202	
Key West	825	419	189	309	496	505	0	383	164	391	777	840	478	382	640	401	
Miami	661	255	27	152	332	341	164	219	0	229	598	673	305	225	478	273	
Orlando	440	57	206	156	112	142	391	55	229	0	376	452	105	130	257	84	
Pensacola	380	445	683	556	341	366	840	490	673	452	100	0	400	518	196	470	
Tallahassee	270	251	456	298	149	163	640	272	478	257	118	196	200	325	0	275	
Tampa	459	140	268	129	130	202	401	33	273	84	394	470	189	58	275	0	
West Palm Beach	596	192	43	130	270	277	229	198	66	165	533	608	240	199	414	226	

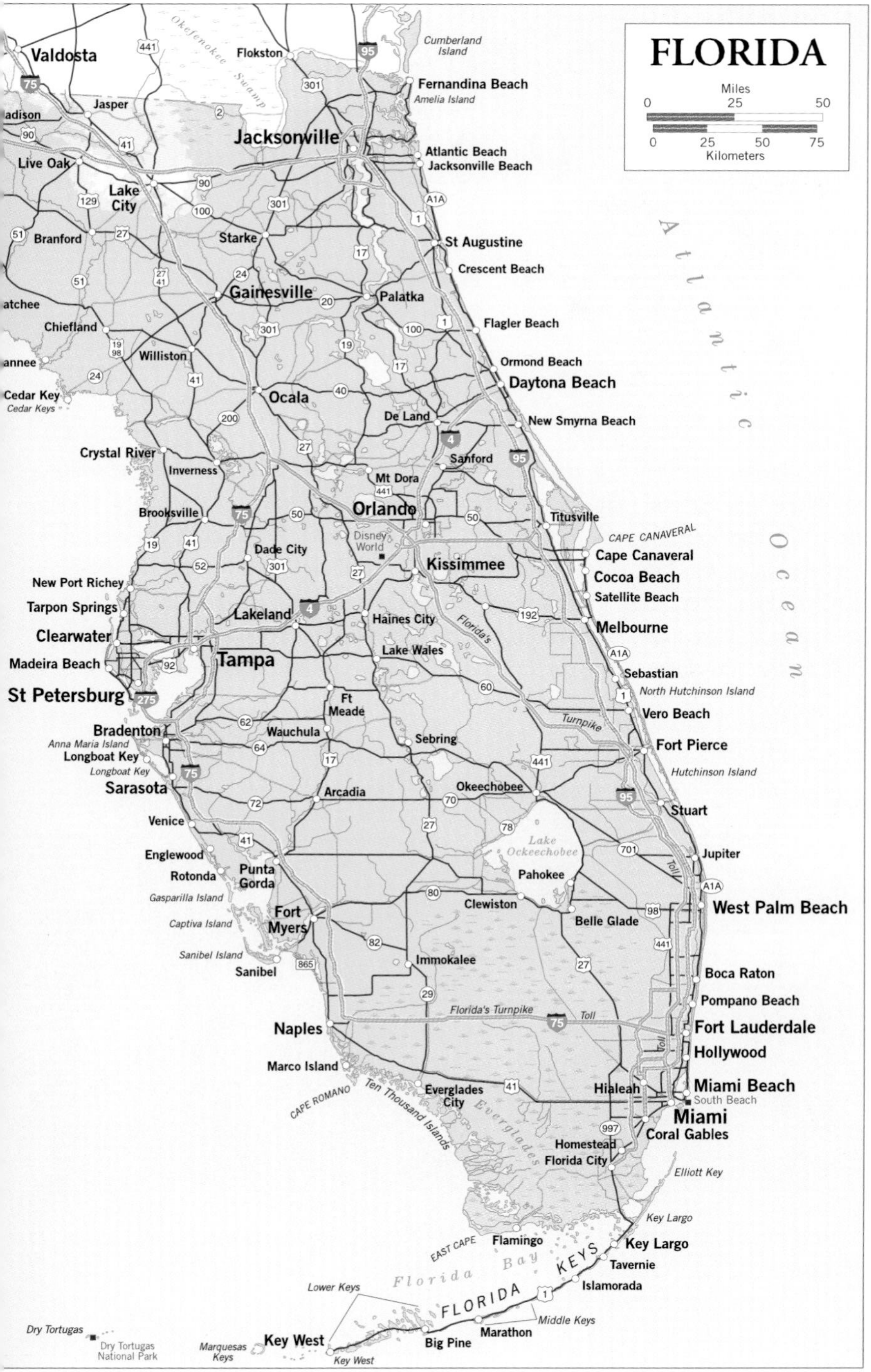
FLORIDA
Miles
0 25 50
0 25 50 75
Kilometers
Atlantic Ocean
Valdosta
Flokston
Cumberland Island
Okefenokee Swamp
Fernandina Beach
Amelia Island
Jasper
Madison
Jacksonville
Atlantic Beach
Jacksonville Beach
Live Oak
Lake City
Branford
Starke
St Augustine
Crescent Beach
Gainesville
Palatka
Flagler Beach
Chiefland
Williston
Ormond Beach
Daytona Beach
Cedar Key
Cedar Keys
Ocala
De Land
New Smyrna Beach
Crystal River
Inverness
Sanford
Mt Dora
Orlando
Brooksville
Titusville
Disney World
CAPE CANAVERAL
Cape Canaveral
Dade City
Kissimmee
Cocoa Beach
New Port Richey
Satellite Beach
Tarpon Springs
Lakeland
Haines City
Melbourne
Clearwater
Florida's Turnpike
Tampa
Lake Wales
Madeira Beach
Sebastian
St Petersburg
North Hutchinson Island
Ft Meade
Vero Beach
Bradenton
Wauchula
Anna Maria Island
Sebring
Fort Pierce
Longboat Key
Hutchinson Island
Sarasota
Arcadia
Okeechobee
Stuart
Venice
Lake Okeechobee
Englewood
Jupiter
Rotonda
Punta Gorda
Pahokee
Gasparilla Island
Clewiston
West Palm Beach
Captiva Island
Fort Myers
Belle Glade
Sanibel Island
Immokalee
Sanibel
Boca Raton
Pompano Beach
Florida's Turnpike
Toll
Naples
Fort Lauderdale
Hollywood
Marco Island
Hialeah
Miami Beach
South Beach
CAPE ROMANO
Ten Thousand Islands
Everglades City
Everglades
Miami
Coral Gables
Homestead
Florida City
Elliott Key
Key Largo
EAST CAPE
Flamingo
Key Largo
Tavernie
Florida Bay
FLORIDA KEYS
Islamorada
Lower Keys
Middle Keys
Dry Tortugas
Dry Tortugas National Park
Marquesas Keys
Key West
Big Pine
Marathon
Key West

L A N D S C A P E

Florida. . . by its very peninsular curve whimsically terminates the
United States in an interrogation-point.

— Sidney Lanier, *Florida: Its Scenery,*
Climate, and History, 1875

It just dangles out there, unprotected, open to the whims of the sea. Nothing solid to hold it in place. Shorelines shift with the movement of tides and winds. A hurricane creates entirely new islands in a flash of its eye. The peninsula we call Florida has continually narrowed and widened her shorelines over a period of 20 million years, rising from the sea and then plunging beneath again as Ice Age glaciers grew and then melted. The geography of the state has maintained, more or less, its thumbs-down shape for the past 30,000 years. The Floridian plateau, as

View of the St. Johns (1875), *by Christian Eisele. (Sam and Robbie Vickers Florida*
Collection)

White ibis fly across Eco Pond in the Everglades.

geologists refer to this broad shelf that protrudes southeastward from the continent, has a limestone base, layered with sand, silt, shells, and bones.

Most of Florida is a low-lying plain with an average elevation of less than 100 feet above sea level. Even so, this flat land supports a richly varied landscape of brackish estuaries, sand dunes, and ridged hardwood hammocks.

■ WETLANDS

Though scattered throughout the state, Florida's wetlands are largely in the southern third of its peninsula, where a 150-mile-long and 50-mile-wide sheet of moving water stretches from Lake Okeechobee to Florida Bay. These swampy regions, which the first settlers were determined to make habitable, are now recognized for their enormous ecological importance. Efforts have been launched to preserve the region as a natural resource, and to stop the drainage and canal building that were part of that early effort to inhabit the area. Wetlands once covered 60 percent of the state; today, they occupy 15 to 20 percent. Within the wetlands are habitats that include mangrove forests, salt and freshwater marshes, and cypress lowlands.

Living within each is a diverse wildlife population that includes alligators, mana-tees, indigo snakes, and a vast array of birds, from the rare wood stork to ospreys, egrets, and herons.

■ BEACHES

A thousand miles of beaches cloak the state's 1,350 miles of coastline. The west coast, especially the Panhandle, is a seemingly endless stretch of powder-soft sand, its brightness caused by high concentrations of pure quartz, scrubbed snow-white by centuries of water and wind. On Atlantic Coast beaches, the sand is coarser and gold- or coral-color. Along both coasts, native plants—such as palm trees, sea oats, and sea grape trees, to name but a few—flourish thanks to their ability to with-stand salt, sandblasting, and hurricanes.

Florida beaches vary in width from year to year. Up to 28 feet of sand may dis-appear due to erosion, and though the sea might give back as much as 16 feet, the state's beaches are still eroding at an average of 3 feet per year.

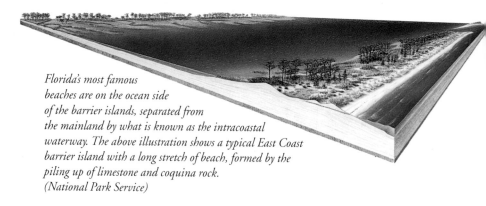

Florida's most famous beaches are on the ocean side of the barrier islands, separated from the mainland by what is known as the intracoastal waterway. The above illustration shows a typical East Coast barrier island with a long stretch of beach, formed by the piling up of limestone and coquina rock. (National Park Service)

The barrier islands strung along both coasts are created when drifting sandy material piles up against underwater rises, usually of limestone or coquina rock. During hurricanes, or over a period of many years, waves continually deposit sand.

■ Caves and Springs

The highly porous limestone that supports Florida's surface has been eroded by eons of fluctuating sea levels and by the carbonic acid from decaying vegetation. The result of this erosion is a subterranean maze of rivers and caverns. When the roofs of underground caverns collapse they form sinkholes, wide depressions in the earth. Sinkholes are so common—there are currently about 150 in the state—they've become a popular tourist attraction. Underwater caves have been made accessible by scuba diving. The largest aboveground cave system is Florida Caverns, west of Tallahassee in the Panhandle.

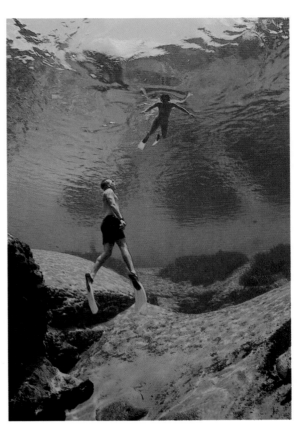

Diving in Alexander Springs.

Florida's 320 natural springs release crystal-clear water that remains at a constant temperature. The springs, a favorite haunt of the endangered manatee, pump minerals to the surface that enrich the soil and create a paradise of green fields, wildflowers, and forests.

Supplied by underground aquifers, Florida springs fall into two categories: artesian springs and seepage springs. Artesian springs form when water is forced up through deep fissures from depths of 100 or more feet below the surface. Seepage springs are caused when the ground surface depresses and falls below the water table. Offshore submarine springs are often large enough

Florida pine forest.

to create a boil at the water's surface. Several such springs can be found in the Gulf of Mexico and in the Atlantic Ocean southeast of St. Augustine.

■ FOREST, HAMMOCKS, AND SCRUBLAND

Jungle and forest once covered most of Florida, where 50 percent of the tree species found in the United States grow naturally. Here, jungles are more commonly called hammocks, a Native American designation that refers to the rounded islands of hardwood trees that rise above wetlands. Live oak and sabal palm (the state tree), gumbo-limbo, pigeon plum, soldierwood, crabwood, and white stopper are common hammock trees. Gulf Hammock, in Levy County, is the state's largest stretch of hammock land. In the drier, forested tracts of the northwest, pine trees flourish. Overall, pines cover 50 percent of the state's land area. At least half of these trees will be logged and processed as pulp. Between forest and coastline lies scrubland habitat, stretches of sandy soil from an ancient dunes system, where saw palmettos thrive.

One of Florida's 7,712 lakes.

■ LAKES AND RIVERS

Florida contains 7,712 lakes of 11 acres or more, many of them formed by sinkholes. More than 2,000 miles of river waters run through the state. The most notable ones are the St. Johns, running from central south Florida to Jacksonville, and the Suwanee and Apalachicola Rivers, which stretch from Georgia to the Gulf. Among Florida's great natural wonders is 448,000-acre Lake Okeechobee, one of the nation's largest freshwater lakes. Most of Florida's lakes are in the central highlands.

Mangrove Islands in the Everglades.

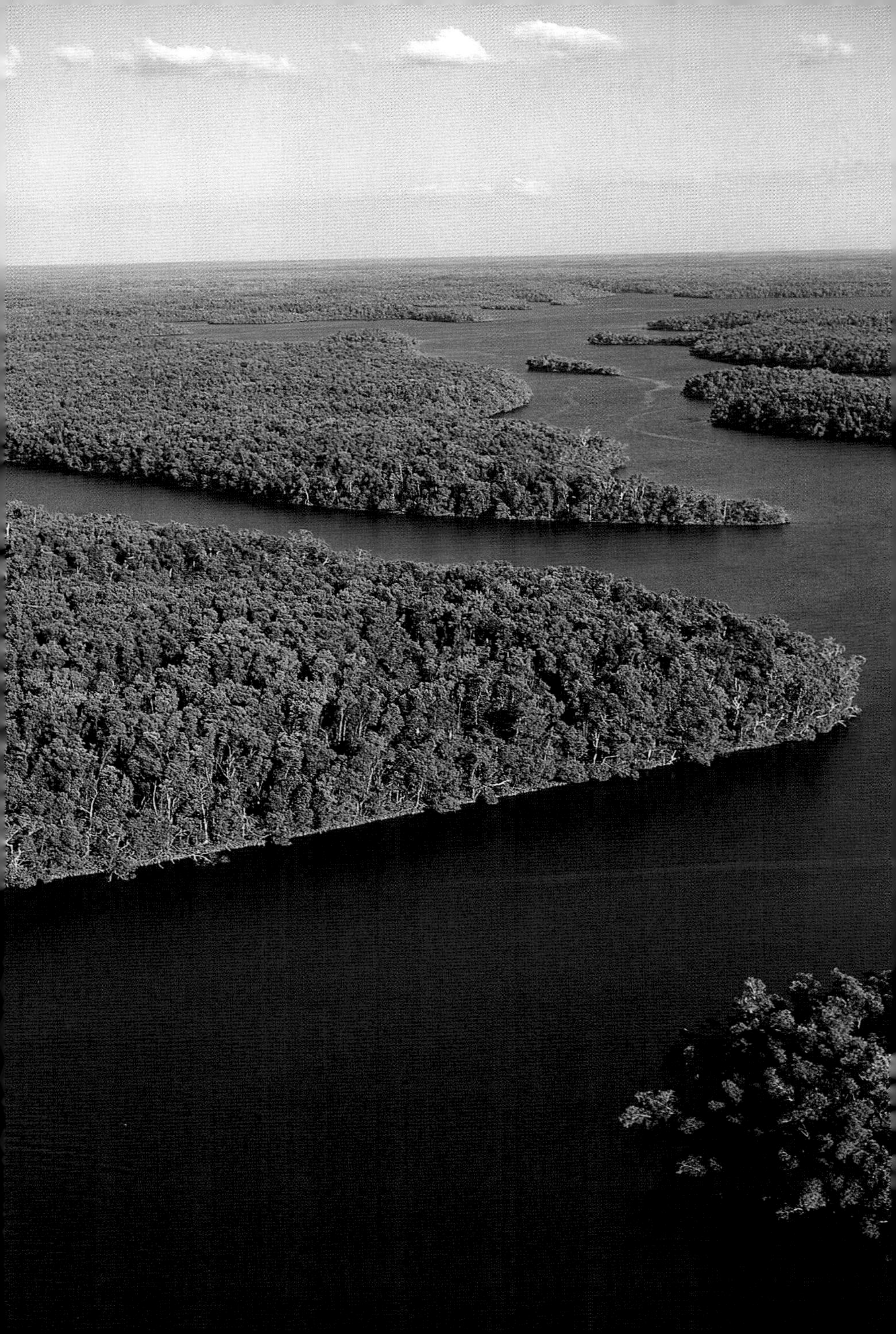

H I S T O R Y

■ EARLY PEOPLE

Much of what we know about the first inhabitants of North America and Florida, the Paleo-Indians, is recent history, and discoveries are still being made. Anthropologists surmise that the land bridge from Asia to North America opened up several times in the past 30,000 years, and that migrations of very different tribal groups continued into the continent through the millennia. As these earliest people spread across North America, they merged, diverged, battled, and regrouped again. About 10,000 to 12,000 years ago, when people arrived at the Florida peninsula, they came to hunt the huge mammals of the late Paleolithic era, collect seafood, and forage for wild berries and seeds. About 4,000 years ago, people

This 16th-century etching, made from a drawing by Jacques Le Moyne, depicts Timucuan Indians taking crops to a granary. (St. Augustine Historical Society)

Jacques Le Moyne accompanied René Laudonnière's expedition to establish the French colony of Fort Caroline. This etching, based on Le Moyne's painting, shows how the Indians hunted alligators. (St. Augustine Historical Society)

began to make pots in which to store supplies, and agriculture was introduced roughly 3,000 years ago.

The first tribes to farm and develop stratified societies lived north of Tampa Bay and along the St. Johns River. They traded with people to the north and built temple mounds at ceremonial centers still visible today. Their descendants were the Timucuan tribes that settled in northeast Florida, the Tocobagas of Tampa Bay, and the Apalachees of Tallahassee.

The tribes in the south remained separate from their northern counterparts, trading and interacting with peoples from the Caribbean and Mexico. Since migration of Indian groups in the Caribbean was common, it is possible that some of Florida's later tribal groups arrived from the south. The Calusa, who occupied the region from Tampa Bay to Cape Sable (and at times the Everglades), subsisted mainly on shellfish. They made ornaments and tools from shell and bone, and crafted boats, boxes, bowls, and masks from wood. Fish and fowl were abundant,

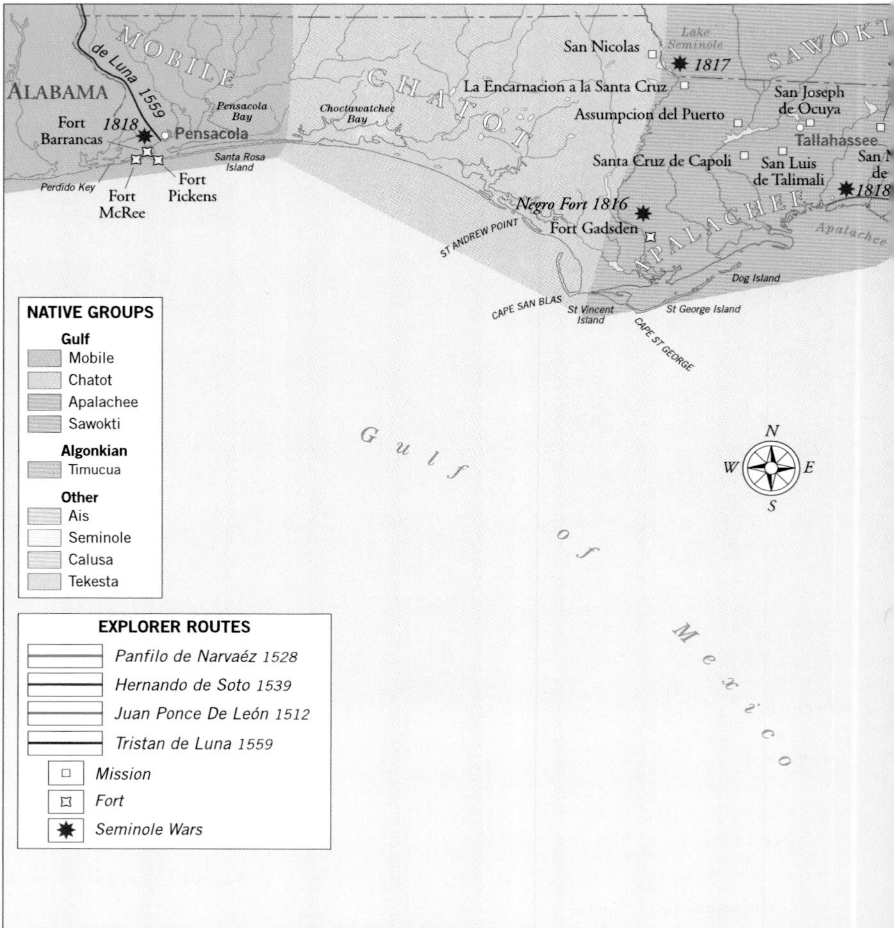
MOBILE
CHATOT
APALACHEE
SAWOKTI
ALABAMA
de Luna 1559
Fort Barrancas
1818
Pensacola
Pensacola Bay
Choctawatchee Bay
Santa Rosa Island
Perdido Key
Fort McRee
Fort Pickens
San Nicolas
Lake Seminole
1817
La Encarnacion a la Santa Cruz
Assumpcion del Puerto
San Joseph de Ocuya
Tallahassee
Santa Cruz de Capoli
San Luis de Talimali
1818
Negro Fort 1816
Fort Gadsden
ST ANDREW POINT
Apalachee
Dog Island
CAPE SAN BLAS
St Vincent Island
St George Island
CAPE ST GEORGE
Gulf of Mexico
N
W
E
S
NATIVE GROUPS
Gulf
Mobile
Chatot
Apalachee
Sawokti
Algonkian
Timucua
Other
Ais
Seminole
Calusa
Tekesta
EXPLORER ROUTES
Panfilo de Narvaéz 1528
Hernando de Soto 1539
Juan Ponce De León 1512
Tristan de Luna 1559
Mission
Fort
Seminole Wars

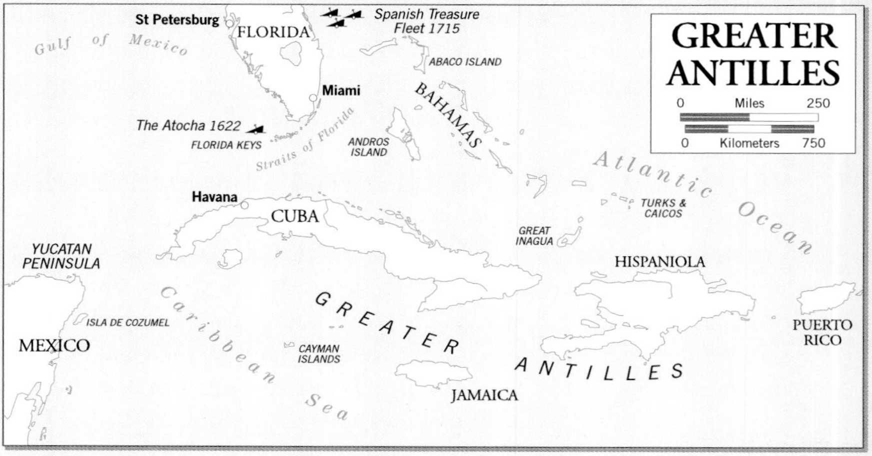
GREATER ANTILLES
0 Miles 250
0 Kilometers 750
St Petersburg
FLORIDA
Gulf of Mexico
Spanish Treasure Fleet 1715
ABACO ISLAND
Miami
BAHAMAS
The Atocha 1622
FLORIDA KEYS
Straits of Florida
ANDROS ISLAND
Atlantic Ocean
Havana
CUBA
TURKS & CAICOS
GREAT INAGUA
YUCATAN PENINSULA
HISPANIOLA
ISLA DE COZUMEL
GREATER ANTILLES
PUERTO RICO
MEXICO
CAYMAN ISLANDS
Caribbean Sea
JAMAICA

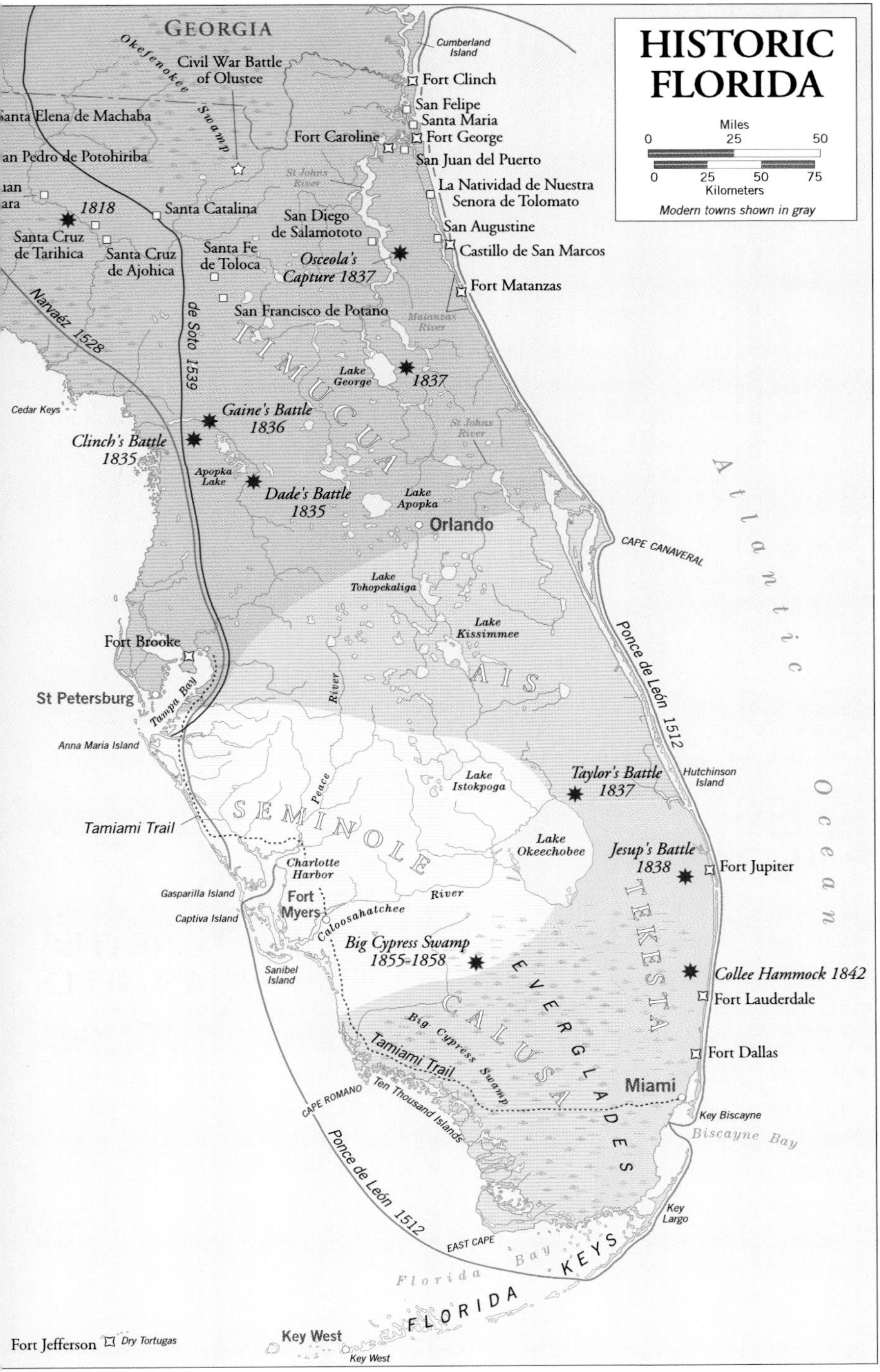
HISTORIC FLORIDA
Miles
0 25 50
0 25 50 75
Kilometers
Modern towns shown in gray
GEORGIA
Okefenokee Swamp
Civil War Battle of Olustee
Cumberland Island
Fort Clinch
San Felipe
Santa Maria
Fort George
Fort Caroline
San Juan del Puerto
St Johns River
La Natividad de Nuestra Senora de Tolomato
anta Elena de Machaba
an Pedro de Potohiriba
1818
Santa Catalina
San Diego de Salamototo
San Augustine
Castillo de San Marcos
Santa Cruz de Tarihica
Santa Cruz de Ajohica
Santa Fe de Toloca
Osceola's Capture 1837
Fort Matanzas
Narvaéz 1528
de Soto 1539
San Francisco de Potano
Matanzas River
TIMUCUA
Lake George
1837
Cedar Keys
Gaine's Battle 1836
Clinch's Battle 1835
St Johns River
Apopka Lake
Dade's Battle 1835
Lake Apopka
Orlando
Atlantic Ocean
CAPE CANAVERAL
Lake Tohopekaliga
Lake Kissimmee
Ponce de León 1512
Fort Brooke
AIS
St Petersburg
Tampa Bay
River
Anna Maria Island
Peace
Lake Istokpoga
Taylor's Battle 1837
Hutchinson Island
SEMINOLE
Tamiami Trail
Lake Okeechobee
Jesup's Battle 1838
Fort Jupiter
Charlotte Harbor
Gasparilla Island
Fort Myers
River
Caloosahatchee
Captiva Island
TEKESTA
Big Cypress Swamp 1855–1858
Sanibel Island
EVERGLADES
Collee Hammock 1842
Fort Lauderdale
CALUSA
Big Cypress Swamp
Tamiami Trail
Fort Dallas
Miami
CAPE ROMANO
Ten Thousand Islands
Key Biscayne
Biscayne Bay
Ponce de León 1512
Key Largo
EAST CAPE
Bay
KEYS
Florida
FLORIDA
Fort Jefferson
Dry Tortugas
Key West
Key West

THE ATTRACTIONS OF FLORIDA

British admiral John Hawkins explored the Florida coast in 1564, following a trading venture in the West Indies. Among those who accompanied Hawkins was John Sparke, who was impressed with the abundance of Florida produce.

The Floridians, when they travel, have a kind of herb dried [tobacco], which, with a cane and cup in the end, with fire, and the dried herbs put together, do suck through the cane the smoke thereof, which smoke satisfies their hunger, and therewith they live four or five days without meat or drink. . . .

The commodities of this land are more than are yet known to any man; for besides the land itself whereof there is more than any king Christian is able to inhabit, it flourishes with meadow, pasture ground, with woods of cedar and cypress, and other sorts, as better cannot be in the world. . . . gold and silver they want not. . . .

—John Sparke, *Principal Navigations*, 1589

and where farming was possible, maize, squash, and beans were grown. The majority of native peoples lived in peace with others.

■ THE SPANISH

Don Juan Ponce de León explored Florida in 1513, searching for the isle of Bimini, which, rumor had it, was blessed with gold. The king of Spain had made Ponce de León governor of the island—should he find it—and gave him the right to exploit it and govern its inhabitants. Ponce de León, a soldier who had accompanied Columbus's second voyage to Hispaniola in 1493, was typical of many well-born Spaniards of that era: eager to make their mark on the world, they found themselves without a war to fight once the Moors were driven from Granada in 1492. The most ambitious among them voyaged west hoping to conquer and rule new lands discovered by Columbus, lands they still believed lay adjacent to India.

Ponce de León landed near St. Augustine on Easter Sunday, 1513, and after claiming the region for Spain and naming it for the Spanish Easter-time holiday

Pascua Florida (Feast of Flowers), he sailed back down the peninsula and around to the west coast. After three weeks, he retreated in the face of native attacks.

Eight years later, Ponce de León sailed for the west coast of Florida once again, with two ships, 50 horses, 200 colonists, livestock, and farming implements. The group had gone ashore and begun building shelters when they were fiercely attacked by Calusas, who may have poisoned their arrows with the juice of the deadly manchineel tree. Ponce de León was mortally wounded, and returned to Havana, where he died. After exploring much of the Florida coastline, Ponce de León reported that Florida was an island.

Pánfilo de Narváez, a battle-hardened conquistador, landed at Tampa Bay in 1528 with 400 men. His mission was commissioned by Charles V of Spain. Narváez promptly tried to extort cooperation from the natives by torturing them. When the natives suggested treasure might be found in neighboring Apalachee territory, Narváez ordered his ships to meet him there as he and his men marched

north. More destruction and enslavement followed. (One especially gruesome account relays how Narváez fed one chief's mother to Spanish war dogs.) When the expedition's ships failed to make the rendezvous, the surviving Spaniards built ships from horse hides and melted-down weaponry and set out for Mexico. Narváez and most of the team perished before reaching Mexico; Cabeza de Vaca, a high-ranking official, survived, and he, along with three other survivors, began walking toward Mexico City. After eight years, they met up with Spanish soldiers in the deserts of northern Mexico.

Cabeza de Vaca wrote Florida's first travel tales in a report to the Spanish king, published in 1542 as *Naúfragios* ("Shipwrecks") *de Alvar Nuñez Cabeza de Vaca.*

Juan Ponce de Léon, the Spaniard who named Florida, was one of the first Europeans to set foot on its soil. (Florida State Archives)

The country where we came on shore to this town and region of Apalachen is for the most part level, the ground of sand and stiff earth. Throughout are immense trees and open woods, in which are walnut, laurel, and another tree called liquid-amber, cedars, savins, evergreen oaks, pines, red-oaks, and palmitos like those of Spain. There are many lakes, great and small, over every part of it; some troublesome of fording, on account of depth and the great number of trees lying throughout them. Their beds are sand. The lakes in the country of Apalachen are much larger than those we found before coming there.

Hernando de Soto, after having made his wealth in the conquest of Peru (for which Charles V appointed him the governor of Cuba), landed in the Tampa area in 1539 with a large expedition. The natives fled. De Soto and his party foraged

and ravaged north in quest of riches, taking slaves and murdering people until they arrived in Tallahassee. During de Soto's first winter in Tallahassee, willing natives showed Spaniards how to make quilted cotton tunics that stopped most arrows and spears. De Soto explored much of the American southeast looking for gold, but was continually disappointed. He died in 1542 of fever near the Mis-

Spanish explorer Hernando de Soto expected to discover great wealth in Florida. He found no gold, but did terrorize the native inhabitants. (Florida State Archives) sissippi River. His companions sank his body in the river, fearing, perhaps justifiably, that the locals might want to desecrate it.

In the years after de Soto's demise, ambitious Spanish colonies in Florida continued to founder. In 1559, Tristán de Luna y Arellano founded a large and initially well-stocked colony at today's Pensacola, but dwindling supplies and a devastating hurricane forced his settlers to leave. In 1565, Pedro Menéndez de Avilés (after attacking French settlers on the east coast) headed west to look for a son who had been shipwrecked. At first on friendly terms with the locals, the elder Menéndez ended up rejecting the chief's proffered sister, beheading the leader he had befriended, and fleeing the tribe's wrath.

■ FRENCH CURIOSITY, NATIVE REBELLION

Of the three contenders for control of the New World—the Spanish, English, and French—France became the next European power interested in Florida. A colony established in 1562 under the leadership of Jean Ribault claimed land on the Atlantic Coast near the mouth of the St. Johns River in modern-day Jacksonville. In 1564, Ribault's second-in-command, René de Goulaine de Laudonnière, erected Fort Caroline and established a French Huguenot colony nearby. (Huguenots, being Protestants, sought refuge all along the east coast of North America.) Unlike the Spaniards, the French were warmly welcomed by the Timucuans, whom the French settlers described as "tawny collour, hawk nosed and of a pleasant countenance."

The French, however, were not to be left in peace. King Phillip II of Spain did not want French settlements along the important Spanish trading route east of Florida, so he appointed Pedro Menéndez de Avilés "Captain General of all Florida" and gave him the task of ridding the possession of Frenchmen. In 1565, with the largest armada yet to set sail for Florida, Menéndez established North America's first European settlement at St. Augustine, which he named for the patron saint of the day on which he landed. The Matanzas River got its name (which translates to "river of massacre") for the slaughter it witnessed as the Spanish crushed the French in a surprise attack. When the dust settled, Spain possessed Fort Caroline, which it renamed Fort San Mateo. Some Huguenots survived by jumping the fort walls onto ships. Among them was Jacques Le Moyne, Ribault's cartographer and the first artist commissioned to make paintings of America's natives. Much of what we know about Timucuans comes from his work.

With the French defeated, Spain seated itself as master over Florida. For the

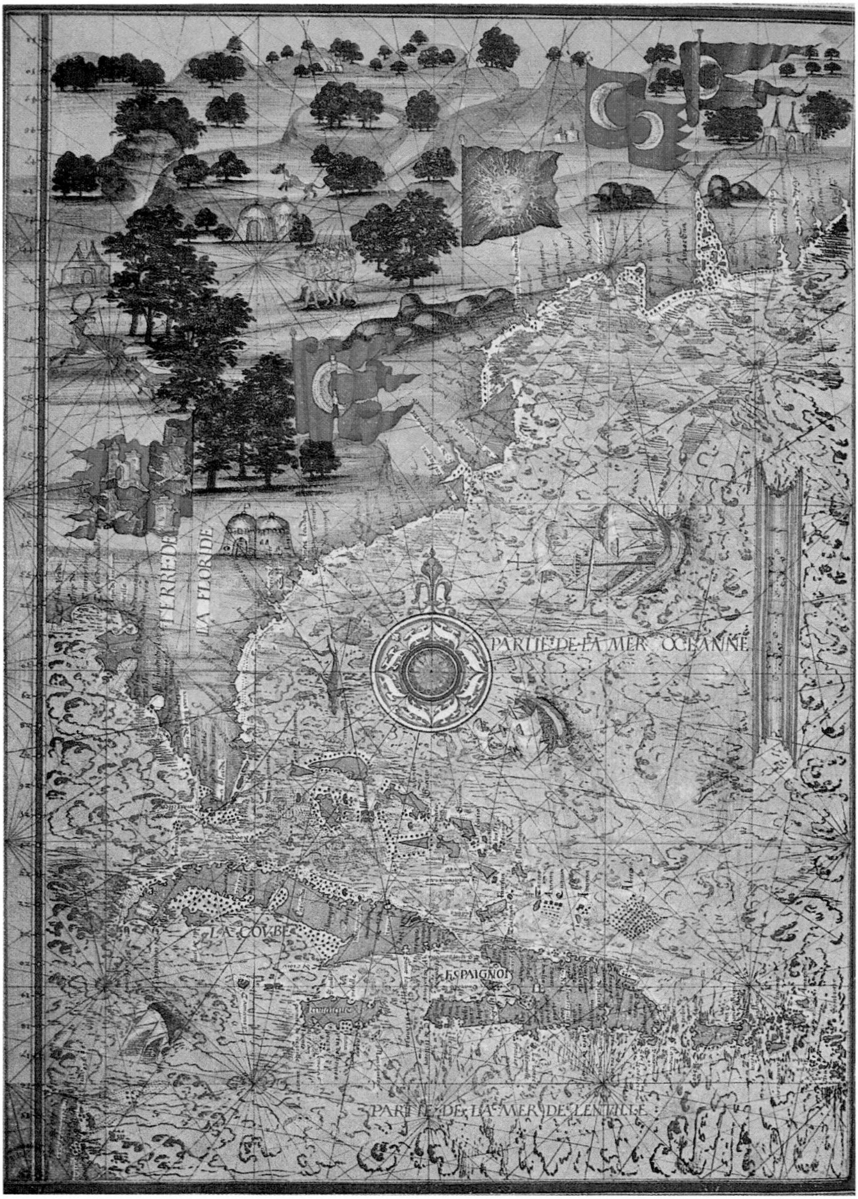
TERRE DE
LA FLORIDE
PARTIE DE LA MER OCEANNE
LA COVBE
ESPAIGNOL
PARTIE DE LA MER DE LENTILLE

Compiled by French chartmaker Guillaume de Testu in 1556, "Terre de Floride" was the most detailed map of Florida at the time, and was used by the French Huguenots when they came to settle in the New World. The map gives many place names, but only Cape Canaveral's remains today. (Ministère de la Défense, Bibliothèque du Service Historique de l'Armée de Terre)

ORIENS
MERIDIES
OCCIDENS.

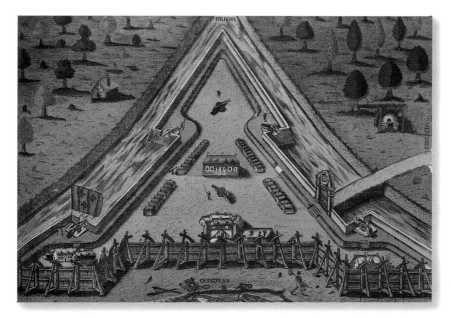

French settlers arrived at the mouth of the St. Johns River in 1562 and erected Fort Caroline, to the consternation of the Spanish. (St. Augustine Historical Society)

century to come, missionaries spread the Catholic faith and colonists busied themselves protecting the eastern shoreline. Forts and missions were built along the northeast coast and westward to Apalachee territory.

In both their ambitions, the settlers met resistance. Natives often rebelled against the abuse they suffered. Attacks were also waged by the French and British against Spanish forts. The most ferocious one was led in 1586 by El Draco—Sir Francis Drake of Britain, the scourge of the Spanish Empire. His St. Augustine raiding party burned down the town. Ten years later, when British buccaneer John Davis succeeded in ravaging St. Augustine's original fort, the Spanish decided to build something that would stop them all dead in their tracks. Castillo de San Marcos was completed 23 years later, an impenetrable monument of coquina rock built by native and slave labor. Never again were the walls of St. Augustine breached by enemy attack.

At the height of Spanish rule, around 1700, St. Augustine was inhabited by native people, blacks—both free and slave—and 5,000 Spanish colonists and soldiers. Spanish women were scarce, and many of the soldiers in the outpost's early days fathered children with natives and blacks.

Spain's other important Florida town, far to the west at Pensacola Bay on the Gulf Coast, had a population of only 300, and often struggled to defend itself against attacks from pirates and French marauders from Louisiana. In the vast acreage between settlements, Franciscan monks operated more than 30 missions, where Indians were brought to be converted to Christianity and where they died by the hundreds of smallpox and measles.

■ THE BRITISH MOVE IN

By the beginning of the 18th century, Spain's power was diminishing rapidly, and the days of its rule in Florida were numbered. The British Crown, which occupied the remainder of the continent's eastern seaboard, wanted to control the entire coast. Its northern colonies were prosperous, and the taxes paid by colonists meant wealth for the Crown. By 1670, British settlers had established Charles Town in the Carolinas, bringing colonists within easy striking distance of Florida. Angered that their runaway slaves were accorded refuge by Florida Indians and the Spanish, English colonists in Georgia and the Carolinas took to raiding and burning Florida's Spanish missions and threatening St. Augustine. When England captured valuable Cuba in 1763, the Spanish handed over Florida to get Cuba back.

England governed Florida as two separate territories, East Florida and West Florida, the boundaries of the latter extending to the Mississippi River. Most of the Spanish settlers fled, and King George III of England wrestled with the task of attracting more people to the area. To do this, he first made peace with the native peoples. Then, in 1767, a Scottish physician named Dr. Andrew Turnbull recruited 1,100 people from Italy, Greece, and Minorca to settle around New Smyrna in East Florida.

When Ponce de León arrived in Florida, its aboriginal people numbered about 350,000, but within a few years their numbers dropped. Some Indian people disappeared in slaving raids, others in battles and skirmishes with the Spanish, but by far the greatest number died from smallpox, measles, and syphilis (which also rendered women sterile). Those who didn't die were absorbed by tribes migrating from the north: the Creeks, Seminoles, Chickasaws, Cherokees, and Choctaws. Miccosukees settled the southern regions, and escaped slaves and Amerindians

In 1586, Sir Francis Drake waged war against the Spanish when he sailed into St. Augustine harbor with 2,000 men and 42 vessels. (Library of Congress)

intermingled with the Seminoles, who had wandered into Florida from Georgia and Alabama.

The state's lower regions were farmed and fished by a class of drifters, who, according to customs inspector Henry B. Crews, lived "in a state of Savage Barbarism with no associate but the Seminole Indians and the lowest class of refugee Spaniards who from crime have been compelled to abandon civilized life."

In 1775, when English colonists from Maine to Georgia rebelled against English rule and established the United States of America, British citizens of the Floridas remained mostly true to the Union Jack. Many northern Loyalists fled to Florida for protection once the British were defeated. They brought with them their wealth and the slaves who built the plantations.

But British rule was not to last, and Florida was continually batted back and forth between major powers and petty potentates in the years to follow. Spain,

England, and France contested its sovereignty, and smugglers and pirates joined with rebellious Indians to make life dangerous for the Florida settlers. The United States tried unsuccessfully to buy Florida so it could secure its southern borders and stop Indian raids. Eventually, Major General Andrew Jackson was sent to subdue the Indians, an act that initiated the Wars of Indian Removal (or Seminole Wars), which raged from 1817 to 1858. Jackson ruthlessly seized St. Marks and Pensacola from the Spanish, then burned homes and villages, murdered Indians, and executed British traders he suspected of being enemy informants. Jackson's behavior was roundly criticized in the U.S. Congress as well as in Spain and Britain, but Spain and the United States eventually settled the matter when the latter agreed to pay off some of Spain's debts in exchange for Florida. As a result, Florida became a territory of the United States in 1821, with Andrew Jackson as provisional territorial governor.

■ PIRATES ON THE SEAS

Bawdy and bloody, dashing yet dastardly, pirates were widely feared in their time, but in Florida today they have been elevated from savage criminal to romantic hero. There's hardly an island or port that doesn't take pride in proclaiming itself an old pirate haunt. Amelia Island lays claim to French privateer Luis Aury, who at one time ruled the island; Black Ceasar and his rough band of outlaws hid in thatched huts on Sanibel Island; Gasparilla, according to legend, enslaved women on Captiva Island; beautiful Anne Bonny had a love tryst at Fort Myers Beach. Tales of pirate escapades still swirl around Florida's coastline, inspiring countless place names, resorts, and theme parks.

For the struggling territory of Florida, however, the piracy of the early 19th century was decidedly unromantic. Pirates sailed up and down Florida's east coast, shuttling back and forth between rendezvous points in the Bahamas and such ports as Charleston, South Carolina, and Ocracoke Island in North Carolina's Outer Banks. Along the way, they plundered merchant vessels, terrorized passengers, and took captives for ransom. Many pirates also patrolled the waterways near Key West, to pick clean the bones of ships stranded on the area's treacherous reefs and shoals. Some deliberately tricked ships onto reefs with false flares and beacons. The constant threat of attack impeded settlement and nearly ruined commerce along the coast.

In Key West, by 1820, 3,000 acts of piracy had been counted since the island was first settled. In 1822, U.S. Commodore David Porter was sent to Key West to suppress piracy, and by 1830, his 14-vessel squadron had accomplished this goal by bloody battle and capture, and with the cooperation of six American warships. Florida waters became safe to travel for the first time in 300 years.

■ EAST-WEST SPLIT

With their new status as American territories, the two halves of British Florida became one. The western half extended along what is now the Panhandle all the way to the Mississippi River, and was not cut to its present size until 1813.

When Florida became a U.S. territory in 1821, its population was less than 8,000, but it grew rapidly. Sugar and indigo plantations were established, and orange trees were farmed along the Indian River and inland, around Ocala. The Panhandle towns of Apalachicola and St. Joseph thrived as ports. Jacksonville, named in honor of Florida's first territorial governor, expanded around a navigable section of the St. Johns River. In 1823, Tallahassee was named capital of Florida. By 1830, the first federal census revealed a population of 34,730, of which 18,395 were white and 16,335 nonwhite.

■ SEMINOLE WARS

The years from 1817 to 1858 were marked by sporadic violence, as settlers and the soldiers who protected them battled with the Indians and escaped slaves of the Florida Seminole tribe. The First Seminole War (1817–1818) led to a peace treaty in 1819 that offered reservation land to the Seminole Indians. The Second Seminole War commenced in 1835 and initiated a seven-year period of bloodshed, sparked after the Seminole nation, under the leadership of Osceola, a respected tribesman, and Chief Micanopy, refused to relocate as specified in the Treaty of Payne's Landing (1832). Things turned nasty, especially after Osceola was captured under the ruse of a white flag sent to him by General Thomas S. Jessup. Jessup imprisoned Osceola with his wives and children at Fort Moultrie in Charleston, where the Seminole warrior died less than four months later. Vicious raids and retaliations by both sides continued for years. The Seminoles retreated into the impenetrable cover of the Everglades, with Chief Billy Bowlegs as leader. Wily and wilderness-wise, the Seminoles were able to evade soldiers unaccustomed to the swamps. Both sides fought with muzzle-loading rifles, and the Indians also

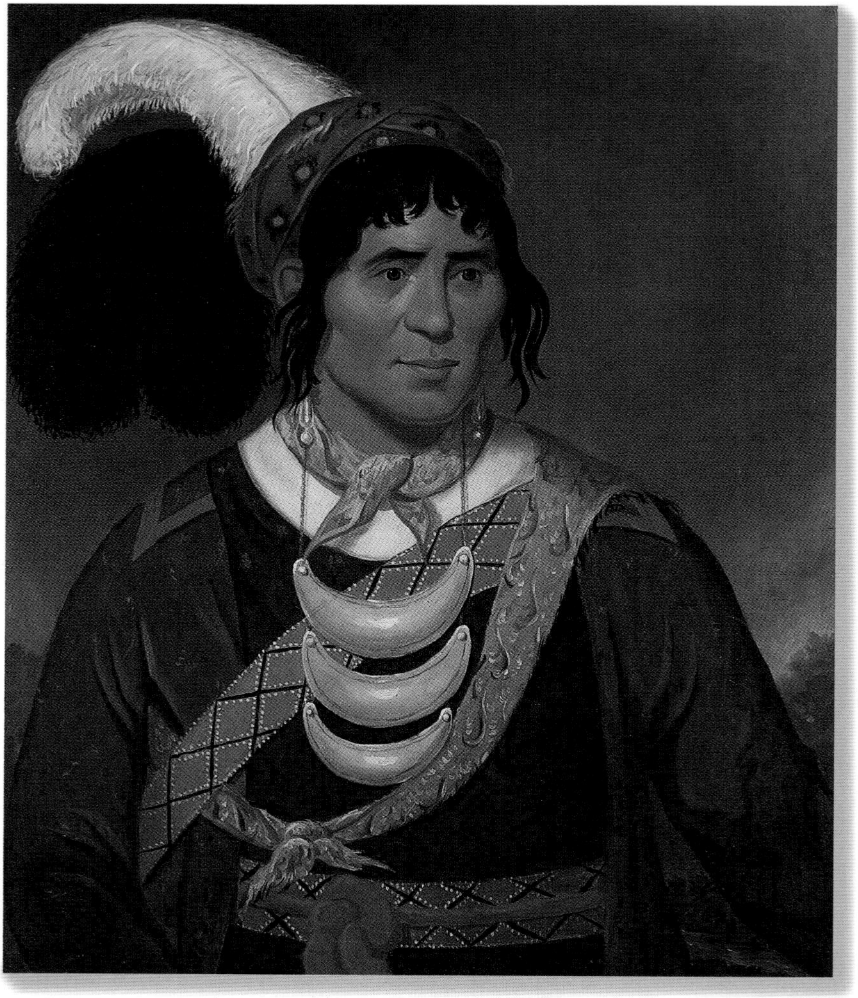

An 1838 portrait of Seminole leader Osceola by Robert J. Curtis. (Sam and Robbie Vickers Florida Collection)

This 1843 painting by John Rogers Vinton portrays a Seminole warrior surveying the ruins of the New Smyrna Sugar House, destroyed by Indians during the Second Seminole War. (Sam and Robbie Vickers Florida Collection)

used bows and arrows. Indians who were captured were shipped west to reservation land in Oklahoma.

A new agreement in 1841 contained the Seminoles along the western shore of Lake Okeechobee, but no mention was made in the treaty of the swampland, which the Seminoles assumed belonged to them.

As the Seminole Wars continued and fighting spread south, Florida's population increasingly included veterans of these wars. The wars also left fort settlements in their wake, including Fort Brooke, built at today's Tampa, and Fort Myers, originally known as Fort Harvie. Florida was granted statehood in 1845, and in 1850 the U.S. government began providing grants for drainage of swampland, making it suitable for farming. Not long after, the Everglades, last retreat of the Seminoles, was drained. Army surveyors destroyed Chief Bowlegs's prize banana grove on a lark, igniting the third of the Seminole Wars. By 1858, U.S. soldiers had captured enough tribe members to force Bowlegs and 165 others to

Pioneer Jacob Summerlin became one of Florida's most prominent stockmen once the threat of Indian raids was removed. Ranging from Fort Myers to Fort Meade, Summerlin's extensive herd supplied both Confederate and Union troops. (Florida State Archives)

relocate to Oklahoma. A few remained, retreating deep into the swamps. From 1817 to 1858, their number within Florida had dropped from 5,000 to 200.

With peace, the state prospered. Farmers and plantation owners, along with their slaves, worked Florida's fertile lands, particularly in the north and southwest around Bradenton. Poorer settlers established subsistence farms in the backwoods, and the fishing industry thrived along the coast. Cattle ranchers and cowboys lived in the interior, raising descendants of the cattle brought ashore by early Spanish explorers. An entire culture arose around this industry, complete with folklore and political power. Cattle barons like Jacob Summerlin in Fort Myers became some of the wealthiest men in the state. Steamboats plied the waterways and railroads connected the state to the industrial North.

■ CIVIL WAR ERA

As Confederate and Union lines were being drawn throughout a nation divided over slavery, Florida seceded from the Union in 1861, the third state to do so. Slave owners had pushed the action through quickly. Politically, the state was divided in its sympathies, not only by area, but within cities, even families. In Pensacola, for instance, Confederate troops occupied Fort McRee on Perdido Key and Fort Barrancas on the mainland, while Union forces held the more spectacular and strategic Fort Pickens on Santa Rosa Island, near today's Pensacola Beach. The two factions fought it out on more than one occasion, and by 1862 the Confederates had withdrawn. Fort Pickens remained Union headquarters in Florida throughout the Civil War.

Federal troops also kept control of two forts on Key West and one in the Dry Tortugas to the south. They later gained control of several important ports, including Fernandina Beach (on Amelia Island), Jacksonville, St. Augustine, Tampa, Cedar Key, Apalachicola, and Fort Myers, from which points they could effectively block supply shipments to interior Confederate outposts. From their inland strongholds, rebel squadrons controlled the flow of food supplies.

Florida's battlefields were confined largely to interior lands, where Union forces marched in search of food. Coastal saltworks were another target. In 1864, at the Battle of Olustee, near Lake City, Union troops tried to cut off northern Florida from food supplies that originated in the south. Union soldiers marched from Jacksonville toward Tallahassee and met Confederates in a six-hour battle from which the Union retreated. The Confederacy held strong in more cases than not, often reinforced by "cradle and grave companies"—the very young and old who were left behind after those of fighting age had enlisted. One such troop defended the Panhandle town of Marianna from a Pensacola-led attack. Tallahassee remained uncaptured, the only Confederate capital east of the Mississippi to do so. It was defended during the Natural Bridge Battle in March 1865. In total, an estimated 15,000 white Floridians joined the Confederates; 5,000 died. About 1,200 whites and 1,000 blacks served the Union cause.

During the war, the Confederacy depended heavily on Florida's cattle industry to feed its armies, but the cattle drivers showed allegiance to no one. They sold to local rebel troops and to Union men. They busted through blockades to ship to other Confederate outposts and to Cuba. After the war, the lure of cattle-ranching attracted young, unattached soldiers in search of adventure and fortune.

The Battle of Olustee on February 20, 1864, was the only major engagement fought in Florida during the Civil War. (Florida State Archives)

■ RAILROADS AND ROUGH RIDERS

Although relatively unscathed during the Civil War, Florida suffered economically during Reconstruction. Still, new industries were established, and Key West diversified into shipwreck salvaging and cigar-making. In the 1880s, cigar-makers moved into Tampa, and Greeks founded a business in nearby Tarpon Springs selling sea sponges.

The Gulf of Mexico, the Atlantic Ocean, intracoastal waters, and such major waterways as the St. Johns, Ocklawaha, Suwannee, Apalachicola, and Caloosahatchee Rivers were the principal routes of transport when the first tourists arrived. Cheap land encouraged railroad companies to lay tracks throughout

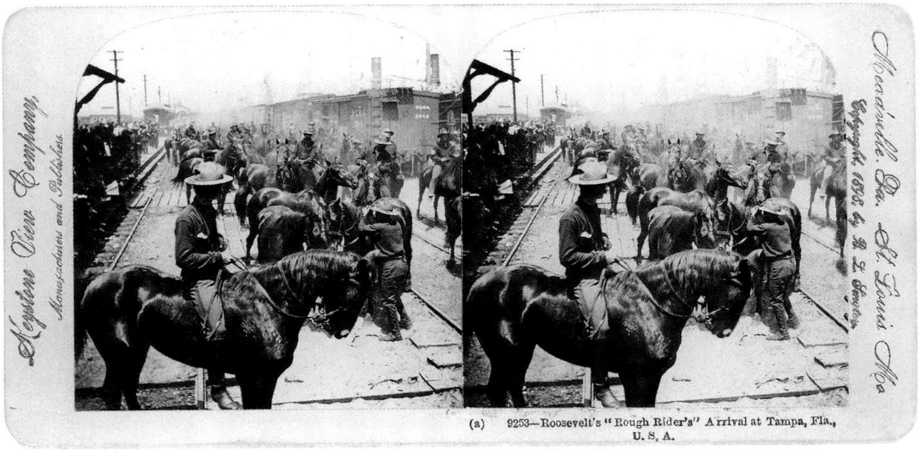
Keystone View Company,
Manufacturers and Publishers.
Meadville, Pa. St. Louis Mo.
(a) 9253—Roosevelt's "Rough Rider's" Arrival at Tampa, Fla., U. S. A.

In 1898, Theodore Roosevelt, worried about military threats from Cuba, stationed 30,000 of his Rough Riders regiment in Tampa. (Library of Congress)

northern Florida and as far south as the fishing village of Miami. Three men are chiefly responsible for the modernization of Florida's transportation in the late 19th century: William D. Chipley, Henry B. Plant, and Henry M. Flagler. Chipley built a railway in the 1880s that connected Jacksonville, Pensacola, and Mobile, Alabama. Plant developed the western portion of the state, and Flagler steamrolled the east. Railroads aided the orange-growing and fishing industries and others, such as pencil manufacturing in Cedar Key. By the end of the 19th century, luxury hotels and resort towns had risen out of the dust of railroad construction, and Florida became a destination for wealthy vacationers looking for adventure in the untamed wilds of St. Augustine, Palm Beach, and Tampa.

In 1898, the Spanish-American War brought attention to the state's more slowly developing south. Teddy Roosevelt stationed 30,000 of his Rough Riders in Tampa. Forts were built around gaping Tampa Bay as a defense against attacks from Cuba, and military bases were built in Jacksonville, Miami, and Key West. Orlando became the hub of central Florida. After the war, soldiers came home with tales of Florida, promoting tourism more effectively than any ad campaign.

In the 1920s, "tin-can tourists" arrived from the Northeast in droves to set up their mobile vacation homes along Florida's sunny coasts. (Florida State Archives)

■ EARLY 20TH CENTURY

At the turn of the 20th century, Florida, with a population of half a million, entered an era of prosperity and growth. Cities built schools, universities, newspapers, and railroad stations. Life eased up on the plucky pioneers who had settled to farm and fish despite mosquitoes, drought, heat, freezes, and hurricanes. The automobile arrived by 1912, and Henry Flagler extended his railroad all the way to Key West. During Prohibition, prime bootlegging operations were established in Florida. Rum was smuggled in from Cuba, and down in the Keys and other far-flung areas, saloons operated as usual.

When the automobile came within financial reach of average Americans in the 1920s, many new roads were built to accommodate the increase in traffic. As a result, people of all economic levels could drive south to Florida for a holiday in the sun. Those who arrived in Model T–towed campers were termed "tin-can tourists." Many who came put down roots. Land-buying prospects were sunny, but dealings often shady. Miami Beach was hailed as the new vacation mecca and compared to the French Riviera. Architectural styles began to imitate Florida's balmy overseas counterparts, with Mediterranean-style arches, red-tile roofs, and wrought-iron balconies. Miami Beach became the chic showplace of a fresh new style known as art deco. The west coast received more attention with the completion of the Tamiami Trail across the Everglades, connecting Tampa to Miami. The stream of wealthy tourists continued to arrive by private coach to Palm Beach and Boca Raton in the east, and to Boca Grande and Naples in the west. Such names as Vanderbilt, Du Pont, Rockefeller, and Mellon showed up on guest lists of Florida's rich and famous. Some enjoyed Gatsbyesque glamour at ostentatious palaces and luxury hotels, where the sound of ice cubes tinkling in glasses and the beachward swish of the sea filled the air. Others built quiet retreats where they could evade the limelight.

When World War II commenced, Florida did its patriotic duty. Whole resort towns, including Miami Beach, were turned over to federal troops for training. The posh Breakers of Palm Beach became a military hospital, and other resorts housed recruits. Naval air stations at Pensacola and Jacksonville shined up their fleets. Air Force headquarters were established in Tampa. Training facilities and

The Breakers Hotel in Palm Beach, the fourth of Henry Flagler's grand resort hotels, opened in 1896 as Florida's tourism boom was getting under way.

military stations popped up everywhere—there were soon 172 such bases in the state. Homeowners on east Florida beaches obeyed lights-out orders when German U-boats were detected close to their shores. Submarines later began torpedoing U.S. vessels traveling Florida's shipping lanes, and there were reports of German military men coming ashore in Ponte Vedra, Palm Beach, and the Panhandle. Florida civilians volunteered as enemy spotters (watching the shores for German vessels) and nurses. The government paid Florida back for its pains by pouring billions of dollars into the economy.

After the war, Florida slipped back into good-times mode. Servicemen again swelled the population, which became more urbanized. Half of the state's full-timers lived in Jacksonville, Tampa, St. Petersburg, Orlando, or Miami, now the state's biggest city. Tourism edged ahead of agriculture as the state's top revenue producer, and to court vacationers in search of paradise, entrepreneurs built motels, hotels, resorts, restaurants, roadside attractions, and gift shops as fast as they could.

■ SPACE FLIGHTS

In 1950, the first missiles and unmanned space rockets lifted off from Cape Canaveral. In 1968, the new Kennedy Space Center sent up *Apollo 8*. Nine subsequent *Apollo* launches followed in the coming years, in addition to all space shuttle launches.

■ CUBAN REVOLUTION

Cubans have been landing in Florida to escape repressive regimes or make a new start for a good 300 years, but no event precipitated a greater influx of refugees than Fidel Castro's takeover of the island in 1959. At first, his daring revolution against a notorious dictator, Fulgencio Batista, was welcomed, but within a few years, as communist rule was established, thousands of refugees began making the journey to Florida, by airplane, ship, and raft. By 1990, more than half a million Cubans had arrived in Florida, and as they gained political power, they began to exert a powerful force in American politics.

Those who arrived in the 1960s are the old elite of the Cuban-American community, people who frequently came with no money, but with excellent entrepreneurial skills and a willingness to work hard. Their achievements are a classic American success story. A second large wave of refugees arrived in 1980, the 125,000 Mariel boat refugees. When he allowed these people to leave, Fidel

From Havana to Miami: Two Stories

The photographer describes a family trip from Cuba to the United States, as well as that of a more recent refugee whom Mr. Arruza met while photographing a magazine story.

What follows are two examples of the Cuban exodus to the United States. Three decades separate these narratives, but both illustrate the instinctive fight for freedom.

The first journey is that of my own family, which was among the mostly upper- and middle-class people who left the island after Castro's revolution in 1959. My father, 31, was employed as a plant manager at a sugar mill. I was seven, my brother six, and together with our parents we boarded a Cuban Airlines plane on October 30, 1960, bound for Miami. We carried a single suitcase filled with clothes and less than $100 in cash.

Father quickly secured employment with the rapidly growing sugarcane industry. After a weeklong stay at the Hotel Liberty in downtown Miami, we rented a home in West Palm Beach before moving to Belle Glade a few years later. Our parents had had the foresight to open a bank account in Miami several years before the revolution, and that helped us through those early days.

Our parent's decision to leave was based on the new regime's control of education. Their children were not to be indoctrinated by communism. We left everything we owned and valued behind us, and though we had hoped to return, as time passed our dreams remained unfulfilled. How my parents coped, I'll never know.

Florida's first wave of Cuban refugees arrived by plane.

The second story is about the human spirit and the willingness to persevere at all cost. Juan Carlos, whom I met on a photo shoot, was a 25-year-old fisherman and diver who left Havana on the night of August 29, 1992, with three other men. Their transportation was a handmade raft. With almost no water or food, they lived on hope alone.

Juan Carlos (red cap), his wife Yaimy, and others when rescued in 1993.

The details of Juan Carlos's escape to freedom would make a stunning motion picture, but what sets Juan Carlos apart from all other rafters who risked their lives in their harrowing journeys (it's estimated that 50 percent of those attempting to cross the Florida Straits by raft perish) is that he did it twice! After crossing to freedom in 1992, he and a friend illegally returned to Cuba a year later on a 26-foot-long boat. They made their way to Havana Harbor at midnight on August 15, 1993. As they approached the shoreline, a Cuban coast guard boat spotted them and the guards aimed AK-47s in their direction. Juan Carlos jumped into the ocean with mask and fins and began swimming underwater until he escaped the searchlight. He then swam about a mile offshore and another couple of miles parallel to the coast before coming ashore. He met a group of teens and traded his mask and fins for shoes and a T-shirt. He escaped the police that same night and afterward went into hiding for a month, as wanted posters for him were placed around the island. During that time, he built another raft.

On the night of September 12, 1993, Juan Carlos, his wife, Yaimy, and four men quietly slipped away on a raft from the shores of Cuba. Yaimy was Juan Carlos's reason for returning and defying the odds of another dangerous crossing. As on Juan Carlos's first trip, he and the others drank but a capful of water three times in a 24-hour period, and twice a day ate a piece of moldy bread. They navigated with a small compass and rowed nonstop, fighting 20-foot seas, strong winds, and lightning storms.

Juan Carlos and Yaimy now live in Lake Worth, Florida. Juan Carlos was lucky enough to find work—at first bagging groceries, then as a gardener. He and Yaimy have learned English and have bought a small house. They are living with the dream of freedom, as are my family and so many other Cubans who have given up so much to make their way to a nearby but very different world.

—Tony Arruza

shipped along with them the occupants of Cuba's prisons and mental institutions, which relieved his island of a great deal of expense and burdened Florida.

People are still trying to escape Castro's Cuba, though one high-profile situation ended in someone who had fled the country—six-year-old Elian Gonzalez—returning to it. The boy, rescued at sea after his mother and nine others perished when their boat sank off the coast of Florida, went to live in Miami with his uncle. But when Elian's father in Havana demanded the return of his son, an ideological battle ensued between Cuban Americans and their relatives in Cuba. The U.S. government ultimately concluded that Elian's natural father had sole authority to make decisions for his son, and Elian was returned to him in June 2000, seven months after he arrived.

With its bizarre twists and turns, the Elian Gonzales story made international headlines for months and turned into something of a political soap opera that brought all the Castro-era tensions back to the surface.

But this wasn't the only high-profile event to take place in Florida that year. In one of the most hotly contested presidential vote counts in U.S. history—it took more than a month for the results to be certified—George W. Bush defeated Al Gore by less than 1,000 votes, thereby securing the presidency. That he did so in the state of which his brother, Jeb Bush, was governor, only heightened the story's inherent drama.

■ THEME PARKS AND NATURAL BEAUTY

The 1970s are remembered as the decade Disney came to town, radically changing Florida. No longer did tourists come for fishing, beaches, and sunshine. They came to have their picture taken with Mickey Mouse. That trend has continued, as one theme park after another has employed the Disney template. The parks have created a sensation, with tourists swarming to the Orlando area from all over the world—indeed, it's the most popular tourist destination in the United States.

In recent years a new trend has surfaced: ecotourism. This hasn't stopped the log flumes and animated bird shows, but has drawn attention to the ancient cypress trees and rare wood storks, and returned focus to what is truly special about Florida. It has made people understand the ephemeral quality of this ever-changing land, and the need to sustain it.

THE PANHANDLE

■ OVERVIEW

Geologically and botanically, Florida's Panhandle resembles its neighbors to the north more than it does the Florida peninsula. This is also true culturally. Panhandle citizens are traditional Southerners. They speak with a pronounced drawl and prefer their fish batter-fried with hush puppies on the side. Mixed into this stew are the men and women who run the military installations all along the coast, and the university students and politicians of Tallahassee.

Along the Panhandle's coastline, there are tourist areas, white-sand beaches, old fishing towns, and fascinating nature areas. The region is home to Florida's capital city, Tallahassee, and its historic port, St. Marks, located 16 miles south on a marshy stretch of coast largely neglected by travelers. Farther west, at the mouth of the Apalachicola River, lies the town of Apalachicola, a major cotton-shipping port in the 19th century that retains its antebellum charm. As the road heads toward Pensacola, beaches become whiter and whiter, the dunes larger and softer.

Panama City Beach is the Panhandle's shamefully overdeveloped vacation headquarters. Around Seaside, things become more exclusive. Destin and Fort Walton Beach are smaller-scale family vacation areas, and, to the west, 52 miles of the region's outstanding coastal landscape are preserved as the Gulf Islands National Seashore. Much of the national seashore lies in the vicinity of historic Pensacola.

■ TALLAHASSEE   *map pages 48–49, E-2, and page 50*

During the 20 years of British rule over Florida, from 1763 to 1783, the area was divided into two administrative sections, with capitals in eastern Florida at Pensacola and St. Augustine. After the United States acquired Florida in 1821, government sessions were held alternately in one city and then the other, but travel was dangerous and time-consuming: it took three weeks to ride the 400 miles from Pensacola to St. Augustine on horseback. By 1824, legislators were in search of a site for a new state capital that would be equally convenient for those living in St. Augustine or Pensacola. Because yellow fever plagued coastal towns, an inland location was desirable.

The Old State Capitol.

PARKHILL

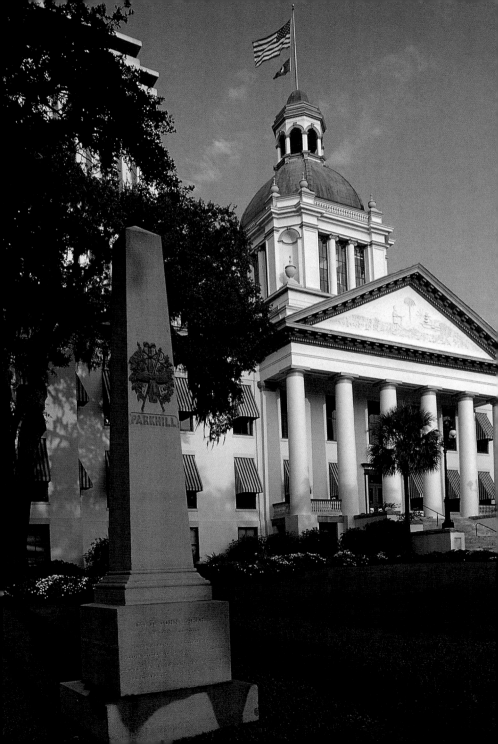

A
B
C
To Montgomery, AL
Atmore
Flomaton
ALABAMA
Florala
Hartford
Gaskin
Pittman
To Mobile, AL
Jay
McDavid
Munson
Prosperity
Liberty
De Funiak Springs
Bonifay
Caryville
Perdido River
Escambia River
Allentown
Galliver
Crestview
Ponce de Leon Springs State Rec Area
Falling Waters State Rec Area
Floridale
Blackwater River State Park
Vernon
Cantonment
Milton
Yellow
Fred Gannon Rocky Bayou State Rec Area
Seminole
Valparaiso
Niceville
Portland
Freeport
Pensacola
Bruce
Ebro
Warrington
Pensacola Village
Pensacola Bay
Mary Esther
Destin
Choctawhatchee Bay
Santa Rosa Beach
Eden State Gardens
Point Washington
Vicksburg
Pensacola Lighthouse
Gulf Breeze
Fort Walton Beach
Henderson Beach
Grayton Beach
West Bay
SANTA ROSA ISLAND
Fort Pickens
Pensacola Beach
Seaside
Gulf Beach
Perdido Key
Perdido State Rec Area
Big Lagoon State Rec Area
Gulf of Mexico
Laguna Beach
Panama City
Panama City Beach
St Andrews State Rec Area
Parker

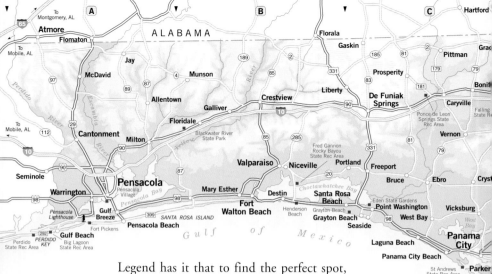

Legend has it that to find the perfect spot, one envoy rode west from St. Augustine and another east from Pensacola, and the site where they met was to be the new capital. A low hill overlooking a flower-filled grassland was chosen as the townsite, and its name, Apalachee, meant "land of the old fields." Thus began Tallahassee. A government center from its founding, the town flourished as the mercantile center of a large cotton-producing area.

Prince Achille Murat, the son of the king of Naples, Italy, established a large plantation here in the 1820s and wrote in his journal that lavish dinner parties took place on adjoining plantations, with "the ladies attending as beautiful and as well dressed as any in New York." The writer Ralph Waldo Emerson was less impressed when he visited in 1827: "Tallahassee [is] a grotesque place, selected three years since as a suitable capital of the territory, and since that day rapidly settled by public officers, land speculators and desperados. . . . Governor Duval is the button on which all things are hung."

During the Civil War, Tallahassee was the only Southern capital not occupied by Union troops. After the war, the town's economy slowed and the population increased by little more than a thousand during the next 100 years. In the late 20th century, the metropolitan area's population mushroomed into the hundreds of thousands.

Tallahassee has the grace of a Southern matron. She likes to show herself off most in the spring, when azaleas, jasmine, oleanders, crape myrtles, and magnolias burst into bloom. The city's old downtown is charming, with its handsome government offices, new and old capitols, cultural center, and active civic life. By day,

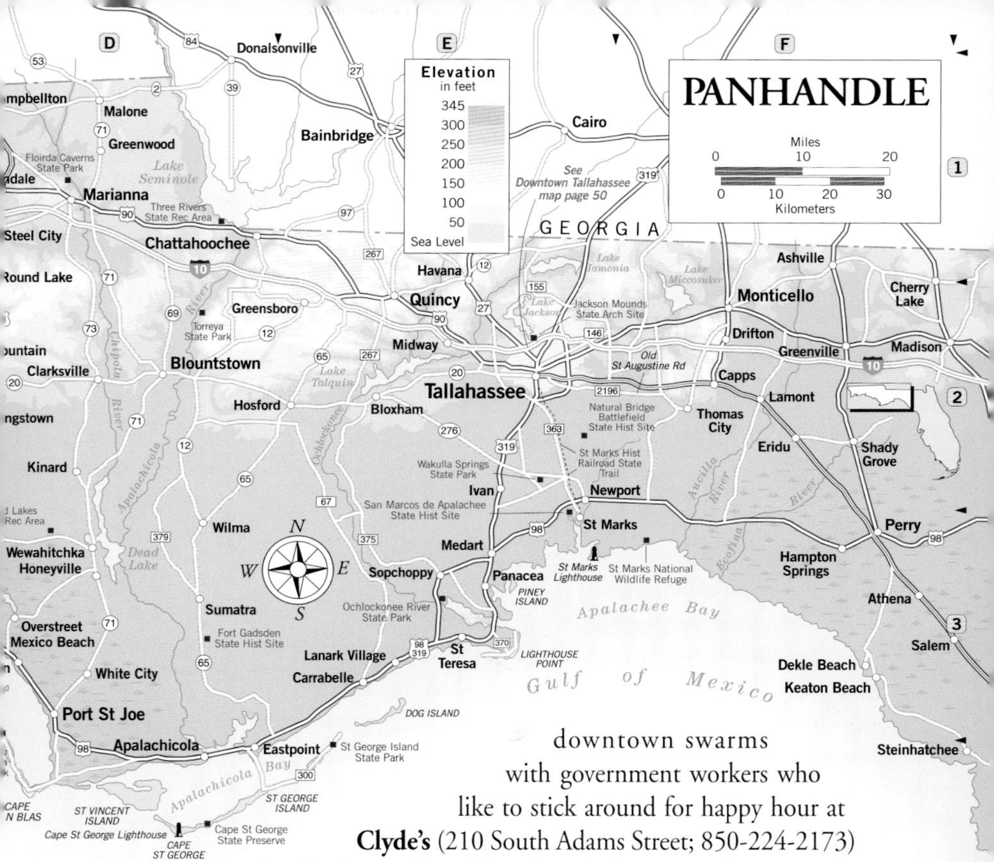
PANHANDLE
Miles
0 10 20
0 10 20 30
Kilometers
Elevation in feet
345
300
250
200
150
100
50
Sea Level
See Downtown Tallahassee map page 50
GEORGIA
D
E
F
1
2
3
Donalsonville
Cairo
Bainbridge
Malone
Greenwood
Florida Caverns State Park
Lake Seminole
Marianna
Three Rivers State Rec Area
Steel City
Chattahoochee
Round Lake
Greensboro
Torreya State Park
Havana
Quincy
Midway
Tallahassee
Lake Talquin
Lake Iamonia
Lake Miccosukee
Lake Jackson
Jackson Mounds State Arch Site
Monticello
Ashville
Cherry Lake
Drifton
Greenville
Madison
Old St Augustine Rd
Capps
Lamont
Blountstown
Clarksville
Hosford
Bloxham
Natural Bridge Battlefield State Hist Site
Thomas City
Eridu
Shady Grove
Kinard
Wakulla Springs State Park
St Marks Hist Railroad State Trail
Ivan
Newport
San Marcos de Apalachee State Hist Site
St Marks
Perry
Wilma
Medart
Wewahitchka
Honeyville
Dead Lake
Sopchoppy
Panacea
St Marks Lighthouse
St Marks National Wildlife Refuge
Hampton Springs
Athena
PINEY ISLAND
Apalachee Bay
Sumatra
Ochlockonee River State Park
Overstreet
Mexico Beach
Fort Gadsden State Hist Site
Lanark Village
St Teresa
LIGHTHOUSE POINT
Salem
Dekle Beach
Keaton Beach
White City
Carrabelle
Gulf of Mexico
Port St Joe
DOG ISLAND
Apalachicola
Eastpoint
St George Island State Park
Steinhatchee
Apalachicola Bay
ST GEORGE ISLAND
CAPE SAN BLAS
ST VINCENT ISLAND
Cape St George Lighthouse
Cape St George State Preserve
CAPE ST GEORGE
Chipola River
Apalachicola River
Ochlockonee River
Aucilla River
Econfina River
N
S
E
W

downtown swarms with government workers who like to stick around for happy hour at **Clyde's** (210 South Adams Street; 850-224-2173) a locally famous bar. After the suits have gone home, students from nearby Florida State University take to the same streets and hangouts.

The boundaries of the old downtown area are the Capitol Square to the south, Adams Street to the west, Monroe Street to the east, and Park Avenue to the north. Most buildings here date from the period immediately following the 1843 fire that destroyed the city.

A good place to begin exploring the area is along the **Adams Street Commons,** a brick-paved and centrally located block between College Avenue and Pensacola Street. Visually arresting landscapes and some of the area's best restaurants await you.

■ Tallahassee Sights *map page 50*

❶ At the **Old Capitol** *(map page 50, B-2),* redesigns, demolitions, and remodels have followed one upon the other for 150 years. The neoclassical 1902 Old Capitol was built over and around the 1845 version, which had replaced the log

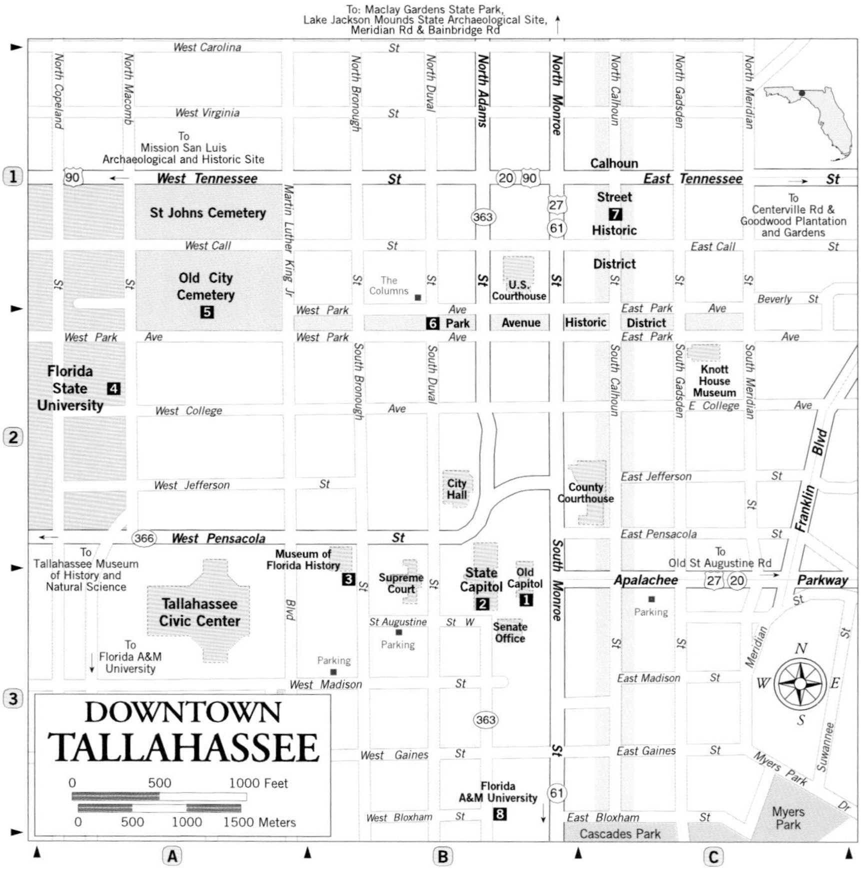
To: Maclay Gardens State Park,
Lake Jackson Mounds State Archaeological Site,
Meridian Rd & Bainbridge Rd
West Carolina
St
West Virginia
St
North Copeland
North Macomb
North Bronough
North Duval
North Adams
North Monroe
North Calhoun
North Gadsden
North Meridian
To
Mission San Luis
Archaeological and Historic Site
90
West Tennessee
St
20
90
Calhoun
Street
7
Historic
District
East Tennessee
St
To
Centerville Rd &
Goodwood Plantation
and Gardens
St Johns Cemetery
Martin Luther King Jr
363
27
61
West Call
St
East Call
St
Old City
Cemetery
5
The
Columns
U.S.
Courthouse
Beverly St
West Park
Ave
6
Park
Avenue
Historic
District
East Park
Ave
Florida
State
4
University
West College
South Bronough
South Duval
South Calhoun
South Gadsden
South Meridian
Knott
House
Museum
E College
Ave
West Jefferson
St
City
Hall
County
Courthouse
East Jefferson
St
Franklin
Blvd
366
West Pensacola
St
East Pensacola
St
To
Tallahassee Museum
of History and
Natural Science
Museum of
Florida History
3
Supreme
Court
State
Capitol
2
Old
Capitol
1
South Monroe
To
Old St Augustine Rd
Apalachee
27
20
Parkway
Tallahassee
Civic Center
Blvd
St Augustine
St W
Parking
Senate
Office
To
Florida A&M
University
West Madison
St
East Madison
St
Meridian
N
W
E
S
Suwannee
DOWNTOWN
TALLAHASSEE
0
500
1000 Feet
0
500
1000
1500 Meters
West Gaines
St
East Gaines
St
Myers Park
Dr
Florida
A&M University
8
West Bloxham
St
East Bloxham
St
Cascades Park
Myers
Park
A
B
C
1
2
3

buildings in which the first territorial government meetings were held in 1824. The 1845 edition was modernized in 1891, when running water was installed, and additions were made to the 1902 structure in 1923, 1936, and 1947. The Old Capitol, saved from the wrecking ball in the mid-1970s, was restored between 1978 and 1982 to conform to the 1902 design.

If you visit, you'll see the governor's suite, supreme court, and legislative chambers, all open to the public. You'll find the **Center for Political History and Governance** here, a permanent exhibit of the Museum of Florida. It relates the state's political history through photographs, videos, books, and artifacts. *South Monroe Street and Apalachee Parkway; 850-487-1902.*

❷ The viewing area on the 22nd floor of the **New Capitol** *(map page 50, B-2)*, adjacent to the Old Capitol, offers a commanding view of the city. On a clear day, you can see all the way to Georgia, 20 miles to the north. Designed by Edward Durell Stone, the architect of the Kennedy Center in Washington, D.C., the New Capitol is an overtly phallic, brutalist structure that not everyone loves.

The **Chapel,** on the first floor, built of quarried coquina rock and tidewater cypress, is worth a look. Brass wall plaques describe the state's religious history. At Tallahassee's **visitors center** (800-628-2866 or 850-413-9200) on the first floor at the West Plaza entrance, you can pick up maps for the historic downtown and the renowned canopy roads. *West of Old Capitol at St. Augustine Street West.*

❸ The star exhibit at the **Museum of Florida History** *(map page 50, B-2)* is the 12,000-year-old skeleton of a 9-foot-tall mastodon found in nearby Wakulla Springs in 1939. A diorama showcases an ancient armadillo large enough to ride. Period clothing from the 19th century, gold, jewelry, and coins retrieved from sunken Spanish galleons, and thousands of other artifacts are also on display. *R. A. Gray Building, 500 South Bronough Street; 850-245-6400.*

❹ To the west of the capitol buildings is the **Florida State University** *(map page 50, A-2)* campus with its gothic twin towers and old oak trees. A map of the campus is available at the Welcome Center in front of the administration center on the east side of campus. *College Avenue and Copeland Street; 850-644-5782.*

Florida State is best known for its football team, the Seminoles, but the university is also the home of the National High Magnetic Field Laboratory, established by the National Science Foundation and operated jointly with Los Alamos National Laboratory in New Mexico.

❺ Stroll through the acres of tombstones at the **Old City Cemetery** and **St. Johns Cemetery** *(map page 50, A-1)* and discover Union and Confederate graves as well as sections set aside for slaves. Originally denoted by wooden markers long decayed, the slave grave sites are mostly unmarked today. *Martin Luther King Jr. Boulevard and Park Avenue.*

❻ The seven-block **Park Avenue Historic District** *(map page 50, B/C-2/1)*, Park Avenue between Martin Luther King Jr. Boulevard and South Meridian Avenue, preserves 64 different sites; 24 buildings are open to the public. The visitor information center in the New Capitol has maps.

The **Knott House Museum** *(map page 50, C-2)* evokes the genteel way of life of the mid-1800s. It was here that the eccentric (or possibly very bored) Luella Knotts wrote poems and attached them to her furniture. The guides let you in on old Southern customs. For example, a person sitting on his or her porch was considered to be in the house. So, a polite passerby would not greet the porch-sitter until acknowledged. *301 East Park Avenue; 850-922-2459.*

❼ **Calhoun Street Historic District** *(map page 50, C-1)*. A drive through the residential district along Calhoun Street reveals how Tallahasseeans lived in the antebellum era, when the town was the commercial center of a thriving cotton-growing region. The architectural styles range from Victorian to Greek Revival and suggest affluence and sophistication.

❽ Founded in 1887 as the State Normal College for Colored Students, **Florida Agriculture and Mechanical University** *(map page 50, B-1)*—better known as Florida A&M, or Fam-U—is the state's oldest black college. This state school is known for its pharmaceutical and engineering departments and its famed Marching 100, one of the best marching bands. The 417-acre campus sits atop the

Moss-draped oaks arch gracefully above a park along Tallahassee's Park Avenue.

highest of Tallahassee's seven hills, directly south of the Florida State University campus off Martin Luther King Jr. Boulevard. The **Black Archives Research Center and Museum** (850-599-3020), housed in Fam-U's Carnegie Library, has an impressive array of artifacts, including 500 Ethiopian crosses. *Off Martin Luther King Jr. Boulevard; 850-599-3860.*

■ GARDENS, PLANTATIONS, AND SIGHTS

The exquisitely designed plantings at **Maclay Gardens State Park** explode with color, especially December through April, when camellias and azaleas bloom. The plantation home, built in 1909, is now a museum showcasing early-20th-century antiques. Nature trails around the park's lake penetrate hardwood and pine forests, where deer, bobcats, and gray foxes live. The lake has a sandy beach and picnic areas. *3540 Thomasville Road; 850-487-4556.*

Six temple mounds at the **Lake Jackson Indian Mounds State Archaeological Site** mark an ancient ceremonial site that may have been occupied by the Southern Cult, an Indian tribe that flourished half a millennium ago across the South. Archaeologists found many bodies buried here, many of them adorned with copper breastplates, cloaks, necklaces, bracelets, and anklets made of shells. The park's nature trails wind through the ruins of a cotton plantation that operated between 1825 and 1860. *3600 Indian Mounds Road; 850-922-6007.*

According to Spanish records, in 1607 Apalachee chiefs asked the Spanish to send missionaries to what is now the **Mission San Luis Archaeological and Historic Site.** By the 1670s, the Apalachee were Christianized. The compound built by the friars was designed like a small village, with separate Spanish and Apalachee living areas, an Indian council house, a Spanish fort, and a plaza. By 1675, more than 1,500 people lived at Mission San Luis, but 29 years later the entire area was burned and abandoned. No Spanish mission survives in Florida, nor do the Apalachee. All that archaeologists have are the objects that Indians and missionaries left behind. Free guided tours are given daily. *2020 West Mission Road; 850-487-3711.*

The mansion that is the centerpiece of **Goodwood Museum and Gardens** is one of those grand architectural confections surrounded by glorious, huge oak trees draped with Spanish moss. If the house could talk, it would tell plenty. The land it sits on was purchased by two brothers from North Carolina in the 1820s. The older one, Hardy Croom, was the first to live on the land. By 1837, having

The Goodwood's main house. (Goodwood Museum and Gardens Archive)

begun construction on a fine mansion, he went north to get his wife and children. The family set sail for Florida on a steamer that sank in a hurricane. Croom's brother, Bryan, took over the land and finished building the house.

By the turn of the 20th century, the estate had passed through the hands of several prominent families and had become a gathering place for Tallahassee society. Goodwood's fortunes rose and fell with its owners' prosperity. The house's last occupants, in the 1920s, were State Senator William Hodges and his wife, Margaret. *1600 Miccosukee Road; 850-877-4202.*

The outdoor **Tallahassee Museum of History and Natural Science** divides its 52 acres into several parts. One section is devoted to Florida's ecology and native creatures, such as the panther and red wolf. A 19th-century farm, schoolhouse, and church evoke pioneer times. On most days, workers in period costumes spin wool and perform other duties typical of the times. Also on the grounds is the **Bellevue Plantation Mansion,** whose exhibits trace the life of the aristocratic Catherine Daingerfield, the great-grandniece of George Washington and the wife of Napoleon Bonaparte's nephew. *3945 Museum Drive; 850-576-1636.*

■ CANOPY ROADS   *map pages 48–49, E-1/2*

Dappled light and aromatic breezes are what you may remember most about the famed canopy roads, so named because of the groves of green oaks that line them. Covered in Spanish moss, the trees look like Southern belles waving lacy handkerchiefs.

Tallahassee's five famous roads have been named among the best byways in America. They thread and twist through Tallahassee and into the countryside, where cotton plantations once thrived. For a copy of the driving tour, visit or call the Tallahassee visitors center in the New Capitol building.

Old St. Augustine Road, the oldest of the canopy roads, was built in the 1600s to connect the area's Franciscan missions with the city of St. Augustine. The road, which travels southeast from Tallahassee, was once the Pensacola–St. Augustine Highway, which was constructed in part by the slaves of a local planter. The nicest stretches lie between Capitol Circle and Williams Road.

Meridian Road (Route 155) starts in Tallahassee at the prime meridian marker (the starting point for all land surveys in the state) and heads north past lakes and

Some of the prettiest drives in the state follow the canopy roads of the Florida Panhandle.

farms to the Georgia border. Twelve miles north of town, on **Centerville Road** (Route 151), you'll find Bradley's Country Store (850-893-1647), famous for its homemade sausage and other specialties.

Miccosukee Road (Route 146), an old Indian footpath, served as a trade route for plantations, including Goodwood Plantation. **Old Bainbridge Road** (Route 361), the least scenic of the bunch, runs northwest toward Lake Jackson and the ancient Indian mounds.

■ WAKULLA SPRINGS *map pages 48–49, E-2*

> The Wakully River rises about ten miles N.W. of St. Mark's, from one of the finest springs in Florida, or perhaps in the world. It is of an oval form, the largest diameter of which is about six rods. It is of an unknown depth and perfectly transparent. In looking into it, the color resembles a clear blue sky, except near the border, where it has a slight tinge of green from the reflection of the surrounding verdure, which hangs over it in drooping branches and waving festoons.
>
> —John Lee Williams, *The Territory of Florida*, 1837

Wakulla Springs, south of Tallahassee, takes its name from the Amerindian word for "mystery." One of the many pure and beautiful springs of north Florida, it pumps 400,000 gallons of 70°F water per minute into the Wakulla River. At 360 feet deep, it's one of the world's largest and deepest freshwater springs. It is also one of the clearest, with visibility ranging up to 100 feet. According to Indian legend, "small water people, four inches tall, with long hair, once held dances in the depths of the springs on moonlit nights, and at a certain hour a warrior appeared in a stone canoe, frightening them away."

The spring waters are enjoyed by creatures great and small. The river into which it flows is lined with cypress, pine, beech, and majestic live oaks wearing shawls of tattered Spanish moss. Alligators swim in the river, and birds—ruby-throated hummingbirds, purple gallinules, and anhingas, among others—are

Many springs feed the region's freshwater lakes, including bucolic Lake Talquin, west of Tallahassee.

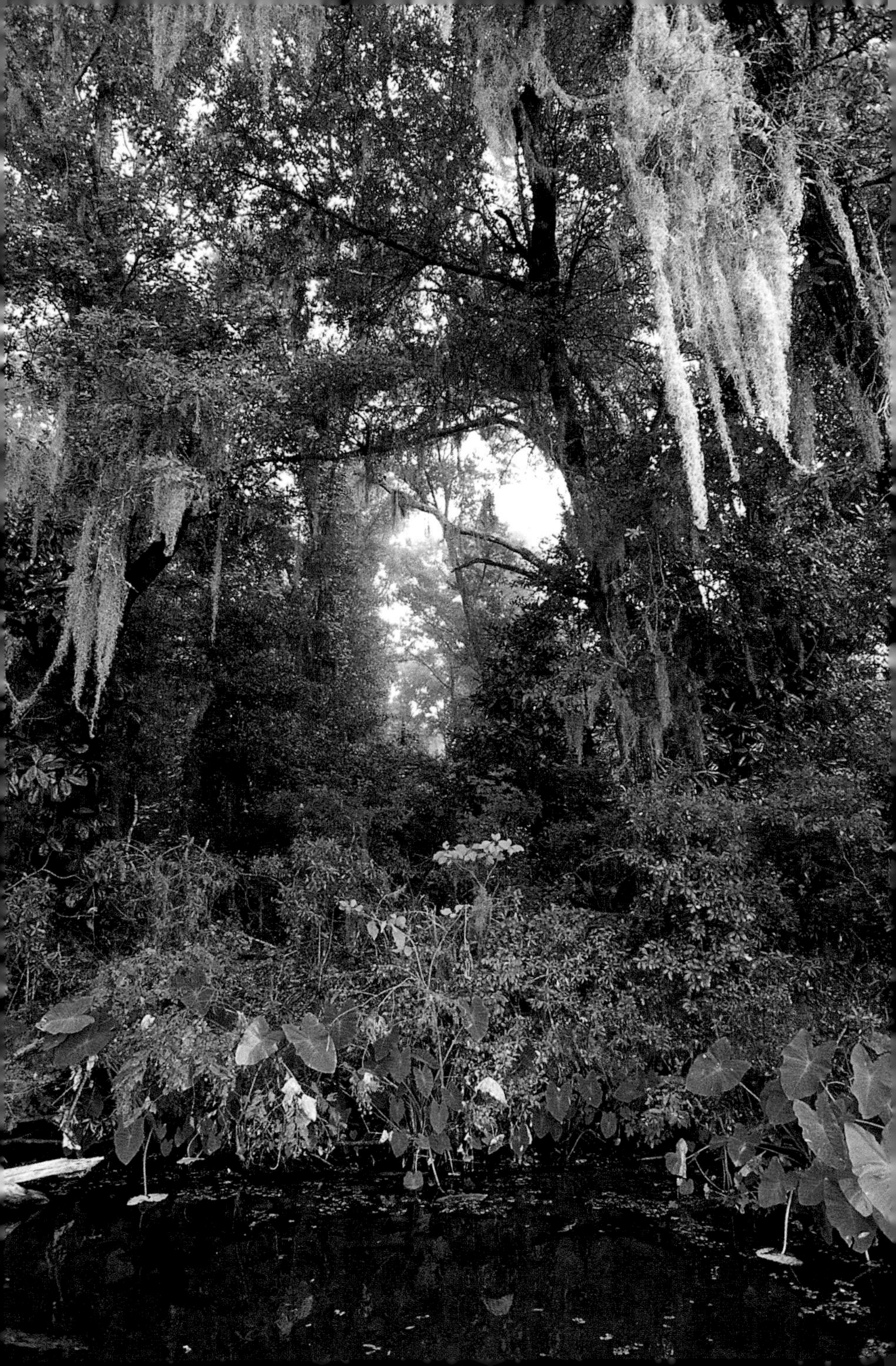

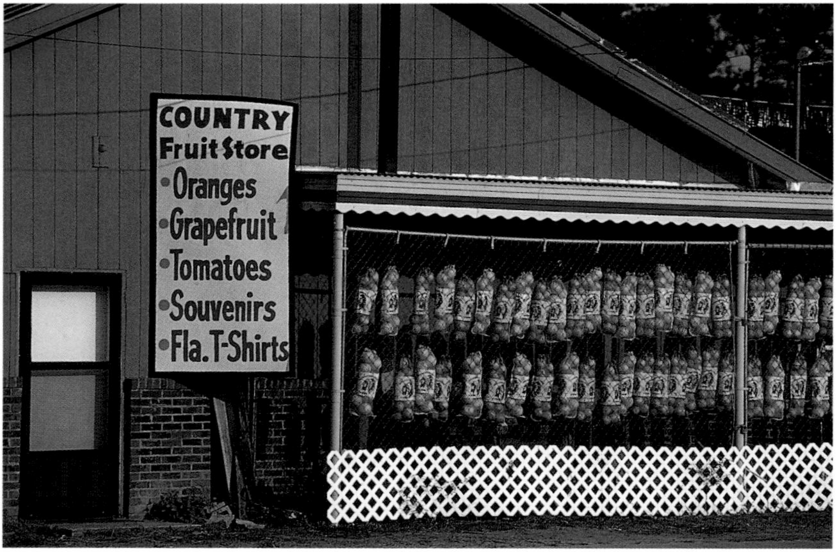

A fruit stand along a quiet back road.

abundant. (Anhingas are easy to spot out of the water, as they have a snakelike neck and are usually perched on a branch or piling with their wings hung out to dry.) Not surprisingly, Hollywood filmed two Tarzan movies here.

In 1937, at the edge of Wakulla Springs, a railroad magnate named Edward Ball built himself a magnificent lodge with marble floors and hand-painted cypress beams. Today, Wakulla Lodge is open to the public and provides lodging and food. The lodge is fronted by a cypress-rimmed beach—climb the diving platform for an unforgettable view. Glass-bottom boats run daily tours of the spring and the river. *Fourteen miles south of Tallahassee at State Road 267 and State Road 61; 850-224-5950.*

←🚗→*Route 363 between Tallahassee and St. Marks is an interesting and lovely forested drive. The Tallahassee–St. Marks Historic Railroad State Trail follows Route 363 from Capital Circle (State Road 261) south out of Tallahassee for 20 miles to St. Marks, and is used by cyclists, hikers, skaters, and horseback riders.* *See map pages 48–49.*

■ SAN MARCOS DE APALACHEE HISTORIC SITE

map pages 48–49, E-3

Apalachee Indians once raised corn, beans, and squash at the confluence of the Wakulla and St. Marks Rivers, 20 miles south of Tallahassee. When the Spanish built missions here, they traded for these foods and shipped them to other Spanish settlements. A fort from the 1600s, San Marcos de Apalachee, remains on the spot. The museum here has artifacts and other materials that relate the early importance of the town. *South end of Route 363; 850-922-6007.*

History in this region is so rich that a timeline is helpful:

1528   Pánfilo de Narváez arrives with 400 men, looking for gold; he finds none.

1539   Hernando de Soto arrives with 600 men. In 1679, the Spanish governor of Florida constructs a fort on the site. Four years later, pirates burn and loot it.

1739   A new fort is built. The British own it briefly, then return it to the Spanish.

1800   British officer William Augustus Bowles, leading a band of Creek Indians, takes control of the fort, but the Spanish send a fleet to retake it.

1818   U.S. General Andrew Jackson takes over the fort from the Spanish to fight the Indians and English. He returns the fort to the Spanish later that year.

1821   The fort, along with Florida, becomes a U.S. possession.

1861   The Confederate army takes the fort and names it Fort Ward.

1865   The fort reverts to U.S. authority.

An 1842 lithograph of the Magnolia Plantation in St. Marks. (Florida State Archives)

■ ST. MARKS NATIONAL WILDLIFE REFUGE
map pages 48–49, F-3

St. Marks National Wildlife Refuge is a 70,000-acre marsh and woodlands preserve renowned for its monarch butterfly migrations and marvelous bird life. There are 75 miles of trails. *Route 363; 850-925-6121.*

A century ago, this area became the home of Charles Pennock, a Philadelphian who settled into a small shack here to observe egrets, herons, swallow-tailed kites, and gray kingbirds. Such a pursuit takes patience, as does reading some of his observations. But his anthropomorphic musings, reprinted in the refuge's newsletter, convey the liveliness of the skies above him.

> At time while passing high overhead, a flock will perform evolutions seemingly in dispute as to a course to be pursued, and a general circling and counter circling will continue for two or three minutes, when perhaps a direct flight will ensue for a few minutes, and again more confusion and circling, the whole performance enlivened by most emphatic demands and protests by apparently every member of the flock.

(above) A sparrow alighting on a lily pad in the St. Marks National Wildlife Refuge.
(opposite) St. George Island monarch butterfly.

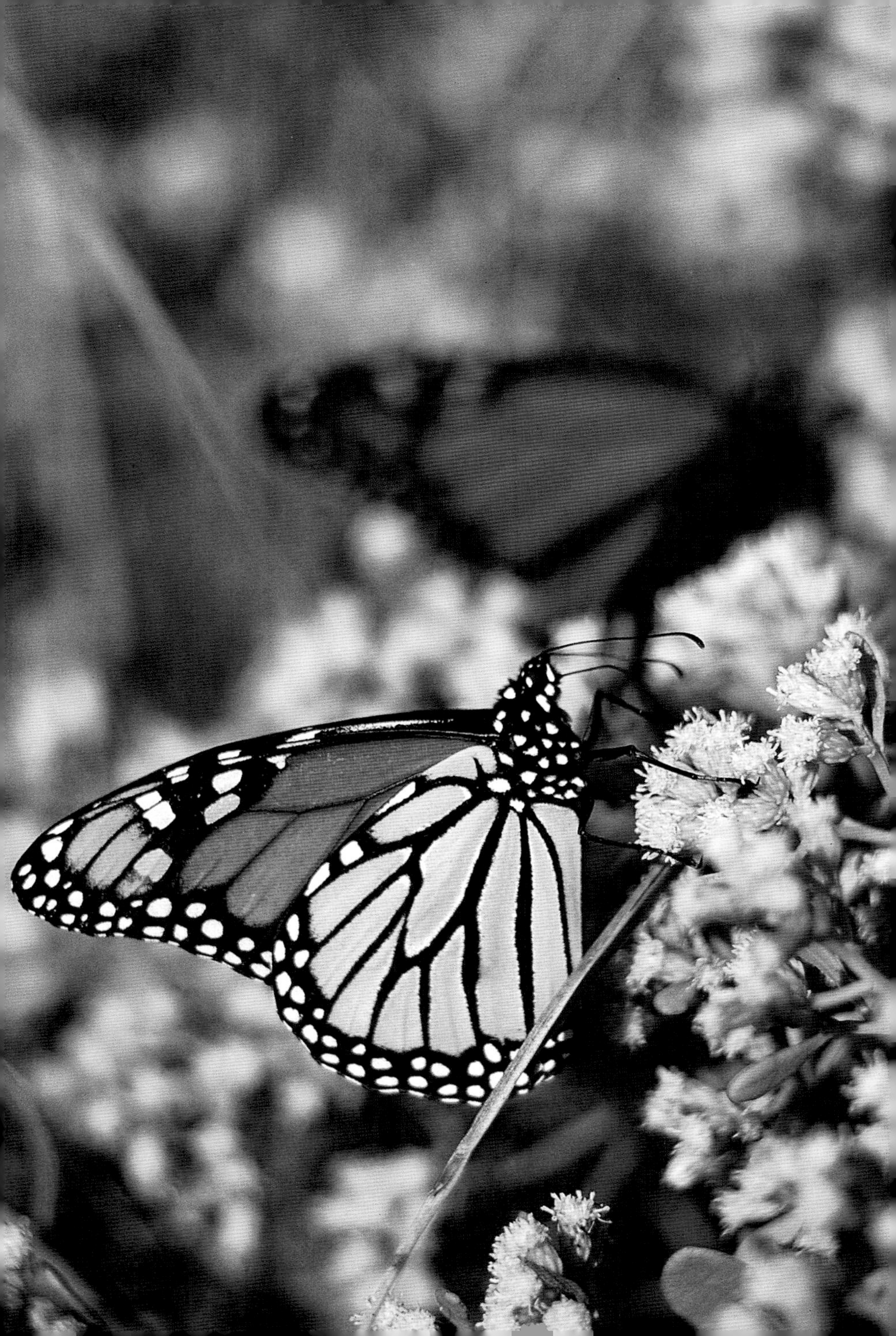

Funky fish houses selling oysters and other seafood line Highway 98 as it heads west along the Gulf Coast from Carrabelle and Eastpoint en route to Apalachicola.

■ CARRABELLE *map pages 48–49, E-3*

Though the Chamber of Commerce promotes this tiny bayside hamlet as the Pearl of the Panhandle, locals know it as the "drinking village with a fishing problem." In addition to having the world's smallest police station (a phone booth off U.S. 98), this oddball port town of 1,600 has something much harder to capture on a postcard: a limited shelf life. Proposed luxury developments in the area have speculators gobbling up waterfront real estate, and shiny new sportfishing boats and motor yachts are becoming familiar sights among the rusted shrimp boats that line the sagging docks. There's even a gourmet coffee shop, **Carrabelle Junction** (88 Tallahassee Street; 850-697-9550), whose proprietor, Ron Gempel, is convinced he'll soon have a run on lattes. "It could be 15 minutes or 20 years," he says of the impending economic boom, "but everyone knows it's going to happen sooner or later."

Oyster boats and oystermen of Apalachicola Bay.

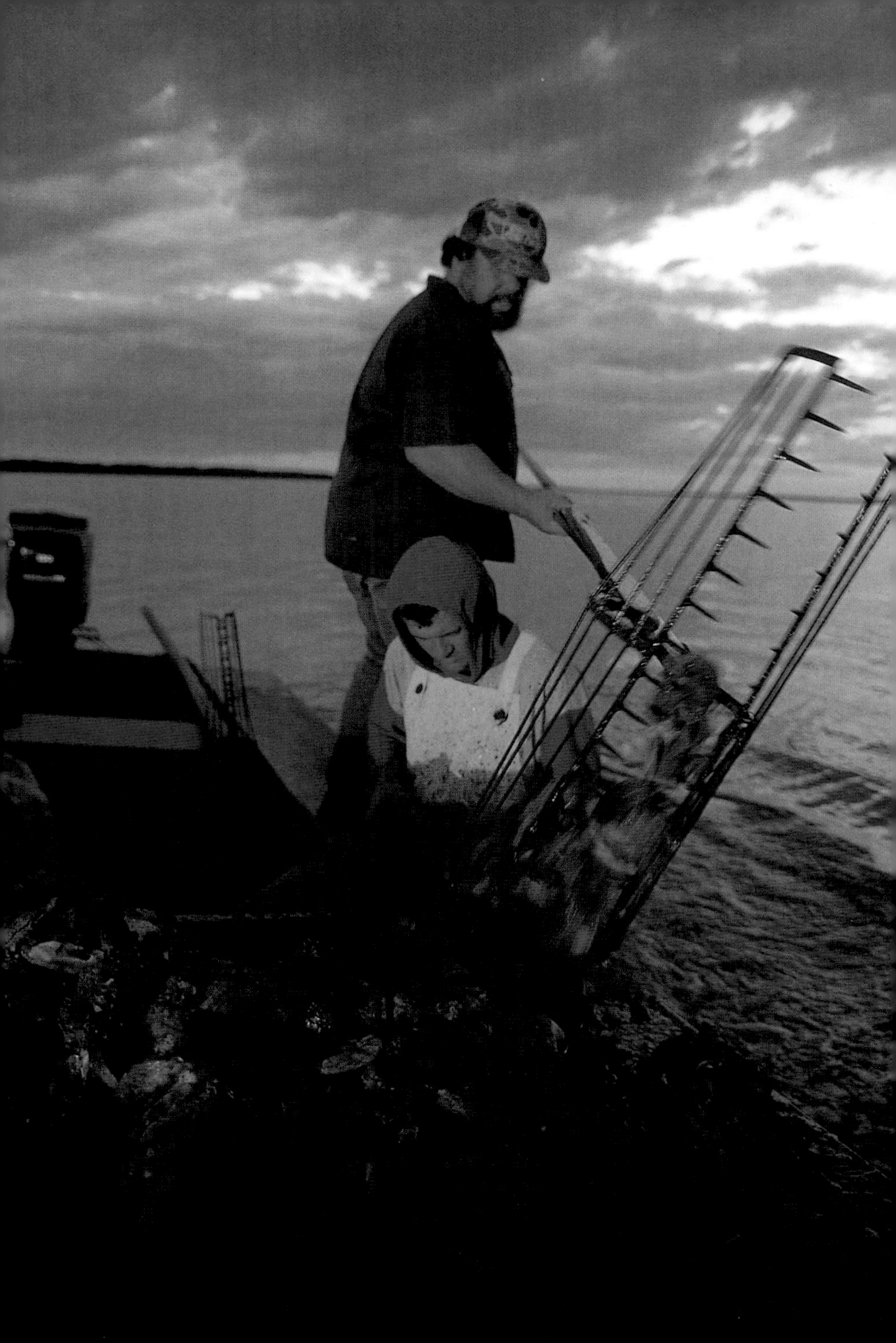

■ St. George Island *map pages 48–49, D/E-3*

St. George Island, reached by bridge from Eastpoint, is best known for **St. George Island State Park,** on Gulf Drive East at the island's eastern point. Here, flat sands gradually rise into low dunes and scrub vegetation. Twisted, weather-beaten magnolias and pines, looking like elaborate twigs buried in snow drifts, dot the landscape. At wide points in the island, slash pines and live oaks grow to full size, surrounded by wild rosemary, reindeer moss, and wildflowers. Leeside, salt marshes support reeds, snakes, turtles, and fish. You can fish, hike, sea kayak, or camp. In summer, loggerhead and green sea turtles lay their eggs on the beach. To the west is a small commercial district with restaurants, an ever-growing number of condos, and a small public beach.

■ Apalachicola *map pages 48–49, D-3*

Apalachicola is one of those small towns that everyone seems to fall in love with. Each time I cross the bridge over the river from Eastpoint, I am once again enchanted by the historic riverfront warehouses, the three-story 1907 **Gibson Inn**

Apalachicola on the Apalachicola River.

(51 Avenue C; 850-653-8282), and the clapboard houses along Chestnut Street, some with pillars and porches, some with gingerbread molding.

The Greek Revival–style **Trinity Episcopal Church,** built in the late 1830s, has been holding services in its original building for more than 150 years. The church was built in sections in New York and then shipped via schooner to "Apalach" and assembled. The handsome columns at the entrance are handcrafted, and the grounds are a nature lover's paradise. Trinity Episcopal is listed on the National Register of Historic Places. *79 Sixth Street; 850-653-9550.*

Buildings throughout the compact historic district are fun to tour and help tell the story of Apalachicola, which, over the past century and a half, has been an important cotton-shipping port, sponging center, and lumber center. Folks boast that the town, which was blockaded by Yankees during the Civil War, has more antebellum architecture than anywhere else in Florida.

On Water Street, you'll find mountains of sun-bleached oyster shells, monuments to the area's biggest commercial enterprise. Apalachicola Bay oysters are among the best anywhere. Surrounding Franklin County claims to harvest most of Florida's oyster supply. The industry employs more than a thousand county residents.

■ **CAPE SAN BLAS** *map pages 48–49, D-3*

West of Apalachicola, U.S. 98 takes a turn away from the coast into a cathedral of pines, an especially scenic drive along County Road C-30 that extends to remote Cape San Blas. The reward for this out-of-the-way foray is **St. Joseph Peninsula State Park,** at the end of Route 30E, where dunes hide beachcombers from the world and where a wildlife refuge provides protection for coyotes, sea turtles, and more than 200 bird species. Cape San Blas is ghostly quiet, except when a squadron from the nearby air force base swoops by. Camping and cabins accommodate those who wish to linger in the restful state park. *8899 Cape San Blas Road; 850-227-1327.*

■ **PANAMA CITY BEACH** *map pages 48–49, C-2*

Ever since MTV started broadcasting its spring-break special from here in the mid-1990s, Panama City Beach's reputation as the University of Sun and Fun has grown exponentially. Unless you're an all-night party type (or are in the market for a pierced eyebrow), avoid this town in March and April. The rest of the year, it's a

Panama City Beach has become the most popular spring-break party scene in the state.

good value, known for wall-to-wall miniature golf courses, race-car tracks, video arcades, kiddie parks, and miles of motels and condos.

St. Andrews State Recreation Area, at the eastern extreme of Panama City Beach, is a 20-mile-long stretch of voluptuous dunes and beaches. Fishing is great on all sides—Gulf, bay, and at the pass—and piers are provided on the Gulf and bay sides. At the pass, rock jetties accommodate anglers trying to snag whatever comes in or out with the tides. Snorkelers dive to watch the marine parade in warm, turquoise waters.

Shell Island, an uninhabited barrier island across the pass, is part of the recreation area. Tours leave from the Jetty Dive Shop and take day-trippers to the island for beachcombing, shell-hunting, and snorkeling. You can also take one of the commercial charters outside of the park. *Shell Island Boat Tours; 850-234-7245.*

The mainland campground has sites near the water, and a reconstructed turpentine still recalls the region's earliest industry. Nature trails wind off into the wilds. Marinas along Thomas Drive offer dolphin-spotting charters, dive boats, sight-seeing excursions, and nature tours in glass-bottom boats. *St. Andrews Recreation Area, Panama City Beach; 850-233-5140.*

←🚗→*Northwest of Panama City Beach, the coastline breaks from the mainland where the wide Choctawhatchee Bay creates a peninsula that stretches for 20 miles to Destin. Follow scenic route signs off of U.S. 98 along County Road C-30A to find two neighboring coastal towns, Seaside and Grayton Beach, that have been getting a lot of attention in recent years.*

■ SEASIDE *map pages 48–49, B-2*

Seaside came into existence in 1982 as the result of one man's nostalgia for his childhood. Developer and New Urbanist Robert Davis envisioned a coastal town where people could sit on front porches, stroll down quiet lanes, and take their children for picnics on the beach. Sounds simple, but Seaside is anything but. Strict building codes require that home builders use only tin roofs and wood siding. Victorian-style homes, all painted like colorful Easter eggs, are standard-issue, but no two on the same street can look alike, which is more than can be said of Florida's countless other subdivisions.

Homes in Seaside.

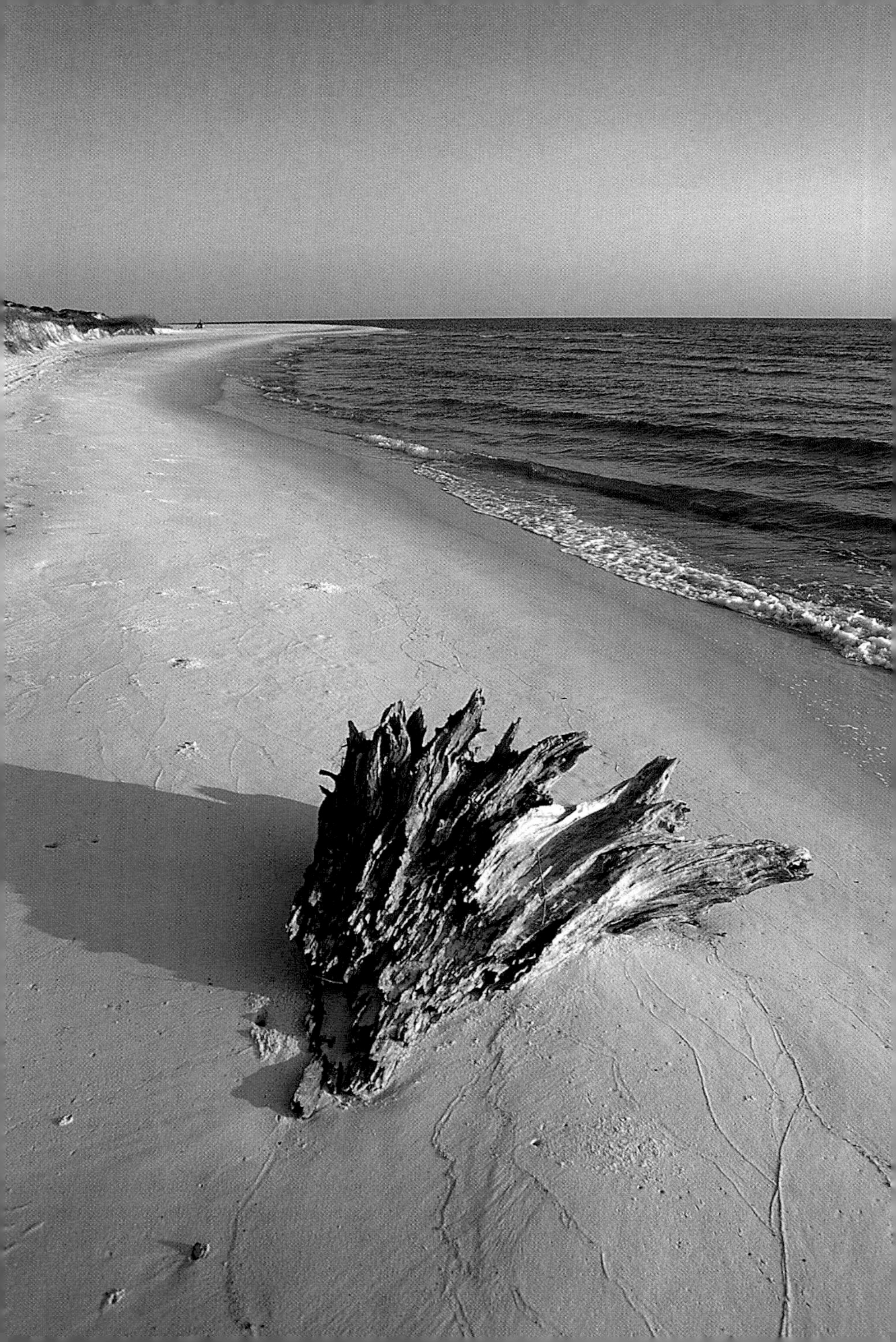

Cars are banned from some streets, and there are high-end shops and restaurants and a market. Visitors can't help but stop to look around, and some actually recognize it as the set for the 1998 movie *The Truman Show.* The residential resort is complemented by the **Seaside Institute** (30 Smolian Circle; 850-231-2421), which hosts seminars, workshops for writers and artists, and children's activities.

Seaside is a magnet for artists. Ruskin Place, at the town's center, is a plaza with galleries and craft shops where you can get complimentary coffee or sign up for painting lessons. In 2002, Seaside proved its commitment to the arts by sponsoring its first annual **Florida Jazz Festival** (877-352-5299) in April at the Seaside Lyceum. The three-day festival drew eager crowds and jazz luminaries, such as Al Jarreau and Diane Reeves. Years ago, Seaside stood out like some sort of gingerbread mirage. Now, it more or less blends in with its many imitators.

■ GRAYTON BEACH *map pages 48–49, B/C-2*

Grayton Beach, a few miles west of Seaside, is a hippie artist town that appears to be struggling with its current, trendier look. People pass through on their way to **Grayton Beach State Recreational Area,** with its white sands and aquamarine waters. The park's pine-fringed lake, set all around with snow-white sand, can fool you into thinking you've stepped into a mountain scene. Visitors come to swim, sunbathe, picnic, fish, and camp. *County Road 30A off U.S. 98; 850-231-4210.*

In town, roads front old cottages and their modern counterparts built up on stilts. But don't let the folksiness throw you. Grayton Beach's restaurants include **Criollas** (170 East County Road 30A), whose Caribbean-influenced fare is some of the best in Florida.

■ DESTIN AND THE EMERALD COAST *map pages 48–49, B-2*

Okaloosa County and Walton County quibble over rights to their emerald-color coastal waters. Okaloosa County claims the water for itself, but many people use the name to describe the length of the entire western Panhandle coast.

In the late 1970s, Destin, in Okaloosa County, underwent a radical transformation from a quiet fishing village to a tourist destination. Today, it's buried under a welter of family amusement centers, like **Big Kahuna's Lost Paradise** (1007 Highway 98 East; 850-837-4061), a 23-acre water park with a 54-hole tropical golf course, body flumes, pools, slides, and white-water tubing.

St. Joseph Peninsula State Park, south of Panama City, on the Gulf of Mexico.

The beach at Destin.

The beaches of the Emerald Coast are gorgeous, with sand so bright it hurts to look at it. The best beach access is at the east end of Destin, at **Henderson Beach State Recreation Area** (17000 Emerald Coast Parkway) and at **James W. Lee Park** (Scenic Highway 98).

On the west end of town, you'll see advertisements for snorkeling, diving, shelling, fishing, sight-seeing tours, party boat tours, and charter boats. All manner of saltwater fish get pulled out of the sea, but the billfishing is the most celebrated. Destin's grandest event is the **Fishing Rodeo** and attendant **Seafood Festival,** held every October.

■ FORT WALTON BEACH *map pages 48–49, B-2*

Across the high bridge from Destin, you enter Okaloosa Island via its backyard and most attractive face, a dunes area run by the U.S. Air Force and Gulf Islands National Seashore. It looks at times like a set for *Star Wars,* especially where odd domed structures rise out of the tufted sand mounds. **Beasley County Park,** at the edge of civilization, is the best place for beach-bumming.

Fort Walton Beach's main beach is a tangle of kiddie castles, racetracks, putt-putt golf, roller-coasters, bumper cars, and the usual assortment of singles-oriented bars you'd find in any city with a large military population.

The popular **Gulfarium** presents dolphin and sea lion shows daily, and has a dolphin interaction program that allows guests to get up close and personal with Kiwi and Daphne, two pantropical spotted dolphins. *1010 Miracle Strip Parkway SE, Fort Walton Beach; 850-244-5169 or 850-243-9046.*

Every June, the town celebrates a **Billy Bowlegs Festival** in honor of William Augustus Bowles. This is somewhat confusing since the real Billy Bowlegs and William Augustus Bowles were two very different people—the former a Seminole Indian chief, the latter a British adventurer.

Eglin Air Force Base, across the bridge on the mainland, is one of the largest air force bases in the world—roughly the size of Rhode Island. Its **Air Force Armament Museum** displays 20th-century bombs and bomber aircraft. *100 Museum Drive, off Route 85; 850-882-4062.*

Indian Temple Mound and Museum provides evidence of a much earlier presence in these parts. It took 100,000 cubic feet of soil to build the 12-foot-high mound that rests here, a labor-intensive undertaking carried out by the Native Americans who lived here 600 years ago. The museum has a large collection of Southeastern Indian pottery. *139 Miracle Strip Parkway SE; 850-833-9595.*

■ **PENSACOLA BEACH** *map pages 48–49, A-2*

Pensacola Beach shares the narrow barrier island of Santa Rosa with the community of Navarre Beach, at the island's eastern end. Pensacola Beach is more attractive than its neighbor, in part because Navarre Beach suffered the brunt of Hurricane Opal in 1995.

I am always dazed by the otherworldliness of the white dunes here, which are made brighter by the green and blue hues of the water. The more remote section of the park sweeps across miles and miles between Pensacola Beach and Navarre Beach, a stretch of wide-open space, low vegetation, and soft, bright sand. The water is a luminous green in the warmer months (from April through September), and deep blue in the winter (from November through March). A sign at the Santa Rosa Day Use Area reads "OPAL BEACH," a tribute to the beach-relocation job achieved by Hurricane Opal. Next to a "NO ROADSIDE PARKING" sign, you may see a hapless motorist trying to extricate his car from a sand drift.

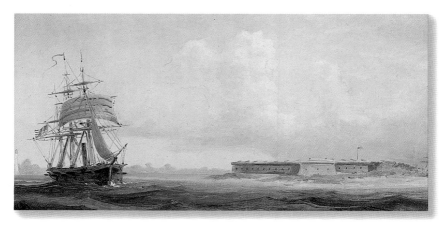

Xanthus R. Smith painted this scene of Fort Pickens, Pensacola, in 1864, soon after his discharge from the Union army. (Sam and Robbie Vickers Florida Collection)

■ **FORT PICKENS AREA**   *map pages 48–49, A-2/3*

Fort Pickens, built between 1829 and 1834, was one of three forts on the Gulf of Mexico that remained in Union hands throughout the Civil War, and it served as Florida's Union headquarters. In 1861, troops at the fort exchanged cannon fire once with Confederate forces occupying the two forts on the other side of Pensacola Bay; the forts were heavily damaged in the exchange, and the Confederates eventually fled. Later, between 1886 and 1888, the Apache warrior Geronimo and his band were kept here under house arrest in a shameless, albeit successful, ploy to attract tourists: you can still buy a postcard with his image on it at the smart little gift shop. The compound itself is a mishmash of fortifications dating from the Civil War through World War II, but the view across the bay is worth the drive. The museum here displays Civil War–era weaponry, and there's a fishing pier. Guided tours are available. *End of Fort Pickens Road, Gulf Islands National Seashore; 850-934-2600.*

■ **DON TRISTAN DE LUNA'S LANDING PLACE**

En route to Fort Pickens, at the island's western extreme, stands a rather haunting white cross on the slope of a steep dune. This marks the spot where Don Tristan

THE ADVENTURES OF WILLIAM BOWLES

Toward the end of the 18th century, a colorful adventurer named William Augustus Bowles, along with a band of Creek Indian warriors, raided Spanish settlements between St. Marks and Pensacola. Dismissed from the British navy for insubordination, he moved to Georgia, where he married a Creek princess and became commander-in-chief of the tribe's warriors. Bowles attempted to establish a multiracial, independent state called Muskogee, which was populated by Indians, escaped slaves, and white settlers. In 1793,

William Augustus Bowles. (Florida State Archives)

Bowles was captured by the Spanish and imprisoned in Madrid. After six years, he escaped by jumping off a prison ship near the coast of Africa and swimming to Sierra Leone. In 1799, he returned to Florida and continued looting Spanish settlements and ships. He was captured again in 1803 and imprisoned in Havana, where he died two years later.

de Luna and his settlers celebrated Mass in August 1559. De Luna, a wealthy Spanish nobleman, had been part of the explorer Francisco Vasquez de Coronado's expedition to the southwestern United States to locate the fabled seven cities of Cibola (the golden cities sighted by survivors of the Narváez expedition, which turned out to be Indian pueblos "gold-plated" by the light of the setting sun).

In 1548, de Luna had directed the "pacification" of the Mitla Indians of Oaxaca, Mexico. In 1559, he gathered 500 soldiers and 1,000 settlers, including Spanish farmers, Indians, blacks, artisans, women, and children, and embarked from the east coast of Mexico in 13 ships, with 240 horses, weapons, farm tools, and seeds. Earlier, de Luna had written glowingly of the Pensacola area:

> Seamen say that it is the best port in the Indies, and the site which has been selected for founding the town is no less good, for it is a high point of land which slopes down to the bay where the ships come to anchor. Concerning the country…it seems to be healthy. It is somewhat sandy, from which I judge that it will not yield much bread. There are pine trees, live oaks, and many other kinds of trees. Until now, there have appeared in this bay a few Indian fishermen only.

De Luna's colonists met with one disaster after another, including shipwrecks, hurricanes, and hunger. They eventually abandoned the area.

■ MAIN BEACH AND QUIETWATER BEACH

A couple of beaches in Pensacola Beach proper provide all the amenities you'll need for a day at the shore. There are shops, food concessions, bandstands, and places to rent gear for various water sports. Main Beach, which some locals still call Casino Beach, is the center of town. Surfers and their fans head there. Quietwater Beach lines bay waters, making it the

(above) Fort Pickens National Park.
(opposite) A lithograph depicting the Pensacola dock in the 1880s, when it was one of the busiest ports in the southeastern United States. (Florida State Archives)

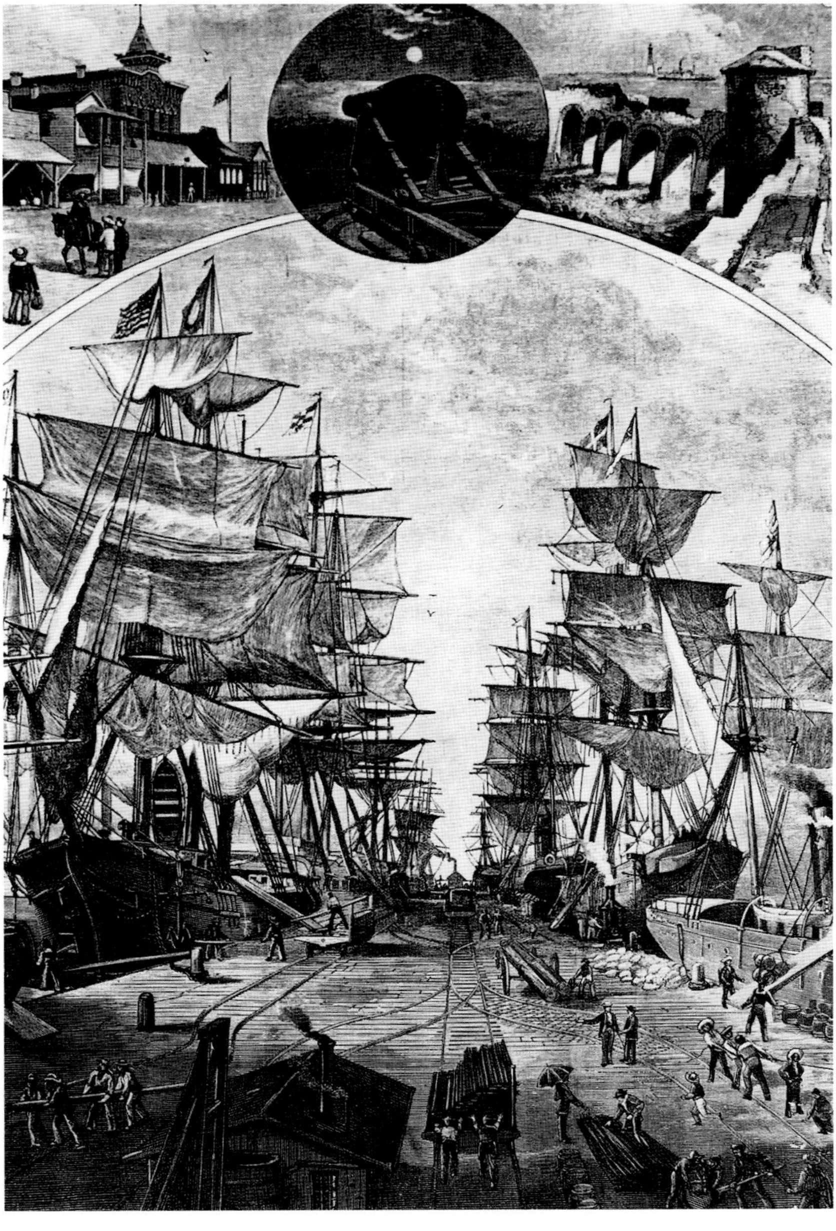

A local relaxes on the front porch of her Pensacola home.

preferred choice of small children and jet skiers. The **Pensacola Beach Gulf Pier** (41 Fort Pickens Road; 850-934-7200) purports to be the longest fishing pier on the Gulf of Mexico, but when it comes to watching sunsets, size doesn't matter. The view from the pier is the next best thing to witnessing the sun sink below the horizon from the prow of a great ship.

■ PENSACOLA *map pages 48–49, A-2*

The buildings in downtown Pensacola tell the story of this town's checkered past. The region was passed among Spain, France, England, and the United States. Unlike Mobile, Alabama, 59 miles west along the coast, Pensacola is not known for long avenues of oak trees or lush Southern gardens. What it does have is a blend of French, Spanish, and Georgian architecture that you can appreciate by visiting the historic districts of Seville, Palafox, and North Hill.

The **Historic Pensacola Village,** a complex of buildings in the Seville Historic District, provides a glimpse into the city's past. You can pick up a walking-tour map in the office of the T. T. Wentworth, Jr. Florida State Museum (330 South Jefferson

An example of folk Victorian architecture in the Seville Historic District.

Street), described below. The tour includes the **Museum of Industry** (200 East Zaragoza Street), which traces Pensacola's history through eras of fishing, brick-making, railroading, and lumbering; the **Museum of Commerce** (201 East Zaragoza Street), which houses an 1890s trolley car and a collection of horse-drawn buggies; and **Julee Cottage** (210 East Zaragoza Street), the home of an early-19th-century free black woman, Julee Paton, that is now a museum of local black history.

The **T. T. Wentworth, Jr. Florida State Museum** houses the oddities of Wentworth, a politician and tax collector who caught the collecting bug the day he found a gold coin along the waterfront. In time, his vast holdings took on a Ripley's Believe-It-or-Not quality and included a shrunken head, the world's largest pair of shoes, and a petrified cat. Wentworth left his curiosities to the state, which now displays them along with more traditional exhibits. *Historic Pensacola Village; 850-595-5985.*

The small **Civil War Soldier's Museum** addresses Pensacola's role in the war with exhibits of uniforms, photographs, and weaponry. *108 South Palafox Street; 850-469-1900.*

The Blue Angels perform air shows in November at Pensacola Naval Air Station.

One of the town's finest attractions, the Pensacola Naval Air Station's **National Museum of Naval Aviation,** illustrates the important role the armed forces have played in the local economy. Suspended from the glass-and-steel ceiling of the seven-story atrium are four aircraft set in diamond formation. Three are F-4 Skyhawks flown by the famous navy stunt fliers, the Blue Angels. A full-motion flight simulator, a test-cockpit trainer, and anti-aircraft guns add a hands-on dimension to the museum. The seven-story IMAX theater shows films shot from the cockpit of some of the world's fastest aircraft. The Pensacola Lighthouse and Fort Barrancas—a temporary Confederate stronghold, now a scenic park—are also here. *Eight-and-a-half miles south of town on Blue Angel Parkway; 850-452-3604.*

■ BIG LAGOON STATE RECREATION AREA
map pages 48–49, A-3

This 700-acre park on the Alabama state border provides a home for gray foxes, cardinals, and nuthatches on the mainland shore. There are camping and picnic facilities, and nature programs interpret life on the beach and along the trails. *12301 Gulf Beach Highway; 850-492-1595.*

■ **PERDIDO KEY** *map pages 48–49, A-3*

Shared between Florida and Alabama, Perdido Key presides over the westernmost stretch of Florida's portion of Gulf Islands National Seashore. Visitors crowd the parking lot at Perdido Key State Recreation Area, which provides beach conveniences and bayside bird-watching. The Alabama state line is marked with a sign, but the **Flora-Bama Lounge** is a more familiar landmark, as it's the site of the annual (in April) Interstate Mullet Toss, in which folks are given trophies for how far they can throw a fish into Alabama. This is also the site of the Frank Brown International Songwriters Festival in November, when more than 150 professional minstrels fill the island and its town with music. *17401 Perdido Key Drive; 850-492-0611.*

■ **TRAVEL BASICS**

Getting Around: Interstate 10 cuts through the breadth of the Panhandle—roughly midway between the Gulf and the Alabama border—and is the route of choice if you're trying to get somewhere quickly. For the most part, it traverses open country and is fast and pleasant. U.S. 98 curves along the shore, passing through the area's most tourist-heavy towns and skirting its glorious beaches, but traffic is slower. Radiating in all directions from Tallahassee are the famous canopy roads.

Climate: The Panhandle, unlike much of the state, has four distinct seasons. Winters are cool (40°–65°F), the temperature dropping below freezing about 20 nights out of the year. Inland, it even snows about once every seven years. Summers are muggy and hot (75°–90°F), with thunderstorms about every other day. Fall is the driest time of year, with mild temperatures. The interior of the Panhandle experiences the widest range of temperatures in the state: from a record high of 109°F at Monticello to a record low of -2°F at Tallahassee. Hurricanes strike the coast of the Panhandle, sometimes with devastating effect. Hurricane season is from June through September.

CENTRAL GULF COAST

■ OVERVIEW

The Gulf Coast between Cedar Key and Weeki Wachee is full of natural beauty. Manatees, black bears, alligators, and bald eagles live in and around the region's wetlands and rivers. Fishing towns are found along the northern coastal area. Farther south, large residential and resort communities have been built on the barrier islands west of urban Clearwater, Tampa, and St. Petersburg. The emphasis in this region is on the beach; millions of people come here to swim, fish, sail, and play volleyball.

Two big cities face each other across Tampa Bay: St. Petersburg, a popular tourist town and retirement area, has art galleries, a lively downtown, and good shopping. Tampa, a center for communications, transportation, and tourism, preserves its Latin roots in historic Ybor City, once known for Cuban-cigar manufacturing, and now a place to come for food, drink, and nightlife.

Fishing boats on the Steinhatchee River.

The entire southern third of the Tampa peninsula is occupied by MacDill Air Force Base, home to the United States Central Command, which coordinates all U.S. military operations in Africa and the Middle East.

■ Big Bend Area

map this page, A/B-1

The Panhandle meets the peninsula at the Big Bend region, whose coast is characterized by marshy shores, turtle-grass flats, and fishing towns. Local promoters call it the Nature Coast. The 91-mile **Historic Big Bend Saltwater Paddling Trail** (904-838-1306) follows the Gulf Coast from St. Marks to Cedar Key and attracts canoeists, who camp at sites along the way and spend the days gliding along the Big Bend River, hearing only the flap of egret wings and, in summer, the buzz of mosquitoes.

■ Keaton Beach and Steinhatchee

Most residents of Keaton Beach and Steinhatchee like to fish, and recreational scalloping is allowed in these sleepy towns from July through September. Many others snorkel for scallops, which are found in the sand of shallow bays and inland waters.

The village of Suwannee lies where the Suwannee River—of "way down upon" fame—ends its 200-mile journey from Georgia's Okefenokee Swamp and empties its waters into the Gulf of Mexico. In Suwannee, you can rent a houseboat for a voyage upriver through clear waters, and alongside riverbanks lined with moss-draped cypress, cedar, and oak.

CENTRAL GULF COAST
0 10 20 Miles
0 10 20 30 Kilometers
Salem
Cooks Hammock
Dekle Beach
Keaton Beach
PINEY POINT
Steinhatchee
Jena
Shamrock
Old Town
Big Bend Paddling Trail
BLAIR POINT
Manatee Springs State Park
Horseshoe Bay
HORSESHOE POINT
Horseshoe Cove
Fowler Bluff
Suwannee
HOG ISLAND
Rosewood
Gulf Hammock
Waccasassa Bay State Preserve
Waccasassa Bay
Cedar Key
Cedar Key State Museum
CEDAR KEYS
Cedar Key National Wildlife Refuge
Gainesville
Trenton
Chiefland
Archer
To Stephen Foster St Folk Culture Center
Raleigh
Williston
Otter Creek
Morriston
Lebanon
Dunnellon
Inglis
Yankeetown
Citrus Springs
Red Level
Crystal River State Archaeological Site
Crystal River
Crystal Bay
Crystal River Nat'l Wildlife Refuge
Beverly Hills
Lecanto
Inverness
Homosassa Springs
Yulee Sugar Mill Ruins
Homosassa
Floral City
Chassahowitzka
Withlacoochee State Forest
Gulf of Mexico
Bayport
Brooksville
Weeki Wachee Spring
Weeki Wachee
Spring Hill
Aripeka
Masaryktown
Hudson
Darby
Bayonet Point
Port Richey
New Port Richey
Anclote
Denham
Anclote Island State Preserve
Odessa
Tarpon Springs
Palm Harbor
Honeymoon Island State Park
Oldsmar
Caladesi Island State Park
Dunedin
Clearwater
Largo
Indian Rocks Beach
Tampa
Redington Beach
St Petersburg
Madeira Beach
Treasure Island
St Pete Beach
Tampa Bay
Ruskin
Sun City
MULLET KEY
Egmont Key Lighthouse
EGMONT KEY
Sunshine Skyway
Gillette
Parrish
Palmetto
Lake Manatee State Rec Area
ANNA MARIA ISLAND
Holmes Beach
Bradenton
Samoset
Bradenton Beach
Longboat Key
LONGBOAT KEY
Sarasota
LIDO KEY

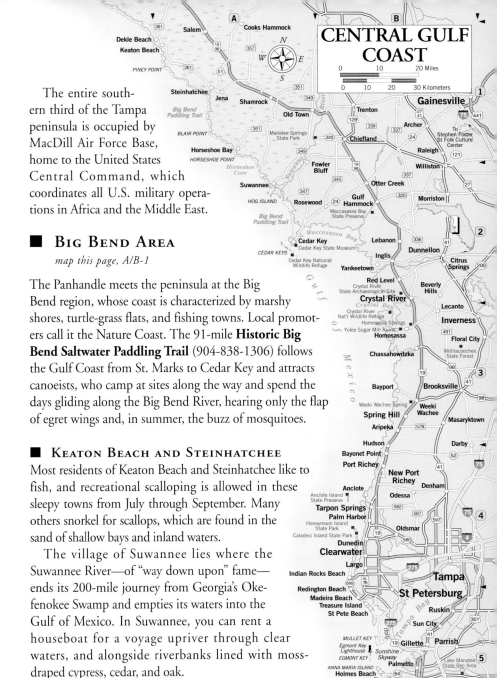

Canoeing in Manatee Springs, by the Suwannee River.

■ MANATEE SPRINGS STATE PARK   *map page 81, A-1*

One of the springs that feeds the Suwannee River is found at Manatee Springs State Park. This spring is one of the nation's 75 first-magnitude springs (27 are in Florida), a term used to describe an average flow of more than 100 cubic feet per second. Swimmers, snorkelers, and cave divers enjoy the spring's cool, azure waters, and hikers and bicyclists make use of a pleasant 8-mile trail. Manatees, which are best seen from the viewing platform or boardwalk, are usually here November through April, when the 72° springwater is warmer than the Gulf or river. Turtles, fish, egrets, and other wildlife, as well as the park's lush flora, can be enjoyed year-round. *County Road 320, 6 miles west of Chiefland; 352-493-6072.*

■ STEPHEN FOSTER STATE FOLK CULTURE CENTER
map page 81, B-1

The center is dedicated to the songwriter who penned the state song, "Old Folks at Home." The 97 tubular bells in the carillon tower ring out Foster's famous song, among others. At the park, artisans demonstrate pottery, stained glass, wood-carving, quilting, and candle-making. *White Springs; 386-397-2733.*

■ CEDAR KEY *map page 81, A-2*

Approximately 100 low-lying keys or islands surround the historic town of Cedar Key, but only one, Way Key, is inhabited and bridged to the mainland. Cedar Key, the island's single town, is relaxed, with a population of about 800 permanent residents, less than half of what it was in the 19th century. The town got its name from the regal cedar forests that once stood here. They were heavily logged from the 1860s to the 1880s.

In the 1860s, Cedar Key became the western terminus of Florida's first trans-state railroad, and over the next few decades it flourished as one of the largest shipping and logging centers in the state. Three of the nation's biggest pencil factories carved pencil stock from the area's red cedars and used the Florida Railroad to ship their goods across the state to the port at Fernandina. Steamboats loaded with merchandise plied the Suwannee River, including elegant stern-wheelers like the

By the time this photograph was taken, in 1916, the cedar stands in Cedar Key had long been depleted, yet logging continued to be a thriving industry in other parts of the region. (Tampa-Hillsborough County Public Library, Burgert Brothers Collection)

Belle of the Suwannee and the *Eagle Pencil,* which had mahogany-paneled passenger quarters and served haute cuisine.

Today, Cedar Key's industry is limited to fishing, clamming, and tourism. Writers, artists, and musicians have always been attracted to this place, the luminaries including the author Pearl S. Buck and Jimmy Buffett, the singer-songwriter who immortalized the town in his song "Incommunicado." The annual Cedar Key Sidewalk Arts Festival, in April, is one of the island's biggest events. The town of Cedar Key is divided into two sections. The main part contains the historic district, waterfront shops, and art galleries. Half of the **Cedar Key Historical Society Museum** is housed in a circa-1870 residence. Artifacts, photos, and newspaper clippings trace the town's history as a center for turtling, sponging, fishing, and pencil-making. Pottery shards and fossilized prehistoric finds open a window on the region's past. You can pick up a walking-tour map of the town at the museum. *609 Second Street; 352-543-5549.*

Town life centers around The Dock, a collection of art galleries, gift shops, and seafood restaurants that lines the waterfront. The seafood is generally deep-fried. Hearts-of-palm salad is a specialty in these parts, and you'll find the preparations as imaginative as they are delicious. The ingredients of one include raw cabbage-palm buds, iceberg lettuce, canned peaches and pineapples, dates, and a scoop of peanut butter ice cream.

West of The Dock is a mostly residential area. At the **Cedar Key State Museum,** attractive dioramas document Cedar Key's various incarnations as naval base, lumber town, shipbuilding center, and fishing port. The museum has an extensive seashell collection. *12231 SW 166 Court; 352-543-5350.*

Five miles offshore is a group of 12 islands set aside by the U.S. Department of the Interior as the **Cedar Keys National Wildlife Refuge.** Rimmed with rookeries and nesting areas for several species of birds, these islands, which have scattered patches of sand rather than real beaches, are also popular with cottonmouth snakes and diamondback rattlers. Seahorse Key has a small sand beach and an 1850s lighthouse used by the University of Florida as a research facility. The island is a nesting place for brown pelicans, comic-looking birds that can fly up to 35 miles per hour and hold up to three gallons of water in their bills. During their nesting season (from March through June), visitors are not allowed within 300 feet of the island; at other times, people are limited to the beach area. *Levy County, along the Gulf Shore, accessed via State Road 24; 352-495-0238.*

■ **CRYSTAL RIVER** *map page 81, B-2/3*

Communities along this part of the coast are less commercialized than other Florida beach towns. Crystal River, a town of about 4,000, is typical of the region. There are no fancy restaurants, amusement parks, or snake-oil stands. Visitors are drawn here by the natural beauty of the place, its warm springwaters, and winter manatee migration.

Manatees, a species more than 60 million years old and related to the elephant, swim through the warm waters of Florida's bayous and canals. The **Crystal River National Wildlife Refuge** has one of the largest concentrations of manatees in Florida—about 300 between January and March. Gentle, bulbous vegetarians, manatees eat from 100 to 200 pounds of aquatic plants daily and can weigh up to 1,500 pounds. Although graceful in the water, they are not swift enough to avoid speedboats, and are often killed or wounded by boat propellers.

Snorkelers and divers comprise the bulk of visitors to Crystal River. I found out about the town when my scuba certification dives took me there. It was in Febru-

Crystal River is known for the manatees that live in its warm springwaters.

ary, and the waters were chilly. My buddy and I were flipping around a channel when a huge blimplike form appeared below us. My first reaction was fear—this thing was mammoth! The manatee approached us, which made it legal for us to interact with her. I looked into her doleful right eye, petted her burlaplike skin, and she rolled over, like a dog begging for a tummy rub. We obliged. And then, with a flip of her powerful tail, she was gone. The refuge is accessible only by boat. Visitors are encouraged to make reservations in advance with local dive shops or marinas in the town of Crystal Springs. Some parts of Crystal River are off-limits to divers and snorkelers, and there are stiff penalties for violations. *1502 SE Kings Bay Drive; 352-563-2088.*

Six huge mounds of dirt and debris are the main attraction at **Crystal River Archaeological State Park.** It's believed that Indians lived here between 2,000 and 600 years ago and built the mounds for religious purposes. The visitors center exhibits pottery, arrowheads, and other artifacts unearthed at the site, and a half-mile-long trail winds through the complex. Guides lead a once-a-week Heritage Eco-Tour, a 90-minute boat trek on which they explain the area's cultural and natural history. *3400 North Museum Point; 352-795-3817.*

■ HOMOSASSA SPRINGS   *map page 81, B-3*

Homosassa Springs State Wildlife Park is a small zoo where animals live in their natural habitats. Among wetlands, hydric hammocks, and springs are white-tailed deer, alligators, river otters, bobcats, and birds. Visitors can take a 20-minute pontoon boat ride through the park and then wander around on picturesque foot trails. One of them incorporates a short span of elevated boardwalk several feet above the water—and a good thing too—as the waters below teem with wild alligators.

Until 1989, rangers would lead visitors to the end of the boardwalk and, while delivering a lecture on alligators, dangle fish over the railing. In response, a behemoth would leap out of the water and snatch the fish with a thunderous clap of its jaws. The park stopped offering this tour after visitors took it upon themselves to feed the alligators, and the spoiled creatures became dangerously aggressive.

Most animals here are native Floridians, except for a hippopotamus that was eventually granted Florida citizenship by former Governor Bob Martinez. The park is an old-Florida sort of attraction: not too fancy or sophisticated. *4150 West Suncoast Boulevard; 352-628-2311.*

From Homosassa Springs, Route 490 leads to Old Homosassa and **Yulee Sugar Mill Ruins State Historic Park.** David Levy Yulee, founder of the first trans-Florida railroad and the first U.S. senator from Florida, constructed a 35,000-acre plantation and sugar mill on this site in 1851. Yulee's operation was one of several large sugarcane plantations along the Florida coast, all of which were destroyed during the Civil War. Union troops burned Yulee's plantation in 1864, but left the mill intact. *Route 490 west of U.S. 19; 352-795-3817.*

■ WEEKI WACHEE SPRING *map page 81, B-3*

Back in 1947, a high-spirited Floridian named Newt Perry decided that a perfectly beautiful springhead needed something extra to make it a bigger attraction. What he created was a spectacle that you almost certainly cannot experience anywhere else on earth, at least not since the last Esther Williams movie. At show time, the audience sits in a small auditorium in front of a huge glass panel, behind which are the blue waters of the spring itself. An ensemble of "mermaids" (they even fill out their W-2s as such) then begins an elaborately choreographed underwater ballet. Weeki Wachee has offered this submerged rarity for decades. The shows last from 30 to 45 minutes,

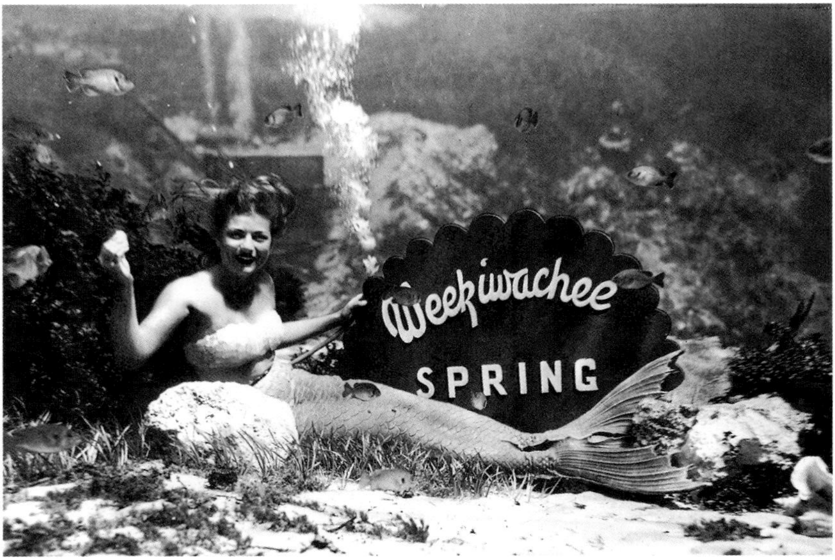
Weekiwachee
SPRING

The mermaids of Weeki Wachee. (Florida State Archives)

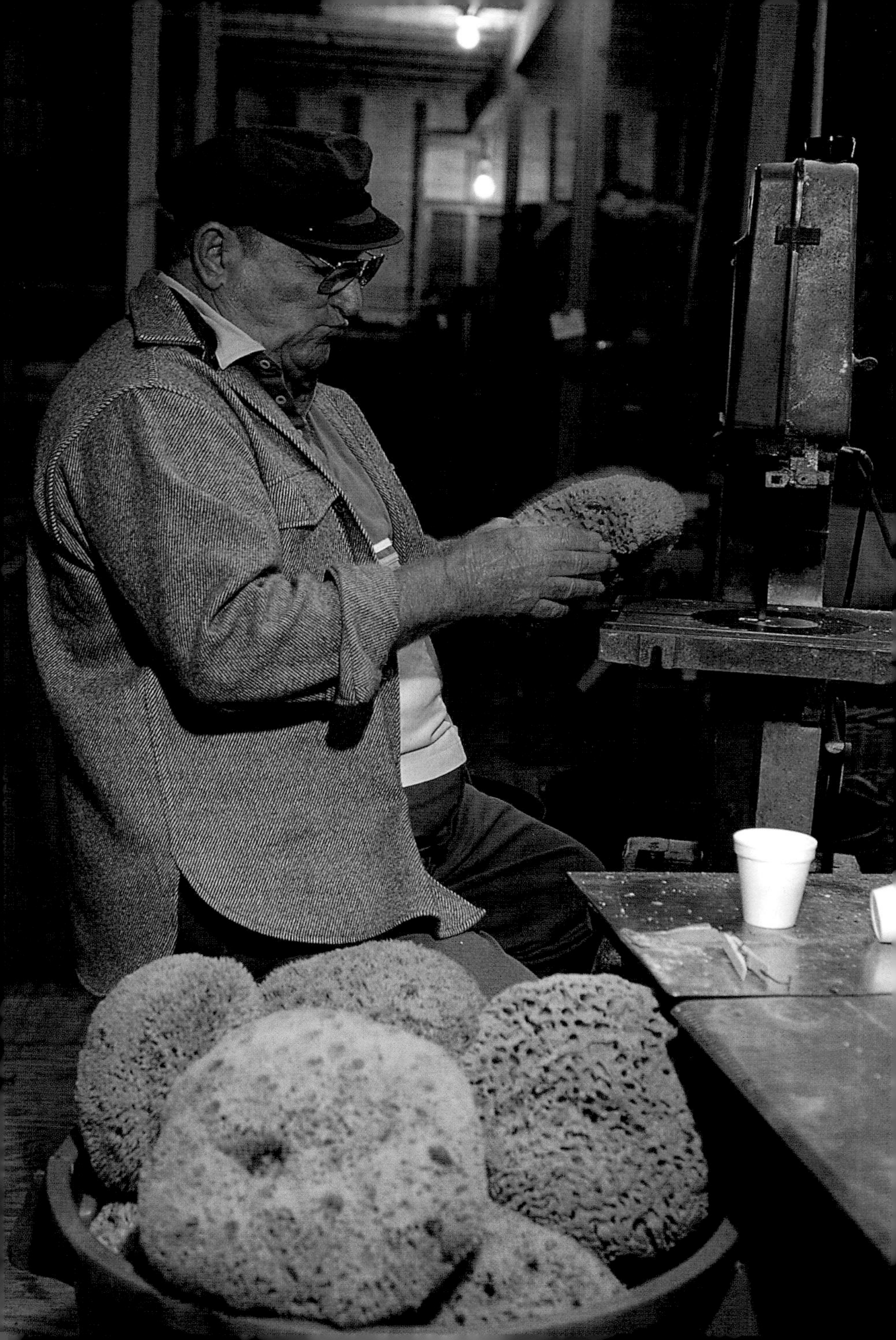

which means that the choreography must include opportunities for the mermaids to catch a breath from air hoses half-hidden by water flowers.

At Weeki Wachee, you can also take a wilderness cruise, see a bird show, and visit the petting zoo. Buccaneer Bay, a water park, has a sand beach as well as water slides. *6131 Commercial Street; 352-596-2062 or 800-678-9335.*

■ Tarpon Springs *map page 81, B-4*

When banker John K. Cheyney set out to develop this area in the 1890s, he discovered sponges growing in the Gulf waters off the shores of Tarpon Springs. Soon, professional spongers from Greece were donning 200-pound diving suits, walking along the sea floor, hook in hand, and plucking off sponges. A sponge fungus wiped out much of the supply and new synthetic sponges eventually took over the market, but the Greek immigrants stayed and their culture continues to flourish. In recent years, sponging has experienced a resurgence.

The quiet, compact town of Tarpon Springs is filled with galleries and antique stores. Dodecanese Boulevard, named for the islands where most of the first spongers originated, is patterned after the waterfront of a typical Greek island village, with white and blue buildings, sponge shops, cafés, and Greek bakeries. (Tacky souvenir shops are also in evidence.)

Facing Dodecanese Boulevard are the old sponge docks, where charter boats offer trips to sponge beds and to Anclote Key, an offshore refuge. To entertain passengers on boat trips, a Greek diver will suit up in heavy, old-time diving

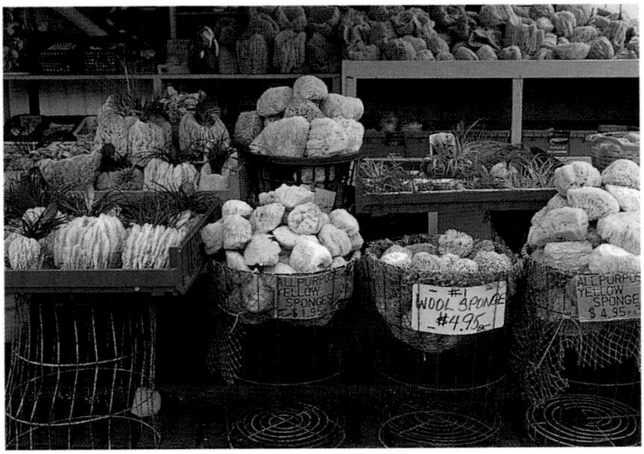
WOOL SPONGE
#4.95

(above) A sponge market on Dodecanese Boulevard sells the most noteworthy wares in Tarpon Springs.
(opposite) George Billiris trims sponges in a Tarpon Springs factory.

gear and helmet, and bring up a sponge the old way. Linger in Tarpon Springs beyond nightfall and you will find locals patronizing tiny cafés and bars ringing with the music of the Greek isles.

Tarpon Springs Aquarium, a small family-run attraction on the sponging docks, doesn't try to compete with the newer aquariums cropping up around the country. The most popular attraction here is shark feeding. Divers enter the 120,000-gallon glass tank and rouse nurse sharks and other varieties of cartilaginous fishes into a frenzy. There's also a touch tank with "destingered" stingrays and other unusual creatures. *852 Dodecanese Boulevard; 727-938-5378.*

The most impressive building downtown is **St. Nicholas Greek**

St. Nicholas Greek Orthodox Cathedral in Tarpon Springs.

Orthodox Cathedral (18 Hibiscus Avenue North), with its distinctive dome and tower. Inside are stained-glass windows, painted icons, gilded frames, and glossy marble. Enter the church only when services are not in session. St. Nicholas looms over the **historic downtown,** a renovated district with good restaurants and several antique shops.

Tarpon Springs is most crowded during the Christmas season, as preparations begin for January 6, the Feast of the Epiphany and the Twelfth Day of Christmas. On the inevitably gray morning, a visiting archbishop is rowed to a spot in the middle of the harbor. Every male child of the Greek Orthodox community under the age of confirmation comes out to meet him on anything that will float. After being blessed by the archbishop, the boys stand on their boats and watch as he throws a cross into the brackish water. The boys then dive into the water, and the one who retrieves the cross receives a special blessing from the archbishop, a year of good luck, and generous media coverage. The town spends the rest of the day celebrating with a huge parade and dancing.

The paved, 34-mile **Pinellas Trail** runs from St. Petersburg to Tarpon Springs, following a former railroad route. Walkers, joggers, cyclists, skaters, and plenty of birds and butterflies can be seen on the trail, which runs through the center of Tarpon Springs.

■ **DUNEDIN** *map page 81, B-4*

Many of Dunedin's citizens are of Scottish descent, which explains the annual Highland Games in April. Participants compete in piping, drumming, hammer-throwing, and *clachneart* ("stone of strength"). Springtime also brings an exceptionally good antiques fair. *727-733-3197.*

Honeymoon Island, just northwest of Dunedin, got its name in 1939 when a New York developer ran magazine ads extolling a Gulf Coast resort with thatched-roof huts as the perfect getaway for newlyweds. World War II put an end to the romance. The island now belongs to **Honeymoon Island State Recreation Area** (727-469-5942), a refuge for ospreys, which nest in virgin slash pines. The rocky beach is beautiful, but not suited for swimming.

A 15-minute ferry ride connects Honeymoon Island to its more secluded southern neighbor, **Caladesi Island State Park.** The two islands formed one barrier island before a 1921 hurricane opened a channel between them. The wide beach, with its white sand and warm, turquoise Gulf waters, puts this spot on many people's lists of finest beaches anywhere (it's the poster child of the local convention and visitors bureau). There are miles of trails, a picnic pavilion, primitive camping sites, and a 99-slip marina. This island is a must-see. *West of Dunedin in the Gulf of Mexico; 727-469-5918; 727-734-5263 for ferry information.*

■ **GULF BEACH COMMUNITIES** *map page 81, B-4*

Curving along Florida's west coast, the Pinellas Sun Coast is a 30-mile strand of barrier islands with gorgeous beaches and good weather. Causeways link beach communities to the mainland. To get there, it's necessary to drive through urban **Clearwater,** known for a Christmastime apparition of the Virgin Mary, who apparently appeared here in the window of an office building. Throngs of people showed up to see the miracle, and a few years later the episode inspired author Carl Hiaasen's novel *Lucky You.*

The northernmost resort is **Clearwater Beach** (connected to downtown Clearwater by Memorial Causeway), which might just be the beach volleyball capital of the world, the sport is so popular here.

Clearwater Marine Science Center Aquarium is primarily a research facility dedicated to the rescue and rehabilitation of injured or sick marine mammals. Downstairs, exotic fish are on display; the space upstairs is devoted to native species. A mangrove exhibit demonstrates the role of estuaries in marine survival, and huge cement tanks hold dolphins, river otters, and sea turtles. *249 Windward Passage, Clearwater Beach; 813-447-0980.*

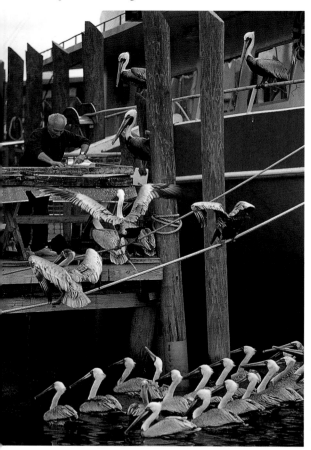

Pelicans queue up for fish scraps on a Gulf Coast pier.

At **Gulfview Beach/Pier 60,** mobs come daily to play in the soft sands of this wide beach. Fishing figures as prominently as volleyball, as anglers congregate atop the pier in pursuit of their catches. A nightly sunset celebration on the pier features acrobats, clowns, and musicians. *Memorial Causeway and Gulfview Boulevard.*

The village of Clearwater Beach stretches across two islands: Clearwater Beach Island and the northern portion of **Sand Key.** The latter, a long slender island, holds a string of small residential communities. My favorite of these is **Indian Rocks Beach.** There's nothing much to do here but visit the beach and drop by **Indian Rocks Area**

Historical Museum (727-593-3861). I like the two-lane road with its bay views, the simple little motels and cottages, and the feeling of community.

Suncoast Seabird Sanctuary, at Indian Shores, is a refuge for injured or orphaned birds. Established by zoologist Dale Shields in 1971, the sanctuary has become one of the nation's largest wild-bird hospitals. *18328 Gulf Boulevard; 813-391-6211.*

Madeira Beach, Sand Key's southernmost community, lies near **John's Pass,** a break in the barrier island created by storm surges from an 1848 hurricane. Today, John's Pass Marina caters to deep-sea fishing boats that head out in search of grouper, a type of sea bass that can grow up to 200 pounds and whose flesh is a local favorite (more grouper is said to be brought in here than anywhere else in Florida). The pass is flanked by a handful of bars and nightclubs on one side and a rustic-looking waterfront village of retail shops on the other. October brings the John's Pass Seafood Festival, which draws as many as 100,000 people.

South of Treasure Island is **Sunset Beach,** an eclectic neighborhood of old beach cottages and million-dollar homes. One of the city's most popular gay establishments was razed a few years back to make room for a new (and some say unneeded) beach pavilion at its southern tip, but this hasn't stopped the local gay community from enjoying the beachfront. There are free showers and bathrooms, but you'll have to feed the meter to park your car.

■ ST. PETE BEACH *map page 81, B-5*

To distinguish itself from the convalescent reputation the city of St. Petersburg garnered in the years after World War II, the city of St. Petersburg Beach shortened its name to the sexier, more casual St. Pete Beach in the 1980s. Perhaps city officials were trying to recapture the racy image the area enjoyed in the 1920s and '30s, when luminaries like Scott and Zelda Fitzgerald, Al Capone, Lou Gehrig, and Franklin D. Roosevelt flocked to the **Don CeSar Beach Resort.** The Don, as locals call it, is a grand, pink palace built by developer Thomas Rowe in 1928. According to local gossip, Rowe, who fell ill and later died in one of the hotel's guest rooms, haunts the hotel alongside his beloved nurse.

After serving briefly as a military hospital in the late 1940s, the Don CeSar fell into disrepair and was virtually abandoned for years. It was on the verge of being demolished when Robert Altman used it as a location for his 1979 film, *Health.* The movie reinvigorated the establishment, and it thrives today as a posh and

The palatial Don CeSar Beach Resort rises above the white sands of St. Pete Beach.

unapologetically kitsch resort. *3400 Gulf Boulevard; 727-360-1881.*

St. Pete Beach itself is graced with 7 miles of soft, white sand lapped by gentle Gulf waters. It is immensely popular with European tourists—British and German in particular.

In the shadow of the Don lies the community of **Pass-A-Grille,** which, according to legend, got its name when smugglers grilled fish near the pass at the southern end of the island. With a mere handful of restaurants and shops, Pass-A-Grille feels more like a small town than many of the overcommercialized municipalities flanking Gulf Boulevard to the north. It's crowded in high season, but even then a relaxed atmosphere prevails. A day at Pass-A-Grille should include breakfast at the **Sea Horse Restaurant** (800 Pass-A-Grille Way; 727-360-1734), some beach time, a visit to the shops along historic Eighth Avenue, a stroll past elegant homes from the early 1900s, and a sunset drink at the open-air bar atop the Victorian-style **Hurricane Seafood Restaurant** (809 Gulf Way; 727-360-9558).

■ **FORT DE SOTO PARK** *map page 97, A-5*

At the southern end of the Pinellas Bayway is the entrance to the 900-acre Fort de Soto Park, which encompasses five small islands. The fine, white sand of Mullet Key is crowned by a dark band of Australian pines that mark the hike to Fort de Soto, where some believe explorer Hernando de Soto came ashore in 1539. You can fish at the bay piers, bike, picnic, sunbathe, swim, or visit the fort ruins, which have cannons and gun emplacements. On the bay side, you can rent a kayak or navigate the shallow mangrove-lined channels, rollerblade, or bike along 6 miles of paved trails. *Follow signs from the Pinellas Bayway; 727-582-2267.*

■ **EGMONT KEY** *map page 81, B-5*

Accessible only by boat (most people leave from St. Pete Beach), Egmont Key is popular with weekend boaters. Despite the crowds, there are still plenty of places here to seek solitude. On the island are the **Egmont Key National Wildlife Refuge,** a lighthouse, and the remains of **Fort Dade,** erected during the Spanish-American War. Fishing and snorkeling are excellent here. *Boats depart from Cortez (southeast end of Cortez Road/Route 684 bridge, on Anna Maria Sound, south of Tampa Bay).*

■ **ST. PETERSBURG** *map page 81, B-4/5*

In 1875, John C. Williams, a farmer from Detroit, Michigan, whose whiskers fell below his belt, invested in a few plots of land surrounding Tampa Bay and decided to build a city. He teamed up with an exiled Russian nobleman, Pietr Dementieff (Peter Demens), who built a railroad to this new city, which he named after the place of his birth.

In 1885, the American Medical Association, citing the abundance of sunshine and opportunities for year-round recreation, named St. Petersburg the "healthiest place on earth," a superlative that brought waves of retirees looking for rest and rejuvenation. This reputation was reaffirmed 80 years later when the *Guinness Book of World Records* named it America's "sunniest city" after it set the record for the longest run of consecutively sunny days (768). Until the mid-1980s, when it ceased publication, the *Evening Independent* newspaper was free any day the sun failed to shine on St. Petersburg—a pretty safe guarantee for a city that still records an average of 361 days of sunshine a year.

The city's green wooden benches, strategically placed so strollers can enjoy sunshine all daylong, have come to symbolize the sleepy old St. Petersburg portrayed in movies like *Cocoon* (1985) and *Cocoon: The Return* (1988). But with million-dollar condos and scores of new establishments, downtown St. Petersburg is breaking out of its old cocoon. **Bay Walk** (151 Second Avenue North), an upscale Mediterranean-style complex of shops and restaurants, is at the heart of this renaissance, and tourists who used to spend entire vacations on St. Pete Beach are now venturing downtown for nightlife, dining, and shopping, or to take an amphibious duck boat or hovercraft tour of Tampa Bay.

St. Petersburg moves at a slower pace than Tampa, but a synergy has developed between the two cities under the general umbrella of Tampa Bay, a metropolitan area whose collective population exceeds 4 million. One such joint venture is Major League Baseball's Tampa Bay Devil Rays, who have Tampa in their name but play at St. Petersburg's **Tropicana Field** (First Avenue South and 16th Street; 888-326-7297), an enclosed, air-conditioned stadium that prevents fans from cooking under all that sunshine. Other major-league exhibition games can be seen at Al Lang Field at **Florida Power Park** (230 First Street South; 727-825-3137).

The city has some surprisingly good museums, such as the **St. Petersburg Museum of Fine Arts** (335 Second Avenue NE; 727-894-1052), a neoclassic structure housing works by Paul Cézanne, Claude Monet, Edgar Degas, Paul Gauguin, Georgia O'Keeffe, and Auguste Rodin, whose *Invocation* graces the sculpture garden. The impressively large **Florida International Museum** (100 Second Street North; 727-822-3693), housed in a former department store, has a life-size replica of John F. Kennedy's White House Oval Office in its permanent Kennedy Gallery. The **Florida Holocaust Museum** (55 Fifth Street South; 727-820-0100) has exhibits and materials that relate the stories of Holocaust survivors living in the area.

The corporate-bland exterior of the **Salvador Dali Museum** belies its contents—the world's largest collection of works by the Spanish surrealist painter. In the late 1970s, Ohio businessman Reynolds Morse sought to donate his personal Dali collection to any American museum that would keep the collection whole, display two-thirds of it at any given time, and never loan the works to other cultural institutions. For years, the museum kept two of the three promises, but in the late 1990s it loaned one of Dali's masterworks. The deal paid off handsomely for the museum, which subsequently ended its no-loan policy. Among the more than 200 paintings in the permanent collection are the famous *Disintegration of the Persistence of Memory* (also known as "The Melting Clocks") and the massive *Hallucinogenic Toreador. 1000 Third Street South; 727-823-3767.*

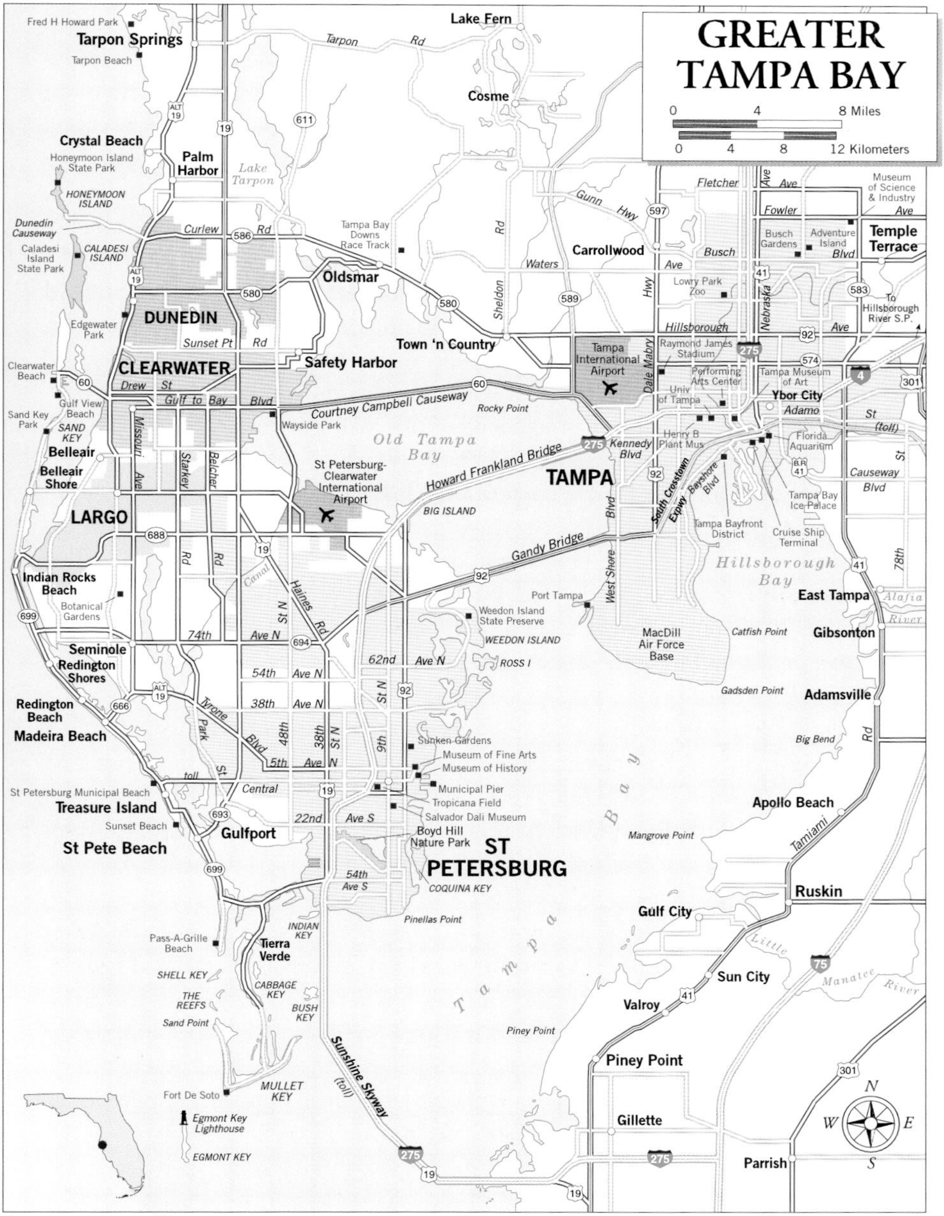
GREATER TAMPA BAY
0 4 8 Miles
0 4 8 12 Kilometers
Tarpon Springs
Fred H Howard Park
Tarpon Beach
Crystal Beach
Honeymoon Island State Park
HONEYMOON ISLAND
Palm Harbor
Lake Tarpon
Dunedin Causeway
Caladesi Island State Park
CALADESI ISLAND
DUNEDIN
Edgewater Park
CLEARWATER
Clearwater Beach
Gulf View Beach
Sand Key Park
SAND KEY
Belleair
Belleair Shore
LARGO
Indian Rocks Beach
Botanical Gardens
Seminole
Redington Shores
Redington Beach
Madeira Beach
St Petersburg Municipal Beach
Treasure Island
Sunset Beach
St Pete Beach
Gulfport
Pass-A-Grille Beach
Tierra Verde
SHELL KEY
THE REEFS
Sand Point
Fort De Soto
Egmont Key Lighthouse
EGMONT KEY
MULLET KEY
CABBAGE KEY
BUSH KEY
INDIAN KEY
Lake Fern
Cosme
Tarpon Rd
Curlew Rd
Sunset Pt Rd
Drew St
Gulf to Bay Blvd
Missouri Ave
Starkey Rd
Belcher Rd
Haines Rd
Tyrone Blvd
Park St
Central
22nd Ave S
54th Ave S
5th Ave N
38th Ave N
54th Ave N
62nd Ave N
74th Ave N
Oldsmar
Tampa Bay Downs Race Track
Safety Harbor
Wayside Park
Courtney Campbell Causeway
Town 'n Country
Rocky Point
Old Tampa Bay
St Petersburg-Clearwater International Airport
Howard Frankland Bridge
BIG ISLAND
Gandy Bridge
Weedon Island State Preserve
WEEDON ISLAND
ROSS I
Port Tampa
Sunken Gardens
Museum of Fine Arts
Museum of History
Municipal Pier
Tropicana Field
Salvador Dali Museum
Boyd Hill Nature Park
ST PETERSBURG
COQUINA KEY
Pinellas Point
Sunshine Skyway (toll)
Tampa Bay
Piney Point
Mangrove Point
Carrollwood
Gunn Hwy
Sheldon Rd
Waters Ave
Fletcher Ave
Fowler Ave
Busch Ave
Busch Gardens
Adventure Island
Museum of Science & Industry
Temple Terrace
Lowry Park Zoo
To Hillsborough River S.P.
Hillsborough Ave
Tampa International Airport
Raymond James Stadium
Performing Arts Center
Tampa Museum of Art
Univ of Tampa
Ybor City
Adamo
Henry B Plant Mus
Florida Aquarium
Kennedy Blvd
TAMPA
Dale Mabry Hwy
Nebraska Ave
Causeway Blvd
Tampa Bay Ice Palace
Tampa Bayfront District
Cruise Ship Terminal
South Crosstown Expwy
Bayshore Blvd
West Shore Blvd
MacDill Air Force Base
Hillsborough Bay
Catfish Point
Gadsden Point
Big Bend
78th St
East Tampa
Alafia River
Gibsonton
Adamsville
Apollo Beach
Tamiami
Ruskin
Gulf City
Little Manatee River
Sun City
Valroy
Piney Point
Gillette
Parrish
N
W
E
S
A
B
C

The verdant **Sunken Gardens,** planted in a sinkhole, is an Old Florida curiosity that once featured alligator-wrestling, bird shows, and countless "creepy-crawly" exhibits that speak to a bygone era. In the late 1990s, the attraction was on the verge of being transformed into a nudist colony when the city purchased the land. The 5,000 varieties of trees and flowers make it a beautiful stop, as do the hundreds of bird and butterfly species that live here. Plans are under way to renovate the attraction and move **Great Expectations,** a fantastic, hands-on children's museum, to the grounds. *1825 Fourth Street North; 727-896-3186.*

Tucked away in south St. Petersburg, on the shores of Lake Maggiore, is **Boyd Hill Nature Park,** a 245-acre green with 3 miles of nature trails and boardwalks. Bike or hike any of the six main trails, and you'll see baby alligators, lizards, bald eagles, snowy egrets, and turtles. A butterfly checklist, provided at the entrance, indicates the various types of lepidoptera that visit the butterfly garden. *1101 Country Club Way South; 727-893-7326.*

At the end of **The Pier,** St. Petersburg's fishing pier, stands an upside-down pyramid, the city's most distinctive landmark. Inside the five-story structure are boutiques, restaurants, an observation deck, and a tropical aquarium. The Pier buzzes with activity during the day: boat charters and bus tours arrive and depart; crowds of shoppers, diners, and sightseers mill about; and anglers fish from the catwalks. At night, bands play beneath twinkling lights. *800 Second Avenue NE; 727-821-6164.*

At the base of The Pier is the **St. Petersburg Museum of History,** which has clever exhibits. As part of one exhibit, you can try on period clothing from the museum's permanent collection. There is also a replica of a circa-1910 airboat that honors St. Petersburg's claim to fame as the destination of the first recorded commercial airplane flight—from Tampa to St. Petersburg. *335 Second Avenue NE; 727-894-1052.*

One of St. Petersburg's most awe-inspiring sights spans the turbulent waters at the mouth of Tampa Bay. The **Sunshine Skyway,** golden as the sun and majestic as a sailboat at sea, was built in the 1980s to replace the original bridge, which was struck by a 35,000-ton ship. The structure's 1,200-foot central section is the largest cement span in the Northern Hemisphere. The remains of the old bridge, which runs parallel to the Skyway, has been transformed into what is billed as the world's longest fishing pier, 1.59 miles in length.

The islands and piers of the St. Petersburg area are favorite fishing spots.

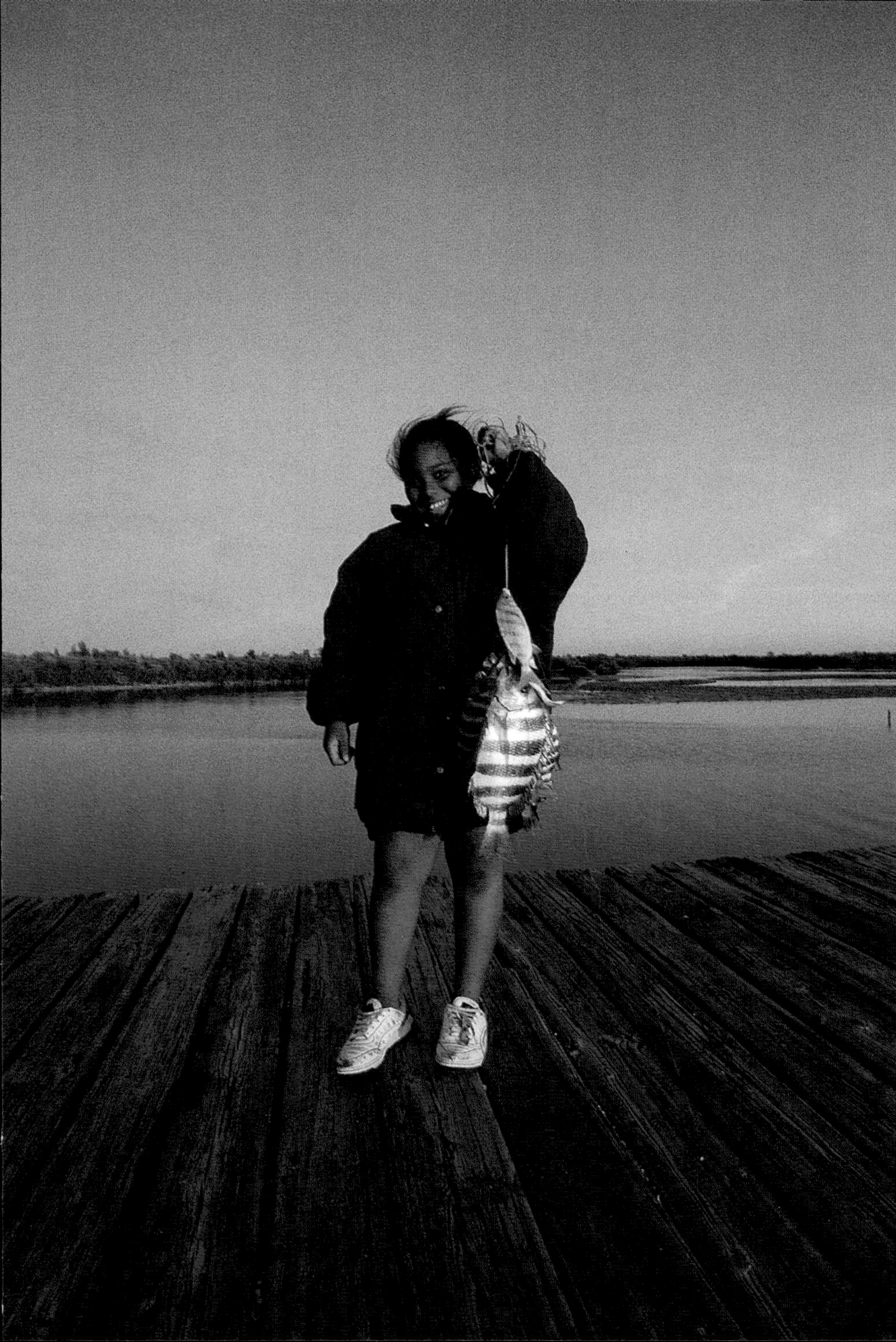

TAMPA *map page 81, B-4, and page 97*

> Tampa is quaint and old-fashioned in appearance, contains about 1,500 inhabitants, and is situated at the upper end of Tampa Bay. It is laid out with considerable regularity into squares, with streets of usual width, level and clean, but very sandy.
>
> —G.M. Barbour, *Florida for Tourists, Invalids and Settlers*, 1882

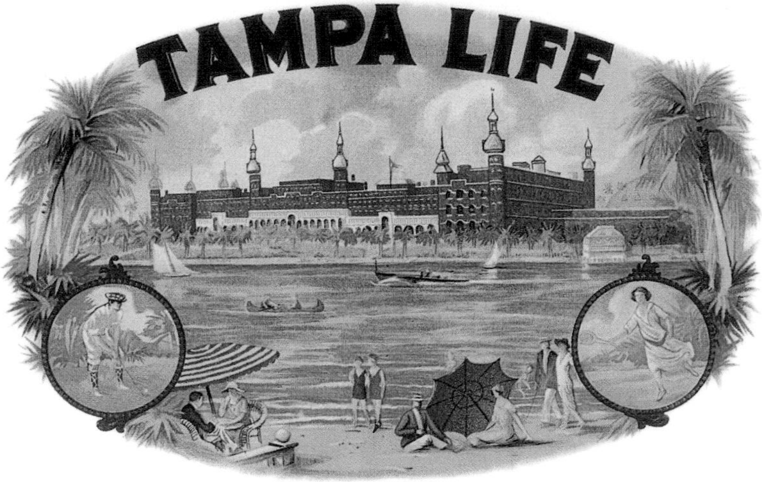
TAMPA LIFE

The Tampa Bay Hotel, built by railroad tycoon Henry Plant in 1891, is now a museum and part of the University of Tampa. (The University of Southern Florida Library, Special Collections)

Barbour published his promotional tract on Florida two years before an economic boom changed Tampa's "quaint and old-fashioned" appearance. Soon after, the wealthy and powerful Henry Plant built a narrow-gauge railroad, bringing with it commerce and tourists. He was followed closely by a cigar manufacturer from Key West, Vincente Martinez Ybor, who opened a factory here in 1888 and staffed it with Cuban nationals fleeing Spanish colonial rule. Soon, Ybor's cigar factory was the largest in the world, employing 4,000 of the town's 20,000 workers. In 1939,

Cigar-makers roll Cuban tobacco at the Cuesta Rey factory in Ybor City in 1929. While they worked, el lector, *a reader hired by workers, read aloud from newspapers, novels, or anarchist treatises, which were also chosen by workers. (Florida State Archives)*

Ybor City, as the area was called, was described by the *WPA Guide to Florida* as a center of Latin culture:

> From Cuba, Spain, and Italy, the Latin-Americans of Ybor City and Tampa have imported their own customs and traditions which survive mostly in annual festivals. The Cubans found good political use for voodoo beliefs brought by slaves from Africa to the West Indies. . . . Prior to the Spanish-American War, Cuban nationalists joined the cult in order to hold secret revolutionary meetings and it then received the Spanish name, *Nanigo.* . . . When the cigar workers migrated from Cuba to Key West and later to Tampa, societies of 'notorious Nanigoes,' as they were branded by Latin opposition papers, were organized in these two cities.

Social clubs, mutual aid societies, Cuban bread, beans 'n' rice, and strong coffee are still conspicuous aspects of life in Ybor City, but the big cigar-rolling businesses have moved on.

In Ybor City, street artists are known to paint with coffee and tobacco juice, to remind us of the city's economic genesis, and a lone cigar roller still plies his trade at Ybor Square. Shops on cobbled streets sell Cuban bread, hand-painted tiles, and trilingual newspapers. A statue of José Martí reflects the enthusiasm of Ybor City's people for this hero of an earlier Cuban revolution.

Ybor City has become the nightlife hub of Tampa, with more than a dozen bars and clubs lining La Septima, or Seventh Avenue, the main drag anchored by Centro Ybor, a city-run retail and dining development designed to blend in with the area's converted warehouses and cigar factories. But with all this growth comes problems: on weekends, when a portion of La Septima becomes a pedestrian mall closed to car traffic, parking becomes scarce and pricey, and crowds can get rowdy in the open-air party atmosphere. The **Ybor City Cigar Museum and Visitor's Center** (1600 East Eighth Avenue; 813-241-8838) offers free historic walking tours of the area.

The Ybor City State Museum keeps heritage and memories alive on a political, social, and cultural level. It occupies an old bakery building where the community's supply of Cuban bread was once baked. **La Casita House,** part of the museum, is a restored cigar-worker's house that shows how people lived and worked in the 19th century. The complex lies on one side of **Preservation Park,** a reconstructed streetscape that evokes the period of Ybor City's cigar-making era. *1818 East Ninth Avenue; 813-247-6323.*

Ybor City has many Cuban sandwich shops. Richard Gonzmart, member of the family that founded Ybor City's landmark **Columbia** restaurant, makes an authentic Cuban sandwich: roast pork, baked ham, Genoa salami, cheese, and pickles stacked between real Cuban bread, which is baked with a palm frond in the loaf. The Columbia claims its Cuban sandwich is best. What Ybor City restaurant doesn't? This has been an ongoing, good-natured competition since the first Latins arrived in Tampa. *2117 East Seventh Avenue; 813-248-4961.*

Downtown Tampa is a thriving commercial area with plenty of high-rises. The Hillsborough River flows through the city, and along the river are the tree-lined drives of the University of Tampa and the outrageous old **Tampa Bay Hotel** (401

Flamenco dancers perform nightly at the lively Columbia restaurant in Ybor City.

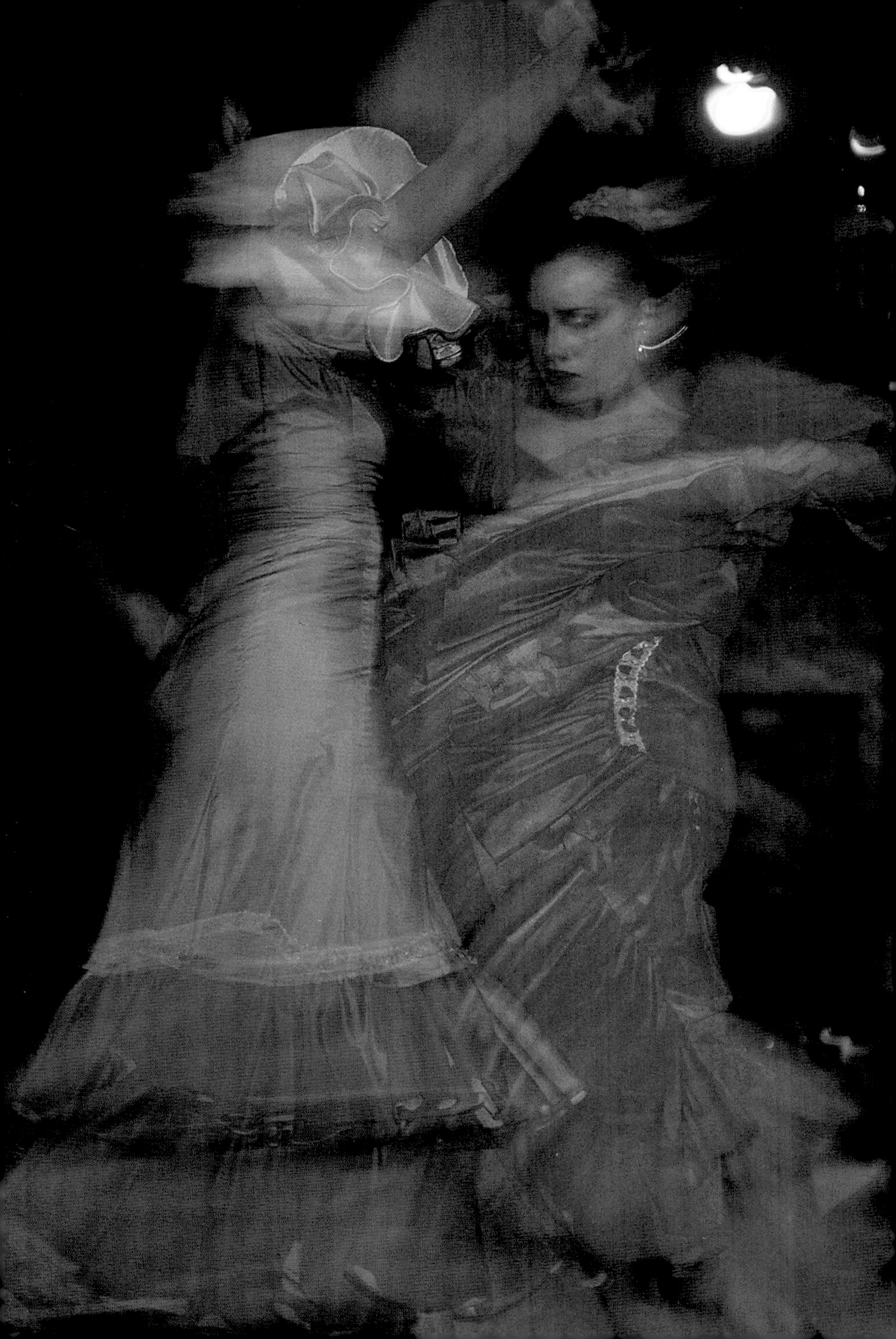

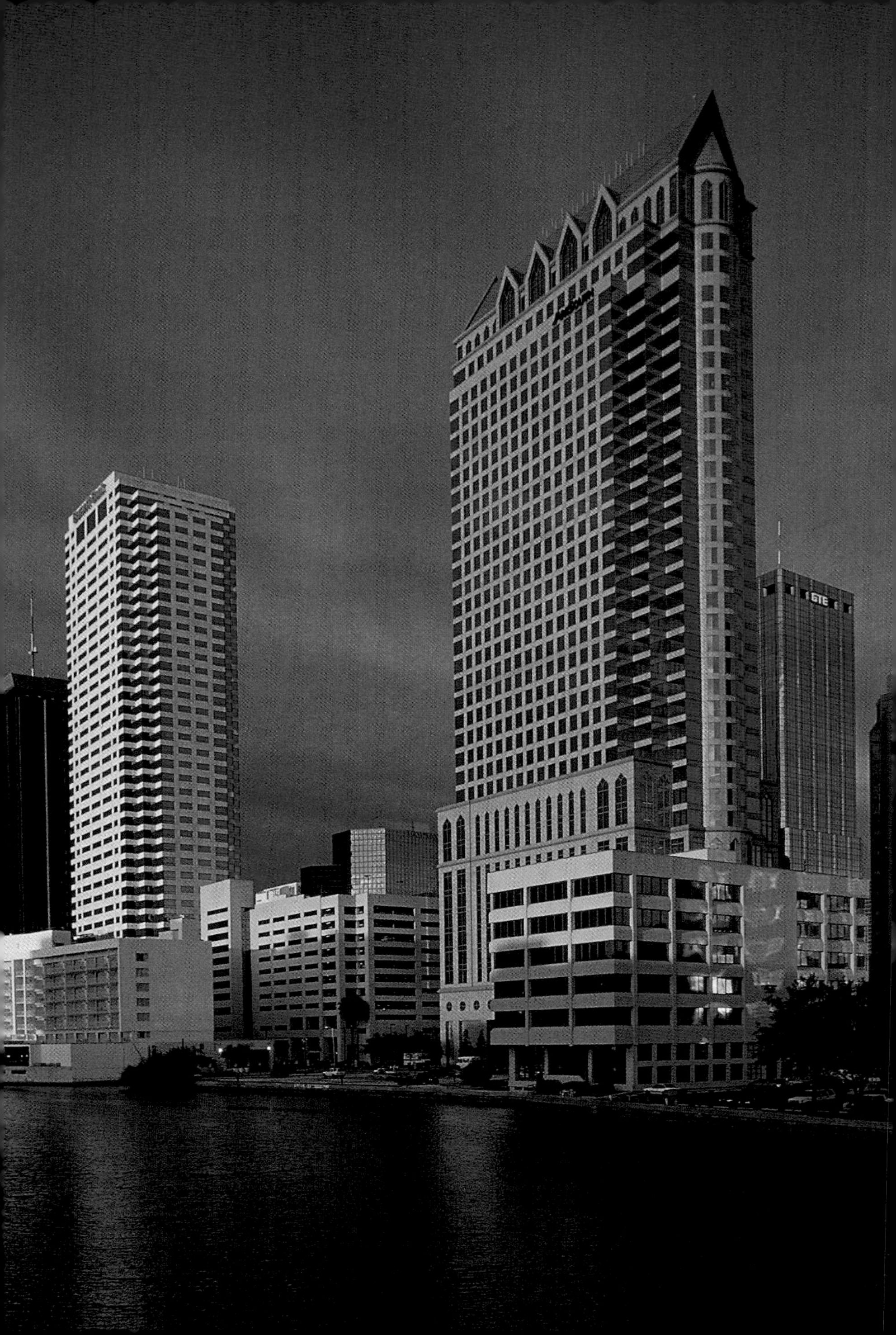
GTE

West Kennedy Boulevard), which also houses the Henry B. Plant Museum (see below). The downtown area is compact and easily explored on foot. Water taxis, ferries, and an old paddle-wheeler offer tours of the bay.

■ **TAMPA SIGHTS** *map page 97*

The fine old **Tampa Bayfront District** has always been a showpiece. Running between downtown Tampa and the bridge to Davis Islands is Bayshore Boulevard, 6 miles of continuous sidewalk popular with rollerbladers, cyclists, and joggers. Bayshore runs through the old Hyde Park neighborhood, providing ideal views of Hillsborough Bay. The old homes here, built before the days of air-conditioning, have ample porches meant to be enjoyed on hot summer nights. A drive through the Beach Park neighborhood will take you along quiet streets lined with enormous oak trees and fine homes built in the 1930s.

The **Gasparilla Pirate Fest,** an elaborate Mardi Gras affair that takes place in February, was started in 1904 when Mary Louise Dodge, then the society columnist for the *Tampa Tribune,* decided to throw a pirate-theme party. Her inspiration was the legendary (or mythical, as many historians claim) José Gaspar, who supposedly seized 400 ships in his lifetime—that is, when he wasn't busy beheading Spanish princesses, terrorizing port towns, or tending to his myriad other antisocial obligations. The highlight of the festival is Invasion Day, when hundreds of swashbuckling "pirates"—businessmen, local celebrities, and civic leaders—raid the city, arriving aboard the three-masted replica of José Gaspar's ship. Once the town has been subdued by cannon fire, the pirates disembark and scatter to the various parade floats of their "krewes," like Ye Mystic Krewe of Venus and Ye Mystic Krewe of Gasparilla. The parade is accompanied by every marching band on the Gulf Coast, a few live alligators, and swamp buggies. Traditionally, the end of the parade marks the opening of the Florida State Fair, at which awards are given to the best key lime pies and barbecued ribs.

When railroad magnate Henry Plant opened the region's most luxurious hotel in 1891, he spared no expense, hiring architect J. A. Wood to create the **Tampa Bay Hotel,** now the Henry B. Plant Museum. A Victorian takeoff on the Alhambra in Granada, Spain, the structure has 13 gleaming minarets (one for each month in the Islamic calendar), Moorish horseshoes, domes, and crescent moons.

(opposite) Bayshore Boulevard affords fine views of Hillsborough Bay and downtown Tampa. (following pages) Feeding giraffes at Busch Gardens. (© Busch Entertainment Corporation)

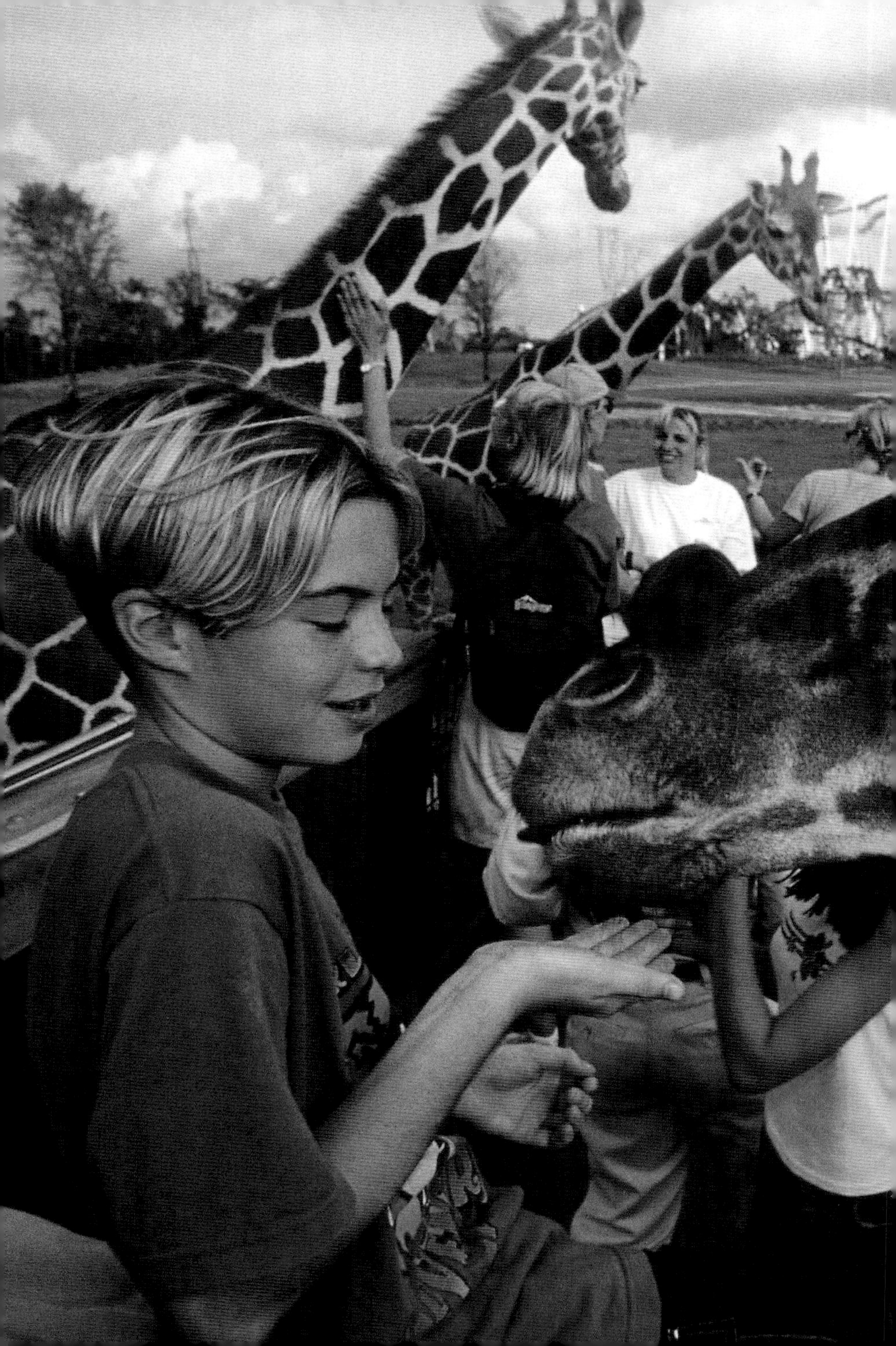

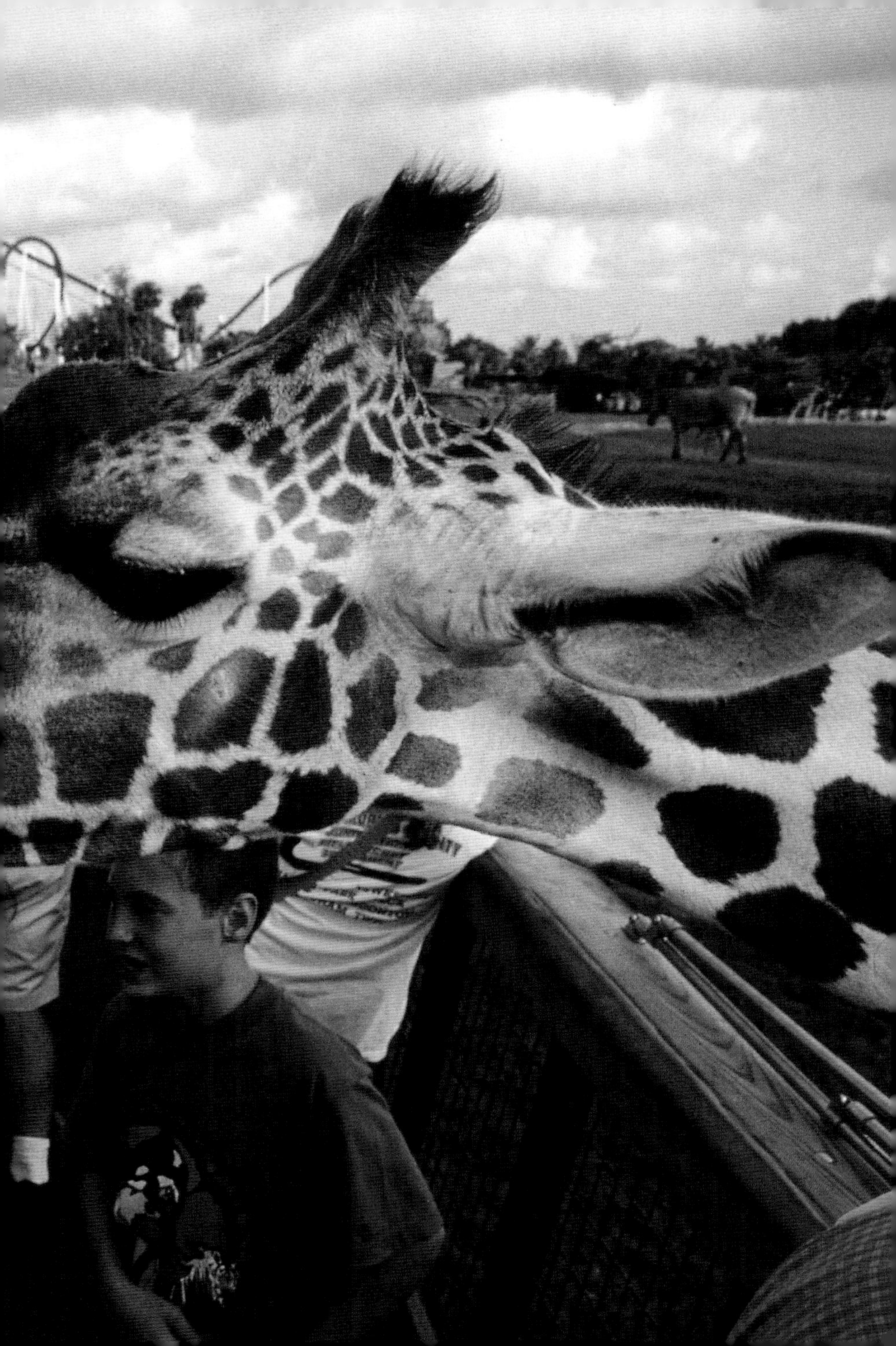

Downtown Tampa rises above the banks of the Hillsborough River.

The interior, equally noteworthy, contains European antiques, furniture, and art reflecting the glamorous tastes of Victorian–era swells. When the hotel opened in 1891, its rooms, priced at $100 a night, served mostly the wealthy, noteworthy, or notorious: heads of state, captains of industry, professional athletes.

Six years after it opened, at the onset of the Spanish-American War, Colonel Theodore Roosevelt set up headquarters for his Rough Riders in the hotel, and Tampa became the staging point for thousands of American soldiers on their way to invade Cuba. Nurses arrived as well, among them Clara Barton, founder of the American Red Cross.

The hotel closed before the turn of the 20th century and in 1930 became part of the University of Tampa. The south wing of the ground floor is preserved today as a museum, with 14 rooms filled with late-19th-century European art and furniture. A pamphlet explains the objects in each room and the significance of the hotel and Henry B. Plant to Tampa's cultural life. There is also a permanent exhibit on the Spanish-American War. *401 West Kennedy Boulevard, on the University of Tampa campus; 813-254-1891.*

The grand **Tampa Theatre** was built in 1926. Its gothic balconies, tapestries, arches, murals, and vaulted ceilings make the perfect setting for a ghost story. Hence the legend of "Fink" Finley, the theater's spectral projectionist, who, long after he had died, continued to jiggle keys, slam doors, and open locked doors. Things got so weird in the projection booth that Finley's replacement finally quit. The 1,400-seat theater hosts concerts, films, and film festivals. Guided tours are offered. *711 Franklin Street; 813-274-8982.*

The waterfront **Tampa Museum of Art** has Greek, Roman, and Etruscan antiquities in addition to 20th-century American art. The museum's new home, with six levels of galleries and exhibition space, opens in early 2004. *600 North Ashley Drive; 813-274-8130.*

The **Tampa Bay Performing Arts Center** is the city's premier venue for dance, opera, ballet, Broadway musicals, cabaret, pop concerts, and jazz. *1010 North MacInnes Place; 813-222-1000 or 800-955-1045.*

Tampa has its own port at **Garrison Seaport Center,** where cruise ships call several times a week. In the shadows of the mammoth ships is the waterfront **Channelside,** a colorful, palm-studded "festival marketplace" with a ho-hum

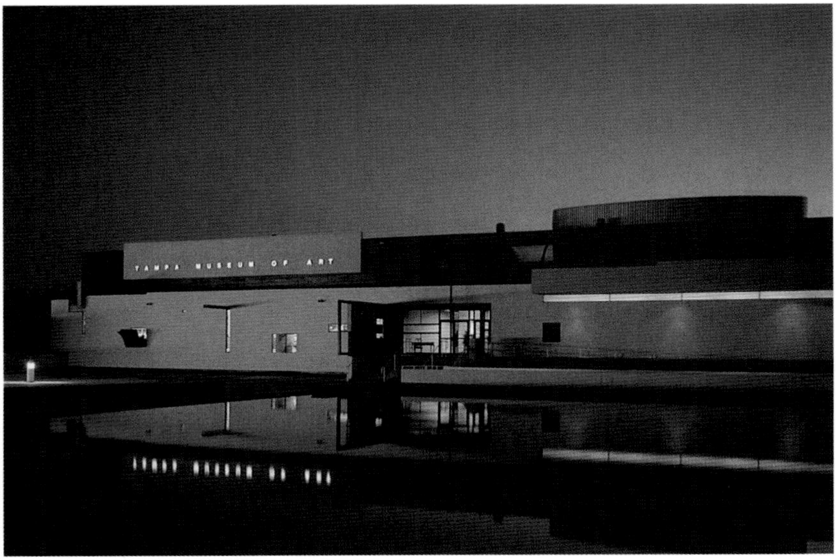
TAMPA MUSEUM OF ART

The Tampa Museum of Art is an impressive waterfront building. (Tampa Museum of Art)

assortment of stores, restaurants, and nightlife destinations. **Howl at the Moon** (615 Channelside Drive; 813-226-2261), a dueling piano bar in which two singers try to out-serenade each other (and the audience) with hits from the 1970s and 1980s, is the best of the bunch. The Tampa Port Authority offers the **Seaport Adventure Boat Tour** (813-905-5131) around the port (it's free). Though not exactly an "adventure," on a nice day taking the tour is a great way to learn about Tampa and enjoy a morning on the water.

The gem of the Channel District is the enormous **Florida Aquarium,** northwest of downtown. Domed with a giant glass seashell, it shows off Florida's aquarian worlds. The mangrove habitat is impressive, with its damp steaminess and exotic birds flapping around, cawing, and hooing. The reef picture-window is also mesmerizing, with whalelike groupers and dainty angelfish. *701 Channelside Drive; 813-273-4020.*

Tampa is big on major-league sports, most of which are played in northwest Tampa. **Raymond James Stadium** is home to the National Football League's Tampa Bay Buccaneers in fall and winter. *4201 North Dale Mabry Highway; 813-879-2827.*

The 10,000-seat **New York Yankees Baseball Complex** is a replica of New York City's Yankee Stadium. It hosts off-season rookie and semiprofessional baseball. *3802 Dr. Martin Luther King Jr. Boulevard; 813-879-2244 or 800-969-2657.*

The **Tampa Bay Ice Palace** is home to the Tampa Bay Lightning hockey team during its season, which runs from October through April. The Tampa Bay Storm, the local franchise of the 16-team National Arena Football League, plays its home games here as well. *501 East Kennedy Boulevard; 813-223-4919.*

Busch Gardens began as a brewery but later became a zoo and amusement park, with areas given African names, such as Egypt, Morocco, Timbuktu, and Nairobi. Soaring over its Serengeti Plains is a monorail that allows visitors to view wildebeests, elephants, zebras, and giraffes. At the Myombe Reserve, gorillas and chimpanzees can be viewed through glass barriers. Thrill rides at the park range from terrifying to merely drenching—roller-coasters like the Kumba and Montu twist you into zero gravity, and the Tanganyika Tidal Wave makes a 55-foot plunge into water. *3000 Busch Boulevard; 813-987-5082 or 888-800-5447.*

Adventure Island, a 30-acre water park owned and operated by Anheuser-Busch, sits just north of the company's flagship amusement park, Busch Gardens, but the water park has some thoughtful touches you won't find at Busch Gardens. Due to the park's cashless payment system, you don't have to worry about your cash getting soggy while riding the Tampa Typhoon. This is a spend-the-whole-day place where people come early with their picnics and save a table while the kids slosh off to the slide or pool. *10001 Malcolm McKinley Drive; 813-987-5600.*

At the **Museum of Science & Industry,** more than 450 exhibits address subjects from flight, space, and Florida weather and ecology to how babies are born. The complex holds a 3-D IMAX theater, with one of those 180-degree screens that are alternately dizzying and fascinating. You'll also find a free-flying butterfly garden and a flight simulator. *4801 East Fowler Avenue; 813-987-6100.*

■ HILLSBOROUGH RIVER

North of town, the Hillsborough River carries canoeists back into old-time natural Florida. Anyone not feeling up to a canoe trip can rent a two-person paddleboat— the current of the river is just lazy enough to allow travel in both directions. You're likely to spy alligators floating in the river, turtles atop logs, ospreys, and herons amid the quiet of cypress and oak trees.

There's camping at **Hillsborough River State Park** as well as hiking and pool swimming. You can rent a canoe at a stand next to the swimming pool. *15402 U.S. 301 North, Zephyrhills; 813-986-1020.*

■ TRAVEL BASICS

Getting Around: U.S. 19/98 South is the original north-south artery between Tallahassee and St. Petersburg. It's slow going most of the way, and south of Weeki Wachee it loses its Old Florida appeal quickly. Interstate 75, which parallels U.S. 19 farther inland, is a fast scenic route that runs through the farmlands and horse ranches outside Gainesville and Ocala. To get to the Tampa Bay area from Tallahassee, take I-10 east to I-75 south. The trip is roughly 4.5 hours. In Tampa, I-75 continues south to Bradenton, while I-275 bridges Tampa Bay to connect to St. Petersburg and the Sun Coast beaches. The best way to travel south from the Tampa airport is to follow I-275 until it connects with I-75, a wide superhighway. On U.S. 41, the Tamiami Trail, the pace is more leisurely.

Climate: The weather is warm year-round and often humid. Spring and fall are relatively dry and warm, with daytime temperatures averaging in the mid-70's F. Summers are wet, with frequent, brief thunderstorms; temperatures range between 75°F and 90°F. Winter temperatures range between 50°F and 70° F. Hurricanes are less of a threat to the west coast.

LOWER GULF COAST
SOUTHWEST FLORIDA

■ OVERVIEW

The lower Gulf Coast of Florida was the last stretch of coastline to be settled. As a result, most of the development here is new. From the coast off Tampa–St. Petersburg, a series of barrier islands extends south 120 miles down the west coast, their white-sand beaches lined with cottages and high-rise hotels. South of Marco Island, the islands blur into a wilderness that is half water, half land: the storied Ten Thousand Islands.

The flourishing cities of Bradenton and Sarasota, south of Tampa Bay, are the region's most interesting historic and cultural centers. Small towns and island enclaves can be found south of Sarasota, along with fishing villages, exclusive retirement communities, and rural getaways.

Hernando de Soto's invasion of Florida in 1539, as illustrated by a Dutch artist. (Florida Historical Society, Alma Clyde Field Library of Florida History)

The twin islands of Sanibel and Captiva are informal and tranquil. Naples, to the south, is concerned with things social. Whereas people on Sanibel are comfortable in T-shirts and sandals, folks in Naples wear suits and Italian pumps. Closer to the Everglades, an earlier culture centered on hunting, fishing, and swamp-buggy racing persists.

On the lower Gulf Coast, the difference between old and new cultures seems most dramatic, because the era of pioneering, with all the hardscrabble living that it suggests, has only recently ended. People in some of these communities still remember the homesteading days, but most have been outnumbered by waves of newcomers, who arrive with a spirit of excitement about starting life anew on Florida's wilder side.

■ BRADENTON *map page 115, A-1*

> The town was of seven or eight houses, built of timber, and covered
> with palm-leaves. The Chief's house stood near the beach, upon a
> very high mound made by hand for defense; at the other end of the
> town was a temple, on the top of which perched a wooden fowl with
> gilded eyes, and within were found some pearls of small value,
> injured by fire, such as the Indians pierce for beads, much esteeming
> them, and string to wear about the neck and wrists.
>
> —André Vasconcelos, 1539

This travel story, told by Hernando de Soto's Portuguese officer, describes the Tocobaga village of Ucita, where the explorers made themselves at home in 1539, on the shores of present-day Bradenton. De Soto's party was not the first to arrive in the village; Pánfilo de Narváez preceded him by 11 years. The natives had already tasted his brand of abuse, so when de Soto and his conquistadors arrived, the locals fled.

De Soto National Park, a tiny, breezy point of land at the mouth of the Manatee River, commemorates de Soto's landing. Take a look at the engraving of de Soto's landing party, then gaze at the mile-wide river. You can almost hear the shouts of the Spanish commanders and the stomping and neighing of warhorses.

In winter, witty and knowledgeable costumed volunteers demonstrate the instruments of conquistador warfare at a living history camp near the visitors center. On the nature trail, horseshoe crabs and egrets are among the many creatures that roam undisturbed, and mangroves barricade the breeze. The park is the northernmost growing region of the beautiful gumbo-limbo tree, a subtropical species whose waxy trunk exudes an aromatic sap and whose leathery leaves were once used to make tea. *75th Street NW, 3 miles north of Route 64; 941-792-0458.*

Route 64, also known as Manatee Avenue, takes you into downtown Bradenton, which was a thriving urban center when river travel was the only way to go. Along **Old Main Street** are some inviting antique shops and art galleries housed in historic brick buildings. Bradenton Waterfront Park, along the Manatee River, is a fine place for a stroll or bike ride. Bradenton's old neighborhoods feel like the Old South. Maybe it's all that Spanish moss on the trees, or perhaps the lived-in look of the houses. In any case, a drive through a neighborhood such as **Point Pleasant** takes you out of Gulf Coast Florida and into places where the ghosts of slaves, Amerindian women, and conquistadors dwell.

A walk on sunny Bradenton Pier.

■ Bradenton Area Sights

The Spanish colonial design of the **South Florida Museum**—courtyard fountains, wrought iron, and stone floors—tells only part of the story of what's inside. Of course, the requisite conquistador history is rehashed, but much more attention is paid to the Seminole and Calusa Indians, prehistoric animals, and endangered wildlife. One of the highlights is Snooty, the oldest manatee in captivity, who has his own digs on the second-floor Parker Aquarium. He doesn't do any tricks—unless you consider eating 100 pounds of lettuce a day a trick—but he's worth visiting if you've never seen a manatee. So large, yet so gentle and vulnerable. In 2001, a fire destroyed part of the museum, including the Bishop Planetarium, and at this writing, museum officials have not set a date for reopening. *201 10th Street West; 941-746-4131.*

Gamble Plantation State Historic Site is a relic of the town's 19th-century sugar days, an era that proved not so sweet for planters, whose crops were continually destroyed by hurricanes and freezes. Most planters succeeded despite their troubles, and many became affluent enough to build opulent mansions, some of which still stand today. Major Robert Gamble, a successful Virginia planter who arrived

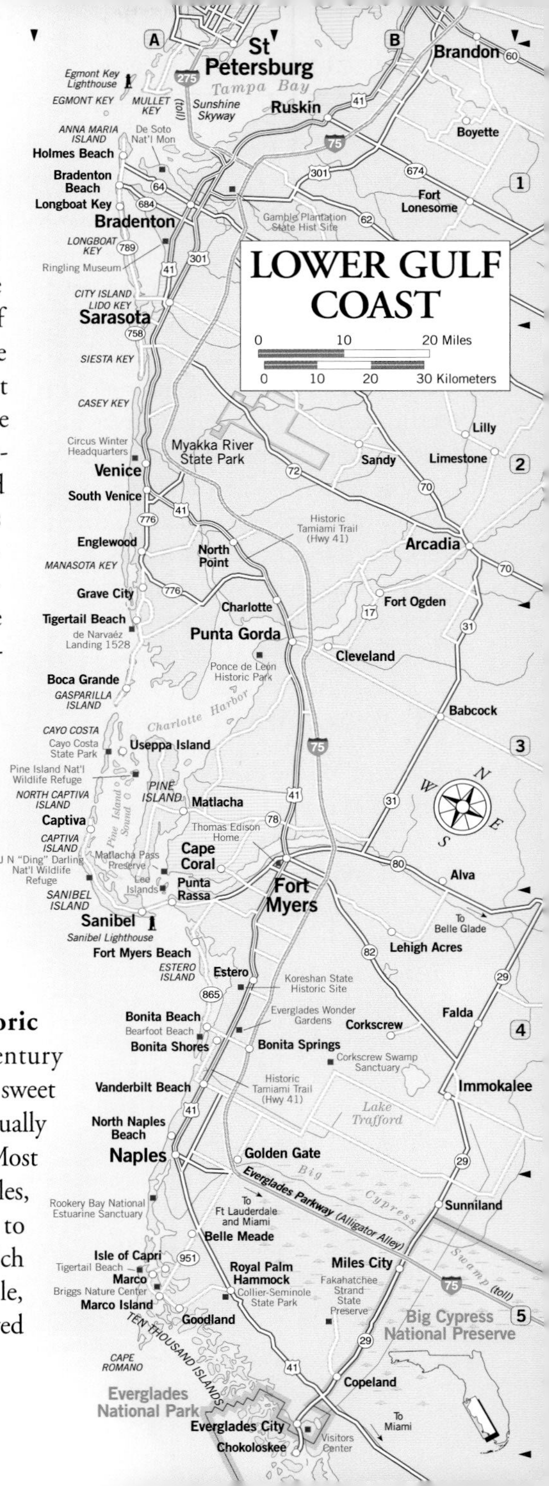

LOWER GULF COAST
0 10 20 Miles
0 10 20 30 Kilometers
St Petersburg
Tampa Bay
Brandon
Ruskin
Boyette
Egmont Key Lighthouse
EGMONT KEY
MULLET KEY
Sunshine Skyway
ANNA MARIA ISLAND
De Soto Nat'l Mon
Holmes Beach
Bradenton Beach
Longboat Key
Bradenton
Gamble Plantation State Hist Site
Fort Lonesome
LONGBOAT KEY
Ringling Museum
CITY ISLAND
LIDO KEY
Sarasota
SIESTA KEY
CASEY KEY
Circus Winter Headquarters
Myakka River State Park
Lilly
Sandy
Limestone
Venice
South Venice
Historic Tamiami Trail (Hwy 41)
Englewood
North Point
Arcadia
MANASOTA KEY
Grave City
Charlotte
Fort Ogden
Tigertail Beach
de Narvaéz Landing 1528
Punta Gorda
Cleveland
Ponce de León Historic Park
Boca Grande
GASPARILLA ISLAND
Charlotte Harbor
Babcock
CAYO COSTA
Cayo Costa State Park
Useppa Island
Pine Island Nat'l Wildlife Refuge
NORTH CAPTIVA ISLAND
PINE ISLAND
Matlacha
Captiva
Pine Island Sound
Thomas Edison Home
CAPTIVA ISLAND
J N "Ding" Darling Nat'l Wildlife Refuge
Matlacha Pass Preserve
Cape Coral
Lee Islands
Punta Rassa
Fort Myers
Alva
SANIBEL ISLAND
Sanibel
Sanibel Lighthouse
To Belle Glade
Fort Myers Beach
Lehigh Acres
ESTERO ISLAND
Estero
Koreshan State Historic Site
Everglades Wonder Gardens
Falda
Bonita Beach
Bearfoot Beach
Corkscrew
Bonita Shores
Bonita Springs
Corkscrew Swamp Sanctuary
Vanderbilt Beach
Historic Tamiami Trail (Hwy 41)
Immokalee
Lake Trafford
North Naples Beach
Naples
Golden Gate
Big Cypress Swamp
Everglades Parkway (Alligator Alley)
Rookery Bay National Estuarine Sanctuary
To Ft Lauderdale and Miami
Sunniland
Belle Meade
Isle of Capri
Tigertail Beach
Royal Palm Hammock
Miles City
Marco
Collier-Seminole State Park
Fakahatchee Strand State Preserve
Briggs Nature Center
(toll)
Marco Island
Goodland
Big Cypress National Preserve
TEN THOUSAND ISLANDS
CAPE ROMANO
Copeland
Everglades National Park
To Miami
Everglades City
Visitors Center
Chokoloskee

in the 1840s via Tallahassee, set about clearing 1,500 acres of jungle for sugar cultivation. Using 191 slaves, Gamble built a Greek Revival–style estate whose design was drawn from memories of his Virginia days. He built the nearly 2-foot-thick walls out of red brick, which was brought from Florida's northwest coast as ship ballast. The mansion's crowning touch—its eighteen 25-foot exterior columns—were constructed of an oyster-shell-based mortar known as tabby. After the Civil War, the Confederate Secretary of State Judah P. Benjamin took shelter here. The mansion had fallen into disrepair by 1925, when the United Daughters of the Confederacy stepped in to restore it. *U.S. 301 off I-75 Exit 43; 941-723-4536.*

The county's oldest buildings can be found in **Manatee Village Historical Park.** Most of these structures date from the late 1880s. The buildings stand beneath the arms of massive oak trees dripping with Spanish moss. Brick-paved pathways take you to the doorsteps of the frontier village and a white clapboard church. Sit, have a picnic outside the old church, and imagine a time when days passed languidly. *604 15th Street; 941-749-7165.*

■ **ANNA MARIA ISLAND** *map page 115, A-1*

Manatee Avenue delivers you to Anna Maria Island, the destination for most visitors to Manatee County. What draws them here? The beaches, of course. Anna Maria Island will seem pleasantly underdeveloped if you've just come from St. Pete Beach and Clearwater Beach to the north. Height restrictions limit buildings to five stories, and the garrison of Australian pines that backs the beach hides many structures from view. The island holds three communities—Anna Maria, Holmes Beach, and Bradenton Beach—all of which blend into one another with little delineation. Just across Anna Maria Bridge is the town of Holmes Beach, with its storefronts that display inflatable alligators and boogie boards. Hotels and restaurants line the sand, and surf music spills from clubs and bars.

The island's casual charm is on display at places like the **Holmes Beach Pier,** where local surfers hang out waiting for the tide to change and fishermen gab with curious onlookers. Near the city fishing pier in **Bradenton Beach** is the Historic Bridge District, which has retail shops, a German bakery, and a few bars and restaurants, including the waterfront **Bridge Street Café** (200 Bridge Street; 941-779-1706), where you're likely to share your table, if not your lunch, with Tyson, the resident egret. A few artsy, whimsically decorated older homes front the bay, as

(top) Plenty of white sand beaches are the main attraction on Anna Maria Island. (bottom) Recreational water sports are popular at Manatee Beach.

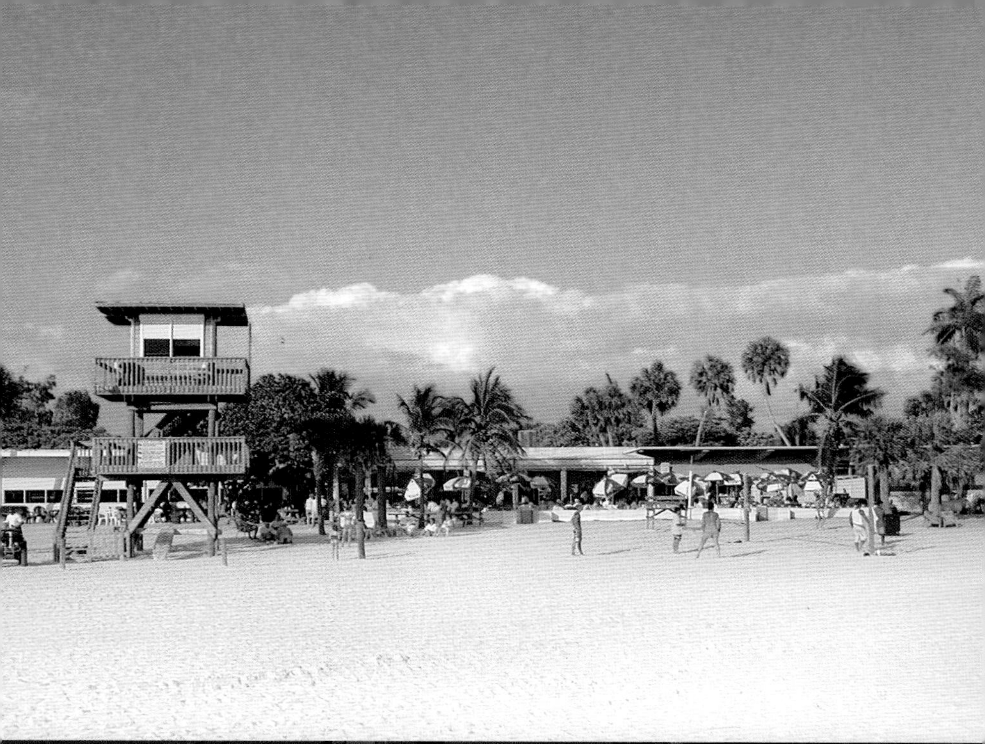

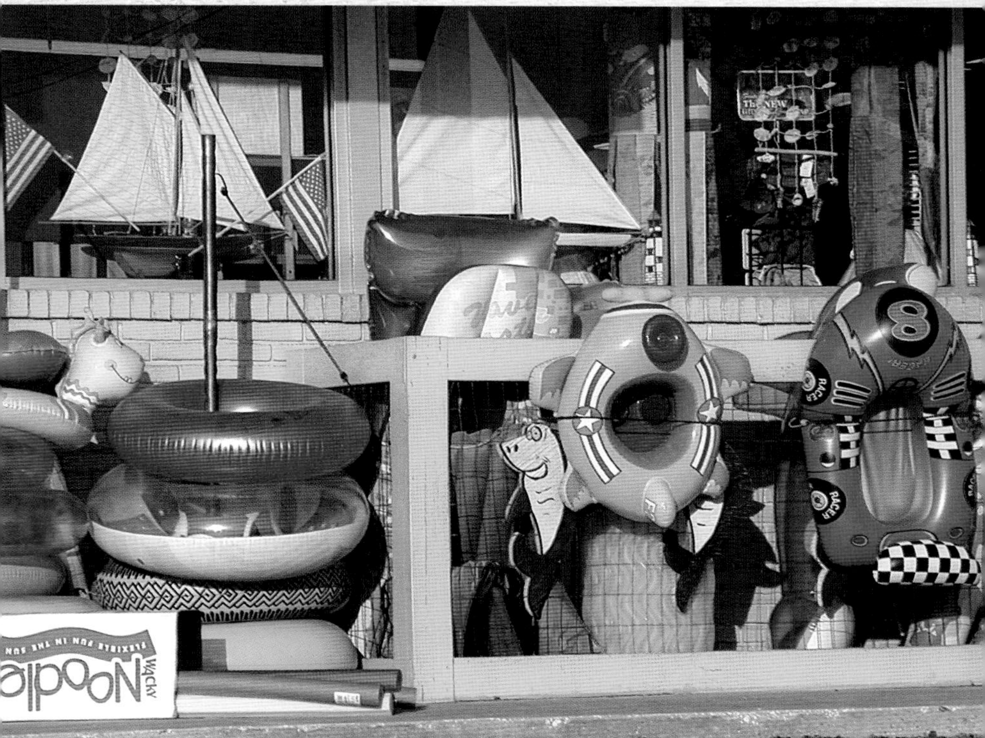
Wacky Noodle
FLEXIBLE FUN IN THE SUN
RACER

does Bradenton Beach Marina, the headquarters for boating and fishing charters, rentals, and tours. Coquina Beach, at the south end of Bradenton Beach, has boating and fishing facilities as well.

■ SARASOTA *map page 115, A-1/2*

The Tamiami Trail binds Bradenton and Sarasota seamlessly. The two used to be billed as sister cities, but today theirs has become more of a grandmother-granddaughter relationship. With its old, wrinkled beauty, laid-back Bradenton relishes history and nostalgia. Sarasota, on the other hand, with gleaming downtown highrises and cultural diversity, has grown into a junior varsity Miami, exuding a youth and energy that puts cutting-edge before quaint. The city regularly makes annual lists of best places to live due to its climate, commitment to the arts, and its school system, which is ranked among the best in Florida.

Paradoxically, the cultural reputation of which Sarasota is so proud was made possible by the circus—Ringling Brothers, to be exact. John Ringling downplayed his circus connections when he came to Sarasota, figuring people wouldn't take him seriously in his new career as a real-estate developer. Writes David C. Weeks in *Ringling, the Florida Years, 1911–1936:* "When the *Sarasota Times* ceased to identify Ringling as 'the well-known circus man,' he was pleased. He had never been apologetic about his circus career and wealth, but his activities in Sarasota required a change in emphasis. Until 1927, there were no visible signs of Ringling Bros. and Barnum & Bailey in Sarasota. There was only the millionaire entrepreneur."

Not that his opulent estate wasn't untouched by Big Top razzmatazz. **Ca' d'Zan,** or "House of John," styled after an Italian palazzo, fairly drips with embellishments that recall calliope wagons and trapeze costumes. Elephants, it's said, were used as work animals during the building of the Ringling Causeway, which connected the circus master's island kingdom to mainland Sarasota. Even Ringling's fabulous art collection, which he willed to the state of Florida, focuses on the large and the baroque-wall-size, richly colored paintings that fill cavernous, light-filled chambers.

By 1927, Ringling had decided to make Sarasota winter headquarters for his circus. Over the course of nine winters, Ringling's circus had a showbiz effect on the city. Today, Sarasota manifests its own version of showmanship in a theater scene that is the boast of the coast.

Sarasota's beaches are among the best in the state.

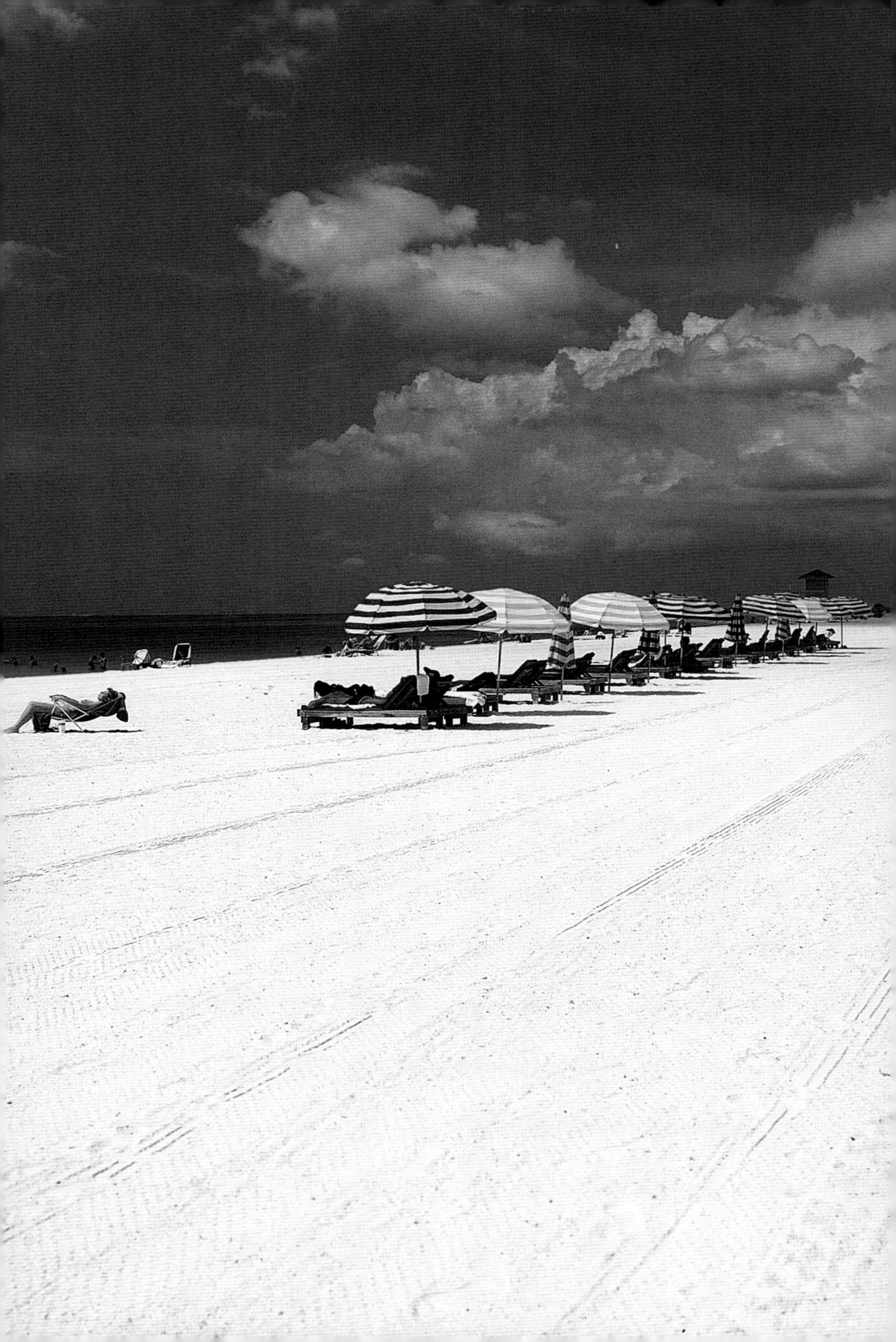

■ SARASOTA SIGHTS

The **Ringling Estate** is Sarasota's premier tourist attraction. Besides the 30-room Ca' d'Zan mansion, you'll find the eminent **John and Mable Ringling Museum of Art,** where you can see stellar baroque paintings like Peter Paul Rubens's *The Triumph of the Eucharist* and Diego Velazquez's *Philip IV of Spain.* Works by Nicolas Poussin, Frans Hals, and Sir Edward Burne-Jones are here, too, in addition to ancient and decorative arts and paintings by 20th-century artists. The Ringling Museum of the Circus displays antique circus wagons and vintage posters.

This is also the site of the **Old Asolo Theatre.** In the 1940s, Ringling heirs heard that in Asolo, Italy, a beautiful theater, built in 1798, was about to be demolished. Believing the theater's baroque Italian style suitable for the Ringling Estate, Ringling had the building dismantled and sent to Sarasota to be reconstructed and used for professional theater productions. (By the early 1980s, the historic theater became inadequate for the Asolo Theatre troupe's growing popularity, and a new center was built.) A magnificent banyan tree and rose garden highlight the landscaping of the gracious waterfront estate. *5401 Bay Shore Road, off the Tamiami Trail (U.S. 41); 941-359-5700.*

The area around Main Street and Palm Avenue is the lively theater and arts district. The **Sarasota Opera House** mounts opera productions in February and March in its 1920s Spanish mission-style building. The fare runs from light to dark, a typical season including such works as Strauss's *Die Fledermaus* and Verdi's *Macbeth. 61 North Pineapple Avenue; 941-366-8450.*

The **Florida Studio Theater** deals exclusively in new plays, accepting only those works that have been produced on Broadway or in Off-Broadway venues within the last five years. The theater has a Parisian-style cabaret restaurant, too, which is used mostly for one-man musical theater productions and monologuists. *1241 North Pineapple Avenue; 941-366-9000.*

Theater Works (1247 First Street; 941-952-9170) presents five productions each year, ranging from musicals to serious drama, in the historic and intimate Palm Tree Playhouse. The **Golden Apple Dinner Theater** (25 North Pineapple Avenue; 941-366-5454) serves up such crowd-pleasers as *Camelot* and *Phantom of the Opera* along with prime-rib dinners.

Along **Palm Avenue,** antiques shops and art galleries stand shoulder to shoulder with cabarets, pubs, restaurants, and cigar bars. Downtown meets Sarasota Bay at

The sculpture garden courtyard at the John and Mable Ringling Museum of Art in Sarasota. (John and Mable Ringling Museum of Art)

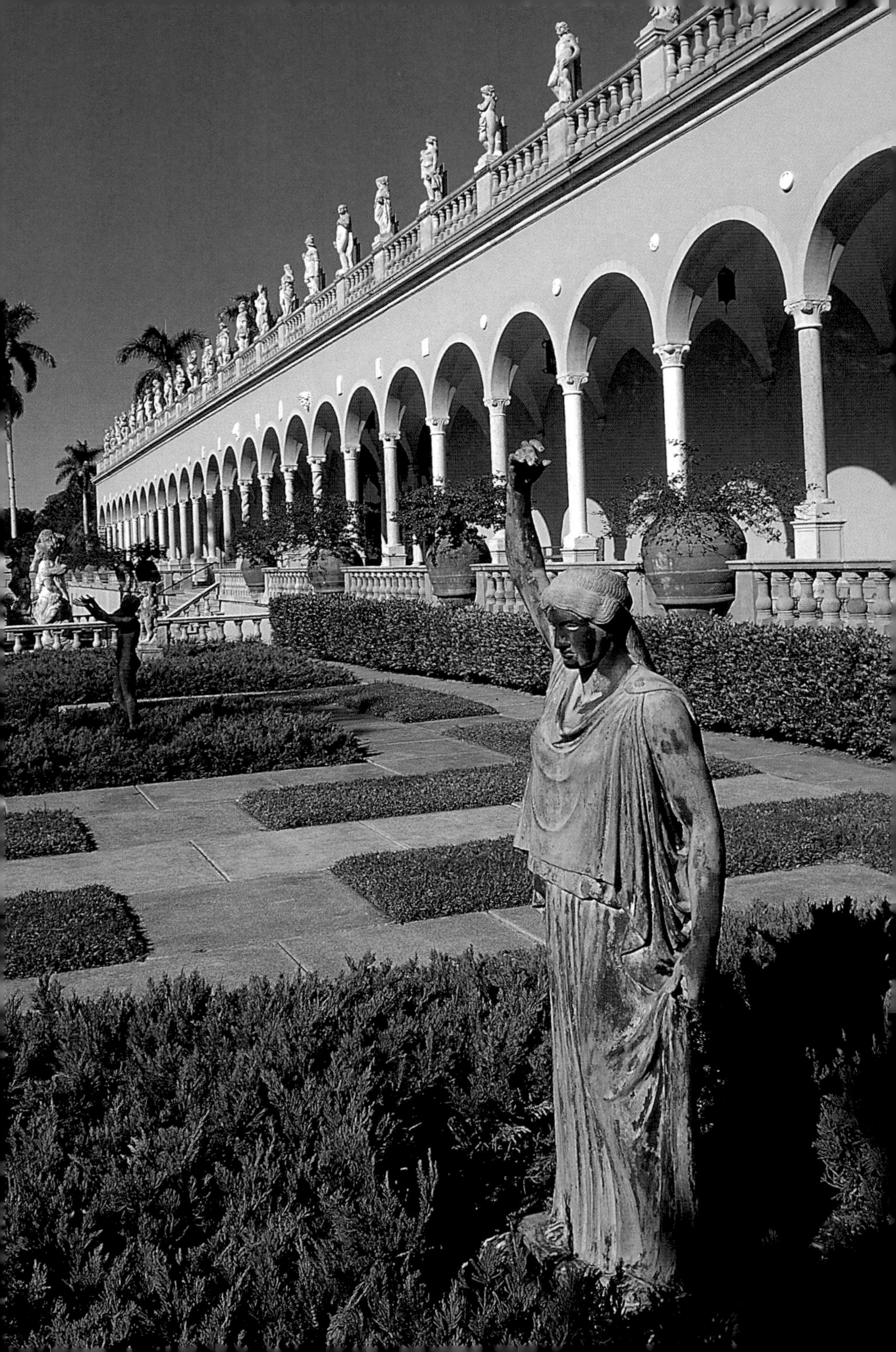

Bayfront Park, the place to go if you're looking to take a fishing, sight-seeing, or party-boat charter.

Slightly north of downtown, **Sarasota Quay** is a flashier nightlife quarter. One club hypes video and laser shows; another boasts jazz and fine cigars. *Fruitville Road at the Tamiami Trail.*

The Frank Lloyd Wright Foundation designed the hard-to-miss **Van Wezel Performing Arts Hall,** which sits near the waterfront north of downtown, like a giant purple clamshell that washed out of Sarasota Bay. Though the funky design has its detractors, critics and musicians agree that the hall's unusual shape is what makes it one of the most acoustically perfect auditoriums in the country. People come from around the state to see performances here, which range from Bob Dylan to Broadway touring productions to the Boston Pops. *777 North Tamiami Trail; 941-953-3366 or 800-826-9303.*

In recognition of Sarasota's Scottish roots, the architects who designed the Asolo Center for the Performing Arts incorporated elements from a circa-1900 Scottish opera house, including carved box fronts, friezes, and ornate cornices. The **Asolo Theatre Company** performs classical and contemporary plays from mid-November through May; you can tour the building for free year-round when rehearsals are not in session. *5555 North Tamiami Trail; 941-351-8000.*

Fans of Old Florida kitsch will get a kick out of Sarasota's **Jungle Gardens,** a 1940s-era tourist attraction where creatures from squirrel monkeys to Asian leopards to alligators live among 30 acres of palm-dappled, breathtakingly beautiful gardens. A few of the older exotic birds, allegedly trained by prison inmates, appeared on the *Ed Sullivan Show* in the 1960s. Disney this ain't, but in a state of corporate-run megaparks, this charmingly dated, family-run attraction is a breath of fresh air. *3701 Bay Shore Road; 941-355-5305.*

■ **SARASOTA'S ISLANDS** *map page 115, A-1/2*

> And I love the beaches too, out beyond the cottage colony, where
> they are wild and free still, visited by the sandpipers that retreat
> before each wave, like children, and by an occasional hip-sprung
> farmwife hunting shells, or sometimes by a veteran digging for
> *Donax variabilis* to take back to his hungry mate in the trailer camp.
>
> —E. B. White

E. B. White found Sarasota's barrier islands a warm and inviting world. During the 1940s and '50s, he made frequent visits to the then mostly unpopulated islands. The *Donax variabilis* he describes is more commonly known as a coquina—tiny bivalves found at the sea's edge. Old-timers like to harvest coquinas, stew them, and drink the broth. The shells appear in an infinite variety of colors and patterns, and veteran beachcombers know that if they plant their feet where the sea laps the coquina-strewn shore, they can experience a most delightful foot massage.

Sarasota's beaches are well populated and offer little peace and quiet. You may find sandpipers, but you're more likely to see hip-slim sunbathers in bikinis than E. B. White's hip-sprung farmwives.

←🚐→ *The most scenic route to Sarasota's islands is Route 789, which travels across the bridge to Longboat Key and then runs south to Lido Key. From downtown Sarasota, cross Ringling Causeway to St. Armands Key, which is tucked into Lido's "belly" and is accessible to Longboat Key as you head north.*

■ St. Armands Circle

You're more likely to hear St. Armands Key referred to as St. Armands Circle. A brainchild of developer John Ringling, the Circle, as it's known, consists of shops, galleries, restaurants, and clubs. If you're a shopper, you'll not want to miss it. Locals compare it to Rodeo Drive or Palm Beach's Worth Avenue, but its retail establishments, from Jamaican Me Crazy to Little Bo-Tique, are nowhere near as exclusive.

■ Lido Key

Ringling also had a hand in Lido Key, which he bought, dredged, and filled. The beach is still the island's long suit. Three separate parks allow public access. You'll see the first one as you head west out of the Circle on John Ringling Boulevard. **North Lido Beach** has few amenities or parking, hence fewer people. The beach scene becomes more frenzied at the main **Lido Beach,** where there's a swimming pool, beach volleyball courts, and a snack bar. **South Lido Beach** is a 130-acre park with nature and canoe trails, a beach, and athletic facilities.

■ CITY ISLAND

The **Mote Marine Laboratory and Aquarium,** on City Island north of St. Armands Circle, is a research facility that focuses on the restoration of fragile Gulf Coast ecology. The 135,000-gallon shark tank, filled to the rim with nurse sharks, stingrays, tarpon, jewfish, amberjack, and barracudas, has been a popular attraction for years. Hugh and Buffett, two West Indian manatees who loll around their tank, are popular, as is Contact Cove, where you can interact with creatures ranging from stingrays to sea anenomes. The Mote Center for Shark Research's hands-on internship program receives hundreds of applications every year from college students interested in the summer of a lifetime. *1600 Ken Thompson Parkway; 941-388-4441 or 800-691-6683.*

■ LONGBOAT KEY

City Island perches at the edge of the pass that separates Lido Key from Longboat Key. Twelve miles long, the island, which was used as a bombing range by the Florida Air National Guard in the early 1940s, is shared by Sarasota and Manatee Counties. The southern, Sarasota section is manicured to perfection. There's not much in the way of sight-seeing, unless you love gaping at fine homes hidden behind iron fences. Beach access is pretty much saved for residents and resort guests.

The Manatee end of the island is less like a movie set. The Village, which was Longboat's original community and sits at the island's northern threshold, is relaxed and unpretentious. Take Broadway Street (south of the bridge to Anna Maria Island) to get there, and stop in at one of two local fish houses. Then drive around the neighborhood looking for wild peacocks perched atop houses and strolling through yards. One public beach is located nearby, but there are no rest rooms or other facilities.

■ SIESTA KEY

Technically part of Sarasota but geographically separate, Siesta Key has resisted being bridged to the chain of islands above it. Two bridges do, however, link it to the mainland south of downtown Sarasota. Siesta Key, like Sarasota's other islands, has its gate-guarded mansions, but it's more welcoming.

Water lettuce clogs the Corkscrew Swamp Sanctuary.

The beaches here are unlike others in southwest Florida, where the sand is generally tan in color and rough with seashell fragments. Here, the sand is pulverized quartz, like that on Panhandle beaches (geologists believe that Siesta Key's beaches were formed by sand migrating from the Panhandle). However it happened, the sand at Crescent Beach, a beach town often confused with one of the same name on Florida's Atlantic coast, is brilliantly white and feels soft as silk between the toes.

Siesta Key County Beach is a huge park that accommodates lovers of surf, sun, and sand. The beach has concessions, tennis courts, ball fields, volleyball courts, a fitness trail, a playground, and a soccer field, plus picnic tables and shelters, a pavilion, two places to eat, a souvenir shop, and lifeguards. For more privacy, try the smaller accesses along Beach Way and Midnight Pass Road. If you like to snorkel and fish, Access #11 puts you at Point of Rocks, which is good for both. Parking at these spots fills up fast.

My favorite time to go to this beach is at sunset. The last time I witnessed one here, the sun wore its clouds like a sweatband as it dropped below the horizon. For a moment I forgot the high-rises, absorbed by this final blaze of nature. *Midnight Pass Road at Beach Way Drive.*

Roseate spoonbills wait in the shallows of the Myakka River State Park.

■ INLAND NATURE PRESERVES

■ MYAKKA RIVER STATE PARK *map page 115, A-2*

Within these 28,875 acres of hammocks and wetlands the most popular activities are camping, canoeing, biking, and touring the park via tram or boat. White-tailed deer, bobcats, red-shouldered hawks, and packs of indigenous Boy Scouts perfecting the art of tent-pitching can all be found here. *Route 72, southeast of Sarasota; 941-361-6511.*

■ CORKSCREW SWAMP SANCTUARY *map page 115, B-4*

The National Audubon Society operates this 700-acre refuge of bald cypress trees, the largest pure forest of the specimen found anywhere in the world, and one of America's largest colonies of nesting wood storks. You can penetrate the swamp via boardwalk and often spy alligators, limpkins, deer, and river otters. *846 Immokalee Road, north of Naples, 21 miles east of U.S. 41; 941-348-9151.*

■ BIG CYPRESS PRESERVE *map page 115, B-5*

The 716,000 acres of Everglades here protect the state's largest population of the endangered Florida panther, as well as a beautiful stand of bald cypress that survived post–World War II clear-cutting. (Outside the park, you'll still see vendors hawking cypress-stump coffee tables, clocks, and assorted cypress folk art.) *U.S. 41, northwest of Everglades City; 941-695-4111.*

■ VENICE *map page 115, A-2*

Venice, Sarasota's little sister, emulates her sibling in a quieter, more small-town way. Hundreds of fossilized shark's teeth wash up on Venice beaches each year, and shark-tooth hunters gravitate toward the Venice Fishing Pier at Brohard Park on Harbor Drive at Center Road to collect them. Working with implements called "Florida snow shovels"—mesh baskets attached to poles—and sometimes wearing carpenter's aprons with pockets to hold their finds, they poke around the black-flecked sand looking for treasure. In August, Venice hosts the **Shark's Tooth Festival** down by the pier. (Don't let all this talk about sharks' teeth keep you out of the water, because there aren't as many sharks in the Gulf as you might think. Sharks lose and replace teeth on a regular basis. One shark can shed more than one hundred teeth in its lifetime.)

A red-bellied woodpecker at the Myakka River State Park.

In the 1920s, the Brotherhood of Locomotive Engineers chose the town of Venice as a retirement community and built a model city in an architectural style to match the town's name. That's why Venice's buildings have Italianate arches, red barrel–tile roofs, stucco walls, and molded detailing. Many original structures can be found along West Venice Avenue, Harbor Drive, and Tampa Drive. Some of the old buildings along date palm–lined West Venice Avenue now hold shops and cafés. On Tampa Avenue, the old Kentucky Military Institute has been turned into a stylish indoor shopping arcade.

■ CHARLOTTE COUNTY *map page 115, A-2/3*

Much of what is worth seeing in Charlotte County can be found in the fishing villages and hidden towns that lie well off the main thoroughfares. Make your way on through the stretch of urban sprawl called Port Charlotte to reach some barrier island gems.

■ **MANASOTA KEY** *map page 115, A-2*

A slice of island on Route 776, Manasota Key contains two communities in two counties. The northern, Sarasota County portion is almost entirely a wildlife preserve. Along the road, you'll see luxurious homes spaced far apart, a few lodgings, and two public beaches. **Manasota Beach** is the more popular of the two beaches, with extended facilities and easier access.

As you cross the Sarasota County line and enter **Englewood Beach,** the mood becomes more low-key. The resort scene here consists of fishermen, families, and vacationers on a budget, making for a relaxed atmosphere where strangers wave to you from their cars in the middle of high season (at which time people in some resort communities are more likely to be making other hand gestures at one another). It's less pretentious here than at Sarasota's playgrounds and feels like a true beach resort, where fun is what matters most.

■ **GASPARILLA ISLAND** *map page 115, A-2/3*

Gasparilla Island, the second reward in backroads Charlotte County, stretches into two counties as well. Gasparilla's north end lies on the other side of Stump Pass from Englewood Beach, a hot fishing spot.

The first inhabitants of Gasparilla Island were the Calusa Indians, who fished here a thousand years ago. In the 1870s, Cubans and Spaniards established camps on the northern end of the island, and when phosphate was discovered inland before the dawn of the 20th century, a railroad was built to transport the phosphate from the mines to deep Boca Grande Pass. The railroad enabled wealthy industrialists to discover Boca Grande, sealing its fate as an exclusive winter camp for such 14-karat names as Vanderbilt, Du Pont, Morgan, Crowninshield, Astor, and Eastman.

Many of them came to pay homage to the silver king, or tarpon—the prize of all prize fish. The well-to-do winterers, called "beachfronters" by locals, built their homes along the Gulf, or stayed at the elite **Gasparilla Inn** (500 Palm Avenue at Fifth Street; 941-964-2201), the still-reigning grande dame of the southwest coast. Since those early days, heirs and developers have broken the grip the beachfronters held on the island. Though still somewhat exclusive, the island is being discovered more and more by visitors who come to shop and dine at some of the fine eateries, or sunbathe on the beach at the 135-acre **Gasparilla Island State Recreation Area** (941-964-0375 or 941-964-0600), 135 acres along the Gulf. In summer, tarpon season, visitors still come to do battle with the feisty silver king.

■ **PUNTA GORDA** *map page 115, A-3*

The town of Punta Gorda hugs the Tamiami Trail and the wide mouth of the **Peace River,** where Ponce de León is said to have made his first stop on the Gulf Coast and been hit by the arrow that eventually killed him. In the past decade, Punta Gorda has been nearly overwhelmed by the sprawl along the Tamiami Trail and has had to fight for its life. Many fine mansions along Retta Esplanade and other neighborhood streets have been restored, most of them looking like valentines from a more gracious era. Marion Avenue holds some resurrected commercial buildings of yore. If you follow one-way Marion to its end, you'll come upon **Ponce de León Historical Park,** a lovely waterfront park with the implicit lesson that searching for youth can kill you.

■ **FORT MYERS** *map page 115, A/B-3/4*

Inventor Thomas A. Edison loved Fort Myers. You can visit the **Thomas Edison Winter Home and Museum,** where he spent most of his winters between 1886 and 1931. The home he built on the shores of the Caloosahatchee River was actually composed of two identical houses, which were prefabricated in Maine and shipped to Fort Myers in pieces. The river was Edison's driveway, and the cow path that was to become the town's showy McGregor Boulevard separated his home from his laboratory. He planted his extensive Seminole Lodge estate with rare and exotic plants, which he used for experiments in creating lightbulb filaments, and rubber for the tires his friend Harvey Firestone produced. Henry Ford built his humble home, **the Mangoes,** next door. The two estates form the most remarkable attraction in Fort Myers. You'll need a few hours to take the guided tour, which leads through the estates, gardens, laboratory, and museum. *2350–2400 McGregor Boulevard; 941-334-3614.*

■ **LEE ISLANDS** *map page 115, A-3/4*

Along the shores of Lee County, a stretch the local tourism bureau calls the Lee Island Coast, several islands seem to float in their own little worlds. Easily accessible by boat from Sanibel and Captiva Islands (also part of the Lee Islands), they're distant enough from the mainland to feel far from the hubbub.

■ **UPPER CAPTIVA** *map page 115, A-3*

Upper Captiva was separated from Captiva during a hurricane in the 1920s. Known as North Captiva on nautical charts, it is a long, skinny stretch of island partially owned and protected by the state. Most of the island has been tastefully developed with homes and town houses available for vacation rental. Owners and renters drive golf carts on the island's sand streets. Upper Captiva is known to recreational boaters for its remote beaches and funky restaurants.

■ **CAYO COSTA** *map page 115, A-3*

An even less developed place just one island to the north, Cayo Costa is practically all state park. Pine woods and palmetto cover much of the 1,600-acre island, which is without most conveniences—though there is running water for showers. Humans are few; there's only a ranger or two. Campers come to use the rustic cab-

Henry Ford's winter home, the Mangoes, Fort Myers.

ins or to stake a tent; day-trippers bike and hike the 5 miles of trails. Beachers, shellers, and picnickers wander the unspoiled beach; in summer, loggerhead turtles lay their eggs here.

■ **USEPPA ISLAND** *map page 115, A-3*

In the early 1960s, soldiers trained for the Bay of Pigs invasion in nearby Useppa Island. Overall, though, the island has been used for the more refined pursuits of the leisure class. During the 1930s, developer Barron Collier established the exclusive Izaak Walton Club for tarpon fishermen, a group that at different times reportedly included Zane Grey, Shirley Temple, and Theodore Roosevelt. The island's newer buildings were built in Old Florida–style for members of the private club that now owns the island.

One regular visitor to Useppa, novelist Mary Roberts Rinehart, purchased a tiny island nearby, in Pine Island Sound, and named it **Cabbage Key** for the type of palms that grow here. The humble home she built for her son and his bride is now a small inn, an unpretentious restaurant famous for seafood and key lime pie, and a tiny bar where boaters continue the Caribbean tradition of signing dollar

A private home on Useppa Island.

bills and then taping them to every imaginable surface. It's supposed to bring good luck, but the luckiest person around might be the bar owner who gets to keep this wallpaper (to date, tens of thousands of dollars have been left here). There are a few modern cottages for rent, and a wooden water tower that rewards climbers with magnificent views of neighboring islands. *Cabbage Key Inn; 941-283-2278.*

■ SANIBEL ISLAND *map page 115, A-3/4*

Sanibel Island divides its history into B.C. and A.C.—Before Causeway and After Causeway. Fiercely independent, Sanibel's residents refused to allow their island to suffer from the shortsighted development that they had seen ruin the fragile ecology of other Florida islands. When Lee County officials insisted on replacing the ferry shuttle with a causeway in 1963, Sanibel Islanders rebelled by incorporating and enforcing a model rate-of-growth ordinance.

Such actions were hardly new, however. Since the 1930s, when Captiva visitor and political cartoonist J. N. "Ding" Darling laid groundwork for a national wildlife refuge here, islanders have been committed to balancing the island's resort potential with their belief that its wilderness should be protected.

The subtly beautiful **J. N. "Ding" Darling National Wildlife Refuge** covers a good half of Sanibel Island. Wetlands and mangroves provide habitat for some of Florida's most prized creatures: manatees, roseate spoonbills, ospreys, brown pelicans, anhingas, bobcats, river otters, alligators, one crocodile (once relocated, it later found its way back), and herons and egrets. Mangroves appear to walk on their tiptoes. Pelicans balance on flimsy mangrove branches. Fiddler crabs move their homes with the tides.

A 5-mile road paved with seashells travels past the 20-foot observation tower, where birds feed in the morning and at sunset. Spotting an alligator is also possible, though when one driver pulls over next to a stream of water, every driver behind follows suit, believing a gator's been sighted. You can almost hear the lens caps click off in unison. Short trails delve into the mangrove world. The best way to experience Ding Darling is by canoe or kayak, which you can rent from a concession at the refuge's fringe, then take on the 6 miles of marked canoe courses. The operators of the same concession conduct narrated tram tours.

The new Ding Darling Education Center is a 4,000-square-foot facility that uses interactive exhibits and multimedia displays to promote estuary conservation. When the federal government refused to build the park a center, the Ding Darling

Wildlife Society raised $3.5 million to complete the project, which speaks volumes about how dearly locals hold this area in their hearts. *Sanibel-Captiva Road, 3 miles from the end of Periwinkle Way; 941-472-1100.*

The **Sanibel-Captiva Conservation Foundation** owns more than 1,800 acres on and around Sanibel. Much of the land is at a nature center where visitors can hike along the Sanibel River, climb a bird observation tower, walk through a butterfly house, buy native plants, and dip their fingers into a touch tank. The center also hosts island boat tours and interpretive beach walks. *3333 Sanibel-Captiva Road; 941-472-2329.*

Sanibel is the best seashelling island in Florida, perhaps in all of the continental United States, because the island's east-west turn at its south end allows it to catch more shells as they wash up from the Caribbean Sea. The late actor Raymond Burr, an enthusiastic sheller, was among the founders of Sanibel's **Bailey-Matthews Shell Museum.** The 25,000-square-foot facility plays an active role in education, environmental preservation, and research. Its two floors hold 2 million shells—from land, freshwater, and sea—that represent a third of the world's 100,000 species of living mollusks. *3075 Sanibel-Captiva Road; 941-395-2233.*

A number of shell shops sell seashells (say that three times) on the island, along with shell crafts and shell art, from tacky little elephants to an elegant brand of Sanibel-born calligraphy art known as "shelligrams."

Bowman's Beach is the island's longest and most secluded beach park, so the shells are less picked over. Be careful about what you pick up, though. In a recent groundbreaking and controversial movement, islanders crafted and got the state legislature to pass a law forbidding the collection of shells on Sanibel with a live animal inside. Protected species include starfish, sea urchins, and sand dollars. Bowman's was long known as a nude beach. Nudity is illegal, of course, but authorities have had difficulty redressing the problem. Patrollers used to ride the beach to arrest offenders, but today they're more likely to be on the lookout for collectors with live shells. *Sanibel-Captiva Road.*

At Sanibel's southeastern end, you'll find a popular sunning and shelling spot, Lighthouse Beach, the site of the Sanibel Lighthouse, built in 1884. This is the most developed of Sanibel's beaches, with a fishing pier, nature trail, and interpretive station. The beach, heavily used in season, is favored by teens and springbreakers. *Southeastern end of Periwinkle Way.*

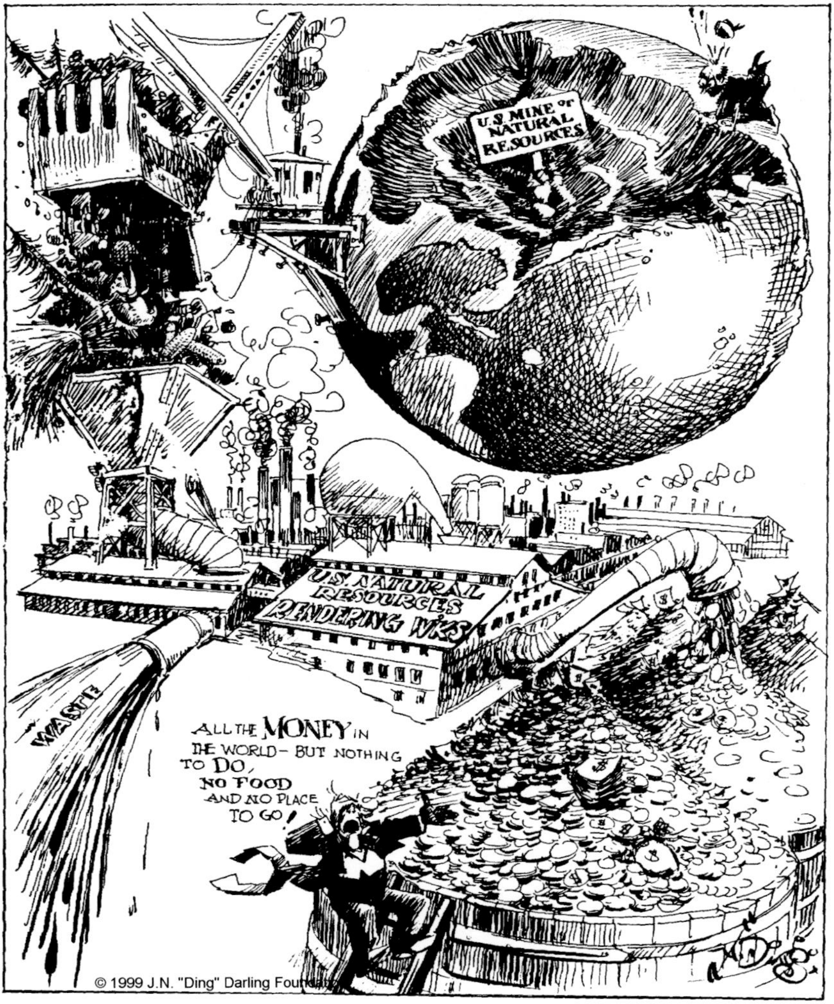
U.S. MINE OF NATURAL RESOURCES
U.S. NATURAL RESOURCES RENDERING WKS
WASTE
ALL THE MONEY IN THE WORLD – BUT NOTHING TO DO, NO FOOD AND NO PLACE TO GO!
© 1999 J.N. "Ding" Darling Foundation

The editorial cartoonist J. N. "Ding" Darling, a major proponent of conservation, tweaked short-sighted industrialists in his 1938 cartoon "How Rich Will We Be When We Have Converted All Our Forests, All Our Soil, All Our Water Resources and Our Minerals Into Cash?"

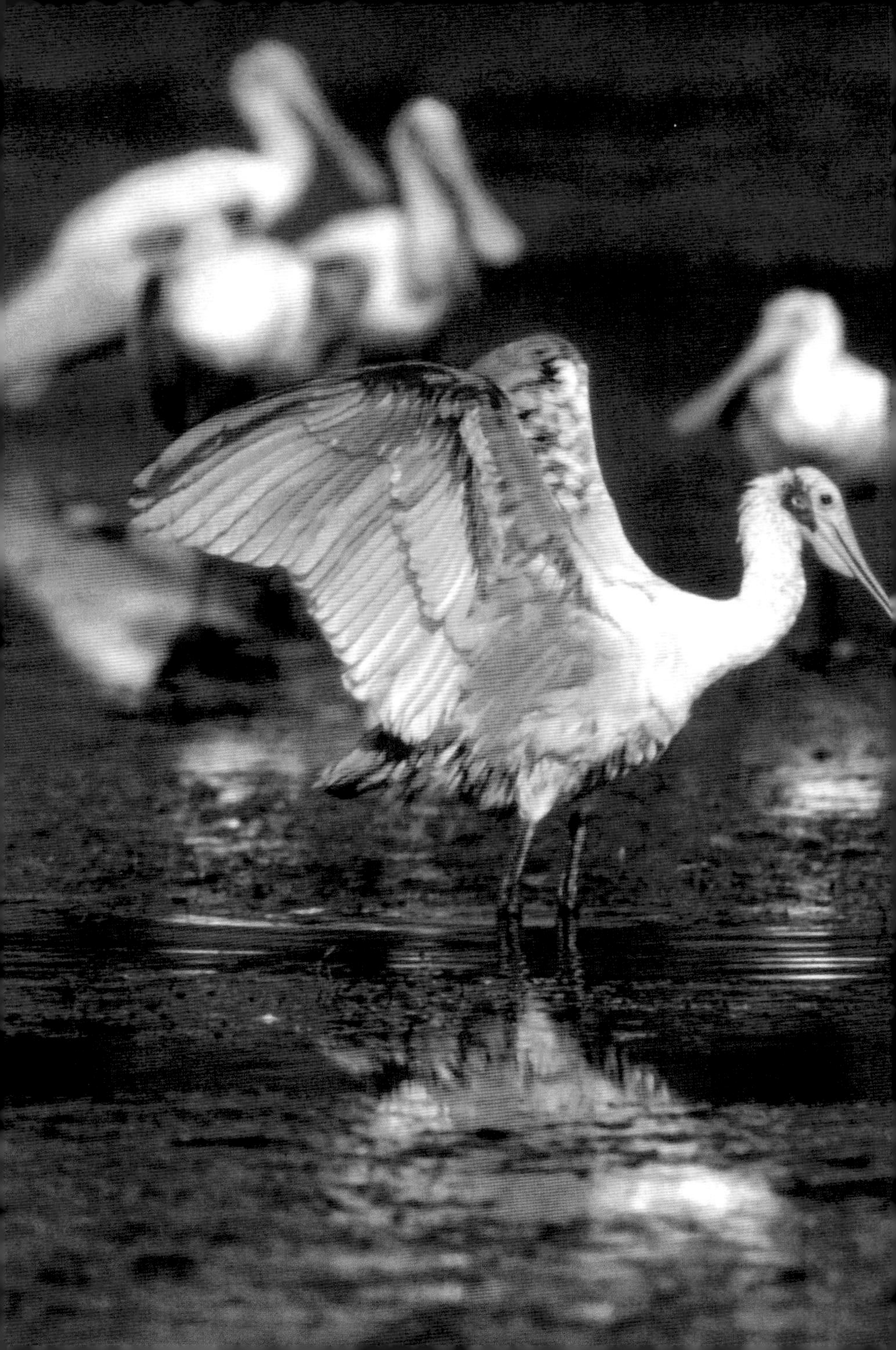

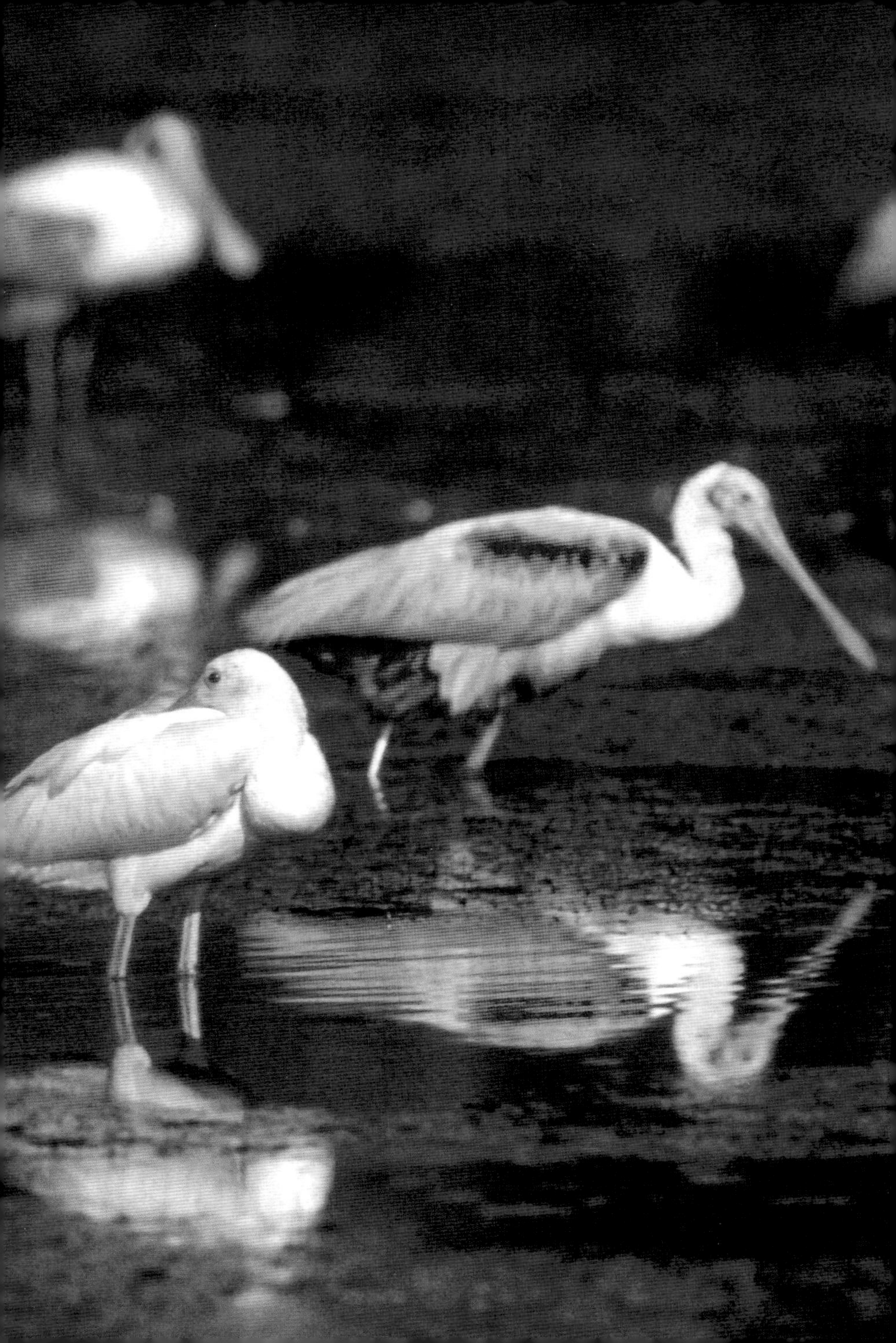

■ CAPTIVA ISLAND *map page 115, A-3*

Captiva lies at the northern end of Sanibel-Captiva Road. Captiva Drive, flat and lined by lush vegetation, makes for a pretty, seaside ride. Captiva is known for its white clapboard cottages and good, if somewhat expensive, restaurants. The waters surrounding the island are warm and blue-green. Boating, fishing, sailing, and kayaking can be enjoyed at **'Tween Waters Inn Marina** (15951 Captiva Road; 941-472-5161).

The island's most famous residents were aviator Charles Lindbergh and his wife, Anne, who wrote of Captiva:

> How wonderful are islands! Islands in space, like this one I have come to, ringed about by miles of water, linked by no bridges, no cables, no telephones. An island from the world and world's life.

The Lindberghs first came to Captiva Island in 1941 to flee the throngs that initially idolized Charles, then criticized him for his isolationist views during World War II. Wrote Charles in one of his journals:

> We went to sleep with the wind blowing softly through the bending boughs and long needles of the Australian pines, and with the odor of semitropical land and sea coming through the window and relaxing all the tension one has gathered through the weeks of a New York winter.

Anne, a poet, continued to visit Captiva Island on her own in years to come. Captiva was probably the source of inspiration for her coming-of-age book, *Gift from the Sea.* She wrote that living on the island seemed to foster among its residents the respect for privacy she had so long sought:

> People, too, become like islands in such an atmosphere, self-contained, whole and serene; respecting other people's solitude, not intruding on their shores, standing back in reverence before the miracle of another individual.

(preceding pages) Exotic birds take the waters at J. N. "Ding" Darling National Wildlife Refuge.

■ ISLAND ROUTE 865 *map page 115, A-4*

Florida's west coast lacks an equivalent to the east coast's seaside scenic Route A1A, but you get glimpses of coastal resort towns and lonely, uninhabited waterfront stretches along some sections of Route 865. It begins in Fort Myers Beach, the beach town to which college kids flock for spring break and families arrive in summer. Less expensive than its northern island neighbors, Fort Myers Beach is also more heavily developed. Residents are trying to put the brakes on development.

Activity centers around Times Square and the fishing pier, where the high bridge lands. If all the commotion bothers you, head south. Stop in at **Matanzas Pass Preserve** (end of Bay Road) for a glimpse of the wilderness that Fort Myers Beach strives to recapture. The 56-acre preserve has nature trails, interpretive areas, a canoe launch, and a boardwalk that traverses mangrove swamps. The end of Estero Island gets quieter and quieter until you reach the pass at Lover's Key.

The wedding gazebo at **Lover's Key State Park** (8700 Estero Boulevard; 941-463-4588) capitalizes on the romantic name, but nature lovers are drawn to the area, too, for its natural beauty, solitude, and mangrove-lined tidal lagoons, where

Along the Gulf, beaches are awash in myriad treasures.

osprey, dolphin, and manatee live undisturbed. Bicycling, sea kayaking, and canoeing are popular pursuits here; call Tarpon Bay Recreation (941-765-7880) to rent equipment or to book a tour.

Route 865 ends at Bonita Beach on Little Hickory Island. Bonita Beach can best be described as a scaled-down, residential version of Fort Myers. The southern end of Bonita Public Beach is somewhat built up with shops and restaurants, but the beach beyond it, 342-acre **Barefoot Beach,** has been left in its natural state.

■ NAPLES *map page 115, A-4/5*

Over the course of 120 years, adventurers and ambitious businessmen have crafted a town that fairly glows with quiet glamour. Some call it the Palm Beach of the west coast, but Naples is more demure. The town's backwoods history is so recent that the "old" rich of Naples are inclined to tell you about the city's rough-and-ready roots, rather than boast about its sparkle.

The short history of Naples holds less interest for travelers than do the city's 55 golf courses, shops, art galleries, and 9 miles of white, warm-water beaches, some of them part of **Delnor-Wiggins Pass State Park.** The beaches at the town's north end have been left pretty much in their natural state. In summer, the staff gives beach talks about the loggerhead sea turtles that nest here. *1100 Gulf Shore Drive North; 941-597-6196.*

Naples's frontier history is told at **Naples Pier,** where locals gather to watch the sunset. The 600-foot-long wooden pier was first built in 1888; after Hurricane Donna demolished it in 1960, it was rebuilt and lengthened. *12th Avenue and Gulfshore Boulevard.*

The 13 acres of the **Conservancy of Southwest Florida,** smack in the center of town, is kept impressively pristine. You can get away from it all on canoe tours and nature trails, or at the aviaries and serpentarium. *1450 Merrihue Drive North; 941-262-0304.*

Perhaps because Naples has always been populated by the well-to-do, downtown Naples, or **Old Naples,** is well preserved; it's never suffered from severe deterioration, the way other Florida downtowns have. Within the historic district, where many buildings are almost a century old, several streets offer especially scenic strolls.

Feeding sea gulls at sunset along Sanibel Island.

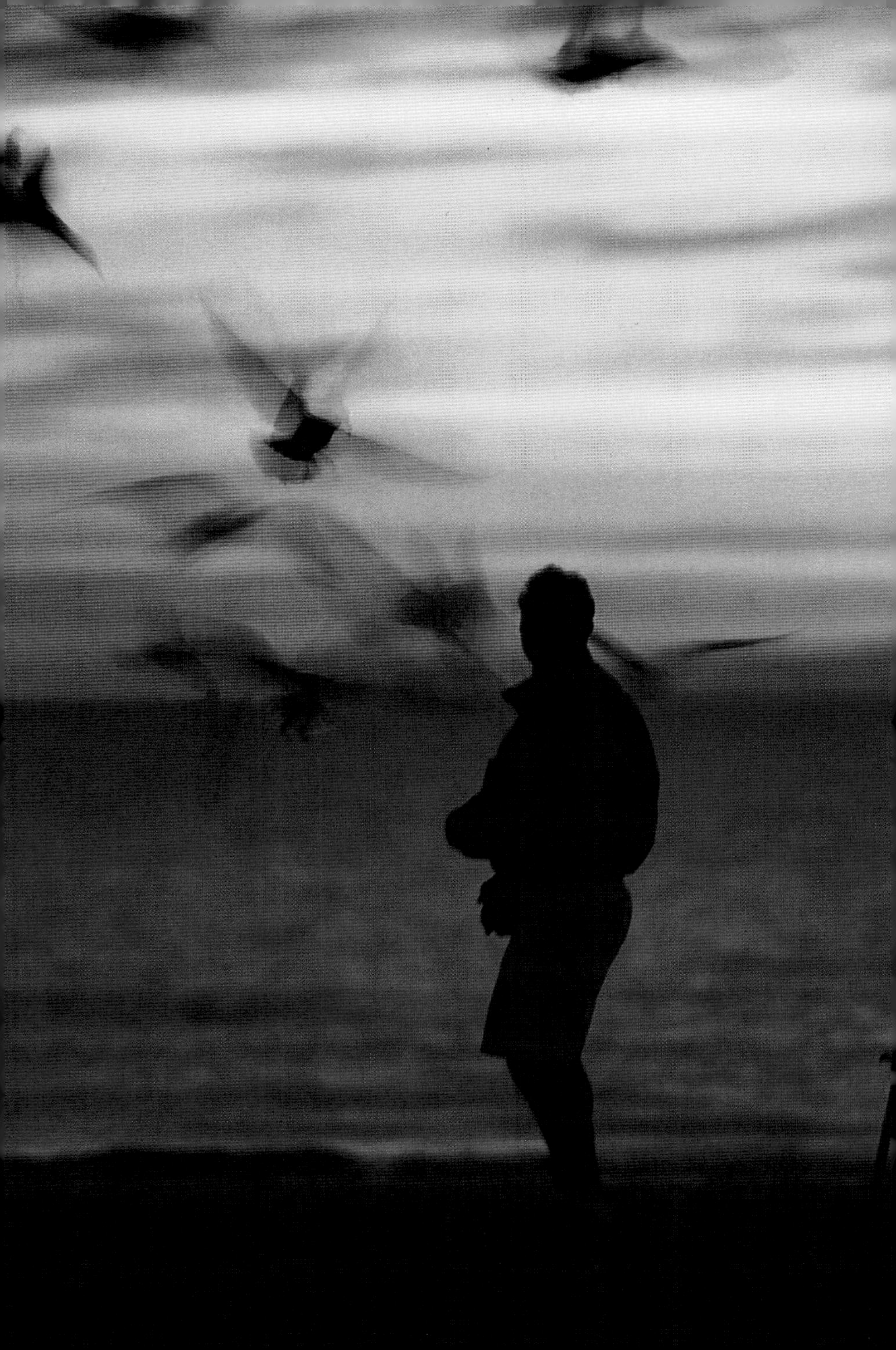

On **Third Street South,** pastel buildings house galleries and shops with art objects and gifts for the person who has everything. Chic restaurants and boutiques line **Fifth Avenue South.** Tin City (at the eastern end of downtown, along the harbor) is a converted oyster-processing plant now full of shops and cafés. Along **Gulfshore Boulevard,** palm trees and beaches provide the backdrop to manicured mansions and elegant town houses.

As you head south on Route 951 to Marco Island, watch for signs for the **Briggs Nature Center.** Though not a dazzling facility, it supplies a good introduction to the 8,000-acre Rookery Bay Estuarine Preserve, where a boardwalk loops through an estuary wetland habitat. The butterfly garden is a nice touch. In winter, when mosquitoes and other party-killers are at a minimum, the center offers boat tours of the area aboard the *Sea Queen.* To understand the often-hidden value and beauty of Everglades ecology, sign up for one of Briggs's tours. On the Beach Night-Seining tour on Marco Island, participants drag seine nets across the beach at low tide and study the collected contents. We came up with a lizard fish, a baby horseshoe crab, a dwarf seahorse, a spider crab, sea stars, a ribbonlike pipefish, a

This region's many islands have popular resorts, such as South Seas Plantation on Captiva Island (right), where patrons can rent jet skis (above) along the beach.

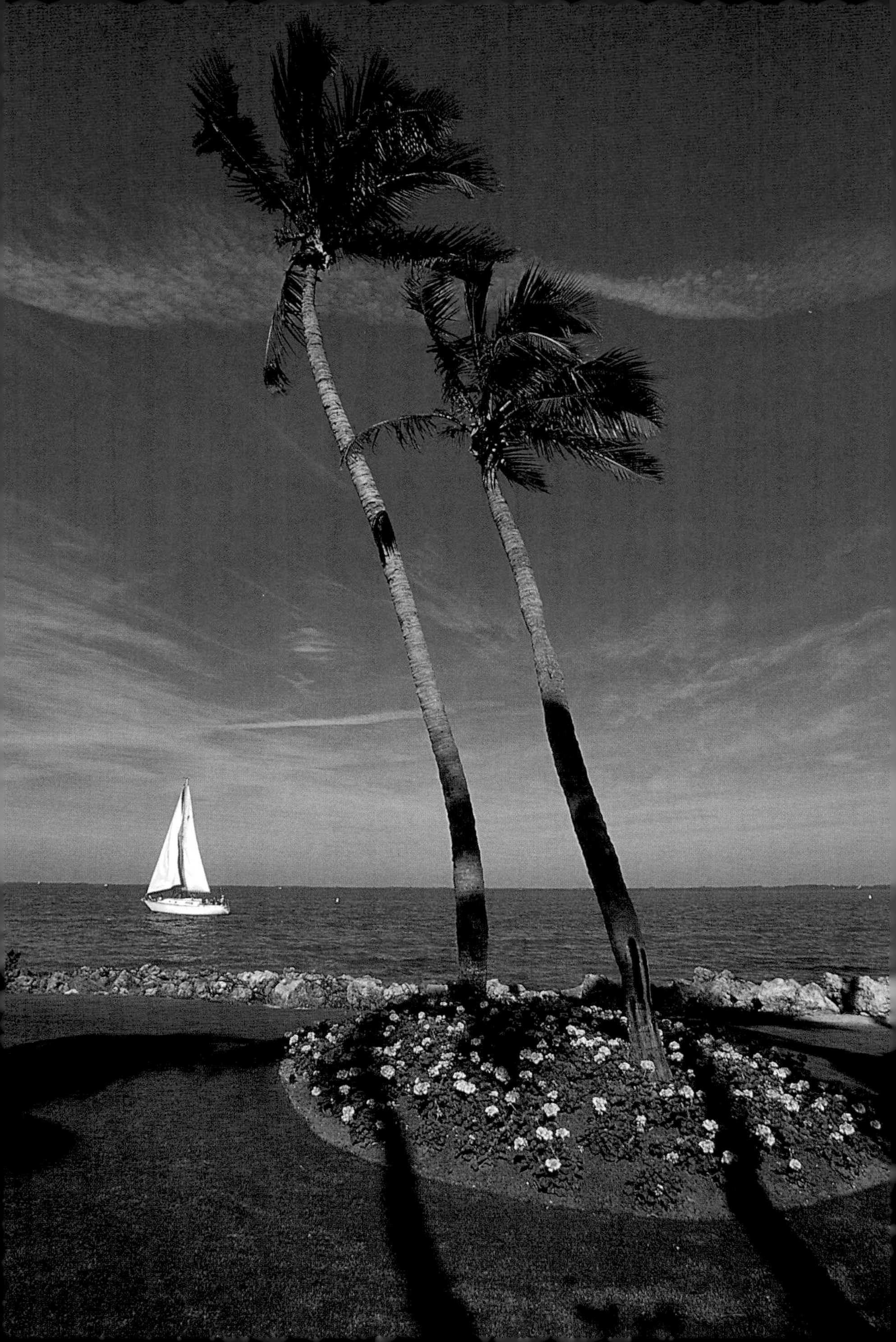

Swamp-Buggy Racing

Expensive foreign cars may be more representative of Naples today, but it's the old-fashioned swamp buggy that is still the town's trademark. Resident Ed Frank invented it back in the 1940s for Everglades swamp travel and hunting. Fellow hunters borrowed from his big-tire design to convert their own Jeep-style vehicles. Each designer added his own hood decoration to see who could come up with the most practical, if not decorative, vehicle.

Soon, the sport of swamp-buggy racing was born, originally timed with the opening of hunting season. As that day approached, hunters fine-tuned their awkward creations, making ready not only for the hunt, but for the parade and inevitable race that came first. As competition flared, and prizes (turkeys and money) began to be offered, speed became the primary objective in building swamp buggies. Clumsy wooden buggies were streamlined and hyper-propelled.

Swamp-buggy races are held three times a year at Florida Sports Park and are broadcast on national television. "In my estimation, it is imperative to keep the old tradition of our town, lest we lose our identity," writes publisher Peter Stone. "Must we become a new city and sacrifice our charm? I feel that the development of Naples needs to slow down long enough for the history of the area to catch up with it."

A stubborn, good-old-boy tradition, swamp buggies remain a practical means of Everglades travel. *Florida Sports Park, Route 951 south of I-75; 941-774-2701 or 800-897-2701.*

baby spadefish, and a live lightning whelk with its curlicue egg case. *401 Shell Island Road; 941-775-8569.*

■ MARCO ISLAND *map page 115, A-5*

Away from the island's hub is **Tigertail Beach,** at the end of Hernando Drive. It's especially nice at the lowest tides, when birds feed in a series of narrow sandbars separated by tidal pools.

In Goodland, and only in Goodland, can you believe that Marco Island is one of the Ten Thousand Islands. The town comes alive on Sundays, when the "Buzzard King," Stan Gober, the colorful owner of **Stan's Idle Hour Restaurant** (221 Goodland Drive; 941-394-3041), hosts the Buzzard Lope bash, a party named after a peculiar dance he invented to go with an even stranger song he wrote about a dead buzzard. The Goodland Mullet Festival, held the week before the Super Bowl, attracts more than 5,000 revelers, who feast on fried and smoked varieties of the fish before getting down to business and electing a new Buzzard Lope Queen. Goodland is a refreshing change from the tourist-crowded beaches of the lower Gulf Coast.

■ TRAVEL BASICS

In general, the hustle and bustle of urban Tampa Bay dissipates the farther south you go, which you'll learn if you drive down the Tamiami Trail (U.S. 41), the best introduction to the coastal towns and beaches of the lower Gulf Coast. Zip through on I-75 and you'll miss most of these; on the other hand, I-75 is fast, with forest views on either side of the roadway.

Climate: Winters are a delight: sunny, and bug-free. In summer, afternoon rain showers are normal, and evening thunderstorms provide spectacular light shows.

The Venetian Bay at Naples.

H E A R T L A N D

■ OVERVIEW

Florida's heartland is just that, the true beauty and heart of this state. It's a region brimming with lush hammock jungles, crystal-clear rivers, and deep blue lakes. When summer thunderstorms turn the sky a luscious deep purple, crickets turn up their volume and grand oaks sparkle with raindrops. In spring, wildflowers blanket grassy plains fed by underground mineral springs.

The architecture and ambience in some small towns here take you back in time to the lazy days of Southern living. Away from Orlando, folks speak with a rural twang or a Hispanic accent. They like grits and strong Latin coffee with their morning eggs, and they continue to make a living off the land, growing citrus and raising cattle and horses. Orlando and Disney's theme parks, which lie in this area, are described in the next chapter.

■ ALACHUA COUNTY *map page 147, A-2/3*

Along rural roads in north-central Florida, where vendors hawk boiled peanuts from the backs of trucks and Native Americans sell souvenirs at roadside stands, is where "Cracker" life once thrived. That life was well described in *The Yearling*, *Cross Creek*, and other works by novelist Marjorie Kinnan Rawlings, who might be described as the patron saint of this area.

In 1997, the first Cross Creek Summer Festival was held throughout Gainesville and Alachua County, focusing on history and the literary arts. Local restaurants added dishes to their menus from Rawlings's *Cross Creek Cookery*, a treasury of recipes for alligator steak, grapefruit marmalade, swamp cabbage, and other dishes. Swamp cabbage, known as hearts of palm in modern cookbook vernacular, was once a staple of early Indian and pioneer diets. The main ingredient is harvested by cutting the bud out of cabbage (sabal) palm trees. Since this usually kills the palm, which is Florida's state tree, the practice has been curtailed.

Memories of Gainesville's back roads and nearby villages surface for me when life seems too hectic. Then Marjorie Rawlings's words come to mind: "There is time in summer to lie idly on the veranda and observe a thousand minute things that through the busier part of the year have gone unnoticed." Rural Alachua is like that: a place for slowing down to an era past, for sipping homemade lemonade, for taking a slow drive down country lanes. The region's central city is Gainesville.

■ Gainesville

map page 147, A-3

Gainesville (pop. 96,000) is a college town, and like other college towns it's variously described as artsy-craftsy, highbrow, hippie, bohemian, radical, and party happy. To more conservative types, it's simply known as Sin City, a fitting description for a place that hosts one of the most notorious Halloween celebrations in the South.

Gainesville is relatively young, having been platted as a convenient railroad stop in 1853. For many years, citrus and strawberries were the main exports; now archery equipment is a key product.

In recent years, Gainesville has begun to show signs of overdevelopment, but downtown, and in the city's five historic districts, you'll find elegant homes and new shops in old brick buildings. The most interesting historic districts are the Northeast Historic District (northeast of Main Street and University Avenue) and Courthouse Square (SE First Street and Uni-

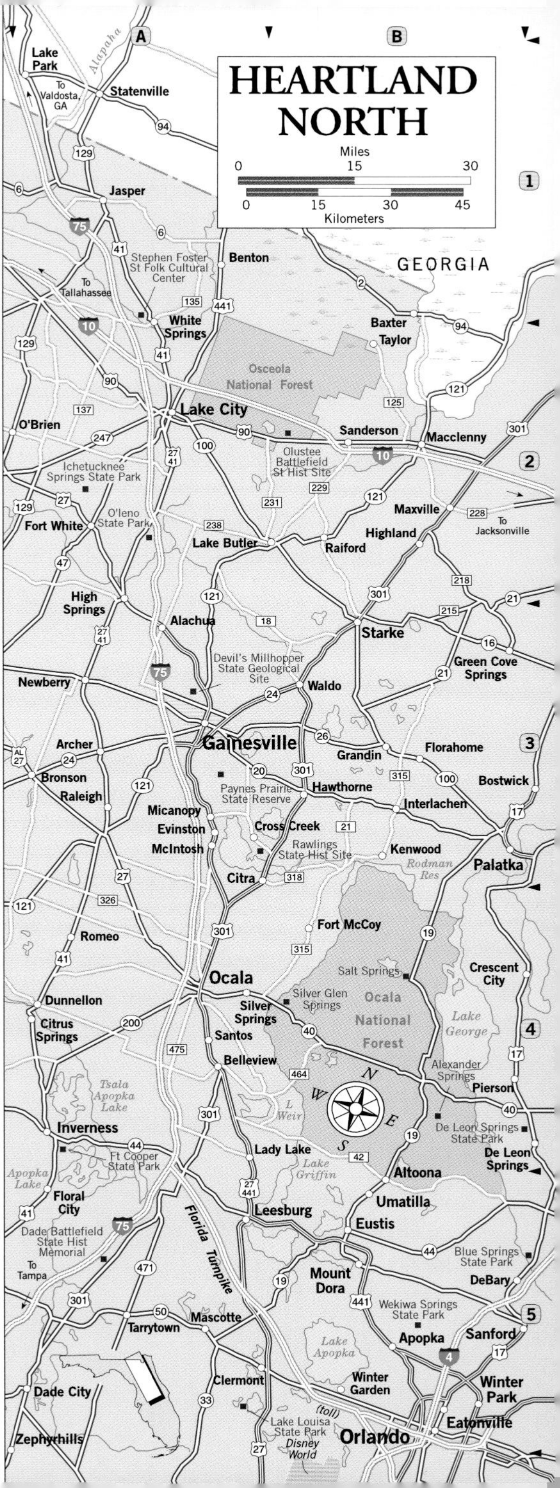

HEARTLAND NORTH
Miles
0
15
30
0
15
30
45
Kilometers
A
B
1
2
3
4
5
GEORGIA
Lake Park
To Valdosta, GA
Statenville
Alapaha
Jasper
Benton
Stephen Foster St Folk Cultural Center
To Tallahassee
White Springs
Baxter
Taylor
Osceola National Forest
Lake City
O'Brien
Sanderson
Macclenny
Olustee Battlefield St Hist Site
Ichetucknee Springs State Park
O'leno State Park
Fort White
Maxville
To Jacksonville
Highland
Lake Butler
Raiford
High Springs
Alachua
Starke
Green Cove Springs
Devil's Millhopper State Geological Site
Newberry
Waldo
Archer
Gainesville
Grandin
Florahome
Bronson
Raleigh
Paynes Prairie State Reserve
Hawthorne
Bostwick
Interlachen
Micanopy
Evinston
McIntosh
Cross Creek
Rawlings State Hist Site
Kenwood
Rodman Res
Palatka
Citra
Romeo
Fort McCoy
Salt Springs
Crescent City
Ocala
Dunnellon
Silver Glen Springs
Silver Springs
Ocala National Forest
Lake George
Citrus Springs
Santos
Belleview
Alexander Springs
Pierson
Tsala Apopka Lake
L Weir
Inverness
De Leon Springs State Park
Ft Cooper State Park
Lady Lake
De Leon Springs
Apopka Lake
Lake Griffin
Altoona
Floral City
Umatilla
Leesburg
Eustis
Dade Battlefield State Hist Memorial
Florida Turnpike
Blue Springs State Park
To Tampa
DeBary
Mount Dora
Wekiwa Springs State Park
Mascotte
Tarrytown
Apopka
Sanford
Lake Apopka
Clermont
Winter Garden
Winter Park
Dade City
(toll)
Eatonville
Lake Louisa State Park
Orlando
Disney World
Zephyrhills

versity Avenue). The crown jewel of Courthouse Square is the **Hippodrome State Theatre** (25 SE Second Place; 352-375-4477), in a former post office. You can catch new and classic dramas here, in addition to musicals, comedies, concerts, and films.

The **University of Florida,** the state's oldest and largest university, with 44,000 students, is near the center of town. Exhibits at the **Florida Museum of Natural History** examine, among other things, the ecosystems of a coral reef, savanna, and temperate and tropical hammocks. There are also displays of fossils, among them the jaw of an extinct great white shark. *34th Street and Hull Road; 352-846-2000.*

If you've heard the word sinkhole over and over again and still have only the vaguest idea what one might be like, then **Devil's Millhopper State Geological Site** is definitely worth a visit. Possibly the most spectacular sinkhole in the state, it measures 120 feet deep and 500 feet wide. A winding staircase leads to the mossy bottom, which, in summertime, is the coolest place in town.

■ **GAINESVILLE AREA SIGHTS**

Devil's Millhopper, named after an Indian legend that told of the devil hurling human bodies into the cavity, was created when rainwater seeped into substrata limestone, forming an underground cavern. About 14,000 years ago, the cavern roof collapsed, leaving a massive depression. *4732 Millhopper Road, off NW 53rd Avenue; 352-955-2008.*

Paynes Prairie State Preserve centers around an irregularly shaped 8-mile-wide basin that supports a wet prairie marsh where alligators and sandhill cranes live. On the higher ground around it are pinewoods, hammocks, and ponds. Three hundred years ago, during a long dry spell, the basin was the site of the largest cattle ranch in Florida, but in the late 19th century, it became a lake served by a steamboat.

Because the state park system is trying to return preserves to their original state, they have reintroduced bison—which lived here in prehistoric times—and feral horses, descendants of those introduced by the Spanish in the late 1500s. Climb the 40-foot observation tower for a great view of the herds in action.

The preserve has been named for a Seminole, King Payne, and several skirmishes were fought here with the U.S. Army during the Second Seminole War.

The University of Florida Gators leaving the field after a victorious game.
Legend has it that Gatorade was invented for these Gators,
either to give them an extra boost on the field or to cure hangovers.

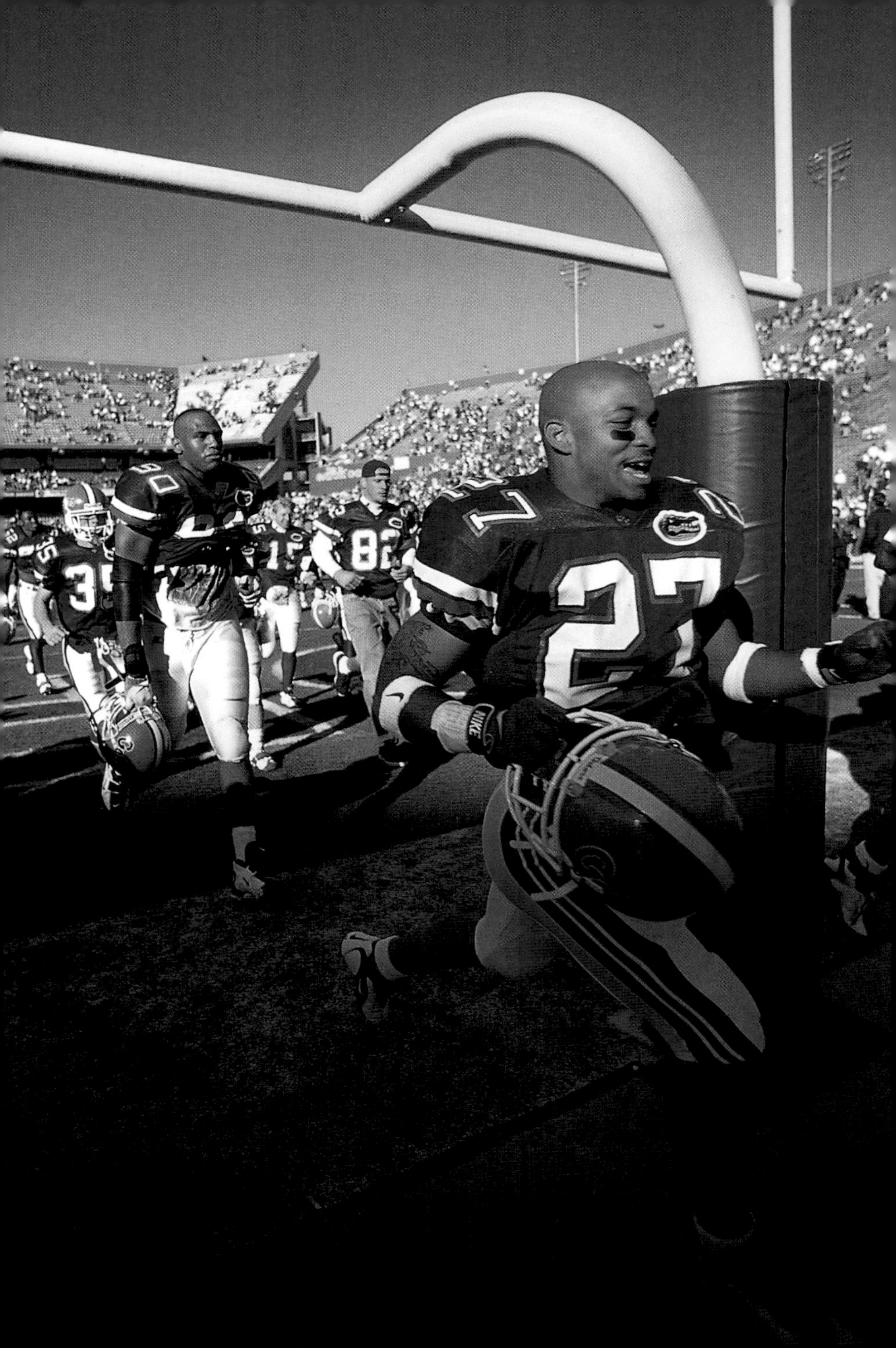

Ranger-led tours reveal the natural wonders of the area in addition to wading birds, eagles, alligators, aquatic snakes, deer, and wild turkeys. *U.S. 441, 10 miles south of Gainesville; 352-466-3397. For tour reservations, call 352-466-4100.*

Twenty miles south of Gainesville, you'll find the **Marjorie Kinnan Rawlings State Historic Site.** The writer lived here from 1928 until her death in 1952. Rawlings's "Cracker shack" is in a citrus grove dominated by an enormous magnolia tree. On her 72 acres, she gardened, gossiped with neighbors, and wrote novels and a recipe book. *County Road 325, off State Road 20, Cross Creek; 352-466-3672.*

The minuscule town of **Evinston,** not much more than a general store and post office, feels more authentically Rawlings to me now than does the historic site. She often bought supplies here. The last time I visited, I stopped to buy a soda and smell the sweet honeysuckle bush outside. "Oh boy, tourists!" exclaimed a feisty elderly woman who was leaving the store. She said our sunglasses gave us away.

Browsing and shopping for artisan wares and vintage collectibles is the thing to do in **Micanopy.** Cholokka Boulevard, running parallel to U.S. 441, is the little town's one main road. Oak trees arch over old buildings and the town's Classic Revival treasure, the **Herlong Mansion Bed-and-Breakfast** (402 NE Cholokka

Locals fish on one of central Florida's quiet rivers.

THE WIDOW'S BOY

Marjorie Kinnan Rawlings at Cross Creek.
(University of Florida Special Collections)

In her novel Cross Creek, *Marjorie Kinnan Rawlings describes the lives of the plucky but desperately poor family of the Widow Slater. When the widow moves away, she leaves behind a teenage son to fend for himself. His employer talks about him in this passage, first published as a short story in 1933.*

I left a note pinned on the sacking. The next day he came to work, his face pinched from privation, his overalls shabby. He walked the two miles back and forth each day, and while the wages I could pay shamed me to offer, they were standard in the section. His lean grave young face filled out, and his loose-limbed frame, and decent shirt and cap and breeches replaced the soiled raggedness. He was a fine grove man and we began a relationship somehow beyond that of employer and employee. A bond was forged that will last as long as either of us lives. Yet he was plainly unhappy. . . . At long last the truth came out. He was one of those who pined for his own piece of land, and he should never be content until he tilled his own acres, had his own house, and a wife to bring him the cheeriness the widow had brought to her brood. His wages only fed and clothed him. He could not save for his dream in a whole life's span.

We both admired the rich hammock land near his palmetto shack, and one day he came to report that thirty-five acres of the best could be bought for taxes. I sent him to the tax sale, and he came back with the tax certificate to the land.

—Marjorie Kinnan Rawlings, *Cross Creek,* 1942

Boulevard; 352-466-3322). This handsome two-story Victorian-style abode has leaded-glass windows, maple inlaid floors, 12-foot ceilings, an elegant dining room and parlor, and a garden filled with oak and pecan trees. The film *Doc Hollywood,* with Michael J. Fox, shows off many of the town's other grand houses, and a fair amount of Micanopy's natural beauty.

This is an excellent area for biking. The oak-shaded roads are relatively flat and easy to navigate. From Micanopy, you can take a good dirt road to McIntosh on Orange Lake; continue to Island Grove and return going past Marjorie Rawlings's place. Then bike on to Evinston to see the little post office and return to Micanopy.

At **McIntosh,** the road divides and goes around a venerable old oak tree. McIntosh was a boomtown tied to the railroad, which shipped oranges out and tourists in during the early 20th century.

Five hundred years ago, Timucuan Indians lived in **Silver Springs,** in a hammock of huge live oaks surrounding 150 natural springs at the head of the Silver River. Timucuans believed the springs held mystical powers, and they worshiped the aqua waters as the shrine of the water gods. Of their lost world, we have only

A time-worn barn in Columbia County, near Ichetucknee Springs.

the notations of Hernando de Soto, who, when he came through the area in 1539, recorded that he found more than 600 horses but no pearls, silver, or gold.

This most appealing of places was one of the state's first tourist attractions, drawing people who arrived by stagecoach, steamboat, and train. The commercial sideshow began almost immediately as entrepreneurs began exploiting the area's reputation for exotic jungle flora and fauna. In the 1940s, when the Florida Reptile Institute was located here, its catalog enthused: "A box of 8 assorted snakes, all more than 4 feet long, can be purchased for $10." The Institute's catalog advises that it does not send poisonous snakes to minors.

Silver Springs has starred in more than 30 films, including six Tarzan movies, *The Yearling, Moonraker,* and more than 100 episodes of the old Lloyd Bridges television series, *Sea Hunt.*

The springs are the centerpiece of **Silver Springs,** a 350-acre wildlife theme park that is equal parts natural beauty and tourist haunt. Curiously, all the glass-bottom tour boats here are named after Indian leaders, most of whom died fighting the U.S. government for control of lands they once owned. The cruises are beautiful,

Fishing in the Santa Fe River in Alachua County.

and when you get a look at the lush vegetation, alligators, fish, and bones of ancient sea creatures, you'll understand why the tribes were willing to sacrifice their lives to retain this place. But the presence of snack stands, a shopping strip by the main entrance, and Wild Waters, a seasonal water slide park, will make you wish the Indians had triumphed. *5656 East Silver Springs Boulevard; 352-236-2121.*

Within the nearly 400,000-acre **Ocala National Forest,** four major springs flow among sand pines, oaks, sweet gums, and palmettos. In addition to all the swimming and snorkeling opportunities here, there are excellent hiking trails and campsites, making this one of Florida's most popular national forests. Alexander Springs is popular with canoeists, campers, snorkelers, and scuba divers. Silver Glen Springs is where snorkelers find large schools of fish. At Salt Springs, a combination of salt and fresh water flows into Salt Springs Run, which merges with the St. Johns River at Lake George. The mill and natural swimming pool formed by Juniper Springs are a picturesque spot, with cool, clear, oak-shaded waters filled with fish and turtles. A 7-mile canoe trail leads down Jupiter Creek. *Ocala National Forest; 352-669-3153.*

Myriad fish inhabit the clear waters of Alexander Springs, where the visibility is 100 feet.

The ruins of a plantation and sugar mill are preserved at **De Leon Springs State Park,** where you will also find a mill-theme restaurant (with griddles for make-'em-yourself pancakes), Spanish-style buildings, and mammoth oaks surrounding the picturesque swimming area. *U.S. 17, east of Ocala National Forest; 386-985-4212.*

Known for its manatees, **Blue Springs State Park** hosts a manatee festival each January. The animals can be seen close up on some winter days by snorkeling or diving, or you can view them from the deck of a boat. The park is a popular stop for houseboats, which come in from nearby Lake George. Things get hectic on summer weekends and holidays. *2100 West French Avenue, Orange City; 386-775-3663.*

In the language of the Timucuans, the word for "bubbling water" is *wekiwa,* and the word for "flowing river" is *wekiva.* These ideas merge at **Wekiwa Springs State Park,** where natural springs pump 42 million gallons of water a day into the Wekiva River. The park, on 7,000 acres of wild scenery, is great for swimming, hiking, canoeing, camping, and horseback riding. *Wekiva Road, north of Orlando in Apopka; 407-884-2009 or 407-884-2008.*

The natural springs of the Heartland are surrounded by profuse vegetation.

Young's Paso Fino Ranch in Ocala.

■ OCALA AND MARION COUNTY *map page 147, A-4*

Fast-growing Ocala, a town of about 46,000, has a compact downtown and a residential historic district of brick commercial buildings and Victorian homes. Ocala experienced a population boom in 1935, when Congress authorized the Army Corps of Engineers to dig a canal from Jacksonville to the Gulf Coast town of Yankeetown via Ocala. Thousands arrived to take up construction jobs. World War II and escalating costs halted the project, but many who came here to work stayed on. Downtown Ocala, known as Brick City, has a lively commercial area with an Irish pub, a New Orleans–style grill, delis, taverns, and shops.

At Ocala's **Appleton Museum of Art,** you'll find an 8th-century, Tang Dynasty earthenware horse; a 19th-century bronze horse sculpture; and Islamic pottery and other artifacts. *4333 NE Silver Springs Boulevard; 352-236-7100.*

The town's **residential historic district,** along Fort King Avenue between Third and 13th Streets, has more than 200 wooden steamboat-era mansions that range in style from gothic to Italianate to Queen Anne Revival.

If you talk to folks in Ocala, it doesn't take long before conversation gets around to horses. You almost need a working knowledge of breeding techniques, racing history, and training methods just to live here. In the area are more than 600 horse farms, raising Thoroughbreds, quarter horses, Clydesdales, and Arabians. Raising horses is a billion-dollar business in Florida, and about 70 percent of the state's horse farms are in Ocala's Marion County, which has produced many Breeders' Cup champions and several Kentucky Derby winners.

The Ocala Stud Farm, the state's oldest breeding facility and birthplace of Needles, winner of the 1956 Kentucky Derby, is no longer open to the public. If you drive past the farm, you'll see barns, pastureland, and a 2-mile training track. *4400 SW 27th Avenue.*

■ North of Orlando *map page 147*

Between Ocala and Orlando, billboards let you know you're nearing Disney territory, the land of full-time amusement. Lakes rimmed with palms, oaks, and fish camps keep the tempo slow.

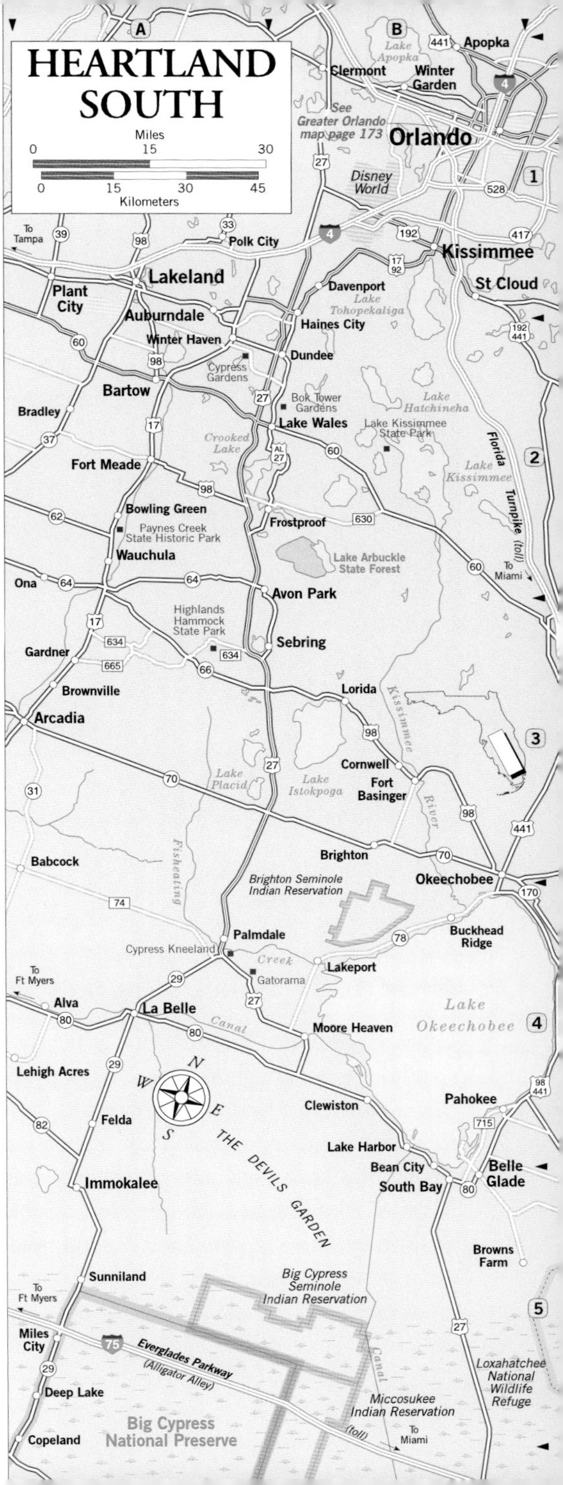
HEARTLAND SOUTH
Miles
0 15 30
0 15 30 45
Kilometers
A
B
Lake Apopka
Apopka
Clermont
Winter Garden
See Greater Orlando map page 173
Orlando
Disney World
Kissimmee
St Cloud
To Tampa
Polk City
Lakeland
Plant City
Davenport
Lake Tohopekaliga
Auburndale
Haines City
Winter Haven
Dundee
Cypress Gardens
Bartow
Bok Tower Gardens
Lake Hatchineha
Bradley
Lake Wales
Lake Kissimmee State Park
Crooked Lake
Florida Turnpike (toll)
Lake Kissimmee
Fort Meade
Bowling Green
Paynes Creek State Historic Park
Frostproof
Wauchula
Lake Arbuckle State Forest
To Miami
Ona
Avon Park
Highlands Hammock State Park
Gardner
Sebring
Brownville
Lorida
Arcadia
Kissimmee River
Cornwell
Fort Basinger
Lake Placid
Lake Istokpoga
Fisheating
Babcock
Brighton
Brighton Seminole Indian Reservation
Okeechobee
Palmdale
Cypress Kneeland
Creek
Gatorama
Buckhead Ridge
Lakeport
To Ft Myers
Alva
La Belle
Canal
Moore Heaven
Lake Okeechobee
Lehigh Acres
N
W
E
S
Clewiston
Pahokee
Felda
THE DEVILS GARDEN
Lake Harbor
Bean City
Belle Glade
South Bay
Immokalee
Browns Farm
Sunniland
Big Cypress Seminole Indian Reservation
To Ft Myers
Miles City
Everglades Parkway (Alligator Alley)
Canal
Loxahatchee National Wildlife Refuge
Deep Lake
Miccosukee Indian Reservation
Copeland
Big Cypress National Preserve
(toll)
To Miami
1
2
3
4
5

In this serene 1915 landscape, artist George Cope depicts the semitropical vegetation of central Florida. (Sam and Robbie Vickers Florida Collection)

■ **MOUNT DORA**   *map page 147, B-5*

Quiet, oak-studded Mount Dora, at the threshold of its namesake lake, is considered hilly, even though its elevation is only 190 feet. Every third weekend in October, Mount Dora hosts a bike race and "antique strolls" that showcase the town's small shops, many of which sell one-of-a-kind collectibles. There's a park here where folks lawn bowl and play shuffleboard, some impressive mansions, and a boardwalk leading to a nature island on the lake. Along Fifth Avenue and Donnelly Street, there are enough cafés and restaurants to have lunch somewhere new each day of the week.

■ **SIGHTS IN THE MOUNT DORA AREA**

From an Indian word meaning "potato-eating place," **Apopka** sits alongside U.S. 441 south of Mount Dora, close to two spring-fed parks: Kelly Park, where Rock Spring creates a swimming hole, and Wekiwa Springs State Park.

Another lake town, **Sanford,** is off I-4. Sanford is a perfect starting place for an exploration of the St. Johns River and nearby Lake George. Houseboats are rented here, and the shallow, easily navigable waterways make boating an option even for novices. With sandy bottoms and a lazy current, the river's only real obstacles are the behemoth barges that carry oil down to central Florida from distribution facilities upriver in Jacksonville. Call **Canal Houseboat Rentals** (407-424-2564) for information on rentals.

Eatonville, founded in 1887, was the childhood home of author Zora Neale Hurston and America's first municipality governed by African Americans. The **Zora Neale Hurston National Museum of Fine Arts** mounts exhibits, one each season, by artists of African descent. To better understand the museum's mission, take the guided tour of historic Eatonville, which makes you realize that the city itself is a living museum. *227 East Kennedy Boulevard; 407-647-3307.*

Winter Park is known for its scenic lake and fashionable downtown shopping

---

THE EATONVILLE ALLIGATOR

They call this part of town Mars Hill, as against Bones Valley to the right of the road. They call the tree-shaded land that runs past the schoolhouse West Street, and it goes past several small groves until it passes Jim Steele's fine orange grove and dips itself in Lake Belle, which is the home of Eatonville's most celebrated resident, the world's largest alligator.

This legendary alligator, it is said, is no other than a slave who escaped from a Georgia plantation and joined the Indians during the Seminole War. When the Indians retreated, he did not follow but instead made "big medicine" on the lake shore, for he had been a celebrated conjuring man in Africa. He transformed himself into an alligator, the god of his tribe, and slipped into the water. Now and then he resumes human form, so people say, and roams the country about Eatonville. At such times all the alligators in the surrounding lakes bellow loudly all night long. "The big one has gone back home," whisper the villagers.

—Zora Neale Hurston, *Their Eyes Were Watching God,* 1937

and dining district centered around Rollins College, at Fairbanks and Park Avenues. A boat tour of the town's old logging canals, which once connected all the lakes in the Winter Park area, is a pleasant way to spend an afternoon while learning local history. Pontoon boat operators narrate a slow-moving, 12-mile trek through Spanish moss–draped secret passages, sometimes no more than 8 feet wide, passing cypress-fringed lakefront mansions, Rollins College, and Kraft Azalea Gardens along the way. **Winter Park Scenic Boat Tours** (407-664-4056), which has introduced visitors to the area's beauty since 1938, is the most popular of the bunch.

The **Charles Hosmer Morse Museum of American Art** houses the world's most comprehensive collection of works by Louis Comfort Tiffany, among them stained-glass windows, glass buttons, mosaics, watercolors, and jewelry. Tiffany's chapel for the 1893 Columbian Exposition has been reconstructed here, in accordance with Tiffany's original, exacting requirements. The museum also has American art pottery, decorative arts, and paintings. *445 Park Avenue North; 407-645-5311.*

Florida cowboys have long been known as "Crackers," the name referring to the cracking noise of the whips they used to herd cattle.

■ Kissimmee and Cowmen *map page 157, B-1*

The interesting part of this town sits next to the lake, where the noble profession of cow handling is celebrated at the **Kissimmee Rodeo** every Friday. Roping, barrel racing, and steer wrestling take place, along with good food and drink. *Kissimmee Sports Arena, 1010 Suhls Lane; 407-933-0020.*

Long the center of the state's cattle industry, the area around Kissimmee is for the most part swampland interspersed with timberland. The cowboys who worked it were called cowhunters since much of their time was spent hunting for cattle in the woods. They were tough hombres, these cowhunters, accustomed to 18-hour days of riding on equally resilient "Cracker" (or marsh) ponies descended from those used by Spanish rancheros. At the end of a long day, cowhunters settled down for grub that consisted of biscuits, bacon, lard, salt pork, syrup, and coffee. Says one source: "When a drive ended, cowmen would take their pay in gold, drink Cuban rum, and fire their revolvers through the floors of their lodgings."

Kissimmee today is only a mile from U.S. 192 and the entrance to Disney World. Roads are lined with motels, amusement parks, and miniature golf courses.

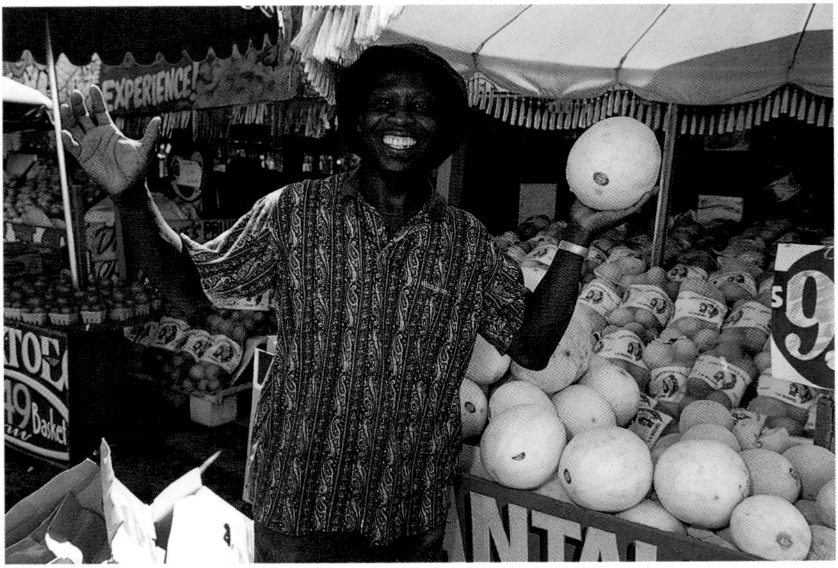
EXPERIENCE!

Dr. Fergie's Fruit Stand is a local landmark in Leesburg, Lake County.

Along Broadway Avenue, south of U.S. 192 via Main Street, is Kissimmee's old downtown, lined with attractive, century-old storefronts. The town's interesting sites include the **Pioneer Museum,** comprising a 1905 "Cracker house," a country store, and a boardwalk leading into an 8-acre nature preserve shaded by old oaks. *750 North Bass Road; 407-396-8644.*

Lake Tohopekaliga, known to locals as Lake Toho, is where people in the area come to sail, jet-ski, and take airboat tours. It's also known as a great fishing area, especially bass fishing. The 18,810-acre lake is connected to the Chain of Lakes leading to Lake Okeechobee and the Everglades.

■ CYPRESS GARDENS *map page 157, A-2*

Just outside the town of Winter Haven, south of Orlando, is Cypress Gardens, where tourists have come for years to see floral beds, Southern belles in hoop skirts that make them look like blooming flowers, and daring water-skiers sometimes dressed in poodle skirts. There's also a butterfly exhibit, reptile display, aviary, ice show and Russian acrobatics. The large, intact cypress head (watershed) is integral to the local ecology and geology. *2641 South Lake Summit Drive; 863-324-2111.*

■ LAKE WALES *map page 157, A/B-2*

> One may loiter along, flanked on either side of the road by lush orange groves heavy with golden fruit, catch glimpses of clear lake waters at nearly every turn of the winding roads through the center of the state, or you may speed along at your own gait on trunk highway. . .
>
> —J. N. "Ding" Darling, *The Cruise of the Bouncing Betsy: A Trailer Travelogue,* 1937

I have one word to describe Lake Wales: eccentric. What else would you call a town that claims as its star attractions a spooked hill, a singing tower, and an elaborately priced inn that resembles a dollhouse?

Chalet Suzanne Country Inn, the town's most popular accommodation, looks

Cypress Gardens near Winter Haven.

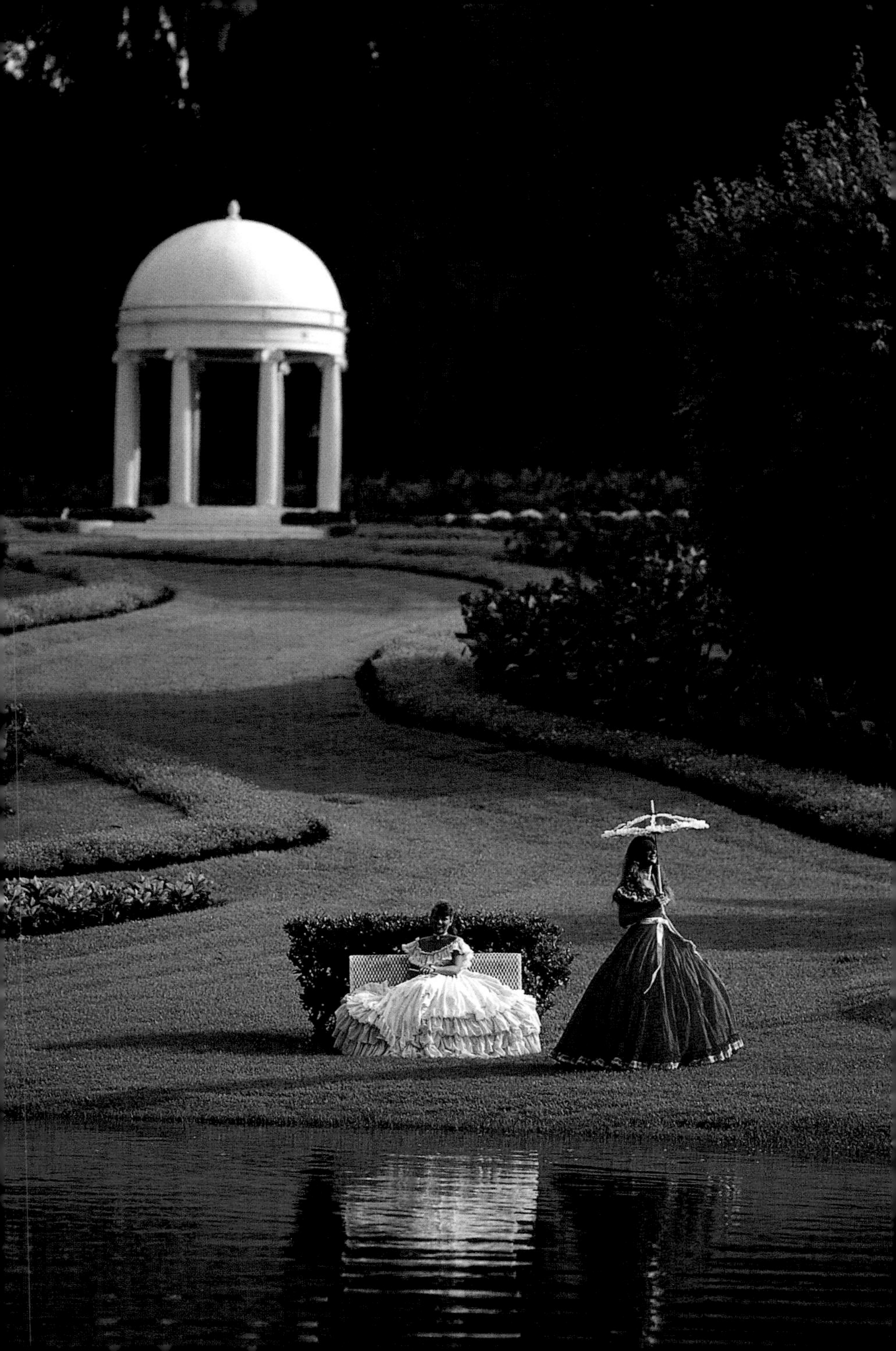

like a jumble of Scandinavian and Mediterranean building blocks squeezed between citrus groves. At the inn's ultraexpensive, uneven-floored restaurant, chairs don't match and each table is set with different tableware. The signature romaine soup is locally famous, not just because it tastes great but because it went to space aboard *Apollo 15* and *Apollo 16*. Guest rooms are in storybook-style buildings along twisting paths that look like something out of *The Sound of Music*. Visitors often come just to look and wander into the little ceramics and antique shops. *Off U.S. 27, 4 miles north of Lake Wales; 863-676-6011 or 800-433-6011.*

The first thing you notice about **Bok Tower Gardens** is the 200-foot-tall carillon tower, built of marble and pink coquina stone. Its bells chime classic tunes on the half hour. The tower and gardens were built by a Dutch immigrant in 1929 as a shrine to America's beauty. Edward Bok planted the gardens—157 acres of them—around the tower with thousands of magnolias, camellias, azaleas, ferns, oaks, palms, pines, and exotic plants. More than 127 wild bird species are known to frequent the gardens, including a colony of wood ducks. The carillon tower contains 57 bronze bells weighing between 17 pounds and 12 tons each. Bok Tower Gardens sits on 295-foot Iron Mountain, peninsular Florida's highest elevation. Bok, once the editor of the *Ladies Home Journal,* is buried beneath his tower. *U.S. 27 and Route 60; 863-676-1408.*

Alternate U.S. 27, also known as the Scenic Highway, crosses the historic section of Lake Wales and provides a refreshing break from four-lane U.S. 27, which connects with it 15 miles later. Visual vitamin C comes in megadoses down this twisting road lined with citrus groves. In spring when the trees blossom, the air is dense with the sweet, tangy odor of citrus. Citrus is a billion-dollar industry in Florida, which produces 70 percent of the nation's oranges. Orange trees were first introduced by the Spanish, but the trees suffered in winter frosts. The solution to this problem was found by a Chinese immigrant, Lue Gim Gong, who developed a hardier variety of the fruit.

■ **SEBRING** *map page 157, A/B-3*

Sebring was founded in 1912. In the mid-1920s, an official "greeter" was hired whose job was to wander around town shaking hands with people. Nowadays, the town is most famous for its 12-Hour Endurance Race, held each March at **Sebring International Raceway.** *113 Midway Drive; 863-655-1442.*

The Singing Tower at Bok Tower Gardens perches on the highest hill on the Florida peninsula.

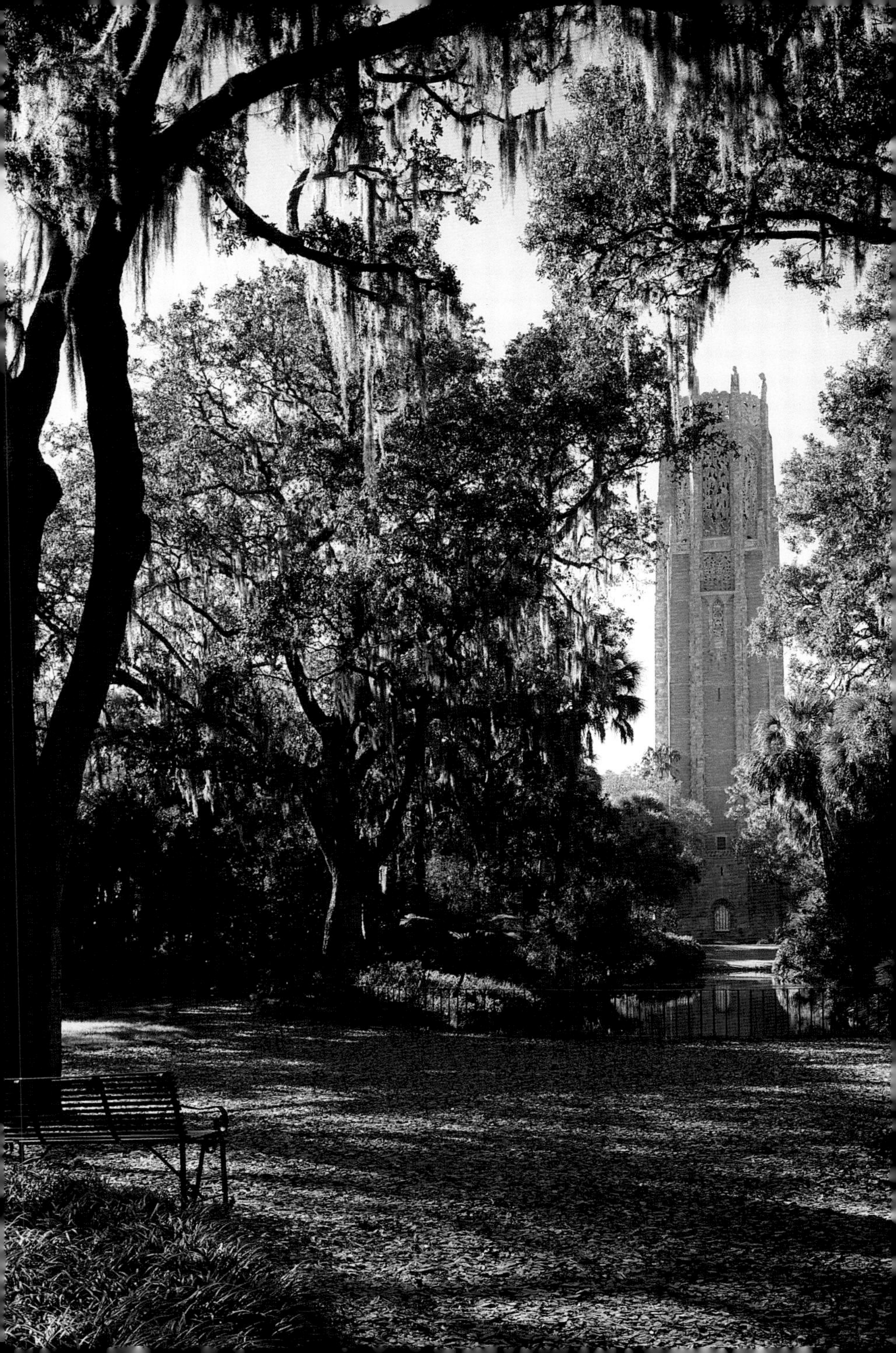

As a family, we often head to the racetrack's antithesis, **Highlands Hammock State Park,** where bicyclists get close to nature in cypress swamps and hardwood hammocks running wild with alligators, bald eagles, deer, and scrubjays. The park has bike rentals, tram tours, picnic grounds, and camping. *State Road 634 off U.S. 27, 4 miles west of Sebring; 863-386-6094.*

■ **ARCADIA** *map page 157, A-3*

Route 70 branches off in two directions from U.S. 27. To the west lies Arcadia. The town is a throwback to the cowhunting era, but there's more to do here than look for cowboys. In downtown Arcadia, visitors can buy a pair of cowboy boots in the historic shopping district and eat country-fried steak at the local café.

In March and July, folks gather for the **Arcadia All-Florida Championship Rodeo** (800-749-7633). Year-round, the **Peace River State Canoe Trail** is a fine place to come and paddle. Canoe Outpost (863-494-1215) supplies outfitting and livery service for day and overnight trips.

Wandering the deserted back roads around Arcadia, you'll pass orange groves,

The Heartland produces the majority of Florida's oranges.

Citrus fruit is Florida's leading agricultural product, with sugarcane a close second.

stands of oak shrouded in Spanish moss, and pastures of cows with cattle egrets poised on their backsides. In the midst of it all rises **Solomon's Castle.** Here, "King Solomon" (a wisp of a man named Howard Solomon) has created a castle made from aluminum offset plates that were discarded by a local newspaper. It's equal parts roadside attraction, art gallery, and high camp. The owner has also built a Boat in the Moat restaurant, constructed to the dimensions of Columbus's *Santa Maria*—65 feet long. *Off Route 665; 863-494-6077.*

■ LAKE OKEECHOBEE *map page 157, B-4*

Eastbound, Route 70 arrives at the northernmost tip of one of the continent's largest lakes: Lake Okeechobee, or the Big O, as locals affectionately call it. The lake connects Kissimmee's Chain of Lakes in the north to the Everglades in the south. By river and canal, the Okeechobee Waterway links the Gulf of Mexico and the Atlantic Ocean. The 152-mile waterway provides commercial and recreational passage between Florida's coasts. Lake O's largemouth bass, bluegills, catfish, and black crappies bring fishermen out in force.

Bald eagles, wood storks, snail kites, manatees, and alligators count among the

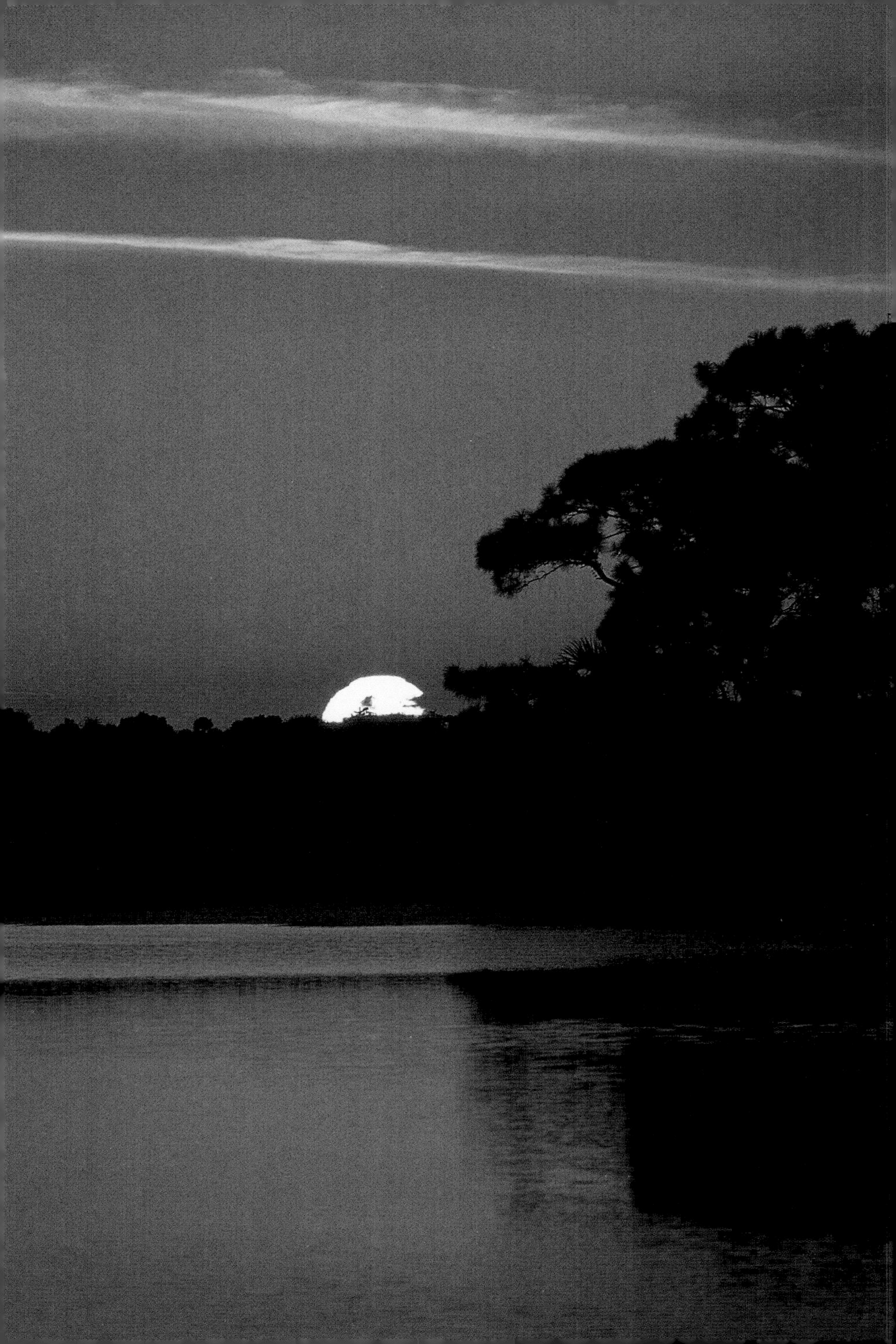

rare fauna of the Big O, which anchors a 28,500-acre National Audubon Society wildlife sanctuary. Many fishing guides offer their services at Lake Okeechobee, which was diked after a 1928 hurricane-induced flood killed 2,000 people. The victims were either drowned or, because they climbed trees to escape the high water, died from the bites of snakes that had the same idea. Atop the dike, the **Lake Okeechobee Scenic Trail** gives cyclists more than 100 miles of panoramic pathways around Florida's "inland sea."

■ LOXAHATCHEE NATIONAL WILDLIFE REFUGE

map page 157, B-5

Five counties and two Indian reservations surround Lake Okeechobee. East of the shores on the Palm Beach County side lies Loxahatchee National Wildlife Refuge. Vast and often forbidding, the 146,000-acre refuge is similar in ecology to the sawgrass marshes seen throughout the northern Everglades. Given its size and density, the preserve is best seen by guided tour. Nature enthusiasts will have plenty of opportunities to view unusual birds and other wildlife in their natural habitats.

(above) Lake Okeechobee at Port Mayaca, where the locks open into the St. Lucie Canal.
(opposite) The lake at sunset.

This 1852 illustration shows Billy Bowlegs with his chiefs. Bowlegs is reclining on the left; sitting beside him are Chocote Tustenuggee, Abraham, John Jumper, Fasatcheee Emanthla, and Sarparkee Yohola. (University of South Florida Library, Special Collections)

The visitors center has information and audio-visual programs. Walking trails and a 5.5-mile canoe trail reveal the rare ecology of this land at the inside edge of the Everglades. *Off U.S. 441, 2 miles south of Boynton Beach Boulevard; 561-734-8303.*

This is the area where the famous Seminole chief Billy Bowlegs lived and fought American troops during the Seminole Indian Wars. In one engagement, on Christmas Day, 1837, Bowlegs attacked Colonel Zachary Taylor, future president of the United States. Eventually, Bowlegs's position was overrun by U.S. forces—which had a two-to-one advantage—but not without heavy losses. American casualties numbered 138; the Indians, 14. The *WPA Guide to Florida* relates, "Years later Billy Bowlegs visited Washington and on being escorted through the buildings of the Capitol and viewing many statues and paintings with lackluster eye, he suddenly halted before a portrait of Zachary Taylor, grinned and exclaimed: 'Me whip!'"

■ **TRAVEL BASICS**

Getting Around: Interstate 75 runs through the northern Heartland. The Florida Turnpike peels off from I-75 above Orlando, traveling in a southeasterly direction. Interstate 4 begins at Daytona Beach, runs through Orlando, and ends in Tampa. For a more scenic drive, get off the interstates whenever possible and travel on side roads. A favorite route from north to south starts out in Gainesville on U.S. 441, which connects in Ocala to U.S. 27/301. U.S. 27 then threads through Orlando outskirts clear to Lake Okeechobee. This chapter roughly follows that route. It takes a few back roads, however, as these reveal the true nature of Florida's Heartland.

Climate: Hot in the summer and cooler in the winter than coastal areas, interior Florida is otherwise similar in climate to its coastal counterparts of the same latitude. Temperatures average 71°F, with summer highs in the 90s and winter lows in the 40s. The southern interior receives more thunderstorms than any other region in North America. These occur mostly in summer but are common anytime of the year.

A Seminole Indian of the Okeechobee area with his three-month-old son. About 1,800 Seminoles live in Florida today on five reservations.

ORLANDO AREA
THEME PARKS

■ OVERVIEW

In 1939, Orlando, population 27,330, boasted a total of 17 hotels. Then in 1965, Walt Disney, Hollywood mogul and modern theme-park pioneer, snatched up 27,500 acres of pinewoods, cattle pastures, citrus groves, and swamplands. It was a move that ultimately transformed this inland city, in a state best known for its white-sand beaches and warm, blue waters, into one of the most popular destinations for overseas travelers to the United States. Orlando now has the highest concentration of hotel rooms in the country and is host to 44 million visitors every year.

■ ORLANDO AND DISNEY *map page 173*

Decades before the Orlando area earned the dubious distinction of hosting the densest concentration of theme parks in the world, it was an agricultural area whose claims to fame revolved around bushels of citrus fruits grown and number of cattle raised. Then, in 1971, the gates to Walt Disney World swung open, enveloping tourists in an insulated world of fairy-tale pleasures, a dreamlike fantasyland where vacationing mortals could temporarily escape the unpleasant realities of daily life. Here, there were no panhandlers, rude waitresses, dust, dirt, or mildew. Within a few years, droves of Disney-inspired peddlers of family fun had descended on the state—Orlando in particular—forever altering the face of Florida tourism.

While many Orlandoans credit Disney with bringing a clean, profitable industry to the area (more than 50,000 people, or about 20 percent of Orlando's population, are employed by the company), there's no shortage of vocal Mickey Mouse bashers lamenting that their homeland has become a gaudy maze of amusement parks, theme restaurants, and roadside attractions. The Disney dynasty still lords over the territory, but some keen competition has cropped up over the years, most notably Universal Orlando and SeaWorld. Disney has taken its share of local criticism for its corporate secretiveness (park attendance figures are never disclosed), among other things, but the simple fact is that Orlando would have never become

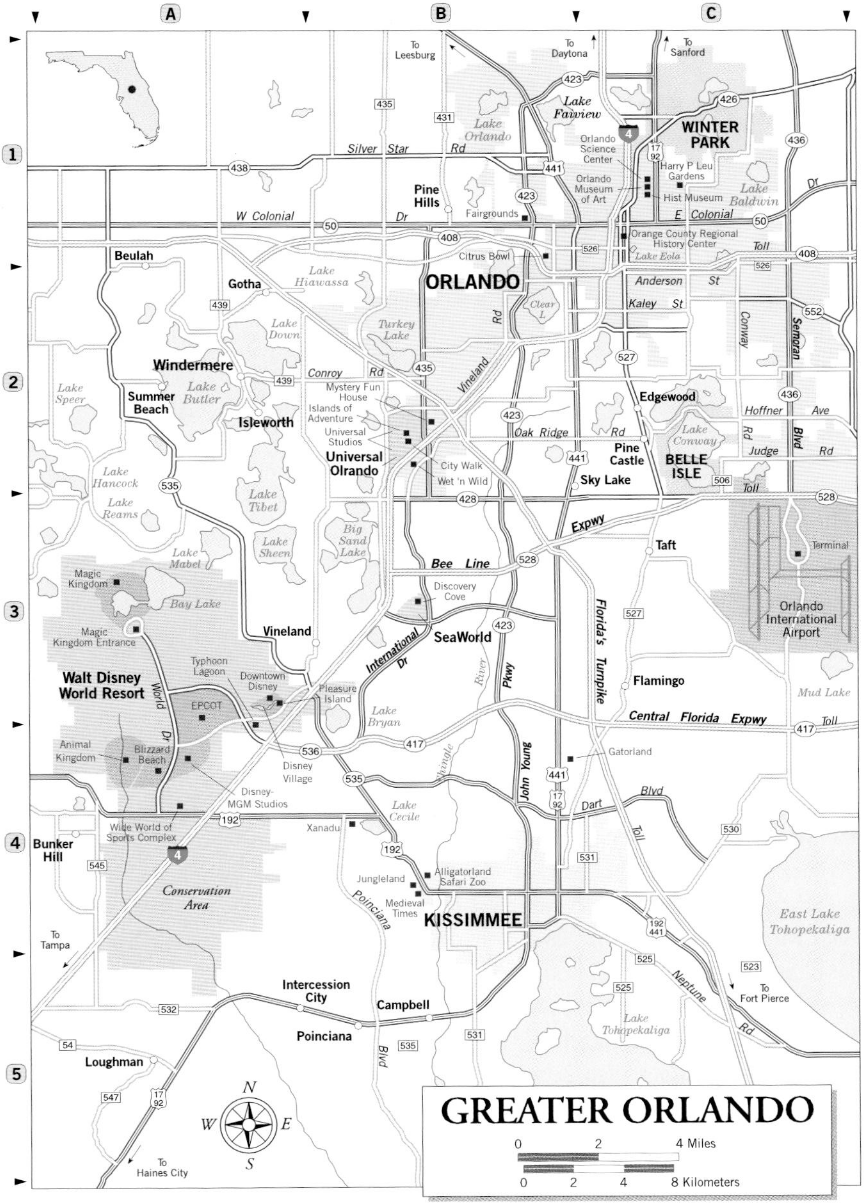
A
B
C
1
2
3
4
5
To Leesburg
To Daytona
To Sanford
Lake Fairview
WINTER PARK
Lake Orlando
Orlando Science Center
Harry P Leu Gardens
Orlando Museum of Art
Hist Museum
Lake Baldwin
Silver Star Rd
Pine Hills
Fairgrounds
W Colonial Dr
E Colonial
Orange County Regional History Center
Lake Eola
Toll
Beulah
Citrus Bowl
ORLANDO
Anderson St
Kaley St
Gotha
Lake Hiawassa
Lake Down
Turkey Lake
Clear L
Conway
Semoran
Windermere
Conroy Rd
Vineland
Rd
Lake Speer
Summer Beach
Lake Butler
Mystery Fun House
Islands of Adventure
Universal Studios
Isleworth
Universal Olrando
City Walk
Wet 'n Wild
Edgewood
Hoffner Ave
Oak Ridge Rd
Lake Conway
Pine Castle
BELLE ISLE
Judge Rd
Blvd
Sky Lake
Lake Hancock
Lake Reams
Lake Tibet
Big Sand Lake
Lake Sheen
Lake Mabel
Expwy
Taft
Terminal
Bee Line
Magic Kingdom
Bay Lake
Discovery Cove
Florida's Turnpike
Orlando International Airport
Magic Kingdom Entrance
Vineland
SeaWorld
International Dr
Typhoon Lagoon
Downtown Disney
Pleasure Island
Walt Disney World Resort
World Dr
EPCOT
Flamingo
Mud Lake
Lake Bryan
River
Pkwy
Central Florida Expwy
Animal Kingdom
Blizzard Beach
Disney Village
Gatorland
John Young
Shingle
Disney-MGM Studios
Lake Cecile
Dart Blvd
Wide World of Sports Complex
Xanadu
Bunker Hill
Conservation Area
Jungleland
Alligatorland Safari Zoo
Medieval Times
Poinciana
KISSIMMEE
East Lake Tohopekaliga
To Tampa
Neptune Rd
Intercession City
Campbell
Poinciana
To Fort Pierce
Lake Tohopekaliga
Blvd
Loughman
N
W
E
S
To Haines City
GREATER ORLANDO
0 2 4 Miles
0 2 4 8 Kilometers

the country's—and by some estimates, the world's—most popular tourist destination without the Mouse.

■ WALT DISNEY WORLD *map page 173, A-3*

In 1971, the name Walt Disney World was coined to distinguish Disney's new Orlando park from the original Disneyland in Anaheim, California. But in 1982, Walt Disney World went through a kind of corporate mitosis, splitting into two organisms with the opening of EPCOT Center and renaming the original park the Magic Kingdom in the process. The two parks were then collectively referred to as Walt Disney World, an umbrella title that grew to include Disney-MGM Studios and, eventually, Disney's Animal Kingdom. To this day park patrons get confused by the monikers, and most wind up referring to the Magic Kingdom as Walt Disney World, proving that there are some things even Disney can't control.

Like any enterprise that reaches the status of an icon, Walt Disney World has a devoted subculture of fans who simply can't get enough of all things Disney. These folks collect commemorative lapel pins—you'll see them for sale at kiosks throughout the parks—and feverishly trade them on the Internet and at Disney-sponsored pin-trading events. Another fan obsession centers around "hidden Mickeys," obscured mouse-ear images that Disney "Imagineers" have designed into background details ranging from the constellations inside Space Mountain to the carpet inside the Animal Kingdom Lodge. An unofficial and downright goofy Web site, *www.hiddenmickeys.org*, keeps a detailed list of hidden Mickey sightings worldwide. It's a hoot.

■ MAGIC KINGDOM *map page 173, A-3*

Physically, this is the smallest of the four Walt Disney World theme parks, but it's by far the biggest for those who make the pilgrimage to have their pictures taken with Mickey Mouse, whose favorite haunt seems to be the Magic Kingdom. This is the park for the whole family—small children, jaded teens, and even the most cynical of adults will be hard-pressed not to get in the spirit of things. At the epicenter of the park is Cinderella Castle, where, in a secret room high up in a gilded turret, Walt is rumored to be freeze-dried in a cryogenic chamber. The various lands—**Main Street U.S.A., Adventureland, Frontierland, Liberty Square, Fan-**

Fireworks over Cinderella Castle. (The Walt Disney Company)

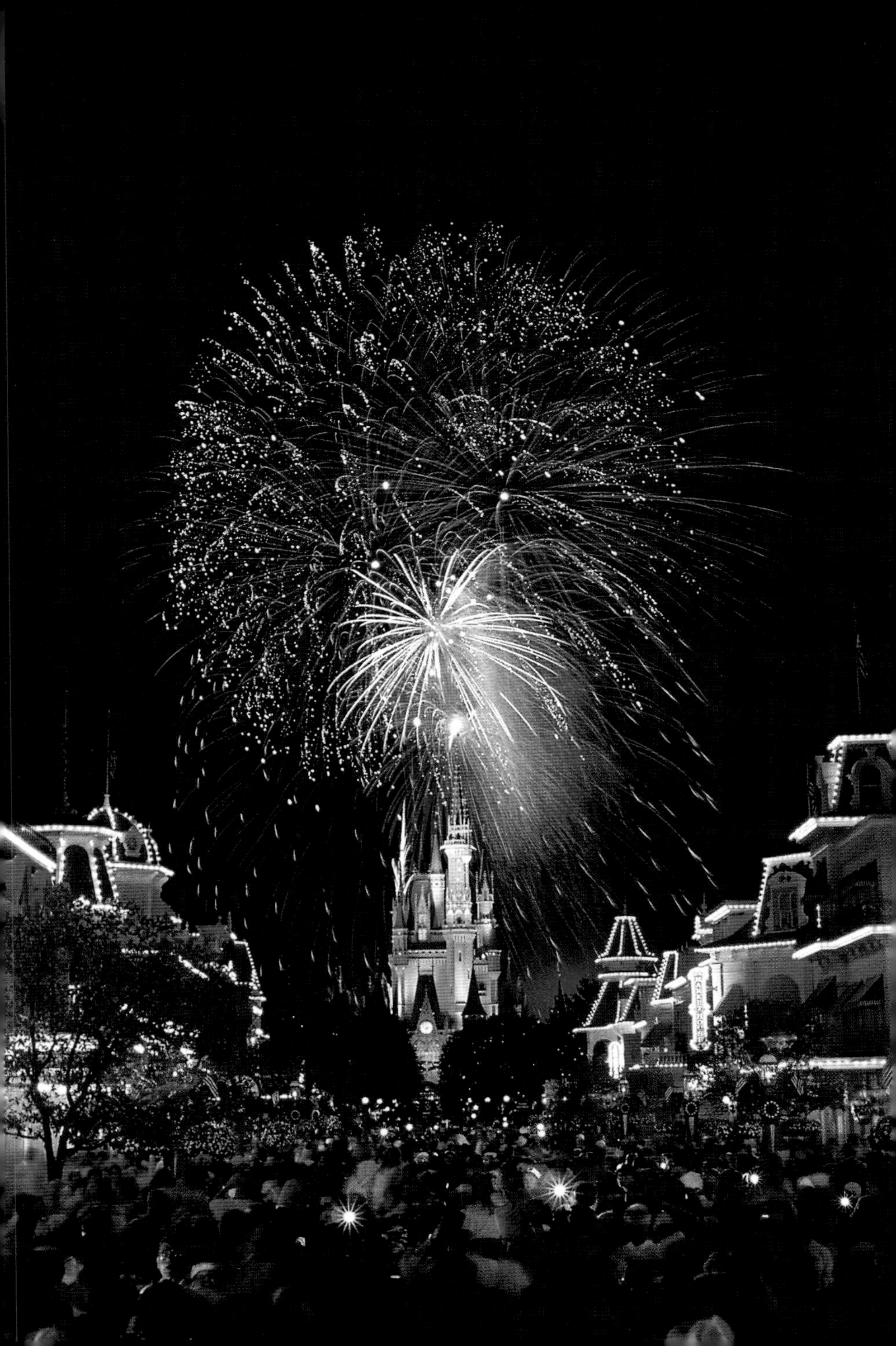

tasyland, and **Tomorrowland**—surround the castle in a broad circle. It takes at least one full day to experience the Magic Kingdom, more if you have small children. *Take I-4 to Exit 25B, follow World Drive to entrance gate; 407-824-4521.*

Highlights
Kids and adults love the **Swiss Family Treehouse,** the Taj Mahal of tree forts. Its many rooms are spread throughout the branches of a massive, albeit fake, banyan tree. (Its 800,000 leaves are made of vinyl and cost $1 each.) The **Jungle Cruise** is a river odyssey where you'll dodge hippos, tourist-eating headhunters, and the often cornball but usually funny spiel of the tour guides.

One of the park's most imaginative rides is the **Pirates of the Caribbean,** a slow-moving boat ride that wends through subterranean canals where mechanical pirates raise untold Cain; the nonstop "Yo-ho! Yo-ho!" soundtrack will stay in your head for days. The classic **Haunted Mansion,** whose once-special effects haven't been updated since the park opened, still gets points for its spooky innocence and humor (dour attendants dare guests to step into the "dead" center of the room). Though **Space Mountain** is no longer the most imaginative or fastest roller coaster in town, it was the first, so its charm and mystique are legendary. Devotees of the ride are legion, forever debating points such as which of the two tracks is superior (the right track, say most folks) and whether the asteroids projected onto the ceiling are actually blown-up images of chocolate-chip cookies (your call). **Thunder Mountain Railroad,** a Wild West train ride gone awry, tears its way down a giant mountain whose highest point affords a great view of the park. **It's a Small World,** a favorite attraction of toddlers, is an engaging (albeit not always politically correct) 11-minute sampler of international cultures: you'll be humming that song for months.

■ **EPCOT** *map page 173, A-3/4*
EPCOT was Walt Disney's vision for a planned community of the future, a utopian paradise enclosed in a climate-controlled dome that would harbor 20,000 people from poverty, pollution, and other contemporary social ills. After Disney died, the Disney Corporation went ahead with EPCOT—an acronym for Experimental Prototype Community of Tomorrow—but they scrapped Walt's grandiose plans for a real-life, inhabited, futuristic city in favor of a more financially viable,

Thrill-seekers enjoy the Countdown to Extinction ride at Disney's Animal Kingdom.
(The Walt Disney Company)

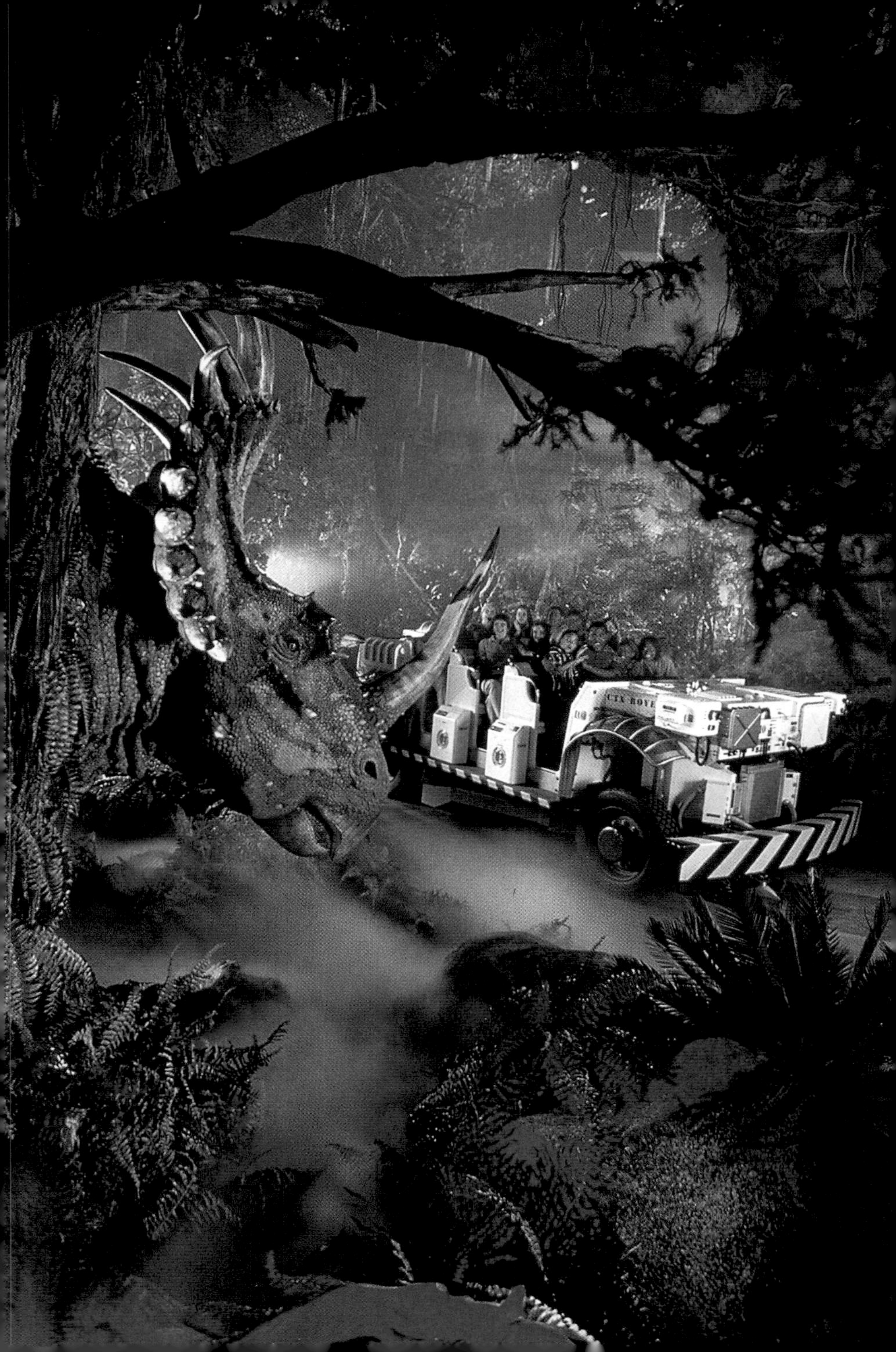

watered-down, theme-park version. The end result is a part educational, part entertaining, 260-acre "thinking-man's theme park" divided into two major areas: Future World and World Showcase. *Take I-4 to Exit 26B, follow EPCOT Center Drive to entrance gate; 407-824-4521.*

Highlights
Future World might as well be called Corporate World. American industrial giants, such as Exxon, General Motors, AT&T, Kodak, and Nestlé, engage in shameless self-promotion by sponsoring most of the pavilions, which are dedicated primarily to tooting the horn of technological progress.

Spaceship Earth, which traces the evolution of human communication (you guessed it, sponsored by AT&T), is housed in a 17-story-high geosphere that shimmers in the bright Florida sun like a giant, silver disco light. **Honey, I Shrunk the Audience** is an interactive 3-D film extravaganza with amazingly real special effects, such as a giant dog that sneezes, and hordes of mice that run rampant under your chair. **GM's Test Track** is a newer attraction in which the car you ride in is put through a series of tests before it goes through a wall and speeds

A tunnel into the future at EPCOT. (The Walt Disney Company)

around an elevated exterior racetrack, where it reaches speeds of 75 miles per hour.

World Showcase celebrates the cultural, architectural, and culinary highlights of a dozen countries, from the United Kingdom to China to Morocco. Each national pavilion is staffed by a person who sells indigenous handicrafts and prepares authentic cuisine. The restaurants in the Mexican, French, Italian, and Japanese pavilions have some of the best dining in town (call 407-939-3463 for reservations). The scaled-down re-creations of China's Temple of Heaven, Venice's St. Mark's Square, and Paris's Eiffel Tower are particularly impressive, and the native performing troupes, such as the gravity-defying Chinese acrobats, are both educational and entertaining—exactly what Disney wanted EPCOT to be.

To that end, the park succeeds, but think twice about visiting EPCOT if you have only one day in the area; it's really more of an ancillary destination that enhances the other offerings at Walt Disney World. At nighttime, **Tapestry of Dreams,** a musical parade filled with giant, colorful figures, and **Illuminations,** a water-based laser and fireworks show, are great ways to end a day.

■ DISNEY-MGM STUDIOS *map page 173, A/B-4*

Opened in 1989, the third installment of the Disney domain isn't a fantasy affair like the Magic Kingdom, or as earnestly educational as EPCOT, but it does offer a pleasant mix of both, wrapped up inside the magic of a working TV and movie studio. Though it pales somewhat in comparison to Universal Studios Florida, and is only one-fourth that park's size, the Disney-MGM effort is enjoyable. *Take I-4 to Exit 26B, follow EPCOT Center Drive to Lake Buena Vista Drive to entrance gate; 407-824-4521.*

Highlights

We liked the slapstick adventure of **Jim Henson's Muppet Vision 4-D** attraction, with its flying trombones, cars, and rocks, and special effects, such as cannons blowing holes in the walls of the theater. The tranquil **Voyage of the Little Mermaid** is a song-and-dance show based on the blockbuster movie and performed by cartoon, human, and audio-animatronic characters. One of the most thrilling rides is **Star Tours,** an unbelievably real-seeming space adventure based on *Star Wars*. In a flight-simulator virtual spaceship, you dodge meteors and engage in intergalactic warfare. Housed in a full-scale reproduction of Mann's Chinese Theatre is the **Great Movie Ride,** an intriguing look at scenes from such films as *Casablanca, Raiders of the Lost Ark*, and *The Wizard of Oz*.

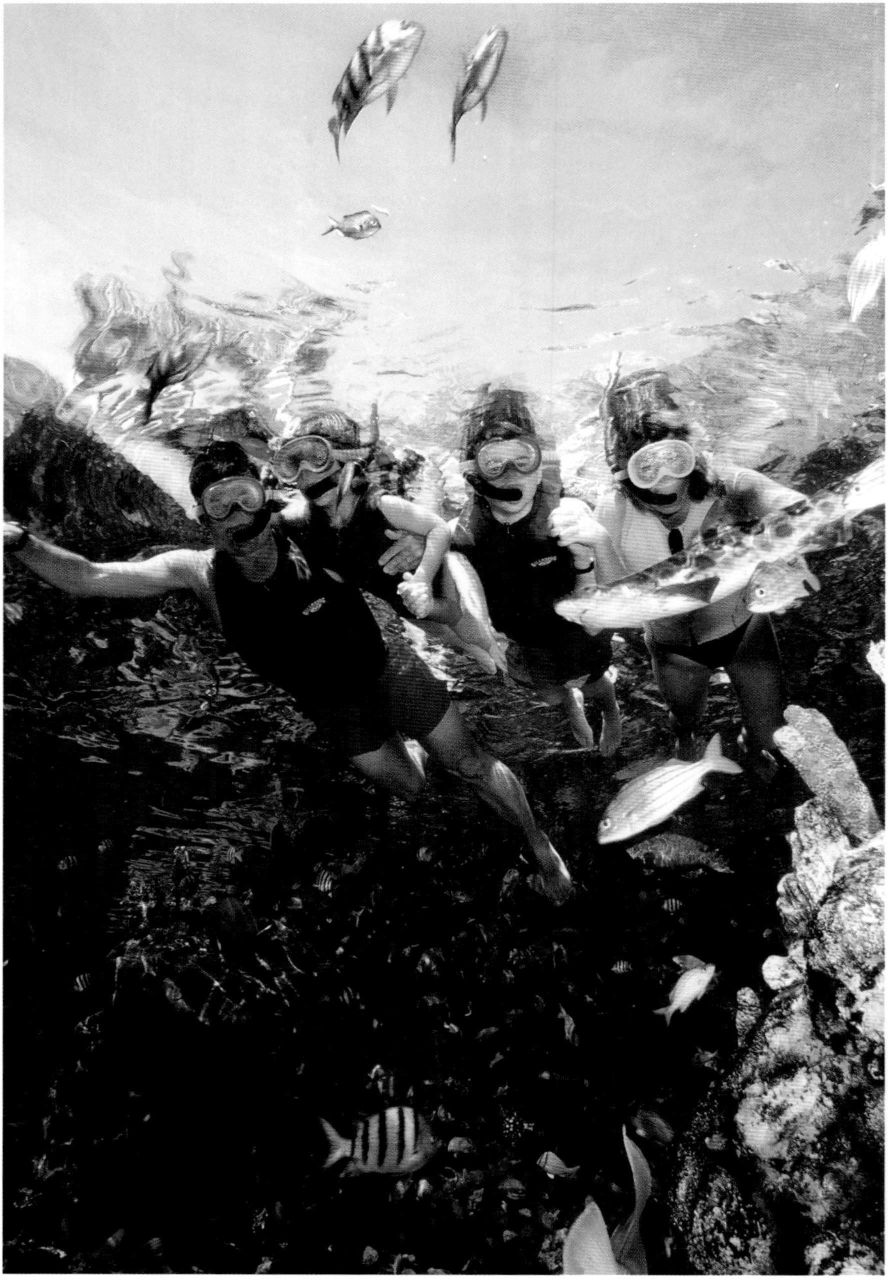

One of Orlando's scariest rides is **Twilight Zone Tower of Terror,** set in a haunted Hollywood hotel whose decrepit service elevator sends riders plummeting 13 stories to their demise. (The original ride had only one drop, but Disney added more after guests complained that the experience was too short and the line too long.)

The initial acceleration of the all-indoor **Aerosmith's Rock 'n' Roller Coaster** is so powerful you'll spend the remainder of the ride trying to catch your breath. The ride, aboard a "stretch limo," whisks you past a series of familiar Southern California landmarks (the Hollywood sign, Roxy Theater) before depositing you at a concert setting. The namesake band provides both the music and a hokey video introduction.

The Tower of Terror and the Rock 'n' Roller Coaster, as well as every other popular attraction throughout all Disney parks, come equipped with Fastpass, a time-saving computer reservation system that allows guests to return at a designated time when they'll experience little or no wait. It's an ingenious system, but the drawback is that you can only get one Fastpass ticket at a time, so choose carefully.

Disney-MGM's *Fantasmic!* show, produced in a semicircular waterfront venue, is one of the most dazzling productions in all Orlando. Images are projected onto screens of mist, water catches fire, and characters magically appear and disappear, all to a perfectly synchronized soundtrack so dynamic it sounds like live accompaniment. Kids are mesmerized by the action; parents are dumbfounded by the sheer technical wizardry. There are several shows (weather permitting) every night; seating is first-come, first-served, but they usually fill up at least 45 minutes before shows begin.

■ DISNEY'S ANIMAL KINGDOM *map page 173, A-4*

The 500-acre Disney's Animal Kingdom is an ambitious conglomeration of wild animal park, exotic zoo, educational adventure, and theme park. The attraction is so massive it straddles two Florida counties, which makes the sales tax on one side of the park different from the other. Within its borders, visitors can cruise on riverboats and shoot rapids, ride battered safari trucks, or hike along jungle trails to observe wildlife in a natural setting. The park's conservationist slant is admirable, exposing guests to the dangers facing wildlife worldwide. *Take I-4 to Highway 192 West, exit World Drive to entrance gate; 407-938-2784.*

The shark reef at Typhoon Lagoon. (The Walt Disney Company)

Highlights

Africa is a stunningly convincing re-creation of an African savanna, modeled after Kenya's Masai Mara Preserve. At the Disney version, you can join Kilimanjaro Safaris on a trip through rivers, forests, and rocky hills and get a close-up look at lions, giraffes, elephants, and zebras. The **Gorilla Falls Exploration Trail** leads past two troops of lowland gorillas, hippos, and scores of exotic birds. At **Conservation Station,** you can meet animal experts and get a behind-the-scenes look at park operations.

Near the park entrance, you can board a riverboat for a trip on the man-made **Discovery River,** which circles the area. At the center of the park in **Safari Village** is the **Tree of Life,** which isn't really alive. Inside the enormous "tree," you get a bug's-eye view of life in the excellent 3-D insect film.

Dinoland USA has a roadside-attraction feel. Here, you can go face-to-face with snarling, audio-animatronic dinosaurs in the **Countdown to Extinction** ride and along the **Cretaceous Trail,** where you can meander through forests of palms and vines and discover alligators, turtles, and creatures of the prehistoric past. Budding paleontologists will find plenty of hands-on stuff to play with, and there's a **Boneyard Playground** for the little ones.

■ DOWNTOWN DISNEY *map page 173, A-3*

When you've taken all the rides and seen all there is to see, head over to **Pleasure Island** and the retail and dining development called Downtown Disney. Pleasure Island is an adult-oriented nightlife destination where you'll find everything from a 1970s dance club to a bar where assorted character actors interact with the crowd (Adventurer's Club, 407-934-7781).

Although it was created exclusively for Walt Disney World, **Cirque du Soleil's** *La Nouba* transcends mere entertainment. On one hand, you have high-concept performance art set to music; on the other, a display of world-class acrobatic feats performed by a cast of 100 athletes from around the globe, many of them former Olympians. Housed in a building that resembles a futuristic-looking circus tent, this production of the famed "human circus" includes aerial ballet, superhuman trampoline tricks, and stunts with bikes and several unique vehicles that defy description. This feast for the senses and the mind puts the theme park productions to shame, and with good reason: You will pay about twice the cost of a theme park admission to see it. *Downtown Disney; 407-939-7600.*

The ride Men in Black: *Alien Attack is based on the Universal film. (Universal Orlando)*

■ UNIVERSAL ORLANDO *map page 173, B-2*

Universal Orlando is actually two separate theme parks: Universal Studios and the newer Islands of Adventure. The former is a 400-acre park with attractions based on popular Universal movies, such as ***Men in Black***; the latter is a highly entertaining, open-air park filled with amusements and plenty of fast rides. It's possible to visit both in one long day, but regardless of how long you stay at each, you'd better visit Universal Studios first: if you don't, you might never leave the more exciting Islands of Adventure.

■ UNIVERSAL STUDIOS *map page 173, B-2*

This 400-acre park, built around a man-made lake, is divided into six neighborhoods, but the only one whose name tells you anything about its attractions is Woody Woodpecker's Kid Zone, an interactive playground where everyone from Barney to E. T. has an attraction. The World Expo neighborhood's newest draw is

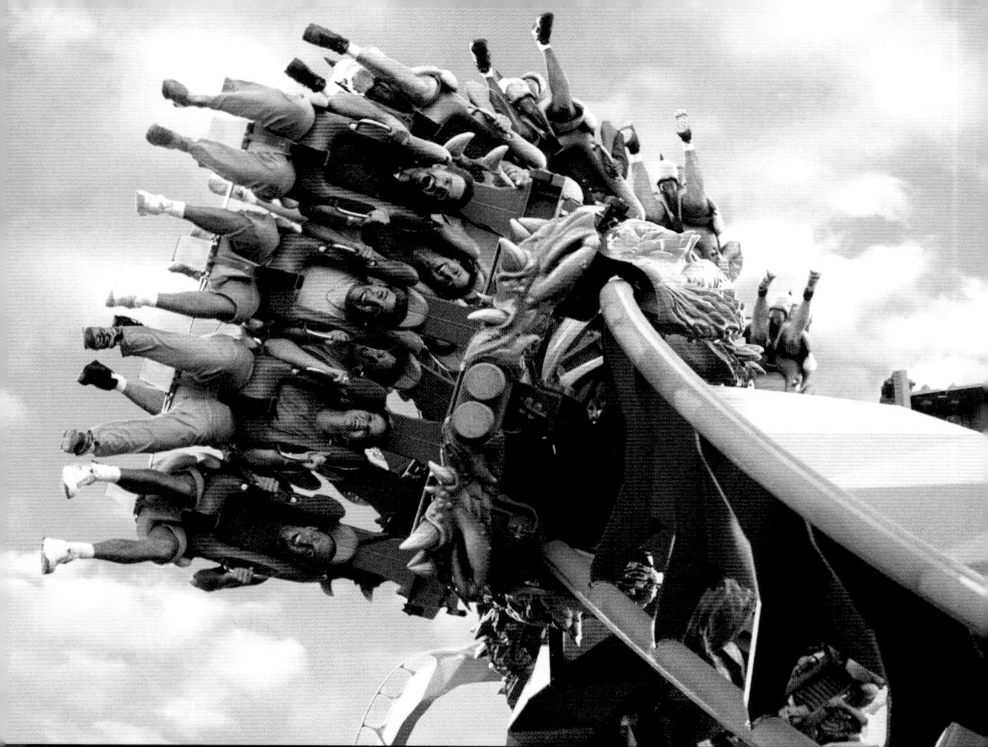

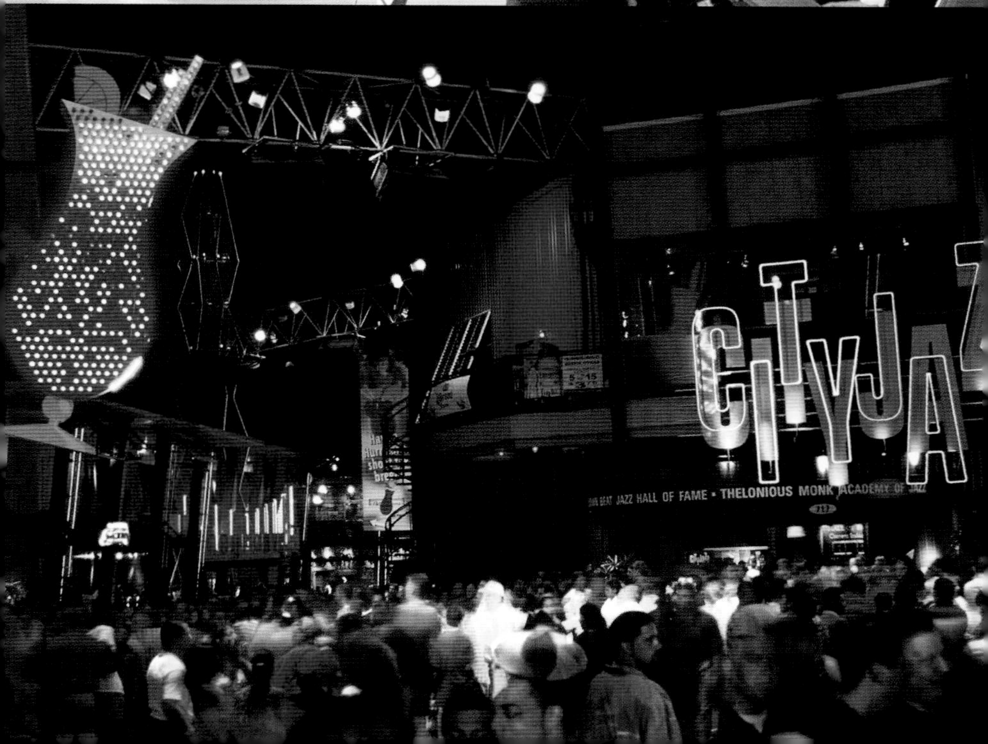
CITYJA
JAZZ HALL OF FAME • THELONIOUS MONK ACADEMY OF JAZZ

Men in Black: **Alien Attack,** where riders get spun and knocked around while firing lasers at scores of aliens. ***Back to the Future*: The Ride** is a jostling, rollicking time-travel journey in a silver DeLorean, the ill-fated sports car that in reality never made it out of the early 1980s.

Arnold Schwarzenegger is back in ***Terminator 2* 3-D,** a technologically advanced attraction accentuated with digital composite computer graphics and a mix of live-action and 3-D cinematography. On *Jaws,* a huge mechanical shark threatens to turn you and your brood into gooey saltwater taffy. As if the state of Florida didn't already have enough experience with natural disasters, *Twister* puts you through a five-story-high funnel cloud. Hang on to those hairpieces! It's big-time monkey business in **Kongfrontation,** where an enormous King Kong assaults your graffiti-covered, circa-1976 New York subway car. Rounding out Universal's disaster triumvirate is **Earthquake—The Big One,** yet another ride that traps you in a subway, then shakes you about in the turmoil of an 8.3 Richter-scale quake. *Take I-4 to Exit 29, take Sand Lake Road to Turkey Lake Road, follow to entrance gate; 407-363-8000.*

■ **ISLANDS OF ADVENTURE** *map page 173, B-2*
Islands of Adventure is an adrenaline junkie's dream. The array of roller coasters, from the gravity-defying steel twists of the mammoth **Incredible Hulk Coaster** to the game of high-speed chicken played by the twin-track **Dueling Dragons,** is unequaled in Orlando; even the **Flying Unicorn,** the supposed "kiddie coaster," is thrilling, though you're unlikely to ever see a kid on it. Other highlights include the **Jurassic Park River Adventure,** where dinosaurs loom overhead and a jarring, flumelike plunge soaks you clear through, and the harrowing, 10-story drop of **Doctor Doom's Fearfall. Seuss Landing,** a real-life cartoon fantasyland filled with rides for young children, is impressive. Upon request, attendants at the **Cat in the Hat** ride will turn off the spin feature on your vehicle to keep uneasy toddlers happy during the ride. It is probably the only attraction in town that allows the rider to control the intensity of the experience.

Islands of Adventure can't match Walt Disney World's famous attention to detail, and its employees don't exude the esprit de corps that Disney's "cast members" do, but when it comes to the basics of entertainment, this place gives the Mouse a run for its money.

(top) Dueling Dragons at Islands of Adventure. (Universal Orlando)
(bottom) City Jazz at Citywalk is a magnet for jazz aficionados. (Universal Orlando)

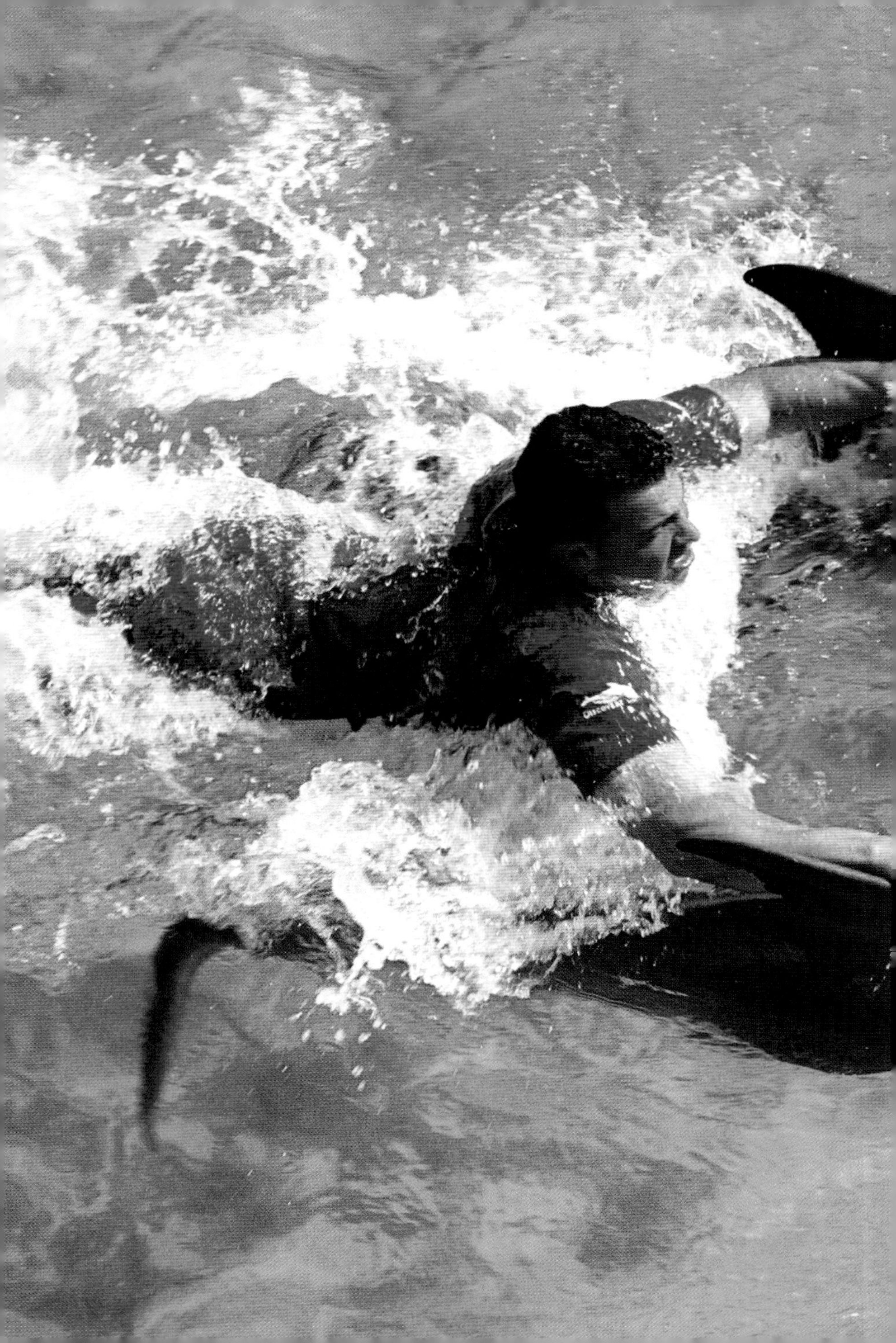

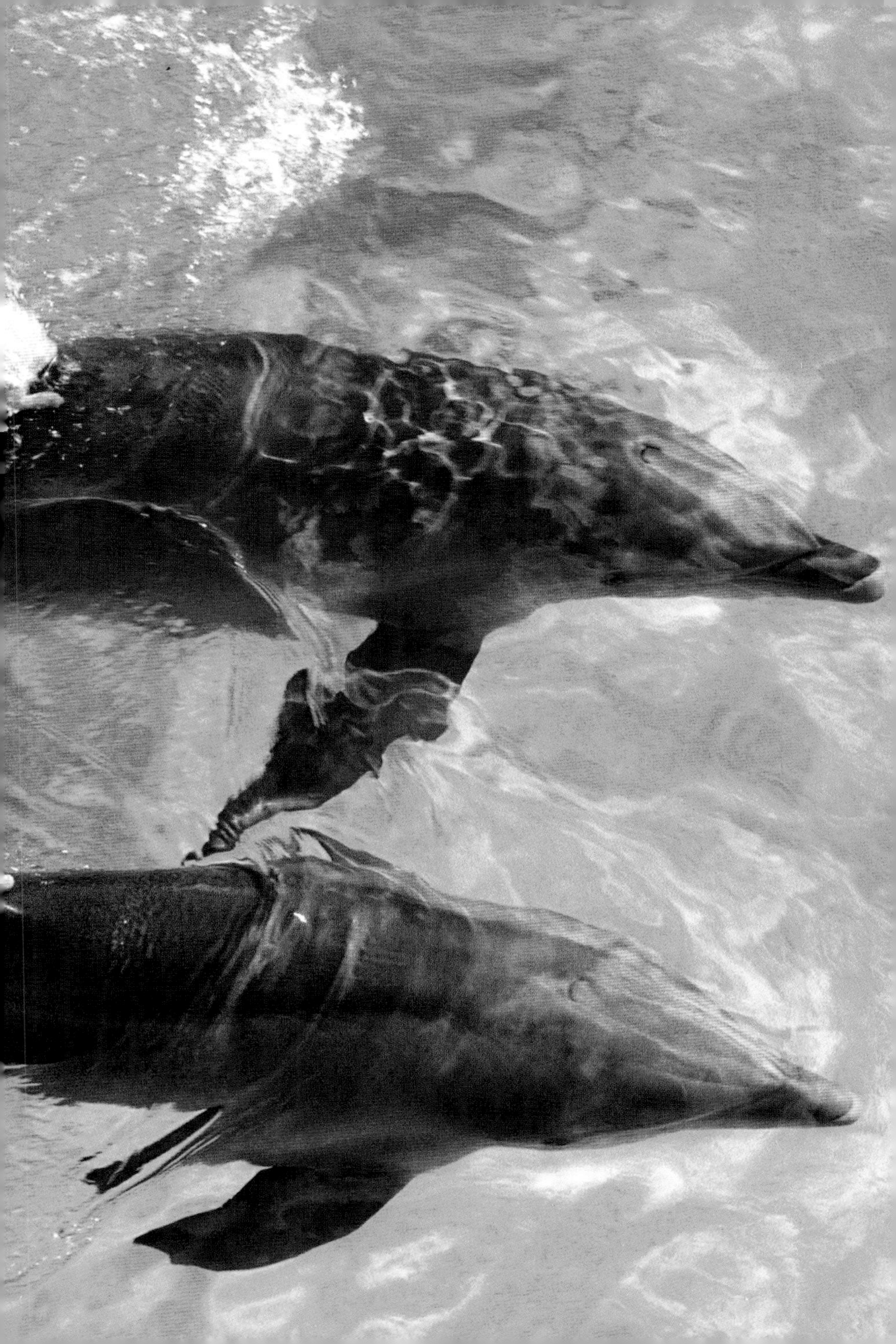

Universal's answer to Disney's Pleasure Island is **Citywalk** (407-224-2692), an array of shops, restaurants, a movie theater, clubs, bars, and arcades. This is where you'll find **Hard Rock Live!** (407-351-5483), a venue for musical performances, from blues to swing to rock.

■ SEAWORLD OF FLORIDA   *map page 173, B-3*

This 200-acre marine park seems to exist as a conflation of two contradictory goals: providing entertainment for people and protecting wild animals. The first is achieved by corralling animals and making them do tricks for paying customers; the second by making SeaWorld of Florida one of the most respected marine research and breeding centers in the world. Its renowned Beached Animal Rescue and Rehabilitation Program has saved literally thousands of animals, including endangered manatees, dolphins, sea turtles, and whales. *Take Exit 28 off I-4, follow the signs to the parking lot; 407-351-3600.*

(preceding pages) A trainer rides with dolphins at Discovery Cove. (Discovery Cove Orlando)
(above) Tropical Oasis at Discovery Cove. (Discovery Cove Orlando)

Highlights

Disney has a talking mouse, but SeaWorld has a dancing, leaping, irresistibly lovable 4-ton killer whale, Shamu. (There are actually five different Shamus that alternate performances.) In **Shamu Adventure,** a selected Shamu and one of his protégés join acrobatic trainers in a 5-million-gallon aquarium for a thrilling show. Arrive early, as the stadium fills even on slow days.

Wild Arctic is part ride, part educational adventure, in which you can observe polar bears, walruses, and beluga whales. **Key West** is a re-creation of the famous Florida island, complete with dolphin shows and a white-sand beach. The park's excellent wildlife-focused exhibits include **Manatees: The Last Generation,** the **Terrors of the Deep** shark tank, **Penguin Encounter,** and **Stingray Lagoon.**

Kraken is a state-of-the-art steel roller coaster that claims to be Orlando's tallest, longest, and fastest, reaching speeds of 65 miles per hour and turning upside down seven times as it descends from a height of 15 stories. It's not for the fainthearted, and the absence of a floor (your feet just dangle) makes it an even more outrageous experience. **Journey to Atlantis** is a flume-style ride built to resemble a huge pyramid. You'll probably be prepared for the drenching you'll receive, but the steepness of the final 60-foot drop never fails to shock.

■ DISCOVERY COVE *map page 173, B-3*

This intimate, lushly landscaped tropical oasis limits daily admission to 1,000 visitors, who relax on white-sand beaches, explore waterfalls and caves, and frolic with sea creatures in man-made lagoons. At an underwater cavern, an invisible glass wall separates live sharks from guests (the effect is chilling), and a freshwater river circles through a jungle where peacocks and two-toed sloths hold court.

But the winner of the day—and the reason guests fork over more than $200 for the experience—is the **Dolphin Swim,** a 30-minute session with one of 32 bottlenose dolphins who live and work here. The animals are amazingly gentle up close, and until you've been dragged across the pool by one of them (on purpose—it's part of the experience), you're bound to take their power for granted. The entrance fee includes both lunch and admission to neighboring SeaWorld, which owns the attraction. If you don't want to swim with the dolphins, you pay half price, but once you see them in action, you'll want to get closer to these wondrous creatures at any cost. *Take I-4 east (toward Orlando) to Exit 27A; 877-434-7268 for reservations, 407-370-1280 for information.*

■ ORLANDO *map page 173, B/C-1/2*

Orlando's first white settlers trickled into the area at the close of the Seminole Wars. Cattlemen, such as Aaron Jernigan, benefited from the government's native relocation program, and, in 1842, he arrived in the area with his family, herds, and slaves. Other ranchers followed, establishing themselves in the vicinity of Fort Gatlin. In 1850, the settlement was granted a post office and the town was named Jernigan in honor of its founder. Some believe it was renamed Orlando by Judge V. D. Spears after the hero in Shakespeare's *As You Like It*, though many assert it was named for settler Orlando Reeves, who was killed by Indians.

Henry Plant's railroad chugged into town in 1880, fostering a citrus boom, and by the early 1890s orchards, along with cattle, became the area's dominant economic venture. Despite the disastrous freeze of 1895 and a crippling fruit-fly infestation in 1929, citrus remained Orlando's biggest industry well into the late 1960s, when Florida's biggest boom to date scurried into town on mouse paws.

Most of the theme parks actually lie outside Orlando, which is by no means an entirely Mickey Mouse town. Starting in the '50s, with the heating up of the Cold War and the dawn of the space race (nearby Cape Canaveral saw its first guided

An early morning view looking across Lake Eola at downtown Orlando.

missile launch on April 24, 1950), Orlando has steadily managed to establish itself as a high-tech hot spot. Recently, it has become a sort of Silicon Valley of Florida, with NASA, the Kennedy Space Center, and private companies fueling a need for the rapidly advancing field of simulation technology.

Though most Floridians can't fathom why anyone would want to live in Orlando, 200,000 people do. When asked why, locals tick off such things as the Orlando-UCF Shakespeare Festival, Southern Ballet Theatre, the Civic Theatre, art museums, the weather, and the reasonable cost of living. Downtown's glass-sided high-rises glitter with the reflection of sparkling Lake Eola. A stroll in **Lake Eola Park,** which surrounds the lake, is a perfect way to idle away an afternoon.

■ ORLANDO SIGHTS *map page 173*

The **Orlando Museum of Art** is proof that Orlando isn't a one-mouse town. The impressive permanent collection includes works by artists ranging from John Singer Sargent and George Inness to Georgia O'Keeffe, Andy Warhol, and Jasper Johns. Extensive pre-Columbian and African holdings provide a counterpoint to more modern offerings. *2416 North Mills Avenue; 407-896-4231.*

C. japonica *"Emily Wilson" at the Leu Gardens. (Harry P. Leu Gardens)*

American art on display at the Orlando Museum of Art. (Orlando Museum of Art)

At **Harry P. Leu Gardens,** you'll find a 50-acre botanical preserve filled with rare camellias and the state's largest rose garden. Two miles of walkways wind throughout the property. *1920 North Forest Avenue; 407-246-2620.*

The promotional literature for the **Orlando Science Center** invites kids to "build a bridge, fire a laser, and touch an alligator—all in one day." There's that and more to do, but what makes this hands-on museum a cut above similar facilities is how beautifully it demonstrates cause and effect in the natural world, especially in the human body. Such exhibits as Healthy Living, where kids learn the physical effects of smoking by pedaling an oxygen cycle, and BodyZone, which explores the food-body relationship (you enter by walking into a huge, open mouth), are educational without being didactic. The dinosaur skeletons and fossils at the new Dino Digs exhibit are replicas donated by Disney's Animal Kingdom, which explains why they look like the real thing. *777 East Princeton Street; 407-514-2000.*

Central Florida has stunning natural beauty, and local entrepreneurs offer some unusual ways to experience it. For a unique perspective on everything from old-growth cypress stands to seemingly endless orange groves, get up early and rise above it all in a hot-air balloon. Don Edwards, owner and operator of **Blue Water Balloons,** is an experienced pilot who offers his otherworldly excursions whenever the weather allows. You'll get a panoramic view of Florida wildlife, from alligators to the occasional eagle's nest, but in more populated areas, the sight of the balloon makes dogs bark and truckers honk. It's a kick, and it gives you a good idea of what the entire place looked like pre-Disney. *800-586-1884 or 407-894-5040.*

If you want to see an alligator close up, head outside Orlando to **Lone Cabbage Fish Camp** and climb aboard an airboat, a flat-bottom, aluminum craft pushed by an airplane propeller mounted on its stern. It's the opposite of a balloon ride—fast and loud—but you'll see gators, especially if you go in the early morning or at night, when guides shatter the darkness of the marshes with spotlights and glowing red eyes stare back at you unflinchingly. It's wonderfully spooky, and when the engines cut off, the sounds of the swamp critters can be just as deafening as the boat engines. After the ride, stop in at the restaurant for a basket of fried gator tail, a Florida Cracker delicacy that sounds more exotic than it tastes. *In Cocoa, on the St. Johns River, State Road 528 South to State Road 520 West; 321-632-4199.*

Orlando County Regional History Center is an entertaining jaunt through central Florida history, starting with Paleo-Indians and ending with the space shuttle and beyond. The museum, housed in a 1927 courthouse, doesn't dwell too heavily on any one era, which might render it superficial were it not for the well-chosen, interesting tidbits, such as the fact that pioneer mattresses were filled with Spanish moss, or that oranges are actually harvested twice a year. Special exhibits explore the local civil rights movement and popular music in the Sunshine State. *65 East Central Boulevard; 407-836-8500.*

■ TRAVEL BASICS

Getting Around: Interstate 4 connects the Gulf Coast of Tampa to the Atlantic Coast at Daytona Beach, cutting through the core of the heartland and Disney country on the way. From Miami, the Florida Turnpike runs north along the coast before breaking inland to Orlando at Fort Pierce. Back roads lace the area. Explore them for an un-Disneyfied look at rolling hills, citrus groves, and open pastures.

Climate: The state's interior is warmer in summer and cooler in winter than coastal areas of the same latitude. The average high in Orlando in January is 70°F; April, 81°F; July, 90°F; and October, 83°F. Southern Florida experiences more thunderstorms than any other region in North America (over 100 days out of the year). They are common year-round, but most occur in summer.

UPPER ATLANTIC COAST

■ OVERVIEW

Northeastern Florida is a lowland plain where pine forests once grew to the edge of the sea. Most visitors stay at the edge of the water, especially on the barrier islands that line the coast from the Carolinas to Georgia. Waterways are filled with a spectacular array of birds and with pleasure boats, commercial, and naval vessels. Along this route are long, flat beaches edged in dunes, fine, protected beachfronts, and St. Augustine, the oldest European city in North America. Inland, the flat plain is traversed in the north by the wide St. Johns River, which creates a grassy floodplain filled with more clamoring birds and thick vegetation.

In places, northeast Florida is industrialized (Jacksonville); elsewhere it is historic (St. Augustine); and in other areas it is hip (Melbourne and Cocoa Beaches). In the far north, plants and flowers resemble those in South Carolina and Georgia; at Vero they are subtropical, like Miami's. The state's central-coast ecology is preserved at Cape Canaveral Seashore; beyond that lies the Kennedy Space Center, the launchpad for America's space programs.

■ AMELIA ISLAND AND FERNANDINA BEACH
map page 196, A-1

In 1736, the governor of Georgia, General James Oglethorpe, sailed a gunboat into Old Town Fernandina's harbor, hoping to extend Georgia's boundaries. Oglethorpe found the island so beautiful that he decided to name it after British King George II's lovely daughter, Amelia Sophia Eleanora.

The princess herself suffered from an unrequited love for her cousin and confidant, Frederick the Great of Prussia, and she never married. Her island, however, was awash in suitors, and it wasn't because of its idyllic beaches. Rather, those who wanted it were impressed by its harbor, which, until the advent of dredging, was the deepest on the southeast coast of North America (17 feet at low tide). The harbor was spacious enough to hold 400 ships and had direct access to the ocean and to freshwater. Because of the freshwater, ships that moored here were protected from the saltwater teredo mollusk, which ate through wood at a terrific rate, rendering finely made hulls into spongy, waterlogged lumber after nine or 10 years on the high seas.

In other words, Amelia had everything, and because of that, her past is a trail of broken hearts and conflicting loyalties. Thirteen miles long and 2.5 miles wide, the island has seen no less than eight flags raised over it in a period of 250 years.

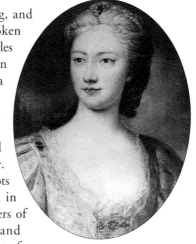

Princess Amelia. (Amelia Island Museum of History Collection)

The Spanish built three missions here and called the island Santa Maria. The English later burned down one mission and attacked the island regularly thereafter. American sympathizers, known as the Patriots of Amelia Island, overthrew the Spanish in 1812 and raised the American flag. Soldiers of fortune sailed in on several occasions and declared the island's independence, the first of these being a 31-year-old Scot, Gregor MacGregor, who raised his own flag, the Green Cross of Florida, in 1817.

Not long after, Luis Aury, a Frenchman by birth and a privateer by inclination, sailed into town with four ships: a 12-gun flagship, two more brigs, and a prize ship valued at $60,000. Aury, who had been the naval commander of Mexican rebel forces, took over the fort and established a state under the Mexican rebel flag. He is credited with importing more than a thousand Africans to Amelia and smuggling them into slavery in Georgia, a profitable tack favored by pirates after 1807, when the U.S. Congress made it illegal to import slaves into the country.

During this period, the region developed a seamy reputation. In 1817, President James Monroe declared it a "festering fleshpot," where unscrupulous bootleggers, smugglers, and painted ladies sauntered the streets. This opinion laid the groundwork for his secret plan to take over Florida once and for all. He sent the U.S. corvette *John Adams* into Fernandina's harbor in 1817, landed troops, met with no resistance, raised the American flag, and that was that. By this time, pirate Aury had sailed quietly into the sunset.

The Spaniards' attempt to recapture their former possession was unsuccessful, and in 1821 they ceded all of Florida to the United States and left for good. The last takeover attempt of Amelia was in 1861, when Confederate forces took over

UPPER ATLANTIC COAST

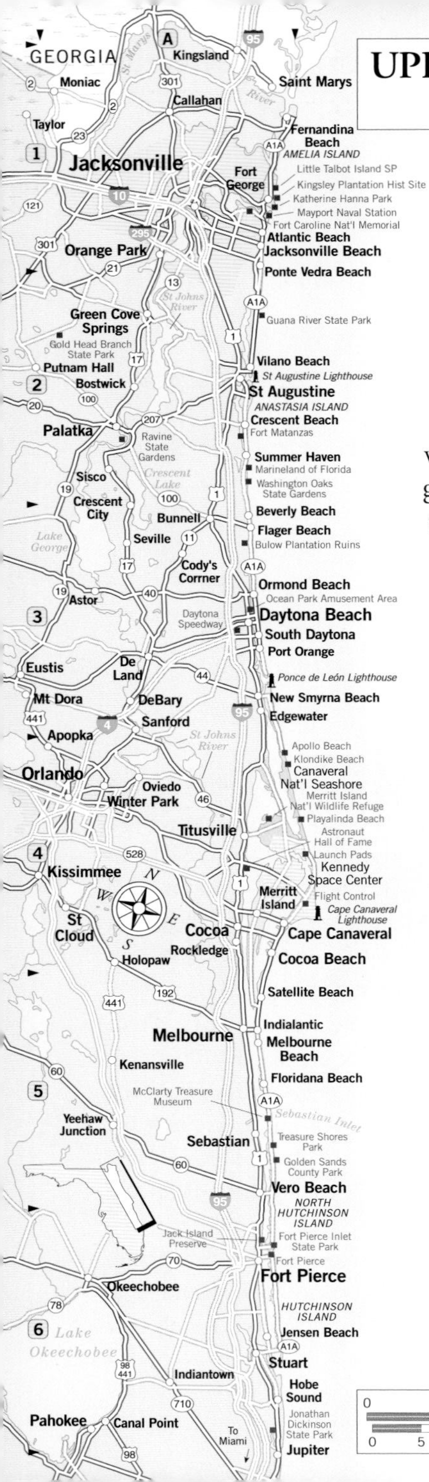

GEORGIA
A
Kingsland
Saint Marys
Moniac
Callahan
St Marys River
Taylor
Fernandina Beach
AMELIA ISLAND
1
Jacksonville
Fort George
Little Talbot Island SP
Kingsley Plantation Hist Site
Katherine Hanna Park
Mayport Naval Station
Fort Caroline Nat'l Memorial
Atlantic Beach
Jacksonville Beach
Orange Park
Ponte Vedra Beach
St Johns River
Guana River State Park
Green Cove Springs
Gold Head Branch State Park
Putnam Hall
Vilano Beach
St Augustine Lighthouse
2
Bostwick
St Augustine
ANASTASIA ISLAND
Crescent Beach
Fort Matanzas
Palatka
Ravine State Gardens
Summer Haven
Marineland of Florida
Sisco
Crescent Lake
Washington Oaks State Gardens
Crescent City
Beverly Beach
Bunnell
Flager Beach
Lake George
Seville
Bulow Plantation Ruins
Cody's Corrner
Ormond Beach
Ocean Park Amusement Area
Astor
3
Daytona Speedway
Daytona Beach
South Daytona
Port Orange
Eustis
De Land
Ponce de León Lighthouse
Mt Dora
DeBary
New Smyrna Beach
Sanford
Edgewater
Apopka
St Johns River
Apollo Beach
Klondike Beach
Orlando
Canaveral Nat'l Seashore
Oviedo
Merritt Island Nat'l Wildlife Refuge
Winter Park
Playalinda Beach
Titusville
Astronaut Hall of Fame
4
Launch Pads
Kissimmee
Kennedy Space Center
N
W
E
S
Merritt Island
Flight Control
Cape Canaveral Lighthouse
St Cloud
Cocoa
Cape Canaveral
Rockledge
Holopaw
Cocoa Beach
Satellite Beach
Indialantic
Melbourne
Melbourne Beach
Kenansville
Floridana Beach
5
McClarty Treasure Museum
Sebastian Inlet
Yeehaw Junction
Treasure Shores Park
Sebastian
Golden Sands County Park
Vero Beach
NORTH HUTCHINSON ISLAND
Jack Island Preserve
Fort Pierce Inlet State Park
Fort Pierce
Okeechobee
HUTCHINSON ISLAND
6
Lake Okeechobee
Jensen Beach
Stuart
Indiantown
Hobe Sound
Jonathan Dickinson State Park
Pahokee
Canal Point
To Miami
Jupiter
0 15 30 Miles
0 5 30 45 Kilometers

Fort Clinch; they were routed by federal troops in 1862.

Between 1875 and 1910, steamers and railroads brought wealthy tourists here in style. They made Amelia Island and its northernmost town of Fernandina Beach one of the finest resort areas in Florida. Ulysses S. Grant came to visit, as did the Vanderbilts, Du Ponts, and Carnegies. More importantly, the town was a major center of commerce, and 14 foreign consulates were stationed here.

What the railroad giveth, the railroad can take away, and so it did when developer Henry Flagler built the East Coast Railway in the 1890s and bypassed Amelia Island. Some say it was Flagler's decision, others claim the town refused to have his railroad. One islander told me, "There's only one F word on Amelia Island, and that's 'Flagler.'"

The bypass turned out to be a blessing, as it meant the island avoided the overdevelopment that soon plagued other parts of the state. In any case, the local economy continued to thrive as the area became an offshore shrimping port. Canneries were established, too, and most of them flourished until the Great Depression of the 1930s. In the late '30s, pulp mills were built, and the island rebounded economically.

■ Amelia Island and Fernandina Beach Sights

Centre Street forms the heart of the 50-block **Fernandina Beach Historic District,** where you can see hundreds of structures from the 18th and 19th centuries. Vintage buildings now hold coffee shops, boutiques, and seafood restaurants. The Palace Saloon (117 Centre Street) was the haunt of the Carnegie family crowd, and, legend has it, is still haunted by a ghost named Charlie, a former bartender. If you look fixedly in the massive back-bar mirror, Charlie will supposedly appear. Murals on the walls depict pirate tales and scenes from Dickens and Shakespeare.

Nineteenth-century homes built in a range of styles—Queen Anne, Italianate, and Florida vernacular—line the roads that branch out from Centre Street. Many of these attractive abodes have been turned into inns. Centre Street ends at the harbor, where shrimp boats bob in the swells.

Enthusiastic docents lead the tours at the **Amelia Island Museum of History,** inside the old brick county jailhouse. The museum bills itself as Florida's only oral history museum, and the guides' folksy sense of humor is not only entertaining but necessary for the task at hand—rehashing 4,000 years of history. Walking tours of the island can be arranged here, and the museum also offers lectures on island history and architecture. *233 South Third Street; 904-261-7378.*

Buried at **Fernandez Reserve at Villalonga Park** is Amelia's most famous cou-

The marina on Amelia Island.

Fort Clinch on Amelia Island.

ple, Maria Mattair and her husband, Don Domingo Fernandez. In the late 1780s, Maria's mother was a penniless widow left with nothing more than a plot of land on which to support a son and daughter. In 1783, when the second Treaty of Paris was signed, and the English turned the area over to the Spanish, most settlers left. The widow, however, did not. When Spanish soldiers began to rebuild the fort, they decided to expand it onto the widow's land. Reluctantly, she traded her plot for large properties on Amelia Island and the mainland, properties which became prosperous plantations.

The widow died when Maria was only 13; the Protestant, English-speaking orphan was then married at 16 to Don Domingo Fernandez, a navigator. She never learned to read or write, but ably ran the land she inherited from her mother and the two lands granted to her husband by the Spanish government. She died a wealthy woman. One of the couple's two daughters, also named Maria, fell in love with one of her family's plantation overseers, Villalonga. Despite her father's vigorous opposition to the union, Maria nonetheless married Villalonga. *North Fourth and Broome Streets.*

An oak-canopied drive leads to **Fort Clinch State Park,** which was held by Union forces during the Civil War. On the first weekend of each month, volunteers dress up as Union soldiers and go through Civil War–era drills. Candlelight tours of the fort are given on weekend nights from May through Labor Day, by reservation.

The park surrounding the fort is rich in plant and animal life. Along the nature trail, you can see maritime hammocks and tidal marshes teeming with life. On any given day, gopher tortoises, deer, raccoons, bobcats, and many other smaller animals can be seen. Alligators patrol Mosquito Ditch, and snakes are a common sight.

Near the fort and within the 1,100-acre park are uncrowded beaches that need to be "renourished" every decade or so as currents and wind reshape the island. It's a simple but tedious process: sand is dredged up from the ocean floor offshore and piped back to the coastline. The problem of erosion is not unique to this part of the state. Most of Florida's barrier islands are heavily developed and need to be renourished regularly to keep houses and condos from washing away.

The park is one of the island's many quiet places, where you can walk for miles in solitude and revel in the beauty of a barrier-island beach. *At the end of Atlantic Avenue, 2 miles north of downtown; 904-277-7274.*

Popular and crowded Main Beach has grassy picnic areas, volleyball courts, a playground, a miniature golf course, a game room, and, across the street, the **Eight Flags Water Slide.** *35 North Fletcher Avenue; 904-261-8212.*

Hurricane lilies bloom beneath the drooping beard of Spanish moss.

The south end of Amelia Island, a place of great natural beauty, contains a forest of oaks shawled in Spanish moss. "The waving drapery of the live oak trailing long and low/Noiselessly waved by the wind. . . ." wrote Walt Whitman of Florida's Spanish moss. The plant, according to legend, originated when a Spanish explorer chased an Indian maiden up a tree and fell to his death in the pursuit. His head remained lodged between branches, and his beard continued to grow.

Spanish moss isn't actually a moss, it's a member of the epiphyte family of air plants, kin to the orchid and pineapple, that are fed by organisms in the air. Natives wove it into cloth. Henry Ford stuffed his first car seats with it. Moss is picked out of the oaks when it gets too thick, because it causes decay and disease.

Oceanside, the wide, caffe latte–color beaches stretch on endlessly. Scrub vegetation and pink-flowering castor bean crisscross dunes that reach up to 40 feet high. A popular thing to do here is to take a 5-mile horseback ride offered by **Seahorse Stables**. *7500 Route A1A; 904-879-9383.*

←🚐→ **Buccaneer Trail:** *South of Amelia Island, where Route A1A crosses over the Nassau River estuary onto Big Talbot Island, the road becomes Buccaneer Trail, in deference to the region's seafaring traditions. Talbot Islands State Parks preserve white, wind-sculpted dunes and bristling marsh grass. More than 190 bird species have been observed here.*

■ KINGSLEY PLANTATION NATIONAL HISTORIC SITE
map page 196, A-1

In 1814, Zephaniah Kingsley established a plantation on Fort George Island and began producing Sea Island cotton, citrus, sugarcane, and corn. Active in the slave trade, he brought hundreds of Africans to Florida, among them his wife, Anna Madgigine Jai, whom he freed in 1811. According to some accounts, Anna was the daughter of a Senegalese chief whom Kingsley met on a slave-buying trip. The two were married in a native ceremony.

Anna Madgigine Jai and her children occupied the whitewashed house known as Ma'am Anna's House, immediately behind the Planter's Residence. Anna herself had many slaves but apparently still served guests personally as dictated by Senegalese custom. Her children became Zephaniah's heirs, and Zephaniah continued to buy property and expand his holdings. Eventually he owned 32,000 acres and more than 200 slaves.

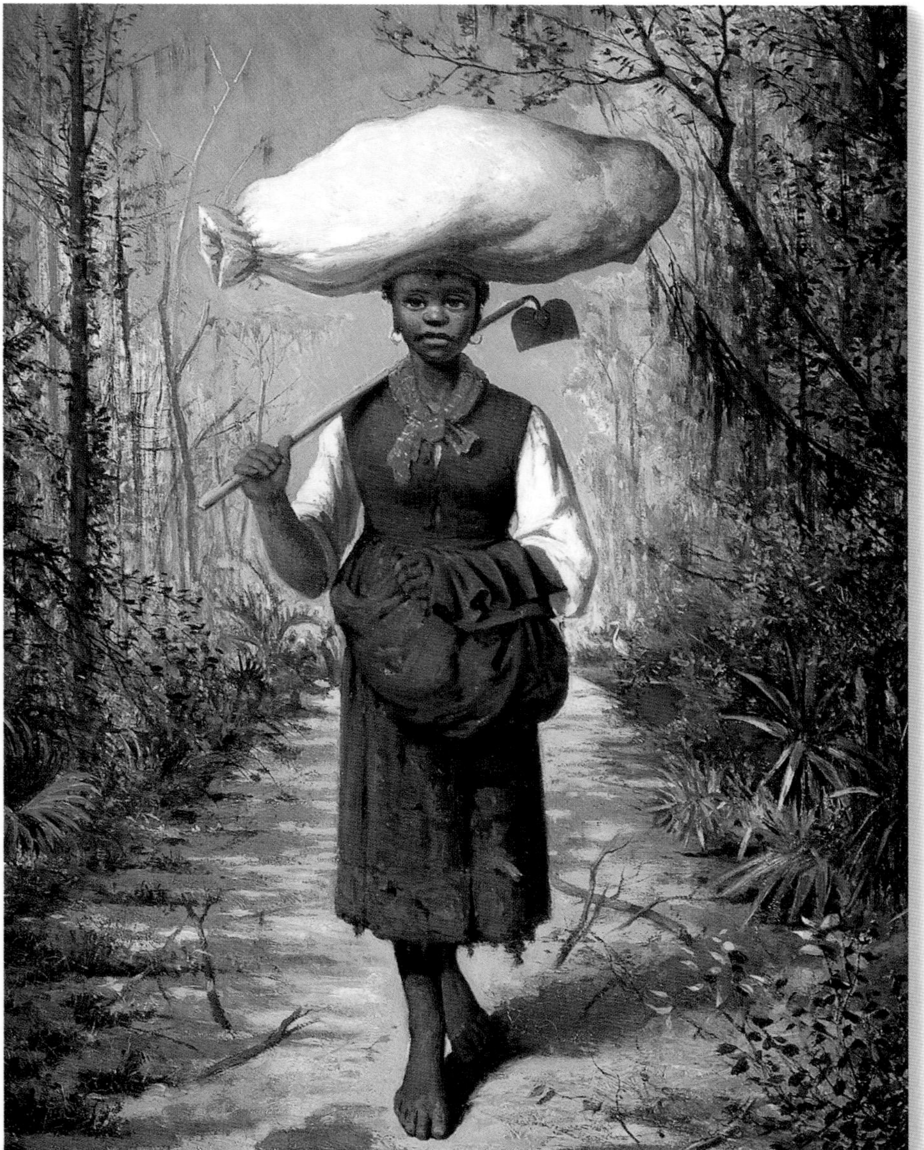

Return From Harvesting *(1874), by James Well Champney.*
(Sam and Robbie Vickers Florida Collection)

The lives of several of the slaves who lived at Kingsley Plantation are known to us. Gullah Jack, stolen from Kingsley by the Seminole Indians, escaped and made his way to the free black community in Charleston, South Carolina, where he helped to plot a slave uprising with Denmark Vesey. Both were caught and hung. Zephaniah's slave Abraham Hanahan was a skillful farmer and manager who ran the Fort George Island plantation in his master's absence.

After the United States purchased Florida from Spain in 1821, life for people of African descent became increasingly restricted. In 1837, Anna Madgigine Jai and the Kingsley children left for Haiti to escape what Kingsley called a "spirit of intolerant prejudice." In Haiti, Kingsley set up a plantation for his wife and some of his former slaves, including Abraham Hanahan.

■ VISITING THE KINGSLEY PLANTATION

I vividly remember my first trip to the Kingsley slave huts. I had turned off the main road and was driving down a narrow, unpaved lane, thinking I'd made a mistake, when I caught sight of the small ruins. I knew slaves had lived here, and the ghostly presence of that history multiplied the eeriness of the drive. The huts were built of tabby, a material created by the labor-intensive process of mixing water with mortar, whole seashells, and burnt seashells ground into lime, then pouring the mixture into wooden forms to harden.

Your experience as a visitor here will depend a great deal upon the enthusiasm and knowledge of your guide. I was fortunate to have a guide who had studied the diaries of Zephaniah Kingsley and, as a result, she knew how to communicate the rigors of slave life and frontier living.

The Planter's Residence has a small visitors center that stocks books on slavery, local wildlife, and the plantation's history. You'll find a few exhibits there and in the nearby Kitchen House, and there's a tabby barn for lectures and a garden where Sea Island cotton is grown. But the ruinous slave quarters, set away from the house and looming as solemn and gray as tombstones in the distance, remain the most poignantly educational structures on the site. *St. George Island, turn left one-half mile north of the Mayport Ferry Landing on Route A1A and follow signs to the plantation; 904-251-3537.*

Aerial view of Kingsley Plantation.

■ JEAN RIBAULT FERRY AND ST. JOHNS RIVER
map page 196, A-1/2

The Jean Ribault Ferry crosses the mouth of the St. Johns River between Fort George (on the north) and the naval station and fishing town known as Mayport. The quarter-mile journey across the river takes less than five minutes, which leaves many impatient visitors wondering why folks here don't build a bridge. The answer is twofold: this is not a busy section of Route A1A (most locals take I-95), and a bridge would have to be tall enough to allow the constant parade of cargo ships headed to the South Atlantic's largest deepwater port to pass underneath. Besides, it's a refreshing speck of Floridiana left untouched by time, and a favorite part of the Buccaneer Trail. In 1790, when American naturalist William Bartram first saw the St. Johns, he wrote of it:

A steamer travels up the St. Johns River in the late 19th century. (Florida State Archives)

> How shall I express myself so as to convey an adequate idea of it to the reader, and at the same time avoid raising suspicions of my veracity? Should I say that the river (in this place) from shore to shore, and perhaps near half a mile above and below me, appeared to be one solid bank of fish, of various kinds, pushing through this narrow pass of St. Juan's into the little lake, on their return down the river, and that the alligators were in such incredible numbers, and so close together from shore to shore, that it would have been easy to have walked across on their heads, had the animals been harmless.

From the mid-1800s until railroads replaced water navigation in the 1900s, rivers like the St. Johns were Florida's most important transportation routes, their waters plied by steamships carrying citrus, farming supplies, and passengers from the state's northeast coast to its heartland. At 310 miles long, the St. Johns is the longest river in Florida, and one of only a handful of rivers in the world that flow from south to north. From its source in a marshy area north of Indian River County to its terminus near the ferry crossing, it drops only 30 feet—about an inch per mile—which also makes it one of the world's slowest-flowing rivers. *Ferry departs every half hour from Mayport and Fort George; both landings are extensions of Route A1A; 904-241-9969.*

■ **KATHRYN ABBEY HANNA PARK** *map page 196, A-1*

This huge, woodsy park south of the naval station is loved by bicyclists, nature hikers, lake and surf fishermen, volleyball players, boogie boarders, and kayakers. The wide beach, more than a mile long, is carpeted in light-tan sand that drifts into dunes around cabbage palms. *Wonderwood Drive off Route A1A; 904-249-4700.*

■ **JACKSONVILLE** *map page 196, A-1*

Jacksonville was once described as the "working son in the Florida family of playboys." Its first resident was Lewis Zachariah Hogans, who built a cabin in 1816 and tilled soil in what is now the heart of town. Cattle forded the St. Johns River here, and, consequently, the village that developed was called Cowford. The name stuck until 1822, when the town was renamed Jacksonville, in honor of then territorial governor, General Andrew Jackson.

Around the turn of the 20th century, as Jacksonville was rebuilding from the Great Fire of 1901, a conflagration that destroyed 400 acres and 2,400 buildings in a single afternoon, movie makers came to town. Within a few years of their arrival, Jacksonville had earned the title "Hollywood of the East" due to the proliferation of silent-film studios—30 in all—that sprang up. By 1916, however, conservative public sentiment had started to turn against the budding industry, which had developed a reputation for unsavory characters and annoying antics, such as setting off false fire alarms to get footage of fire brigades in action. After the election of a mayor who promised to rid the city of the scourge of the studios, Jacksonville said goodbye to its dreams of stardom.

Eventually, Jacksonville settled back into the port town existence it knew before the studios arrived. Its location at the mouth of the St. Johns River made it a historically important stop on trade and navigation routes, providing easy access both to the open ocean and Florida's inland waterways. It's also been a strategic location for military installations for more than 400 years, so it came as no surprise when, in 1942, the mammoth Mayport Naval Station was constructed here. Today, more than 60,000 active-duty personnel, military dependents, and civilian employees make the base—the third largest in the continental United States and home to the aircraft carrier USS *John F. Kennedy*—a city unto itself.

In the late 1960s, a county-wide consolidation referendum designed to streamline local government turned the whole of Duval County into the City of Jacksonville. Overnight, Jacksonville became the world's largest city, in area. Although that distinction now belongs to a city in China (depending on your definition of city), the "Bold New City of the South," as Jacksonville is known, remains America's largest metropolis to this day, all 800 square miles of it. The city is so big that once you enter the city limits, you have to drive through 20 miles of pine forests before you see civilization.

In the mid-1990s, the creation of the National Football League's expansion team, the Jaguars, set into motion a renaissance that is bringing Jacksonville into the national spotlight. The NFL chose the city to host the 2005 Super Bowl festivities, reportedly won over by the city's innovative plan to moor cruise ships along the downtown riverfront for use as hotels during the event. The role the St. Johns River plays in Jacksonville's development never seems to diminish.

■ JACKSONVILLE AREA SIGHTS

The river makes a logical starting point for exploring Jacksonville. On the **Southbank,** have a quick look at Friendship Fountain, whose spectacular 150-foot plumes of water will more than mist you if the wind is right. Then stop in at the adjacent **River City Brewery** for a bite and beer with a view. Water taxis run across the river to the **Northbank,** where you can peruse the waterfront shops of the **Jacksonville Landing,** a large, semicircular marketplace whose orange roof has become a downtown landmark. At the very tip of the Northbank, you'll find **Alltel Stadium,** home of the Jacksonville Jaguars, and riverfront **Metropolitan Park,** whose distinctive, white canvas band shell is fittingly reminiscent of a schooner under full sail. The park hosts a jazz festival and has a Kids Kampus, a beautifully kept, 10-acre recreational facility where climbing, sliding, and other kiddie activities have an educational twist.

Jacksonville's most beautiful neighborhoods can be explored on a leisurely drive. Start on the Southbank in San Marco, an upscale neighborhood of restored homes from the 1920s and '30s. Stop in at San Marco Square, at the intersection of Atlantic Boulevard and Hendricks Avenue, and visit the fashionable boutiques and cafés that line tiny Balis Park. From the square, head south down River Oaks Road and you'll pass a row of impeccably kept riverfront estates that quietly announce you are in the South. Directly across the river from San Marco, over the Fuller Warren Bridge, you'll find the Riverside-Avondale neighborhood, an older version of San Marco's oak-draped avenues and waterfront estates—it's as if the river cut one large neighborhood in half. Jacksonville's "old money" lives here, and posh St.

Johns Avenue is the address of choice. The Shops of Avondale, a smaller version of San Marco Square, and the funkier, trendier Five Points area are the neighborhood's retail and nightlife meccas.

The **Museum of Science and History** is a worthwhile stop. At one exhibit, you can listen to the squeak of a manatee (it sounds like a rusty door opening), track the migrations of whales in the local waters, or admire the backbone of a humpback whale. Other museum highlights include a Kidspace for tots, an allosaurus skeleton, and a live alligator turtle. *1025 Museum Circle, off I-95, San Marco Exit; 904-396-6674.*

"Find Us," reads the cover of the **Cummer Museum and Gardens'** brochure. Doing so is not easy, but is worth the effort. The museum, set in beautiful gardens that lead down to the St. Johns River, is known for its impressive collection of Renaissance, baroque, impressionist, and 20th-century paintings. The kids interactive section enthralls most youngsters, as it uses optical illusions, computer finger painting, holograms, and fiber-optic design to teach art principles. *829 Riverside Avenue; 904-356-6857.*

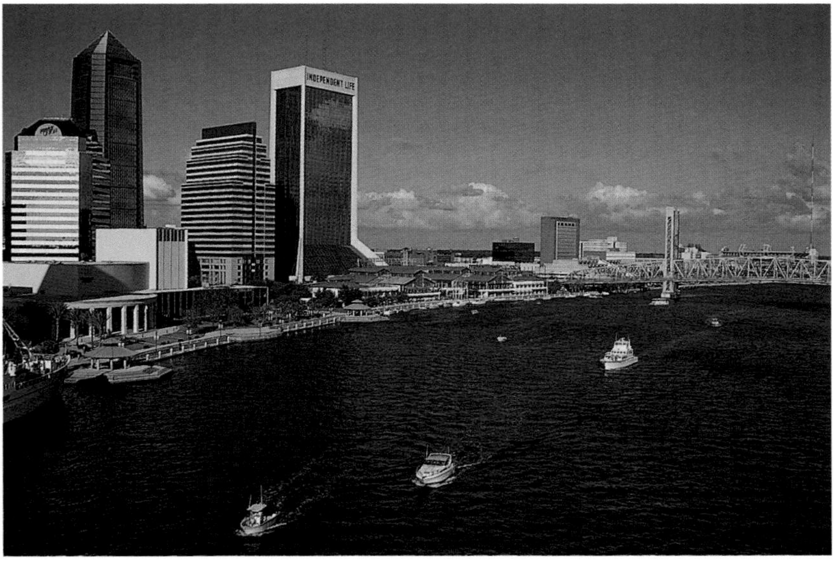
INDEPENDENT LIFE

A view of downtown Jacksonville and the northern bank of the Riverwalk.

The **Fort Caroline National Memorial** commemorates the brief presence of the French along the Florida coast. Under the leadership first of Jean Ribault, then of René de Goulaine de Laudonnière, groups of Huguenots came ashore in search of religious freedom. Unlike the Spaniards, the Huguenots were befriended by the native Timucuans.

French artist Jacques Le Moyne traveled with the Huguenots who built Fort Caroline, and he made many beautiful illustrations of the Timucuan villages and customs. Most agree that the tribe's members were much taller than the Europeans. Ribault described them as "tawny collour, hawk nosed and of a pleasant countenance."

The Spaniards resented the presence of the French, and a battalion led by Pedro Menéndez de Avilés ruthlessly slaughtered the Huguenots. The fort is located east of Jacksonville and operates under the auspices of the National Park Service and the Timucuan Ecological & Historic Preserve. *12713 Fort Caroline Road; 904-641-7155.*

■ JACKSONVILLE BEACHES *map page 196, A-1*

Sixteen miles due east of Jacksonville, across the bridges that span the saw-grass estuaries and the tea-color Intracoastal Waterway, Atlantic Boulevard dead-ends into its namesake ocean. The beach area actually comprises three separate towns—**Atlantic Beach, Neptune Beach,** and **Jacksonville Beach,** from north to south—whose prouder residents take the bridge back to the mainland as infrequently as possible. In truth, many people work in Jax, as locals call it, and live at the beach, and the distinctions between the two get blurrier every year. But the beach has a laid-back culture all its own, as well as a concentration of nightlife venues that bring the townies out to party.

In Atlantic Beach, at the corner of First Street and Atlantic Avenue, you'll find the **Ragtime Tavern** (904-241-7877) and **Sun Dog Cafe** (904-241-8221), two veteran drinking and eating establishments that present some of the best live music around. Farther down First Street, at First Avenue, is a city-backed retail and nightlife development zone that is breathing new life into Jacksonville Beach, the least glamorous of the three communities. Also in Jax Beach is the **J. Johnson Gallery** (177 Fourth Avenue North; 904-435-3200), a New York–style showcase for contemporary art that seems almost too marvelous for this unsuspecting beach town (though perhaps it's a sign of things to come).

Ponte Vedra Beach, land of increasingly congested luxury, lies between Jacksonville Beach and St. Augustine. The town is most famous for its golf courses, namely the Tournament Player's Club's famed stadium course, home to the PGA's Tournament Player's Championship. Its chic homes and resorts eventually give way to **Guana River State Park** (904-825-6877), a 2,400-acre expanse of low shrubs and rolling dunes bisected by the scenic coastal road, Route A1A. Both sunrise and sunset are spectacular here because the park lies between the Atlantic Ocean and the Guana River, which isn't really a river but a brackish section of the Intracoastal Waterway that functions as a tidal estuary. The dunes in the north beach area rise to 40 feet, making them among the tallest in the state. Climb the observation deck, and you will be amazed by how thin this sliver of land looks against the expanse of ocean, and even more amazed that people dare to build homes on it.

■ ST. AUGUSTINE *map page 196, A-2, and page 211*

The faint traces of romantic things
The old land of America
I find in this nook of sand
The first footprints of that giant grown.

—Ralph Waldo Emerson,
"An Unfinished Poem on St. Augustine," March 1828

I often hear St. Augustine described as touristy, and it is. How could it be otherwise, given that the 18,000 people who live here are visited by 2 million people a year, all eager to see the oldest European city in North America? The town lives and breathes history. St. Augustine was claimed by Spanish settlers in 1565—39 years before English settlers arrived in Jamestown. It has been coveted and fought over by the kings of Spain and Britain, the fledgling United States of America, and the Confederacy. Within it have lived a heady mix of Spanish soldiers and notorious pirates, Spanish ladies and British adventurers, free blacks and slaves, Minorcan immigrants, and Gilded Age tourists.

Set on a peninsula, the city is bordered by two marshy rivers: the San Sebastian (to the west) and the Matanzas (to the east). In some sections, the rivers become saltwater estuaries fringed by vast marshlands of smooth cordgrass, which is home to migrating birds using the Atlantic Flyway between temperate and tropic zones.

■ HISTORY

Ponce de León arrived in St. Augustine in 1513. He was probably the first European to land here. He had been along on Columbus's second voyage and was given a mandate by the king of Spain to explore and settle Florida. Ponce didn't stay on, however, and the area was left to itself for another 52 years, after which five Spanish ships and 600 settlers under the command of Pedro Menéndez de Avilés entered the harbor. Menéndez was "Captain General of all Florida," a title conferred by Philip II of Spain. His job was to rid the territory of the Protestant French Huguenots living just to the north, at Fort Caroline near modern-day Jacksonville. Menéndez did so, slaughtering them and then setting sail for Florida's west coast. After that, the Spanish paid little attention to the colony, sending few supplies and little food. Colonists began robbing Indian stores to feed themselves. Hungry and poorly equipped, the Spanish settlers were in no position to defend themselves when, in 1586, English privateer Sir Francis Drake sailed into the harbor, chopped down the orange trees, destroyed the crops, and burned the buildings.

Life in the settlement during the following years was uneasy, if not chaotic. The settlers were under constant threat from British colonies to the north, and they suffered through hurricanes and fires.

St. Augustine *(1890), by Robert S. German. (Sam and Robbie Vickers Florida Collection)*

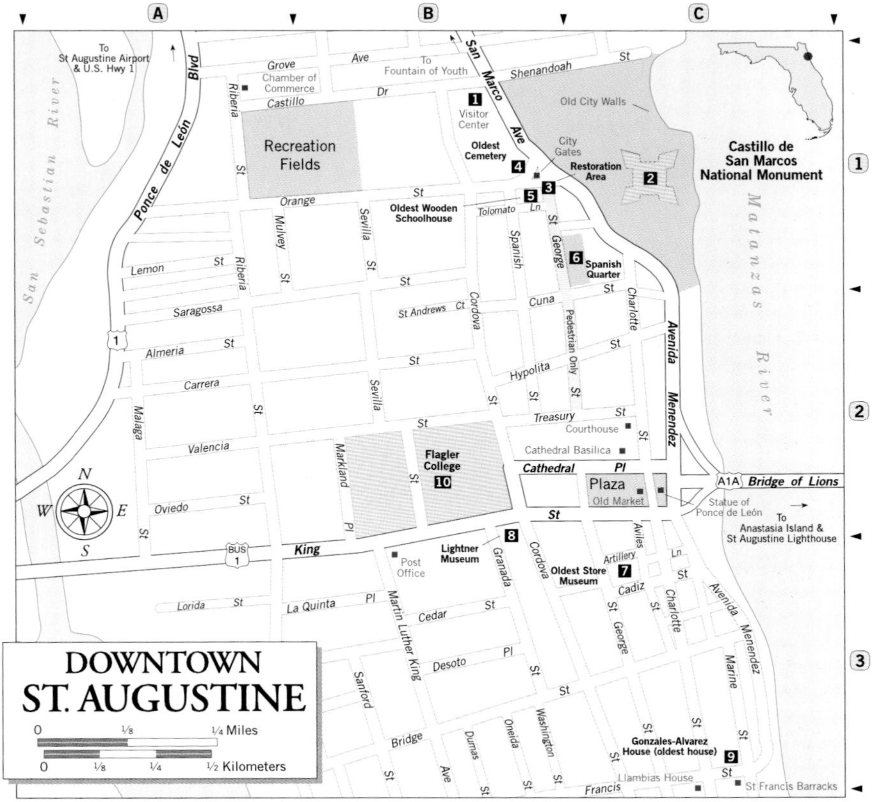
DOWNTOWN
ST. AUGUSTINE
0 1/8 1/4 Miles
0 1/8 1/4 1/2 Kilometers
A
B
C
1
2
3
To St Augustine Airport & U.S. Hwy 1
To Fountain of Youth
Chamber of Commerce
Recreation Fields
Visitor Center
Oldest Cemetery
City Gates
Restoration Area
Old City Walls
Castillo de San Marcos National Monument
Oldest Wooden Schoolhouse
Spanish Quarter
Courthouse
Cathedral Basilica
Flagler College
Plaza
Old Market
Statue of Ponce de León
To Anastasia Island & St Augustine Lighthouse
Bridge of Lions
Lightner Museum
Post Office
Oldest Store Museum
Gonzales-Alvarez House (oldest house)
Llambias House
St Francis Barracks
San Sebastian River
Matanzas River
Ponce de León Blvd
San Marco Ave
Avenida Menendez
King
Cathedral Pl
N
S
E
W

In 1702 and again in 1740, the city was attacked by English forces from South Carolina and Georgia, but the Spanish successfully repelled these advances and retained control of Fort Caroline. What the English couldn't take by battle, though, they eventually acquired through barter. In 1763, Spain agreed to trade the city of St. Augustine for the island of Cuba, which the British had captured a few years earlier. After years of warring over the port town, the two parties reached a peaceful settlement and the Spanish settlers sailed away, leaving the city to some English-speaking settlers from the north, who established plantations manned by slaves. Forests were cut, swamps drained, and rice and indigo planted. But 20 years later, under terms agreed upon in the Treaty of Paris, the British handed the city, together with the Empire's other holdings in Florida, back to Spain.

This time, the British settlers prepared to leave. No amount of energy, it seemed, led to prosperity, because the great powers kept transferring settlers' lands back and forth. Spain tried to persuade the previous settlers to return, but they were uninterested in starting over again. During the following years, St. Augustine began to fill up with European immigrants, slaves and free blacks, and Indians.

In the early 1800s, as Spanish power continued to decline, American expansionism surged, challenging Spanish and Mexican settlements in California, New Mexico, and Florida. St. Augustine's population was demoralized and the city in shambles when the state was purchased by the United States in 1821. After an outbreak of yellow fever and sporadic confrontations with local Indian tribes during the Seminole Indian Wars, the city regained a sense of direction; stability and prosperity eventually ensued. New settlers arrived, and so did the first tourists, who continued to come until the Civil War started.

■ St. Augustine Sights *map page 211*

❶ North of downtown and adjacent to the great lawn of the Castillo de San Marcos, lies the **Visitor Information Center,** where you can park all day for a small fee. The center has historical dioramas and video presentations, and racks filled with informational brochures and coupons for discounts on area attractions. Tickets are sold here for sight-seeing tours, which leave from a stop adjacent to the center. *10 Castillo Drive, off San Marco; 904-825-1000.*

Castillo de San Marcos, also known as Fort Marion. (Library of Congress)

❷ Just outside the Old City Gate, along San Marco Avenue, is the **Castillo de San Marcos National Monument,** one of the nation's oldest masonry forts and a fine place to begin exploring the city. Completed in 1695, the Castillo de San Marcos took 23 years to build and effectively protected the citizens of St. Augustine for 235 years. The fort was built of the same coquina stone as the old city wall, and its four outer walls are 12 feet thick.

Protected by a drawbridge and wide moat, the Castillo de San Marcos overlooks Matanzas Bay. In 1702, these waters protected the town from being sacked by the English General James Moore, and in 1740 General James Oglethorpe, the governor of the state of Georgia, was turned back. At certain times of the year, the old cannons here are fired to celebrate those achievements. *1 Castillo Drive, at Orange Street; 904-829-6506.*

❸ Inside the city gates, in the **St. Augustine Restoration Area,** practically every building is of historical interest. Shops, galleries, and restaurants line the pedestrian-only St. George Street, the heart of the colonial district, and King Street, which intersects the south end of St. George. The north end of St. George Street (at the corner of Orange Street) runs to Old City Gate, a remnant of the wall that once encircled the city. The gate, once the only entrance to the city, is supported by pillars of coquina, a porous limestone rock formed by the sedimentation of seashells. The coquina in this area was quarried at nearby Anastasia Island.

❹ The **Oldest Cemetery,** also known as the Huguenot Cemetery, can be visited on a tour. "A Ghostly Experience" adds hair-raising drama to a visit as part of its 90-minute nighttime city tour. *Orange Street and Avenida Menendez; 904-471-9010 or 888-461-1009 for tours.*

❺ Built as a home in 1804 during the second Spanish Period, St. Augustine's **Oldest Wooden Schoolhouse** was put to use as a school in the early 20th century. An audio-animated schoolmaster and dunce explain elementary schooling procedures in colonial days. *14 St. George Street; 904-824-0192.*

❻ Occupying most of a city block, the delightful **Spanish Quarter Living History Museum** encompasses preserved and reconstructed homes set in gardens enclosed by a low wall. Here, the rather simple lives of the mid-18th-century Spanish and Minorcan inhabitants are examined and preserved. As we approached the first building, the Gomez House, a young man dressed up as a soldier greeted us and invited us in. He showed us around and explained the difficulties of life for a commissioned military man suddenly shipped off far from home. At the Gallegos House, a Minorcan home, we were greeted by the smoky, wholesome smell of food cooking on the hearth. Two costumed women demonstrated cooking practices typical in the home of an artillery sergeant. A carpenter repaired furniture beneath the woodworker's *bohio,* a thatched shelter. The soldier's wife at the De Hita home taught a young girl how to spin from flax the thread she used for her mending. *53 St. George Street; 904-825-6830.*

❼ At the **Oldest Store Museum,** a circa-1800 enterprise, you can browse among button-clasp shoes, an Edison phonograph, corsets, woodstoves, patent medicines, old farm equipment, kitchen wares, a Conestoga wagon, and a slew of other items from different periods. *Four Artillery Lane; 904-829-9729.*

❽ The **Lightner Museum** is at the old Hotel Alcazar and gardens, one of several magnificent hotels Henry Flagler constructed to establish St. Augustine as the American Riviera. The museum's three floors concentrate on America's Gilded Age, with outstanding displays of antiques, mechanical musical instruments, and Tiffany stained glass. Christmastime, when the museum is decked out in Victorian-era holiday decorations, is a good time to visit. *75 King Street; 904-824-2874.*

A narrow street in the St. Augustine Historic District.

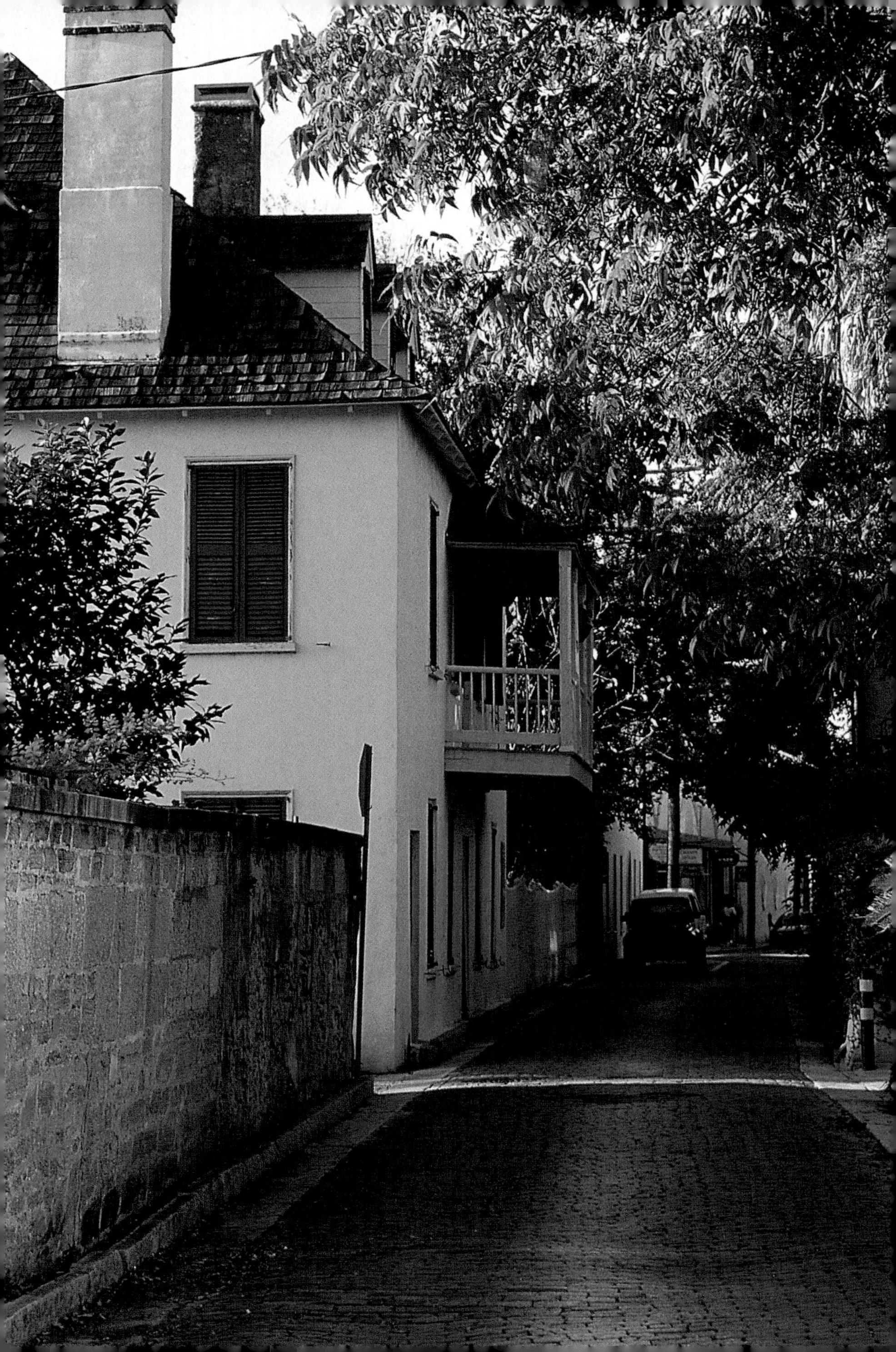

❾ Built in 1727 of coquina and hand-hewn cedar beams, the **Gonzalez-Alvarez House** is believed to be the oldest house in St. Augustine. The architectural elements, furnishings, and paintings reflect nearly 400 years of Spanish, British, and American influences. *14 St. Francis Street; 904-824-2872.*

❿ In 1888, oil and railroad magnate Henry Flagler built the grand, Spanish Renaissance–style **Hotel Ponce de León** in the heart of downtown for $2 million. Its terra cotta–topped turrets, ornate balconies, gold-leaf details, and grand arches made it one of the poshest resorts of its day, drawing luminaries whose names— Rockefeller, Astor, and Roosevelt—were synonymous with American wealth and power. It was the first major structure in the United States to be constructed of poured concrete, and its mezzanine has windows designed by Louis Comfort Tiffany, who was responsible for the interior. In 1968, the then-struggling hotel was transformed into **Flagler College,** a four-year liberal-arts college known more today for its architectural rather than academic reputation. Guided tours of the restored areas are offered in summer only, but a simple walk around the exterior of this masterpiece never fails to impress. *King and Sevilla Streets; 904-823-3378.*

Adjacent to the college is the **Flagler Memorial Presbyterian Church,** another of Henry Flagler's ornate wonders. Constructed in 1889 as a memorial to his daughter, the Venetian Renaissance structure, loosely modeled after St. Mark's Cathedral in Venice, took one year and cost $1 million to complete. A massive pipe organ, a 150-foot-high tower with copper dome, ornate terra cotta friezes, and hand-carved mahogany details make this a monument fit for a king. Or, in this case, a tycoon: Flagler himself was laid to rest here upon his death in 1913. *32 Sevilla Street; 904-829-6451.*

To make the best of a two-day exploration of the city, take the **St. Augustine Sightseeing Train.** You can board at several locations around town and get off and on at will, which makes it easy to see things at your own pace. Don't worry about looking like a tourist riding around town in a little, red choo-choo, because in St. Augustine most everyone is a tourist—it's just that some of them bought houses and stayed. *170 San Marco Avenue; 904-829-6545 or 800-226-6545.*

If you're looking for an alternative to the tram tour, rent a moped from **Solano Cycle** (61 San Marco Avenue; 904-825-6766) and explore on your own. With slow-moving traffic, good weather, and narrow streets, the city is a relatively safe place to putt-putt around.

During the three-month **Nights of Lights Festival,** around the Christmas holidays, more than a million twinkling lights lend the old town even more of a fairytale atmosphere. Highlights of the festival include a lighted boat parade, a candlelight procession, and Fire and Ice, a combination chili cook-off and ice-sculpting competition. *904-829-1711 or 800-653-2489.*

Ponce de León might have landed in 1513 on the site of what is now called the **Fountain of Youth Archaeological Park,** establishing the first European settlement at the Timucuan village of Seloy. It wasn't a permanent settlement, and a half-dozen more Spanish expeditions would be needed before the city of St. Augustine would be founded in 1565. But Ponce de León is more likely to have landed here than at the countless other alleged landing sites throughout Florida and the Caribbean. A planetarium, exhibits, and a natural spring whose waters just might restore your youth make this a fun and educational stop. *11 Magnolia Avenue; 904-829-3168.*

World Golf Village, a billion-dollar undertaking, includes three golf courses, luxury condos, the Golf Hall of Fame, the Golf Museum, and a large convention center. *21 World Golf Place; 904-940-4000.*

Route A1A resumes its island-hopping on the east side of St. Augustine's Bridge of Lions, whose lions were carved from Carrera marble. You can charter a boat for fishing or nature-watching at the Municipal Marina, at the western base of the bridge.

■ ANASTASIA ISLAND *map page 196, A-2*

Anastasia Island, across the bridge, has wide, hard-packed beaches where the sport of paddle tennis was born. At **Anastasia State Recreation Area,** on 4 miles of sandy beach, you can swim, surf, sailboard, and fish. The beach is great, and never too crowded. *904-461-2033.*

One of the area's oldest brick structures, the **St. Augustine Lighthouse,** built in 1875 and rising 165 feet, provides those ambitious enough to scale its 219 steps with a sweeping view of town and beach. *81 Lighthouse Avenue; 904-829-0745.*

■ MARINELAND *map page 196, A-2*

A half-hour's drive south of St. Augustine Beach, along the coast, a blue steel structure arches up out of the surrounding landscape like the backbone of a dinosaur. It's a fitting image, because **Marineland,** the facility the structure

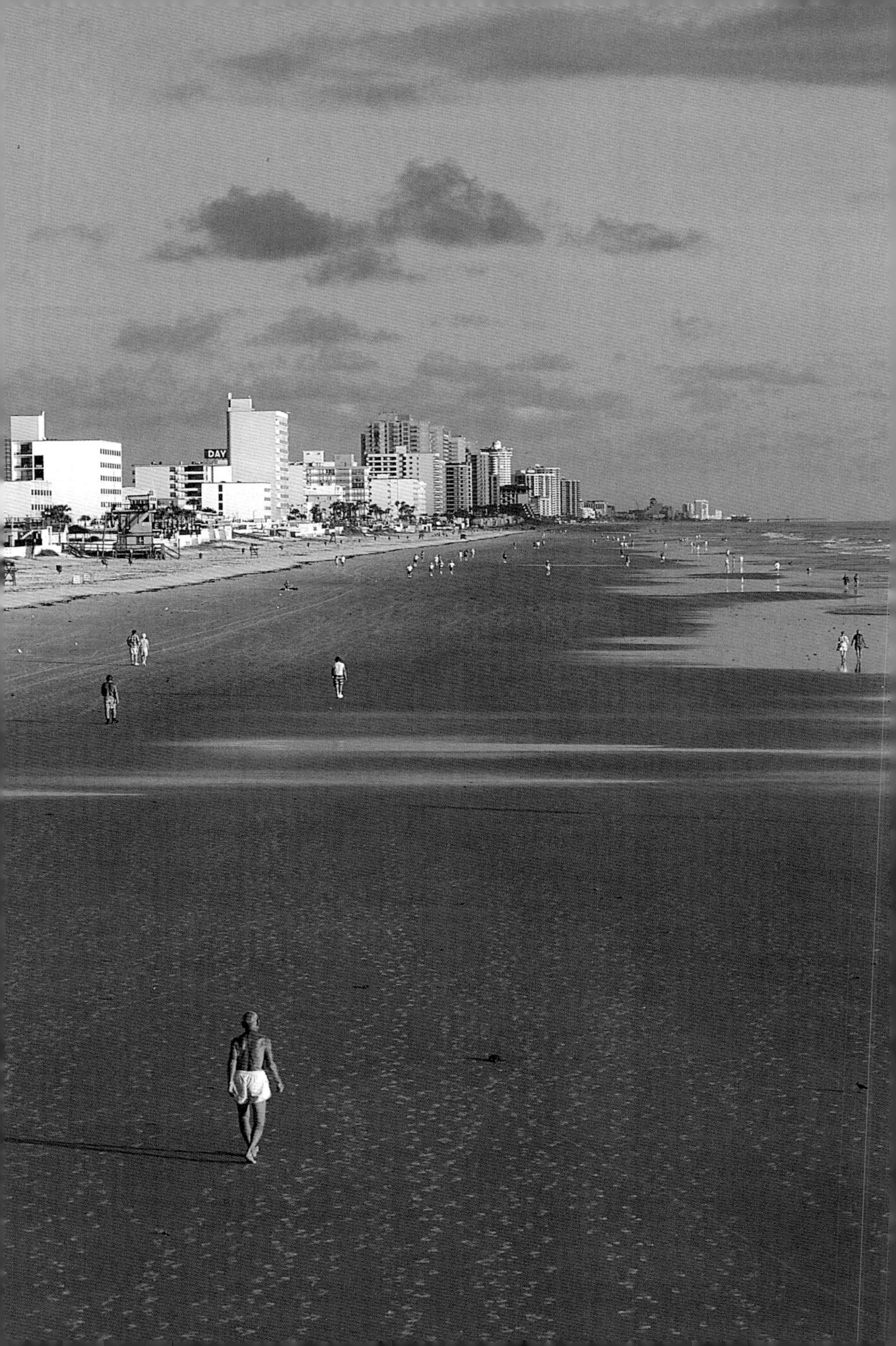
DAY

houses, has itself become something of a dinosaur. The world's first oceanarium, Marineland roared to life in 1938 with much fanfare, thriving on a steady diet of tourists heading down Route A1A to points south. Then, in the 1950s, I-95 opened farther inland, and in the 1970s, Orlando's newborn tourism behemoths began eating up its food supply. By the early 1990s, the forgotten attraction was teetering on the verge of extinction, and in 1998 it closed its doors altogether. Marineland has since reopened in a scaled-down version—the restaurant and hotel are gone—but you can still swim with dolphins as part of the Dolphin Encounter, or view the exotic sea creatures that make their home in the 450,000-gallon oceanarium. *9600 Ocean Shore Boulevard, Marineland; 877-326-7539.*

■ **DAYTONA BEACH** *map page 196, A-3*

Daytona Beach is a city of events. At intervals throughout the year, the place swells with tourists, then empties out just as quickly, like the tide that laps against the hard-packed sand on its beachfront. The motorcycle mania of Bike Week, the roaring crowds of the Daytona 500, and the youthful revelry of spring break are the big three breadwinners, bringing in millions of dollars in tourist revenue to this town of 64,000 people. But much of the rest of the year this is a slow-moving spot that can't seem to shake its image as Party Town, USA.

Many local businesses flounder in this feast-or-famine environment—shops open and close here on an alarmingly regular basis—but in recent years city officials have courted a steadier stream of older tourists and families rather than rowdy college kids. Still, between the megaevents and the migratory population of snowbirds flocking to and from their beachfront condos, Daytona Beach sometimes feels rented rather than owned.

When the joint is jumping, the party culminates at Ocean Park Amusement Area (Ocean Avenue), with video games, rides, and the Victorian-style Main Street Pier. Streetside, along Ocean Avenue and Route A1A, miniature golf courses, go-cart racetrack parks, a horror house, T-shirt shops, bars, and fast-food restaurants cater to the young.

Daytona Beach, with its 23-mile stretch of sand, is among the most developed beaches in the state of Florida.

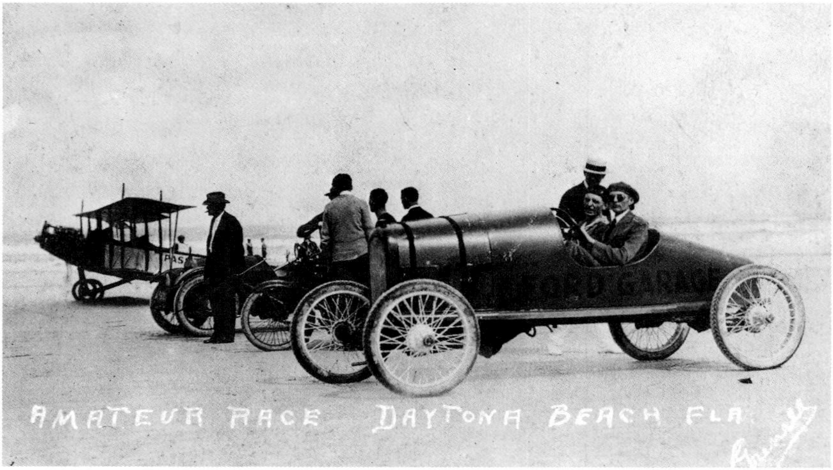
AMATEUR RACE DAYTONA BEACH FLA

Amateur car race, Daytona Beach, ca. 1926. (Florida State Archives)

■ Beach Driving

Cars have been cruising on the hard sands of the coast here for nearly a hundred years. In the early 1900s, such folks as Henry Ford and Louis Chevrolet began test-racing on the pavement-firm sands of Ormond Beach, known as the "Birthplace of Speed," and of Daytona Beach to the south. They reached the dizzying speed of 68 miles per hour in 1902. Henry Ford's car broke down once, and because he couldn't afford to repair it, he withdrew from a race. In 1935, Sir Malcolm Campbell propelled the world's most expensive automobile across packed sands at a speed of 276 MPH. Car-racing is still big, and on an 18-mile stretch of Daytona Beach, cars still drive along the sand, making it a treacherous place for slow walkers, young or old. Partyers, on the other hand, thrive on the action.

■ Lighthouse Point Park

At the south end of the beach, the party peters out and vehicular beach traffic is prohibited. On South Peninsula Drive is quiet Lighthouse Point Park and **Ponce de León Inlet Lighthouse.** Florida's tallest, and some say finest, lighthouse is 8 feet thick at the bottom and has 213 stairs leading to an observation deck that

C. P. Morris carrying the stars and stripes at Ponce de León Inlet Lighthouse.

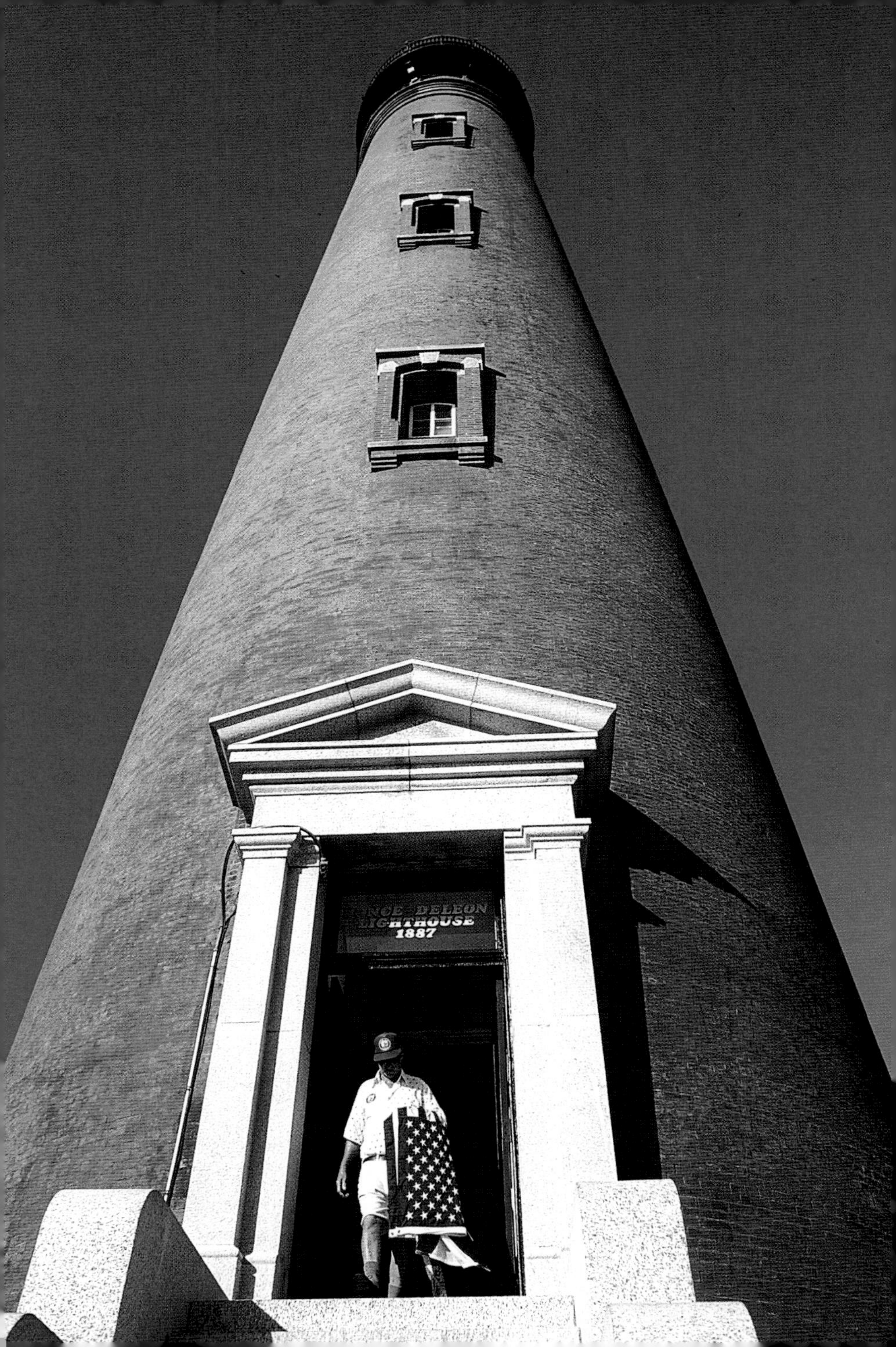
LIGHTHOUSE
1887

Keeping cool on the beach at Daytona.

towers 175 feet over the inlet. You're advised to stop and enjoy the view at every window, which helps you catch your breath and to gaze upon the marshy inlet and the choppy Atlantic.

During the real-estate boom of the 1920s, the area's original name, Mosquito Inlet, was changed to Ponce de León Inlet to help sell mosquito-infested plots to unsuspecting newcomers, even though the namesake explorer likely never stepped foot on the spot. Today, a little village of historic buildings surrounds the base of the lighthouse. The second assistant keeper's cottage houses the original French-cut lighthouse lens, which spins around and throws prism patterns on the wall. *4391 South Peninsula Drive; 386-761-1821.*

■ DAYTONA INTERNATIONAL SPEEDWAY

Practically everything in Daytona is related to race cars. Video games simulate car races; shops sell black-and-white-checkered flags, memorabilia of drivers Richard Petty and Dale Earnhardt, and toy race cars. Restaurants and bars are decorated with racing motifs and museums devote space to Daytona's beach-racing legacy. Every citizen roots for his or her favorite driver, always a favorite topic of conversation.

The quintessential Daytona racing experience takes place at Daytona International Speedway, home of the Daytona 500 NASCAR stock car race in March, the Pepsi 400 NASCAR race in July, and the Daytona 200 motorcycle race in March.

The speedway's **Daytona USA** is an attraction that re-creates the history and hysteria of motor sports with glitzy interactive displays. Visitors can change a tire at the pit stop, broadcast a race, and design and test a stock car. For an added fee, you can drive a race car simulator at 180 miles per hour—thumps, bumps, crashes, and all. *1802 West International Speedway Boulevard; 386-253-7223.*

Daytona 200 is part of Bike Week, a citywide event that attracts thousands of motorcycle enthusiasts, as does Biketoberfest in October. We took the tram tour around the speedway, which is the thing to do when there's no racing. We snapped a lot of pictures from the rim road behind banked Turn Four, from which the view is dizzying even without the interminable circling of speed demons. *1802 West International Speedway Boulevard; 386-947-6800.*

Down the road from the speedway is the **Klassix Auto Museum,** a fantasy showroom filled with Corvettes, race cars, and motorcycles. The displays are dazzling. Chrome and spit-polished paint gleam under bright lights. Murals depicting period vignettes and streetscapes create a backdrop for the vintage autos. *2909 West International Speedway Boulevard; 386-252-3800 or 800-881-8975.*

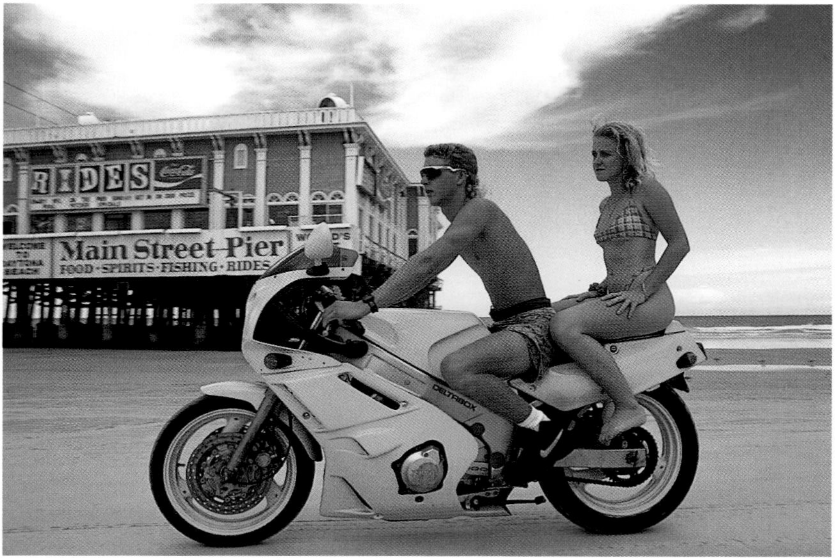
RIDES
Main Street Pier
FOOD · SPIRITS · FISHING · RIDES

Daytona Beach is one of the few beaches in Florida where cars and motorcycles are allowed on the sand.

A pair of 1956 Chevy Corvettes at the Klassix Auto Museum.

The **Museum of Arts and Sciences** is a sophisticated facility that gives space to an impressive collection of Russian, Cuban, and African art in addition to American decorative art. Highlights of the African collection, housed in a 2000-foot-long wing, include ceremonial masks, religious icons, sculptures, fetishes, weaponry, and decorative objects. Outside, you can see a coastal hammock environment and a 13-foot-tall skeleton of a 130,000-year-old giant ground sloth, which was discovered only a few miles from the museum. *1040 Museum Boulevard, off Nova Road; 386-255-0285.*

The stellar **Southeast Museum of Photography** has a simple, two-story-tall space on the campus of Daytona Beach Community College, whose 40-year-old photography program is recognized as one of the finest in the nation. The permanent collection of more than 3,000 photographs includes the work of such American masters as Gordon Parks, Paul Strand, Sally Mann, Arthur Rothstein, and Robert Rauschenberg, as well as historical and experimental photographs. It's one of a small number of arts institutions in the United States dedicated exclusively to

Biking in shallow waters at New Smyrna Beach.

photography, and its changing exhibitions are world-class. A recent show featured works by Steve McCurry, whose *National Geographic* images are some of the best of the 20th century. *1200 West International Speedway Boulevard; 386-254-4475.*

■ NEW SMYRNA BEACH   *map page 196, A-3*

A city neatly divided by the Intracoastal Waterway, **New Smyrna Beach** is a case study in Florida history. In 1867, an experimental and ill-fated settlement of indentured servants from Smyrna, Greece, together with a handful of Italians and Minorcans, attempted to settle here. Cut off from society, many of the settlers died, and the rest of them abandoned the project and eventually moved up the coast to St. Augustine.

Today, this same seclusion has become one of the town's assets. The beach side of New Smyrna Beach escaped Daytona-style overdevelopment because Route A1A hugs the mainland side of town on its way south, taking tourists and traffic along with it. As a result, New Smyrna Beach exudes an Old-Florida appeal that most other coastal cities lost long ago.

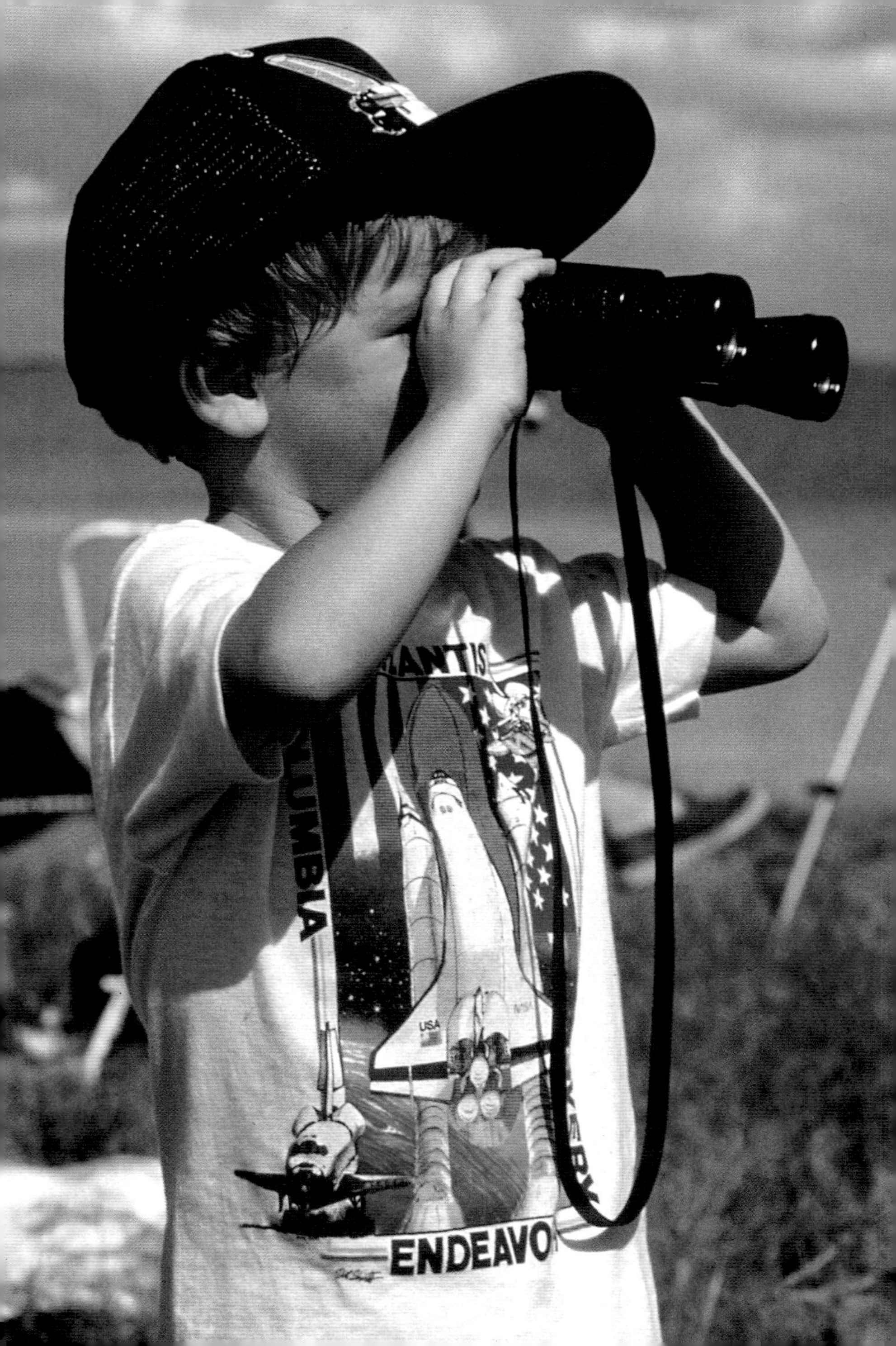

LANTIS
UMBIA
USA
ENDEAVO

From U.S. 1, head east on Washington Street to the North Causeway bridge before the road becomes Flagler Avenue, where the tin-roofed **Riverview Hotel** (103 Flagler Avenue; 386-428-5858) makes for an elegant but casual welcome. The northern end of the island dead-ends into **Smyrna Dunes Park** (2995 North Peninsula Drive; 386-424-2935), whose raised boardwalk commands terrific views of the slate-colored ocean and the Ponce de León Inlet Lighthouse across the water; the southern end leads to the Canaveral National Seashore, which contains some of the most pristine coastline on Florida's east coast.

Although the area in between has not completely escaped the eyes of developers, the town's charms still survive. On Flagler Avenue, between Peninsula Avenue and the ocean, where you can still drive on the beach, you'll find a mix of mom-and-pop-style businesses, from restaurants to art shops to motels, without a chain name in sight. Stop by the **Beacon Diner** (416 Flagler Avenue; 386-428-8332) and see how life here is lived by families, retirees, and local surfers. **Toni and Joe's** (309 Buenos Aires Street; 386-427-6850), a simple beachfront spot that has been in business for more than 40 years, is another good place to pick up the town's often faint pulse. Grab a chair on the patio, order a steak and cheese sandwich, and watch surfers make the most out of even the smallest waves.

■ THE SPACE COAST *map page 196, A-4*

Confusion abounds concerning which space missions begin at Kennedy Space Center and which at Cape Canaveral. The latter, a physical land projection into the Atlantic, holds a U.S. Air Force station that sent some of America's earliest missiles into space. It was renamed Cape Kennedy in 1963, following the assassination of President John F. Kennedy, but in 1973 the State of Florida changed the town's name back to Cape Canaveral, the name it was given in 1572. The newer Kennedy Space Center, several miles north of Canaveral, sent up its first launch, *Apollo 8,* in 1968. Since then, all space-launchings have been at Kennedy. All along the Space Coast, museums devote rooms to rockets and pieces of space shuttles.

Despite all the hoopla of Kennedy Space Center, with its rocket ships and visitors attractions, the Space Coast is a normally quiet spot along Florida's hectic eastern shoreline. But this might be changing. In an attempt to draw more business from day-trippers in Orlando, Space Center officials are considering proposals for con-

Getting a closer look at a shuttle launch. (Kennedy Space Center)

Launchings of the space shuttle have become a Florida tradition. (Kennedy Space Center)

struction of a space-theme amusement park, complete with rides based upon the real rockets that blast off from its launchpads. Given the bureaucratic complexities required to marry a private amusement company with NASA, any decision—let alone a groundbreaking ceremony—is still years off. For now, though, strict governmental regulations protect the shoreline from overdevelopment.

■ CANAVERAL NATIONAL SEASHORE *map page 196, A-4*

Twenty-five-mile-long Canaveral National Seashore begins south of New Smyrna at Apollo Beach, then runs south to Klondike Beach, reachable only by foot. Until a couple of years ago, Klondike unofficially qualified as a nude beach, but county officials put a fig leaf on that tradition a few years ago. People still take their clothes off, though, at remote locations.

At its southern end, Klondike connects to Playalinda Beach, accessible by car well east of the mainland. This is truly out in the middle of nowhere, the only reminders of civilization being the awe-inspiring sight of rocket launchpads in the distance, looking entirely out of context beside the soft, rolling dunes. Sea turtles, mostly loggerheads, but also leatherbacks and green turtles, come ashore in large numbers from May through September. People come here, too, but on the day I visited, I could have been the only person left on earth. *Closes three days before launches; 407-867-0677 or 386-428-3384.*

■ LOGGERHEAD TURTLES

On summer nights, female loggerheads drag themselves onto Canaveral's beaches, above high-tide line, leaving only tiny trails like tractor treads in the sand behind them. They dig nest holes and into them drop 100 or more eggs that hatch about 57 days later. As soon as they hatch, the baby turtles scurry away from the shadows and toward the water, hopefully before birds or raccoons can make a meal out of them. Along the Canaveral beaches, nests are fenced to keep critters from digging up the eggs. Nature organizations conduct evening turtle watches that allow participants to observe this ancient miracle of nature. Between Cape Canaveral and Sebastian Inlet, as many as 14,000 nests are counted each year.

A gopher tortoise at the Merritt Island National Wildlife Refuge.

■ MERRITT ISLAND NATIONAL WILDLIFE REFUGE
map page 196, A-4

The Merritt Island National Wildlife Refuge's 140,000 acres stand between Canaveral Seashore and the other world on the mainland. The two refuges provide habitats for rare and endangered plants, birds, and animals. Among the refuge's residents are the bald eagle, wood stork, manatee, and loggerhead turtle. Walking and driving trails wind past the salt marsh and hardwood hammock habitats of these vast refuge lands. Merritt Island Refuge butts up to the Kennedy Space Center, providing a sometimes shocking contrast between nature and technology. Because of the proximity of the launchpads to the refuge, hours of operation can change at Merritt Island with little or no warning. Call ahead before making the trip. *Visitors Information Center, Route 402, 3.5 miles east of Titusville; 321-861-0667.*

■ KENNEDY SPACE CENTER *map page 196, A-4*

John F. Kennedy Space Center is the main attraction of the Space Coast. Visitors can explore space from terra firma, and most activities are free. In the Gallery of Spaceflight, model spaceships, videos, and artifacts from manned space missions interest kids and adults alike. The center shows films about the space program in its two IMAX theaters, and there are guided bus tours of the launchpad area. The Apollo/Saturn V Center has more space-related movies and interactive displays, and tots enjoy the space-age playground and Lego play area. *Route 3; 321-867-5000.*

Six miles west of the Kennedy Space Center, the **Astronaut Hall of Fame** contains simulators that demonstrate what it's like to be aboard a spaceship in antigravity conditions or in a jet doing 360-degree rolls. Shuttle to Tomorrow provides a multimedia experience aboard a full-scale replica of the space shuttle, and the hall of fame pays homage to the people who pioneered space. The facility is also home to Space Camp Florida, a hugely popular overnight camp at which kids receive hands-on lessons in state-of-the-art simulators. *6225 Vectorspace Boulevard, at U.S. 1 and Route 405; 321-269-6100.*

■ COCOA AND COCOA BEACH *map page 196, A-4*

Two communities south of Cape Canaveral, Cocoa and Cocoa Beach, are considered part of the Space Coast and milk the "final frontier" as a part of their identities. One of the attractions here, the **Astronaut Memorial Planetarium &**

Observatory, has as its stated objective "to preserve the spirit and tradition of the American Space Program on a personal level." To achieve that goal, the facility presents planetarium programs, hosts high-tech stargazing, and plays intergalactic movies on a three-story-high screen. *Brevard Community College, 1519 Clearlake Road, Cocoa; 321-634-3732.*

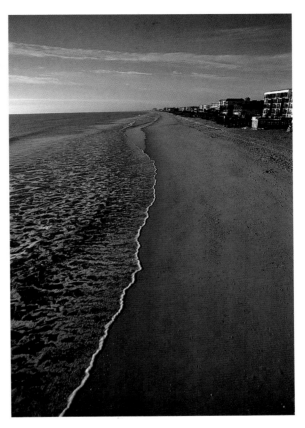

The Space Coast's Cocoa Beach.

Except during space shuttle launches, when its pier provides a fine view of the proceedings, Cocoa Beach is usually oblivious to the area's all-space-all-the-time mind-set. The area's reputation for surfers and surfing is based on the advertising power of **Ron Jon Surf Shop** (4151 North Atlantic Avenue; 321-799-8820), which purveys all manner of surfing accessories and clothing in a 52,000-square-foot emporium (open 24 hours a day, 7 days a week). In-the-know surfers say the waves are better to the south, but Ron Jon draws the faithful with far-flung billboard messages advertising its temple to water sports.

The **Cocoa Beach Pier** is another local landmark and a center of beach activity. People tread its 840-foot length to fish, rent water sports equipment, shop, eat, drink, and dance.

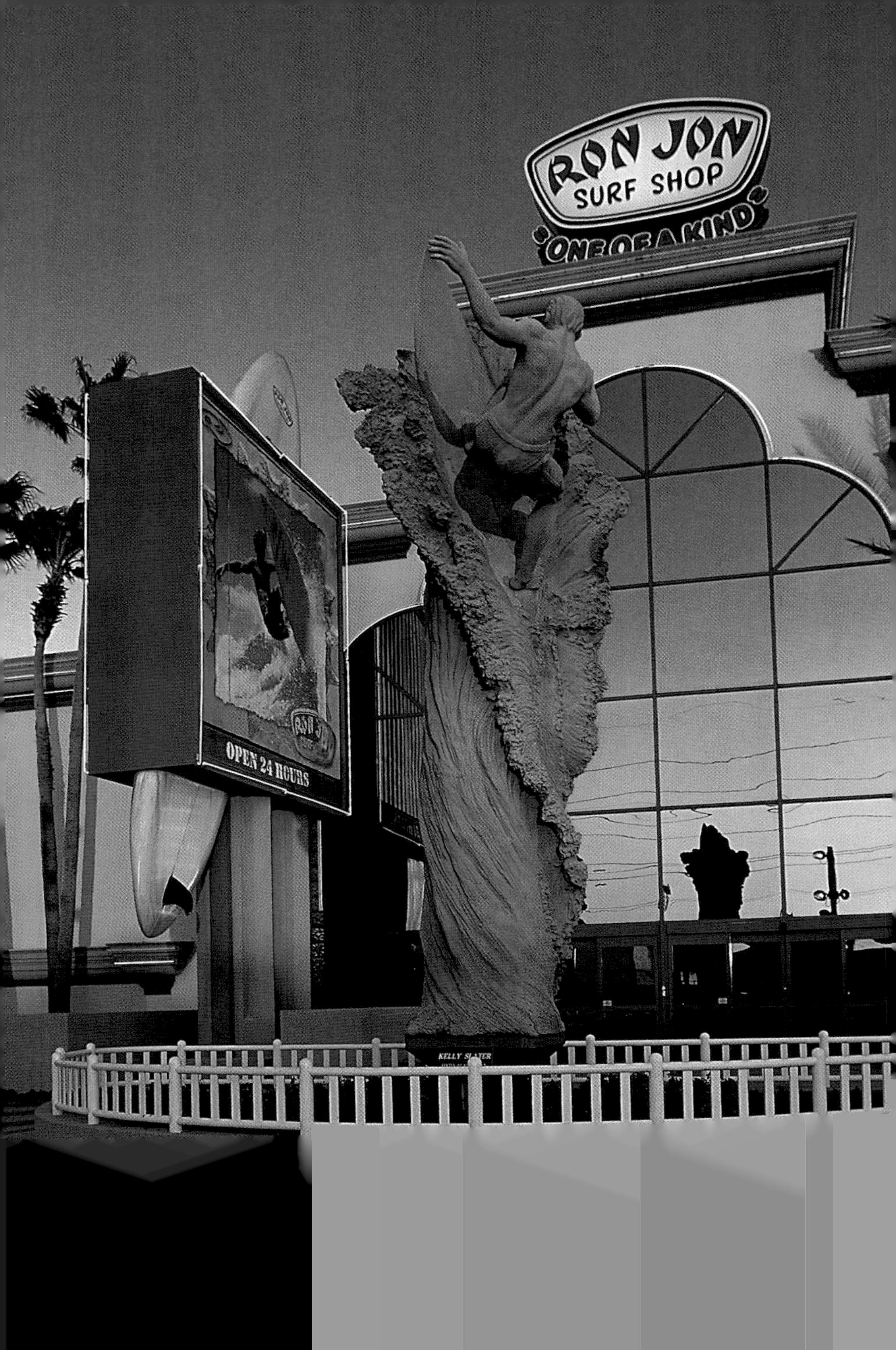
RON JON
SURF SHOP
ONE OF A KIND
OPEN 24 HOURS
KELLY SLATER

■ **MELBOURNE SOUTH**   *map page 196, A-5*

Down around Cocoa Beach and Melbourne, Route A1A becomes congested with resort-town traffic. To escape the commercial beach jungle and get a taste of the past and future, take the Eau Gallie Causeway to Eau Gallie. Here, you'll find a historic district with antique shops and the riverfront Pineapple Park, with picnic facilities and a playground. The **Brevard Museum of Art and Science** (1463 Highland Avenue; 321-242-0737) has a wide-ranging collection encompassing everything from contemporary American paintings to Japanese vases to Tibetan costumes and Chinese porcelain. Kids like the laser magic of the Singing Shadows installation as well as the Science Center's 30 hands-on exhibits designed to demystify the natural sciences.

The run of good waves for surfers pipelines down the beach to **Sebastian Inlet State Recreation Area** (9700 South Route A1A; 321-984-4825), a great destination for serious fishermen, snorkelers, and surfers. Sea turtles favor its relatively undisturbed sands.

The best surfing spots on Florida's east coast are found in Sebastian Inlet (above) and Cocoa Beach, where the famous Ron Jon Surf Shop (opposite) is known to surfers worldwide.

■ Treasure Coast *map page 196, A-5*

South of Sebastian Inlet, Florida's east coast changes its name to the Treasure Coast. The designation makes sense once you've been to the **McLarty Treasure Museum,** where salvaged wreckage and other displays tell the story of 11 Spanish galleons that were dashed onto the rocks here by a hurricane in 1715. The riches-laden wrecks drew salvagers and pirates from throughout the New World and Europe. After they were through, half the booty—coins, jewelry, weaponry, and vases—still lay at the bottom of the sea. Treasure has been washing ashore for decades up and down the coast, usually after a strong storm. Smaller museums in the area display treasures, but the McLarty collection is the most comprehensive. *13180 North Route A1A; 561-589-2147.*

The greatest treasure along this portion of the coast, though, is the natural beauty: long stretches of unpeopled sands alternating with wild greenery and well-maintained beach parks. **Treasure Shores Park** and **Golden Sands County Park** are both lovely, but I prefer the former because of its landscaped native vegetation.

Route A1A carries you to the island segment of the town of Vero Beach, an area worth exploring for its shops and art galleries, beaches, and small restaurants. Running between island and mainland is the Intracoastal Waterway, formed in this area by the Indian River. At mainland Vero Beach, the Los Angeles Dodgers hold spring training at Dodgertown. *3901 26th Street; 561-569-4900.*

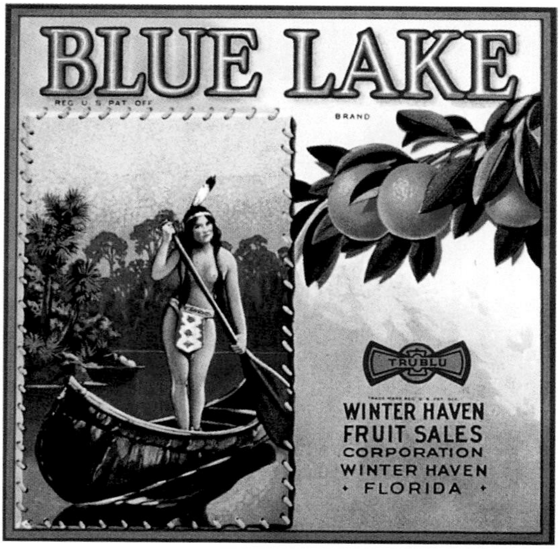
BLUE LAKE
REG. U. S. PAT. OFF.
BRAND
TRUBLU
WINTER HAVEN
FRUIT SALES
CORPORATION
WINTER HAVEN
• FLORIDA •

The area is also famous for its softball-size oranges. Indian River Citrus is hard to beat for the bigness and juiciness of its fruit. Like Vidalia onions, the Indian River Citrus designation is closely monitored. How it came to be so famous is the subject of the **Indian River Citrus Museum**, where photographs, antiques, farm tools, and memorabilia track area history from the early 1800s to the present. *2140 14th Avenue; 561-770-2263.*

Vero Beach boasts a thriving art scene, nourished by its many artists and art galleries. The **Vero Beach Center for the Arts** (3001 Riverside Park Drive; 561-231-0707) has exhibitions of original paintings, sculpture, and drawings by Florida artists in addition to traveling exhibitions, lectures, and performing arts. The **Riverside Theater** (3250 Riverside Park Drive; 561-231-5860 or 800-445-6745) presents musicals like *Damn Yankees* and dramas such as *Dial M for Murder* in its 600-seat theater. A 300-seat theater is used for one-night-only events with stars like Peter Nero, Debbie Reynolds, and Tommy Tune. Vero Beach is listed in the top 100 of John Villani's book *The Best Small Art Towns in America: Where To Find Fresh Air, Creative People and Affordable Living.*

■ NORTH HUTCHINSON ISLAND *map page 196, A-5/6*

Route A1A resumes its leisurely pace as it heads south to quiet North Hutchinson Island, which has more parks than anything else. **Pepper Park** brackets the road with its oceanside and bayside components. The oceanside has obviously been here longer and shows its age in dated pavilions and rest room facilities. Across the road, new construction has created fishing, canoeing, and boating docks. *3300 North State Route A1A.*

The UDT-SEAL Museum honors the birthplace of the frogman program and chronicles the development of Underwater Demolition Teams (UDTs) and the navy's elite Sea Air Land (SEAL) fighters. Museum displays include the weapons, diving gear, demolition apparatus, and submarines used by frogmen in many of their top-secret operations. Films and videos document undertakings in Vietnam and Panama, and the Ship's Store sells T-shirts, books, and videos. *3300 North State Route A1A; 561-595-5845.*

The headquarters and main part of **Fort Pierce Inlet State Park** are at the south end of North Hutchinson Island, where Fort Pierce Inlet separates it from Hutchinson Island. Here, you can beachcomb, fish, surf, and hike.

One beach fronts the inlet and another the Atlantic Ocean. Dynamite Point on the inlet beach marks the training spot for the navy's first underwater demolitionists in preparation for the D-Day invasion in 1944. Today, pelicans and seagulls prevail. The water is clear but swiftly moving, thus a danger to swimmers.

On the other side of the jetty lies the ocean side of the beach, also known as

DREAMY VISIONS OF FLORIDA

Afternoon Savannah *(1997), by James Gibson. (Jacobs Highwaymen Archive)*

If you're poking around a local garage sale and come across an oil painting of a crimson Florida sunset or palm-dappled landscape, take note: if it's by one of the group of artists known as the Highwaymen, you've found a valuable piece of Florida history.

The Highwaymen were a group of young, self-taught African-American painters from the Fort Pierce area who, between 1950 and 1980, sold their works from the backs of their cars along Florida's east coast. Mentored by the prominent white regionalist A.E. Backus, these entrepreneurs were motivated less by artistic statement than by financial profit: one artist might produce as many as 20 paintings in one nocturnal gathering. The artists sold the works with the same fervor, and during the banner days cash fell out of their pockets.

But in their rush to get rich, the Highwaymen inadvertently developed a unique artistic aesthetic. Speed determined their collective style, and the general visual effect of a Highwaymen painting is akin to glancing at the land while tearing down a two-lane highway. This fleeting quality encouraged viewers to find their own meanings in these works, and eager residents snapped up the inexpensive, eye-catching originals, proudly displaying them in their homes like so many picture windows showing Florida as the "dream state."

That teenagers who seemed destined to labor in the citrus fields would leave such a compelling—and prolific—visual testament about postwar Florida is truly remarkable. Because no records were kept, no one knows for sure how many paintings the Highwaymen produced, but some estimates put the number as high as 200,000.

The paintings had faded from view by the mid-1980s, but they came back with a vengeance around the turn of the millennium. Works bearing the names Newton, McLendon, and Hair, among others, that cost $25 when they were new, now fetch hundreds and even thousands of dollars. But even today it's not the inflated price tags that make the Highwaymen's works so sought after: it's the exotic, natural beauty of a vanishing Florida and the sense of comfort and escape the paintings bring to a state in the midst of fast-paced change.

—Gary Monroe

Gary Monroe, a professor of art at Daytona Beach Community College, is the author of *The Highwaymen: Florida's African-American Landscape Painters* (University Press of Florida).

Jetty Park, or, to locals, North Beach. The jetty provides protection from large waves, so this beach is better-suited for swimming. A shady nature walk leading out of the parking lot traverses a coastal hammock. *North Hutchinson Island, north end of U.S. 1; 561-468-3985.*

Jack Island Preserve juts into the lagoon off Route A1A. One hiking trail leads along a peninsular dike and another through a mangrove wetlands habitat, the nursery for an infinite variety of marine and avian creatures.

■ JENSEN BEACH AND STUART *map page 196, A-6*

En route to Jensen Beach, Route A1A travels first through the north end of Hutchinson Island, which is lined with condos, high-rises, and golf courses. South of Fort Pierce, after the overbuilt areas, the drive becomes more enjoyable, with remote, low-key beach access every few miles. At **Sea Turtle Beach** (Jensen Beach Causeway and Route A1A), concessions cater to water sports enthusiasts in a pretty little park.

Ocean Boulevard, another lovely road, leads to Stuart and its popular **Stuart Beach,** which becomes crowded on weekends. **Elliott Museum** (825 NE Ocean Boulevard; 561-225-1961) is named for Sterling Elliott, the inventor of the stamp machine, automatic knot-tyer, four-wheel bicycle, and other curiosities, all of which are on display.

Of the 10 houses built during the late 19th century by the U.S. Life Saving Service for shipwreck victims along Florida's east coast, **Gilbert's Bar House of Refuge** (561-225-1875) alone survives. Along with displays focused on marine life, salvaging, lifesaving, and ships, it has several aquariums. Families may favor the conditions at nearby **Bathtub Reef Beach** (301 SE McArthur Boulevard), where the reef creates a calm, shallow pond of water and the crowds are light.

Downtown Stuart has been reshaped into a place whose personality does not rely solely on restored historic buildings. There's almost a sense of humor about the town, along with some of the trendiness that rejuvenation often brings to the surface. Downtown revolves around Confusion Corner, an aptly named roundabout, and a second such juncture marked by a bronze statue of Lady Abundance, wearing a clingy, revealing gown and bearing water jugs. City planner Andres Duany, instrumental in the design of Seaside, conferred over Stuart's renovation. Once empty and forlorn, downtown now buzzes with activity at such spots as the **Jolly Sailor Pub** (1 SW Osceola Street; 561-221-1111) and the revitalized **1926**

Early-20th-century rendering of Old South Drive, Indian River. (Florida State Archives)

Lyric Theatre (59 SW Flagler Avenue; 561-286-7827), which presents musicals, dramas, children's productions, movies, concerts, and recitals in a 500-seat theater. Bookstores, art and pottery galleries, and boutiques make for great shopping.

■ TRAVEL BASICS

Getting Around: Route A1A is the most pleasing conduit along the coast, but the going can be slow. The same goes for U.S. 1, which takes you through the center of most towns along the east coast. Interstate 95 skirts metropolitan areas. At Jacksonville, I-95 splits into bypass I-295, and then I-10, which goes west.

Route A1A passes through coastal towns from Fernandina Beach all the way to Miami Beach and, along the way, visits reminders of many eras of Florida's history, from the old pirate havens near Fernandina Beach, to Spanish colonial St. Augustine, to Space Age Cape Canaveral.

Climate: The northeast is best in spring, when flowers are in bloom and the temperature is in the high 60s or low 70s. Summer is humid, and the mercury reaches the 90s. Winter can be cold, with temperatures in the 40s or 50s.

SOUTH FLORIDA

■ OVERVIEW

The drive along the coast's best-loved highway, Route A1A, reveals a varied coastline: In some areas, it passes glorious beaches, where a carefree beach-ruled existence is revealed. It moves on to enclaves of affluence, where little of what is enjoyed is visible to the casual observer; then it bows under the weight of the ill-defined, high-spirited, and often confusing metropolis of Miami.

Urban sprawl extends all along this coast, from Jupiter, just north of West Palm Beach, to Homestead, doorstep of the Everglades. On the ocean side, the coast is lined with the winter homes of America's multimillionaires. On the mainland side, along Highway 1, it's one megalopolis as city flows into city.

Of the cities along this route, Boca Raton, with its distinctive Mediterranean architecture, has the most character. Fort Lauderdale, the second-largest city on Florida's east coast, is known from songs and films as the place where college students on spring break let loose—but this is no longer the case. City fathers and residents decided it wasn't worth it living *Where The Boys Are.*

Miami swings to Caribbean rhythms and is often described as the largest metropolis in Latin America. Shopping, dining, beaching, people-watching, boating, and boogying the night away are what Miami and Miami Beach do best.

■ HOBE SOUND NATURE PRESERVES *map page 242, B-1*

Hobe National Wildlife Refuge, on Jupiter Island, preserves 700 acres of coastal wildlife habitat reached via the inlet on Beach Road. This wild and beautiful park occupies the northern end of the island, including over 3 miles of lovely beaches and dunes. Sea turtles nest here, and in the summer, rangers offer nighttime sea turtle walks. A few miles away from the Jupiter Island section of the park, and across Hobe Sound on U.S. 1, lies a second section of the park—200 mainland acres of pine scrub, an environment that resembles desert, with its sandy soil, evergreens, and saw palmetto. Within this area, the **Hobe Sound Nature Center** hosts environmental education programs, nature hikes, exhibits, and camps. *13640 SE Federal Highway; 772-546-2067.*

Small harbor off Jupiter Inlet.

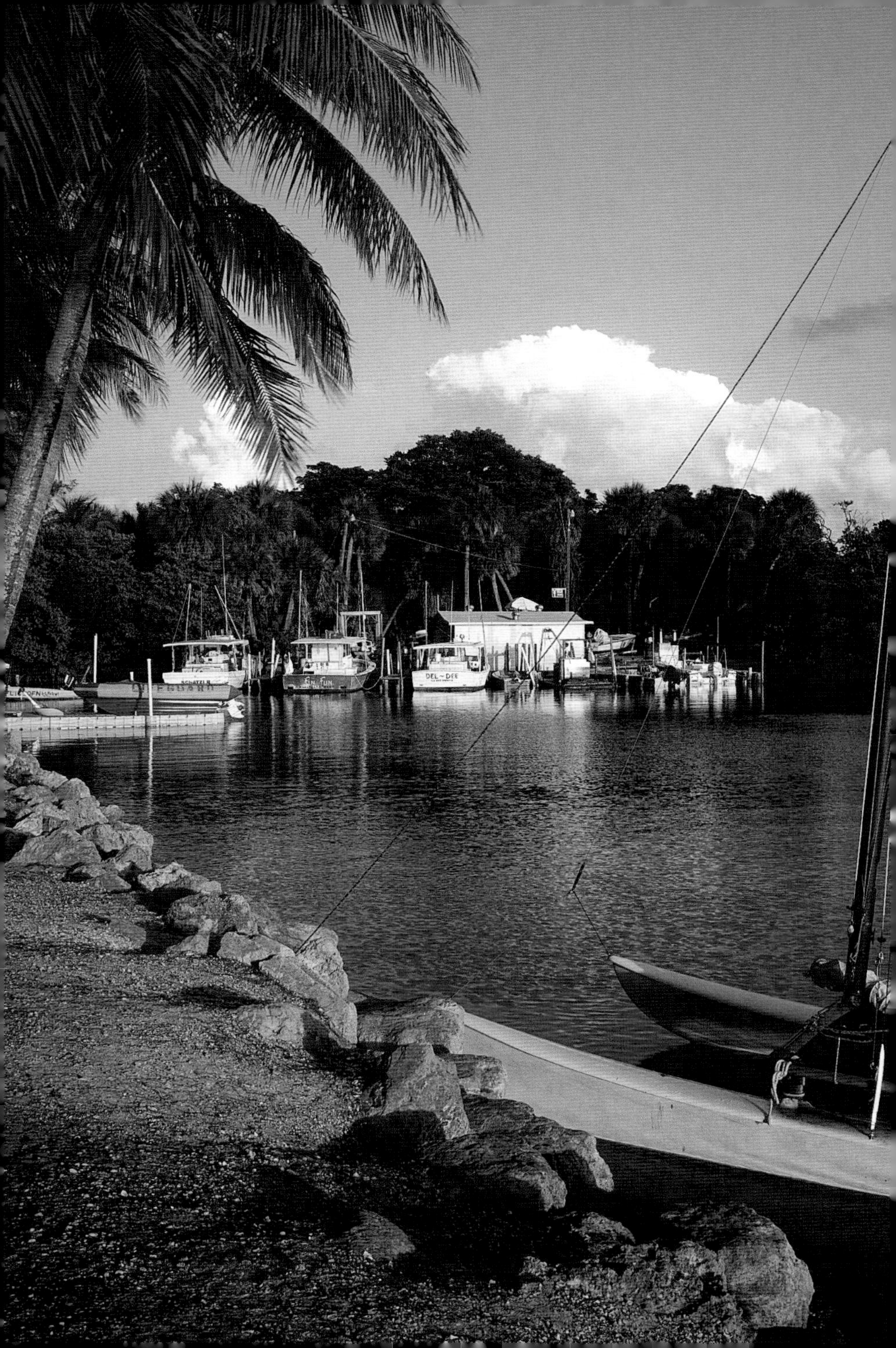
DEL ~ DEE

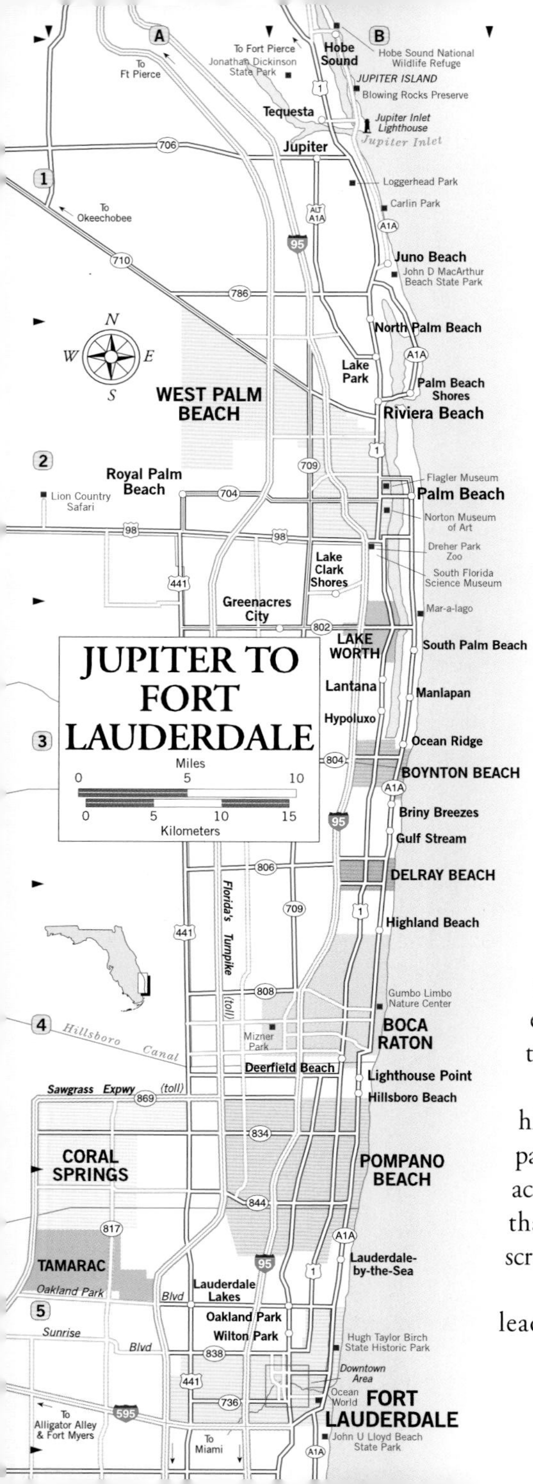
JUPITER TO FORT LAUDERDALE
Miles
0 5 10
0 5 10 15
Kilometers
A
B
To Fort Pierce
To Ft Pierce
Hobe Sound
Hobe Sound National Wildlife Refuge
Jonathan Dickinson State Park
JUPITER ISLAND
Blowing Rocks Preserve
Tequesta
Jupiter Inlet Lighthouse
Jupiter Inlet
Jupiter
Loggerhead Park
Carlin Park
To Okeechobee
Juno Beach
John D MacArthur Beach State Park
North Palm Beach
Lake Park
Palm Beach Shores
WEST PALM BEACH
Riviera Beach
Royal Palm Beach
Lion Country Safari
Flagler Museum
Palm Beach
Norton Museum of Art
Dreher Park Zoo
Lake Clark Shores
South Florida Science Museum
Greenacres City
Mar-a-lago
LAKE WORTH
South Palm Beach
Lantana
Manlapan
Hypoluxo
Ocean Ridge
BOYNTON BEACH
Briny Breezes
Gulf Stream
DELRAY BEACH
Highland Beach
Florida's Turnpike
(toll)
Gumbo Limbo Nature Center
BOCA RATON
Hillsboro Canal
Mizner Park
Deerfield Beach
Lighthouse Point
Sawgrass Expwy (toll)
Hillsboro Beach
CORAL SPRINGS
POMPANO BEACH
TAMARAC
Lauderdale-by-the-Sea
Oakland Park Blvd
Lauderdale Lakes
Oakland Park
Sunrise Blvd
Wilton Park
Hugh Taylor Birch State Historic Park
Downtown Area
Ocean World
FORT LAUDERDALE
To Alligator Alley & Fort Myers
To Miami
John U Lloyd Beach State Park
1
2
3
4
5
N
S
E
W

Blowing Rocks Preserve, on Jupiter Island south of the Hobe National Wildlife Refuge, is a 73-acre park run by the Nature Conservancy. It's reached via Beach Road, which crosses through the preserve. Lining Blowing Rock's beach is a mile-long limestone formation, whose crevices, at very high tides, redirect crashing waves skyward into water plumes up to 60 feet in height. Four distinct ecologies coexist here: mangrove wetlands, coastal hammock, coastal strand, and shifting dune. *South Beach Road on Jupiter Island; 561-744-6668.*

Jonathan Dickinson State Park (south of the Hobe Sound Nature Center on U.S. 1) provides yet another opportunity to foray into nature, this time along the Loxahatchee River. It was on this site that Jonathan Dickinson and 25 Quakers were shipwrecked in 1696 and taken captive by local Indians. Badly treated, they somehow survived, escaped, and eventually made their way to St. Augustine.

Today, you can camp, rent a cabin, hike, canoe, or join pontoon tours of the park's waterways. The park covers 11,500 acres of river and land, including a tract that is home to alligators, bald eagles, scrub-jays, and manatees.

The half-mile **Hobe Mountain Trail** leads up to a sand ridge and a 50-foot observation tower from which you can scan the vast primeval wilderness; to the east, Jupiter Island and the wide Atlantic come into view. *16450 SE Federal Highway; 561-546-2771.*

■ JUPITER ISLAND *map page 242, B-1*

Greeting visitors to Palm Beach County is the cherry-red **Jupiter Inlet Lighthouse,** built in 1860 and designed by George Meade, who would later command Union forces at Gettysburg. One of Florida's 30-plus standing lighthouses, this picturesque structure perches atop a 40-foot hill. Visitors can climb the 105-foot-tall lighthouse; if you're acrophobic—or just curious about lighthouses—you can forego the climb and visit the small museum in the oilhouse at the lighthouse's base. The lighthouse is closed Mondays and Tuesdays. *805 North U.S. 1, about 100 yards north of Indian Town Road; 561-747-6639.*

A fort was established on Jupiter in 1838 during the Seminole Wars. A half-century later came the narrow-gauge train—called the Celestial for its stops in Jupiter, Juno, Neptune, Venus, and Mars. With the arrival of Henry Flagler's railroad, the area began to grow rapidly.

Today, Jupiter and especially Jupiter Island are known for wealth but not for ostentation. Actor Burt Reynolds, who lives here, helped to found **Burt Reynolds Park** (at Jupiter Inlet), home to the **Florida History Center and Museum,** which displays a nicely put-together collection of historic vignettes, exhibits, and artifacts relating how nature shaped the land's history. Outside is the Seminole Living History Village. Also on-site is the county's oldest known home, Tindall House, a Cracker shack built in 1892. *805 North U.S. 1; 561-747-6639.*

■ SOUTH FROM JUPITER: BEACHES AND PARKS
map page 242, B-1/2

A fine array of beaches lines the nearly 16-mile drive between Jupiter and Juno Beach. **Carlin Park,** on Route A1A, is a full-service beach park where special events are staged both indoors at the civic center and outdoors. At **Juno Beach Park,** high dunes protect beachgoers from the traffic and city above.

Among the neighborhood's beaches is **Loggerhead Park** (14200 U.S. 1), with the same dune bluffs as Juno Beach, plus tennis, picnicking, a playground, and the **Marinelife Center** (561-627-8280). Here, a nature trail and indoor displays edu-

THE FLORIDA FLAGLER BUILT

South Florida was made more or less what it is today by Henry Morrison Flagler—the region's first and most important developer. He and his Gulf Coast counterpart, developer Henry Plant, raced down their respective coasts, laying track, building grand hotels, and promoting Florida as a resort for the rich and famous. Flagler won the contest. He made it all the way to Key West by 1912, upgrading and building more than 722 miles of railroad along the way.

Born in 1830, Flagler left home at age 14 and made his way in the world, wheeling and dealing with great success. By age 38, he had met John D. Rockefeller and become a founding partner in Standard Oil. Soon thereafter, he turned to building railroads and resorts.

By 1894, Flagler had extended his railroad—the Jacksonville, St. Augustine & Indian River Railway—to Jupiter Inlet, where the Loxahatchee River empties into the Atlantic Ocean. In time, he reached Palm Beach, a narrow barrier island about 13 miles south of the inlet. Here, he erected first the Royal Poinciana Hotel (since demolished) on the western side of the island, and then, on the eastern side, the Palm Beach Inn—which, after it burned down and was rebuilt *twice,* became known as The Breakers. It is still operated by Flagler heirs. Flagler's railroad brought wealthy northerners to the island to spend the winter. The site remains today the pinnacle of high-society vacationing.

In the winter of 1894–95, freezing temperatures caused Palm Beach guests to shiver, Flagler to quiver, and oranges to die on the tree. Meanwhile, Julia Tuttle, who owned large parcels of land 70 miles south, sent to Flagler's Palm Beach home a nosegay of fragrant orange blossoms in an attempt to interest him in extending his railroad to her warm and tropical, if isolated, settlement. Flagler snapped at Tuttle's bait. In came orange growers and up went Flagler's Royal Palm Hotel, along with the soon-flourishing town of Miami.

Flagler's most ambitious project, however, was the extension of his railroad to Key West. An important seaport island 156 miles south of the Miami terminus, it never before had been linked to land. By 1912, Flagler had completed a remarkable undertaking: a railroad connecting a series of quiet, castaway keys to the then-flourishing mainland, just as Florida's land boom was gaining momentum. This last link in Flagler's railroad was destroyed by the disastrous hurricane of 1935. Flagler's legacy remains and is still celebrated, however—in fine buildings, grand hotels, and prosperous cities.

Henry Flagler's railroad transformed southern Florida from quiet countryside to a bustling resort area. Private railroad cars shuttled tourists from the Northeast to Flagler's Royal Poinciana Hotel (pictured above) in Palm Beach. (Henry Morrison Flagler Museum Archives)

cate beachgoers about local flora and fauna, particularly the turtles for which the park is named. Each summer, loggerhead sea turtles waddle ashore to lay their cache of white, leathery eggs. *For information on all three parks, call 561-966-6600.*

A 2-mile stretch of beautiful sandy beach is the major attraction at **John D. MacArthur Beach State Park,** on **Singer Island.** You get to the beach from the nature center by walking across the 1,600-foot-long boardwalk, which spans Lake Worth Cove. Three species of turtle—leatherbacks, greens, and loggerheads—nest here, and rangers offer some wonderful turtle walks. Rangers also lead tours for advanced snorkelers, or you can take yourself out to the reef close to shore. Along the boardwalk-nature trail that leads to the beach, signs identify various plant species. *10900 Route 703, North Palm Beach; 561-624-6950.*

Charters and water taxis from **Sailfish Marina** (98 Lake Drive; 800-446-4577) in **Palm Beach Shores** provide narrated tours past Palm Beach mansions and yachts (including the home and golf course of Jack Nicklaus), and to Peanut Island, a tiny isle that attained political importance during the Cuban missile crisis, when President Kennedy, who wintered at Palm Beach, had a bunker built here for himself.

On Thursday nights, the marina hosts Sunset at Sailfish, an event featuring the work of local artisans. It's also here that you can try a local specialty, grouper dogs—sandwiches made with fried fresh grouper.

←🚗→ *Water separates Singer Island from Palm Beach to the south, so Route A1A turns inland and blends with U.S. 1, a particularly unattractive stretch of road. Attractive Flagler Drive, a refreshingly green, bayside alternative, is reached via 36th Street in West Palm Beach.*

■ PALM BEACH *map page 242, A/B-2*

It is a place, Palm Beach, unlike any other in the world. And only the other day it was merely sand and marsh and brush, with a few palms that grew from coconuts which drifted ashore from the wreck of a West Indian schooner. Only that and the blue sky and the blue lake and the blue ocean. And Flagler came and saw what there was. And then he saw what there could be.

In restaurants and clubs along the palm-lined roadways of Palm Beach, celebrities rub elbows with kings of commerce. Palm Beach is unquestionably Florida's social capital. It comes alive in winter, when princesses, actresses, presidents, musicians, and industrial wizards close up their northern homes and relocate.

Much of the beach here is privately owned, but the public stretch fronting downtown is beautiful and well maintained. The most popular form of entertainment for visitors is touring residential neighborhoods containing some of the most extraordinary mansions in America. Residents try to protect themselves behind high ficus hedges and fences, but most homes are remarkably visible from the roads. Many were designed and built by architect Addison Mizner and reflect exquisite craftsmanship. (The roof tiles were often formed by molding the clay around the thighs of the roofers!)

At the southern end of Ocean Boulevard sits the spectacular Hispano-Moresque palace known as **Mar-a-Lago.** The home, which has 118 rooms and a staff of 100, was built by Marjorie Merriweather Post (Mrs. E.F. Hutton at the time) and later

Sunset over Palm Beach.

occupied by Donald Trump, who has since transformed it into an ultra-exclusive club whose members (300 to date) fork over more than $80,000 a year each in club dues. The pale-orange-colored castle is surrounded by a 15-foot stone fence and capped with a light tower. The former Kennedy Compound—from which eminent structure numerous tabloid tales have been spun—stands farther north behind a long stone wall. Don't count on seeing the rich and famous on their front lawns. Your chances are better at **Chuck & Harold's** restaurant (207 Royal Poinciana Way; 561-659-1440), or at the lunch counter at **Green's Pharmacy** (151 North County Road; 561-832-0304), a refuge for the local working class and "slumming" elite.

To sightsee and shop, walk along **Worth Avenue,** Florida's answer to Rodeo Drive, where the chic cafés and boutiques cater to those with money to burn. (Frugal shoppers wait for end-of-season close-outs or haunt the thrift shops, where practically new designer clothes occasionally appear.) The bougainvillea-lined street's visual charms, however, are free of charge. Many of Worth Avenue's very attractive, villa-like buildings were also designed by architect Addison Mizner in the 1920s. He and like-minded architects of his day drew from Moorish, Italian

Renaissance, and Spanish colonial architecture for inspiration, creating a style of their own now referred to as Mediterranean Revival. Mizner also designed the street's "vias"—the narrow alleys that lead to picturesque courtyards with fountains and mosaics, art galleries, and open-air restaurants.

■ **PALM BEACH SIGHTS** *map page 242*

The **Henry Morrison Flagler Museum** is the contemporary, fairly mundane name of the opulent Gilded Age mansion that its namesake built in 1902 as a wedding present for his third wife. Then known as Whitehall—and sometimes referred to as "the Taj Mahal of America"—it was the couple's winter home until his death in 1913. Reproductions of period furnishings fill elaborate rooms in styles of the Italian Renaissance and Bourbon kings. "Too elaborate and formal to be a livable place," wrote Flagler biographer Sidney Walter Martin. Carrere and Hastings, the architects responsible for the New York Public Library and the U.S. Senate and House buildings, designed the mansion. Gilded trim is everywhere, and Flagler's bedroom is wallpapered and upholstered in gold-yellow fabrics. Tour

In a city noted for its mansions, Mar-a-Lago surpasses all others. It was originally a private residence with 58 bedrooms, 33 bathrooms, and three bomb shelters, but today it's a private club.

guides rightly describe Flagler—railroad and hotel developer and a founding partner of Standard Oil—as the man who converted Florida from a backwater wilderness to a major tourist destination. Self-guided tours are also an option. *Cocoanut Row and Whitehall Way; 561-655-2833.*

The **Hibel Museum of Art** is devoted to the sculptures, paintings, and lithographs of award-winning American artist Edna Hibel. Traveling exhibits also pass through its galleries. At this writing, the museum was preparing to move into a new facility, so call ahead or check the museum's Web site, *www.hibel.org*, for updates. *5353 Parkside Drive in the Abacoa Town Center; 561-533-1583.*

The historic **Royal Poinciana Playhouse** presents Broadway productions, sometimes starring well-known actors who are wintering in Palm Beach. The season runs from November through July. *70 Royal Poinciana Plaza; 561-659-3310.*

A tour through the Italianate loggias of **The Breakers** resort reveals the poised and cultured character of those Palm Beach vacationers who once called the grande dame home for the winter. It is still owned by the Kenan family, relatives of Henry Flagler's third wife, Mary Lily Kenan, for whom he built Whitehall. The hotel served as an army hospital during World War II, when Palm Beach turned into a military town and a target for the German U-boats that scoured the shoreline. Locals tell tales of torpedoed tankers offshore, blackout orders, submarine crews that sneaked ashore, and social dances where the young women of the community were wooed by the resident servicemen. *1 South County Road; 561-655-6611.*

This part of the coast attracts drift divers, scuba divers who swim into underwater currents that carry them swiftly past reefs and marine life. One great resource for divers and snorkelers is Ned Deloach's *Diving Guide to Underwater Florida.* **Coral Island Charters** (561-832-4800) cruises to the area's best reefs and diving spots.

■ WEST PALM BEACH   *map page 242, A/B-2*

Across the bridge and over Lake Worth—which is not a lake, but rather the Intracoastal Waterway that separates Palm Beach from West Palm Beach—lies the city of West Palm Beach. A booming metropolis in its own right, West Palm also furnishes services to Palm Beach, land of castles and kings. Like its counterpart across the canal, West Palm Beach has a thriving theater and arts scene—the latter centers around the excellent Norton Museum—as well as other hallmarks of affluence, but generally people here work and live a more traditional life. On the first weekend in May, West Palm Beach hosts **SunFest,** an extravaganza of music of all kinds, with an arts-and-crafts show, food, and fireworks. *Call 561-659-5980 for information.*

■ **WEST PALM BEACH SIGHTS** *map page 242*

The **Clematis Shopping and Entertainment District** is between Flagler Drive and Rosemary Avenue. Stylish, brightly painted metal-sculpture palm trees and colorful umbrellas accent a sidewalk bustling with people who pop in and out of galleries and cafés. The district is the site of a Brown Bag Lunch Concert Series and a Saturday Green Market. On Thursday nights, the streets close to traffic. Bands play and people dine al fresco or just stroll. Fun for folks of all ages, this is West Palm Beach at its best.

The Chicago steel magnate Ralph Norton financed the very fine **Norton Museum of Art,** whose collection includes paintings by Matisse, Gauguin, Monet, Degas, Homer, O'Keeffe, and Picasso; sculptures by Rodin and Brancusi;

The concert hall at the Kravis Center for Performing Arts is indicative of the renaissance that West Palm Beach has undergone in recent years.

Just outside West Palm Beach in the town of Wellington, picnickers enjoy the Southern tradition of a crawfish boil.

and Chinese ceramics from the Tang Dynasty (from the 4th to 11th century). *1451 South Olive Avenue; 561-832-5196.*

The 1920s-era **Old Northwood Historic District** is on the National Register of Historic Places. On Sundays, volunteers lead walking tours of the posh neighborhood, which students of architecture will appreciate for its stunning collection of Mediterranean Revival, Mission, and Old-Florida wooden "frame vernacular" buildings. *West of Flagler Drive between 26th and 35th Streets.*

The family-oriented **South Florida Science Museum** has the usual array of gadgets found in today's interactive science museums. Its aquariums, though, are more extensive than most. They hold marine life from the Pacific and Atlantic, from coral reef and mangrove environments. The jawbone of a sperm whale reaches from floor to ceiling. *Dreher Park, 4801 Dreher Trail North; 561-832-1988.*

Palm Beach Zoo at Dreher Park provides a home for more than 400 native and exotic animals, including such endangered species as the Komodo dragon, Florida panther, Bengal tiger, and tamarin. *1301 Summit Boulevard; 561-547-9453.*

At **Lion Country Safari,** far to the west, giraffes, rhinoceroses, zebras, chimps, bison, elephants, ostriches, wildebeest, and lions run right outside the car windows as visitors drive (with windows tightly rolled up) through the 500-acre preserve. Don't bother with the other rides and amusements. *Off Southern Boulevard; 561-793-1084.*

←🚙→ *South of Palm Beach proper, Route A1A passes mansion after mansion as it heads through the small, immaculate beachside towns of South Palm Beach, Lantana, Manalapan, Ocean Ridge, Boynton Beach, Gulf Stream, and Highland Beach. Best beach access is found at Lantana Public Beach.*

■ **DELRAY BEACH** *map page 242, B-3*

What began as a small settlement of Japanese farmers and later became an artists' retreat is now a sophisticated beach town with a successful historic preservation movement. Atlantic Avenue, the main drag, has been transformed into a mile-long stretch of brick sidewalks, lined with stores, galleries, and restaurants. Running east-west and ending at the beach, it's a pleasant place for a stroll day or night. Another pedestrian way begins at the edge of town across Northeast Eighth Street along the broad swimming beach off Atlantic Avenue.

Morikami Museum and Japanese Gardens is a monument to the original Japanese agricultural community here. Museum founder George Sukeji Morikami was one of the few who survived the colony's eventual decline, and he has made this a soothing retreat from the hubbub of the city. Ceremonial demonstrations are held in the Tea Room. In the gardens, native plants have been raised according to Japanese gardening principles. *400 Morikami Park Road; 561-495-0233.*

■ **BOCA RATON** *map page 242, B-4*

Boca, as it is fashionably known, exudes the same affluence that prevails in areas farther north, yet like all the other well-to-do communities along the southern Atlantic shoreline, it's just not Palm Beach. After all, Boca Raton means "mouth of the rat" in Spanish. A snooty spoof in *Palm Beach Illustrated* tells the story of a socially inept Rudolph the Blue-Blooded Reindeer who's not making it in Palm Beach. It advises him: "Look on the bright side, Rudolph, there's always Boca Raton."

Sailfishing off the coast of Florida.

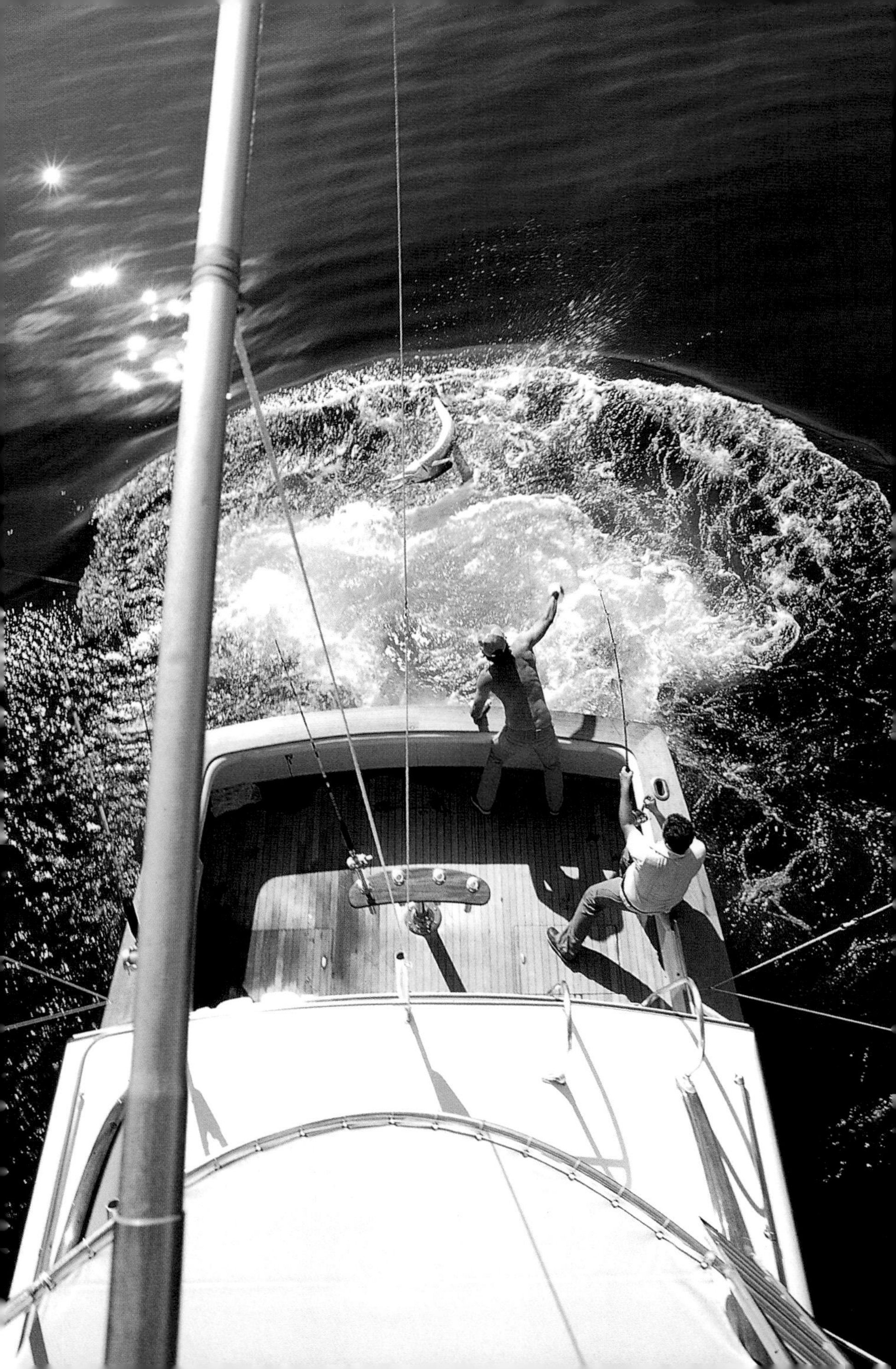

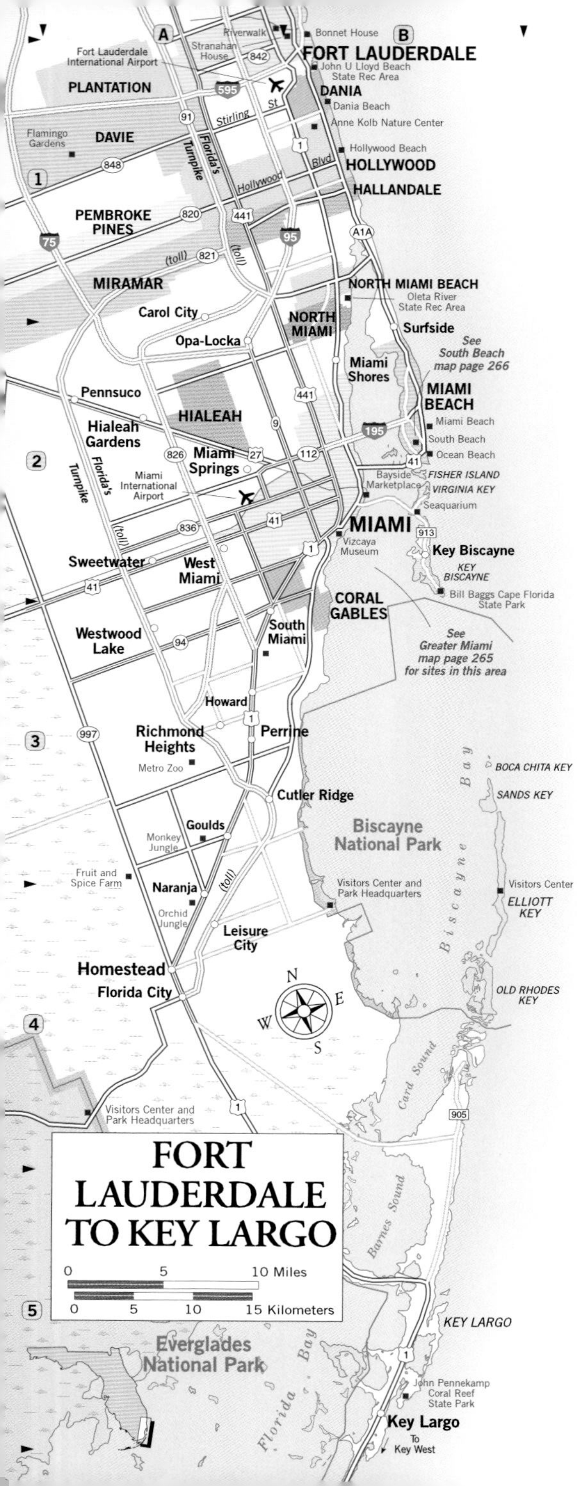
FORT LAUDERDALE TO KEY LARGO
0 5 10 Miles
0 5 10 15 Kilometers
A
B
1
2
3
4
5
Riverwalk
Bonnet House
Stranahan House
Fort Lauderdale International Airport
FORT LAUDERDALE
John U Lloyd Beach State Rec Area
PLANTATION
DANIA
Dania Beach
Anne Kolb Nature Center
Flamingo Gardens
DAVIE
Hollywood Beach
HOLLYWOOD
HALLANDALE
PEMBROKE PINES
MIRAMAR
NORTH MIAMI BEACH
Oleta River State Rec Area
Carol City
NORTH MIAMI
Surfside
Opa-Locka
See South Beach map page 266
Miami Shores
MIAMI BEACH
Pennsuco
HIALEAH
Hialeah Gardens
Miami Beach
South Beach
Ocean Beach
Miami Springs
Miami International Airport
Bayside Marketplace
FISHER ISLAND
VIRGINIA KEY
Seaquarium
MIAMI
Vizcaya Museum
Key Biscayne
KEY BISCAYNE
Sweetwater
West Miami
Bill Baggs Cape Florida State Park
CORAL GABLES
Westwood Lake
South Miami
See Greater Miami map page 265 for sites in this area
Howard
Richmond Heights
Perrine
Metro Zoo
BOCA CHITA KEY
SANDS KEY
Cutler Ridge
Goulds
Biscayne National Park
Monkey Jungle
Fruit and Spice Farm
Naranja
Visitors Center and Park Headquarters
Visitors Center
ELLIOTT KEY
Orchid Jungle
Leisure City
Biscayne Bay
Homestead
Florida City
OLD RHODES KEY
Card Sound
Visitors Center and Park Headquarters
Barnes Sound
KEY LARGO
Everglades National Park
Florida Bay
John Pennekamp Coral Reef State Park
Key Largo
To Key West
Turnpike
Florida's
Stirling
St
Hollywood
Blvd
(toll)

If Addison Mizner helped make Palm Beach what it is today, then he was absolutely key to Boca. In 1925, his corporation bought a patch of what was then barely settled, waterside acreage. With a plan to draw wealthy visitors, the architect built a resort hotel in his signature style: pink stucco, open arcades and arches, and Mediterranean details. He named it the Cloister Inn. The plan worked, and Mizner set about planning an entire city with landscaped gardens, theaters, even a cathedral. Though the Florida land boom went bust, putting an end to Mizner's elaborate plans, much of the city did get built. The Cloister Inn weathered the hurricanes of 1926 and 1928 and operates today as Boca Raton Resort.

Boca's beaches epitomize the best of the east coast's ocean-swept, dune-ridged shoreline, where beachgoers descend flights of stairs to reach the sand. Hefty parking fees keep the beaches safe from the havoc that weekenders can wreak.

■ **BOCA RATON SIGHTS**

South Beach Park (400 North Route A1A) is a beautiful place to spend a day swimming, surf fishing, or walking on the beach. There are three designated beach access areas, and you'll find lifeguards are on duty from 9 AM to 5 PM. **Red Reef Park** (1400 North Route A1A) has picnic facilities equipped with grills and tables on 67 acres of oceanfront.

Gumbo Limbo Environmental Complex educates the public—especially children—about local endangered species and ecology in general, with nature trails, aquariums, videos, interpretive and identification displays, and other nature programs. Outdoor marine tanks hold baby loggerhead turtles and local fish species. One short trail takes visitors through a butterfly garden and to a bayside beach (no swimming allowed). Another travels through a hammock to an observation tower. *1801 North Route A1A (across from Red Reef Park's north entrance); 561-338-1473.*

Mizner Park is Boca Raton's shopping headquarters, but shops, galleries, and gourmet boutiques are scattered all over town. Great buys can be found at the flea markets and at designer sample sales and seconds stores.

The **International Museum of Cartoon Art** chronicles America's cartoon history and displays the works of cartoonists from more than 50 other countries, too. This international angle makes it unique, and its massive collection includes 160,000 original drawings from comic books, cartoons, greeting cards, novels, and more. *201 Plaza Real in Mizner Park; 561-391-2200.*

■ **FORT LAUDERDALE** *map pages 242, B-5, and page 254, B-1*

South of Boca Raton, condos begin to line Route A1A and the road becomes increasingly congested. The highway takes the name of Atlantic Boulevard in Fort Lauderdale.

The trademark of Fort Lauderdale is Fort Lauderdale Beach, made famous by Frankie Avalon, Annette Funicello, and spring-breakers of the 1950s and '60s. College students took wild vacations here well into the 1990s, but these days they usually go elsewhere, discouraged by strict law enforcement and skyrocketing motel rates. Instead, Fort Lauderdale has lately become a highly appealing and comparatively affordable refuge for those weary of the nonstop bustle that enveloped Miami after it was "rediscovered" in the mid-1990s. In fact, Fort Lauderdale seems to have retained a quaintness that Miami has since lost, which might explain why it is referred to in some circles as "Fort La-di-da." The area around Las Olas Boulevard, in particular, with its neatly kept shops and trendy restaurants, is a beautiful place to stroll at a much more relaxed pace than in Miami's South Beach. The best way to see the area is by horse-drawn buggy or water taxi. In the downtown area, you'll find the **Center for the Performing Arts** (201 SW Fifth Avenue; 954-462-0222), the crowning jewel of Fort Lauderdale's Arts and Science District, which hosts traveling shows and Broadway-quality local productions.

An early Fort Lauderdale developer dredged finger canals through town, hence the town's nickname as the "Venice of America." A boat ride through a handful of the fingers reveals the spiffy backyards of those who can afford such property. At one mansion, rare antique cars are on display in a glass waterfront showcase. Any number of tours are available, and the **Water Taxi** (954-467-6677) makes stops at shops, restaurants, resorts, and sights on the water.

From the windows of restaurants along the Intracoastal Waterway are fine views of boats gliding by and, in December, of the nighttime lighted boat parades.

(above) Fort Lauderdale's most magnificent homes lie beside narrow peninsulas—known as the Isles—set in the mouth of the New River.
(opposite) The quintessential beach scene of Las Olas Boulevard in Fort Lauderdale.

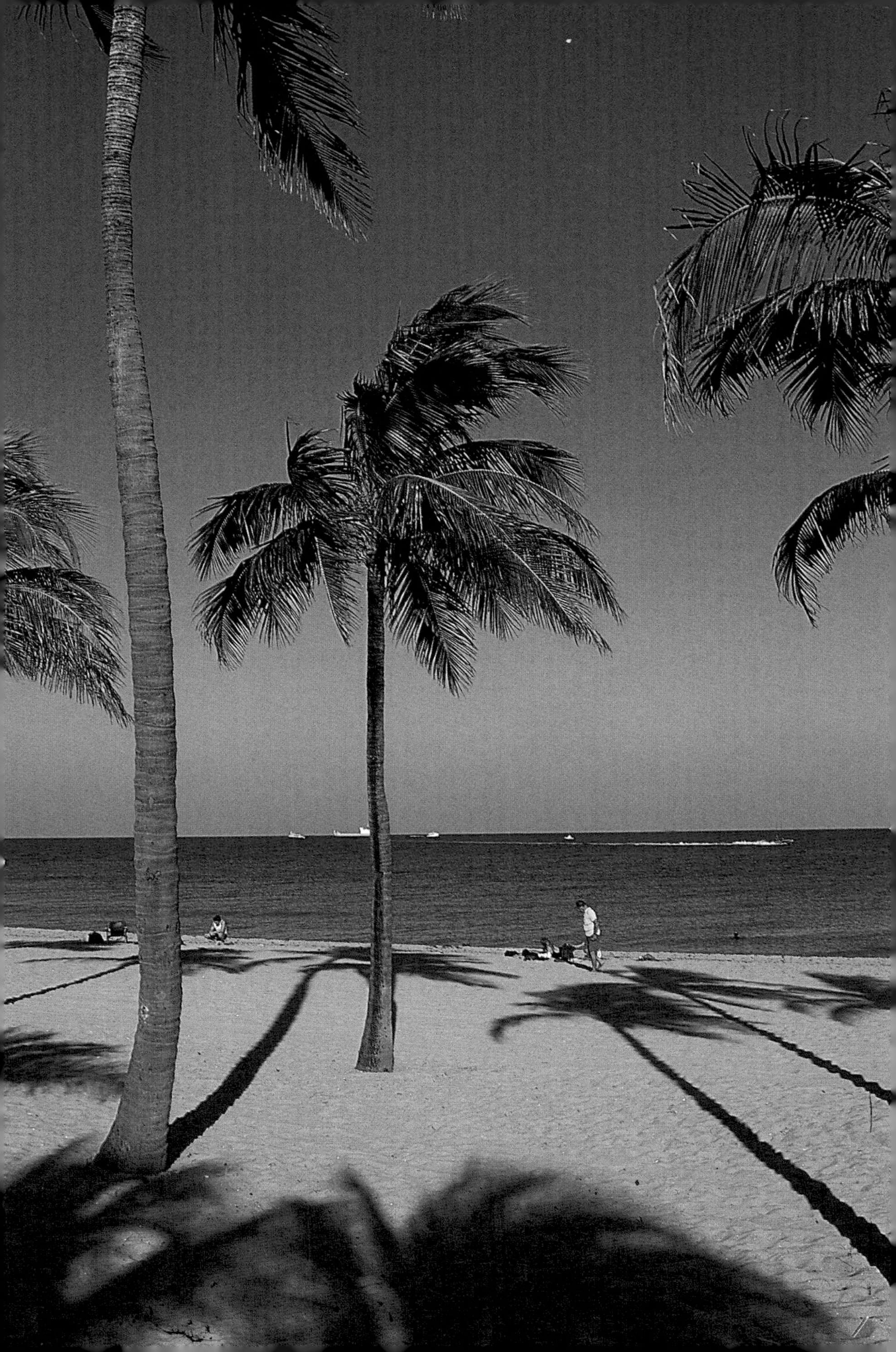

■ FORT LAUDERDALE SIGHTS

At **Fort Lauderdale Beach,** a stylish serpentine wall separates the sand from a busy sidewalk thronged with joggers, cyclists, rollerbladers, and parents pushing strollers. Sidewalk cafés, bars, and T-shirt shops line the opposite side of the street. South Beach Park, at the south end, is quieter and fine for family picnics and the like. Nearer to Port Everglades, you can view the comings and goings of ship traffic. Especially impressive are the enormous cruise liners that berth here.

Hugh Taylor Birch State Park, at the north end of Fort Lauderdale Beach, encompasses 180 acres stretching from the ocean to the Intracoastal Waterway. By foot or canoe, visitors can explore the park's five biological communities: beach, mangroves, freshwater lagoon, coastal strand, and oak hammock. *3109 East Sunrise Boulevard; 954-564-4521.*

A visit to **Bonnet House** combines the delights of art, architecture, and wildlife. In 1920, muralist Frederic Clay Bartlett and his wife, Helen, built this Mississippi River plantation–style home of coral rock and Dade County pine, with wrought-iron detailing. Helen died suddenly in 1925, and Bartlett's second wife, artist Evelyn Fortune Lilly, encouraged him to add an aviary, an elaborate shell inlay, and a ceiling mural of sea life. The 35 acres of lush grounds are graced with countless native plants and include an extensive collection of orchids. Swans navigate the lagoon in the front of the house; the yellow Bonnet lilies for which the house was named still thrive. To visit Bonnet House, you must take a guided tour. *900 North Birch Road; 954-563-5393.*

The city's history unfolds at **Stranahan House,** the county's oldest standing structure, built on the site of a trading post for settlers and Seminoles. City founder Frank Stranahan built his humble two-story house at the turn of the 20th century. The house is made of Dade County pine, also known as Florida or heart pine, which was popular with early home builders because of its resistance to pests. Builders had to chop down the tree, saw the pine boards, and nail them up as quickly as possible, because as soon as heart pine sap sets up, the wood becomes impenetrable. *335 SE Sixth Avenue, at Las Olas Boulevard; 954-524-4736.*

The highlight of the **Museum of Discovery and Science** is a space-flight simulator that lands riders on the moon. During the summer, the museum hosts Ecofloat, environmental boat tours to the beaches, barrier islands, sinkholes, mangrove estuaries, and other local habitats. There's also an IMAX 3-D Theater that's five stories high. *401 SW Second Street; 954-467-6637.*

Across the street from the museum runs **Riverwalk Park,** a recreation area that follows the New River and features educational stations, such as one with hands-on marine navigational instruments. Sunday Jazz Brunches convene here, featuring top artists. The Broward Center for the Performing Arts (box office: 954-462-0222) is also found in the park complex.

The **Old Dillard Art and Cultural Museum,** inside a public school built in 1924 for African Americans, re-creates classroom and home environments in the early part of the 20th century. *1009 NW Fourth Street; 954-765-6952.*

■ HOLLYWOOD AND HOLLYWOOD BEACH
map page 254, B-1

Hollywood is the favored roost of French-Canadian snowbirds—retirees who come here in winter to escape the cold northern climates of Boston, New York, Washington, D.C., and elsewhere. Downtown Hollywood is enjoying a revival, with restaurants, shops, and beautiful streetscapes. Along the Hollywood Beach Boardwalk (a cement walk at sand's edge), sidewalk cafés sell crêpes, and coffee

Much of the coastline from Fort Lauderdale south to Miami is backed by luxury condominiums.

and beer, and provide a comfortable venue for people-watching. At the beach's northernmost extreme, **John U. Lloyd Beach State Park** hides sunbathers from the crowds in a dune-edged refuge with rock jetties and a boat ramp. *6503 North Ocean Drive; 954-923-2833.*

At **Anne Kolb Nature Center and Marina,** nature-seekers may indulge in hiking, biking, birding, canoeing, boat touring, and pier fishing. A five-story observation tower and environmental exhibits present an overview of local wildlife. *West Lake Park, 751 Sheridan Street; 954-926-2480.*

■ MIAMI METRO OVERVIEW *map page 265*

It's hard to believe that this complex, vital, thoroughly urbanized city, with its layers of ethnic diversity, was only a century ago a wilderness swamp dense with mosquitoes. But that's what it was until John Sewell, "Daddy of Miami," floated in to build yet another grand hotel for Flagler's railroad in 1896. Twenty-five years later, he published his pioneer tales—one more who came to visit Florida and never left.

Sewell's name stars in the honor roll of Miami boosters—Julia Tuttle, William Brickell, John Collins, and Carl Fisher—visionaries who helped change a wilderness town named Fort Dallas into a bustling metropolis.

Henry Flagler's railroad opened up Fort Dallas, which changed its name back to Miami, a name probably deriving from an American Indian word for "sweet water." (*Mayami* was originally the local Indians' appellation for the clear spring-waters of Lake Okeechobee.) Flagler dredged the port and introduced electricity. Collins and Fisher built a bridge to Miami Beach and turned that strip of coast into America's Cote d'Azur, hoping to attract tourists. And come they did: first the privileged few, later the Jewish upper-middle class, eventually everyone. They came to this capital of sunshine, sand, and shopping. To them, it represented escape, whether for a month or a lifetime, from winter's punishment.

■ CUBAN INFLUX

To the next human influx, Miami offered a different, more vital definition of escape—escape from the regime of Fidel Castro. After having absorbed several waves of immigration over the last 40 years, the city has become home to the largest Cuban population outside of Havana. From Operation Pedro Pan in the

Regulars meet for a game of dominoes in Little Havana's Domino Park.

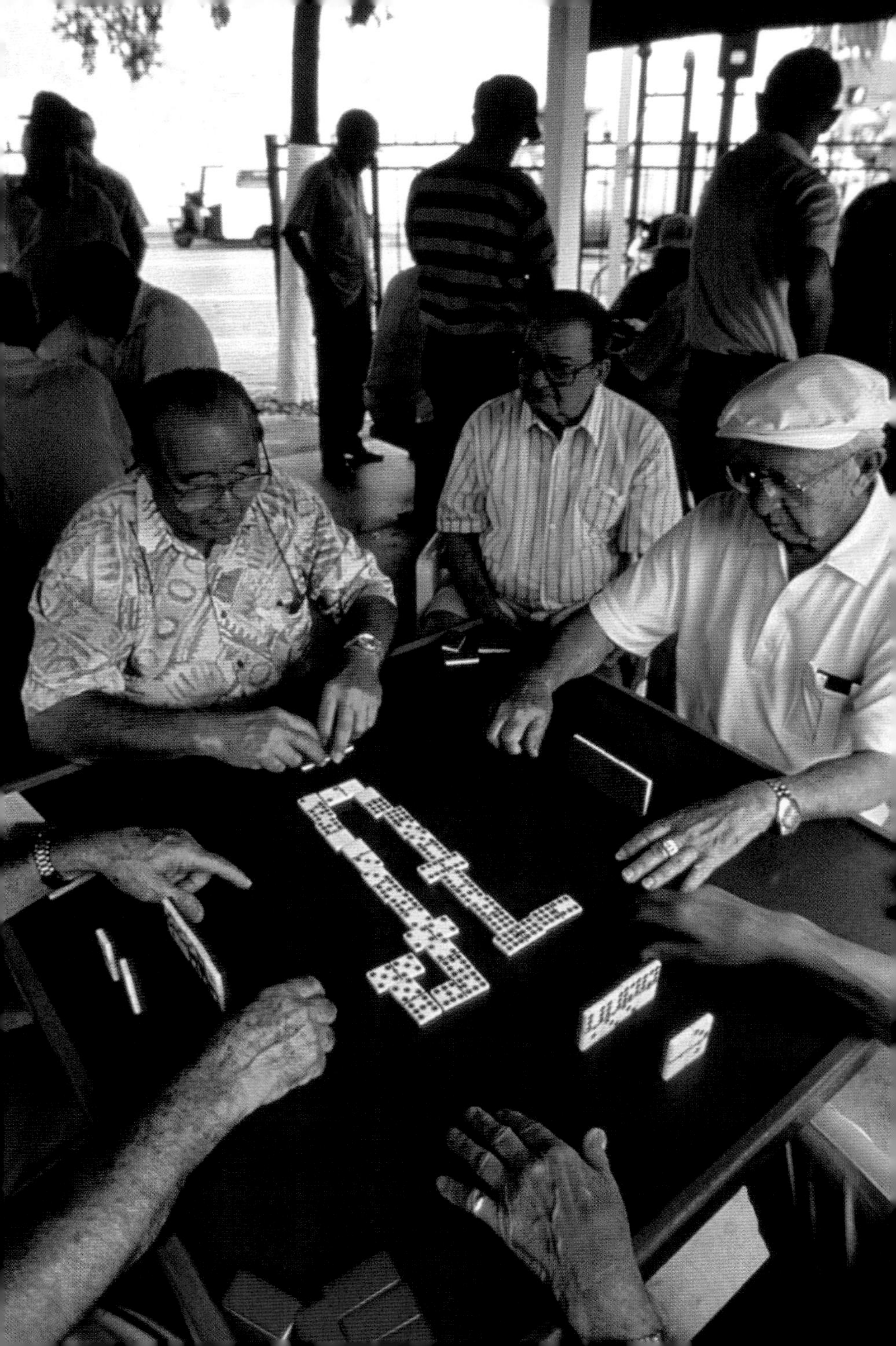

early 1960s, when fearful Cuban parents sent their children alone to Miami to escape Castro's indoctrination, to the Mariel boatlift of the 1980s, which brought more than 100,000 refugees in a matter of weeks, expatriate Cubans have sought refuge on the city's shores. Even today, immigrants continue to arrive on rafts and small boats, a situation that was brought into the international spotlight again in 1999 when six-year-old Cuban refugee Elian Gonzales became the unwitting pawn in a game of international tug-of-war.

Though old-guard Cuban immigrants are staunchly anti-Castro, they take pride in their cultural heritage, even though many second- and third-generation Cuban Americans are more comfortable speaking English than their parents' native tongue. As a result, perhaps the most common language in this city today is Spanglish, the mixture of Spanish and English.

Miami's Cuban influence is evident throughout the area, from salsa classes in Coral Gables and South Beach to art galleries and restaurants on Calle Ocho. Even those Miamians who don't speak Spanish call Southwest Eighth Street, which is the heart of Miami's Cuban culture, by its Spanish name—Calle Ocho.

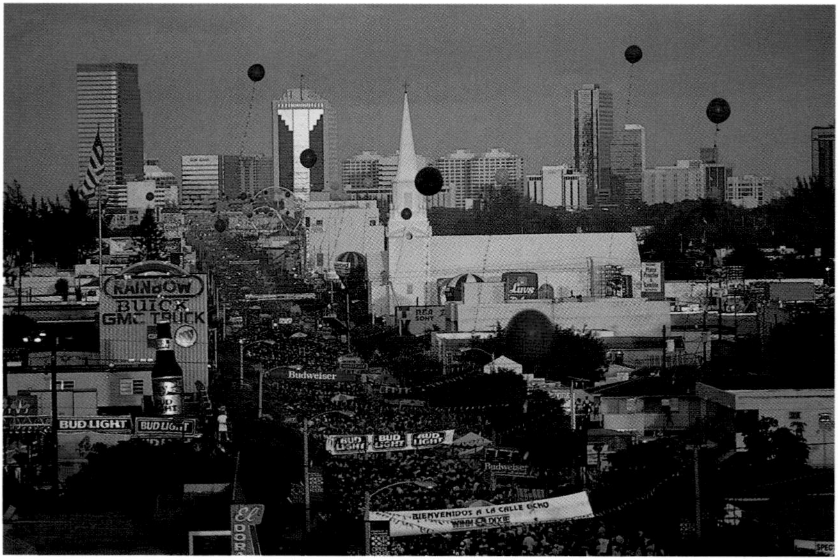
RAINBOW
BUICK
BUD LIGHT
Budweiser

Calle Ocho is the center of Little Havana's street party every March during Miami's Carnaval.

Mid-nineties merengue.

Hot Cuban Miami

The entire tone of the city, the way people looked and talked and met one another, was Cuban. The very image the city had begun presenting of itself, what was then its newfound glamour, its "hotness" (hot colors, hot vice, shady dealings under the palm trees), was that of prerevolutionary Havana, as perceived by Americans. There was even in the way women dressed in Miami a definable Havana look, a more distinct emphasis on the hips and décolletage, more black, more veiling, a generalized flirtatiousness of style not then current in American cities. In the shoe departments at Burdines and Jordan Marsh there were more platform soles than there might have been in another American city, and fewer displays of the running-shoe ethic....

Fête followed fête, all high visibility. Almost any day it was possible to drive past the limestone arches and fountains which marked the boundaries of Coral Gables and see little girls being photographed in the tiaras and ruffled hoop skirts and maribou-trimmed illusion capes they would wear at their *quinces*, the elaborate fifteenth-birthday parties at which the community's female children came of official age. The favored facial expression for a *quince* photograph was a classic smolder.

—Joan Didion, *Miami,* 1987

Here you'll find the city's most famous Cuban restaurant, **Versailles Restaurant and Bakery** (3501 SW Eighth Street; 305-441-2500), where such Cuban staples as arroz con pollo, a traditional chicken and rice dish, or a Cuban sandwich are the specialties. Imaginative, more upscale takes on classic Cuban fare can be found at **Yuca** (501 Lincoln Road; 305-532-9822), whose name is purported to be an acronym for the crowd you'll likely encounter: Young Urban Cuban Americans.

■ MIAMI TODAY

Miami today is a mix of modern metropolis and international playground. On one hand, its beach is a year-round getaway whose natural splendors—sun, sand, surf—make it a prime vacation destination for travelers from around the world. On the other hand, its downtown area, where futuristic-looking people movers snake their way around glass-walled skyscrapers, is a bustling center of commerce, both domestically and throughout Latin America. The city's close ties to Caribbean nations has earned it the unofficial title of "Capital of the Caribbean," and immigrants from both Latin American and Caribbean countries continue to shape its culture.

According to the 2000 census, Miami's population is now more than 60 percent Hispanic, but only half of that population is Cuban. Immigrants from many other Latin American countries have also shaped the city's diverse culture. Wealthy Venezuelans and Colombians have gravitated toward the posh condo developments in the Brickell neighborhood, just south of Miami's financial center. Likewise, from South Beach to South Miami, Nicaraguans, Puerto Ricans, and other Latin Americans have taken root here. Brazilians, in particular, have gained greater visibility in the last decade, adding samba dancing and roasted meat buffets, known as *churrascaria*, to the city's ever-growing list of cultural influences. **Porcao** (801 South Bayshore Drive; 305-373-2777) is the most popular of these all-you-can-eateries, and if you leave the place hungry you've missed the point entirely. Immigrants from Caribbean nations, including Haiti, Jamaica, and the Bahamas, have also contributed to the diversity of restaurants and to the incredible Afro-Latino music scene. **Tap Tap Haitian Restaurant** (819 Fifth Street; 305-672-2898), on Miami Beach, is a great place to sample the flavors, sounds, and poetry of the Haitian community.

With its ever-expanding cultural scene and warm, tropical climate, Miami has also attracted many refugees from America's colder climes, most notably from the

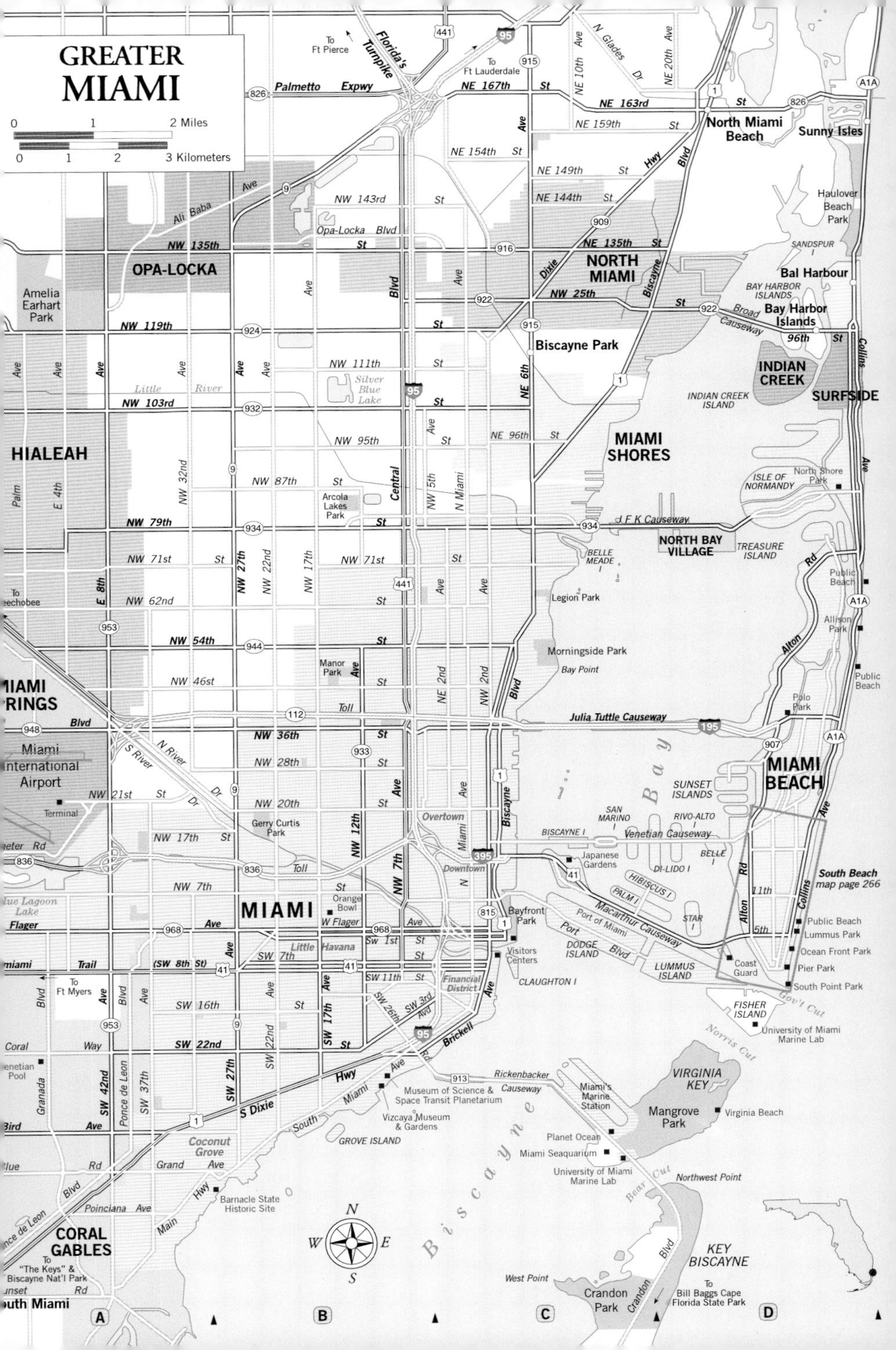
GREATER MIAMI
0 1 2 Miles
0 1 2 3 Kilometers
To Ft Pierce
Florida's Turnpike
To Ft Lauderdale
Palmetto Expwy
NE 167th St
NE 163rd St
NE 159th St
NE 154th St
NE 149th St
NE 144th St
NE 135th St
NE 125th St
NE 96th St
NE 10th Ave
N Glades Dr
NE 20th Ave
North Miami Beach
Sunny Isles
Haulover Beach Park
SANDSPUR I
Bal Harbour
BAY HARBOR ISLANDS
Bay Harbor Islands
Broad Causeway
96th St
Collins Ave
INDIAN CREEK
SURFSIDE
INDIAN CREEK ISLAND
Biscayne Park
NORTH MIAMI
MIAMI SHORES
Dixie Hwy
Biscayne Blvd
Ali Baba Ave
NW 143rd St
Opa-Locka Blvd
NW 135th St
OPA-LOCKA
Amelia Earhart Park
NW 119th St
NW 111th St
Little River
Silver Blue Lake
NW 103rd St
NW 95th St
NW 87th St
HIALEAH
Palm Ave
E 4th Ave
NW 32nd Ave
Arcola Lakes Park
Central Blvd
NW 5th Ave
N Miami Ave
NE 6th Ave
NW 79th St
J F K Causeway
NORTH BAY VILLAGE
TREASURE ISLAND
ISLE OF NORMANDY
North Shore Park
BELLE MEADE I
NW 71st St
NW 27th Ave
NW 22nd Ave
NW 17th Ave
To Okeechobee
E 8th Ave
NW 62nd St
Legion Park
Public Beach
Allison Park
NW 54th St
Morningside Park
Bay Point
Alton Rd
Manor Park
NW 46st
NE 2nd Ave
NW 2nd Ave
MIAMI SPRINGS
Toll
Julia Tuttle Causeway
Polo Park
Blvd
Miami International Airport
NW 36th St
NW 28th St
S River Dr
N River Dr
MIAMI BEACH
SUNSET ISLANDS
Biscayne Bay
NW 21st St
Terminal
NW 20th St
Gerry Curtis Park
Overtown
SAN MARINO I
RIVO-ALTO I
BISCAYNE I
Venetian Causeway
NW 17th St
Japanese Gardens
BELLE I
DI-LIDO I
Downtown
HIBISCUS I
PALM I
South Beach map page 266
NW 7th St
NW 12th Ave
NW 7th Ave
Blue Lagoon Lake
MIAMI
Orange Bowl
W Flagler
Flagler Ave
Bayfront Park
Port of Miami
Macarthur Causeway
11th St
STAR I
5th St
Public Beach
Lummus Park
Little Havana
Sw 1st St
SW 7th St
Tamiami Trail (SW 8th St)
DODGE ISLAND
Port Blvd
Visitors Centers
Ocean Front Park
LUMMUS ISLAND
Coast Guard
Pier Park
SW 11th St
Financial District
CLAUGHTON I
South Point Park
To Ft Myers
SW 16th St
SW 17th Ave
SW 26th Rd
SW 3rd Avd
Brickell Ave
FISHER ISLAND
Gov't Cut
University of Miami Marine Lab
Norris Cut
Coral Way
SW 22nd St
SW 22nd Ave
Venetian Pool
Granada Blvd
SW 42nd Ave
Ponce de Leon Blvd
SW 37th Ave
SW 27th Ave
S Dixie Hwy
South Miami Ave
Rickenbacker Causeway
Museum of Science & Space Transit Planetarium
Vizcaya Museum & Gardens
Miami's Marine Station
VIRGINIA KEY
Mangrove Park
Virginia Beach
Bird Ave
Coconut Grove
GROVE ISLAND
Planet Ocean
Miami Seaquarium
Blue Rd
Grand Ave
University of Miami Marine Lab
Bear Cut
Northwest Point
Barnacle State Historic Site
Poinciana Ave
Main Hwy
Ponce de Leon Blvd
CORAL GABLES
To "The Keys" & Biscayne Nat'l Park
Sunset Rd
South Miami
N
W
E
S
West Point
KEY BISCAYNE
Crandon Park
Crandon Blvd
To Bill Baggs Cape Florida State Park
A
B
C
D

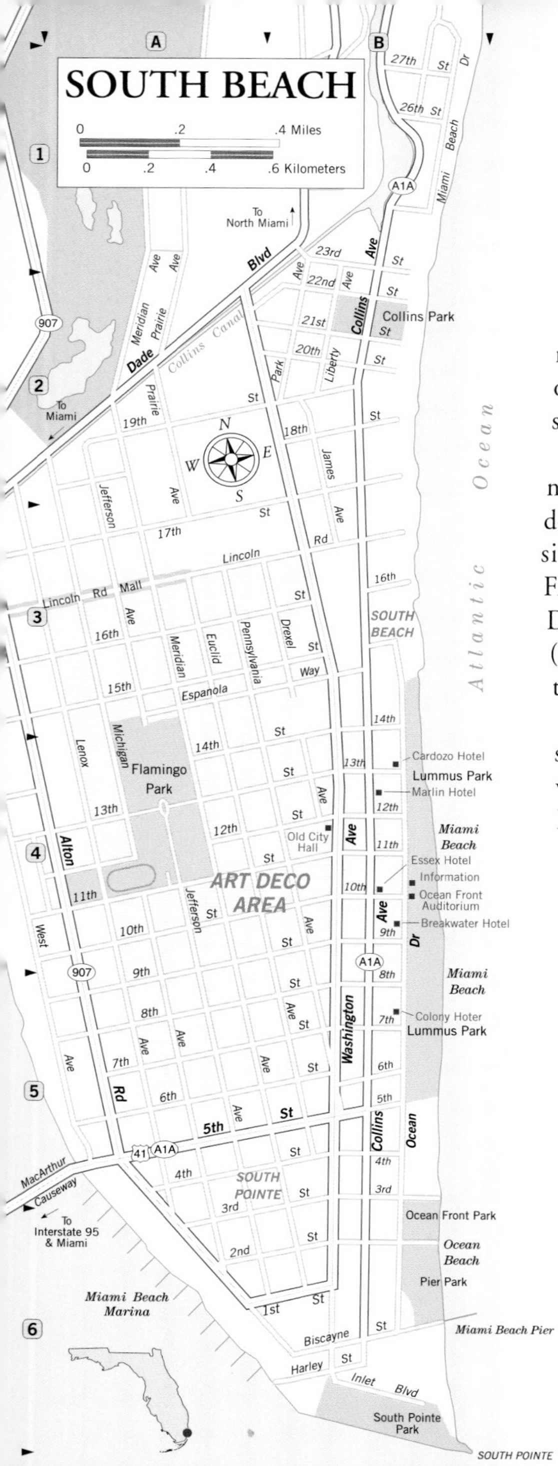
SOUTH BEACH
0
.2
.4 Miles
0
.2
.4
.6 Kilometers
A
B
1
2
3
4
5
6
27th St
26th St
Miami Beach Dr
A1A
To North Miami
23rd St
22nd St
21st St
20th St
Collins Park
Collins Canal
Dade Blvd
Meridian Ave
Prairie Ave
Park
Liberty
907
To Miami
19th
18th
James Ave
N
E
S
W
Jefferson
17th St
Rd
Lincoln Rd Mall
16th St
SOUTH BEACH
Atlantic Ocean
Meridian
Euclid
Pennsylvania
Drexel
Way
15th
Espanola
14th St
Lenox
Michigan
Flamingo Park
13th
12th
Old City Hall
Alton
11th
10th
ART DECO AREA
Cardozo Hotel
Lummus Park
Marlin Hotel
Miami Beach
Essex Hotel
Information
Ocean Front Auditorium
Breakwater Hotel
West
9th
8th
7th
Colony Hoter
Lummus Park
Washington
Ave
6th
5th St
Rd
Collins
Ocean
41
MacArthur Causeway
To Interstate 95 & Miami
4th
SOUTH POINTE
3rd
2nd
1st St
Ocean Front Park
Ocean Beach
Pier Park
Miami Beach Marina
Miami Beach Pier
Biscayne St
Harley St
Inlet Blvd
South Pointe Park
SOUTH POINTE

Northeast and the Midwest. This combined influence of America and Latin America has created another "city that never sleeps," where many restaurants serve dinner as late as midnight and after-hours nightclubs only get the party started at 4 AM and stay open until noon.

But the city isn't all about nightlife and the beach. Miami residents are also proud of their professional sports teams, including the Florida Marlins (baseball) and Miami Dolphins (football), the Miami Heat (basketball), and even a hockey team, the Panthers.

If you prefer to participate in sports you can always find a pick-up volleyball game on the beach, or head to the Atlantic for scuba diving, snorkeling, sea kayaking, jet-skiing, sailing—and every other water sport you can imagine. And a visit to the South Beach area will prove that rollerblading, whether done wearing proper safety equipment or wearing little more than a thong bikini, is still the most popular individual sport in town.

Spectators lay complicated bets at the **Jai-Alai Fronton**. The popularity of jai alai (say "high-lie"), a fast-paced game of Basque origin, has spread throughout the state. *3500 NW 37th Avenue; 305-663-6400.*

■ South Miami *map page 265, B-5*

The brilliant silhouette of Miami's high-rises marks a thriving commercial center. At the city's fringes, along the bay, are surprisingly visitor-friendly parks and the ever-buzzing Bayside Marketplace, on Biscayne Boulevard. Here, one can have a burger at (one more) Hard Rock Cafe, buy a cave-bear skeleton for $45,000, or hop on a tour bus or boat tour to visit the homes of the local rich and famous, who over the years have included Gloria and Emilio Estefan, Rosie O'Donnell, Madonna, and Sly Stallone to name (drop) a few.

Eighth Street, known as **Calle Ocho,** forms the core of Little Havana, the heart of Miami's trademark Cuban-American culture. Fragrant Cuban coffee bars, smoky cigar shops, lively salsa and flamenco bars, and stores selling guayabera shirts and Santeria cult fetishes line the street. Every year in March, Calle Ocho becomes a sea of human bodies, as the world's longest conga line forms during Carnaval.

■ Miami Beach: South Beach *map page 266*

The town of Miami Beach lies on a barrier island 2 miles off the mainland. Much of this narrow, 7-mile-long island was formerly mangrove swamp. The wetlands

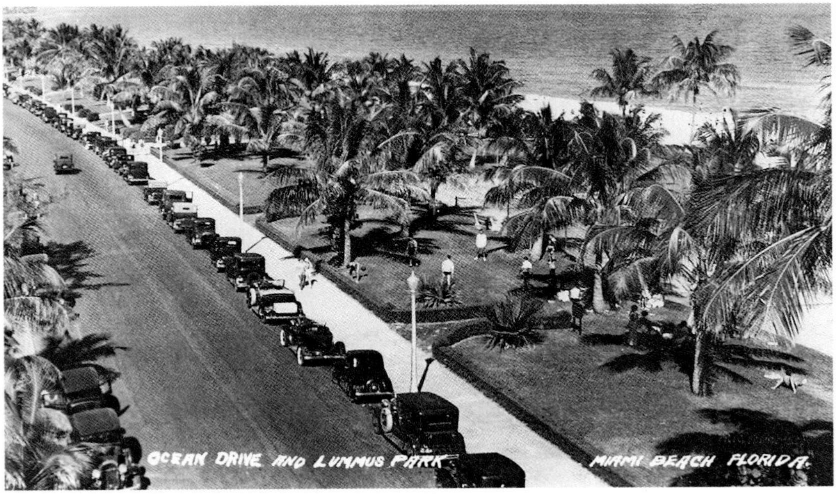
OCEAN DRIVE AND LUMMUS PARK
MIAMI BEACH FLORIDA.

(above) Ocean Drive, Miami Beach, ca. 1925. (Florida State Archives)
(following pages) Ocean Drive at night.

South Beach Art Deco

From the late 1920s to the early '40s, a group of single-minded, immensely talented architects—the most prominent being Henry Hohauser, Albert Anis, and L. Murray Dixon—came to South Beach and designed a mile-square district of 800 Art Deco and some late Mediterranean Revival structures. The South Beach National Historic District provides a unique opportunity to understand and enjoy the art and design movement inspired by the 1925 Paris Exposition International des Arts Décoratifs et Industriels Modernes, which celebrated the union of the decorative arts and technology. (The term "Art Deco" dates from a 1966 retrospective of that show.) Using reinforced concrete, stucco, and glass blocks to realize their designs, the architects were able to construct thoroughly Modern Age–looking structures quickly and inexpensively. To add style and show detail at negligible cost, exteriors were painted in different pastel colors—often blue, green, and white, in keeping with the hues of the sea and the tropical surroundings. Some of the restored hotels have been punched up in even brighter shades of hot pink, turquoise, and citrus yellow—less authentic, but flattering to these fanciful buildings. New man-made materials, such as vitrolite and chrome, allowed designers to create avant-garde interiors for little money. Patterned terrazzo, made with colored stone set in mortar, was a modest alternative to marble flooring.

Revealing the builders' admiration for contemporary skyscrapers, the classic South Beach Art Deco structure is massed symmetrically around a strong vertical center, often a tower or group of columns that stretches above an otherwise flat roof. Balancing this verticality are horizontal ledges over the verandah and sunshades above windows; in some cases, both window and sunshade (or "eyebrow") curve around the corner of the building. These elements fit the Art Deco architectural principle of the "Holy Three"—three stories counterposed by a triptych-like facade. Most hotels on Ocean Drive have three floors. Signage was incorporated into the design to help achieve a desired overall effect: a bold, spare typeface might be used to emphasize a building's Machine Age lines; vertical signs drew the eye up, accenting the structure's upward movement; and neon, also used to highlight structural features, lent a futuristic feel and a dash of urban excitement. The Breakwater and Colony Hotels have striking, effective signs.

Especially intriguing in SoBe architecture is the highly eclectic—though in keeping with Art Deco dictates, sparingly used—ornamentation. Friezes contain the flowery organic forms of Art Nouveau, Egyptian-style figures inspired by the then-recently uncovered Tutankhamen's tomb, and the geometric shapes of Aztec art.

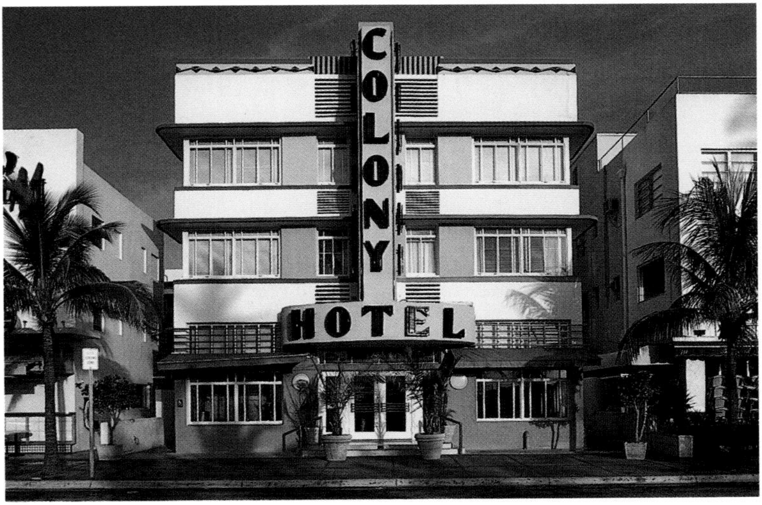
COLONY
HOTEL

One of the splendid Art Deco hotels that have become the hallmark of South Beach.

While these motifs are relatively common in American Art Deco, the SoBe architects also had their own Tropical Deco images—palm trees, sea horses, and ocean waves—which they incorporated into their bas reliefs. At the Beacon Hotel, flamingos are etched into the glass doors.

Some of the buildings constructed after 1935 have a slightly different look—still spare and geometric, but with rounded corners and ledges, horizontal racing stripes, stainless steel accents, and aerodynamic-looking facades devoid of decoration, as at the Marlin and the Cardozo Hotels. Identified as Streamline Moderne, these buildings recall the sleek trains of the day; some, like the 1941 Avalon, have an asymmetric element, such as a tower on only one side. Science fiction touches like antenna poles and Buck Rogers-y parapets further the Machine Age theme. South Beach architects also drew inspiration from the clean curves of ocean liners and added portholes, railings, and columns. Buildings dominated by the cruise liner look, such as the Essex, are often called Nautical Moderne. Another seaside reference appears at Waldorf Towers (1937), which boasts an ornamental "lighthouse" tower at one corner.

—Julia Dillon

were dredged and filled by developers John and James Lummus—with a little cash from Carl Fisher—in 1912–13. Fisher also helped fund John Collins's bridge, now known as the Venetian Causeway, from the mainland to Miami Beach.

Today, Miami Beach is largely known for its **South Beach (SoBe) district,** whose glamorous stretch of wide beachfront is lined by chic Art Deco hotels, bustling nightclubs, fine restaurants, trendy boutiques, and open-air cafés, which are great for people-watching.

■ ART DECO DISTRICT *map page 266, A/B-3/5*

SoBe's renewal began in 1976, when one woman, art historian Barbara Capitman, literally threw herself in front of the bulldozers that threatened to raze the decrepit relics of circa-1920 America. The Art Deco Historic District is today a rectangle bounded by Dade Boulevard on the north, Sixth Street on the south, the Atlantic Ocean on the east, and Lenox Court on the west, comprising a square mile of 800 classic buildings. The most famous strip of them lines Ocean Drive.

Because the neighborhood was so rapidly developed and designed by like-minded architects—Henry Hohauser, L. Murray Dixon, Albert Anis, and their colleagues—it has an amazing stylistic unity. Most of the buildings are splendid examples of the Art Deco style, ranging from angular, vertically emphatic early Art Deco to pared-down, neoclassically influenced Depression Moderne to the glamorous and more curvy, aerodynamic-looking style reminiscent of the era's big ocean liners. About a third of the structures are of the earlier Mediterranean Revival school.

■ OCEAN DRIVE *map page 266, B-3/6*

Ocean Drive is one of the liveliest stretches of roadway in America. Restaurants, hotels, and bars line its length, and pedestrians crowd it night and day. Along the main South Beach drag, traffic inches along from midday to dawn.

The easiest way to park is to turn your vehicle over to one of the many freelance valets who will take care of it for $14 per 24-hour period. A little south down Ocean Drive, a few lots charge half that amount. If you park at a meter, be aware that the meters are patrolled until midnight on South Beach, and at 25 cents for 15 minutes, you'll need a pound of quarters to keep from being issued an unwanted souvenir. At night, Caribbean and Latin music blasts from places like

Art Deco–style hotels line Miami Beach.

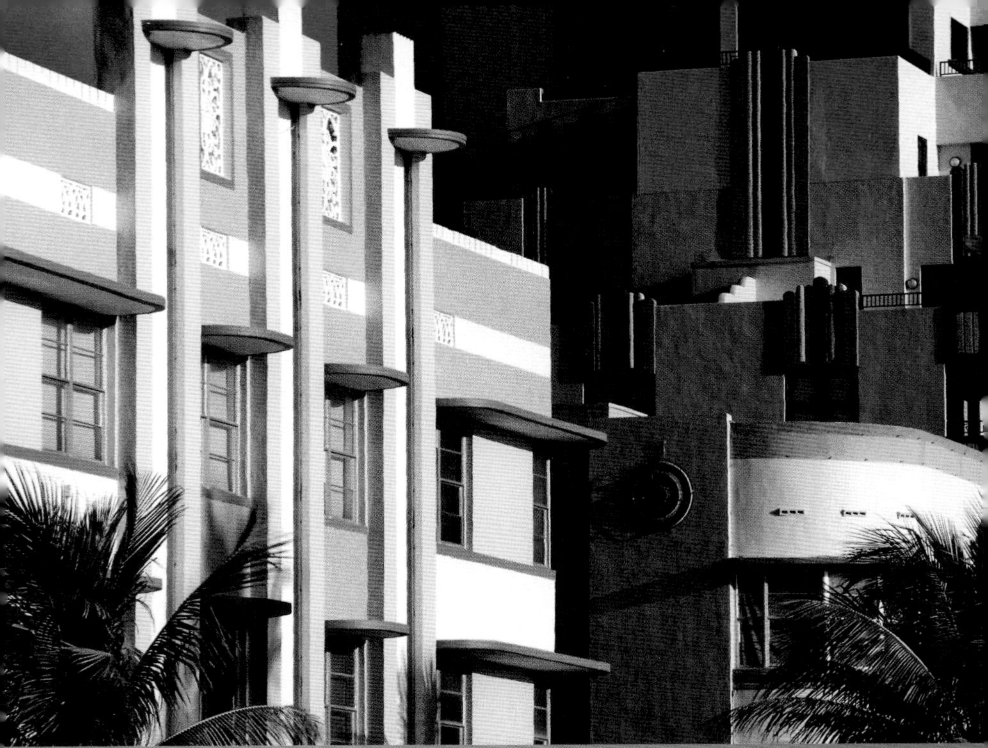
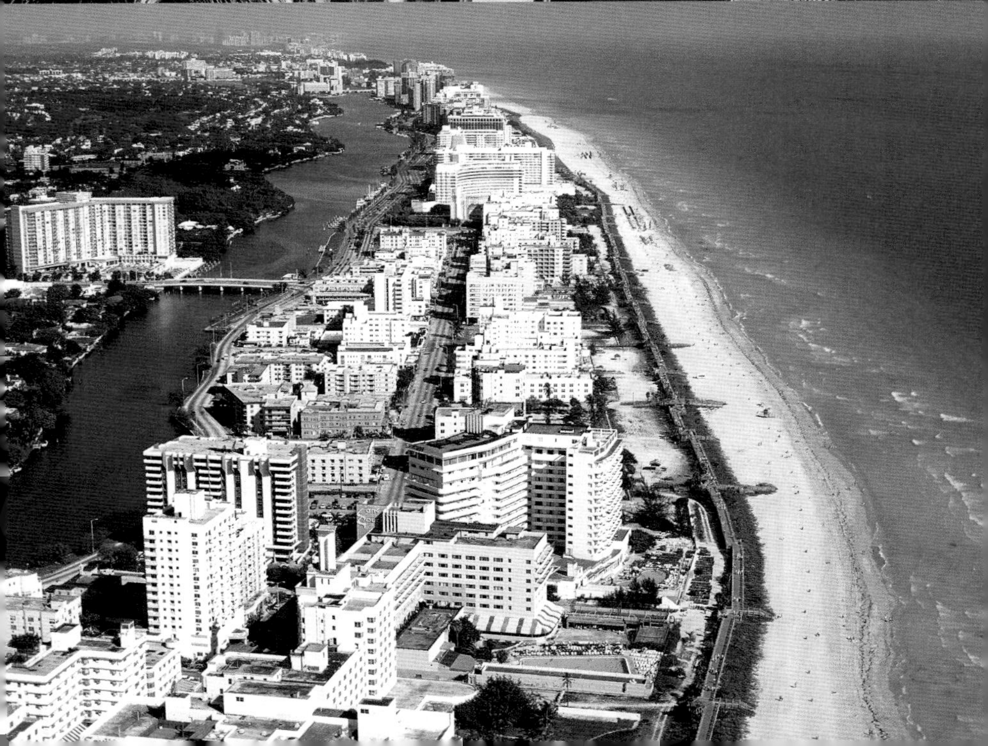

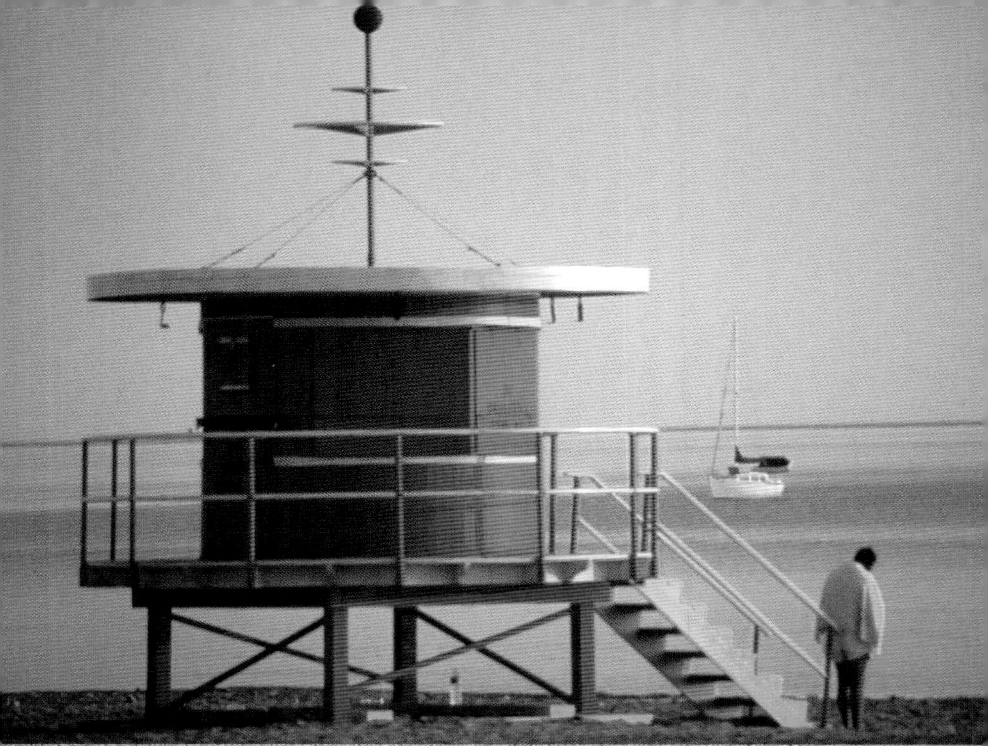
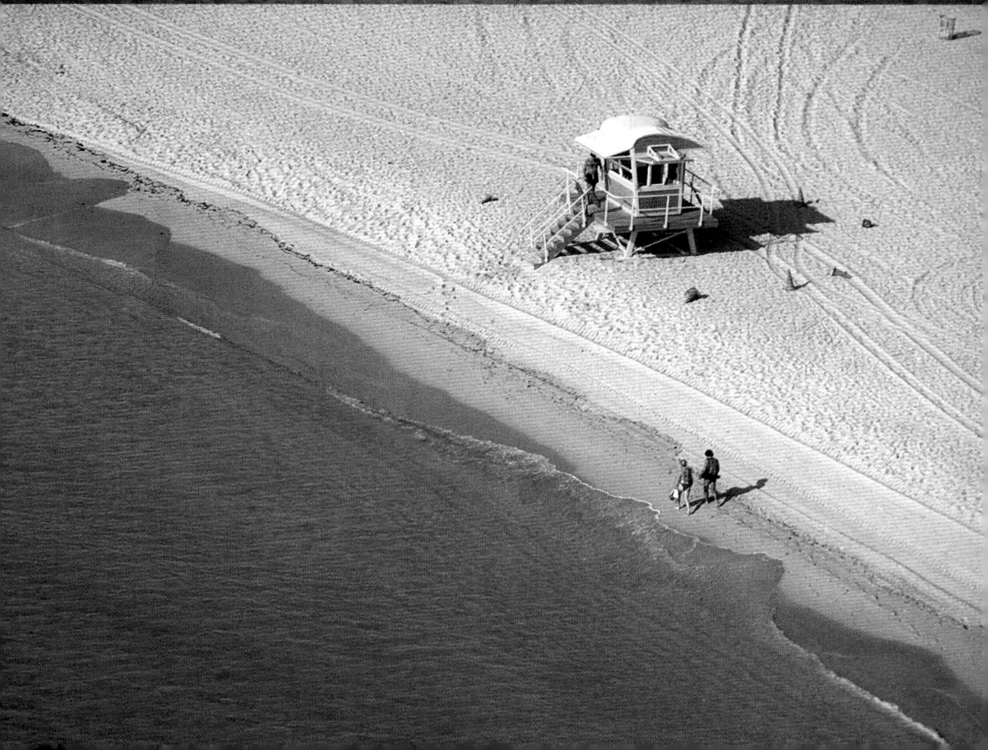

the Mango Bar, while hundreds of young people gather at the corner of 8th and Ocean Drive in front of Wet Willies—which continues to be the center of action. The warm tropical breezes that roll off the ocean just across the street make this one of the nation's preeminent people-watching streets, and it's not surprising that one of the hottest fashion magazines in the United States is named for it.

The road cuts between the famed sands of **Ocean Beach** and the strip of Art Deco structures rejuvenated into sprightly hotels with sidewalk cafés at their doorsteps. On the beach, sportsters parasail and wannabe models strut topless. The scene is reminiscent of Rio's fabled Copacabana. Rollerbladers zip along the sidewalk, sometimes skipping into the road to blade between cars stalled in traffic.

The celebrities who hang out at the cafés and on the beach are generally high-profile movie stars and rock musicians, unlike say, the rich and famous of staid Palm Beach. And those celebrities will likely flock to the newest Ocean Drive hot spot, one that has created an extraordinary buzz even before it opens. The late Gianni Versace's Ocean Drive mansion, **Casa Casuarina,** which was the site of the legendary designer's brutal murder in 1997, is being converted into a super-luxury boutique hotel where room prices will *start* at $2,000 a night.

■ **WASHINGTON AVENUE** *map page 266, B-2/6*
Two blocks west of Ocean Drive, Washington Avenue is alive (and then some) with the rhythms of the city's most popular nightclubs, from the intimate live jazz scene at **Jazid** (1342 Washington Avenue; 305-673-9372) to some of the country's most renowned large-scale dance venues. Two of the hottest dance options are **Crobar** (1445 Washington Avenue; 305-531-5027), the SoBe campus of the same-named Chicago club, and the massive **Level** (1235 Washington Avenue; 305-532-1525), a 44,000-square-foot techno dance cathedral housed in a 1937 Art Deco theater.

Given the area's international clientele and cosmopolitan flair, the line between straight dance clubs and gay dance clubs is blurry at best. One club might host hip-hop parties, gay nights, and retro nights all in the same week. Without a doubt, South Beach has one of the country's most vibrant gay social scenes (although it's often over-hyped in the popular media), which goes into high gear for annual dance music events, such as the Winter Music Conference and Miami's famed White Party. So ingrained in the area psyche is the local gay community

Lifeguards and beaches in South Beach.

that the Loews Hotel in South Beach even offers a new option for convention planners: a drag queen-hosted breakfast buffet.

Also on this street is the **Wolfsonian Foundation,** with its mind-boggling collection of decorative, graphic, architectural, and propaganda art from the late 19th to the early 20th century. *1001 Washington Avenue; 305-531-1001.*

Farther up the street are some impressive public buildings, including the Mediterranean Revival **Old City Hall,** at number 1130; and, at number 1300, the **U.S. Post Office,** whose sharp, square lines and glass-block windows characterize the Depression Moderne style of many WPA projects.

■ LINCOLN ROAD MALL   *map page 266, A-3*

Stretching 12 blocks from Collins Avenue to Bay Road, Lincoln Road is home to nearly 400 businesses, including discount stores on the east end and upscale chain stores and art dealers farther west. Several blocks have been closed to traffic, creating a pedestrian mall where restaurants post their menus out front so you can easily compare options as you stroll. You'll find parking, including a large public garage, along 17th Street, a block north of Lincoln Road.

Many of the old hotels nearby have been reborn in high chic, such as hotel impresario Ian Schrager's **Delano Hotel** (1685 Collins Avenue; 305-672-2000), with its winged towers (inspired by Aztec headdresses) and super-hip, all-white interiors by designer Philippe Starck. The stylish spot adds more than a dash of Manhattan sophistication to South Beach, which makes sense since Schrager's New York properties have become some of that city's hottest nightspots. **The Tides** (1220 Ocean Drive; 305-604-5070), owned by Island Records founder Chris Blackwell, is another stunning transformation. Suites come equipped with telescopes so guests can check out the beach action without leaving their rooms.

■ KEY BISCAYNE   *map page 254, B-2*

On Key Biscayne, Miami's barrier island greenery is once again in evidence. If the area is more exclusive than Miami, it's also more ordinary. The causeway that leads here first crosses Virginia Key and its Hobie Beach, a mecca for windsurfers and sailors. Flipper, the star of the old TV show, performs at the **Miami Seaquarium** with other dolphins in a set from *Flipper.* There are also shark and manatee exhibits and tropical fish aquariums. *4400 Rickenbacker Causeway; 305-361-5705.*

THE MYTH OF LATIN CUISINE

Menus all over South Florida tout something called "Latin cuisine," but there really is no such thing. Each Latin American country has a distinct cuisine, and to group all of them under one term is about as subtle as grouping French, German, Spanish, and Italian food under the heading "European cuisine." The cuisines of Latin America—Cuban, Argentine, Bolivian, Chilean, and so forth—are as different from one another as a Swedish smorgasbord is from Catalonian oxtail stew.

Of course, this mixing is nothing new. Though some celebrity chefs have been credited with creating New World Cuisine, or Nuevo Latino, the truth is that fusion cuisine goes way back. You might say it was invented the moment one of Columbus's sailors added *ajís* (hot peppers) and tomatoes to his salt-cod stew and sopped it up with *casabe* (manioc bread). Five hundred years later, the consequential concoction, *aporreao de bacalao,* is still considered delicious—even though today it's more likely to be sopped up with French bread than casabe.

The current trend has to do with refinement. Take the humble quesadilla, itself a prime example of early fusion cuisine: corn tortillas were native to the Americas before the cheese—which was made from milk from cows imported from Spain—was added. But today, with the addition of sliced duck breast or an infusion of basil, the quesadilla morphs into something quite contemporary, even flashy.

South Floridians can sample authentic Latin American cuisine—rather, the fusion of one or more of these cooking styles—without leaving their own backyards. The large numbers of immigrants who have settled here have brought their cuisines with them, with deliciously unique results. It's no surprise that restaurants heralding Cuban, Nicaraguan, Argentine, Mexican, and even Spanish fare dominate the local scene. Below are some of the major "Latin cuisines" available in Miami.

CUBAN

Spanish immigration into Cuba continued into the late 1950s, so the influence of Spanish cuisine on Cuban dishes is considerable. You'll detect this influence in the heavy soups, hearty stews, and many grain and legume dishes that would otherwise seem out of place in the native cuisine of a tropical island. Cuban meat dishes—usually pork, beef, or chicken—are often flavored with sour oranges, garlic, and spices, and are always served with black beans (the national dish), white rice, and plantains. A must-try is the classic Cuban sandwich, made of roast pork, baked ham, Swiss cheese, and sliced pickles on French bread flattened on a toasting grill. Top it off with a *cafecito,* a high-octane version of espresso.

NICARAGUAN

Nicaragua is famous for beef dishes of all kinds and for its *gallo pinto,* similar to the Cuban *congris,* for which red beans and rice are cooked together. The end result is quite different from the better-known Caribbean version of black beans and rice known as *moros y cristianos.* Nicaraguans also created the voluptuous *tres leches,* a sweet concoction made of cake soaked in a combination of cream, milk, and condensed milk and topped with meringue. Tres leches has replaced flan as the dessert of choice among Latinos.

ARGENTINE

Lean, Argentine-raised beef is world famous for its deep, meaty flavor. Owing to large-scale Italian immigration to Argentina, many Argentine restaurants have an Italian flair. The meal starts with an antipasto, followed by pasta, then moves on to grilled meat accompanied by any of a variety of large salads. After a pause, dessert that involves *dulce de leche* (candied milk), in some form or another, is consumed. (Love of this sweet has moved north: dulce de leche is one of the top-selling Häagen-Dazs ice-cream flavors in the United States.)

BRAZILIAN

The cuisine of Brazil combines African dishes and root vegetables, and there is an indelible Portuguese influence. The food boldly recalls West Africa in its use of *dendé* (orange palm oil), malagueta peppers, and coconut milk, and Portugal in the *linguiça* sausage and kale used in hearty soups. There is also the tradition of the *rodezio,* in which meats of all sorts and styles come to the table skewered on long swords in an endless parade of delicacies. Rodezio-type restaurants also display enormous buffets of salads, vegetables, and other seemingly unrelated side dishes.

CHILEAN

Spanish influences mingle with those of the native Mapuche Indians in Chilean cuisine, which has also been influenced by other European cultures—namely Irish and German—through immigration. Given Chile's 3,000 miles of coastline, it's not surprising that fish and shellfish are dietary staples, and a mild climate and gentle topography mean plenty of vegetables and fruits, too. One of the most delicious dishes in the Chilean repertoire is *pastel de choclo,* a casserole of fresh, tender, creamy ground corn, ground beef, and roast chicken.

PERUVIAN

Potatoes have grown in Peru in infinite variety since the days of the Incas, and the indigenous *papa* (potato) remains a staple in the diet of residents of the high sierra of the Andes. *Papas a la huancaína* combines boiled potatoes with a zesty cheese and chili sauce; *causa limeña* is a combination of mashed potatoes, shrimp, olives, cheese, *yuca* (cassava, or manioc root), and hard-boiled eggs. These dishes combine the ancient papa with ingredients like cheese and olives, unknown in the Americas before the Spanish conquest.

—by Viviana Carballo

Cuban-born Viviana Carballo, a Miami-based food writer and restaurant critic, is a former columnist for the *Miami Herald* and *El Nuevo Herald* and is a regular contributor to *Cooking Light* magazine.

Crandon Park (4000 Crandon Boulevard; 305-361-5421) may well be Miami's best beach. The sand is the whitest, the water the cleanest, the facilities the most complete of any in the area. They include a golf course, tennis courts, baseball fields, soccer fields, bike path, volleyball courts, playground, and marina. The **Tennis Center at Crandon Park** (7300 Crandon Boulevard; 305-365-2300) hosts the Lipton Championships in March. The public can also use its 17 paved, eight clay, and two grass courts.

Another park rounds the south end of the island. **Bill Baggs Cape Florida State Park** may not be as aesthetically and recreationally pleasing as Crandon, but it has a lot to tell about local history. Built in 1846, its **Cape Florida Lighthouse** is South Florida's oldest standing structure and the state's oldest surviving lighthouse. The park itself demonstrates the impact of Miami's most important event in recent history—Hurricane Andrew of August 1992. Key Biscayne took the brunt of the storm's fury. Biscayne's beaches suffered disastrously, but they have come back better than before. Some folks now identify Andrew as a blessing in disguise, because the non-native Australian pines, which were destroying the native fauna, were leveled. Today, the park has been replanted with palms, sea grapes, and other indigenous plants. *1200 Crandon Boulevard; 305-361-5811.*

The beach at Sonesta Beach Resort on Key Biscayne.

■ CORAL GABLES *map page 266, A-6*

The realized vision of developer George Merrick, Coral Gables was one of the world's first fully planned communities. With the **Biltmore Hotel** as its centerpiece, Coral Gables was built of stucco and quarried limestone in Spanish Colonial Revival style during the 1920s. Huge shade trees drape over wide avenues of what is today one of metropolitan Miami's premier restaurant and shopping areas, home to art galleries, theaters, and the University of Miami. Coral gateways mark the town's boundaries.

Exhibits at the **Coral Gables Merrick House** trace the city's history and Merrick's childhood. *907 Coral Way; 305-460-5361.*

Out of the quarry that provided stone for many of Coral Gables's homes, Merrick fashioned the **Venetian Pool.** Listed on the National Register of Historic Places, the 1923 landmark is like a movie set, with its faux-Venice stylings, caves, lush foliage, stone bridges, and waterfalls. William Jennings Bryant once lectured here on the merits of living in Coral Gables, America's new ideal community. *2701 DeSoto Boulevard; 305-460-5356.*

■ COCONUT GROVE *map page 265, B-5*

The Grove, as it's called in Miami-speak, is among the city's most fashionable neighborhoods. Its boutiques, clubs, restaurants, and street festivals make it the chic place to be on Friday night or Saturday afternoon or evening. The Grove began as a community of Bahamian immigrants and was known once as Kebo. The Bahamians are still around, and so are their festivals. The big one is June's **Goombay Festival,** the largest black-culture festival in the United States, featuring a sailing regatta and Junkanoo bands—Bahamian folk groups that parade in elaborate garb while playing whistles and goat-skin drums.

Commodore Ralph Middleton Munroe founded Coconut Grove as a stylish neighborhood in the 1890s. The highlight of the **Barnacle State Historic Site** is Munroe's unusual cone-shaped home. *3485 Main Highway; 305-448-9445.*

The **Museum of Science & Space Transit Planetarium** is known for its bird-rehabilitation facilities, with more than 140 live animals, and other permanent and special exhibits. The planetarium hosts astronomy and laser shows; visitors are also free to use telescopes. *3280 South Miami Avenue; 305-646-4200.*

George Merrick constructed the exquisite Venetian Pool in Coral Gables in 1923.

Vizcaya Museum and Gardens in Coconut Grove reflects South Florida's romance with all things Mediterranean.

James Deering, International Harvester mogul, built a monument for himself here. His **Vizcaya Museum and Gardens** reflect his affection for Italian palazzos. The museum's 34 rooms are dense with art and expensive furniture. Outdoors, sculptured European gardens juxtapose with the gnarled, tangled wildlife of a South Florida hammock. *3251 South Miami Avenue; 305-250-9133.*

■ HOMESTEAD AND BISCAYNE NATIONAL PARK
map page 254, A/B-3/4

The landscape becomes decidedly more rural and agricultural by the time one reaches Homestead, Florida City, and environs. Situated in Florida's warmest and most fertile region, the area is the largest producer of tropical fruits and vegetables in the United States. If tasting is believing, visit the **Fruit and Spice Farm** near Homestead. *24801 SW 187th Avenue; 305-247-5727.*

Homestead is poised on a crossroads between the Keys, the Everglades, and beautiful **Biscayne National Park,** which comprises a strip of coastline, some islands, and more than 170,000 acres of sparkling waters. With its astonishingly clear water and glorious technicolor reefs, Biscayne is a paradise for divers and snorkelers. It's thanks to Biscayne's mangrove coast that the water is so clear: red and black mangroves trap eroded soil in their tangled roots and also protect the mainland from storms and hurricanes. The **Convoy Point Visitors Center** offers guided nature walks and snorkeling, scuba diving, glass-bottom boat tours of the park, and transportation to offshore Elliott Key. *9700 328th Street; 305-230-7275.*

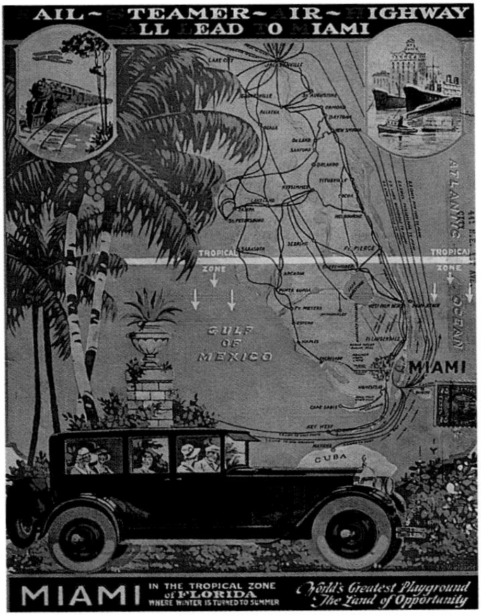
TROPICAL ZONE
GULF OF MEXICO
ATLANTIC OCEAN
MIAMI
CUBA
MIAMI
IN THE TROPICAL ZONE of FLORIDA
WHERE WINTER IS TURNED TO SUMMER
World's Greatest Playground
The Land of Opportunity
A '20s postcard touts Miami as a winter paradise.

South of Homestead on Route 9336, the road traverses the farmlands of southern Dade County. A different kind of farm lies at the edge of the Everglades. **Everglades Alligator Farm** raises alligators for their meat and skin. The farm offers 30-minute airboat rides, which give passengers the opportunity to see alligators, hawks, ospreys, and roseate spoonbills. *40351 SW 192nd Avenue; 305-247-2628.*

■ Travel Basics

Getting Around: Most people visiting South Florida fly into Miami International Airport. Other cities in this part of the state with major airports include West Palm Beach and Fort Lauderdale. U.S. 1 and the more scenic Route A1A run parallel to the coast and are both notoriously slow. The speedier alternatives are inland: I-95 and Florida's Turnpike.

Climate: The subtropical climate of this region imposes long, warm, and very humid summers (75°F to 95°F) and mild, dry winters (55°F to 80°F). Summer is the rainiest season, but precipitation can vary greatly from year to year. Hurricanes are a threat between June and October, although they rarely make landfall. Thunderstorms occur any time of the year but are most frequent during the summer.

EVERGLADES

■ OVERVIEW

The Everglades is a vast expanse of wetland forest and prairie known for exotic flora, marvelous birds, and alligators. Few back roads lead into the Everglades. To see the area, drive to access areas near the Everglades National Park visitors centers, park your car, and hike, canoe, or bicycle out into the wetlands. This is a place of great natural beauty, where you can experience a vast wilderness area unique in the world.

■ LAKE AND LANDSCAPE

The Everglades is, without a doubt, one of the world's most poignantly beautiful landscapes—vast wetlands, part prairie, part forest, stretching as far as the eye can see below an unbroken horizon of translucent sky marked by white and silver clouds. The amount of water varies enormously by season. Archie Carr writes in *The Everglades, The American Wilderness:*

> In the Everglades, the pendulum of the seasons swings in a wide arc between flood and drought, producing alternating periods of fecundity and barrenness. From early spring well into autumn, the Glades are usually kept flushed by ample rainfall, annually averaging about 50 inches. But by November the last drenching tropical storm of the year has gone, and its passage signals the start of the dry season, a time of trial for the creatures of the Glades.

Several different but overlapping environments exist here. In the area just southwest of Lake Okeechobee, cypress "islands" tower over surrounding dwarf cypress. The taller trees grow where the limestone bedrock has crumbled, leaving pockets of soggy, extremely fertile soil.

In the Shark River Slough, a silent, slow-moving river flows through saw grass prairie during the wet season, then dries to a few narrow channels in the winter. Hardwood hammocks of royal palms, mahogany, and slash pines rise above grass, providing habitat for deer, panthers, and bears. The 12-foot-high saw grass is so tough it takes a hurricane to flatten it.

The Unique Everglades Habitat

The Everglades provides the largest wetland habitat in North America, protecting 600 species of animals. ① Wood storks serve as a barometer for the health of the Everglades, as they come to nest only when the water level during the dry season yields enough concentrated food to sustain them. Other signature birds of the Glades are the ② Everglades snail kite, which feeds only on apple snails, and the ③ ibis (called the Chokoloskee chicken by pioneers who liked to eat them). Among the most spectacular birds of this wetland are the ④ great white heron and ⑤ the beautiful roseate spoonbill. The most elusive and endangered species in the Everglades is the sleek ⑥ Florida panther. About 50 of these large cats (relatives of the Western cougar) survive north of Everglades City.

Largemouth bass, crayfish, tarpon, snook, and bluegill, share freshwater saw grass rivers with ⑦ alligators, the largest reptile in North America. Male alligators can grow to 16 feet in length and are known for the ferocious clamp of their jaws. Their saltwater relative, the ⑧ crocodile, lives among the keys at the southern end of the Florida peninsula. The bulbous, gentle ⑨ manatee swims in these rivers and estuaries but is rarely seen because Everglades water is dark. These vegetarians are relatives of the elephants and have been known to reach 3,000 pounds. ⑩ Loggerhead turtles, ⑪ ospreys, and ⑫ southern bald eagles thrive near the dense impenetrable islands formed by ⑬ mangroves, a unique tree that roots on oyster bars and forms islands in salt water.

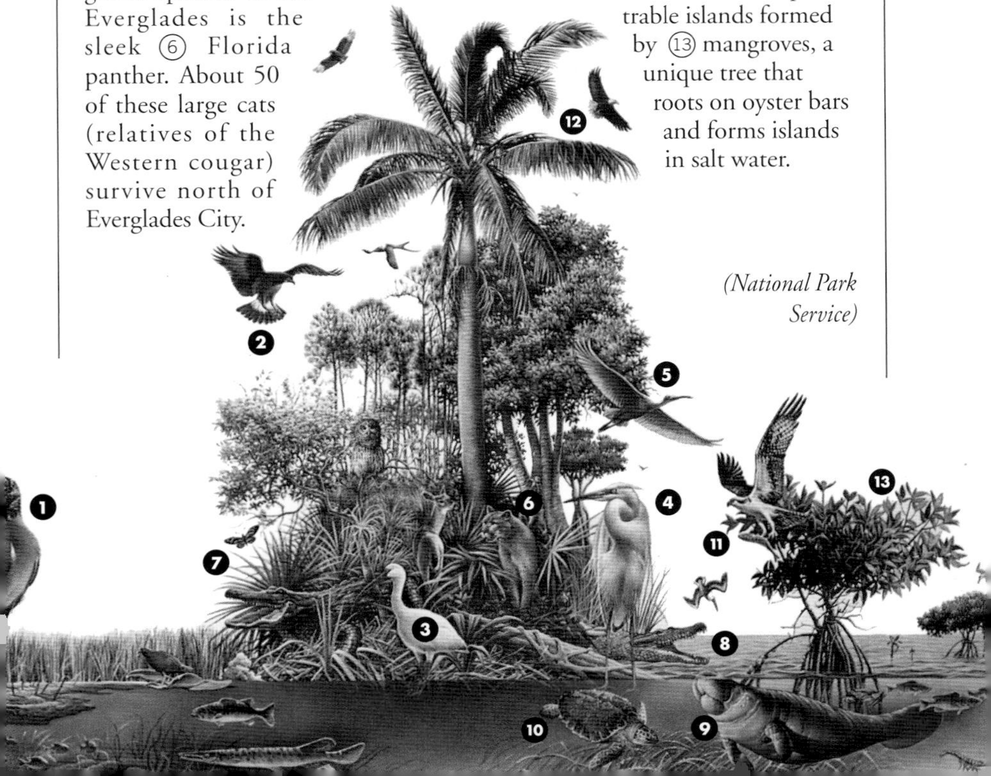
12
2
5
13
1
6
4
7
11
3
8
10
9

(National Park Service)

Along the intricate waterways of the Ten Thousand Islands, at the western perimeters of the park, mangroves pitch their roots on shell bars, forming new islands.

■ FOUNDING OF THE PARK

In 1947, Marjorie Stoneman Douglas penned her influential book *The Everglades: River of Grass,* an examination of what was happening to Florida's "down under" as a consequence of the dredging and draining of wetlands. The book helped convince Congress and President Truman to create what is now the second-largest national park in the contiguous United States and our largest subtropical wilderness. Its 2,100 square miles of wetlands shelter more than 600 types of fish and 300 bird species, and contain the largest mangrove forest in the world. Toxic runoff and habitat degradation continue to take a deadly toll on the fragile Everglades ecology, yet the Glades remains, thanks to the valiant efforts of the National Park Service, an intriguing place to visit.

■ EVERGLADES: EAST   *map page 287, C/D-4*

The **East Entrance** to Everglades National Park lies just southwest of Miami and Florida City on Route 9336. As the view from the Everglades roads is limited by the flatness of the land and car-high grass and shrubs, it's important to follow one of the trails and spend time listening closely to the watery rhythm of the Glades to get a sense of the beauty of this place.

Outside the east entrance gate, the **Ernest F. Coe Visitors Center,** named for the man who proposed making a park of the Everglades, contains exhibits that focus on Glades wildlife. You won't get the mystery here, or the beauty, but you will understand the wilderness better. One exhibit identifies the calls of cricket frogs and limpkins. Another discusses water management from many perspectives, including those of the fisherman, farmer, and conservationist. Pick up a trail map here. *305-242-7700.*

Four miles down the road, take a well-marked turnoff to find The **Royal Palm Visitors Center** and the starting point for two interpretive trails. Less than a mile long, the **Gumbo Limbo Trail** is lined with orchids and royal palms; the equally short **Anhinga Trail** usually provides a chance to spot alligators, turtles, snakes, and anhingas, also known as snake birds because of the way they slither through the water with only their necks exposed.

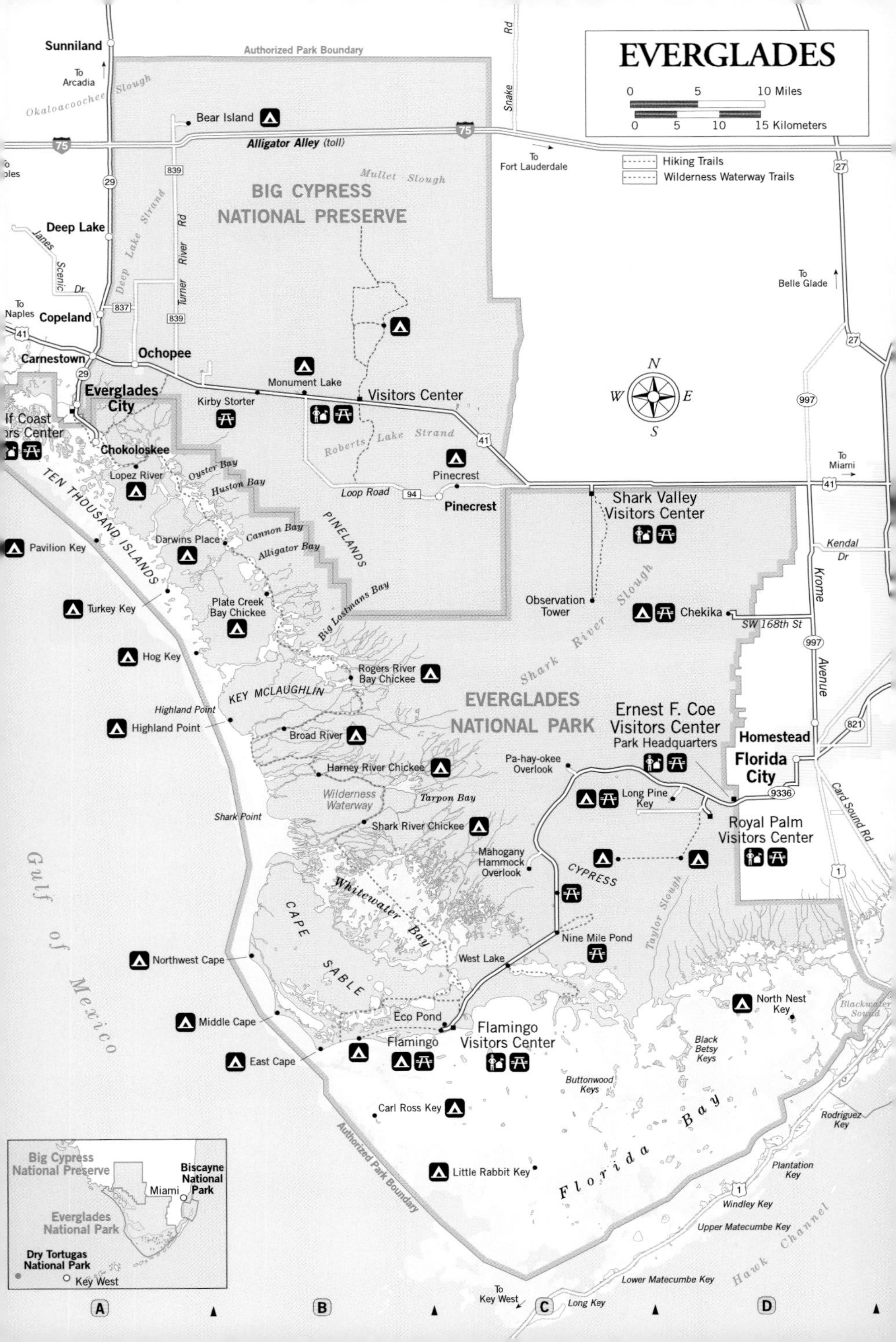

EVERGLADES
0 5 10 Miles
0 5 10 15 Kilometers
Hiking Trails
Wilderness Waterway Trails
Authorized Park Boundary
Sunniland
To Arcadia
Okaloacoochee Slough
Bear Island
Alligator Alley (toll)
To Fort Lauderdale
Snake Rd
Mullet Slough
BIG CYPRESS NATIONAL PRESERVE
Deep Lake
Janes Scenic Dr
Deep Lake Strand
Turner River Rd
To Naples
Copeland
Carnestown
Ochopee
Everglades City
Chokoloskee
Kirby Storter
Monument Lake
Visitors Center
Roberts Lake Strand
Pinecrest
Loop Road
To Belle Glade
To Miami
Shark Valley Visitors Center
Observation Tower
Chekika
SW 168th St
Kendal Dr
Krome Avenue
TEN THOUSAND ISLANDS
Lopez River
Oyster Bay
Huston Bay
Cannon Bay
Alligator Bay
Darwins Place
Pavilion Key
PINELANDS
Big Lostmans Bay
Turkey Key
Plate Creek Bay Chickee
Hog Key
Shark River Slough
Rogers River Bay Chickee
KEY McLAUGHLIN
Highland Point
EVERGLADES NATIONAL PARK
Ernest F. Coe Visitors Center
Park Headquarters
Homestead
Florida City
Broad River
Harney River Chickee
Pa-hay-okee Overlook
Long Pine Key
Wilderness Waterway
Tarpon Bay
Shark Point
Shark River Chickee
Royal Palm Visitors Center
Card Sound Rd
Mahogany Hammock Overlook
CYPRESS
Gulf of Mexico
Whitewater Bay
CAPE SABLE
Taylor Slough
Nine Mile Pond
Northwest Cape
West Lake
Middle Cape
Eco Pond
Flamingo
Flamingo Visitors Center
North Nest Key
Blackwater Sound
East Cape
Black Betsy Keys
Buttonwood Keys
Carl Ross Key
Florida Bay
Rodriguez Key
Little Rabbit Key
Plantation Key
Windley Key
Upper Matecumbe Key
Hawk Channel
Lower Matecumbe Key
To Key West
Long Key
Big Cypress National Preserve
Biscayne National Park
Miami
Everglades National Park
Dry Tortugas National Park
Key West
A
B
C
D

A great white heron rests among hardwood trees and red mangroves.

Three miles past Royal Palm on Route 9336, **Pinelands** is the starting point for a short trail that penetrates towering slash pine habitat.

At **Pa-hay-okee Overlook,** 13 miles inside the park, a boardwalk leads to an observation tower above a saw grass prairie and cypress stands. **Mahogany Hammock,** a boardwalk trail 7 miles down the road from Pa-hay-okee, traverses dense jungle and passes the largest living mahogany tree in the United States.

At **Flamingo Visitors Center**, at the end of the road at Florida Bay, a marina and motel complex have replaced a fishing village once accessible only by boat. You can book sight-seeing cruises, tram tours, and fishing boat charters here and rent canoes, boats, and bicycles. Campgrounds, cottages, motel rooms, and dining at the Flamingo Lodge provide creature comforts in this vast, challenging wilderness. *941-695-2945.*

Wilderness canoeists have access to the 99-mile **Wilderness Waterway** trail through rivers and bays, from Flamingo to Everglades City. Campsites are set up all along the route. *941-695-2945.*

Eco Pond, a short walk west of Flamingo, is the place to go to spy roseate spoonbills and other wading birds.

■ SHARK VALLEY *map page 287, C-3*

Shark Valley is a marvelous wet prairie. A 15-mile loop road into the Shark River Slough extends from the visitors center parking lot. On either side of this flat road is saw grass prairie growing in water; rising above the prairie are hardwood hammocks. Alligators can easily be spotted lying half submerged in the narrow waterway along the west side of the trail. In the trees and walking through the prairie are all manner of waterbirds, including egrets, herons, and ibis. You can take a tram along the route, walk, or rent a bike by the parking lot. Bicyclists are sometimes startled by gators sunbathing right alongside the path. *About 25 miles west of Miami on U.S. 41, the Tamiami Trail; 305-221-8455.*

■ TEN THOUSAND ISLANDS AREA *map page 287, A-3/4*

Ten Thousand Islands refers to a labyrinth of islands extending down Florida's western coast south of Naples and Marco Island. Shallow, dark waters wash against islands formed by mangroves on oyster bars, most of them impenetrable. In the

(above) An alligator lurking in Shark Valley.
(following pages) An aerial view over a typical Everglades landscape.

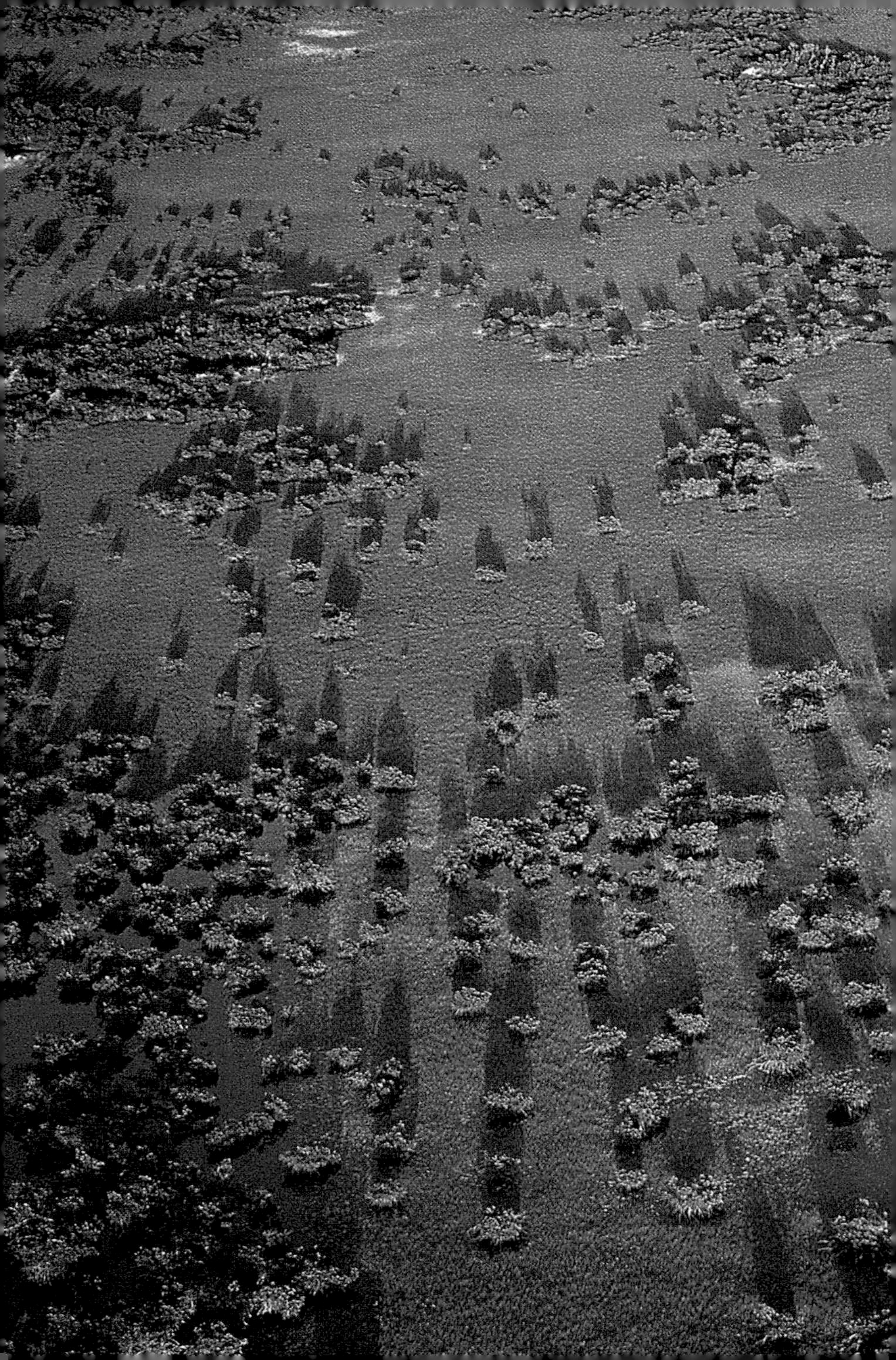

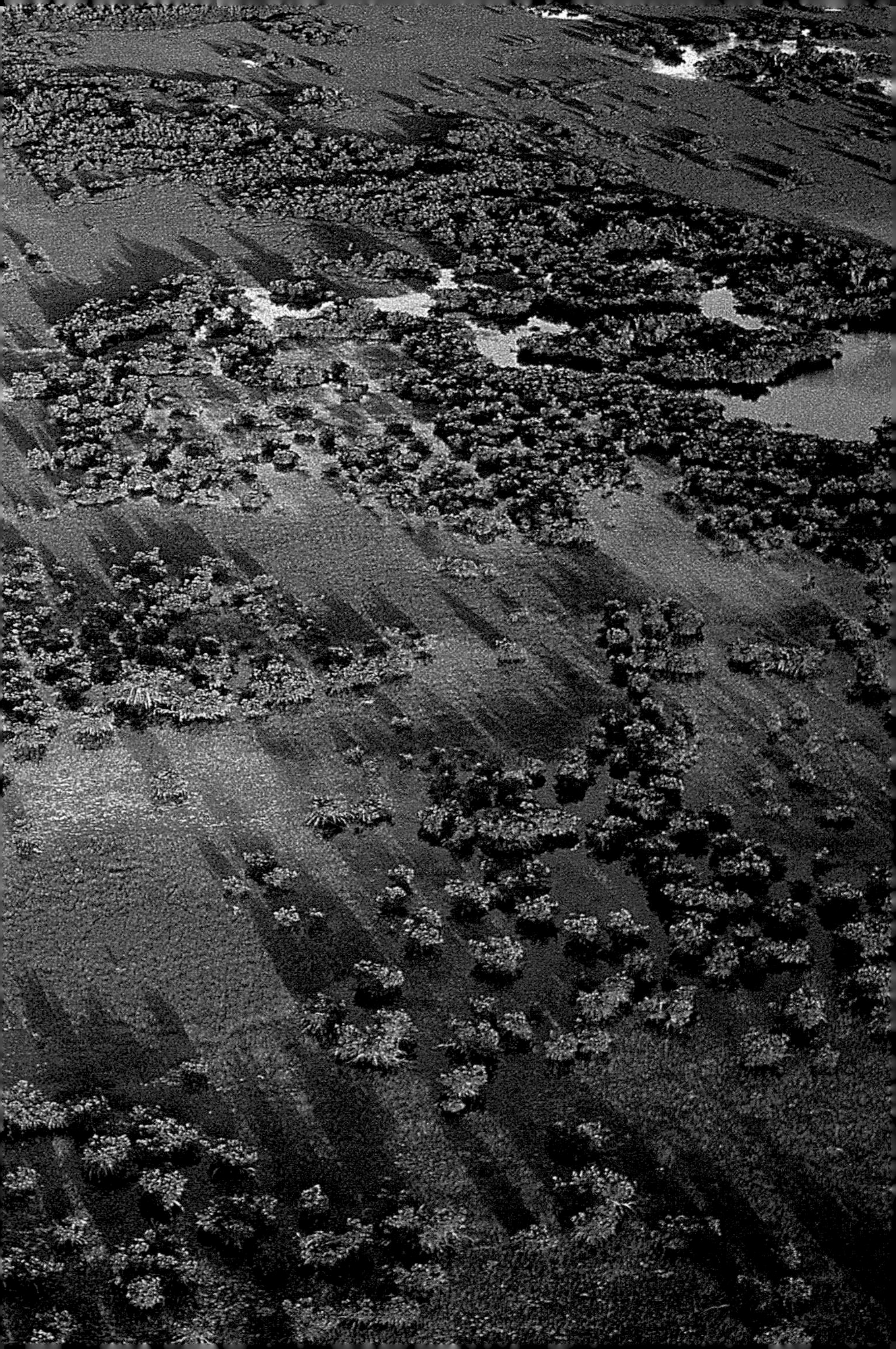

Mangroves have formed many of the islands in the Ten Thousand Islands area.

waters swim stingrays, innumerable fish, and, near the estuaries, alligators and manatees. Exotic birds are easy to spot, as this region is home to herons, ospreys, eagles, egrets, ibis, roseate spoonbills, purple gallinules, and more. The birds come to live among the thick, protective mangroves that thrive here.

The late Totch Brown, a native of this area, once pointed out to me a mangrove island, 20 feet across, in a sea of backwater keys. "When I was 11, I stuck a ring of bobs into an oyster bar and that became Totch Key," he told me.

The formation of an intracoastal island is easily understood. Take one exposed or shallow oyster bar and a few green, torpedolike mangrove tree pods, then bake in the Florida sun for 20 or so years. Just one tree can make an island: as a tree grows, its leggy root structure begins to trap detritus and silt, and barnacles and oysters set up housekeeping there, attaching themselves to roots. As more bobbing mangrove seeds fall from the mature tree and sink their roots into backwater muck at the fringes, the sediment at the forest's center solidifies. Though this process may be simple, it's also a miracle, because the trees that form these islands grow in salt water.

At first glance, mangroves look forbidding—hulking, scraggly shapes whose spiderlike roots arch in impenetrable tangles above the water. Yet their resilience in the face of high winds and waves is far superior to any man-made concrete seawall. Old-timers will tell you that if you don't have time to seek out higher, safer ground, the best place to ride out a hurricane is amid a mangrove forest.

Mangroves also provide shelter and food for the local fauna. One acre of leggy red mangroves drops more than four tons of leaves each year. Once processed by bacteria and fungi, the protein-rich leaves become food for the tiniest crustaceans that find shelter among the roots. These minuscule creatures are in turn food for crabs, beach fleas, shrimp, and barnacles, which themselves make a tasty dinner for the birds that balance on the mangrove's crooked limbs, or the sea creatures that lurk beneath. It has been estimated that up to 98 percent of Florida's commercial fish spend part of their life among the mangroves.

There are three different types of mangrove: red, black, and white. Called "walking trees" by Indians, **red mangroves** have exposed, reddish roots that drop from trunks and limbs above into the water below. Those aerial roots pick up atmospheric oxygen from the air, because there's little to be had in the constantly flooded soil below. The salt-resistant roots branch out farther below the water's surface and interlace, forming a cagelike structure with countless anchors in the mud. Red mangroves have narrow, thick green leaves; in spring, tufted yellow blossoms bloom. By summer, the flowers are replaced by a small fruit that sprouts a foot-long seedling (really a rudimentary tree). These then fall off, ready to root.

Black mangroves usually grow just behind and a foot or so above red mangroves. These shrublike trees have dark brown bark and small white blossoms. Black mangroves adapted to the oxygen-deficient soil by developing the pneumataphore, an extension of the root that reaches above the soil surface to exchange gasses. In the interior of mangrove forests, these black projections can cover the ground. Black mangrove leaves have glands that excrete salt, enabling the tree to grow in saline environments. Early settlers used the leaves to salt their food.

A variety of buttonwood, **white mangroves** usually grow a few feet above red or black mangroves, but like them can tolerate salt water, wind spray, and occasional high tides. Very occasionally, they will sprout pneumataphores and aerial roots under duress. The two salt-excreting glands (petioles) on each leaf stem near the leaf distinguish this tree.

■ EVERGLADES: WEST   *map page 287, A-2/5*

The main access to this area lies through Everglades City, located 3 miles south of the junction of U.S. 41 (Tamiami Trail) and Route 29. The town has long been a sportsmen's haven, a "y'all" kind of place where social status doesn't seem to matter. The area is open, almost parklike, with houses set far apart and built up one story off the ground. Frog legs and alligator tail are served at the local restaurants, including the **Rod & Gun Club** (200 Broadway, off Route 29; 941-695-2101), an Old South survivor, circa 1864. Built as a residence for a pioneer, this three-story white clapboard building later became a prestigious fishing and hunting club; today it's a roomy, comfortable inn, with a wood-panel interior, clubby furnishings, and an alligator hide and a bear skin hanging on the walls. Except for the club, though, the town is mostly down-home.

Drive around the traffic circle in the center of town and on down to the **Gulf Coast Visitors Center** (941-695-3311). If you follow the road across the causeway, you'll arrive on Chokoloskee Island, which still feels like rough-and-ready frontier land. **Ted Smallwood's Store and Museum** (941-695-2989), on Chokoloskee Road, was named for the pioneer who first settled here. The life and times of Smallwood were immortalized by Peter Matthiessen in *Killing Mr. Watson*, a fictionalized account of the slaying of a suspected outlaw on the island's muddy banks.

(above) The Rod & Gun Club in Everglades City. (opposite) Paurotis palms in a mahogany hammock.

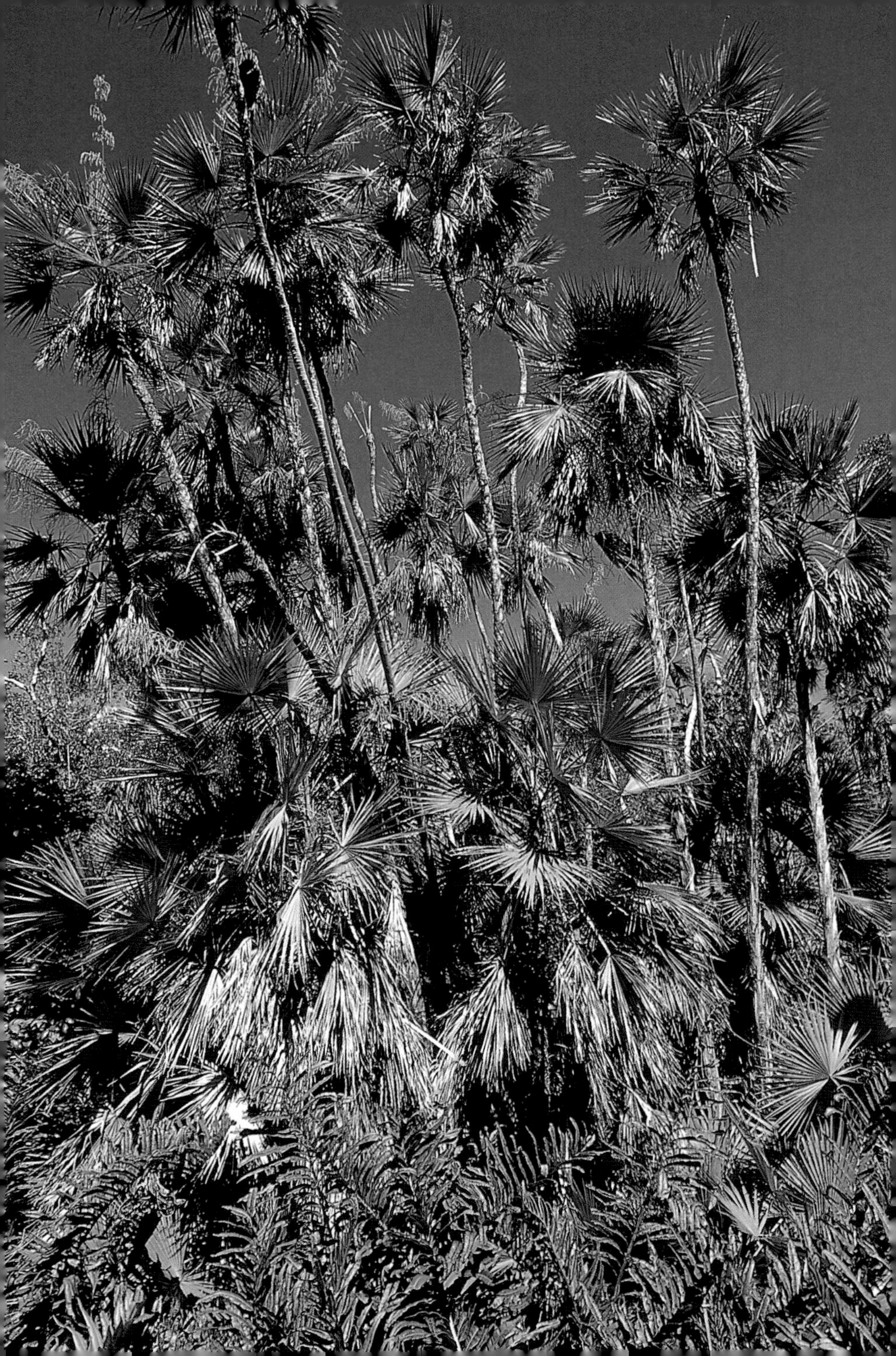

■ TEN THOUSAND ISLANDS BOAT TOURS

Just past Everglades City at the Gulf Coast Visitors Center, you can catch an informative boat tour led by a park ranger. A tour is essential if you want to truly experience this area and see the countless waterbirds that live here, fishing in the brackish, dark waters and living on the mangrove islands. The rangers are enthusiastic and extremely knowledgeable; one even passed out black mangrove leaves for passengers to lick—the salty tang of the leaves demonstrating that this tree's strategy for growth in salt water is to excrete the salt through its leaves. On the same trip, our guide pointed out a bald eagle (they love to eat baby alligators) and a pair of "newlyweds," ospreys who spent all day on a nest. **Everglades National Park Boat Tours** also rents canoes and provides shuttle service. *941-695-2591, or in Florida only 800-445-7724.*

Local outfitters also run guided tours within the park. One of these, **Majestic Everglades Excursions,** taught me more than I could have hoped about Everglades wildlife. On their pontoon boat tour, we passed obscure birding and wildlife-sighting spots. The dolphins we saw on the tour didn't disappoint us either: a playful family of dolphins came alongside, and we began thumping on the sides of the boat. They actually peeked up at us, slapping their bottlenoses against the waves and seeming—as they always do—to smile. In a white mangrove tree, two screeching ospreys were setting up housekeeping in their nest—the same one to which they return every year to raise their young. *941-695-2777.*

■ WILDERNESS WATERWAY *map page 287, B-4*

A marked, 99-mile canoe trail snakes its way from Everglades City to the Flamingo Visitors Center at the south eastside access. It's a grand adventure, but not one to be undertaken lightly. The islands are not rounded in shape, but narrow and twisted, with arms reaching this way and that, meaning that you can't easily navigate around them. They all look alike, and the same on every side: low, green, and covered with dense mangroves. Although a few islands have beaches, most are impenetrable tangles of mangrove roots. There's no freshwater to drink, and tides change radically, which can make paddling back to a landing area close to impossible. These aren't waters you'd want to swim in, as stingrays, sharks, and a few alligators live here. On the other hand, the fishing is excellent. Tarpon, snapper, and snook abound, as do stone crabs (although you'd need a pot to catch the latter).

A wood stork scopes out the Everglades.

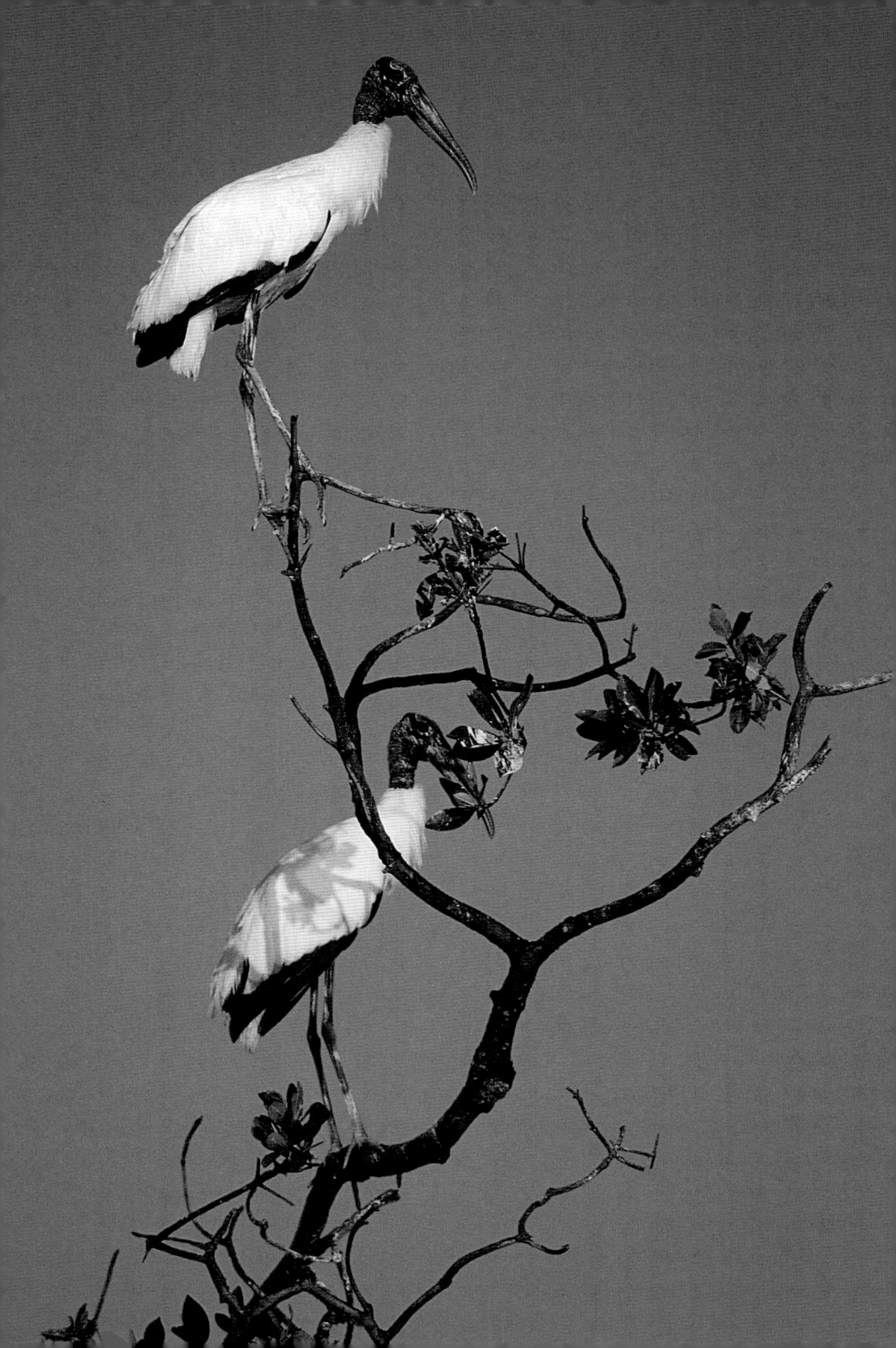

BIRDS OF FLORIDA

Great blue heron

American anhinga

White ibis

On some landing spots, chickee (Indian thatched) huts provide primitive shelter for campers, who must file a plan with the ranger's office before setting out. Those who are less ambitious can rent a houseboat or make shorter small boat trips.

■ SIGNATURE ANIMALS OF THE EVERGLADES

The **panther,** a relative of the Western mountain lion or cougar (distinguished by its cowlick and crooked tail) is rarely sighted, and when it is, it's most often crossing the road at Big Cypress, a sanctuary at the northern end of the Everglades. Panthers are large cats whose fur is the color of a golden retriever. Along Route 29 from I-75 to Everglades City, you'll see many "PANTHER CROSSING" signs, but it's unlikely you'll see any animals crossing the road. Only about 50 members of this endangered species are believed to live in this area.

Lurking in the narrow, dark rivers along the roads, **alligators** are abundant and fairly easy to see in the Everglades, although most of the time they just lie there, unmoving. Adults can measure nine to 16 feet and in the wild live about 35 years. Their feeding mechanism is triggered by the sound of movement—especially flapping or stumbling in water. When they hear this they move close, whack an animal with their tail, and scoop it into their mouth. The snapping and closing power of an alligator's jaws is phenomenal, and yet the opening muscles are relatively

Osprey

Great egret

Wood stork

weak, making it possible for a strong person to hold an alligator's mouth shut.

A female alligator lays eggs in a mound of earth. Few hatch, because eggs (and baby alligators) are a favored food of turtles, ospreys, eagles, male alligators, and raccoons. Small gators can be seen in the pond at the end of the boardwalk at Big Cypress Bend, just west of the Everglades City turnoff on U.S. 41. Large alligators can sometimes be sighted along the Turner River. (Take the unpaved road that leads north of U.S. 41 at the H. P. Williams Roadside Park.)

The saltwater-tolerant **crocodile** is more aggressive than the alligator, but rarely seen.

■ TRAVEL BASICS

Getting There: Parts of the Everglades are within easy driving distance of Miami, making a day trip feasible. To really see the Everglades, however, it's best to stay overnight in one of the small towns near the main park. From the southeast: Route 9336 begins at Florida City and penetrates 40 miles into the park. It passes trailheads and interpretive centers, then dead-ends at Flamingo, on Florida Bay, where you'll find a marina, motel, campgrounds, and restaurants. Shark Valley and the west entrances are reached by I-75 or the Tamiami Trail. At Everglades City, take a boat tour of the islands with the National Park Service.

Climate: October through April is the best time to visit. In summer, the heat, humidity, and bugs are overwhelming.

THE KEYS

Overview

A string of narrow islands lush with tropical vegetation, the Keys curve southwest into the blue waters of the Gulf of Mexico, beckoning divers, snorkelers, fishermen, and an eclectic group of travelers. Physical disconnection from the mainland fosters a psychological disconnection, and the Keys have long emanated a bohemian spirit. Life centers on playing in the sea all day and in bars all night. International tourists and Floridians alike escape here to soak up the scene.

Geographically, the series of islands known as the Florida Keys juts southwestward like a series of ellipses. At the north end, Key Largo is an easy drive from Miami and the site of some of the country's best snorkeling and scuba diving. At the southern end lies Key West, famous for its independent spirit, cozy inns, and historical sites, such as the Ernest Hemingway Home and Museum. At both ends and everywhere in between, you'll find state and national parks where you can swim in clear warm waters, trek through mangrove swamps, and scale observation towers to catch panoramic views of the low-lying islands, which at times look more like clumps of floating trees than solid land masses.

Mentally, the Keys have come to represent a state of mind, a mode of living that has at its core the Caribbean concept of "island time." Here, the rhythm of nature—of the tides, the sun, of seasonal migrations—has more pull than any time clock. It may take you a few visits to figure out how to navigate the region, but once you do, you'll feel like you belong here. Each island is beautiful, the beauty intensified by the encircling green-blue waters.

LOWER KEYS
Great White Heron National Wildlife Refuge
Content Keys
Mud Keys
Barracuda Keys
Turkey Basin
Gulf of Mex
Lower Harbor Keys
Johnston Key
Raccoon Key
Water Keys
To Dry Tortugas
U.S. Naval Air Station
Waltz Key Basin
Snipe Keys
Howe Key
National Key Deer Refuge
Johnson Keys
Horseshoe Key
Key West
Stock Island
Big Torch Key
Big Pine Key
Great White Heron National Wildlife Refuge
Saddlebunch Keys
Sugarloaf Shores
Summerland Key
Little Pine Key
Key West
Key West Airport
Cudjoe Key
No Name Key
Sugarloaf Key
U.S. Naval Air Station
Boca Chica Key
Looe Key National Marine Sanctuary
Summerland Key
Ramrod Key
Little Torch Key
Big Pine
7-Mile Bridge
Moser Channel
Atlantic Ocean
Bahia Honda State Park
Bahia Honda Key
1
A
B
C
N
W
S

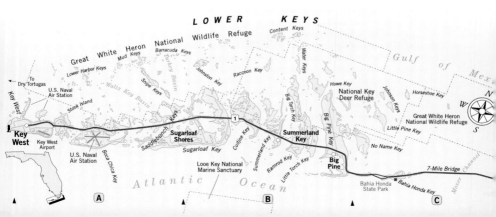

In Key West, sunset is an elaborate celebration, and fishing boats leave when the tide is right. Things happen when they happen, a fitting philosophy for a place that has only one road in and one road out.

Many visitors headed down that road come for the gorgeous waters that surround the islands. But if you come to the Keys expecting miles of sandy white beaches, you'll be disappointed. In many places, leaves from the ubiquitous mangrove trees that thrive at water's edge create a sediment-rich shoreline that is great for wildlife but not great for beachgoers. The clearest water tends to be farther offshore, so most people enjoy the water from boats. Licensed operators offer day trips for fishing, snorkeling, and scuba diving, or you can rent your own boat, canoe, kayak, or wave runner. The selection of shops and restaurants ranges from tacky strip-malls that line U.S. 1 to high-end restaurants and inns housed in beautifully restored homes in Key West. Bird-watching is spectacular in this region, as you are likely to see, among other things, white egrets fishing in the shallow waters and large osprey nests, many of them on man-made platforms built high above the road.

■ Key Largo *map pages 300–301, F-1*

Key Largo's most remarkable feature is the marine life under its blue-green waters, and **John Pennekamp Coral Reef State Park** is a first stop for snorkelers and divers. This is the northernmost park of the Florida Keys National Marine Sanctuary, which protects coral reefs and exotic marine life. At the park, you can follow canoe trails, hike, sail, motor-boat, and camp. To get out on the reef, you'll need to rent a canoe or kayak or go out on a tour boat that stops for diving and snorkeling. You can rent almost everything you need to enjoy the park, including snorkeling equipment. *Entrance at Mile Marker 102.5; 305-451-1202.*

Diver-sightseers head for Key Largo Dry Rocks to see a 9-foot-tall bronze statue, ***Christ of the Deep,*** a replica of the *Christ of the Abysses* statue in the Mediterranean Sea, off Genoa.

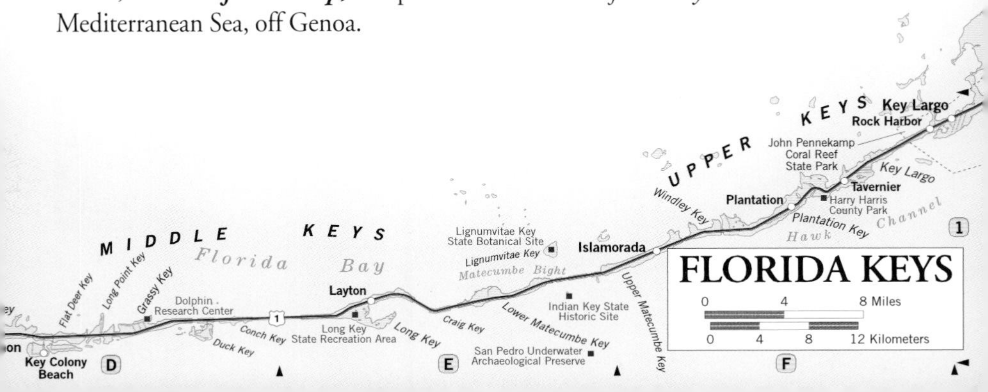
UPPER KEYS
Key Largo
Rock Harbor
John Pennekamp Coral Reef State Park
Key Largo
Tavernier
Harry Harris County Park
Plantation
Windley Key
Plantation Key
Hawk Channel
MIDDLE KEYS
Florida Bay
Lignumvitae Key State Botanical Site
Lignumvitae Key
Islamorada
Matecumbe Bight
Upper Matecumbe Key
Indian Key State Historic Site
Lower Matecumbe Key
San Pedro Underwater Archaeological Preserve
Craig Key
Long Key
Long Key State Recreation Area
Layton
Conch Key
Duck Key
Dolphin Research Center
Grassy Key
Long Point Key
Flat Deer Key
Key Colony Beach
FLORIDA KEYS
0 4 8 Miles
0 4 8 12 Kilometers
1
D
E
F

An Italian industrialist and recreational spear fisherman donated the statue, sunk in about 20 feet of water, as a memorial to all who have died at sea and as a welcome to divers and snorkelers who visit this spot.

Farther along the Overseas Highway, **Plantation Key** is a jumping-off point for the Inner and Outer Conch Reefs, and for the drop-offs and ledges at Davis Reef and Crocker Wall—spectacular diving spots. Giant rays ply the waters at Outer Conch, where sand-floored corridors are walled off by labyrinthine reef ledges.

■ MIDDLE KEYS *map pages 300–301, D/F-1*

The Middle Keys begin at **Windley Key.** Formerly two islands known as the Umbrella Keys, Windley Key was made into one island by builders of the railroad, who filled the space between landforms with fossilized coral rock, which they quarried here. The quarry pit left behind was filled with water, and is today the **Theater of the Sea,** which has dolphin and shark shows and rides in glass-bottom boats. The office here can arrange for you to swim with the dolphins. *Mile Marker 84.5; 305-664-2431.*

Christ of the Deep lies among the reefs at John Pennekamp Coral Reef State Park.

A houseboat on Florida Bay.

The town of **Islamorada** [say "eye-la-mo-RA-da"] calls itself the "Fishing Capital of the World," which is an exaggeration, but the town does have more fishing charter boats than any other in the Keys, and it does host lots of fishing tournaments.

It was in Islamorada that the men building the Overseas Highway met with tragedy in September of 1935. On September 2, after word came that the Keys were about to be hit by a powerful hurricane, a Florida East Coast Railroad train was sent to bring the 700 workers north out of harm's way. But, with debris on the tracks, wind, and delays, the train took hours to travel a few dozen miles. Barometric pressure became so low (26.35 inches) that windows and jars exploded. Residents tried to save themselves by lashing themselves to trees or hiding in their cars. Many might have survived, had it not been for a 20-foot-high ocean surge. Late that night, the wall of water reached the rescue train in Islamorada, uprooted the train tracks, and knocked 10 of the cars over. Hundreds of people died. Upper Matecumbe Key was flattened from end to end, with the exception of the stone angel that marked the grave of 15-year-old Etta Dolores Pinder. The angel stands today on the lawn of Cheeca Lodge; just beyond, at Mile Marker 81.5, is a monument to the victims of the Labor Day hurricane.

Off Lower Matecumbe Key lies government-owned **Lignumvitae Key,** 280 acres of rare virgin forest filled with lignumvitae, strangler fig, and gumbo limbo trees. Most of the other keys have been burned or bulldozed to make room for tropical fruit farms and resort development. Lignumvitae Key managed to avoid any such disaster. The worst it suffered was the harvesting of the island's giant mahoganies in the late 19th century. Lignumvitae Key is accessible only by boat. Fishing is big here, and in Lignumvitae Basin you can often see pods of dolphins and lumbering sea turtles. If you go, bring bug spray.

Traveling by boat to **Lignumvitae Key State Botanical Park** is like traveling back to a time before civilization took its toll on Florida's Keys. Here, you'll find diverse bird life and unusual shade trees, including the poisonwood and pigeon plum. But you won't find many humans, since only 50 people are allowed on the key at any time. Trips can be arranged at the boat ramp at Mile Marker 77.5. *305-664-2540 or 305-664-9814.*

Many of my happiest memories of the Keys are of days spent at **Long Key State Recreation Area,** a skinny key where campers can set up tents along the shoreline (what Keys people call "beaches," but if truth be known, they are but narrow strips of sand). *Mile Marker 67.5; 305-664-4815.*

The 200-mile-per-hour winds of the 1935 Labor Day hurricane blew an evacuation train off its tracks in Islamorada, resulting in the deaths of hundreds of people and permanently destroying Henry Flagler's east coast railway. (Florida State Archives)

Lower Matecumbe Key *by William Akien Walker, 1908.*
(Sam and Robbie Vickers Florida Collection)

■ **LOWER KEYS** *map pages 300–301, A/C-1*

The 7-mile causeway from the Middle Keys to the Lower Keys marks a geologic as well as a geographic change: the Middle Keys are coral, the Lower Keys limestone. The mood changes, too. Life moves at a slightly slower pace in the Lower Keys.

The best of the Keys' beaches, such as they are, can be found at **Bahia Honda State Park.** At its bayside beach, snorkeling, kayaking, and windsurfing are typical pastimes, and a nature trail leads over an old railroad bridge. The oceanside beach is wilder and more appealing to loners and couples than to families and sportsmen. Camping facilities and cottages accommodate overnighters. *Mile Marker 37; 305-872-2353.*

Big Pine Key is the most natural and old-fashioned of the Keys, and its fish camps give it an old-time feel. **National Key Deer Refuge** (305-872-0774), which occupies part of this key and a half-dozen others, prevents excessive development. The 8,000-acre refuge provides protection for the beguiling, miniature key deer, a subspecies of the white-tailed deer whose numbers have been steadily dwindling since the 1970s. This deer faces many obstacles to survival, including losing its habitat to development, motor vehicles, dogs, and fire ants. Key deer can be spotted in the early morning or evening. At Blue Hole, a freshwater lake in an old quarry, alligators, turtles, and fish swim in crystal-clear waters.

Fishing drew vacationers to the Keys early on, and still does. The catch of preference for sports fishermen is bonefish, an elusive flatfish that has sparked the revival of fly-fishing in the Keys. Other game and food fish swim through the Keys, where the water is so clear you can see a fish as it approaches the hook. Dolphinfish, tuna, and wahoo lure blue-water fishermen, while snapper and redfish are found around the flats. (Barracuda can be extremely poisonous—if you catch one, don't eat it.) Fishing charters abound throughout the Keys, and many divers come to enjoy the noncommercial "mini-lobster" season at the end of July.

Ramrod Key has long been loved by divers because of outlying **Looe Key National Marine Sanctuary.** Off Looe Key—really a reef, not an island—gin-clear waters expose technicolor reefs and the bright and flitting fish that live among the coral. The area around Ramrod Key booms in July, when the sport lobster season begins. The regular commercial season runs early August through March.

■ **KEY WEST** *map pages 300–301, A-1, and page 313*

Four miles long and 2 miles wide, Key West is the jewel at the end of U.S. 1—or the beginning, since it is officially located at Mile Marker 0—and is in spirit more Caribbean than American. Gingerbread-trimmed clapboard homes with large airy porches and tropical gardens sit behind white picket fences. On central Duval Street, traffic is often at a standstill, while on the side streets an even slower pace prevails among the locals. The aromas of frangipani, Cuban coffee, and conch fritters float through the humid, salt-heavy air. Of course, you'll see the names of familiar chain establishments and tacky tourist haunts, too, but the city has a laidback pace you won't find anywhere else in the continental U.S.

But don't let the slow pace fool you: Key West has a notorious wild streak that comes out on holidays, like October's **Fantasy Fest** (800-352-5397), for which Halloween provides a perfect excuse for 10 days of costumed bacchanalia, and New Year's Eve. Other festivals and events throughout the year bring a diverse group of revelers to the city.

Because of this festive, tropical atmosphere, Key West has become a popular stop for countless cruise ships, which dwarf the skyline even before they arrive at the dock. Almost every day of the week, cruise passengers flood the city's narrow streets, browsing souvenir shops and crowding into the more famous restaurants and bars, such as **Margaritaville Café** (500 Duval Street; 305-292-1435) and **Sloppy Joe's** (201 Duval Street; 305-294-5717). Because most of the drinking

A boat maneuvers around reefs in blue-green waters.

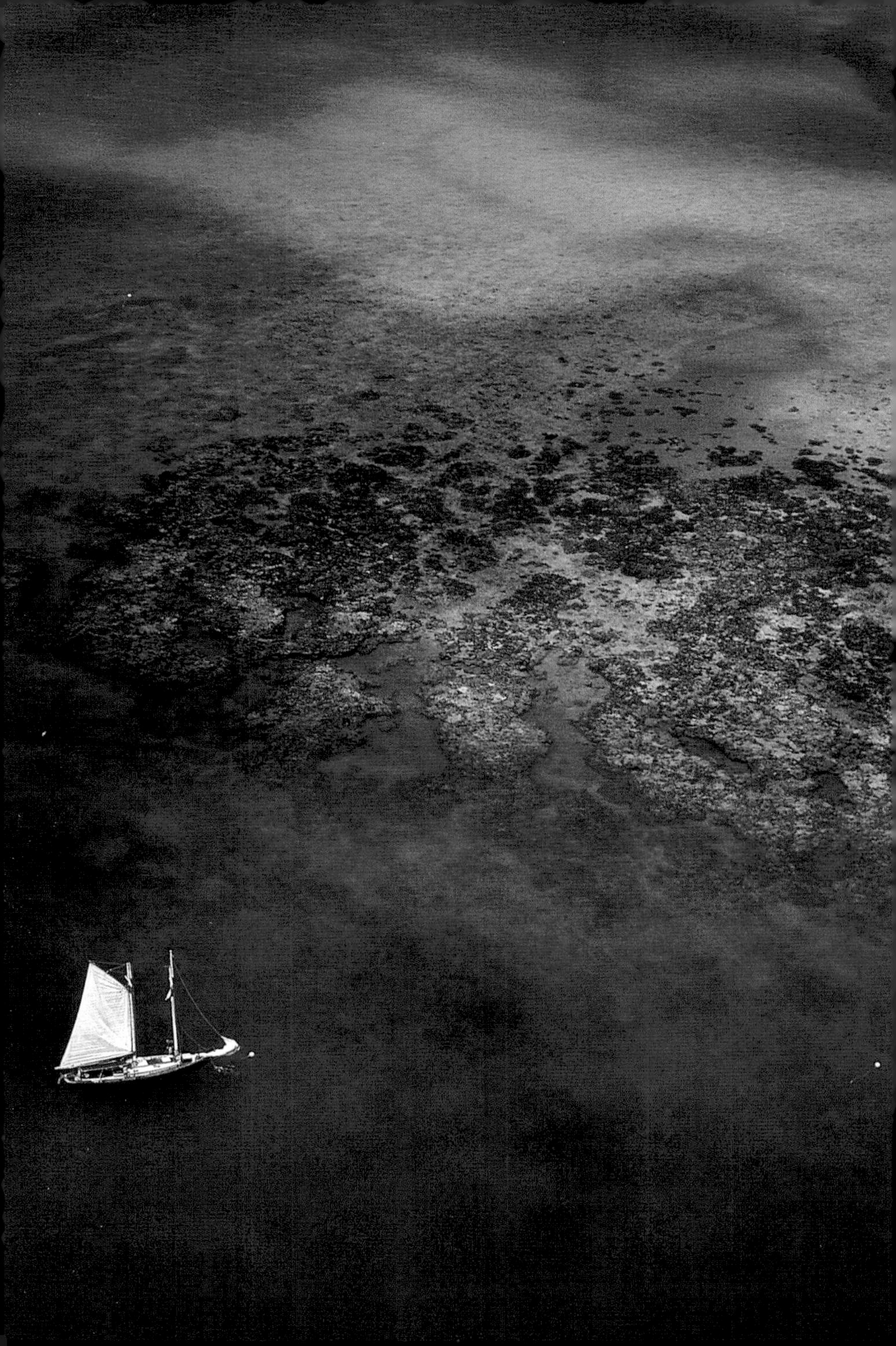

establishments are located on or near Duval Street, and because many patrons tend to overindulge, locals refer to this type of bar-hopping as doing the "Duval crawl." Crawling or not, tourists recede after a few hours when the ships depart and the streets return to relative calm.

Visitors looking to stay overnight will find many major hotels, especially on the outskirts of Old Town, but the quaint B&Bs, many of which are gay-owned or gay-friendly, are considered some of the best places to stay in the Keys. The **Key West Information Center** (1601 North Roosevelt Boulevard; 888-222-5148) maintains an updated list of guest houses and inns and offers a free reservation service for all Key West accommodations.

As you enter Key West on U.S. 1, the highway splits into South Roosevelt Boulevard to the left and North Roosevelt Boulevard to the right. Both will take you into the downtown area, but the left fork will take you past more fast-food restaurants than historical landmarks. Once you get to Old Town, you'll find plenty of restaurants with a Caribbean flavor and some of the freshest seafood you'll ever eat.

Natives of Key West call themselves Conchs [say "Conks"], a name originally applied to Bahamian-born "Key Westers," who loved to eat conch, a big bivalve with a gorgeous pink shell that was once abundant in Key waters. Now the name is bestowed on anyone actually born in Key West. Conch and conch fritters are still associated with Key West cuisine, although harvesting conch has been illegal in Florida since 1985. Most of the conch you eat in Florida restaurants is imported from the Bahamas, but many environmentalists are now concerned about the overharvesting of conch in the Bahamas, as well.

■ KEY WEST HISTORY

When Spanish explorers arrived in Key West in the early 1500s, they found the beach littered with human bones, and they named the island *Cayo Hueso,* "Key of Bones." Five hundred years later, one can only speculate as to whom these bones might have belonged, but it seems likely some small tribal group had been badly beaten in battle. By the time the name *Cayo Hueso* was corrupted to Key West, the island had become a den of pirates and salvagers, who made their fortune from picking clean the bones of ships stranded on offshore reefs.

In 1822, the Spanish sold the island for $2,000 to an Alabama businessman named John Simonton. Later that year, Lieutenant Matthew Perry came down to

WRECKERS' ODD LIVES

Beginning with its settlement in the 1820s, Key West was for thirty years the wrecking capital of the world....

Once a wreck was spotted, the wreckers raced to the reefs; the first boat to reach the damaged vessel and get the captain's permission to board became master of the wrecking operation. The master's first obligation was to see that the passengers and crew were safe. Then the wreckers removed the cargoes.

Wreckers, salvors, auctioneers and wharf owners made fortunes, and they built their houses to reflect their means. Those who chose to be paid in goods rather than auction monies found their homes so full of furniture, dry goods, and grand pianos that their families had to sleep in the kitchen.

There was something strange and sad about the lives these people led. In the best of homes, prominent citizens served tea from silver engraved with the initials of a family unknown to them; and on Sundays, when the men decked themselves out in white suits and gathered in front of the County Courthouse, the ladies of the town glided down the aisle at the beginning of church services in dresses made of water-stained silk. At night these same people are said to have met on the beach. If the weather had improved and business declined, the wreckers would string a rope between two mules and hang it with ship lights. Walking the animals along the beach, they conveyed the impression to a distant ship that another vessel was sailing closer to the shore but still outside the reef. The innocent captains would then steer their boats toward disaster.

—Christopher Cox, *A Key West Companion,* 1983

fly the American flag over its inhabitants: a few West Indian and Cuban fishermen, a handful of settlers, and pirates taking a break from their plunders in the Keys and the Caribbean. A few months later, Naval Commodore David Porter arrived to take care of this last group, and with the use of small, flat-bottomed boats—with names like *Gnat, Midge,* and *Mosquito*—he was able to follow the pirates over reefs and into mangrove coves. By 1830, Porter had routed the scourge from the Keys, but in his fury he pursued the pirates into the Spanish waters of Puerto Rico and Cuba, for which he was eventually court-martialed. The belligerent Porter never liked Key West, nor was any fondness returned, so Porter left to join the Mexican navy, and later the Turkish.

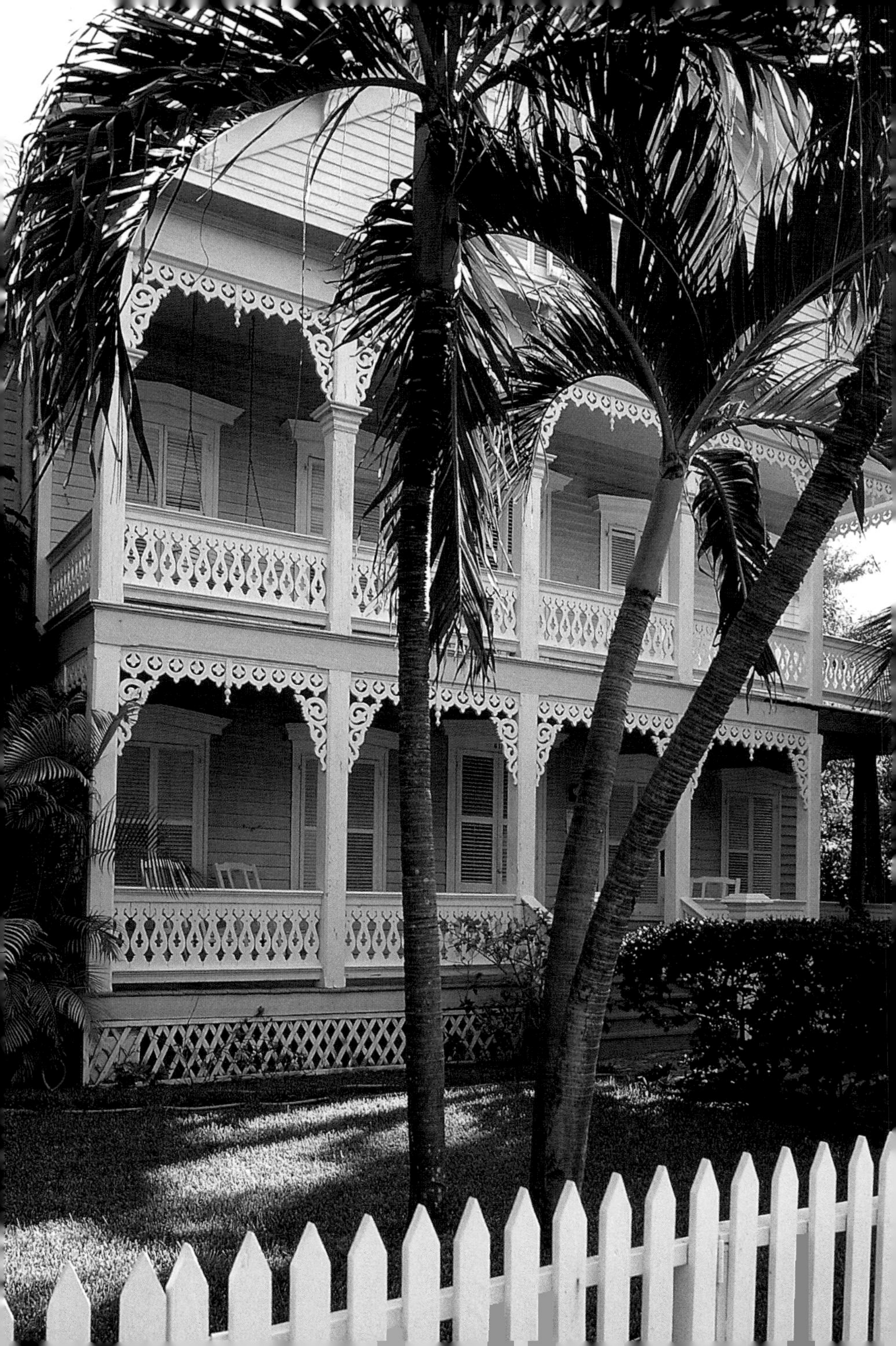

Three decades later, the island's population, comprised largely of English Bahamians, Southerners, and New Englanders, had jumped from 500 to 2,700. Wrecking became a regulated industry in which millions of dollars were made, for while pirates had been driven off, reefs and hurricanes were still destroying ships. Key West became an outpost where (water-stained) silks and velvets were worn every day, and porcelain and silver—no doubt taken directly from vessels run aground—adorned dining room tables.

The building of the reef lighthouses in the late 1850s changed all that, and the economic focus shifted to another sea treasure: sponges. Just as the town's industry was in transition, a fire swept the community in 1859. Homes were rebuilt quickly, many of them more elegantly than before. Meanwhile, Cuban cigar manufacturers were fleeing their war-torn island and arriving on Key West. By the 1880s, Key West was the wealthiest city, per capita, in the nation. When Henry Flagler's railroad rolled in, the town was already an important shipping port, cigar capital, and a Bahamian community with a feisty spirit.

By the 1930s, however, the cigar trade had left for Tampa and the sponge industry was suffering. The railroad did little for the faraway community, and the land boom that swept through Florida fell short of Key West. Then came the Depression. It took a dapper, if somewhat corrupt, New Deal Federal Relief Administrator to see that the answer for this downtrodden, dilapidated town was tourism. In 1934, Julius Stone organized the Volunteer Work Force to clean out the trash, restore the decrepit buildings and piers, open hotels, and rejuvenate the town. He even had a school opened for the sole purpose of training young women to work in hotels and restaurants. For six months, tourists flooded into Key West. Then came the Labor Day hurricane of 1935, and the island had to wait for World War II and the arrival of more sailors to jump-start the town.

Almost from the beginning, and certainly throughout much of the 20th century, the island has had a history of going from rags to riches and back again. Right now, it's riches. What's been consistent throughout is Key West's eccentricity, its spirit of independence. So independent is Key West that in 1982, its residents, annoyed by traffic blockades set up to discourage drug trafficking from Latin America, decided to secede from the Union and form The Conch Republic. They informed the nation that their plan was to declare war on the United States, surrender, then ask for a foreign aid package so they could party.

A classic example of the simple yet elegant architecture that is a trademark of Key West.

■ KEY WEST SIGHTS *map page 313*

Mallory Square

Watching the sunset here is considered a quintessential Key West experience. In the 10 years since I'd done so, the scene had grown from a few jugglers to a regular circus, with silver-painted human statues, tightrope walkers, and sword swallowers.

Yet the brick square is bright and clean, the air soft and warm, and the Gulf's blue-green waters turn gold in the light of the sinking sun. Around the perimeters of the square, trees and white buildings take on a golden hue below a wide arc of translucent sky. As the sun sets in the Gulf, it changes shape, bulging as it sinks below the horizon. Backlit by the sun, mangrove keys just offshore turn a misty gray-green, and when the sun finally disappears below the horizon, the crowd erupts into applause, continuing a tradition allegedly started by Tennessee Williams (who took great care not to spill his gin and tonic while clapping).

In 1984, in response to complaints from local shop owners who claimed that the spectacle was bad for business, Mallory Square's vendors and performers formed a nonprofit organization to preserve the tradition and regulate participation in the event. The organization's Web site, *www.sunsetcelebration.org*, posts lists of current performers and recounts the celebration's colorful early days, when young locals strung out on LSD gathered at the spot to watch what they thought was Atlantis rising out of the clouds at sunset. Of course, you might not be lucky enough to see the lost city reemerge, but at the square's Historic Memorial Sculpture Garden you will see 36 bronze busts of men and women who have made Key West what it is today.

A quieter place to view this spectacle of sinking light is from the top of the old **La Concha Hotel** (430 Duval Street; 305-296-2991). The only high-rise in the area, its rooftop is reached via an elderly elevator behind its street-side restaurant. From this vantage point, the town is laid out in miniature. There's a bar up top, where drinks are served in plastic cups.

Key West's patron saint is Ernest Hemingway. You can visit the **Ernest Hemingway Home and Museum,** an 1851 Spanish colonial–style mansion built of coral rock. Like many other homes on Key West, the house was run-down (and haunted, according to Hemingway's wife) when the Hemingways bought it in 1931. This is where the Nobel Prize–winning author penned such classics as *Death in the Afternoon, The Green Hills of Africa, For Whom the Bell Tolls,* and *To Have and Have Not.*

DOWNTOWN
KEY WEST
A
B
C
D
0
.2
.4 Miles
0
.2
.4
.6 Kilometers
Key West Bight
Garrison Bight
Man of War Harbor
Mallory Square
Chamber of Commerce
Key West Shipwreck Historeum
Key West Aquarium
Audubon House
OLD TOWN
Bayview Park
Lightbourn Inn
Jackson Square
Chelsea House
Hemingway House
Lighthouse Museum
Submarine Basin
U.S. Naval Reservation
Fort Zachary Taylor State Historic Site
WHITEHEAD SPIT
Southernmost Point in U.S.
Southernmost Point Monument
City Beach
South Beach
Dog Beach
Higgs Beach
Atlantic Park
C.B. Harvey Rest Beach
White Street Pier
NEW TOWN
To Miami
To Key West Airport
Atlantic
Ocean
N
S
E
W
Trumbo Rd
Palm Ave
N Roosevelt Ave
Truman Ave
Flagler Ave
Atlantic Blvd
Duval St
South St
Reynolds St
Whitehead St
Simonton St
Eisenhower Dr
1st St
George St
Ashby St
Thompson St
Greene St
Caroline St
Eaton St
Fleming St
Southard St
Angela St
Petronia St
Olivia St
Julia St
Virginia St
Amelia St
Catherine St
Louise St
United St
Washington St
Waddell Ave
Duncan St
Seminary St
Von Phister St
Tropical Ave
Windsor Ln
White St
Grinnell St
Frances St
Margaret St
William St
Elizabeth St
Ash St
Emma St
Fort St
Wall St

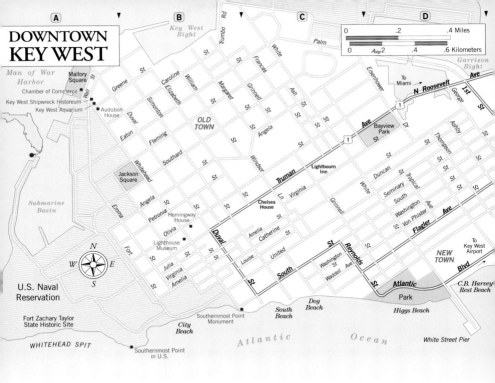

Hemingway family members dispute some of the stories spun by guides during tours, including the one about the six-toed cats around the house being descended from Hemingway's own brood of felines. The Hemingway Festival in July includes a short story competition, Hemingway lookalike contest, and twilight party. *House: 907 Whitehead Street; 305-294-1136.*

Hemingway may get the most press, but Elizabeth Bishop, Robert Frost, Annie Dillard, Richard Wilbur, James Merrill, and Tennessee Williams, among others, also lived in Key West. The **Tennessee Williams House** was the residence of the famous playwright. No doubt Williams was happy in Key West because of its tolerant attitude toward gays, but it's well known that Williams and a companion were jumped here once by two men who didn't like the spin Williams had put on a gospel hymn he was singing. *1431 Duncan Street.*

Off Duval Street, you'll find the **Pelican Poop Shoppe** (314 Simonton Street; 305-296-3887), which single-handedly demonstrates Key West's tolerance for the

A street performer juggles torches at Mallory Square.

irreverent. Formerly named Casa Antigua, it was the guest house where Ernest Hemingway first stayed when he came here. You can buy unique gifts here. Another shop in an old building off Duval makes and sells Kino sandals, Key West's trademark footwear. **Key West Island Bookstore** (513 Fleming Street; 305-294-2904) has an excellent collection of books on Key West.

Touristy as it may be, a ride on the **Conch Train** is a good introduction to Key West, its history and legends. The trip gives an excellent overview of the island—the beguiling old downtown area, the banal chains, and the low-key motels and attractive beachside resorts on the Atlantic side of the island. The "train" passes by all of the important historical sites, and its guide-drivers are entertaining. *The train departs from Mallory Square or North Roosevelt Boulevard; 305-294-5161.*

The naturalist and painter John James Audubon never stayed at the **Audubon House & Tropical Garden,** but Captain John Geiger, who built the home, did, beginning in the 1830s. Geiger introduced the Geiger tree to Key West from the West Indies (known there as cordia); one orange-blossomed specimen stands on the front lawn today. *On Whitehead Street, between Caroline and Greene Streets; 305-294-2116.*

The **Key West Aquarium** (1 Whitehead Street; 305-296-2051) is one of the oldest of its kind—a simple aquarium: no tricks, no shows. Next door to the aquarium, the small **Key West Shipwreck Historeum** (1 Whitehead Street; 305-292-8990) explains how salvaging, which has since been banned due to environmental concerns, contributed to the development and architecture of Key West. Today, those same wrecks that made Key West so wealthy serve as underwater playgrounds for scuba divers.

Despite the island's tropical bent, Key West's beaches are not the sandy open spaces found in places like Miami Beach. Most of the sand on the beaches here is crushed limestone and tiny bits of coral reef trucked in from elsewhere. The most popular and sandiest stretch of coastline is **Smathers Beach** (South Roosevelt Boulevard, opposite the airport).

The old fort at **Fort Zachary Taylor State Park,** a National Historic Landmark, played an important role as a Union outpost in the Civil War and saw action again during the Spanish-American War. Shade trees, picnic and barbecue facilities, and the most uncrowded beach on Key West make this an ideal place to spend a leisurely afternoon. You can take a half-hour tour of the fort, or if you visit in February, you can check out the Civil War Days celebration, which includes costumed reenactments of daily fort life and warfare demonstrations. Nearby is the aptly named Dog Beach (Vernon Street and Waddell), the only beach in Key West where man's best friend is always welcome. *Southard Street at the Truman Annex; 305-292-6713.*

Unique boat trips depart from Key West, from sunset cruises on old sailing ships to snorkeling excursions aboard the ***Conch Queen*** catamaran with Captain Dave. All along Duval Street, you'll find kiosks selling tour-boat tickets.

■ DRY TORTUGAS AND GARDEN KEY *map pages 300–301*

Seventy miles west of Key West is Dry Tortugas archipelago and **Fort Jefferson,** a hexagonal structure on Garden Key. Although never completed, the fort is among the largest brick-and-masonry structures in the Western Hemisphere. The pre–Civil War fortification is most famous for the incarceration in 1865 of Dr. Samuel Mudd, who set John Wilkes Booth's broken leg after Booth assassinated President Abraham Lincoln—and hence the expression "Your name is Mudd." You can charter a seaplane or take a boat out to Garden Key to tour the fort. Sunny Days Catamarans (800-236-7937) offers daily trips that include lunch and snorkeling.

KEY LIME PIE

If you're ever served lime-green key lime pie, send it back. It's not the real thing.

Although many people expect key lime pie to be green, the limes used to create this popular South Florida dessert are actually light yellow, and authentic pies retain this natural color.

The key lime (*citrus aurantifolia swingle*) is a variety of lime brought to the Florida Keys decades ago from Mexico, which is why it's also known as the Mexican lime. These prized fruits range in size from about the size of a ping-pong ball to the size of a golf ball. Seldom growing more than 16 feet tall, key lime trees typically look more like bushes than trees, and their thorny branches and small, pale-green leaves become shrublike if they are not pruned regularly.

The key lime's unique flavor—tart, yet flavorful—has won over chefs, bartenders, gastronomes, and local Key West school kids, who hawk key limeade rather than traditional lemonade from roadside stands. The truth is, on this island you'll find key limes most everywhere: garnishing mixed drinks, replacing lemon in teas, and accompanying fresh seafood and other delicacies.

Specialty stores, such as the **Key Lime Company** (701 Caroline Street; 305-294-6567 or 800-872-2714), sell a dizzying array of all things key lime, from pies to jelly to barbecue sauce to chocolate-dipped key lime dessert bars on a stick. But if you are adventurous, try your hand at making your own pie. The dessert is easy to make, and the principal ingredients (eggs, condensed milk, and key lime juice) can be found in most grocery stores.

Ingredients
4 ounces of key lime juice (preferably squeezed from fresh limes)
3 eggs
1 can (14 ounces) of sweetened condensed milk
1 pie crust (graham cracker or regular)

Combine all filling ingredients in a mixing bowl and pour into piecrust (if you want a little more tartness, add a scraping or two from the rind). Bake at 350°F for 10 minutes, then chill before serving.

And if you are not inspired to make your own, order a slice in most any restaurant in Key West. And don't worry–in Key West, the pie won't be green.

—Janine Warner

The waters off these keys are protected as a national park, a blessing for divers. The islands—named both for the turtles once found here and because there was no potable water—comprises three reefs surrounding a central lagoon that reaches depths of 60 feet; outside this circle, the water drops to 100 feet. This construction makes the coral reefs highly attractive to sea life, and dangerous to ships. More than 250 vessels, from Spanish galleons to clipper ships, have met their doom here.

Diving and snorkeling around the Tortugas require expertise: hazards include powerful currents, fire coral, barracuda, and scorpion fish. The warm waters are also a breeding ground for nurse sharks, a small species that tends to stay near the bottom of the reef and is usually not considered dangerous to divers. There is spectacular reef life in the Keys, but you'll need a good dive guide and a boat to reach the best diving areas. *Dry Tortugas National Park; 305-242-7700.*

■ TRAVEL BASICS

Getting there: The best way to drive to the Florida Keys is to take the Florida Turnpike south to Florida City, where it meets U.S. 1. One of America's most scenic drives, U.S. 1, often called Highway 1, or the Overseas Highway, stretches 126 miles from Key Largo to Key West. This two-lane road connects all of the Keys, and traffic can be slow, especially on weekends. The views are spectacular, though, as the road is lined with mangroves that frame superb views of the ocean and the bay sides. The water that flows under the famous Seven-Mile Bridge is as blue as any in the Caribbean.

Addresses in the Keys are commonly designated by mile marker numbers, found on green signs along the road. Flights to Key West are frequent and offered by major carriers from both Miami International and Fort Lauderdale–Hollywood International Airports. If you prefer a shuttle, you can take the Keys Shuttle (888-765-9997) from both airports to all points in the Keys. The Key West Shuttle (888-539-2628), a high-speed ferry service that runs from Marco Island to Key West, operates October through May only.

Climate: Rainfall averages about 39 inches per year, with summer wetter than winter. Frost is unknown in this subtropical region, and temperatures range between 65°F and 90°F virtually every day. Hurricanes occur from time to time between June and October. Humidity is high year-round.

PRACTICAL INFORMATION

■ AREA CODES AND TIME ZONE

Major area codes are: 850 for the Panhandle; 904 for Jacksonville; 813, 727, and 352 for Gainesville, Tampa, and St. Petersburg; 407, 689, and 321 for Orlando; 785, 954, and 305 for Miami; 305 and 986 for Florida Keys; 941 and 239 for the southwest coast from Bradenton to Naples; and 863, 561, and 772 for the heartland south of Orlando. Most of Florida is within the Eastern time zone. The section of the Panhandle west of Tallahassee is in the Central zone.

■ METRIC CONVERSIONS

1 foot = .305 meters   1 mile = 1.6 kilometers   1 pound = .45 kilograms (kg)
Centigrade = Farenheit temperature minus 32, divided by 1.8

■ CLIMATE

April and October are Florida's most temperate months. Summer months bring afternoon thunderstorms, particularly in the lower half of the state, where the intense heat brings about powerful downpours and fantastic, sometimes deadly, lightning storms. Florida is famous for its humidity, which is no surprise since the state is surrounded on three sides by water.

CITY	FAHRENHEIT TEMPERATURE				RAINFALL
	Jan. Avg. High/Low	Apr. Avg. High/Low	July Avg. High/Low	Oct. Avg. High/Low	Average Rain
Daytona Beach	69 48	80 59	90 72	81 65	48"
Everglades N.P.	76 56	83 65	90 75	85 70	58"
Fort Myers	75 52	85 61	91 74	86 69	53"
Jacksonville	64 42	79 57	92 73	80 59	52"
Key West	75 65	81 71	89 79	80 60	39"
Miami	75 59	82 68	90 76	84 77	57"
Orlando	70 49	81 60	90 73	85 71	47"
Pensacola	60 42	64 44	90 74	83 67	61"
Tallahassee	64 39	79 52	90 70	80 58	64"
Tampa	70 50	81 60	90 75	83 67	47"
West Palm Beach	75 58	81 65	90 75	85 70	60"

Hurricanes and Florida

Florida is invariably associated with hurricanes in the minds of most Americans. Although the state is frequently targeted by these destructive storms, they are not as common as one might expect. An average of nine tropical storms form in the Atlantic Ocean or Gulf of Mexico each year between June and October. Of these, five usually reach hurricane strength (sustained winds of more than 75 miles per hour), and two become major hurricanes with sustained winds of more than 125 miles per hour, capable of producing severe damage. On average, however, Florida is struck by a tropical storm only about twice a year and by a hurricane once every three years. The odds of a hurricane hitting any one section of the state's coastline are as follows (i.e., one might expect hurricane winds to strike Jacksonville once every 50 years):

Jacksonville	1 in 50	Fort Myers	1 in 12
Daytona Beach	1 in 40	Palm Beach	1 in 10
Melbourne-Vero Beach	1 in 20	Pensacola	1 in 10
Tampa-St. Pete	1 in 20	Miami	1 in 7
Apalachicola-St. Marks	1 in 15	Key West	1 in 7

Interestingly, the Outer Banks of North Carolina and the upper coast of Texas are just as likely to be hit by a hurricane as the highest-risk regions of Florida—its South Atlantic coastline and the Keys.

A major storm has not affected the Lower Keys since 1935 and is long overdue. A storm surge of 20 feet, as would occur if a Category 5 storm struck (sustained winds of 155 mph or higher), would completely submerge the islands. An evacuation along the 110-mile-long Overseas Highway would have to begin at least 36 hours in advance to be successful. In 1935, the hurricane that devastated the Upper Keys strengthened from a tropical storm with 60 mph winds into the most powerful storm to have struck North America (with winds of 200 miles per hour) in just 30 hours.

TEN MOST SEVERE HURRICANES OF THE 20th CENTURY

Region	*Date*	*Winds*	*Pressure*	*Deaths*
Panhandle	Sep 1906	130+*mph*	28.55"	164
Keys	Sep 1919	155+*mph*	27.37"	600-900
Southeast-Northwest	Sep 1926	138+*mph*	24.61"	243
Peninsula (Heartland)	Sep 1928	136+*mph*	27.43"	1836
Keys	Sep 1929	150+*mph*	28.00"	3
Keys	Sep 1935	200+*mph*	26.35"	400+
Extreme South	Sep 1945	170+*mph*	28.09"	0
South	Sep 1947	155+*mph*	27.97"	51
South-Central	Sep 1960	140+*mph*	27.46"	13
South	Sep 1992	175+*mph*	27.23"	15

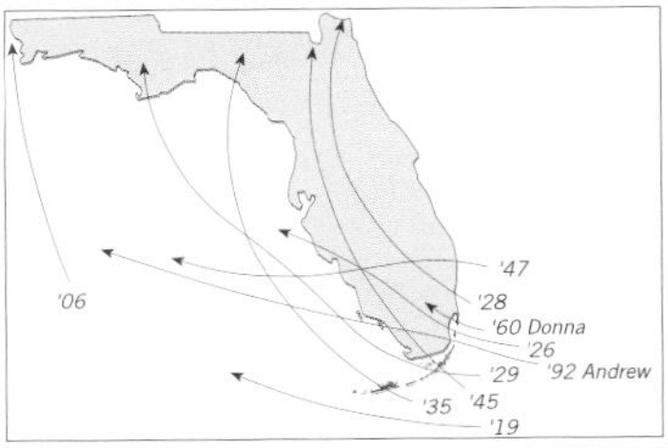
'06
'47
'28
'60 Donna
'26
'29
'92 Andrew
'35
'45
'19

■ GETTING THERE AND AROUND

BY AIR

Fort Lauderdale–Hollywood International Airport (FLL) has daily service from major cities in the eastern United States. *320 Terminal Drive; 954-359-6100.*

Key West International Airport (EYW) receives daily flights from Miami, Fort Lauderdale, Naples, Orlando, and Tampa. *Four miles east of downtown off U.S. 1; 305-296-7223.*

Miami International Airport (MIA) serves more than 100 international and domestic airlines. *Northwest 21st Street, 5 miles northwest of downtown, off I-95; 305-876-7000; www.miami-airport.com*

Orlando International Airport (MCO) receives flights from more than 100 cities in the United States and overseas. *1 Airport Boulevard, off I-4; 407-825-2001; www.orlandoairports.net*

St. Petersburg/Clearwater International Airport (PIE) receives U.S. and Canadian flights. *14700 Terminal Boulevard, off I-275; 727-453-7800; www.fly2pie.com*

Tampa International Airport (TPA) receives flights from East Coast cities as well as Chicago and London. *5507 Spruce Street, off I-275, exit 20; 813-870-8700; www.tampaairport.com*

BY CAR

The main arteries into Florida include I-95, which crosses the Florida-Georgia border just north of Jacksonville and hugs the east coast to Miami, and I-10, which crosses the Florida-Alabama border west of Pensacola and shoots east to Jacksonville. Interstate 75 runs south from Georgia through the state's middle, working its way to the west coast just south of Tampa Bay. Interstate 4 moves southwest across the state from Daytona through Orlando and eventually connects with I-75 in Tampa. Route 417 provides a quicker way across the state.

BY TRAIN AND BUS

Greyhound. Serves most cities in Florida. *800-231-2222; www.greyhound.com*

Amtrak. Serves major cities on both coasts. *800-872-7245; www.amtrak.com*

■ RESTAURANTS

Panhandle cuisine is heavily influenced by traditional Southern and Cajun-style cooking. Po'boys, which are basically baguettes filled with either fried shrimp or oysters, are as common in these parts as a sandwich or a hoagie. Apalachicola, Florida's oyster capital, is known for juicy gems of all sizes. Restaurants in the region serve the freshest oysters anywhere (but don't expect them to be cheap).

Central Gulf Coast restaurants are known for local seafood, including redfish, grouper, Gulf shrimp, oysters, and stone crab. St. Petersburg has a growing selection of upscale dining establishments offering everything from pan-Asian to Continental cuisine. Across the bay in Tampa, you'll find the ubiquitous Cuban sandwich and Cuban coffee, beans and rice in Ybor City, and a vibrant fine-dining scene in Old Hyde Park and downtown.

From the lower Gulf Coast's fertile shrimping grounds come succulent, pink Gulf shrimp, which find their way onto many restaurant menus. In Sarasota, seafood dining ranges from casual beachside eateries to innovative upscale restaurants. The tomatoes, citrus, and other fruits and vegetables grown here are top-notch.

Florida's heartland area is not known for fine dining. Most options are chain franchises located off the major highways. But you're also likely to find small, unpretentious restaurants that serve "Cracker-style" cuisine, the food of Old Florida cowboys and early settlers—alligator tails, smoked fish, and hearts of palm salads.

The upper Atlantic Coast is known for excellent seafood, and Amelia Island, Fernandina Beach, and Atlantic Beach have some of the finest restaurants in the region. Jacksonville, once famous for having more barbecue restaurants per capita than any other U.S. city, is slowly coming out of the barbecue pit, and fine-dining establishments are taking root. The trademark of St. Augustine cuisine is the fiery datil pepper, developed here in colonial times and found nowhere else in the world.

Orlando has more than its share of chain restaurants. But the area's theme parks, Walt Disney World in particular, also cater to refined tastes with high-end restaurants. Likewise, many resort hotels have made their restaurants culinary destinations in and of themselves

Key West is famous for its key lime pie, a regional favorite made from the tiny limes cultivated in the region. The most popular appetizer in these parts is conch fritters, a fitting culinary tribute to a city that once threatened to secede from the United States as the Conch Republic. Cuban sandwiches and strong Cuban coffee are local specialties, and fresh seafood is abundant.

■ ACCOMMODATIONS

In the Panhandle area, smaller seaside towns, beach cottages, and rental homes are popular and relatively inexpensive choices for lodging. In fancier places like Seaside, rental prices are higher, but lodging is generally more affordable in the Panhandle than in other parts of coastal Florida. The larger resort towns, such as Panama City Beach, have chain hotels and motels, and what seems to be an impenetrable line of condos.

On the upper Atlantic Coast, cottages or condos can be rented on Amelia Island, which is also home to luxury resorts, including the Ritz-Carlton. In Jacksonville, both beach areas and downtown have seen major hotel development.

Farther south in Ponte Vedra Beach, lush landscaping hides posh resorts and condo developments from view, and in historic St. Augustine there are quaint B&Bs and comfortable beachfront condos. As you travel farther down the coast, you'll find more of the ubiquitous mom-and-pop motels from the 1940s and 1950s, but by the time you reach Hutchinson Island, luxury resorts are de rigueur.

The Walt Disney Company owns about 35,000 hotel rooms in the Orlando area. But the company has competition from giant non-Disney resort hotels close to the attractions that offer myriad amenities, activities, and opportunities for sports or relaxation. For budget travelers, or those just passing through, there are small hotels, motels, and old-time resorts in the more rural areas of central Florida, and there are plain but affordable accommodations in Kissimmee.

Lodging options on the barrier islands of the central Gulf Coast run from tacky motels to casual summer cottages to high-rise resorts. In the city of Tampa, several higher-end hotels have opened downtown. In St. Petersburg's historic districts, bungalows and two-story houses are being transformed into B&Bs. Sarasota's eclectic lodgings include high-rise hotels, condos, chain motels, cottages, and full-service resorts.

Miami Beach is known for Art Deco hotels. Newer hotels have bigger rooms, and the buildings are often three to four times taller than the older structures. A few high-end hotels in downtown Miami cater to business travelers. Super-luxe resorts can be found in the Florida Keys, including Little Palm Island, which is accessible only by boat. Other options include small hotels, or "boatels," which are little more than overnight accommodations for boaters. Intimate hotels and palm-draped B&Bs are popular in Key West, though familiar chains (with unfamiliar prices) can be found on the outskirts of town.

■ RESERVATIONS SERVICES

Accommodations Express. *800-663-7666; www.accommodationsexpress.com*
Florida Hotel Network. *800-538-3616;* www.floridahotels.com
Florida Sunbreak. *305-532-1516; www.floridasunbreak.com*

■ HOTEL AND MOTEL CHAINS

Best Western. *800-528-1234; www.bestwestern.com*
Days Inn. *800-329-7466; www.daysinn.com*
Hilton Hotels. *800-445-8667; www.hilton.com*
Holiday Inn. *800-465-4329; www.6c.com*
Hyatt Hotels & Resorts. *800-233-1234; www.hyatt.com*
Marriott Hotels. *800-228-9290; www.marriott.com*
Radisson. *800-333-3333; www.radisson.com*
Ramada Inn. *800-272-6232; www.ramada.com*
Renaissance Hotels. *800-468-3571; www.renaissancehotels.com*
Sheraton. *800-325-3535; www.starwood.com*
Westin Hotels. *800-228-3000; www.westin.com*

■ CAMPING IN FLORIDA

Florida is a natural destination for outdoor enthusiasts, especially in winter, when the cooler weather keeps mosquitoes and other insects at bay. Florida is blessed with many gorgeous state parks set in spectacular natural environments ranging from oak-draped natural springs to pristine coastline. In winter, reservations are essential at the more popular parks.

Florida Association of RV Parks and Campgrounds. *850-562-7151; www.floridacamping.com*
Florida Keys National Marine Sanctuary. *305-743-2437; www.fknms.nos.noaa.gov*
Florida Outdoors. *321-725-3456; www.floridacrackeroutdoor.com*
Florida State Parks Department. *850-488-9872; www.dep.state.fl.us/parks*
National Park Service. *404-562-3100; www.nps.gov/parks*
National Recreation Reservation Service. *877-444-6777; www.reserveusa.com*
U.S. Forest Service. *425-775-9702; www.fs.fed.us*

■ OFFICIAL TOURISM INFORMATION

Emerald Coast. *850-651-7131; www.destin-fwb.com*
Jacksonville. *904-791-4305; www.jaxcvb.com*
Key West. *305-296-1552; www.fla-keys.com*
Miami. *305-539-3000; www.miamiandbeaches.com*
Orlando. *407-363-5800; www.orlandoinfo.com*
State of Florida. *850-488-9406 or 888-735-2872; www.flausa.com*
Tallahassee. *850-413-9200; www.seetallahassee.com*
Tampa. *813-985-3601; www.thcva.com*

■ USEFUL WEB SITES

Bay News 9. Web site of the Tampa Bay area's 24-hour news and information channel. *www.baynews9.com*

Florida Beach Directory. *www.beachdirectory.com*

Florida History. *www.floridahistory.org*

Florida Lighthouse Association. *www.floridalighthouses.org*

Florida Scuba News. Dive shops, boats, reefs, and parks. *www.scubanews.com*

Florida Sportsman. Fishing forecasts, and more. *www.floridasportsman.com*

Florida Today. Space Coast–area newspaper site has links to listings of missions, launches, news, and other out-of-this-world features. *www.flatoday.com*

Florida Trail Association. Descriptions, photos, maps. *www.florida-trail.org*

Miami.com. Official site of the *Miami Herald* and the Spanish-language *El Nuevo Herald* has news, features, and information. *www.miami.com*

South Beach Nights. Events, clubs, and restaurant listings for Miami's South Beach. *www.sobenightsonline.com*

Tropical Everglades. Photos, maps, attractions. *www.tropicaleverglades.com*

Walt Disney World. *www.disneyworld.disney.go.com*

INDEX

COMPASS AMERICAN GUIDES

Alaska	Las Vegas	San Francisco
American Southwest	Maine	Santa Fe
Arizona	Manhattan	South Carolina
Boston	Michigan	South Dakota
Chicago	Minnesota	Southern New England
Coastal California	Montana	Tennessee
Colorado	Nevada	Texas
Florida	New Hampshire	Utah
Georgia	New Mexico	Vermont
Gulf South: Louisiana, Alabama, Mississippi	New Orleans	Virginia
	North Carolina	Wine Country
Hawaii	Oregon	Wisconsin
Idaho	Pacific Northwest	Wyoming
Kentucky	Pennsylvania	

Compass American Guides are available at special discounts for bulk purchases for sales promotions or premiums. Special editions, including personalized covers, excerpts of existing guides, and corporate imprints, can be created in large quantities for special needs. For more information, contact your local bookseller or write to Special Markets, Fodor's Travel Publications, 1745 Broadway, New York, NY 10019. Inquiries from Canada should be directed to your local Canadian bookseller or sent to Random House of Canada, Ltd., Marketing Department, 2775 Matheson Boulevard East, Mississauga, Ontario L4W 4P7. Inquiries from the United Kingdom should be sent to Fodor's Travel Publications, 20 Vauxhall Bridge Road, London, England SW1V 2SA.

ACKNOWLEDGMENTS

I begin with love and thanks to my husband, Rob, and son, Aaron, who endured a soggy tent, endless road miles, and lots of leftovers to help and support me. The crew at Compass American Guides became like family through the trials and tribulations of the editing process. I have only gratitude and respect for Kit Duane, the editor of the first edition, with whom I spent one afternoon on Sanibel Island scouting for 'gators. Thanks also to Chris Burt and the rest of the staff.

Then there are all of my Florida friends, old and new, who came to my rescue with answers and assistance. These are in no particular order; just as they come to mind when I think back on the adventure of researching this guide: Beth Preddy Sanz, a dear friend and valuable Naples resource; Ed Carlson at Corkscrew Swamp; Stuart Newman Associates; Dan Ryan in Daytona Beach; Gina Sholtis in Destin; Deborah Roker at Key Biscayne; Kathy Casper in Miami; Anne Hersley in Palm Beach; Frances Borden; Marsha Blasko in Jacksonville; Larry J. Marthaler in Sarasota; Bob and Hannah Spencer on Siesta Key; Bob Burrichter; Julie Root in Seaside; Michael Monahan, who has endured years of questions about Tampa; Debbie Geiger and Traci Greenberg; Michele Holder on Amelia Island; Amy Rankin, who has helped me tremendously with Amelia Island research through the years; Amy Bressler Drake and Alisa Sundstrom Bennett on Longboat Key; Alison L. Roberts at South Florida Museum; Zimmerman Agency; Dawn L. Chesko-Grigsby in Orlando; Wit Tuttell at Universal Studios; Tracy Louthain in Tallahassee; Allison McCoy; Ellen Kennedy in Fort Lauderdale, a longtime associate; Nancy Hamilton, right here in my home stomping grounds; and Lee Daniel in St. Petersburg, who has helped me since I wrote my first guidebook in 1988.

Compass American Guides also wishes to thank Director Ronald H. Kirtz and the staff at the Amelia Island Museum of History; Ranger Adams and staff at the Paynes Prairie State Preserve; Loma Alexander; Viviana Carballo for her essay on Latin cuisine, pp. 277–279; Julia Dillon for the essay about Art Deco, pp. 270–271; Deborah Hansen; Gary Monroe, for his essay on the Highwaymen, pp. 236–237; Wayne Tucker; John Ciavarella, copyeditor; and Ellen Klages, proofreader.

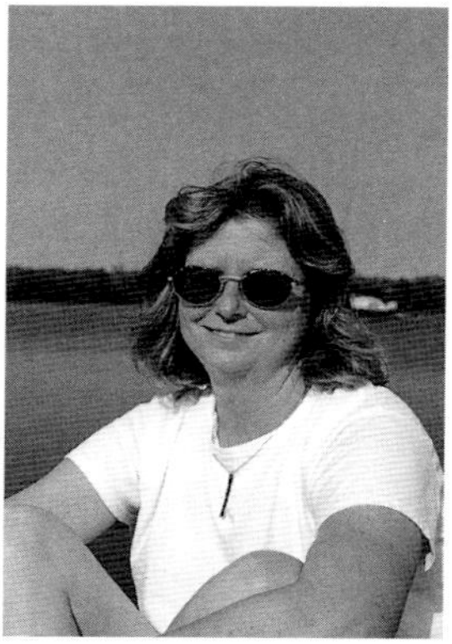

■ About the Author

Chelle Koster Walton, a longtime resident of Sanibel Island, has written many guidebooks about Florida, among them *Fun for the Family in Florida; The Sarasota, Sanibel Island and Naples Book;* and *Caribbean Ways,* which won the Lowell Thomas Bronze Award for Best Guidebook. She has contributed to *Caribbean Travel & Life, Endless Vacations, National Geographic Traveler,* the *Miami Herald, Family Fun,* and other publications.

■ About the Contributors

Florida-raised David Downing balloons over orange groves, sails the Gulf of Mexico, and scours cities large and small to find the best of the Sunshine State. His work has appeared in numerous travel publications, including Fodor's *Florida.* Avid scuba diver Janine Warner is a Miami Springs resident, author, and syndicated columnist whose work appears in the *Miami Herald.* In her spare time she teaches journalism at the University of Miami and explores shipwrecks off the Florida Keys.

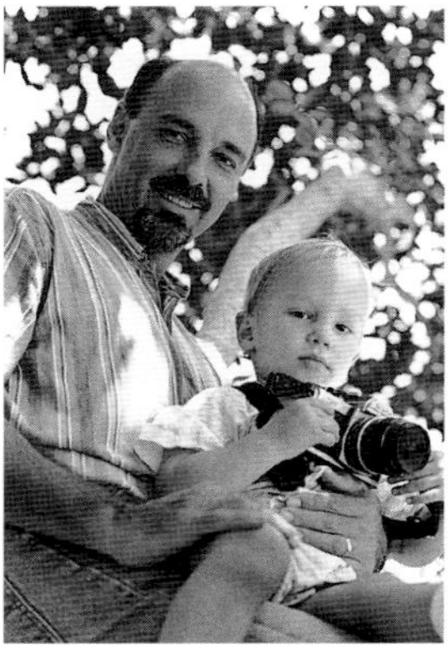

ROBERT SADLER CLARK

■ About the Photographer

Tony Arruza began his career in photography more than two decades ago shooting surfers in Puerto Rico. He has traveled extensively for *Surfing* magazine and now concentrates his energy on travel guides and magazine assignments. His work has appeared in *Audubon, Outside, Smithsonian, Newsweek, Reader's Digest,* the *New York Times,* and many other publications and books. Tony lives in West Palm Beach.

NAGB/17/02

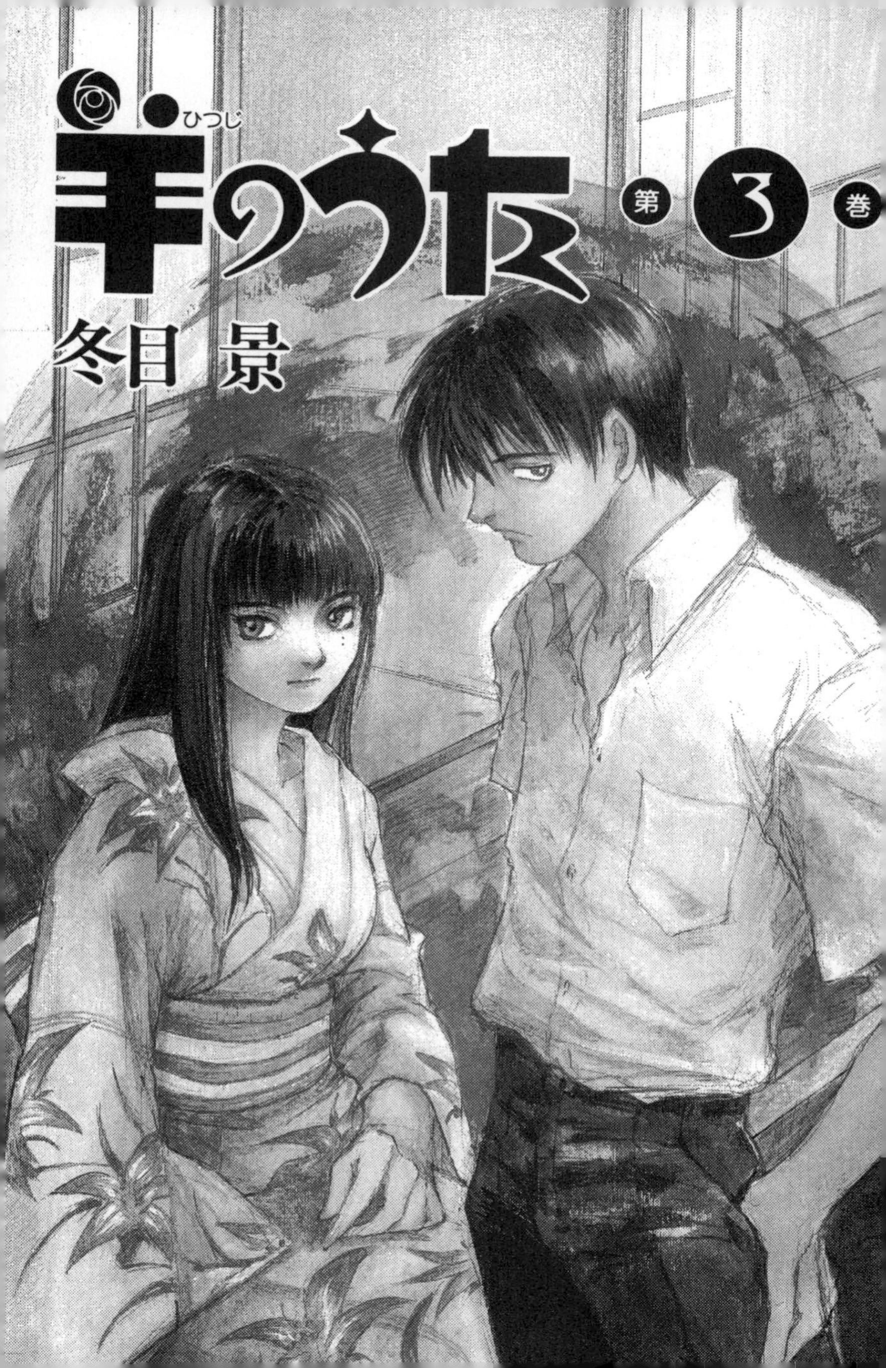
ひつじ
羊のうた
第3巻
冬目景

Lament of the Lamb Vol. 3
Created by Kei Toume

Translation - Ryan Flake
English Adaptation - Jay Anatni
Associate Editor - Alexis Kirsch
Copy Editor - Suzanne Waldman
Retouch and Lettering - Keiko Okabe
Production Artist - Vicente Rivera, Jr.
Cover Design - Gary Shum

Editor - Paul Morrissey
Digital Imaging Manager - Chris Buford
Pre-Press Manager - Antonio DePietro
Production Managers - Jennifer Miller and Mutsumi Miyazaki
Art Director - Matt Alford
Managing Editor - Jill Freshney
VP of Production - Ron Klamert
President and C.O.O. - John Parker
Publisher and C.E.O. - Stuart Levy

A  Manga

TOKYOPOP Inc.
5900 Wilshire Blvd. Suite 2000
Los Angeles, CA 90036

E-mail: info@TOKYOPOP.com
Come visit us online at www.TOKYOPOP.com

ISBN: 1-59182-862-7

First TOKYOPOP printing: September 2004
10 9 8 7 6 5 4 3 2 1
Printed in the USA

LAMENT of the LAMB

VOL. 3

BY KEI TOUME

HAMBURG // LONDON // LOS ANGELES // TOKYO

My name is Kazuna Takeshiro. When I was a child, my mother died and my father disappeared. He took my older sister, Chizuna, with him. But he left me behind, to be raised by his friends, the Edas. I grew up never knowing where my father and Chizuna had gone. One day, in our high-school Art Club, I was hanging out with my friend, Yaegashi, when I caught sight of her blood-red paint. It filled me suddenly with strange, terrifying desires. Oddly enough, it rekindled memories of my family's abandoned home. Soon after, I visited that home and was shocked to find Chizuna living there. Now reunited, my long-lost sister revealed to me the darkest secret of our Takeshiro lineage--generations of our family have been under the curse of a strange disease. It causes an intense, vampire-like craving for blood. In shock and disbelief, I backed away into my old, routine life. But, after I suffered another collapse, I sought out Chizuna again. Only, she found me. I was suffering horribly, and she pacified my vile cravings by feeding me her own blood. She also gave me a mysterious medicine to stave off future attacks, a serum that a doctor, Minase, who was also an old friend of our father's, regularly smuggled in for her.

Chizuna told me how much she loved our father. But Chizuna insisted that Father only returned her affections because she reminded him of our dead mother. Now I suspect that a lonely Chizuna looks to me to fill the emotional void left by Father's suicide. Despite my trepidation, I've decided to live with Chizuna. It's for the best. I can hide from the world, and everyone I love will be safer. Poor Yaegashi. While in the throes of yet another attack, I told her about my strange disease. She was frightened and confused, but insisted that she still cares about me. My only fear is that she cares too much.

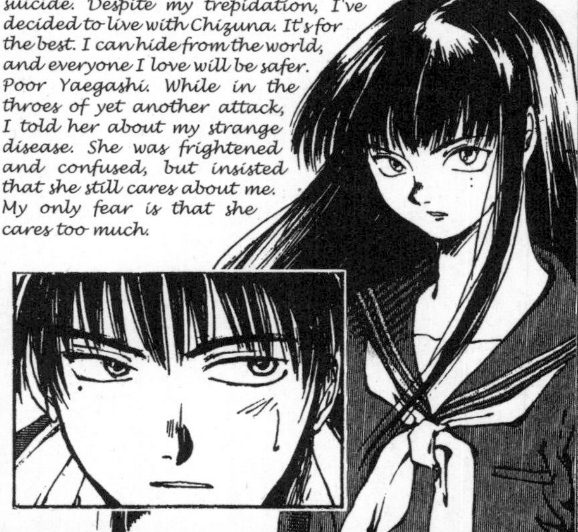

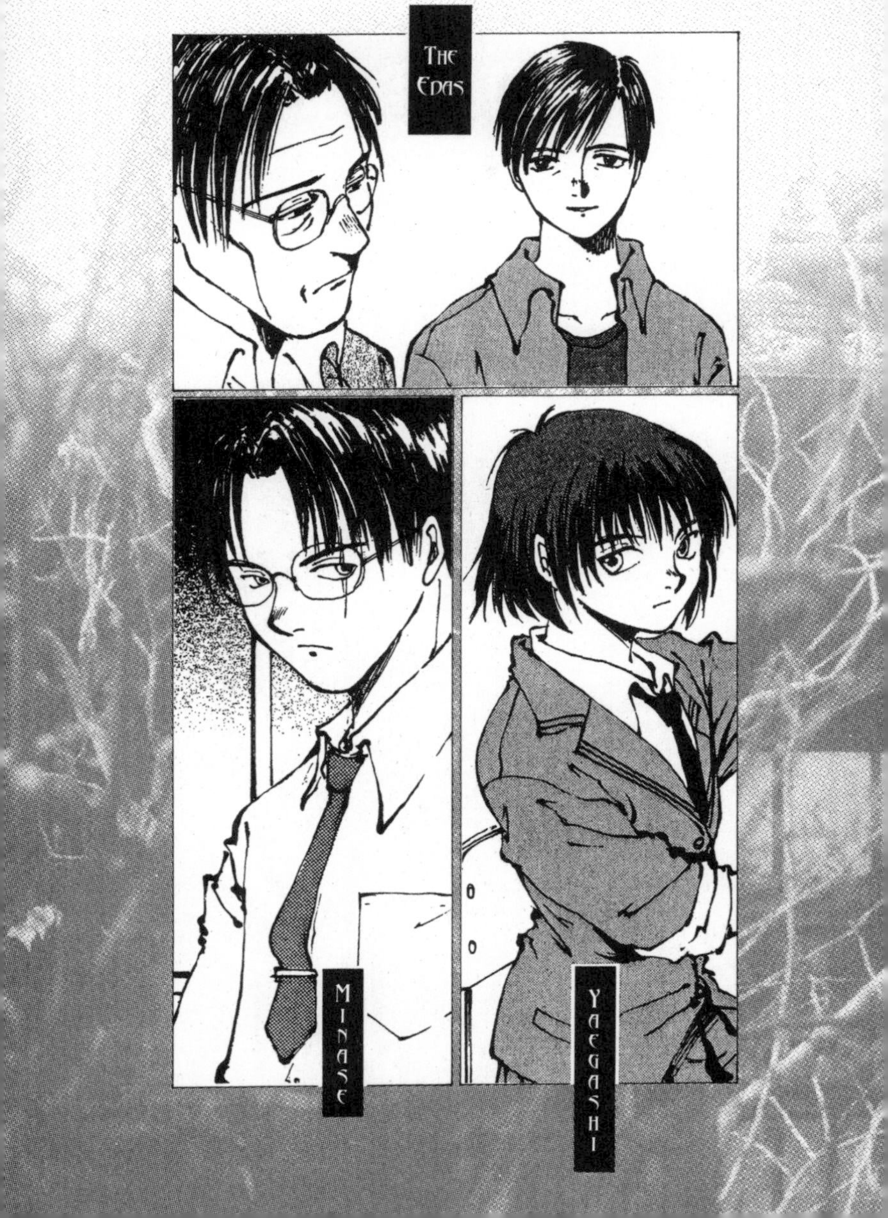
The Edas
Yaegashi
Minase

LAMENT of the LAMB.

羊のうた

第 **3** 巻

Contents

Chapter

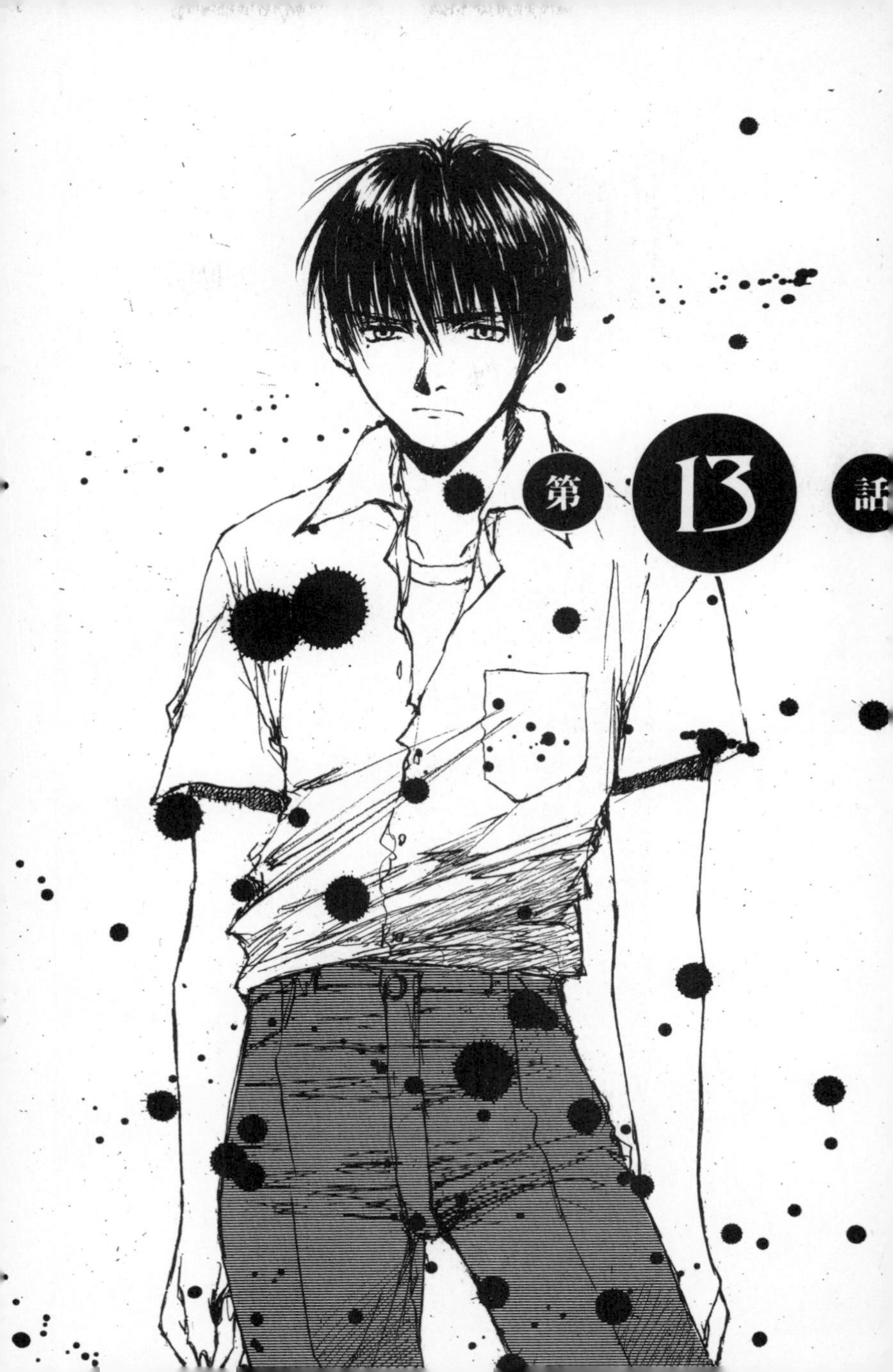
第13話

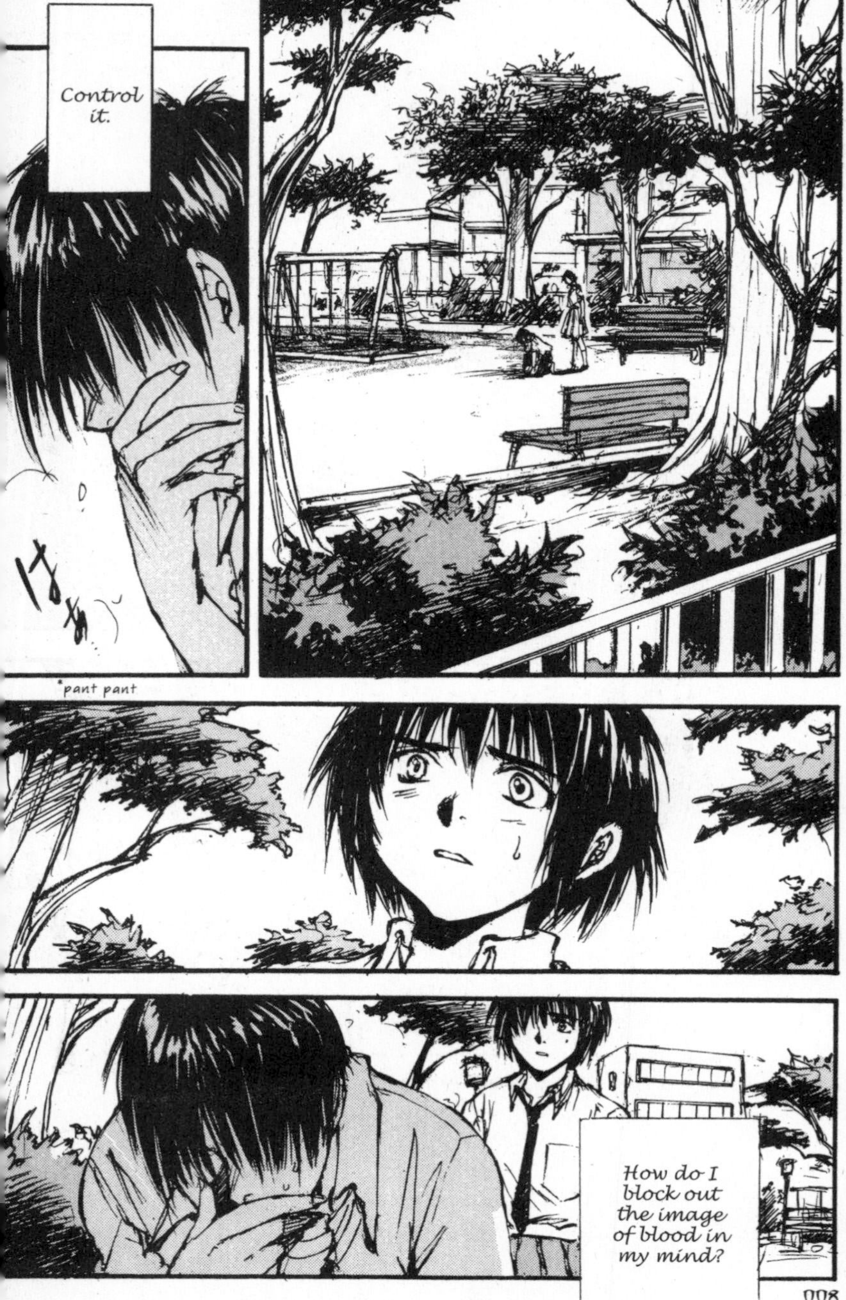
Control it.
*pant pant
How do I block out the image of blood in my mind?

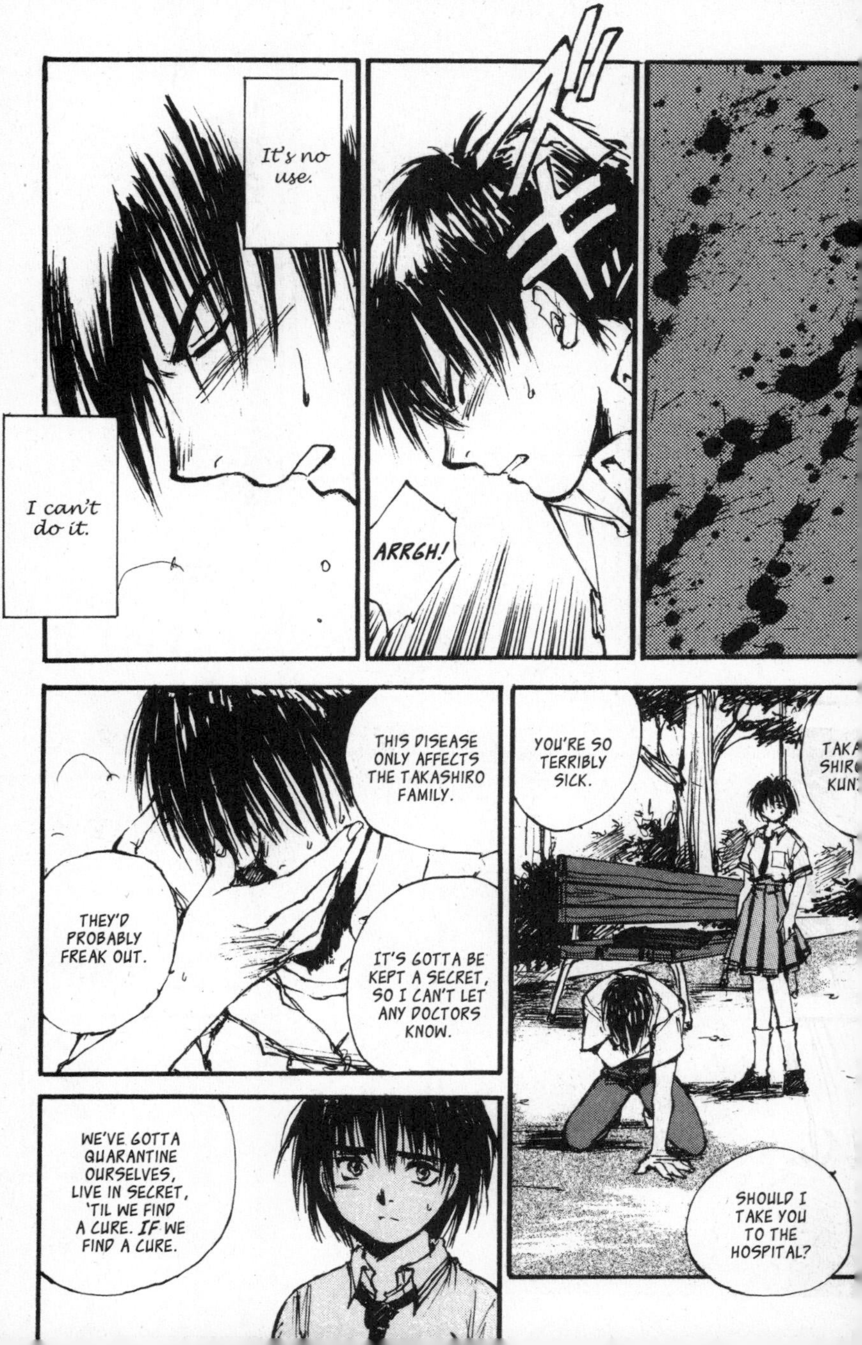
ARRGH!
It's no use.
I can't do it.
TAKA SHIRO KUN
YOU'RE SO TERRIBLY SICK.
SHOULD I TAKE YOU TO THE HOSPITAL?
THIS DISEASE ONLY AFFECTS THE TAKASHIRO FAMILY.
IT'S GOTTA BE KEPT A SECRET, SO I CAN'T LET ANY DOCTORS KNOW.
THEY'D PROBABLY FREAK OUT.
WE'VE GOTTA QUARANTINE OURSELVES, LIVE IN SECRET, 'TIL WE FIND A CURE. *IF* WE FIND A CURE.

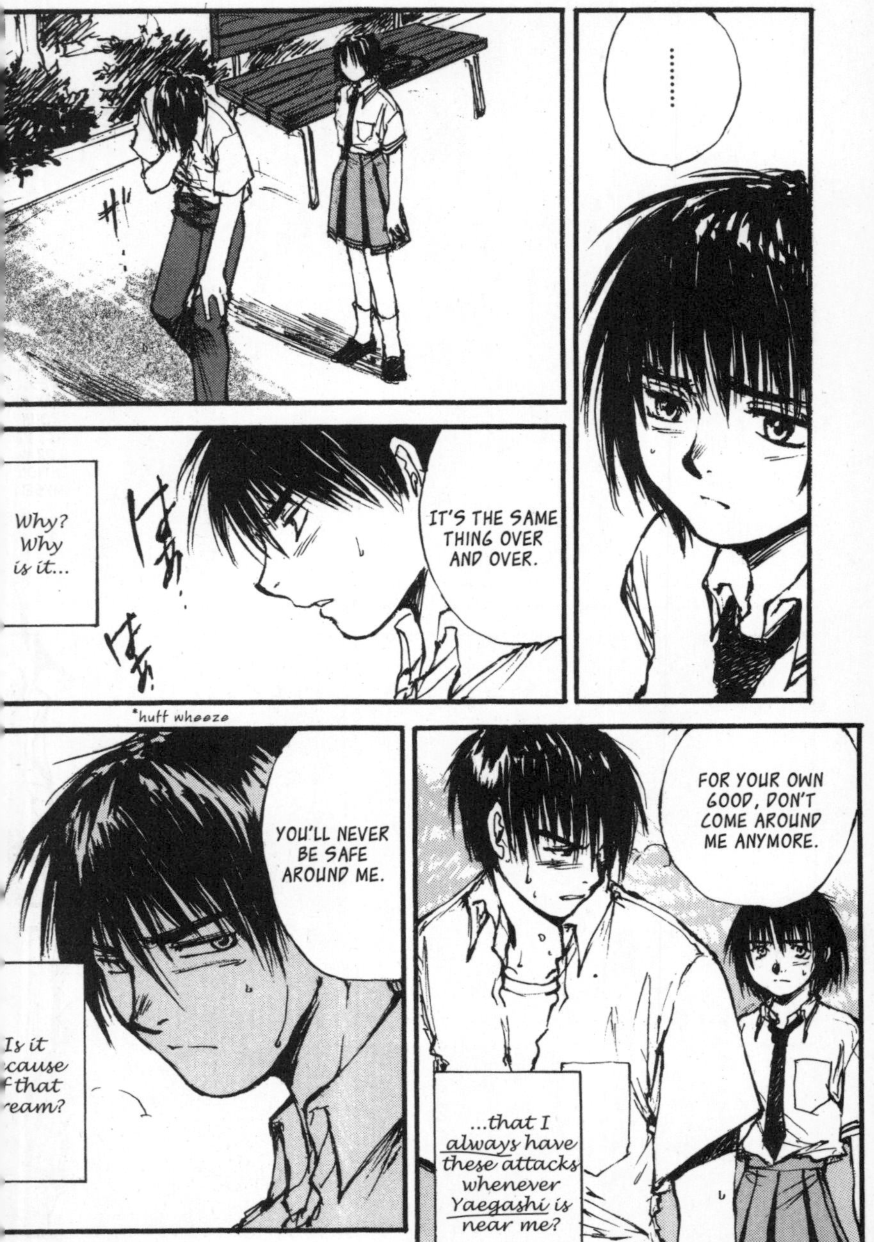
......
IT'S THE SAME THING OVER AND OVER.
Why? Why is it...
*huff wheeze
FOR YOUR OWN GOOD, DON'T COME AROUND ME ANYMORE.
...that I always have these attacks whenever Yaegashi is near me?
YOU'LL NEVER BE SAFE AROUND ME.
Is it cause f that ream?

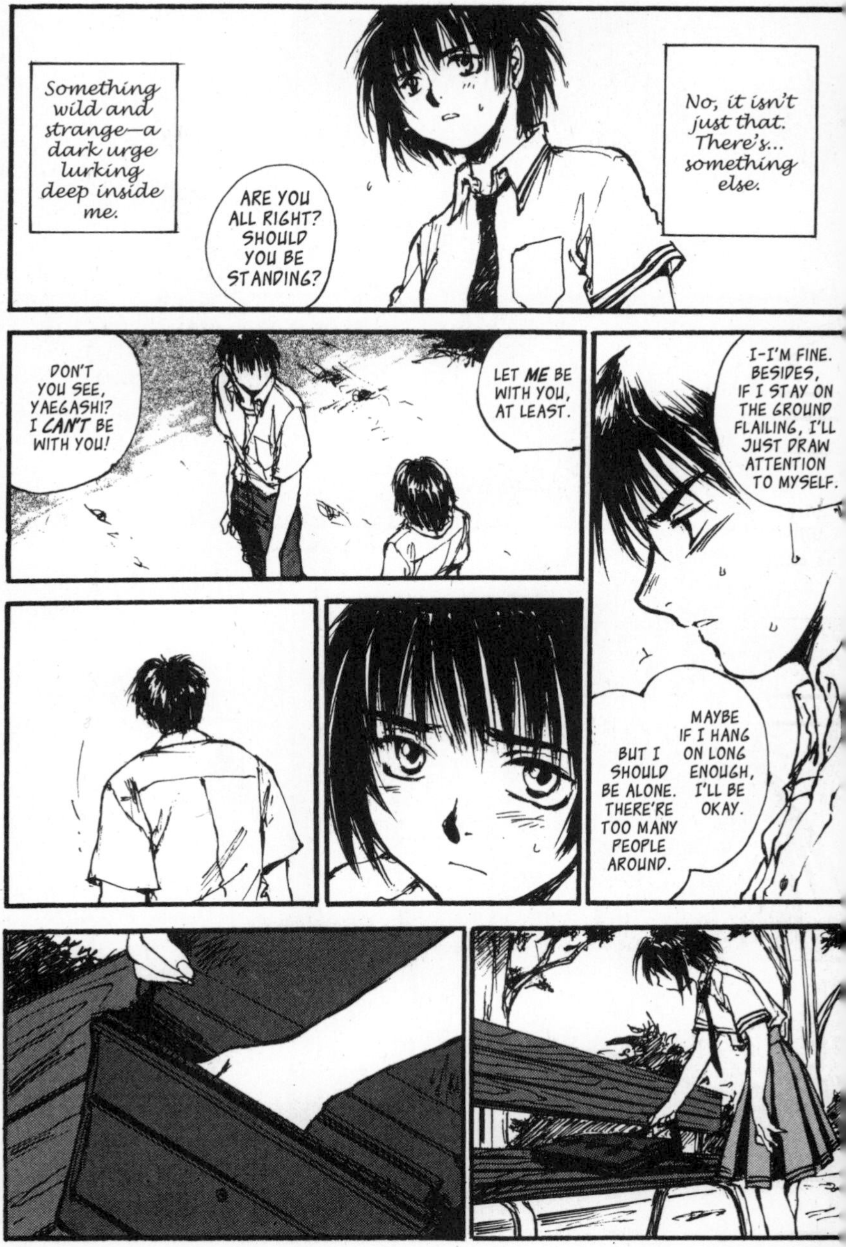
No, it isn't just that. There's... something else.
ARE YOU ALL RIGHT? SHOULD YOU BE STANDING?
Something wild and strange—a dark urge lurking deep inside me.
I-I'M FINE. BESIDES, IF I STAY ON THE GROUND FLAILING, I'LL JUST DRAW ATTENTION TO MYSELF.
MAYBE IF I HANG ON LONG ENOUGH, I'LL BE OKAY.
BUT I SHOULD BE ALONE. THERE'RE TOO MANY PEOPLE AROUND.
LET *ME* BE WITH YOU, AT LEAST.
DON'T YOU SEE, YAEGASHI? I *CAN'T* BE WITH YOU!

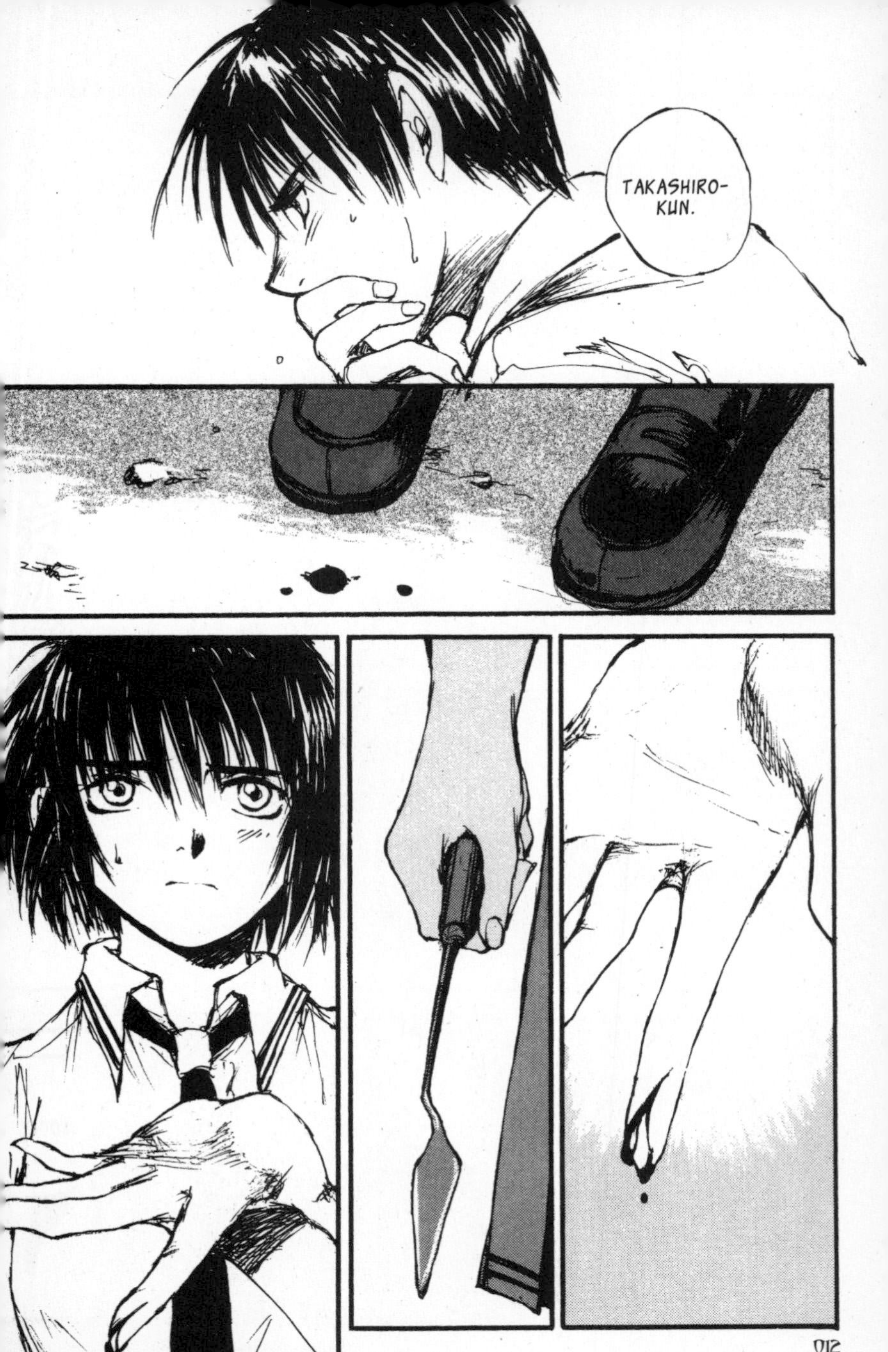
TAKASHIRO-KUN.

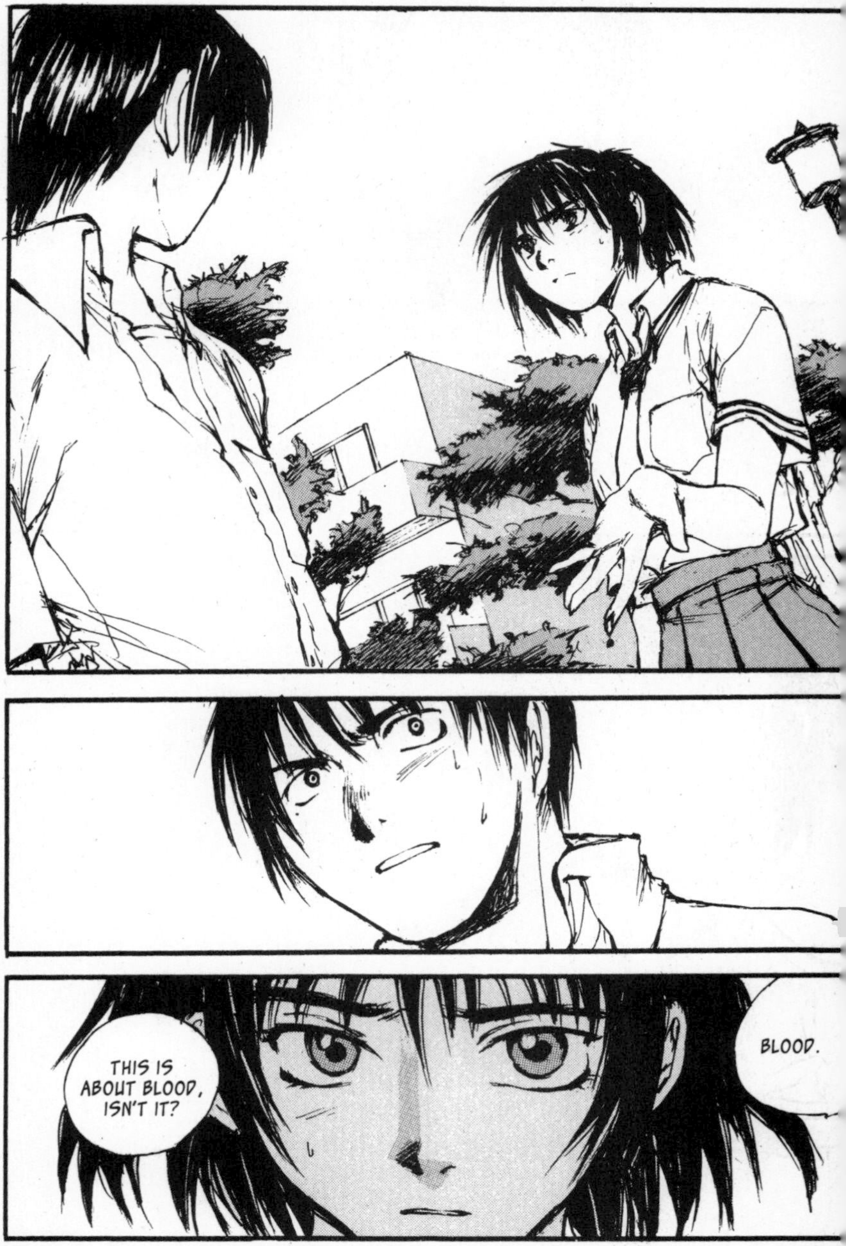
BLOOD.
THIS IS ABOUT BLOOD, ISN'T IT?

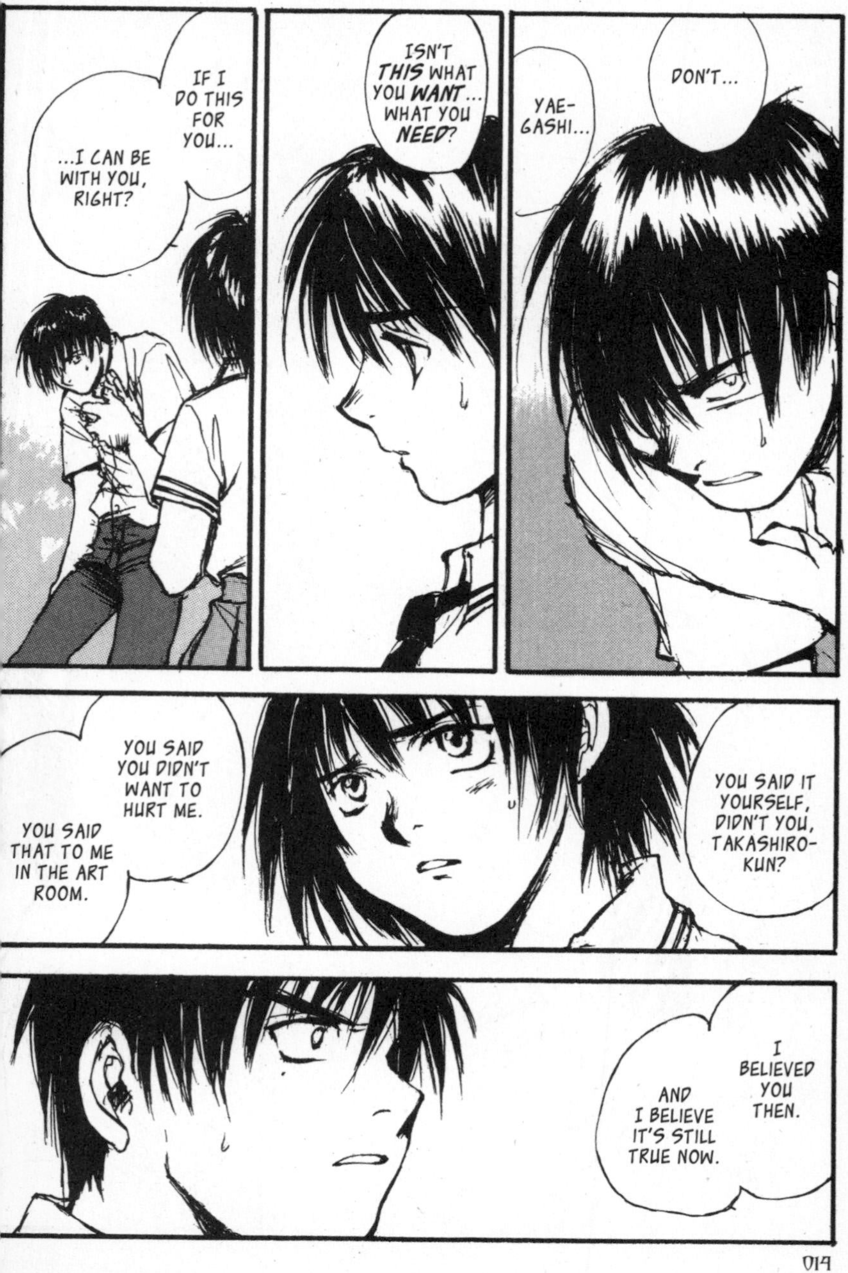
DON'T...
YAE-GASHI...
ISN'T THIS WHAT YOU WANT... WHAT YOU NEED?
IF I DO THIS FOR YOU...
...I CAN BE WITH YOU, RIGHT?
YOU SAID IT YOURSELF, DIDN'T YOU, TAKASHIRO-KUN?
YOU SAID YOU DIDN'T WANT TO HURT ME.
YOU SAID THAT TO ME IN THE ART ROOM.
I BELIEVED YOU THEN.
AND I BELIEVE IT'S STILL TRUE NOW.

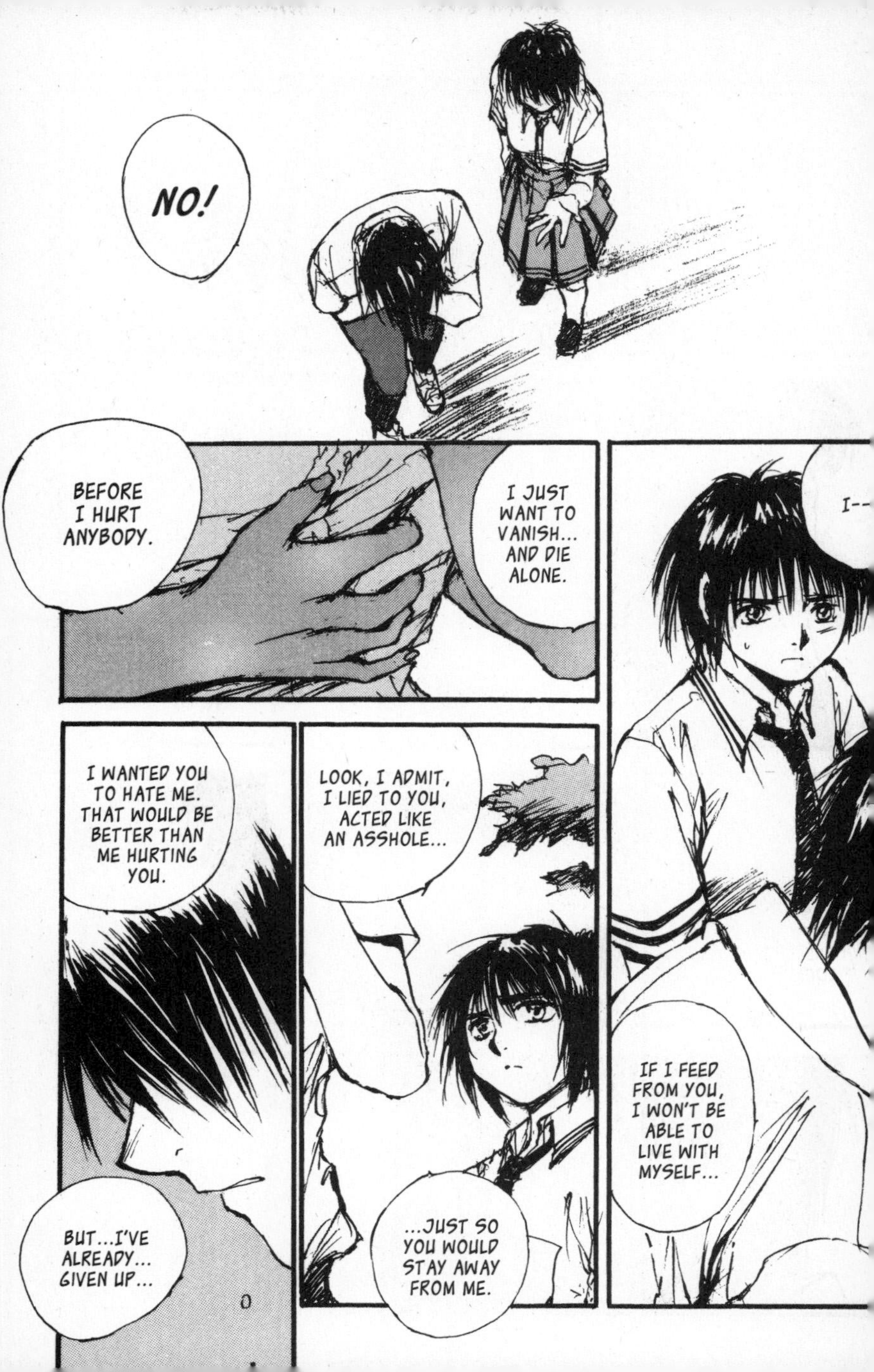
NO!
I--
IF I FEED FROM YOU, I WON'T BE ABLE TO LIVE WITH MYSELF...
I JUST WANT TO VANISH... AND DIE ALONE.
BEFORE I HURT ANYBODY.
LOOK, I ADMIT, I LIED TO YOU, ACTED LIKE AN ASSHOLE...
...JUST SO YOU WOULD STAY AWAY FROM ME.
I WANTED YOU TO HATE ME. THAT WOULD BE BETTER THAN ME HURTING YOU.
BUT...I'VE ALREADY... GIVEN UP...

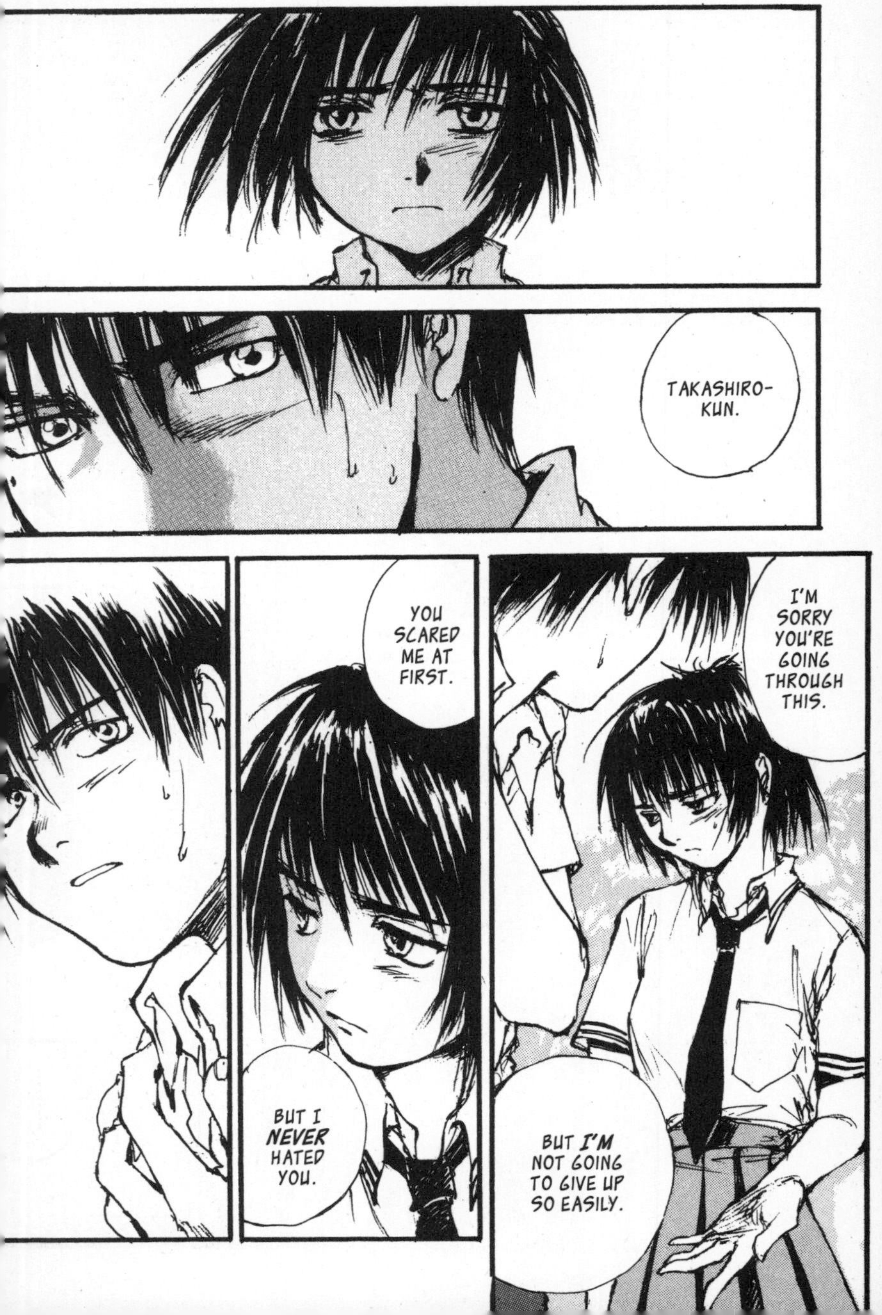
TAKASHIRO-KUN.
I'M SORRY YOU'RE GOING THROUGH THIS.
BUT I'M NOT GOING TO GIVE UP SO EASILY.
YOU SCARED ME AT FIRST.
BUT I NEVER HATED YOU.

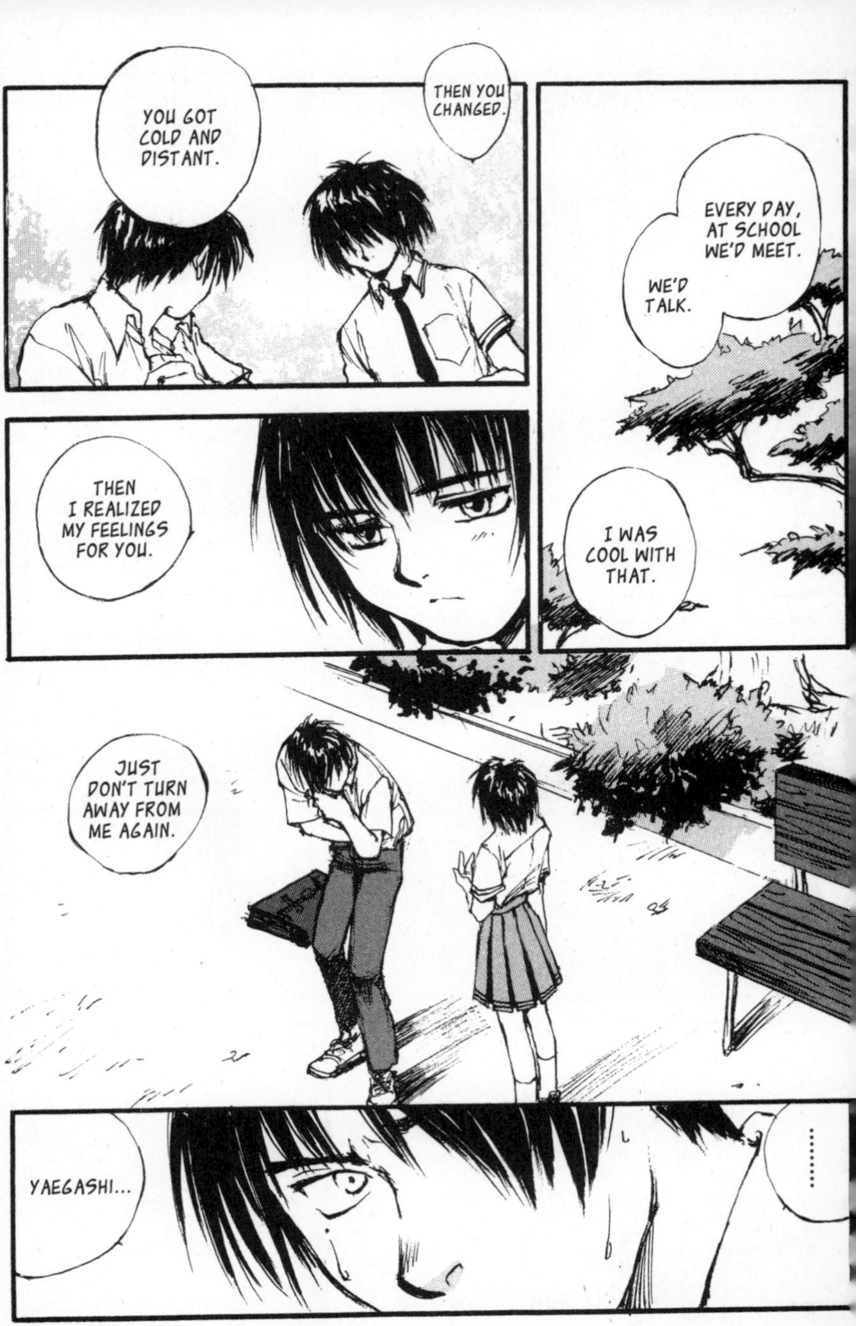
EVERY DAY, AT SCHOOL WE'D MEET.
WE'D TALK.
I WAS COOL WITH THAT.
THEN YOU CHANGED.
YOU GOT COLD AND DISTANT.
THEN I REALIZED MY FEELINGS FOR YOU.
JUST DON'T TURN AWAY FROM ME AGAIN.
....
YAEGASHI...

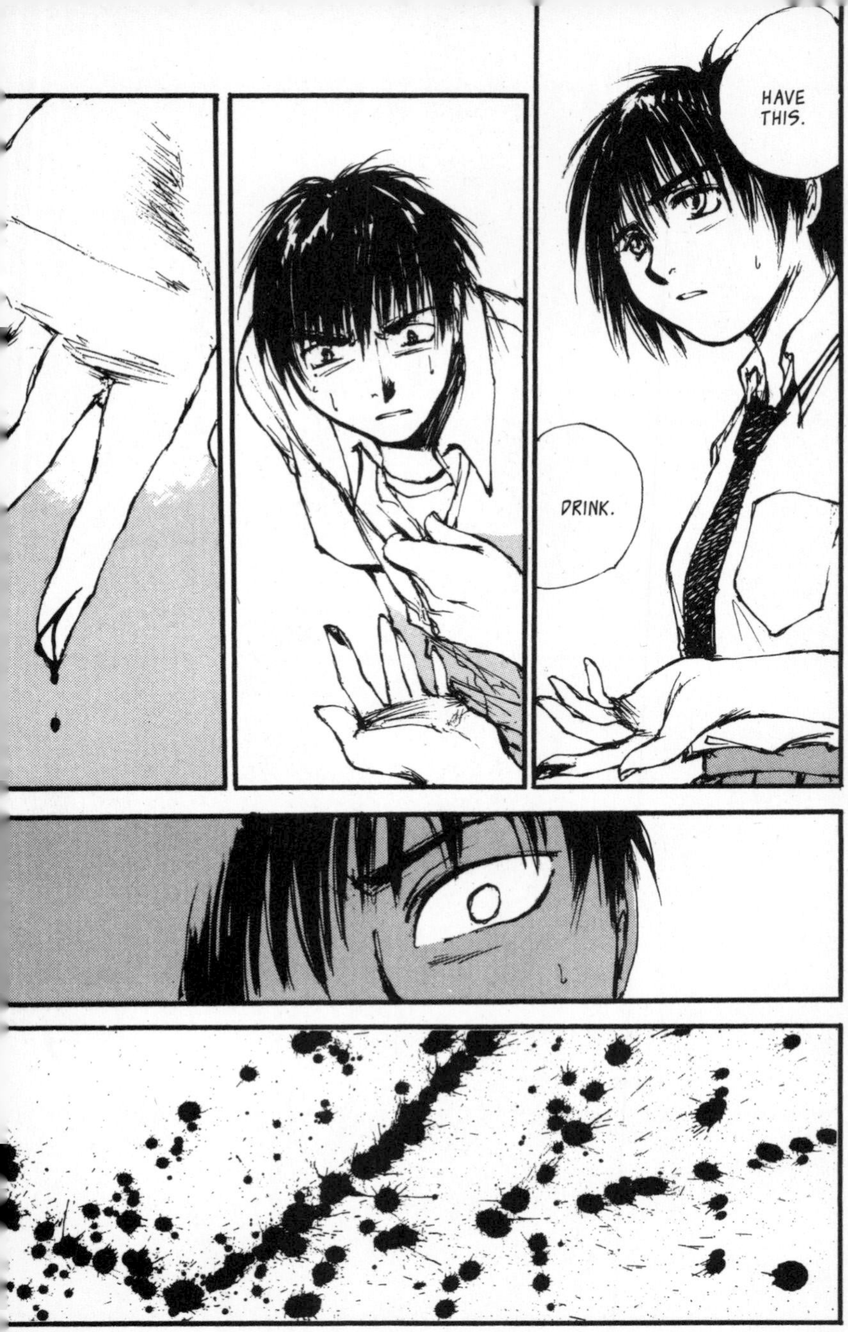
HAVE THIS.
DRINK.

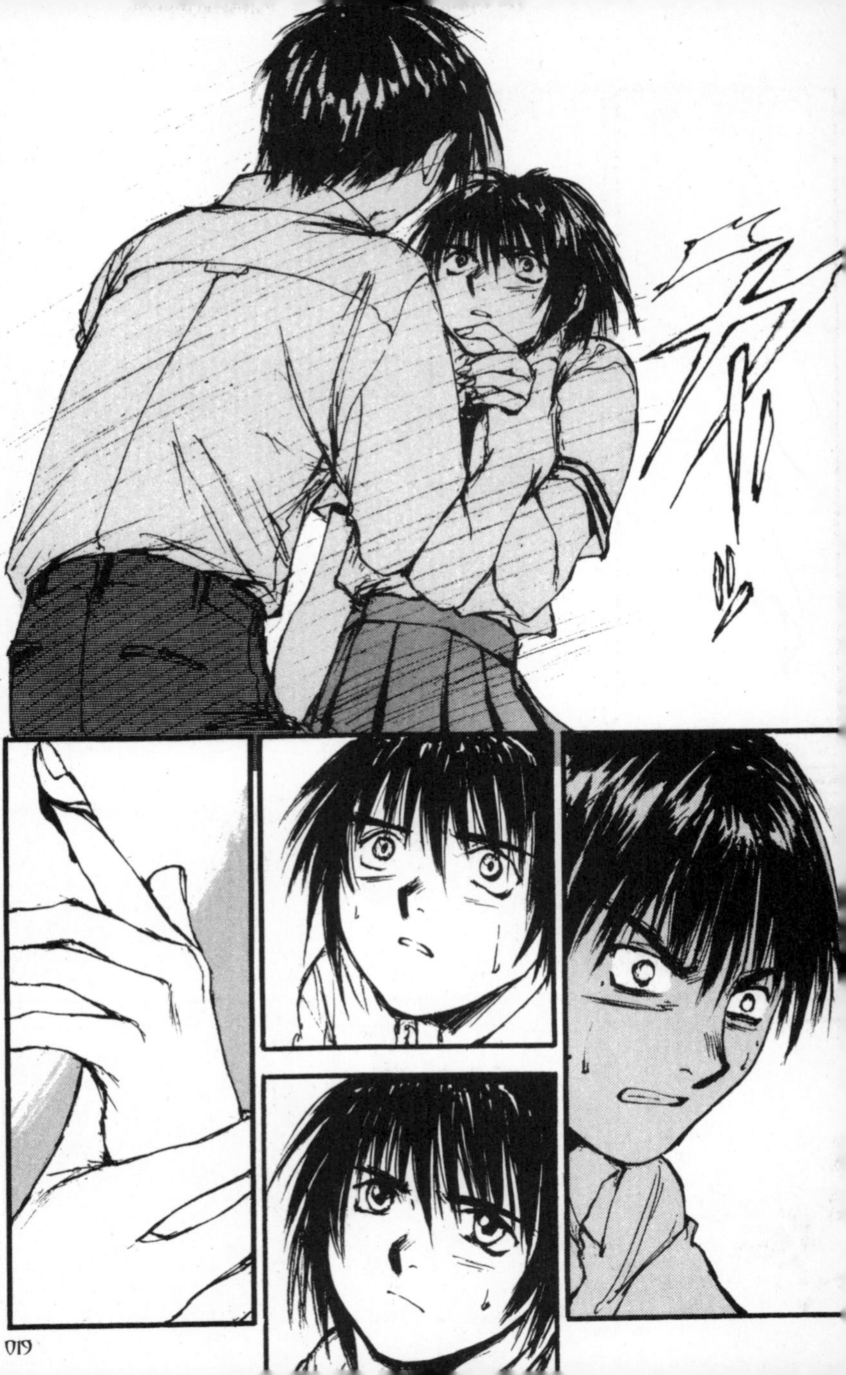

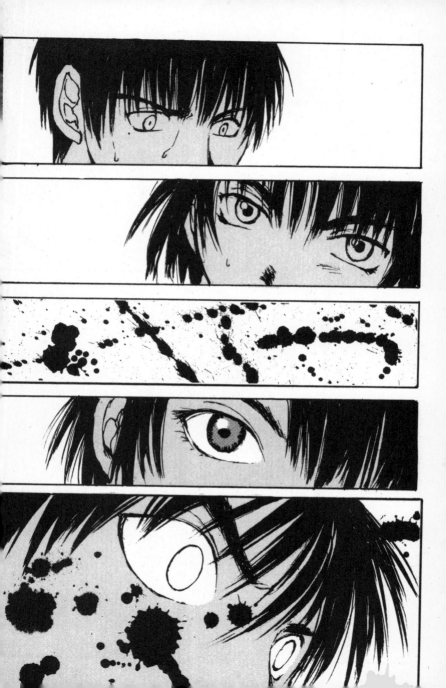

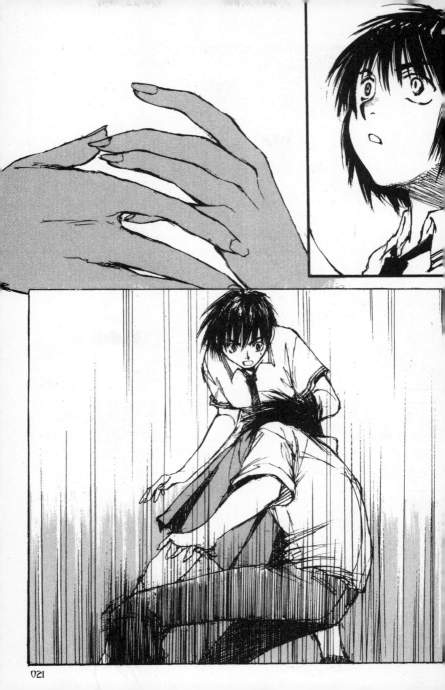

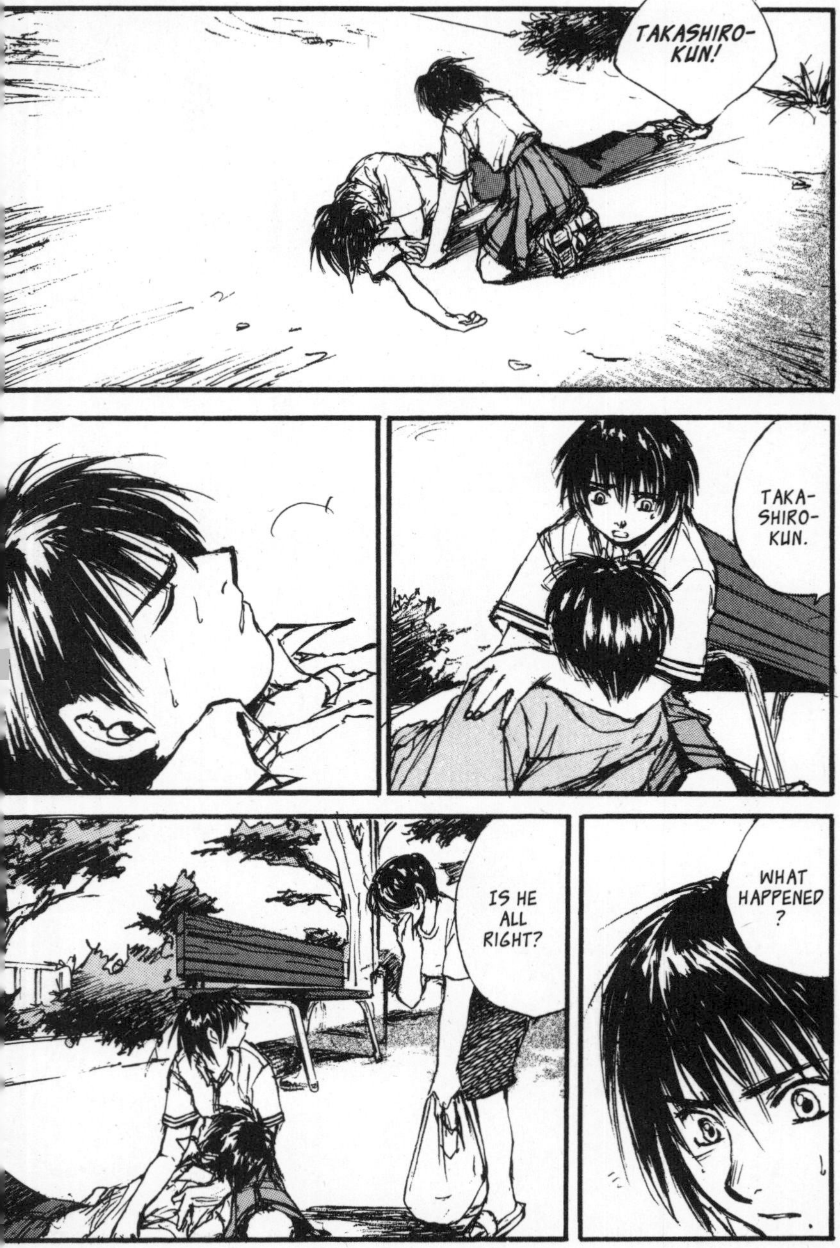
TAKASHIRO-KUN!
TAKA-SHIRO-KUN.
WHAT HAPPENED?
IS HE ALL RIGHT?

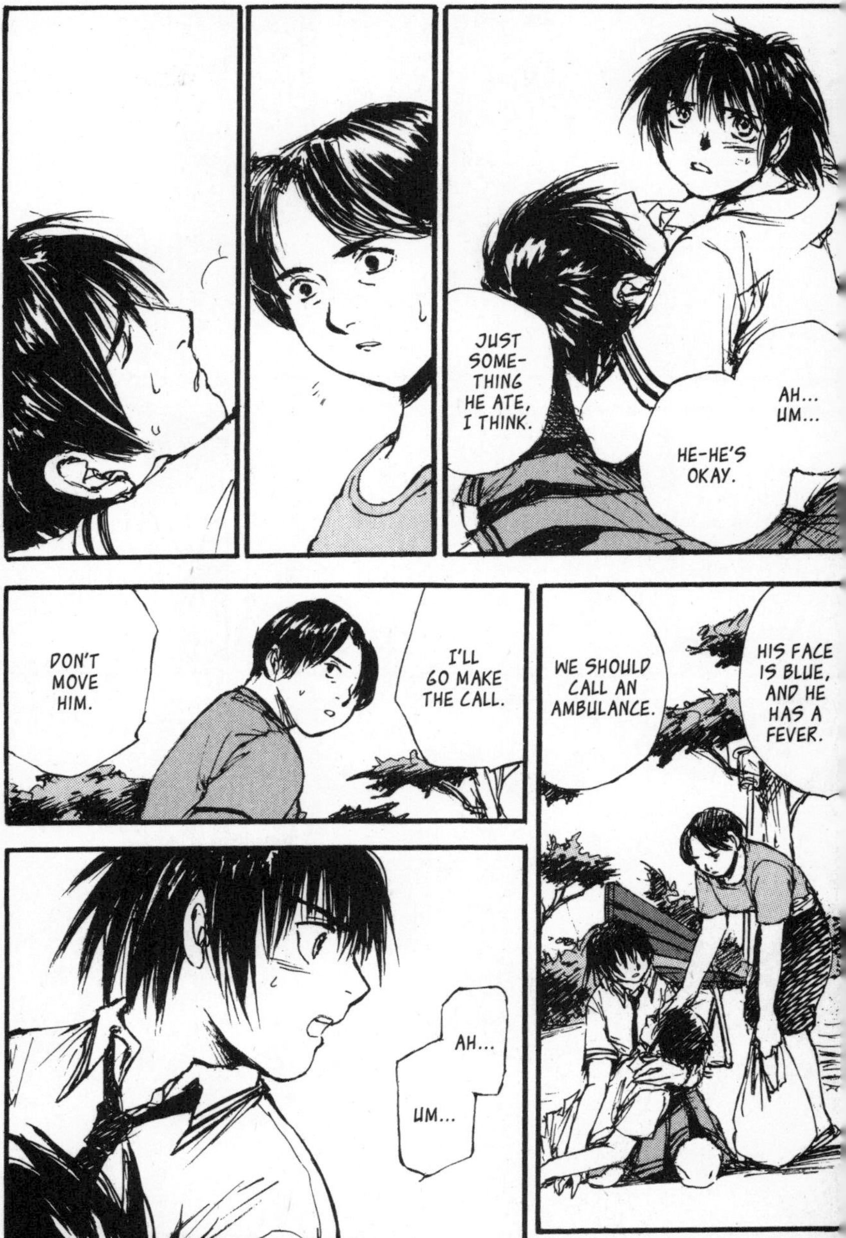
AH... UM...
HE-HE'S OKAY.
JUST SOME-THING HE ATE, I THINK.
HIS FACE IS BLUE, AND HE HAS A FEVER.
WE SHOULD CALL AN AMBULANCE.
I'LL GO MAKE THE CALL.
DON'T MOVE HIM.
AH...
UM...

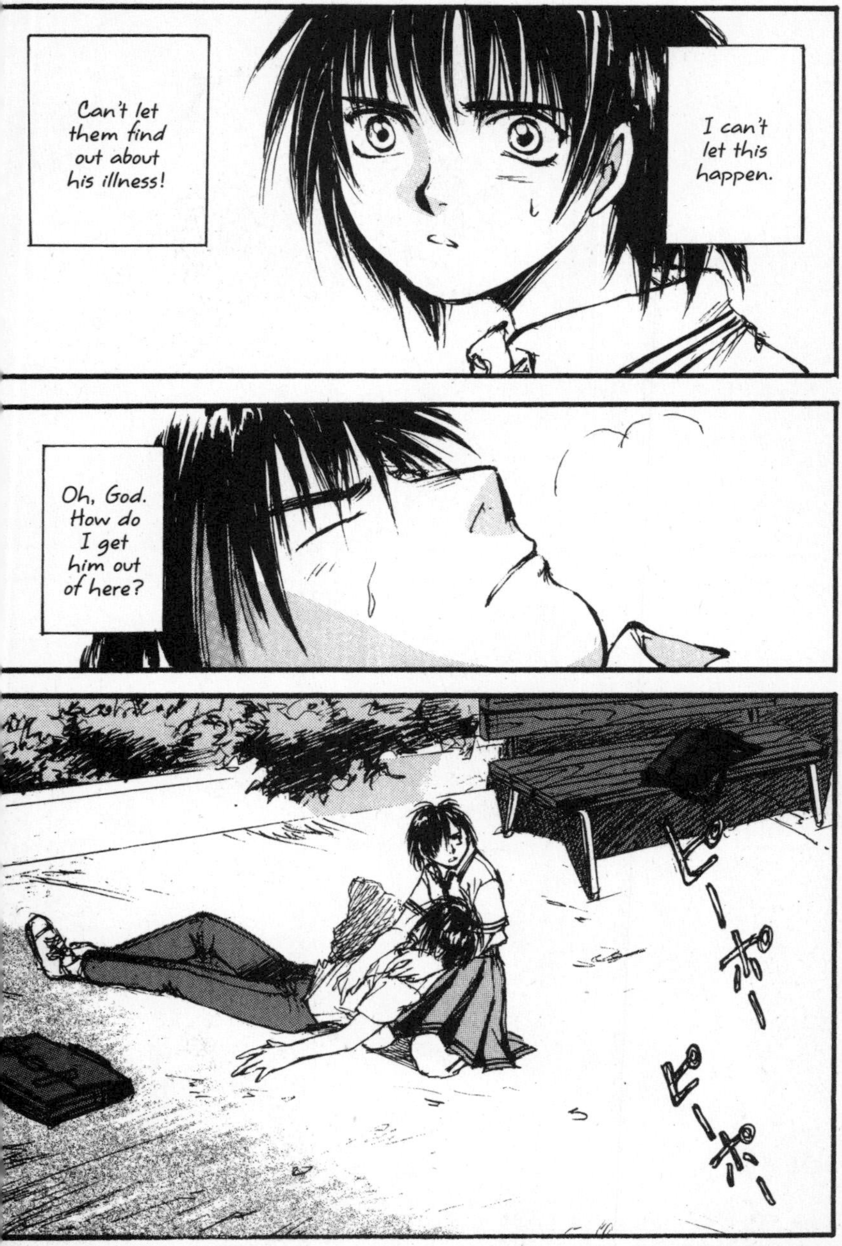
I can't let this happen.
Can't let them find out about his illness!
Oh, God. How do I get him out of here?
ピーポー
ピーポー

*ambulance siren

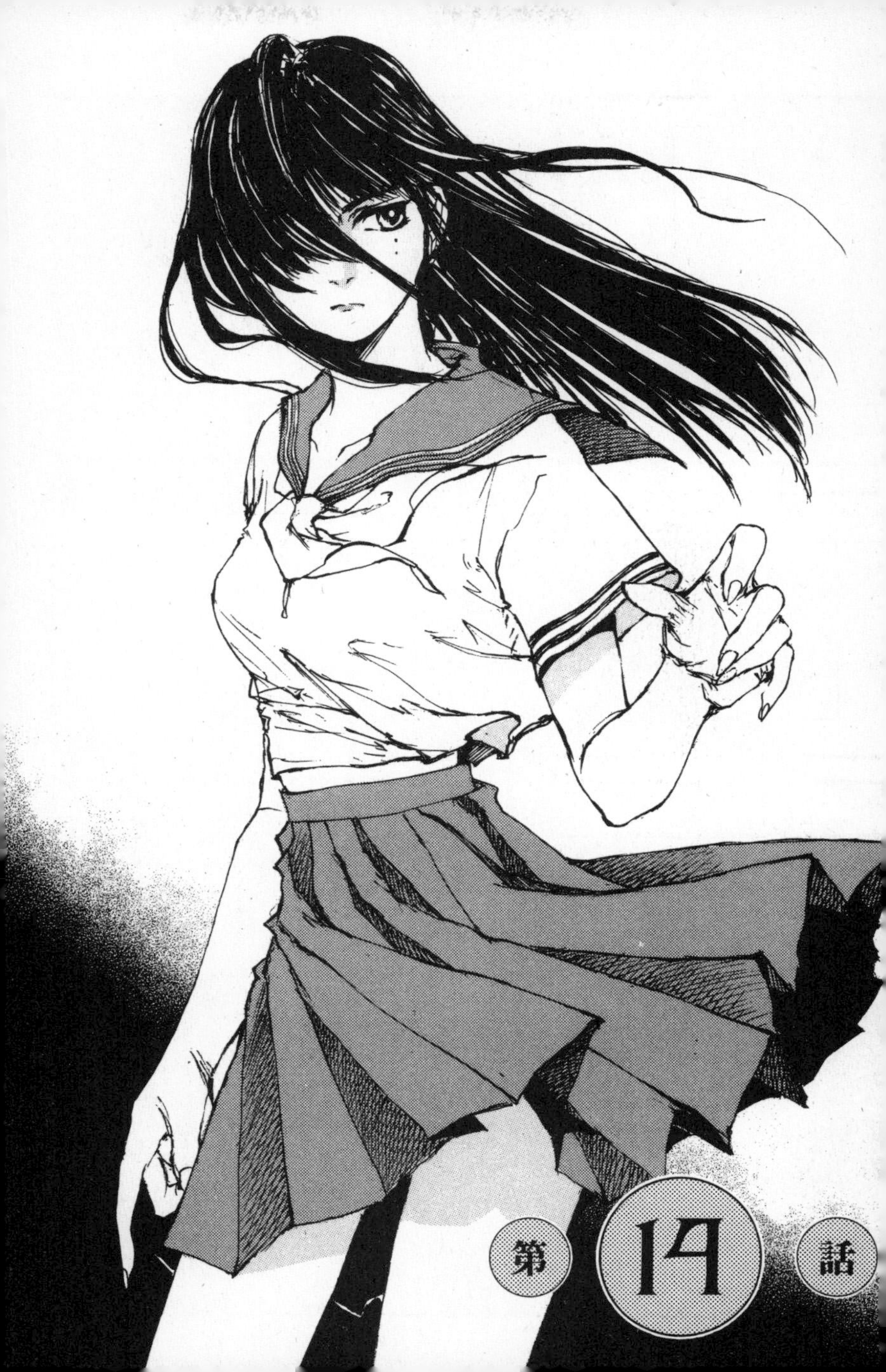
第 14 話

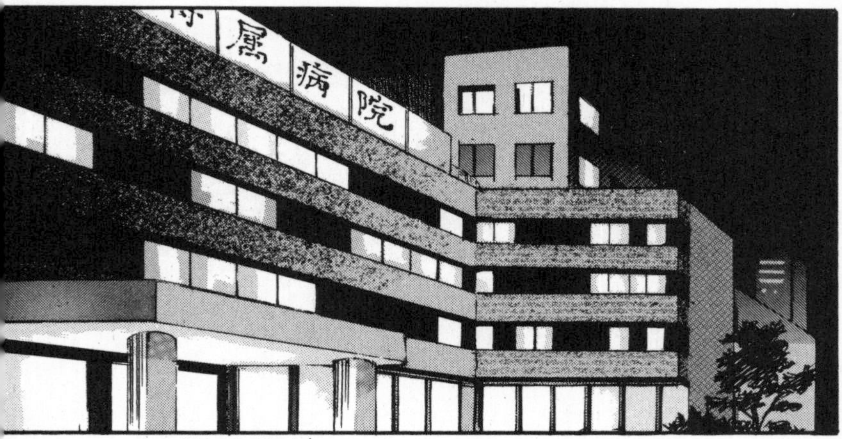
属病院
*University Hospital

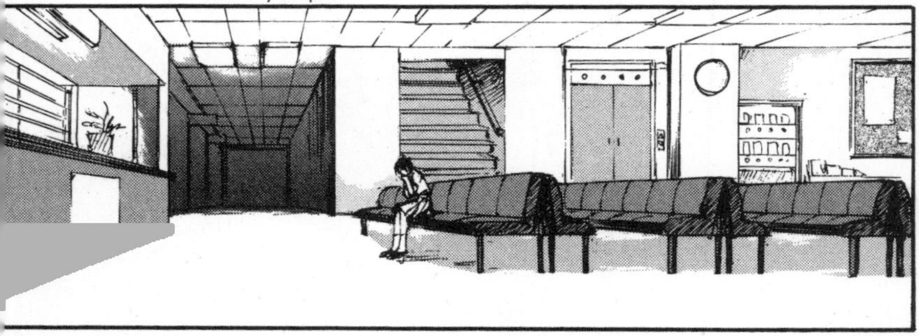

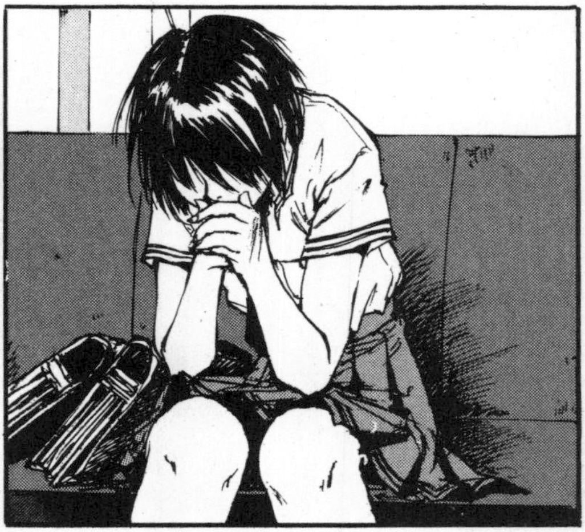

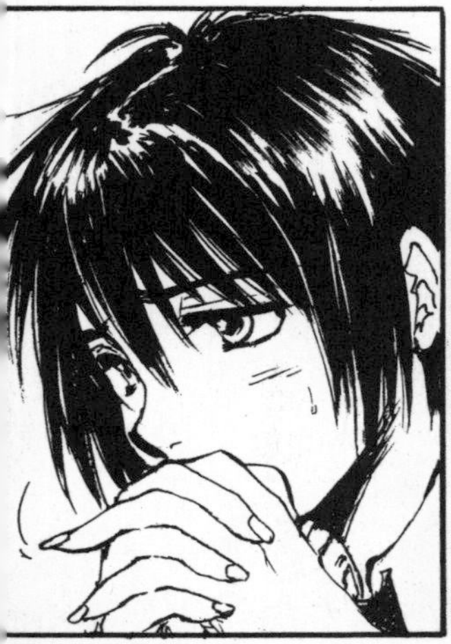

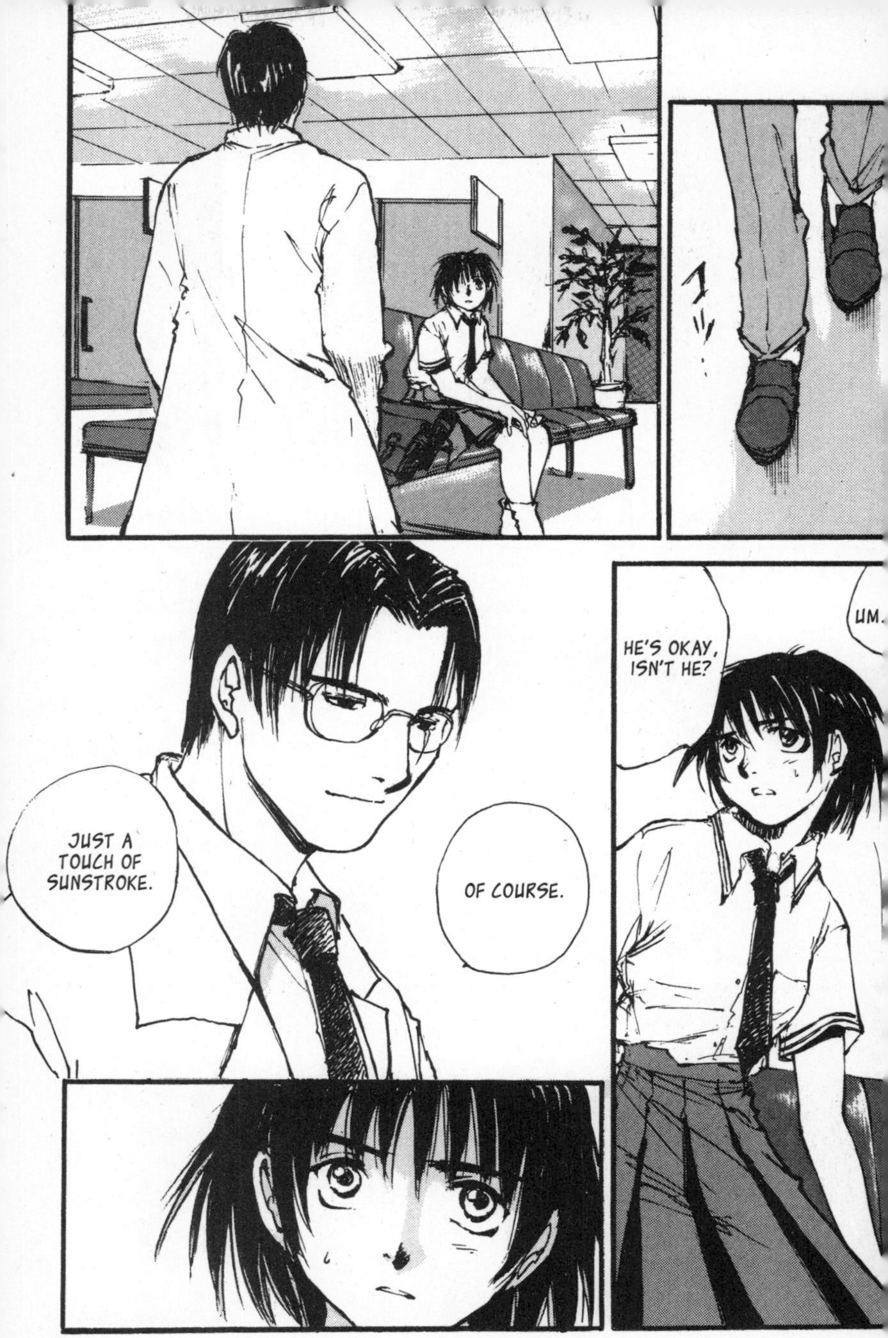
UM.
HE'S OKAY, ISN'T HE?
OF COURSE.
JUST A TOUCH OF SUNSTROKE.

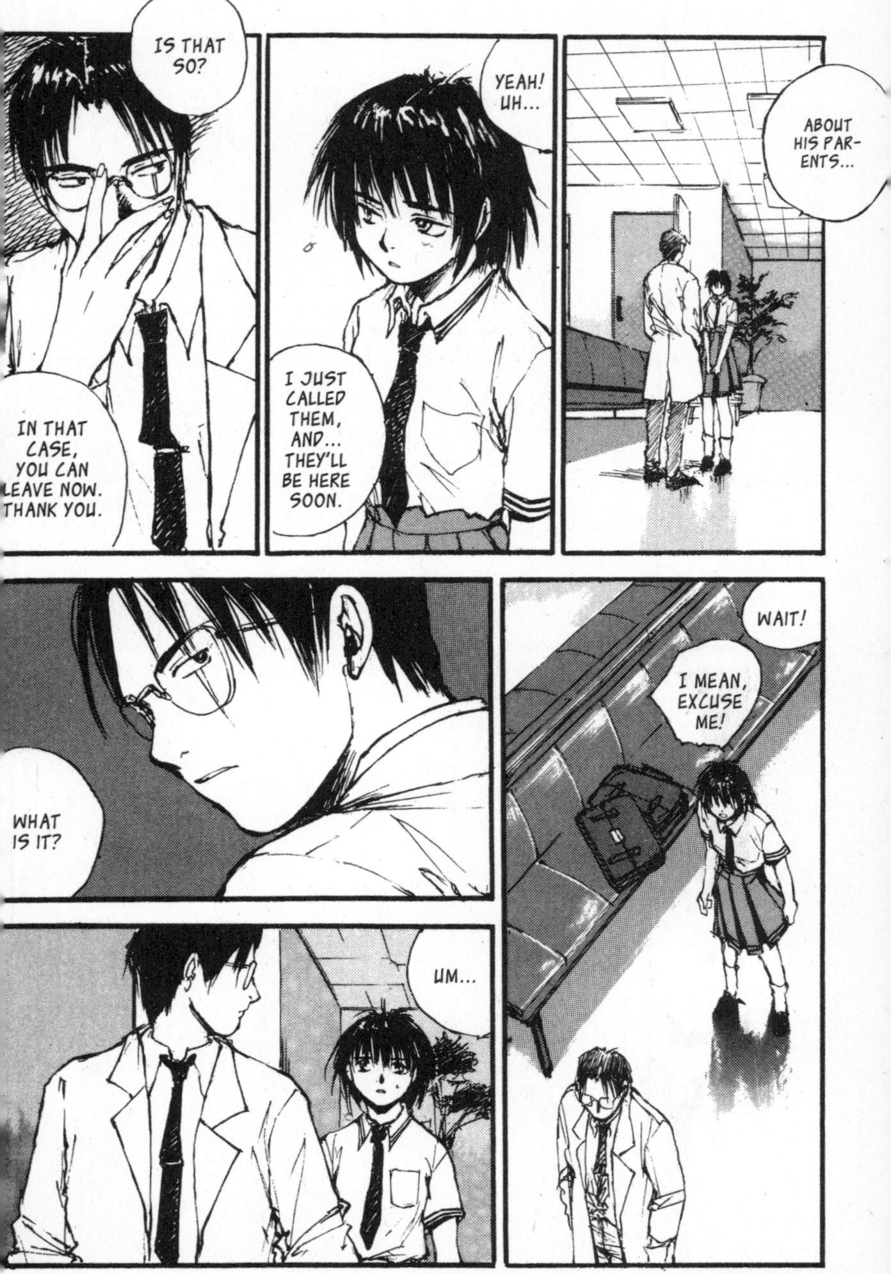
ABOUT HIS PARENTS...
YEAH! UH...
I JUST CALLED THEM, AND... THEY'LL BE HERE SOON.
IS THAT SO?
IN THAT CASE, YOU CAN LEAVE NOW. THANK YOU.
WAIT!
I MEAN, EXCUSE ME!
WHAT IS IT?
UM...

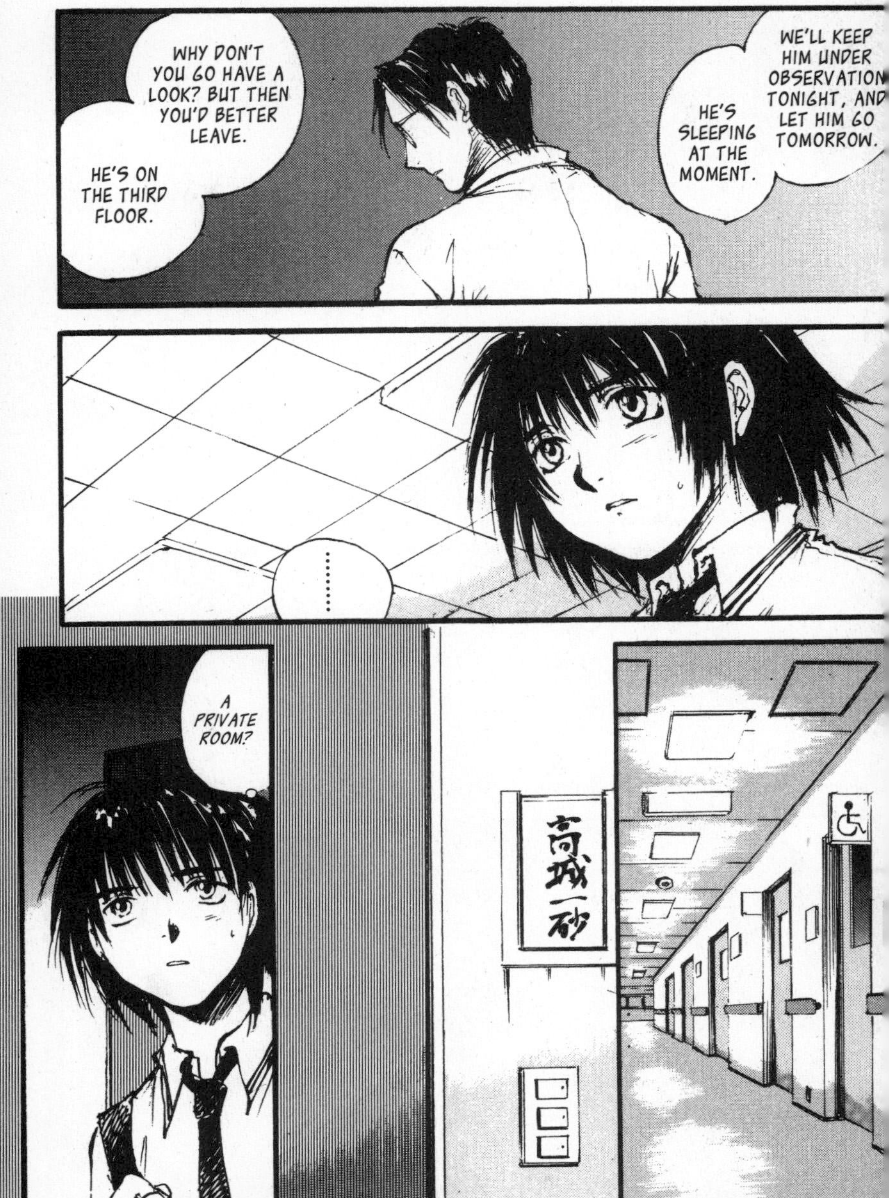
WE'LL KEEP HIM UNDER OBSERVATION TONIGHT, AND LET HIM GO TOMORROW.
HE'S SLEEPING AT THE MOMENT.
WHY DON'T YOU GO HAVE A LOOK? BUT THEN YOU'D BETTER LEAVE.
HE'S ON THE THIRD FLOOR.
……
高城一砂
A PRIVATE ROOM?

* Takashiro Kazuna

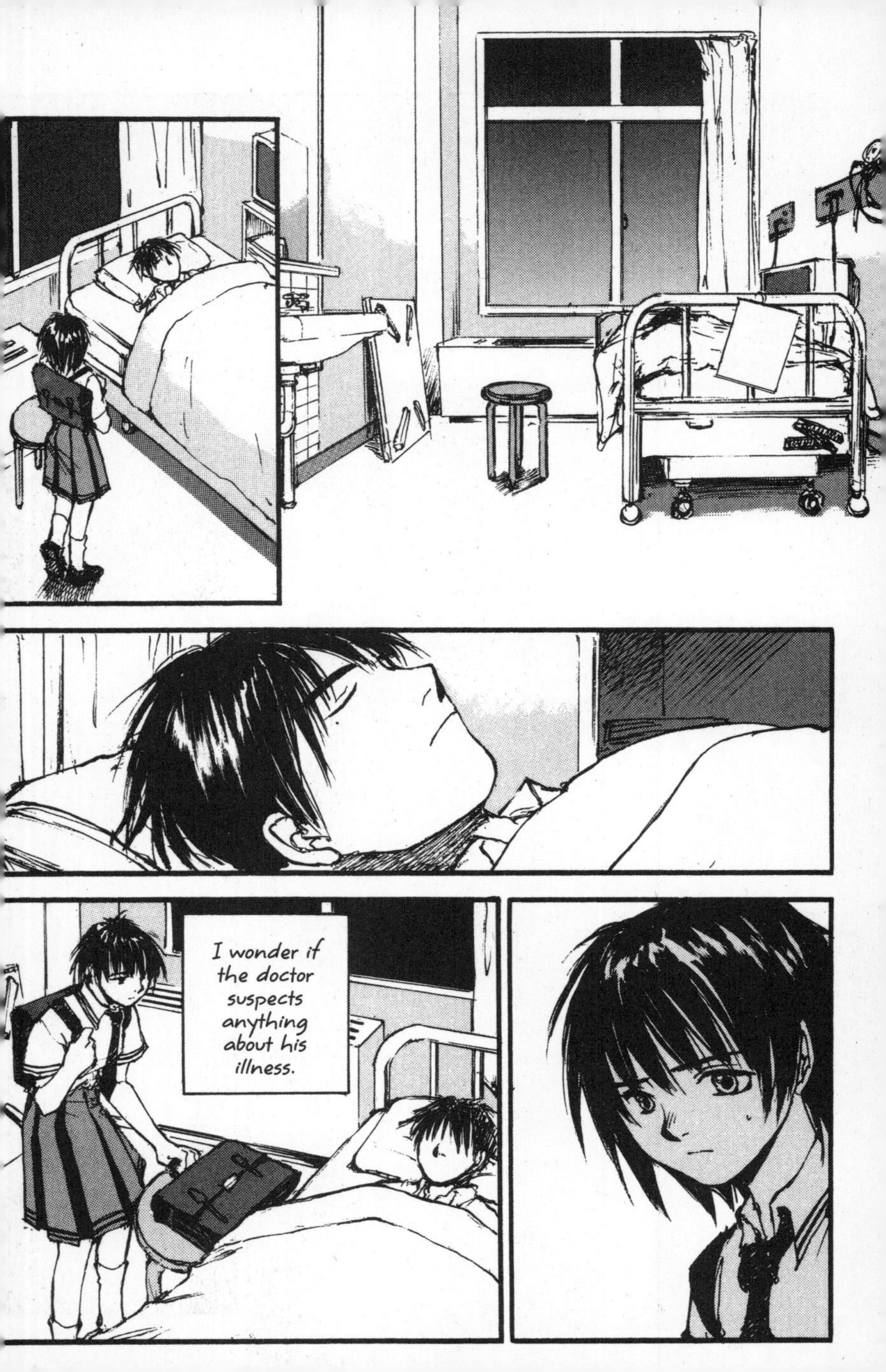
I wonder if the doctor suspects anything about his illness.

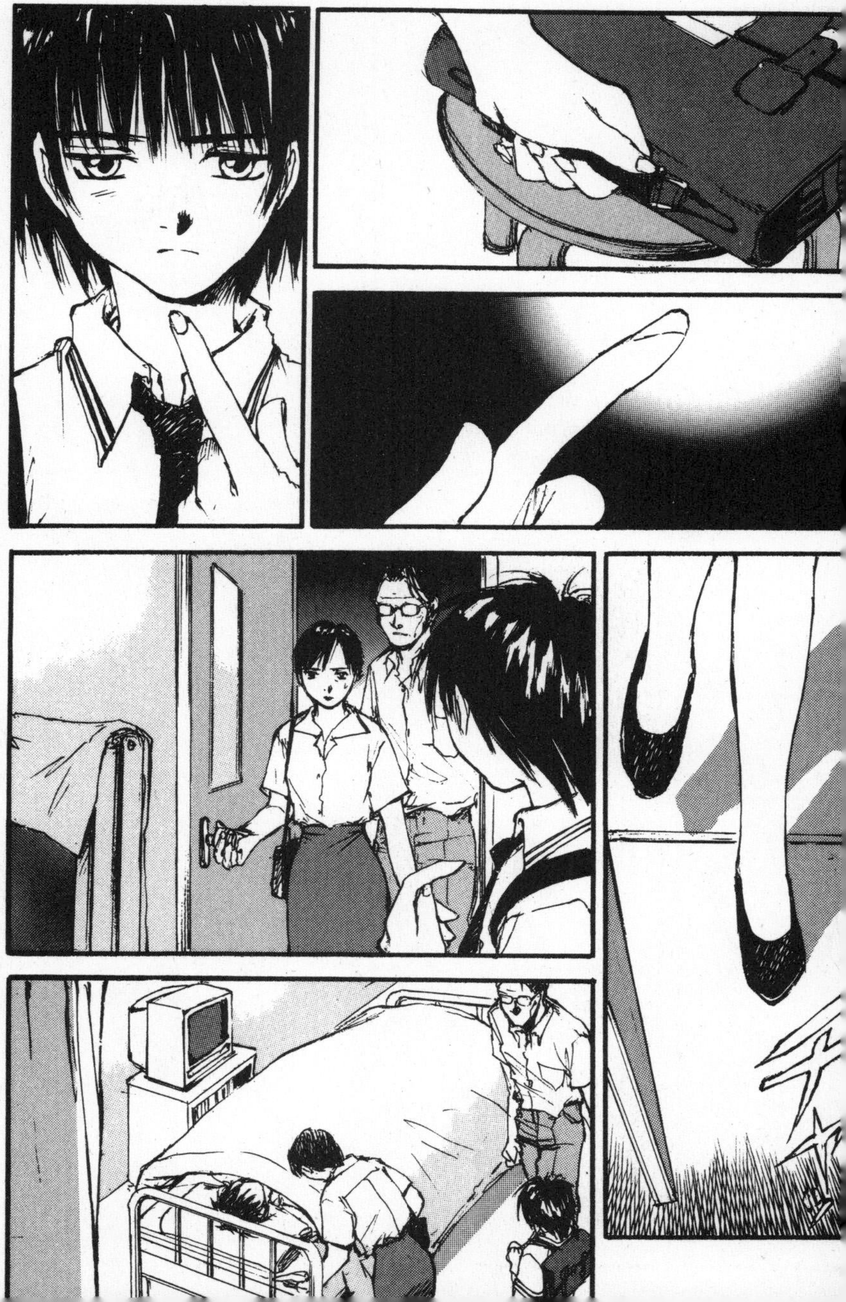

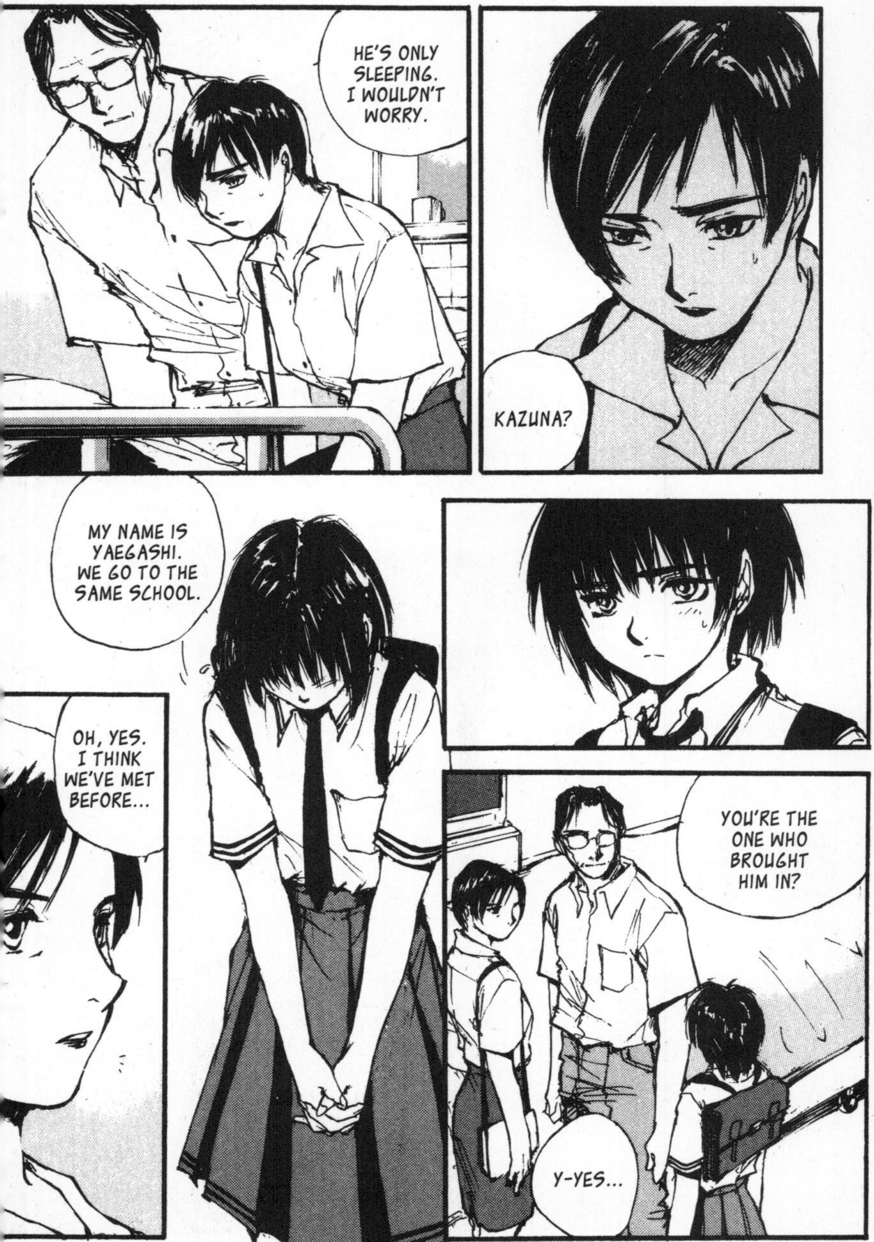
KAZUNA?
HE'S ONLY SLEEPING. I WOULDN'T WORRY.
YOU'RE THE ONE WHO BROUGHT HIM IN?
Y-YES...
MY NAME IS YAEGASHI. WE GO TO THE SAME SCHOOL.
OH, YES. I THINK WE'VE MET BEFORE...

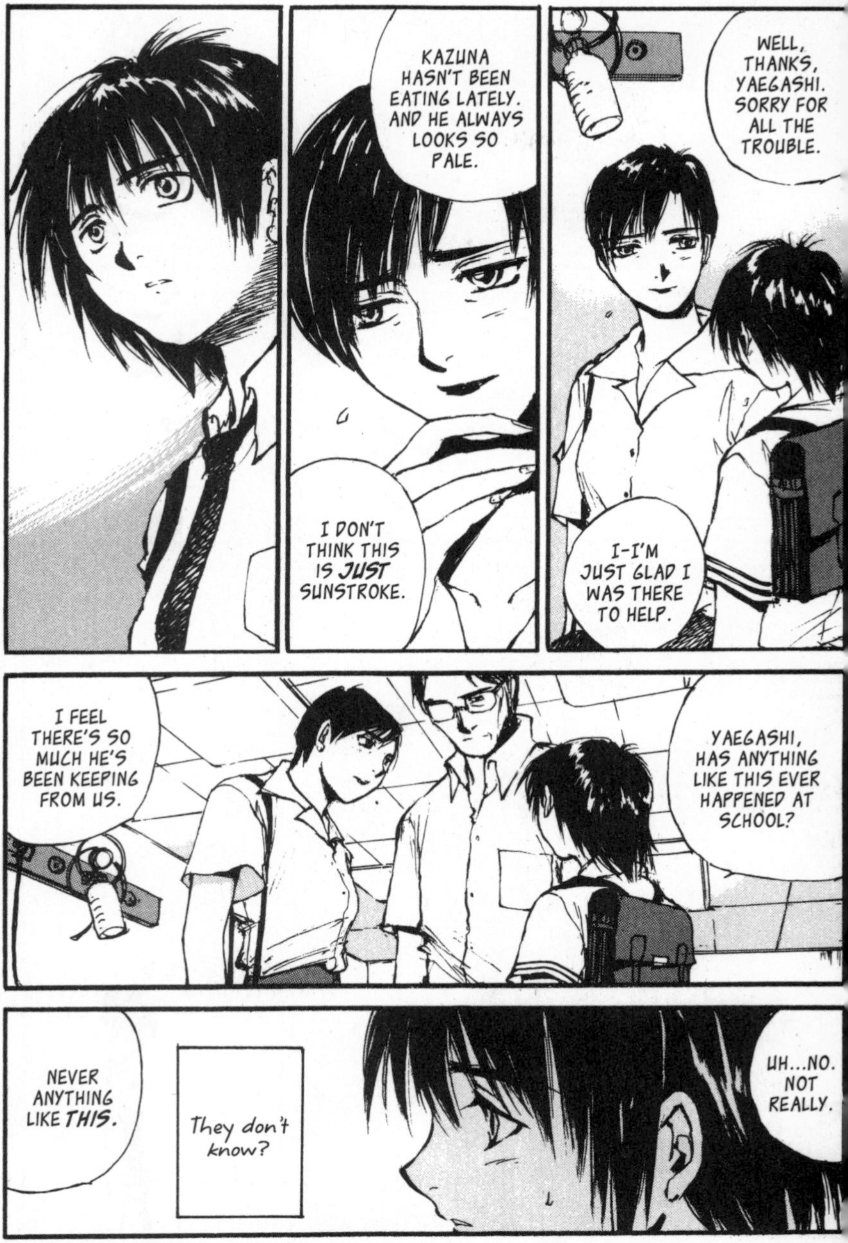
WELL, THANKS, YAEGASHI. SORRY FOR ALL THE TROUBLE.
I-I'M JUST GLAD I WAS THERE TO HELP.
KAZUNA HASN'T BEEN EATING LATELY. AND HE ALWAYS LOOKS SO PALE.
I DON'T THINK THIS IS *JUST* SUNSTROKE.
YAEGASHI, HAS ANYTHING LIKE THIS EVER HAPPENED AT SCHOOL?
I FEEL THERE'S SO MUCH HE'S BEEN KEEPING FROM US.
UH...NO. NOT REALLY.
They don't know?
NEVER ANYTHING LIKE *THIS*.

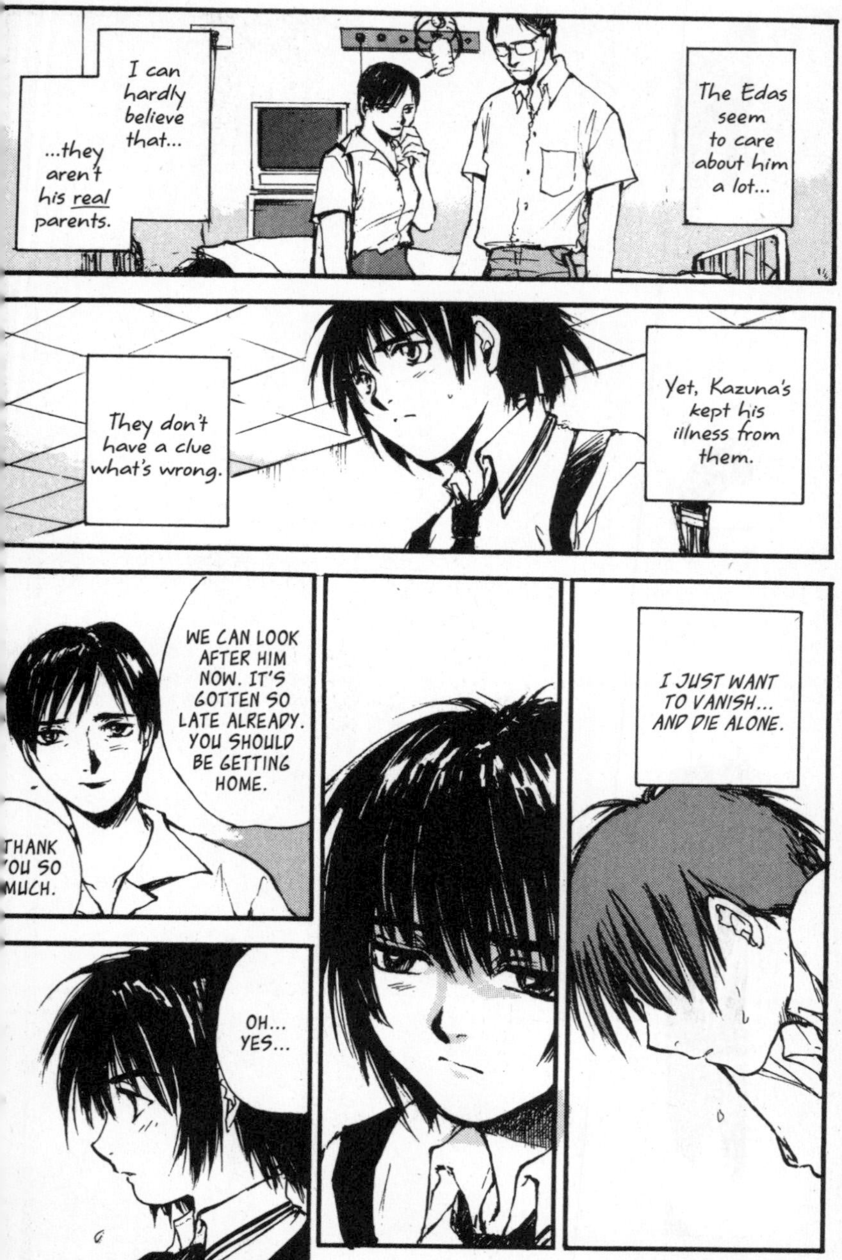
The Edas seem to care about him a lot...
I can hardly believe that...
...they aren't his real parents.
Yet, Kazuna's kept his illness from them.
They don't have a clue what's wrong.
I JUST WANT TO VANISH... AND DIE ALONE.
WE CAN LOOK AFTER HIM NOW. IT'S GOTTEN SO LATE ALREADY. YOU SHOULD BE GETTING HOME.
THANK YOU SO MUCH.
OH... YES...

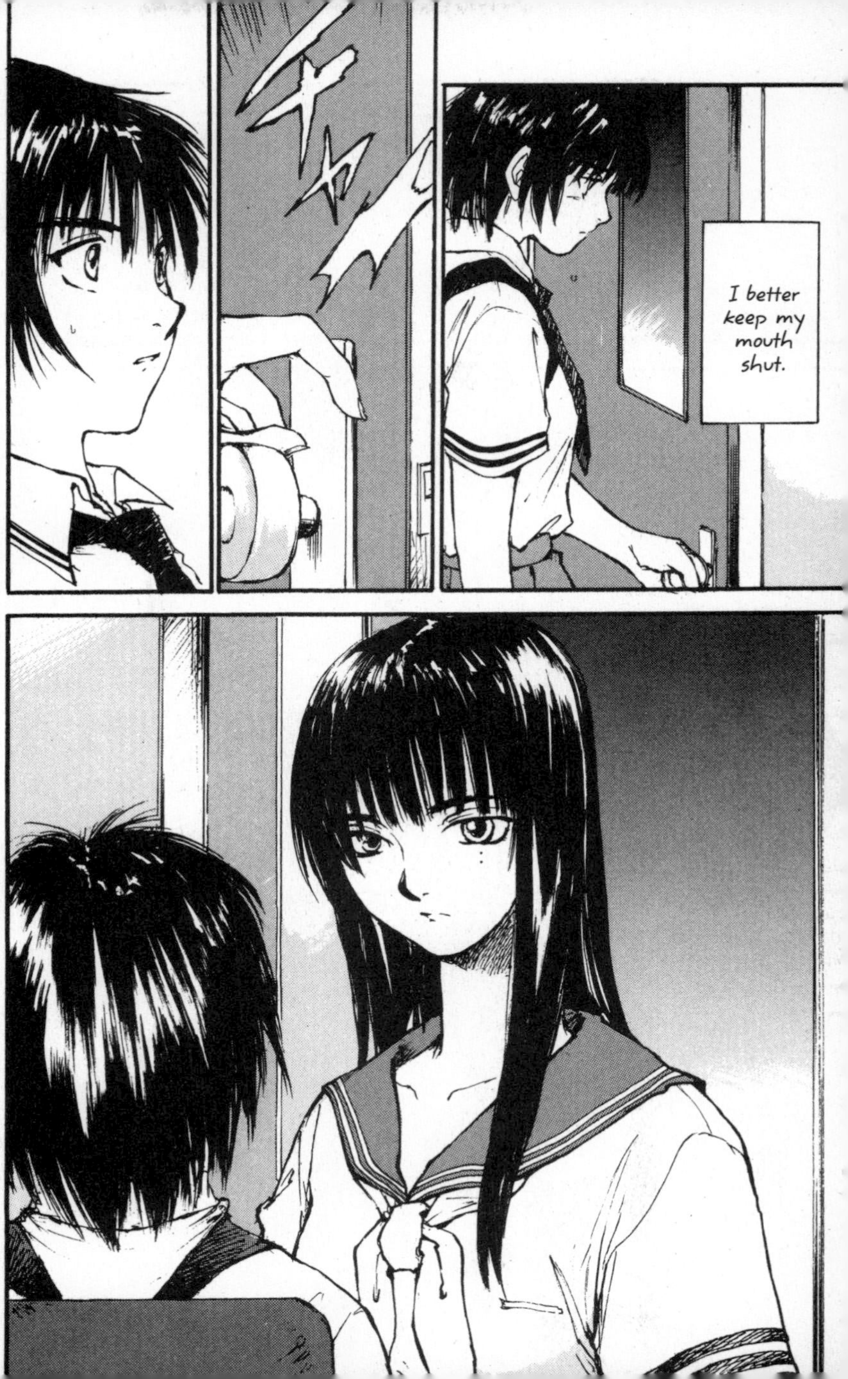
I better keep my mouth shut.

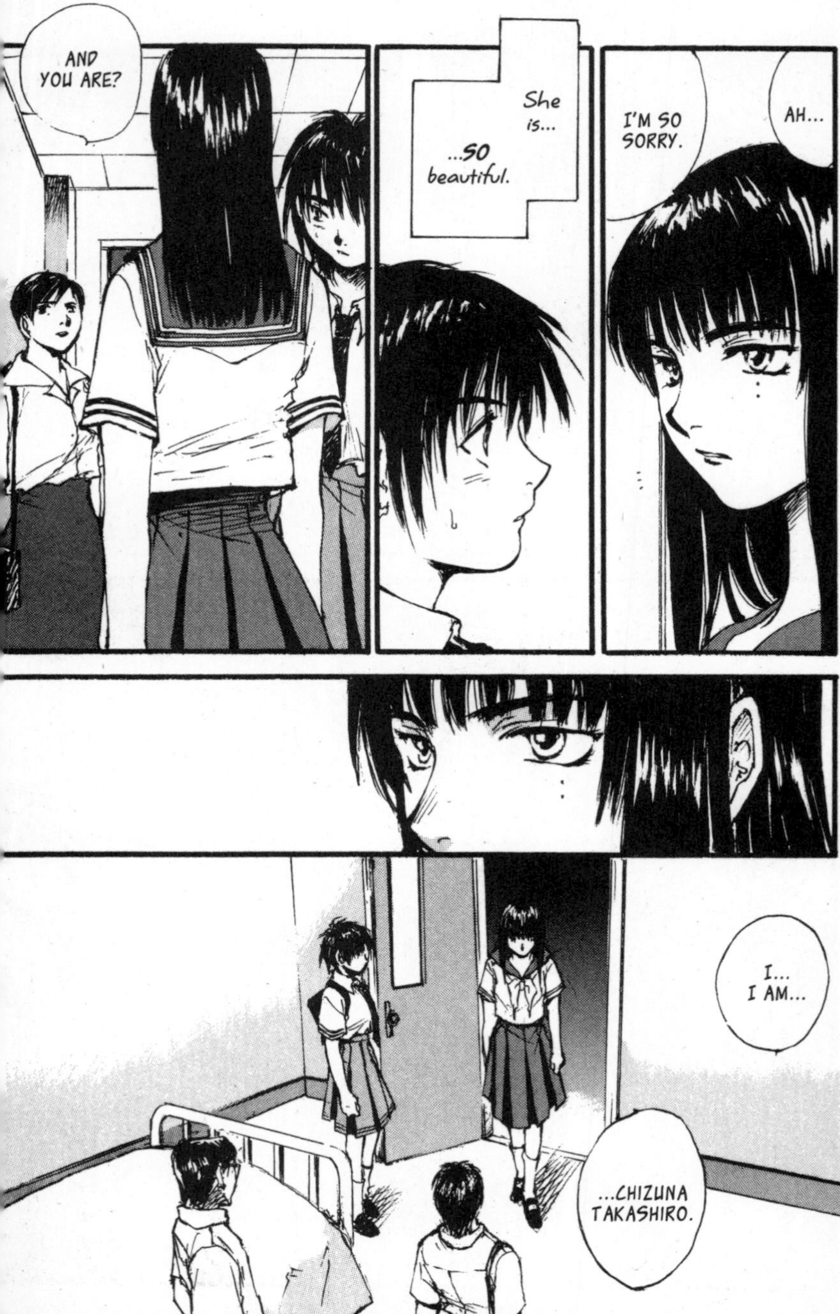
AH...
I'M SO SORRY.
She is... ...SO beautiful.
AND YOU ARE?
I... I AM...
...CHIZUNA TAKASHIRO.

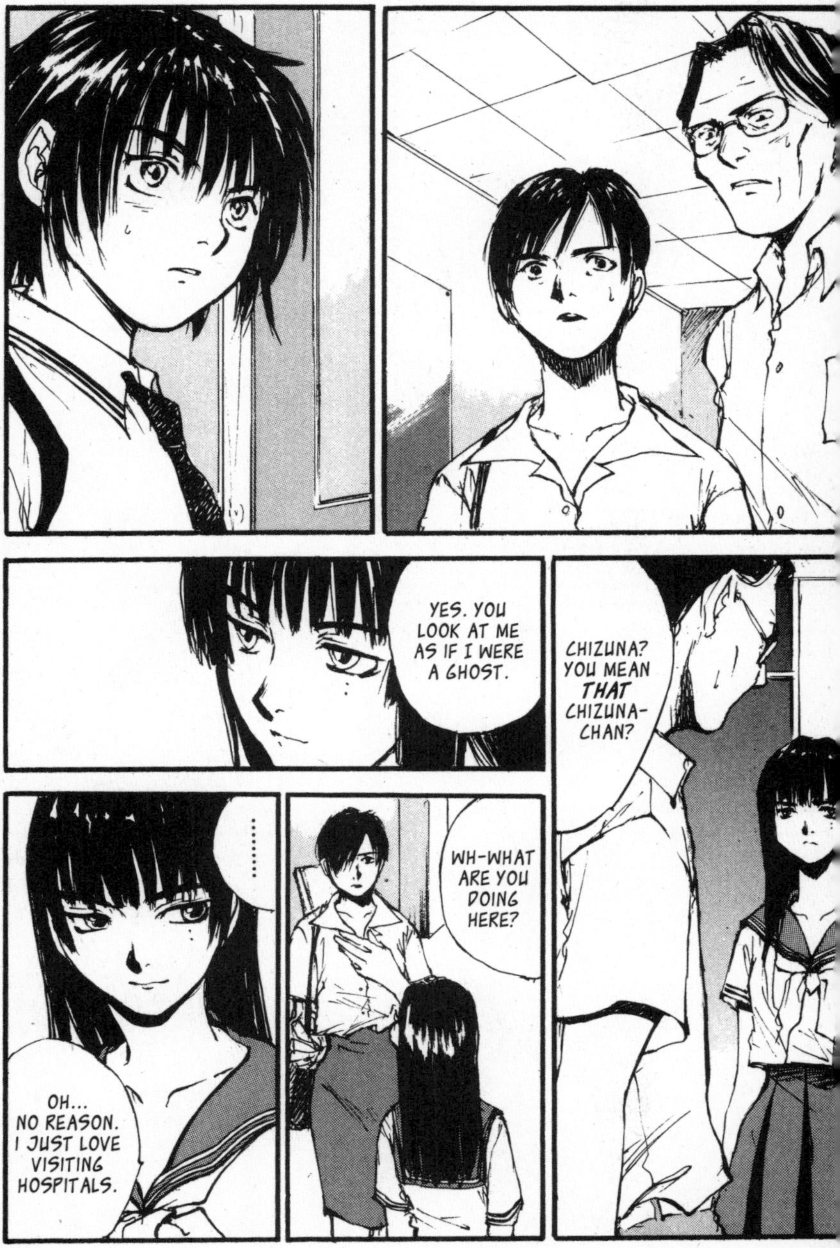
CHIZUNA? YOU MEAN *THAT* CHIZUNA-CHAN?
YES. YOU LOOK AT ME AS IF I WERE A GHOST.
WH-WHAT ARE YOU DOING HERE?
......
OH... NO REASON. I JUST LOVE VISITING HOSPITALS.

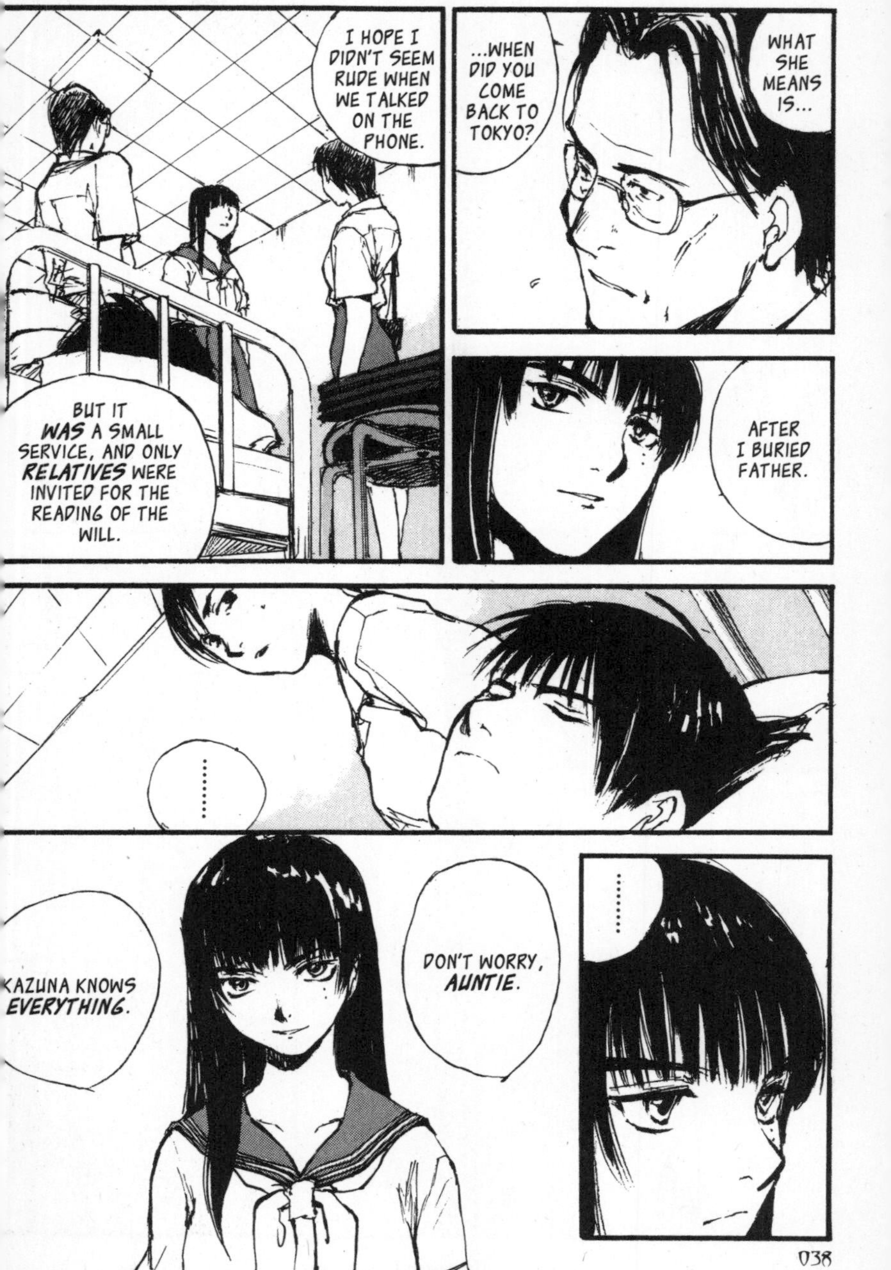
WHAT SHE MEANS IS...
...WHEN DID YOU COME BACK TO TOKYO?
AFTER I BURIED FATHER.
I HOPE I DIDN'T SEEM RUDE WHEN WE TALKED ON THE PHONE.
BUT IT WAS A SMALL SERVICE, AND ONLY RELATIVES WERE INVITED FOR THE READING OF THE WILL.
....
....
DON'T WORRY, AUNTIE.
KAZUNA KNOWS EVERYTHING.

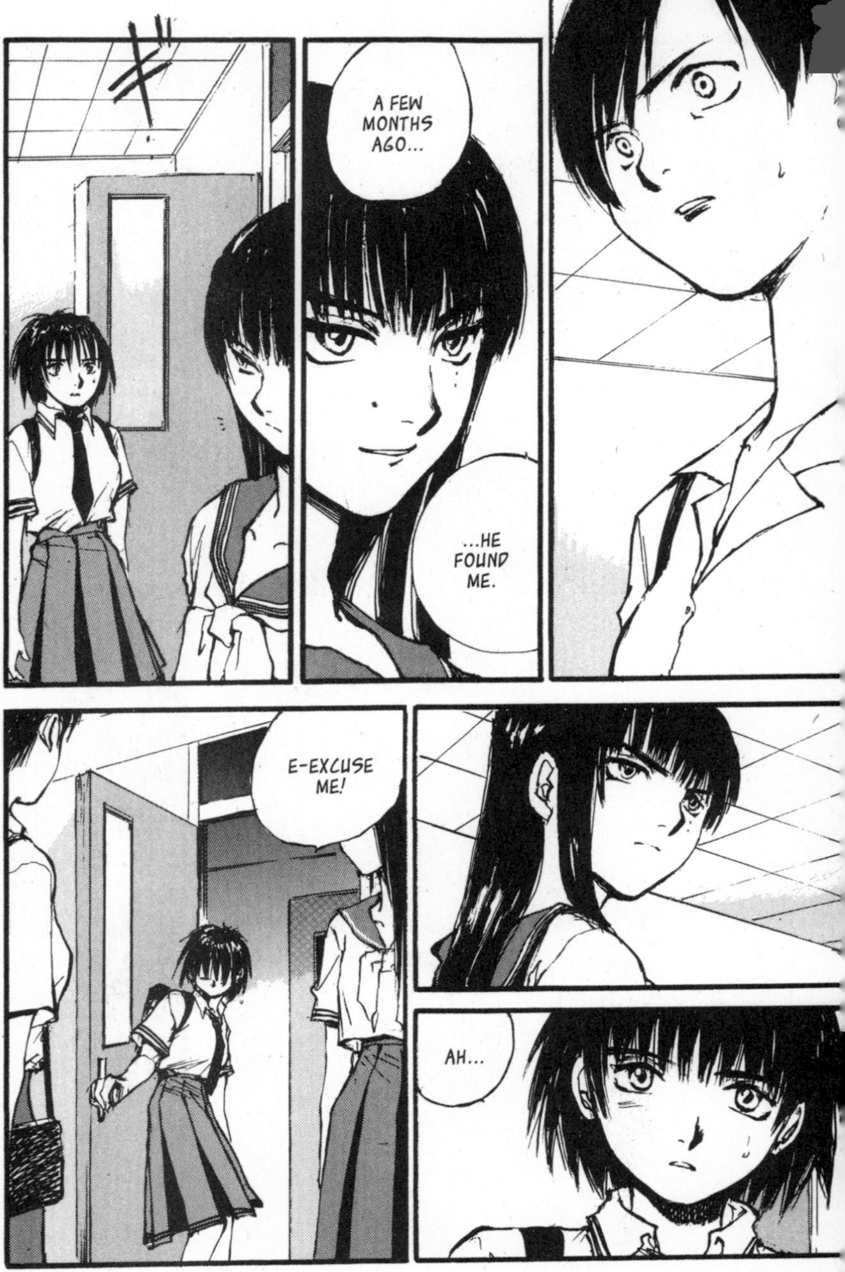
A FEW MONTHS AGO...
...HE FOUND ME.
AH...
E-EXCUSE ME!

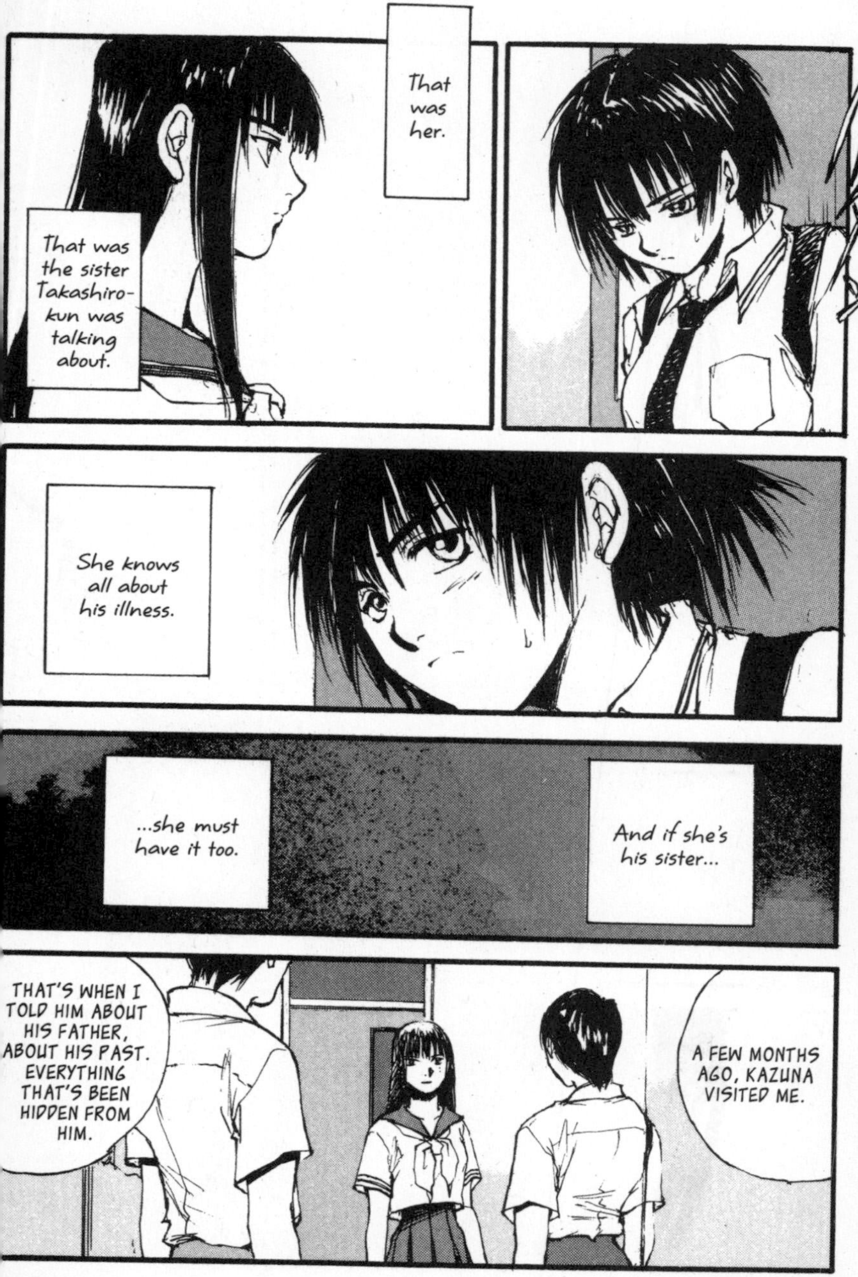
That was her.
That was the sister Takashiro-kun was talking about.
She knows all about his illness.
And if she's his sister...
...she must have it too.
A FEW MONTHS AGO, KAZUNA VISITED ME.
THAT'S WHEN I TOLD HIM ABOUT HIS FATHER, ABOUT HIS PAST. EVERYTHING THAT'S BEEN HIDDEN FROM HIM.

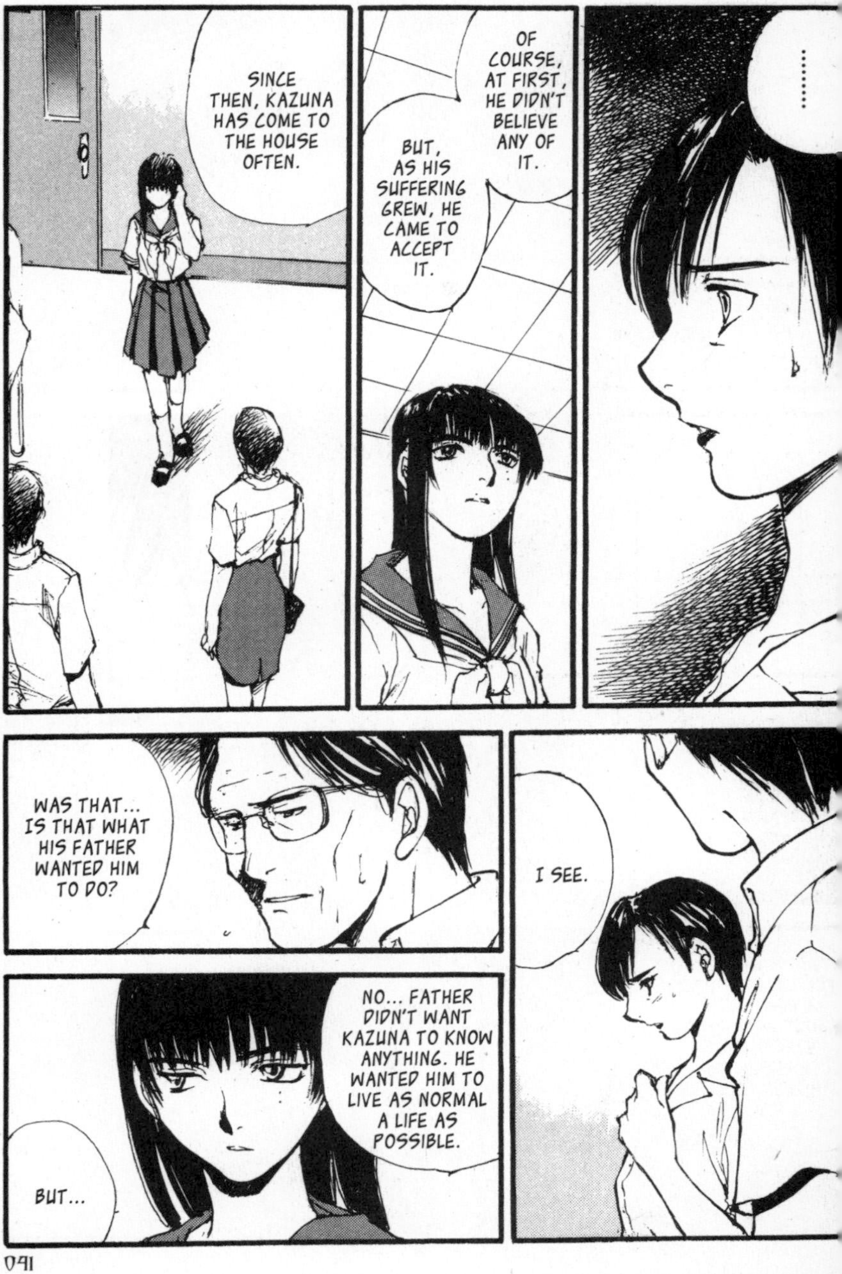
......
OF COURSE, AT FIRST, HE DIDN'T BELIEVE ANY OF IT.
BUT, AS HIS SUFFERING GREW, HE CAME TO ACCEPT IT.
SINCE THEN, KAZUNA HAS COME TO THE HOUSE OFTEN.
I SEE.
WAS THAT... IS THAT WHAT HIS FATHER WANTED HIM TO DO?
NO... FATHER DIDN'T WANT KAZUNA TO KNOW ANYTHING. HE WANTED HIM TO LIVE AS NORMAL A LIFE AS POSSIBLE.
BUT...

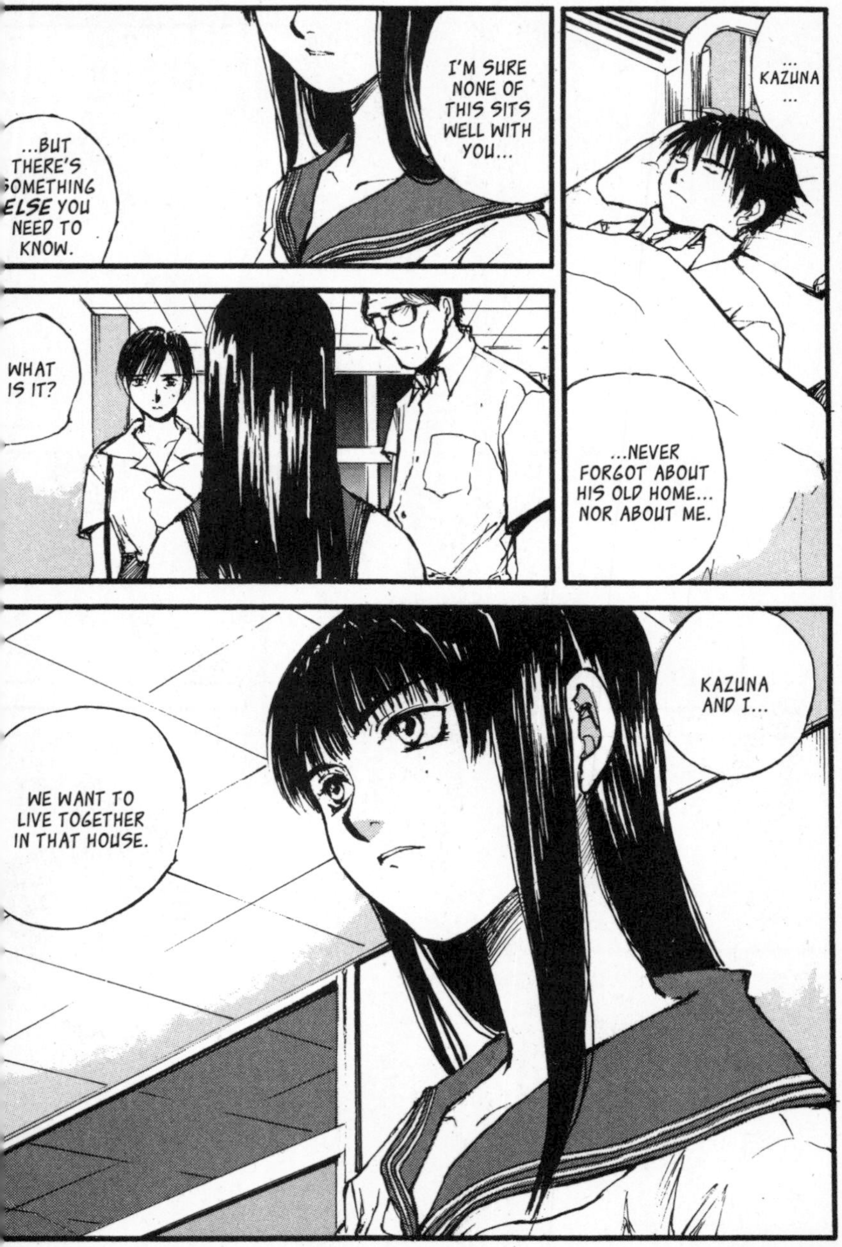
... KAZUNA ...
...NEVER FORGOT ABOUT HIS OLD HOME... NOR ABOUT ME.
I'M SURE NONE OF THIS SITS WELL WITH YOU...
...BUT THERE'S SOMETHING *ELSE* YOU NEED TO KNOW.
WHAT IS IT?
KAZUNA AND I...
WE WANT TO LIVE TOGETHER IN THAT HOUSE.

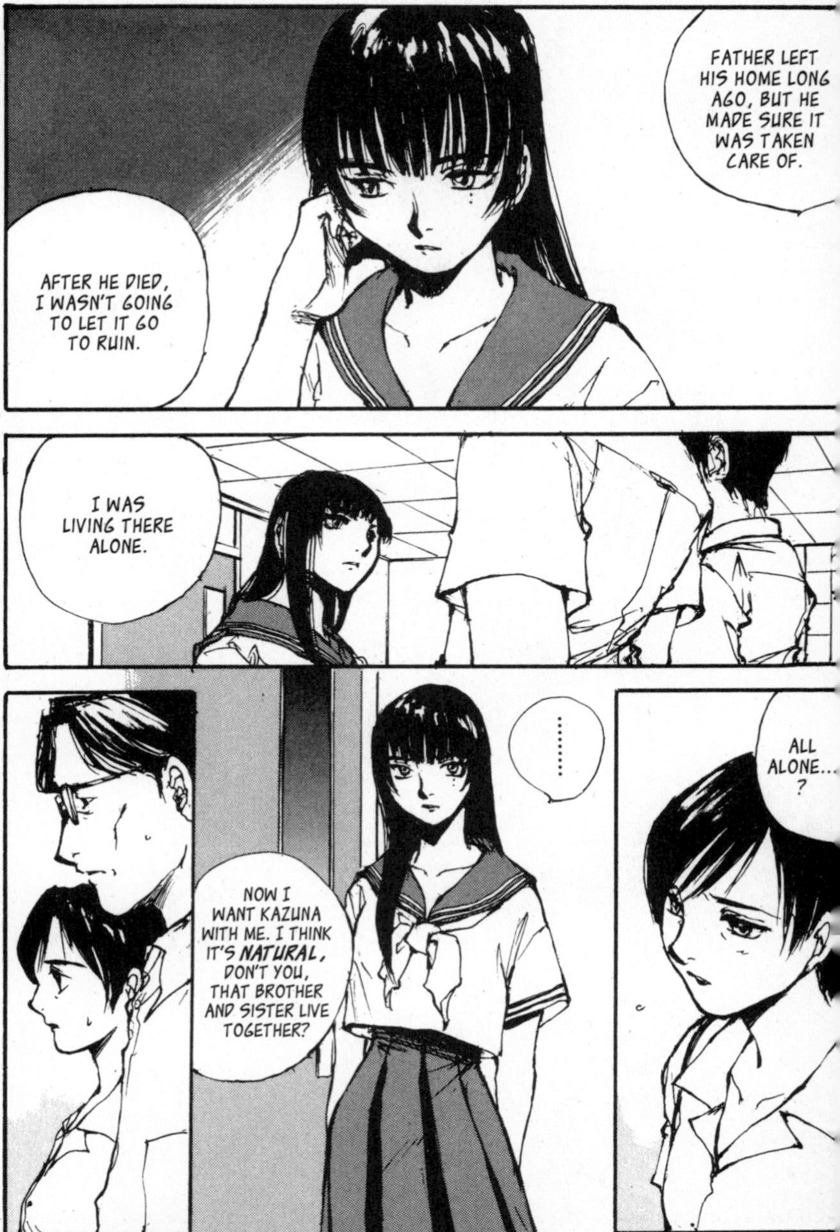
FATHER LEFT HIS HOME LONG AGO, BUT HE MADE SURE IT WAS TAKEN CARE OF.
AFTER HE DIED, I WASN'T GOING TO LET IT GO TO RUIN.
I WAS LIVING THERE ALONE.
ALL ALONE...?
......
NOW I WANT KAZUNA WITH ME. I THINK IT'S ***NATURAL***, DON'T YOU, THAT BROTHER AND SISTER LIVE TOGETHER?

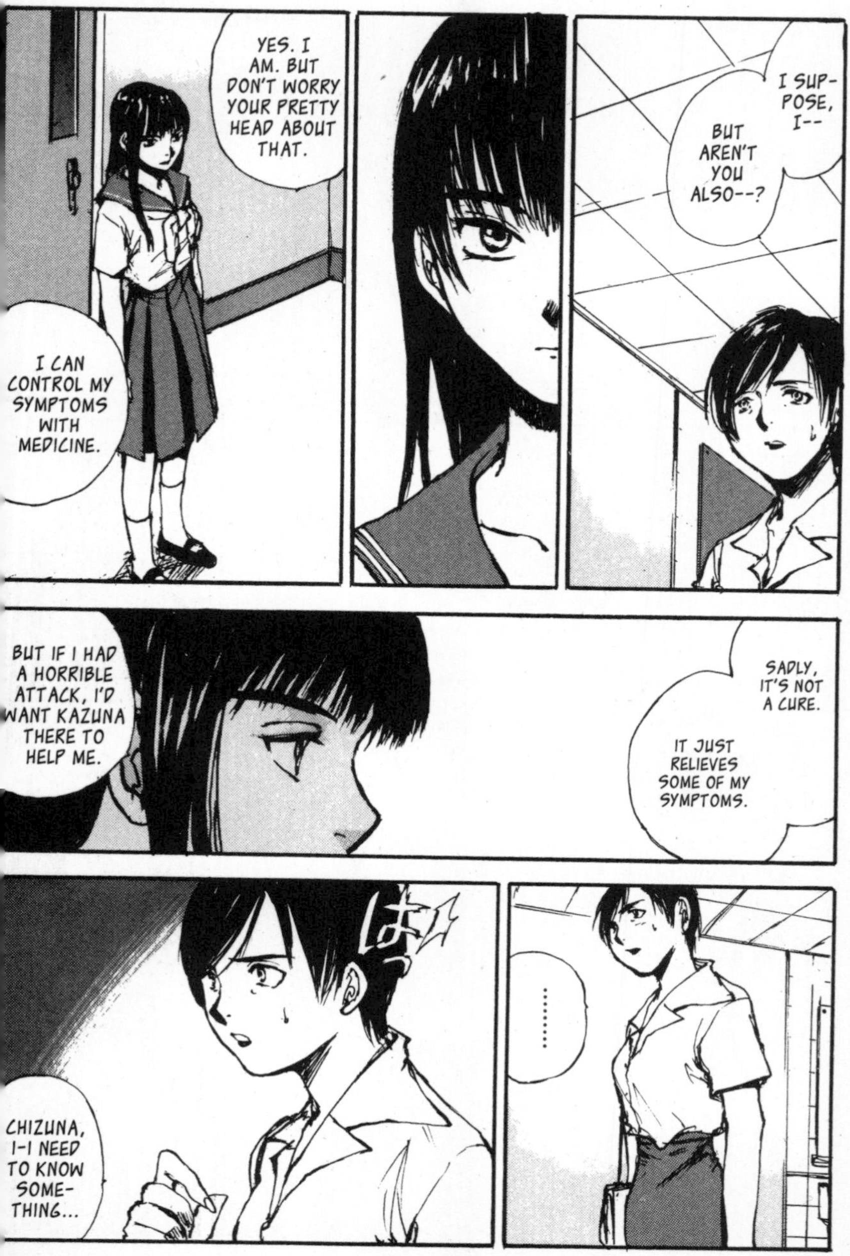
I SUPPOSE, I--
BUT AREN'T YOU ALSO--?
YES. I AM. BUT DON'T WORRY YOUR PRETTY HEAD ABOUT THAT.
I CAN CONTROL MY SYMPTOMS WITH MEDICINE.
SADLY, IT'S NOT A CURE.
IT JUST RELIEVES SOME OF MY SYMPTOMS.
BUT IF I HAD A HORRIBLE ATTACK, I'D WANT KAZUNA THERE TO HELP ME.
......
はっ
CHIZUNA, I-I NEED TO KNOW SOMETHING...

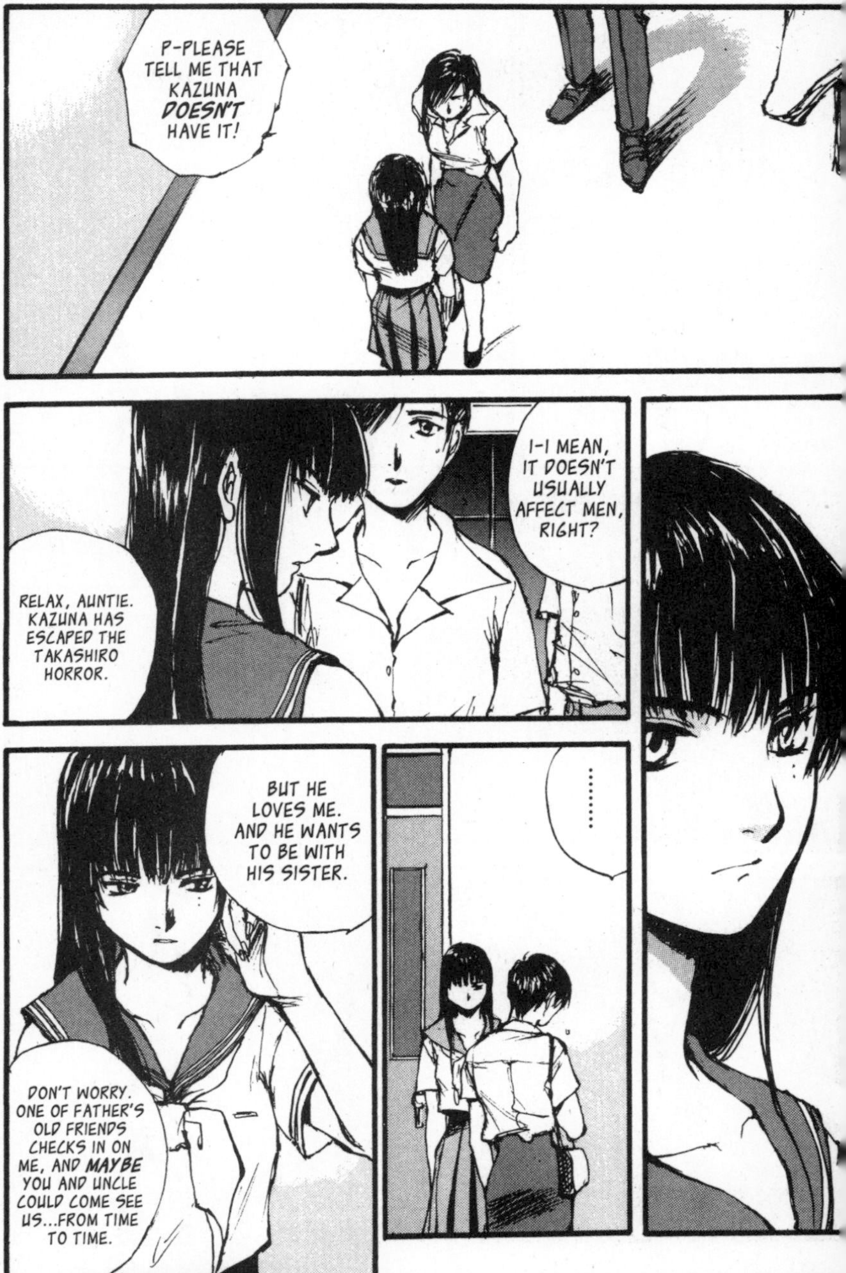
P-PLEASE TELL ME THAT KAZUNA ***DOESN'T*** HAVE IT!
I-I MEAN, IT DOESN'T USUALLY AFFECT MEN, RIGHT?
RELAX, AUNTIE. KAZUNA HAS ESCAPED THE TAKASHIRO HORROR.
......
BUT HE LOVES ME. AND HE WANTS TO BE WITH HIS SISTER.
DON'T WORRY. ONE OF FATHER'S OLD FRIENDS CHECKS IN ON ME, AND ***MAYBE*** YOU AND UNCLE COULD COME SEE US...FROM TIME TO TIME.

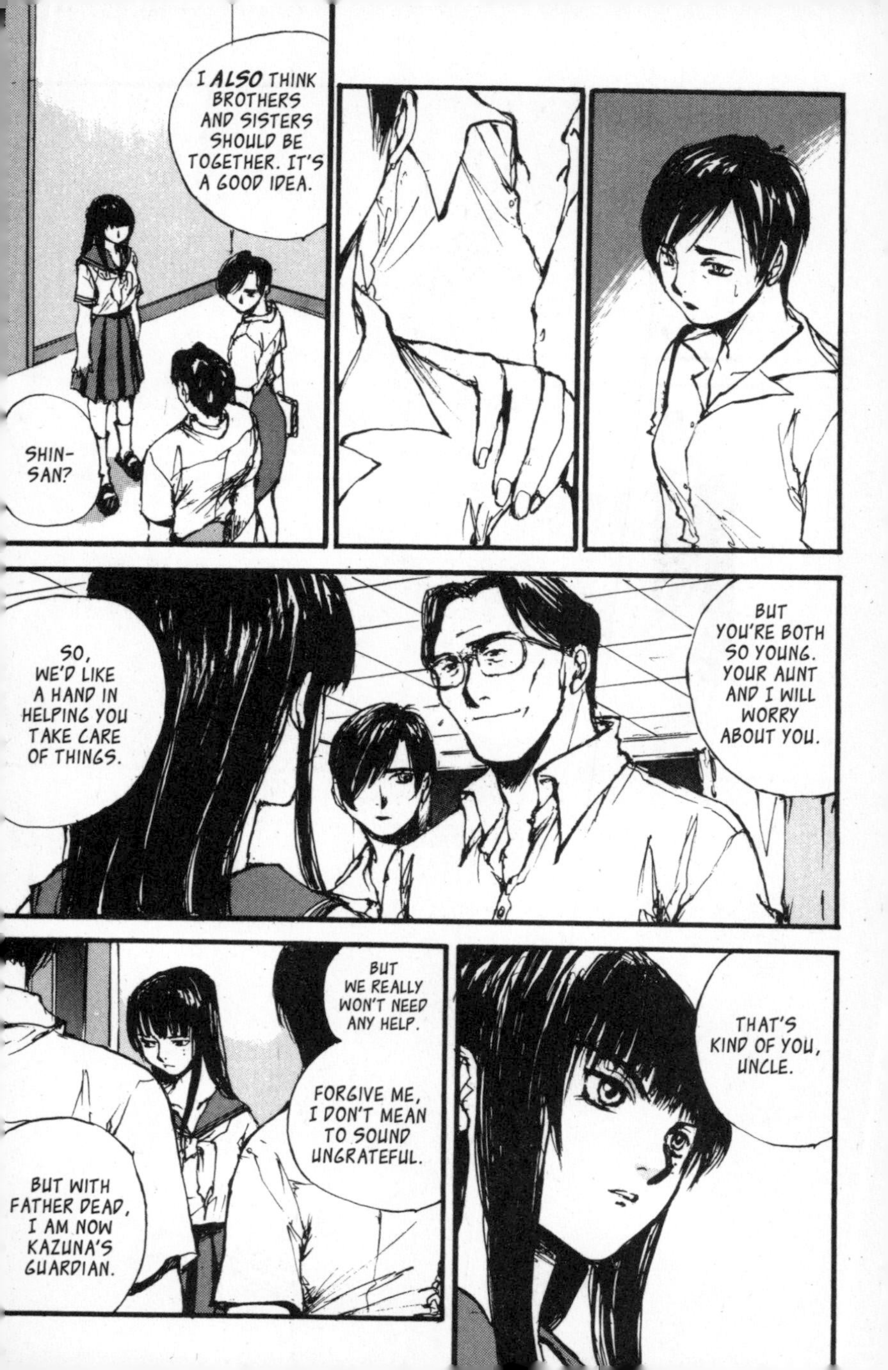
I ALSO THINK BROTHERS AND SISTERS SHOULD BE TOGETHER. IT'S A GOOD IDEA.
SHIN-SAN?
BUT YOU'RE BOTH SO YOUNG. YOUR AUNT AND I WILL WORRY ABOUT YOU.
SO, WE'D LIKE A HAND IN HELPING YOU TAKE CARE OF THINGS.
THAT'S KIND OF YOU, UNCLE.
BUT WE REALLY WON'T NEED ANY HELP.
FORGIVE ME, I DON'T MEAN TO SOUND UNGRATEFUL.
BUT WITH FATHER DEAD, I AM NOW KAZUNA'S GUARDIAN.

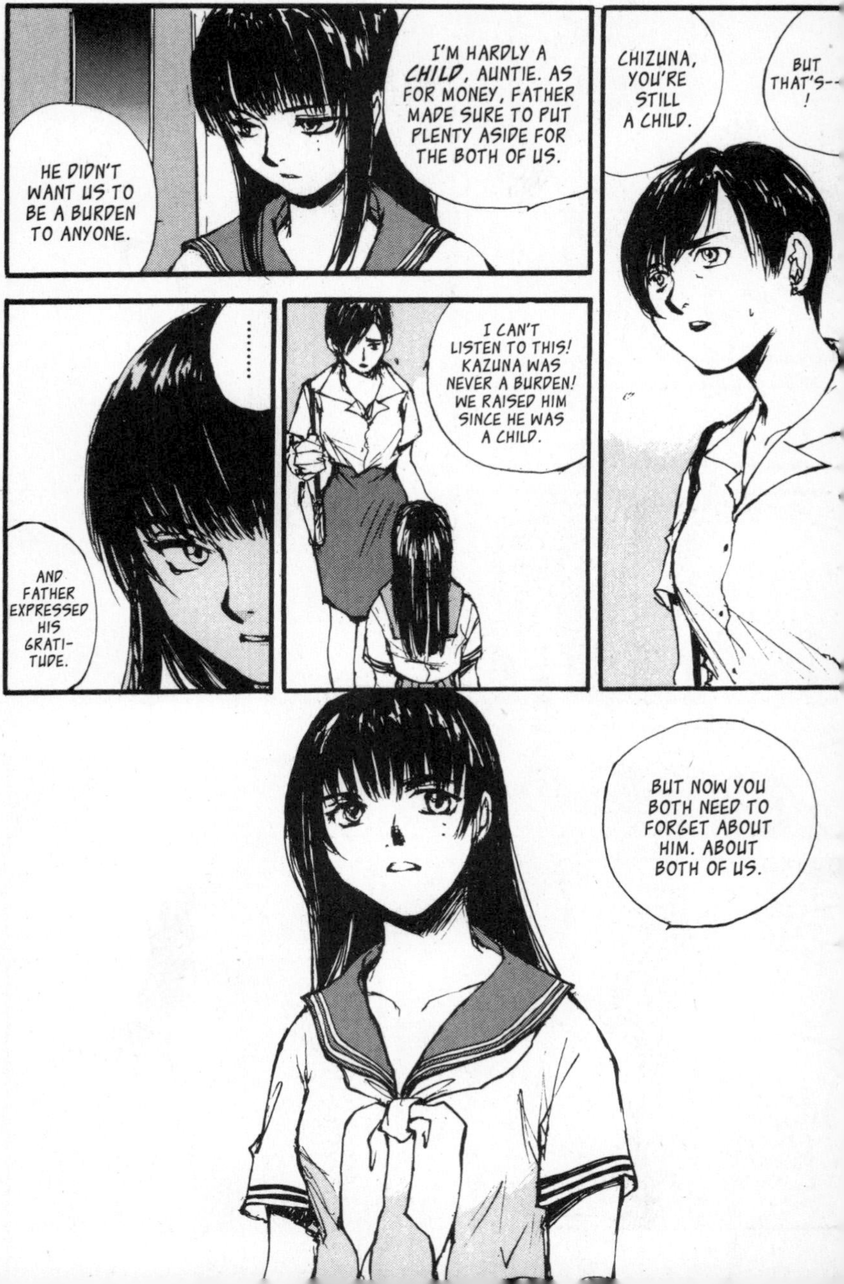

BUT THAT'S--!
CHIZUNA, YOU'RE STILL A CHILD.
I'M HARDLY A CHILD, AUNTIE. AS FOR MONEY, FATHER MADE SURE TO PUT PLENTY ASIDE FOR THE BOTH OF US.
HE DIDN'T WANT US TO BE A BURDEN TO ANYONE.
I CAN'T LISTEN TO THIS! KAZUNA WAS NEVER A BURDEN! WE RAISED HIM SINCE HE WAS A CHILD.
......
AND FATHER EXPRESSED HIS GRATITUDE.
BUT NOW YOU BOTH NEED TO FORGET ABOUT HIM. ABOUT BOTH OF US.

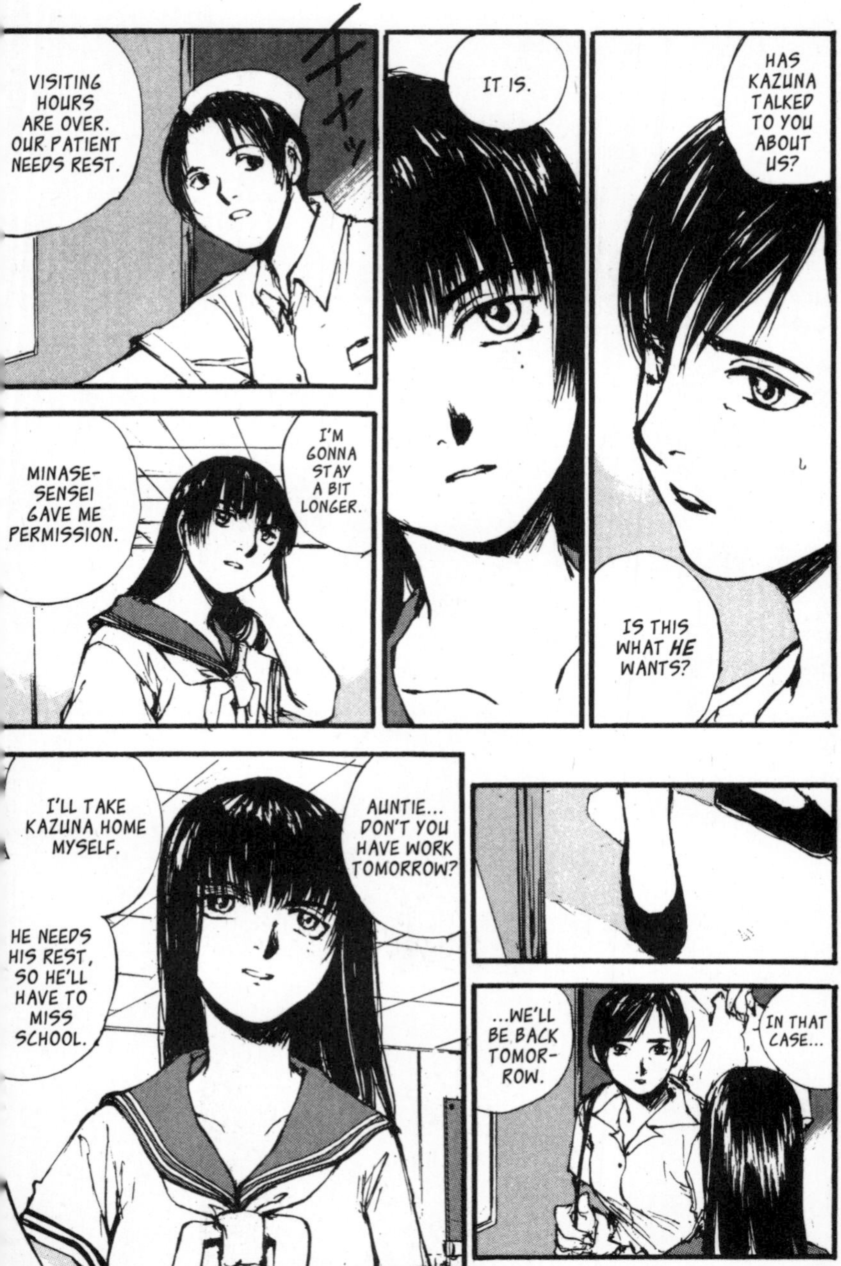
HAS KAZUNA TALKED TO YOU ABOUT US?
IS THIS WHAT *HE* WANTS?
IT IS.
VISITING HOURS ARE OVER. OUR PATIENT NEEDS REST.
I'M GONNA STAY A BIT LONGER.
MINASE-SENSEI GAVE ME PERMISSION.
AUNTIE... DON'T YOU HAVE WORK TOMORROW?
I'LL TAKE KAZUNA HOME MYSELF.
HE NEEDS HIS REST, SO HE'LL HAVE TO MISS SCHOOL.
IN THAT CASE...
...WE'LL BE BACK TOMORROW.

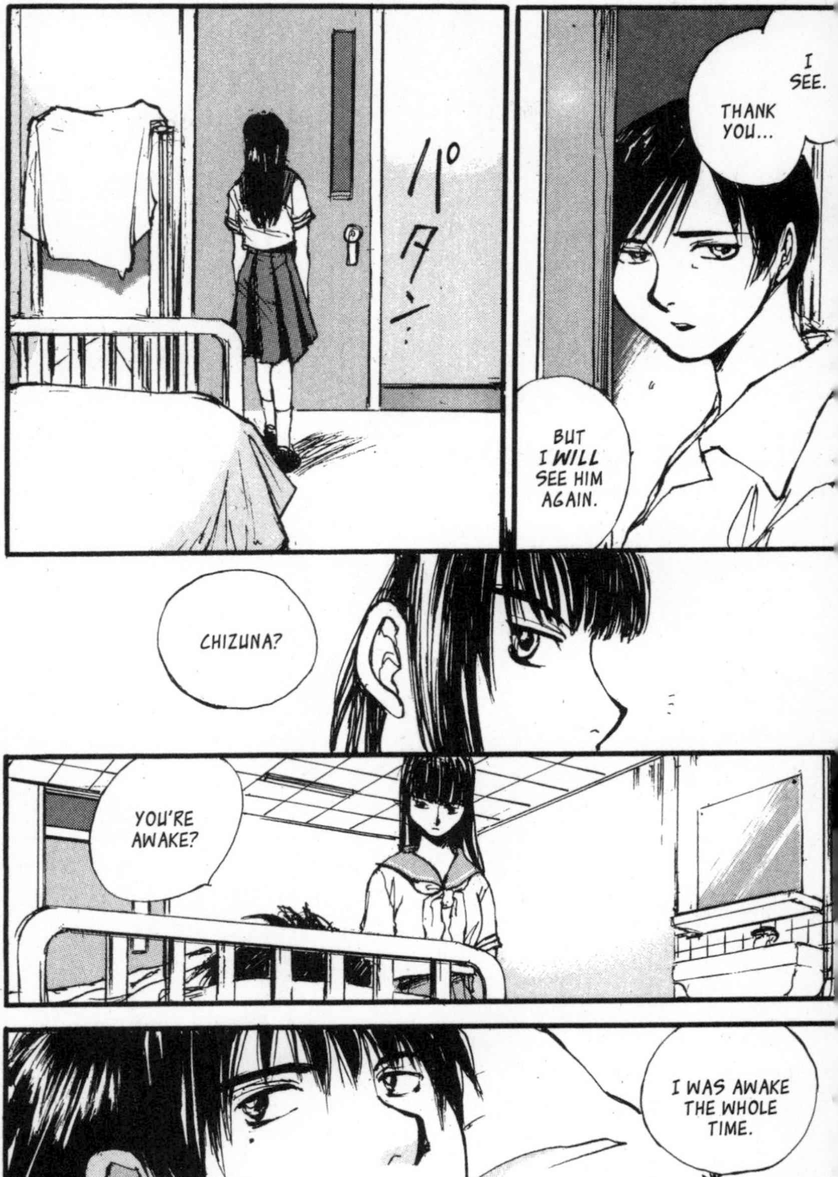
I SEE.
THANK YOU...
BUT I **WILL** SEE HIM AGAIN.
パタン
CHIZUNA?
YOU'RE AWAKE?
I WAS AWAKE THE WHOLE TIME.

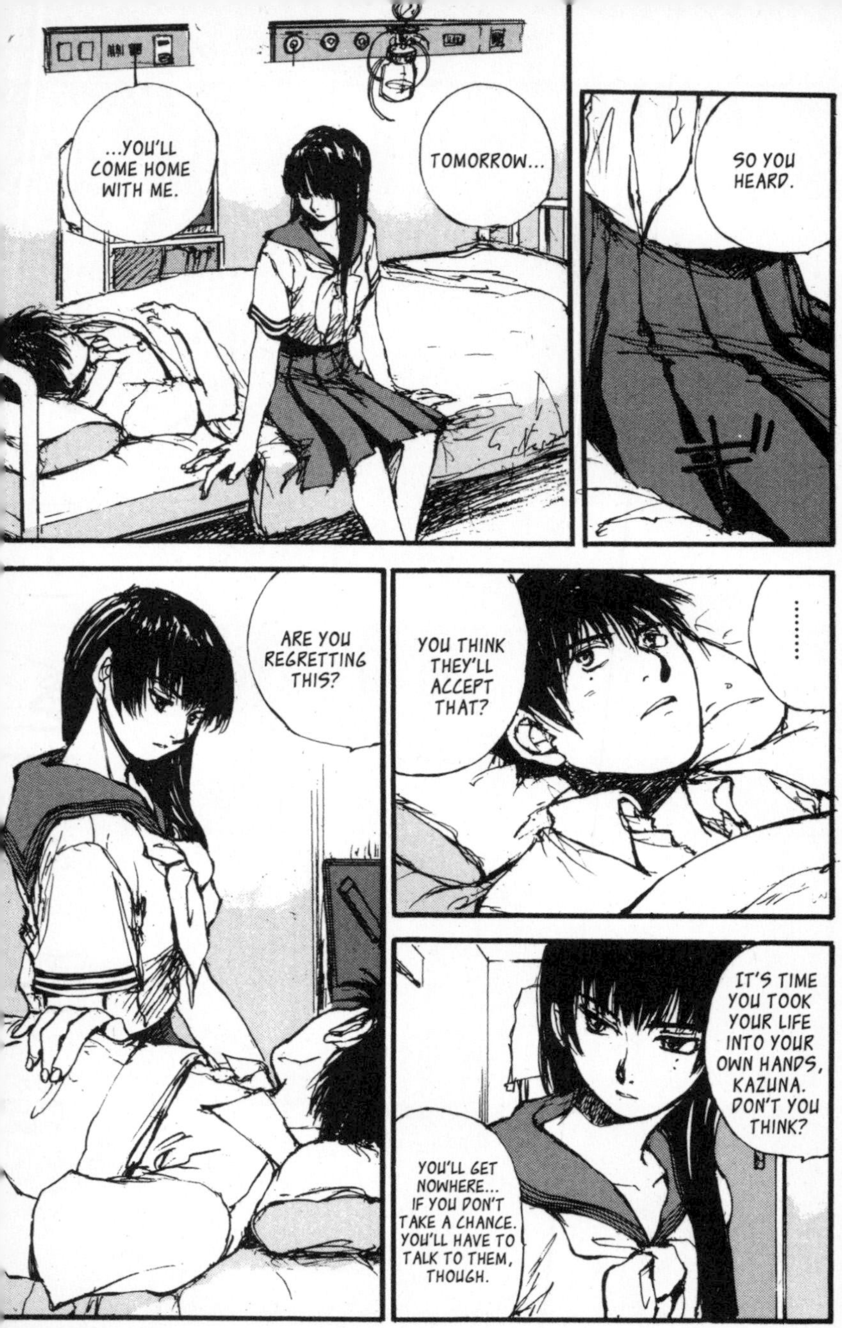
SO YOU HEARD.
TOMORROW...
...YOU'LL COME HOME WITH ME.
......
YOU THINK THEY'LL ACCEPT THAT?
IT'S TIME YOU TOOK YOUR LIFE INTO YOUR OWN HANDS, KAZUNA. DON'T YOU THINK?
YOU'LL GET NOWHERE... IF YOU DON'T TAKE A CHANCE. YOU'LL HAVE TO TALK TO THEM, THOUGH.
ARE YOU REGRETTING THIS?

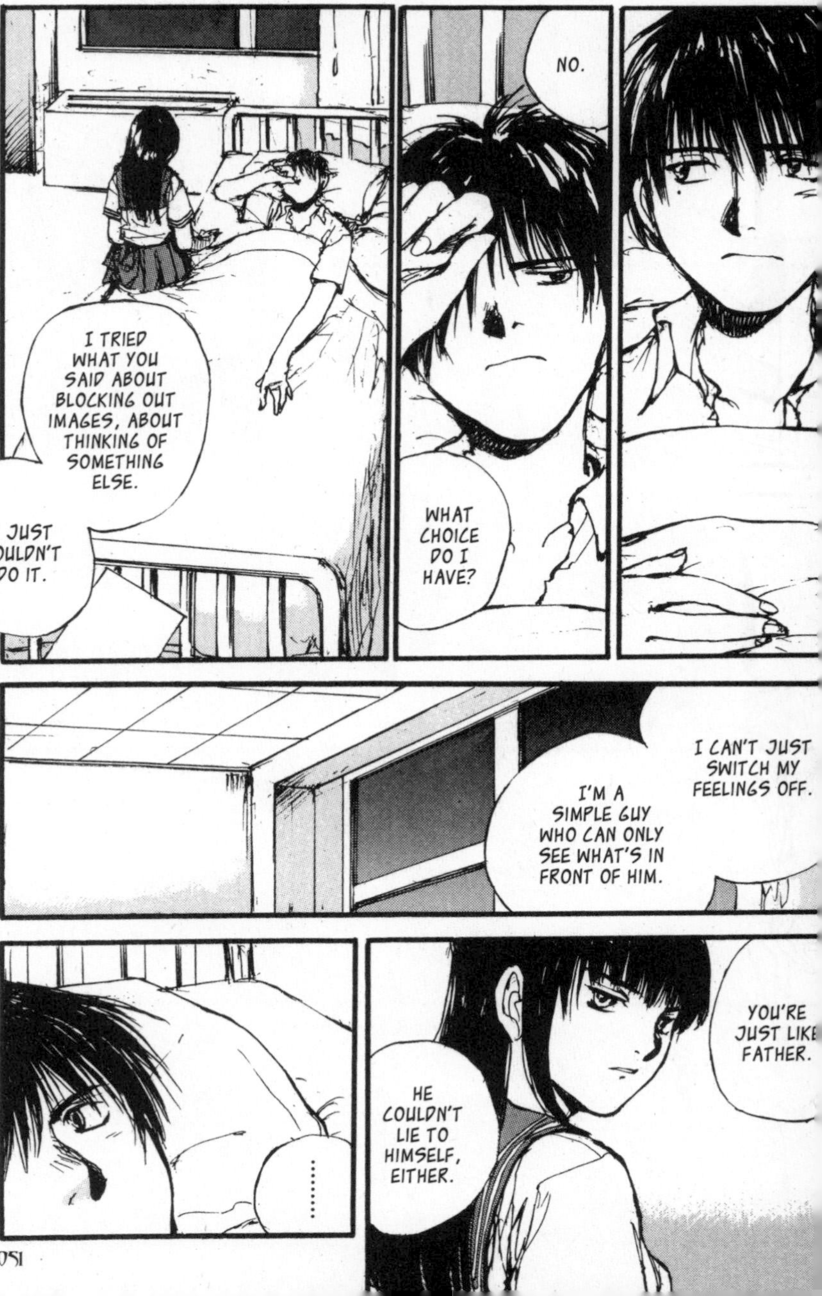
NO.
WHAT CHOICE DO I HAVE?
I TRIED WHAT YOU SAID ABOUT BLOCKING OUT IMAGES, ABOUT THINKING OF SOMETHING ELSE.
I JUST COULDN'T DO IT.
I CAN'T JUST SWITCH MY FEELINGS OFF.
I'M A SIMPLE GUY WHO CAN ONLY SEE WHAT'S IN FRONT OF HIM.
YOU'RE JUST LIKE FATHER.
HE COULDN'T LIE TO HIMSELF, EITHER.
......

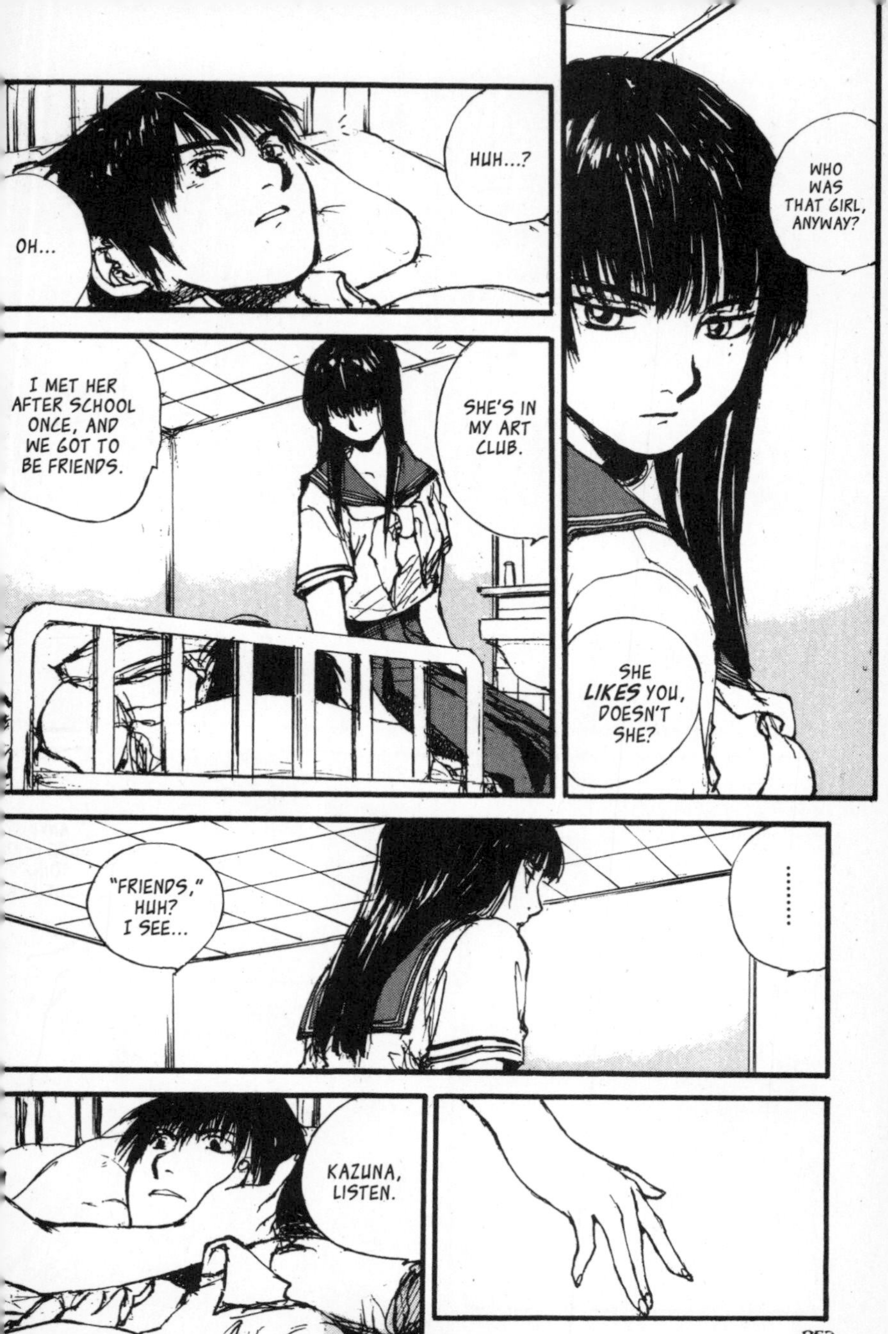
WHO WAS THAT GIRL, ANYWAY?
SHE LIKES YOU, DOESN'T SHE?
HUH...?
OH...
SHE'S IN MY ART CLUB.
I MET HER AFTER SCHOOL ONCE, AND WE GOT TO BE FRIENDS.
......
"FRIENDS," HUH? I SEE...
KAZUNA, LISTEN.

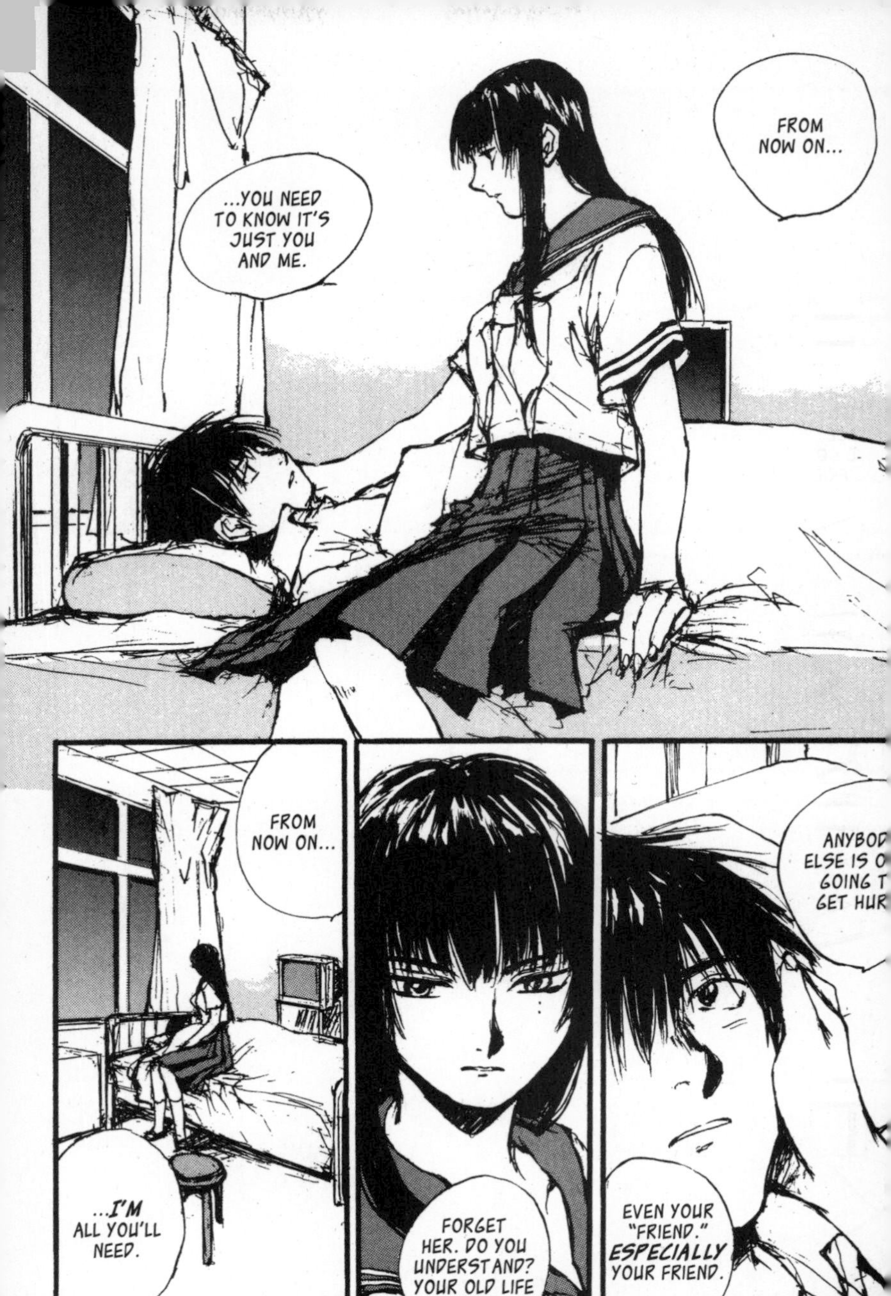
FROM NOW ON...
...YOU NEED TO KNOW IT'S JUST YOU AND ME.
ANYBOD ELSE IS O GOING T GET HUR
EVEN YOUR "FRIEND." ***ESPECIALLY*** YOUR FRIEND.
FORGET HER. DO YOU UNDERSTAND? YOUR OLD LIFE IS ***OVER***.
FROM NOW ON...
...***I'M*** ALL YOU'LL NEED.

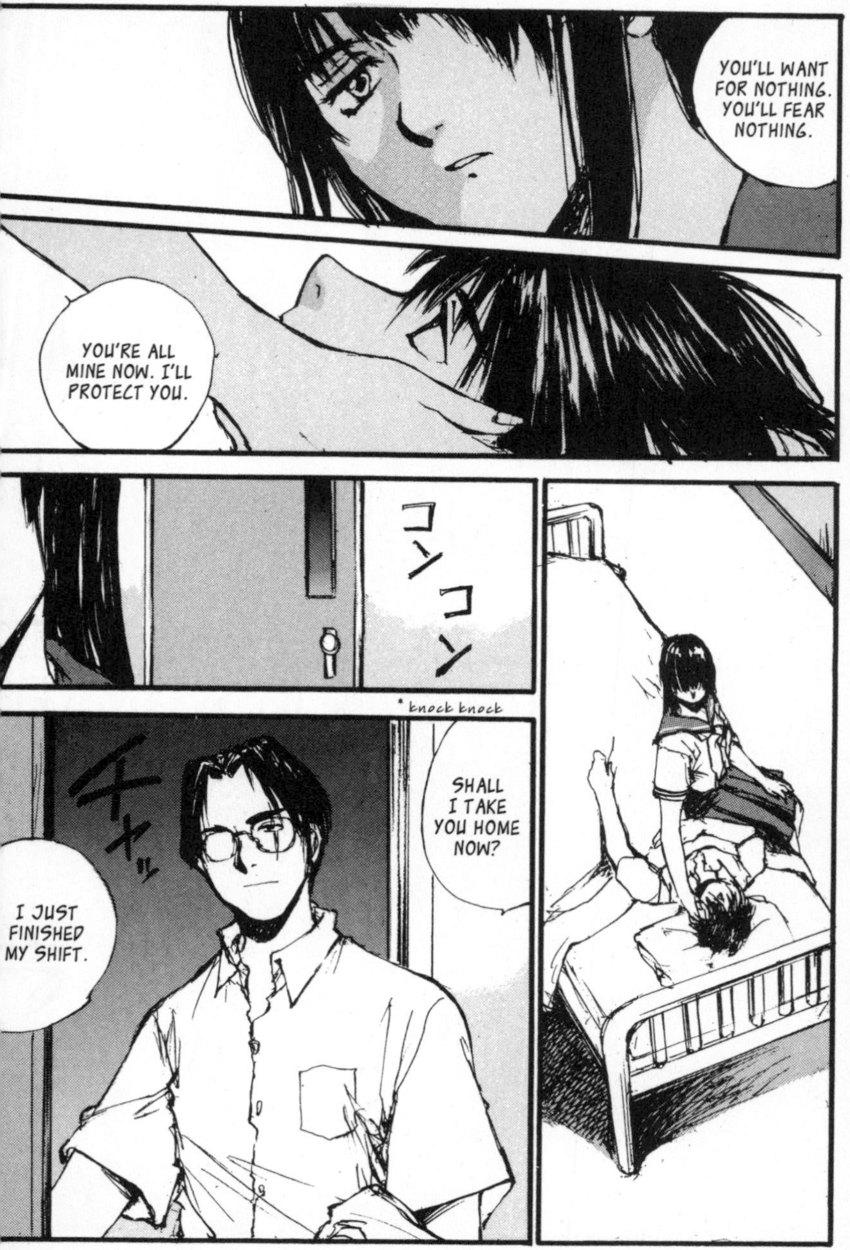
YOU'LL WANT FOR NOTHING. YOU'LL FEAR NOTHING.
YOU'RE ALL MINE NOW. I'LL PROTECT YOU.
コンコンコン
* knock knock
SHALL I TAKE YOU HOME NOW?
I JUST FINISHED MY SHIFT.

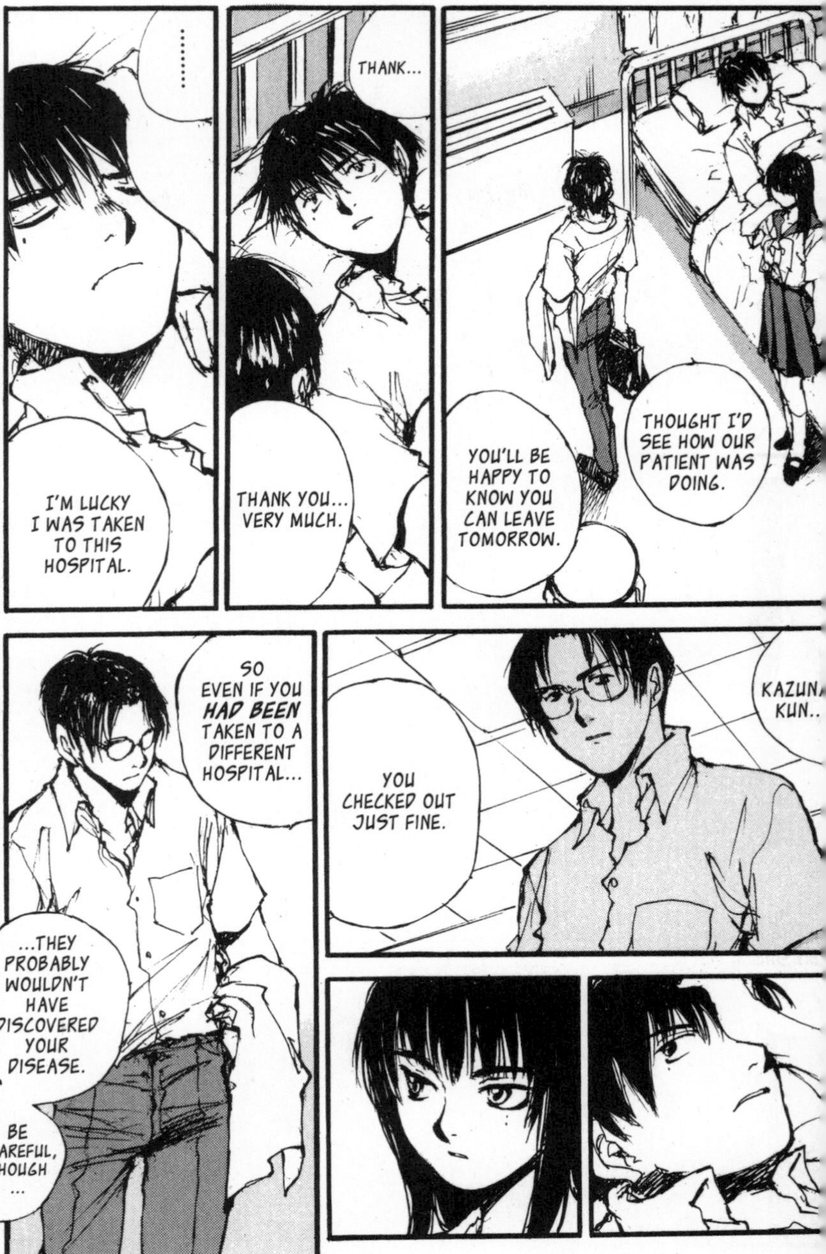

THOUGHT I'D SEE HOW OUR PATIENT WAS DOING.
YOU'LL BE HAPPY TO KNOW YOU CAN LEAVE TOMORROW.
THANK...
THANK YOU... VERY MUCH.
......
I'M LUCKY I WAS TAKEN TO THIS HOSPITAL.
KAZUN KUN..
YOU CHECKED OUT JUST FINE.
SO EVEN IF YOU ***HAD BEEN*** TAKEN TO A DIFFERENT HOSPITAL...
...THEY PROBABLY WOULDN'T HAVE DISCOVERED YOUR DISEASE.
BE CAREFUL, THOUGH ...

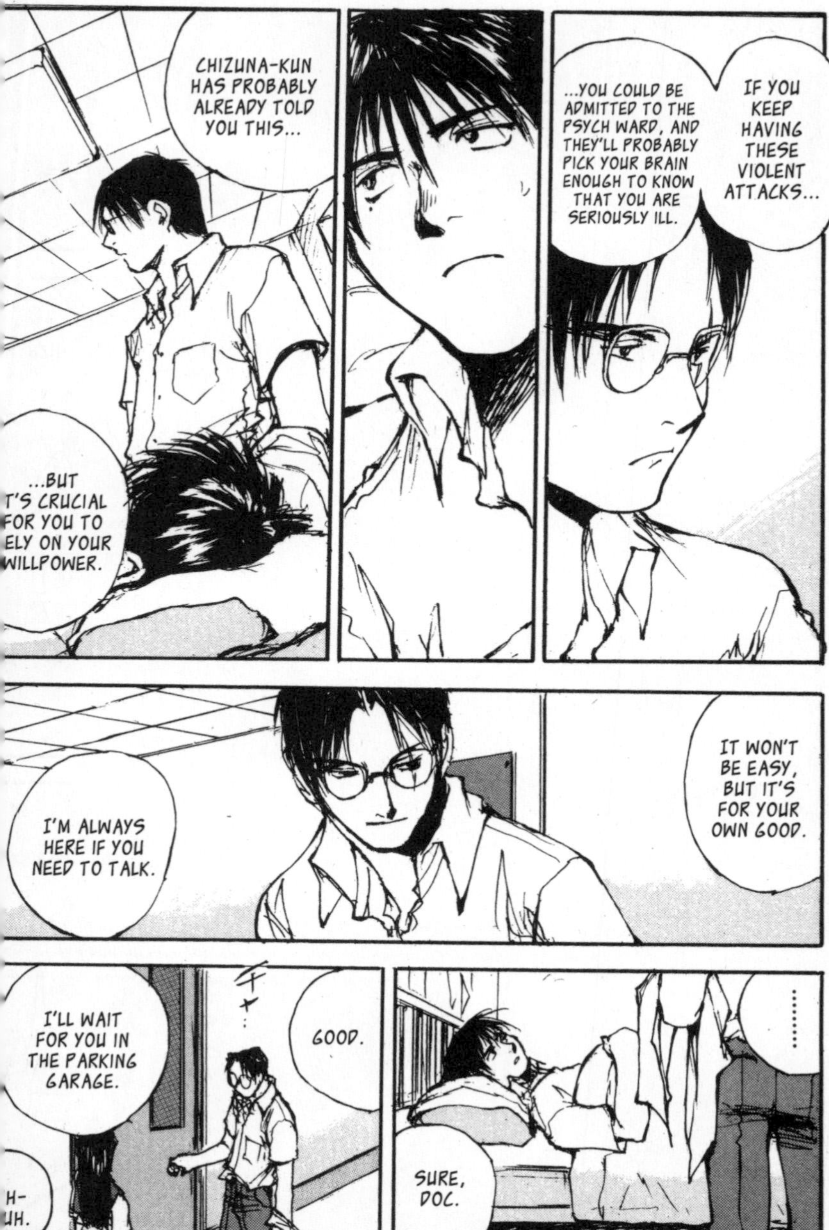
IF YOU KEEP HAVING THESE VIOLENT ATTACKS...
...YOU COULD BE ADMITTED TO THE PSYCH WARD, AND THEY'LL PROBABLY PICK YOUR BRAIN ENOUGH TO KNOW THAT YOU ARE SERIOUSLY ILL.
CHIZUNA-KUN HAS PROBABLY ALREADY TOLD YOU THIS...
...BUT T'S CRUCIAL FOR YOU TO ELY ON YOUR WILLPOWER.
IT WON'T BE EASY, BUT IT'S FOR YOUR OWN GOOD.
I'M ALWAYS HERE IF YOU NEED TO TALK.
......
SURE, DOC.
GOOD.
チャ…
I'LL WAIT FOR YOU IN THE PARKING GARAGE.
H-UH.

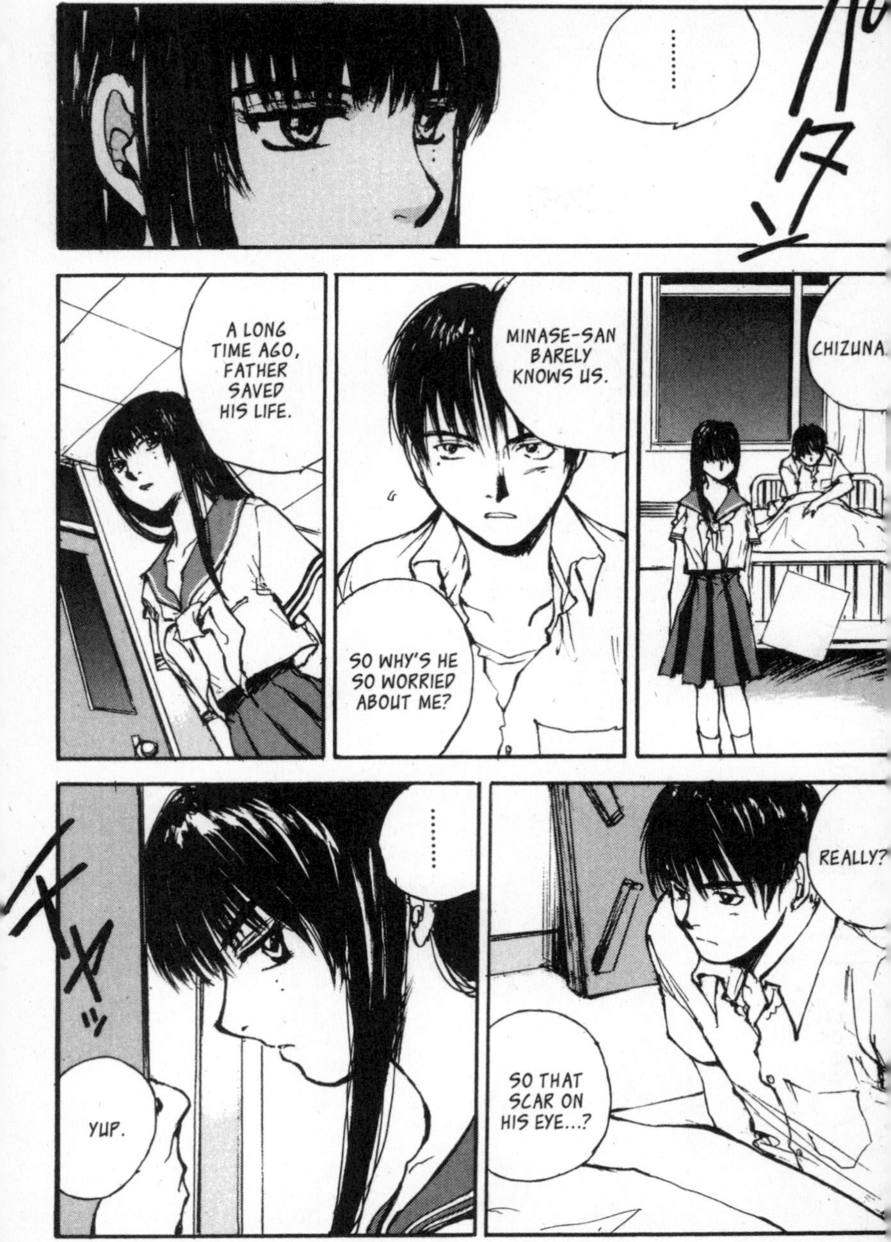
......
パタッ
CHIZUNA.
MINASE-SAN BARELY KNOWS US.
SO WHY'S HE SO WORRIED ABOUT ME?
A LONG TIME AGO, FATHER SAVED HIS LIFE.
REALLY?
SO THAT SCAR ON HIS EYE...?
......
YUP.

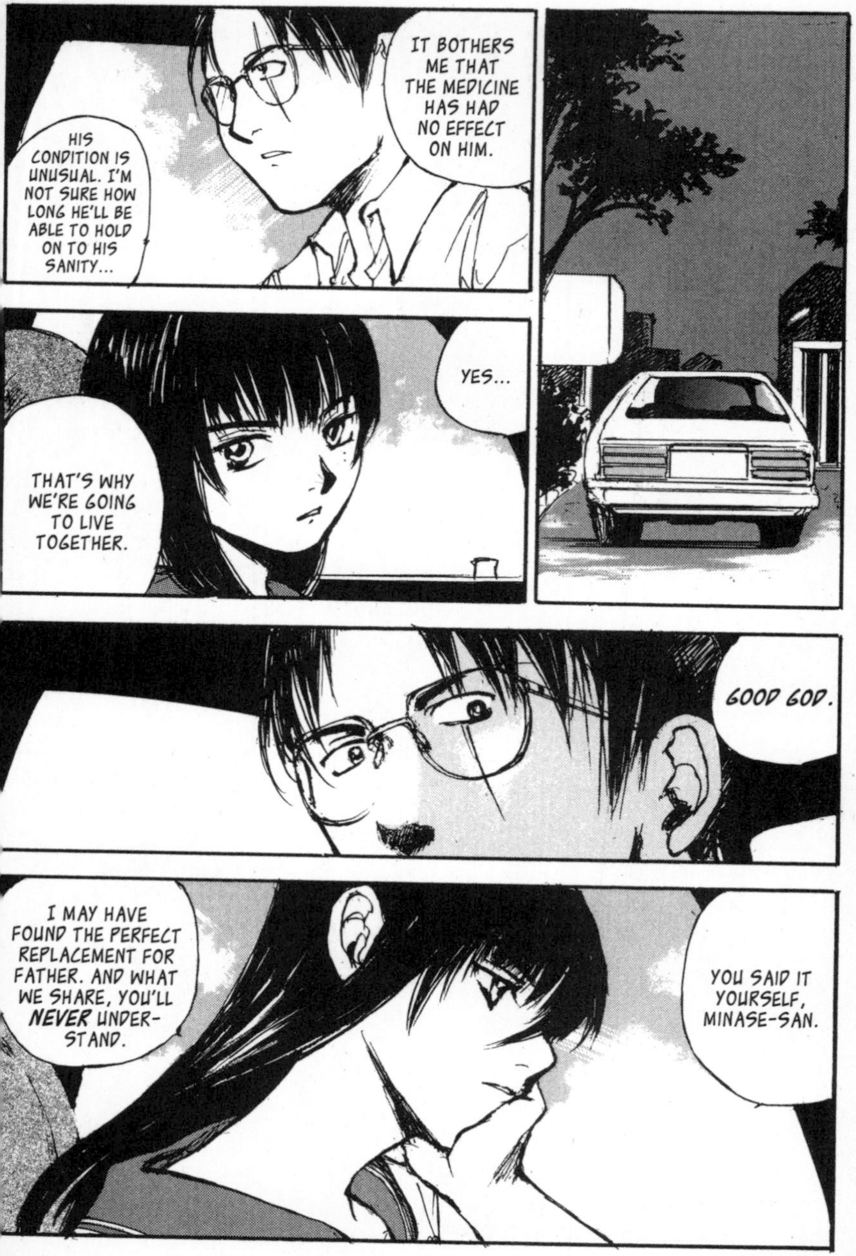
IT BOTHERS ME THAT THE MEDICINE HAS HAD NO EFFECT ON HIM.
HIS CONDITION IS UNUSUAL. I'M NOT SURE HOW LONG HE'LL BE ABLE TO HOLD ON TO HIS SANITY...
YES...
THAT'S WHY WE'RE GOING TO LIVE TOGETHER.
GOOD GOD.
YOU SAID IT YOURSELF, MINASE-SAN.
I MAY HAVE FOUND THE PERFECT REPLACEMENT FOR FATHER. AND WHAT WE SHARE, YOU'LL **NEVER** UNDER-STAND.

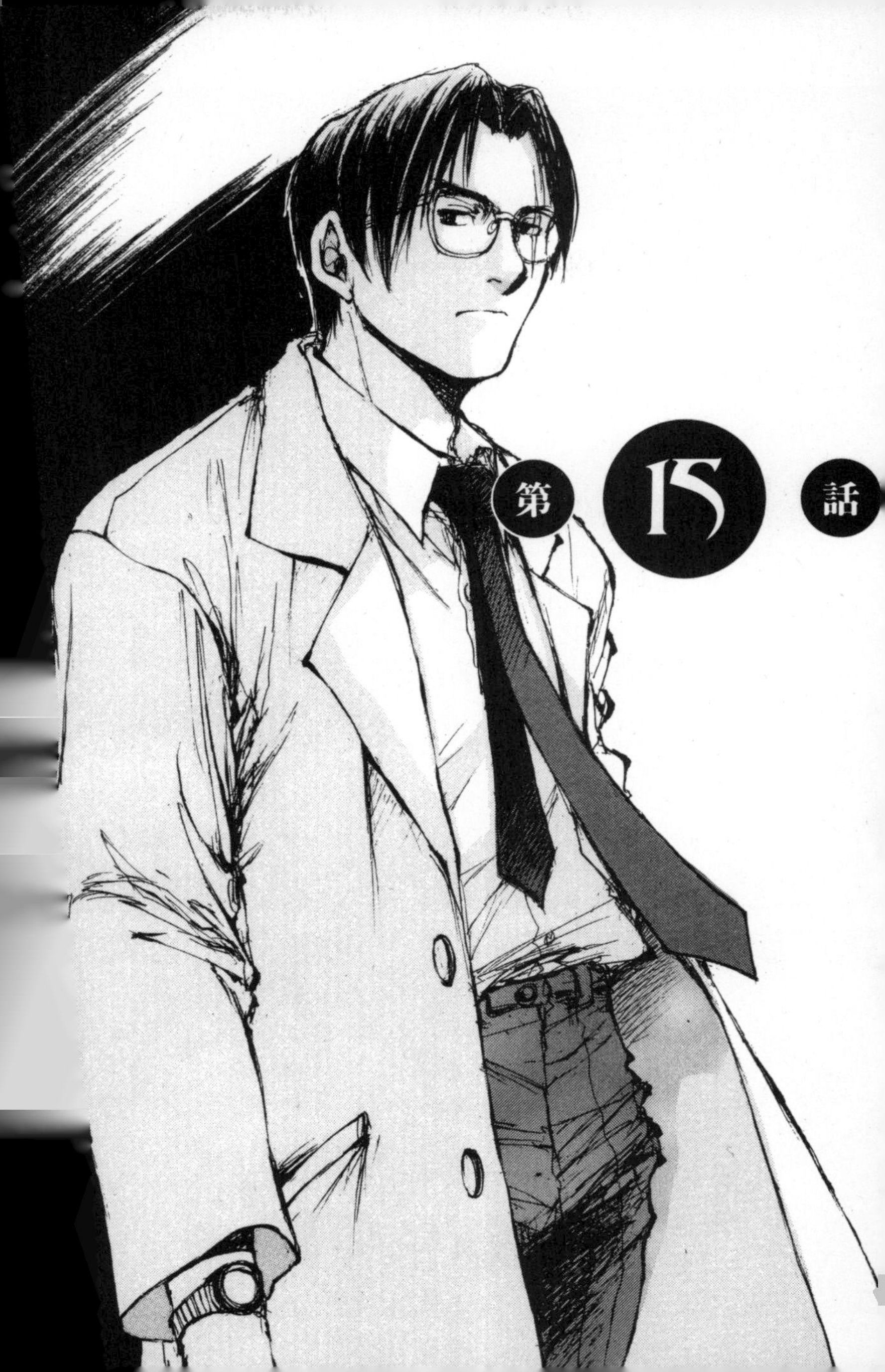
第15話

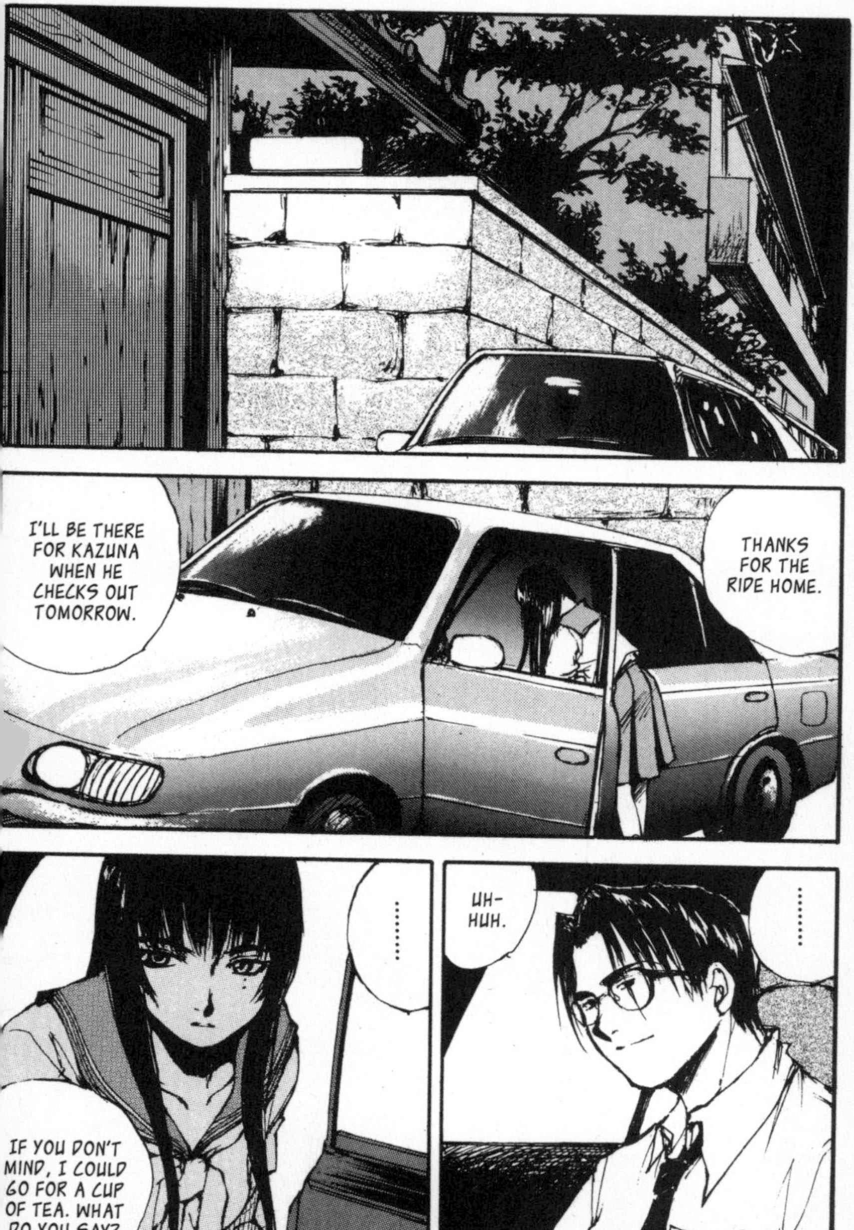
THANKS FOR THE RIDE HOME.
I'LL BE THERE FOR KAZUNA WHEN HE CHECKS OUT TOMORROW.
....
UH-HUH.
....
IF YOU DON'T MIND, I COULD GO FOR A CUP OF TEA. WHAT DO YOU SAY?

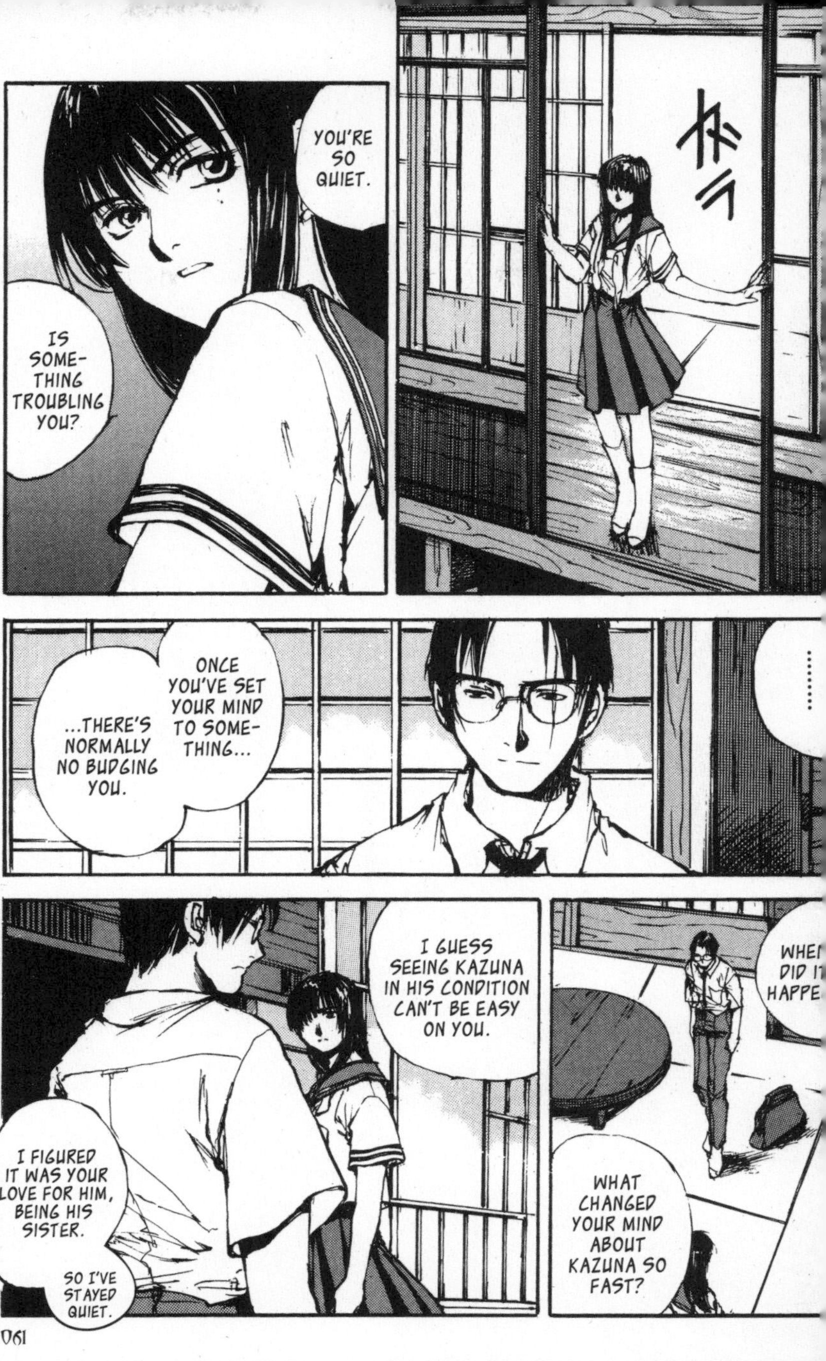
ガラ
YOU'RE SO QUIET.
IS SOMETHING TROUBLING YOU?
......
ONCE YOU'VE SET YOUR MIND TO SOMETHING...
...THERE'S NORMALLY NO BUDGING YOU.
WHEN DID IT HAPPE
WHAT CHANGED YOUR MIND ABOUT KAZUNA SO FAST?
I GUESS SEEING KAZUNA IN HIS CONDITION CAN'T BE EASY ON YOU.
I FIGURED IT WAS YOUR LOVE FOR HIM, BEING HIS SISTER.
SO I'VE STAYED QUIET.

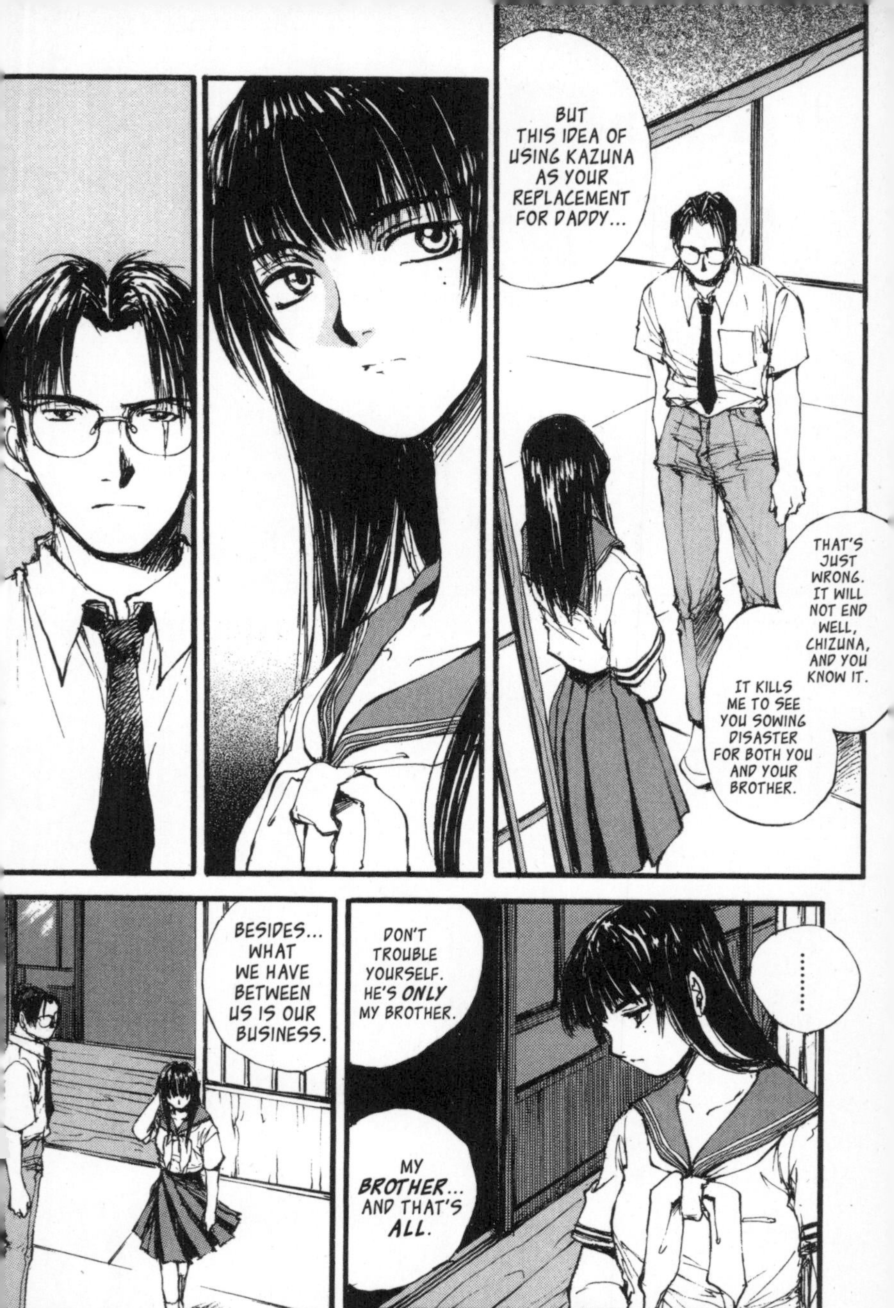
BUT THIS IDEA OF USING KAZUNA AS YOUR REPLACEMENT FOR DADDY...
THAT'S JUST WRONG. IT WILL NOT END WELL, CHIZUNA, AND YOU KNOW IT.
IT KILLS ME TO SEE YOU SOWING DISASTER FOR BOTH YOU AND YOUR BROTHER.
......
DON'T TROUBLE YOURSELF. HE'S ONLY MY BROTHER.
MY BROTHER... AND THAT'S ALL.
BESIDES... WHAT WE HAVE BETWEEN US IS OUR BUSINESS.

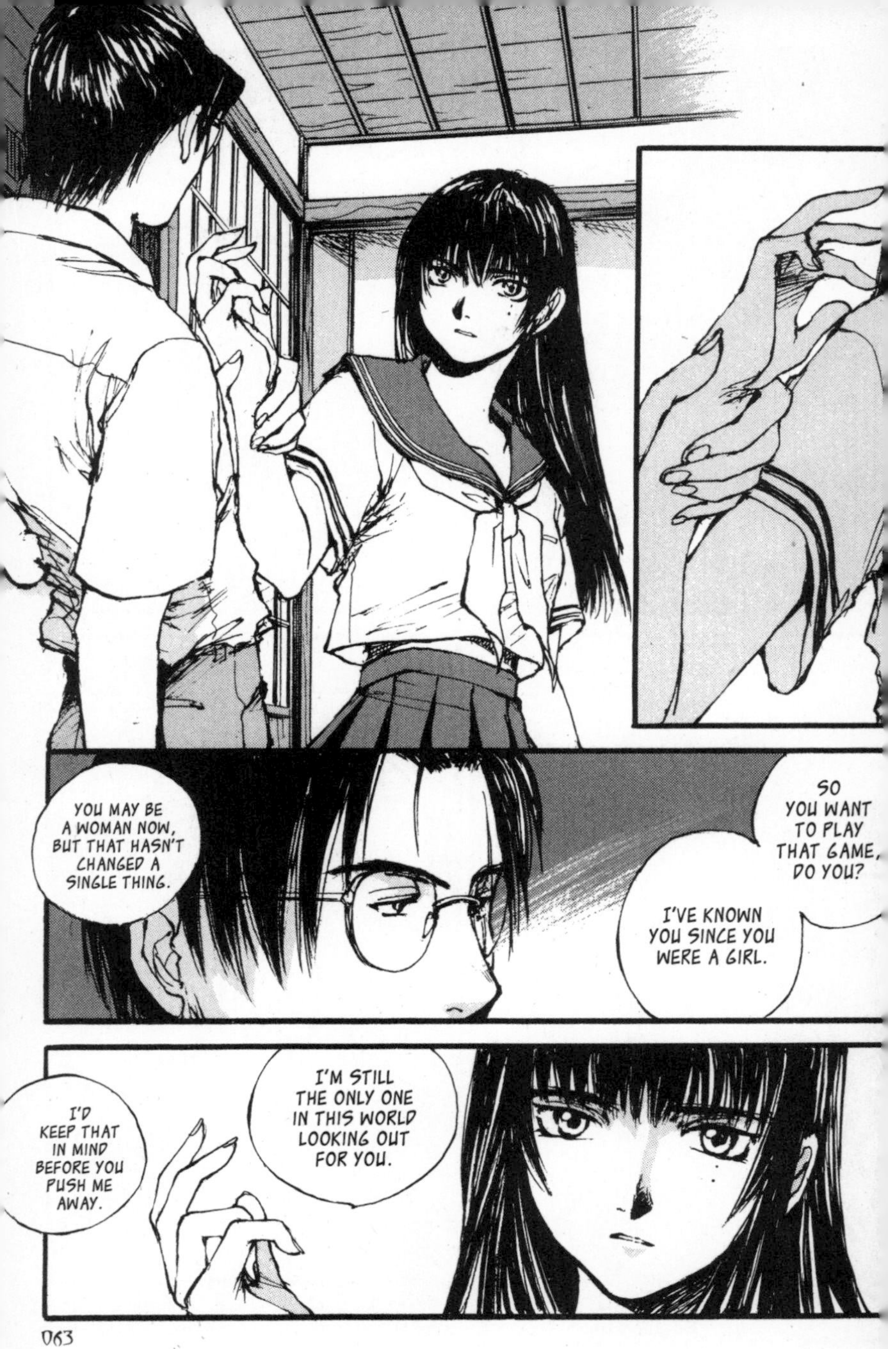
SO YOU WANT TO PLAY THAT GAME, DO YOU?
I'VE KNOWN YOU SINCE YOU WERE A GIRL.
YOU MAY BE A WOMAN NOW, BUT THAT HASN'T CHANGED A SINGLE THING.
I'M STILL THE ONLY ONE IN THIS WORLD LOOKING OUT FOR YOU.
I'D KEEP THAT IN MIND BEFORE YOU PUSH ME AWAY.

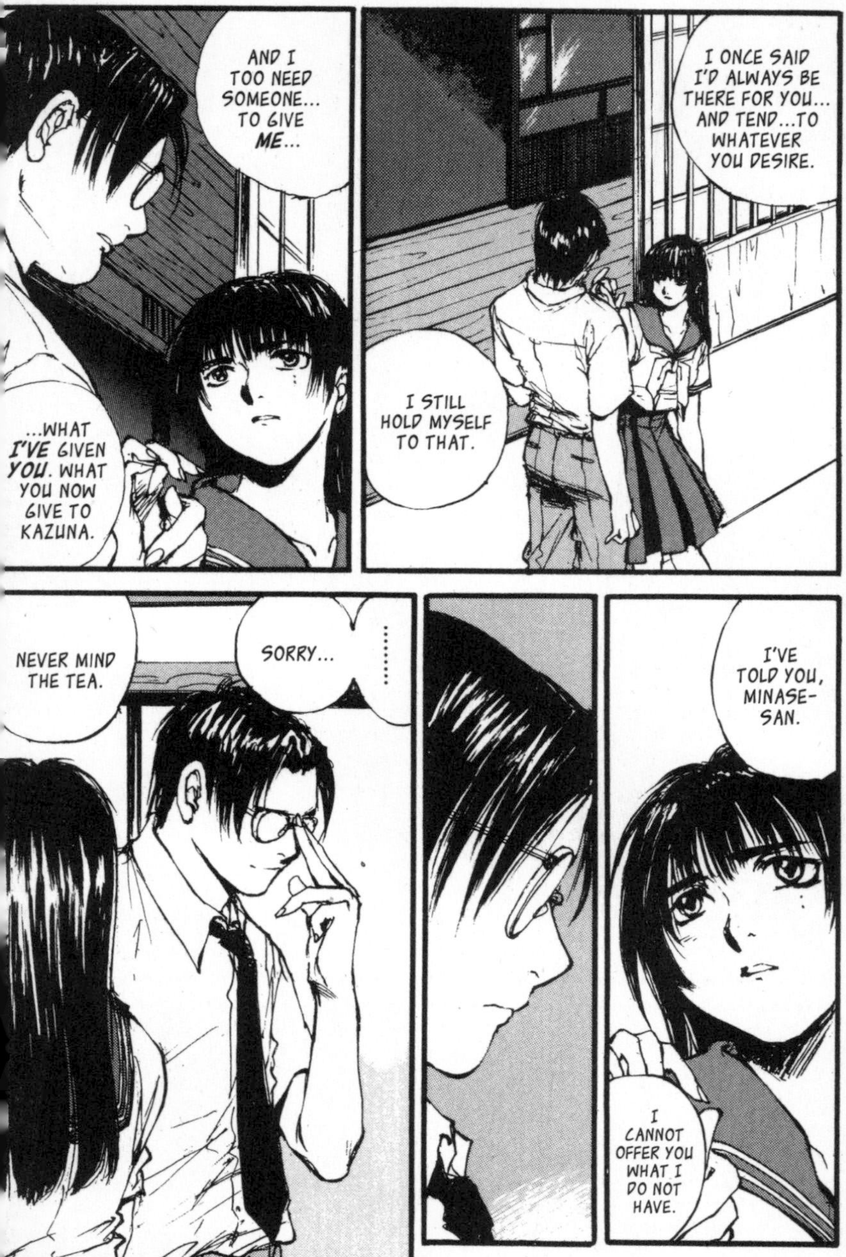
I ONCE SAID I'D ALWAYS BE THERE FOR YOU... AND TEND...TO WHATEVER YOU DESIRE.
I STILL HOLD MYSELF TO THAT.
AND I TOO NEED SOMEONE... TO GIVE *ME*...
...WHAT *I'VE* GIVEN *YOU*. WHAT YOU NOW GIVE TO KAZUNA.
I'VE TOLD YOU, MINASE-SAN.
I CANNOT OFFER YOU WHAT I DO NOT HAVE.
......
SORRY...
NEVER MIND THE TEA.

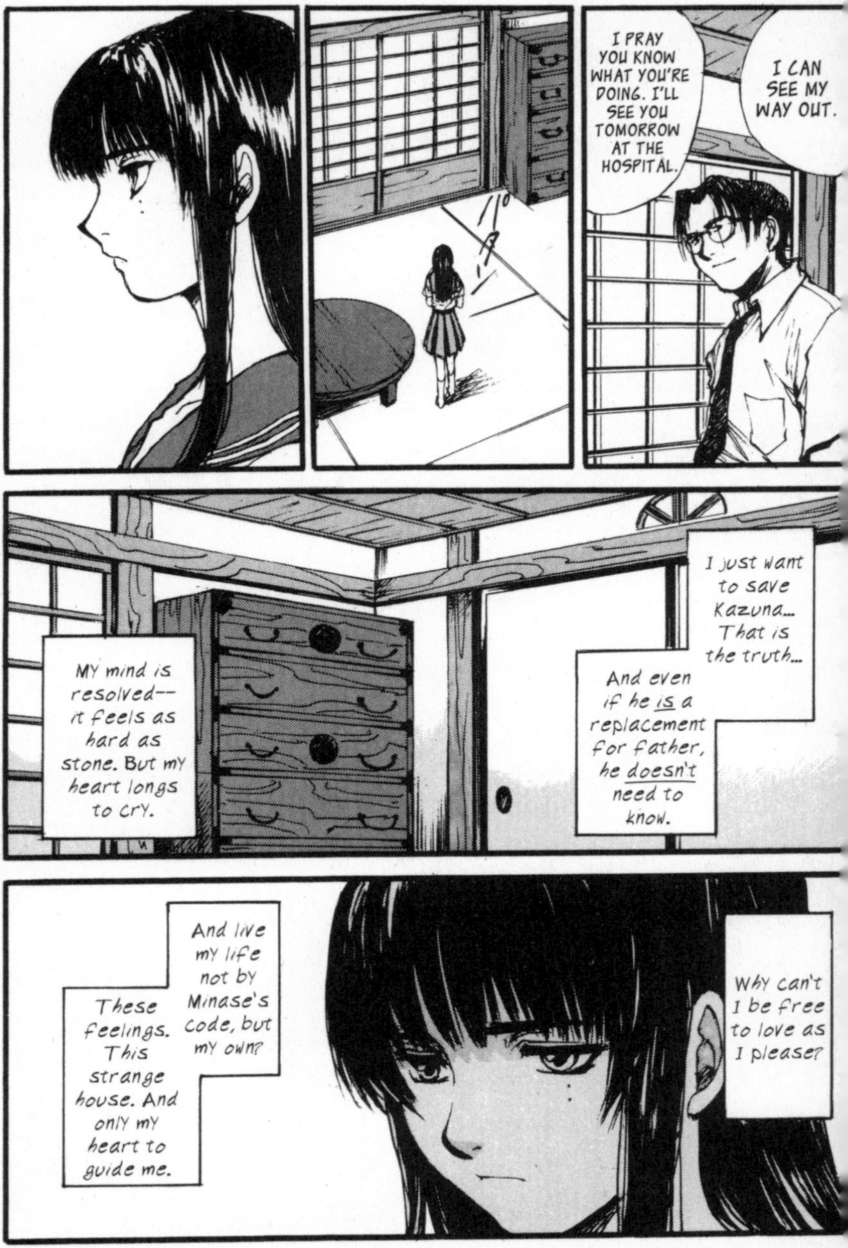
I CAN SEE MY WAY OUT.
I PRAY YOU KNOW WHAT YOU'RE DOING. I'LL SEE YOU TOMORROW AT THE HOSPITAL.
I just want to save Kazuna... That is the truth...
And even if he is a replacement for father, he doesn't need to know.
MY mind is resolved-- it feels as hard as stone. But my heart longs to cry.
Why can't I be free to love as I please?
And live my life not by Minase's code, but my own?
These feelings. This strange house. And only my heart to guide me.

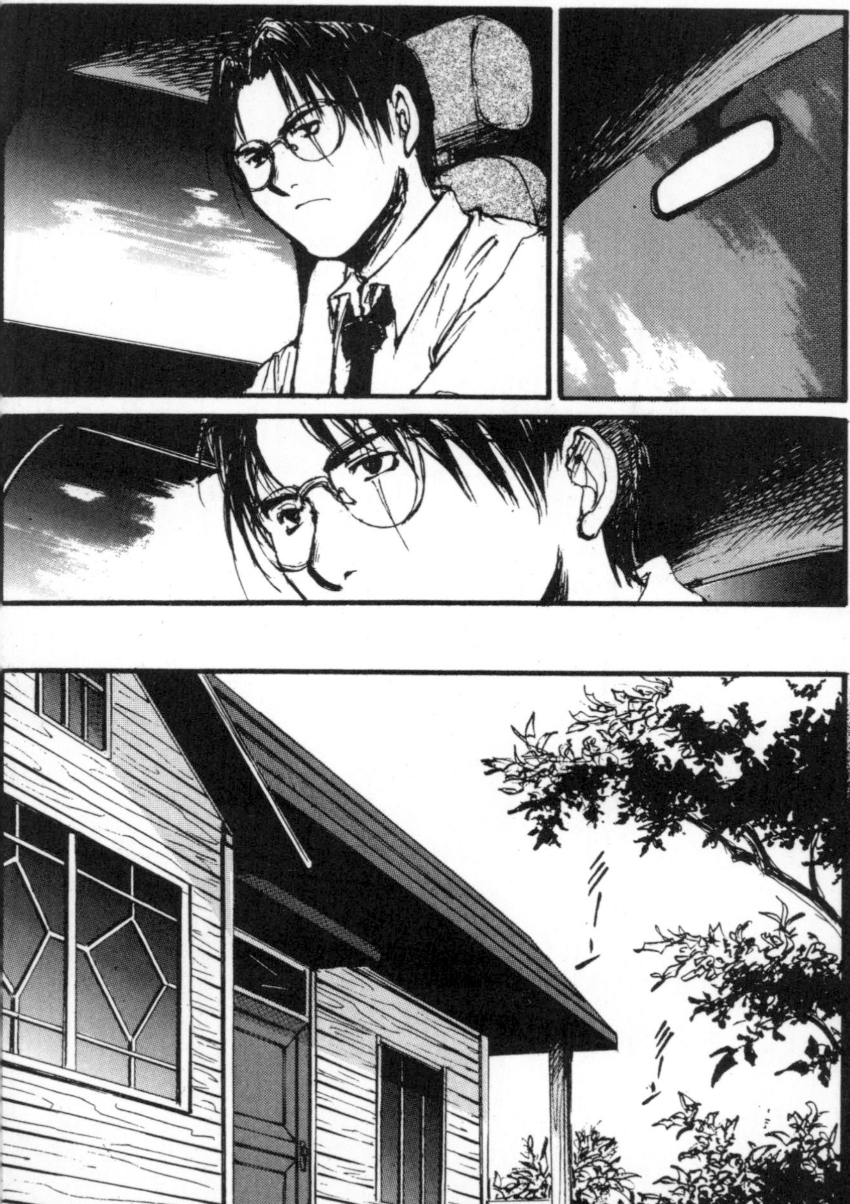

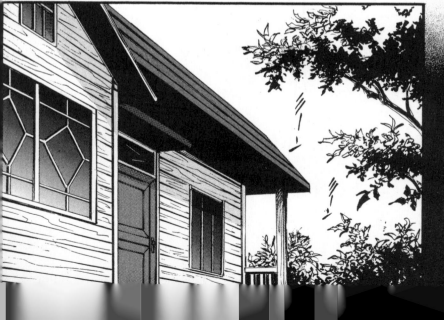

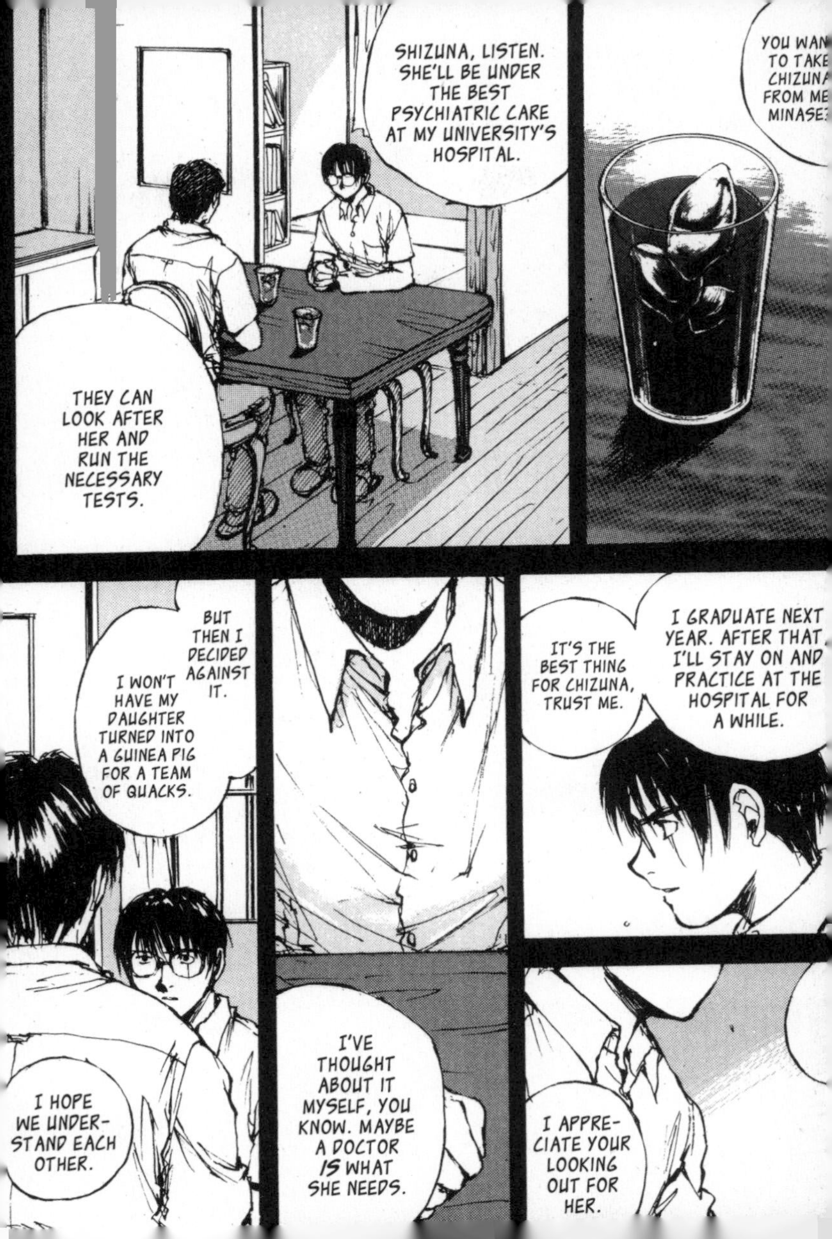
YOU WAN TO TAKE CHIZUNA FROM ME MINASE?
SHIZUNA, LISTEN. SHE'LL BE UNDER THE BEST PSYCHIATRIC CARE AT MY UNIVERSITY'S HOSPITAL.
THEY CAN LOOK AFTER HER AND RUN THE NECESSARY TESTS.
I GRADUATE NEXT YEAR. AFTER THAT, I'LL STAY ON AND PRACTICE AT THE HOSPITAL FOR A WHILE.
IT'S THE BEST THING FOR CHIZUNA, TRUST ME.
I APPRECIATE YOUR LOOKING OUT FOR HER.
I'VE THOUGHT ABOUT IT MYSELF, YOU KNOW. MAYBE A DOCTOR *IS* WHAT SHE NEEDS.
I WON'T HAVE MY DAUGHTER TURNED INTO A GUINEA PIG FOR A TEAM OF QUACKS.
BUT THEN I DECIDED AGAINST IT.
I HOPE WE UNDERSTAND EACH OTHER.

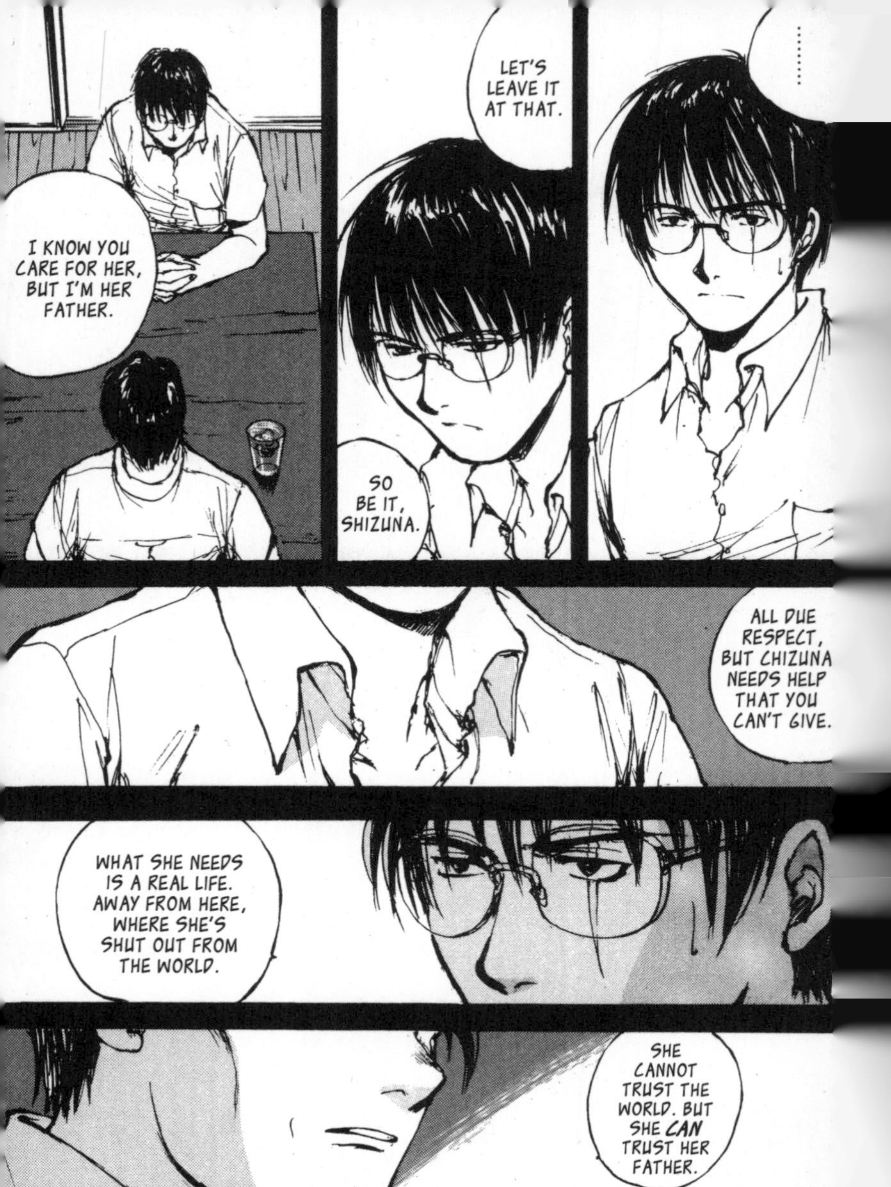
......
LET'S LEAVE IT AT THAT.
SO BE IT, SHIZUNA.
I KNOW YOU CARE FOR HER, BUT I'M HER FATHER.
ALL DUE RESPECT, BUT CHIZUNA NEEDS HELP THAT YOU CAN'T GIVE.
WHAT SHE NEEDS IS A REAL LIFE. AWAY FROM HERE, WHERE SHE'S SHUT OUT FROM THE WORLD.
SHE CANNOT TRUST THE WORLD. BUT SHE *CAN* TRUST HER FATHER.

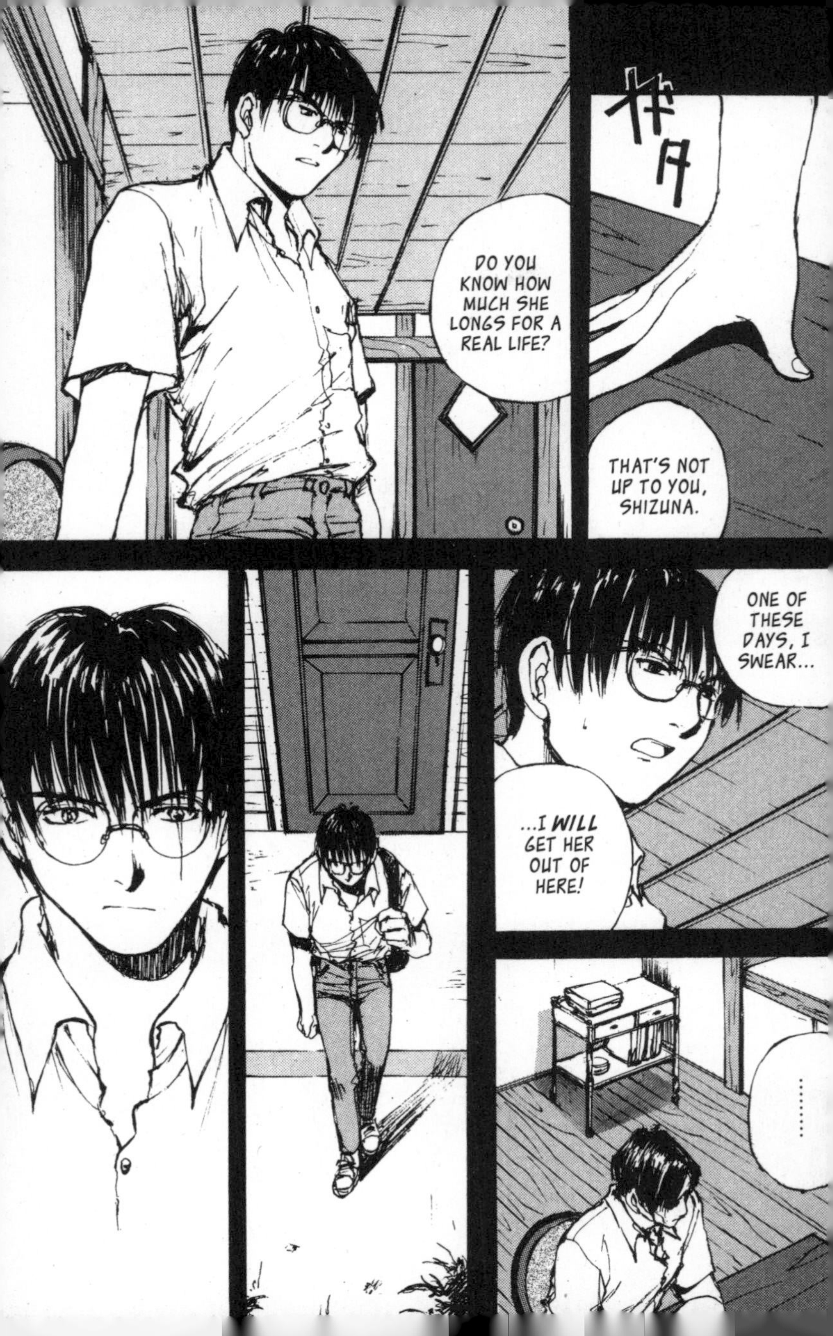
DO YOU KNOW HOW MUCH SHE LONGS FOR A REAL LIFE?
ガタ
THAT'S NOT UP TO YOU, SHIZUNA.
ONE OF THESE DAYS, I SWEAR...
...I **WILL** GET HER OUT OF HERE!
....

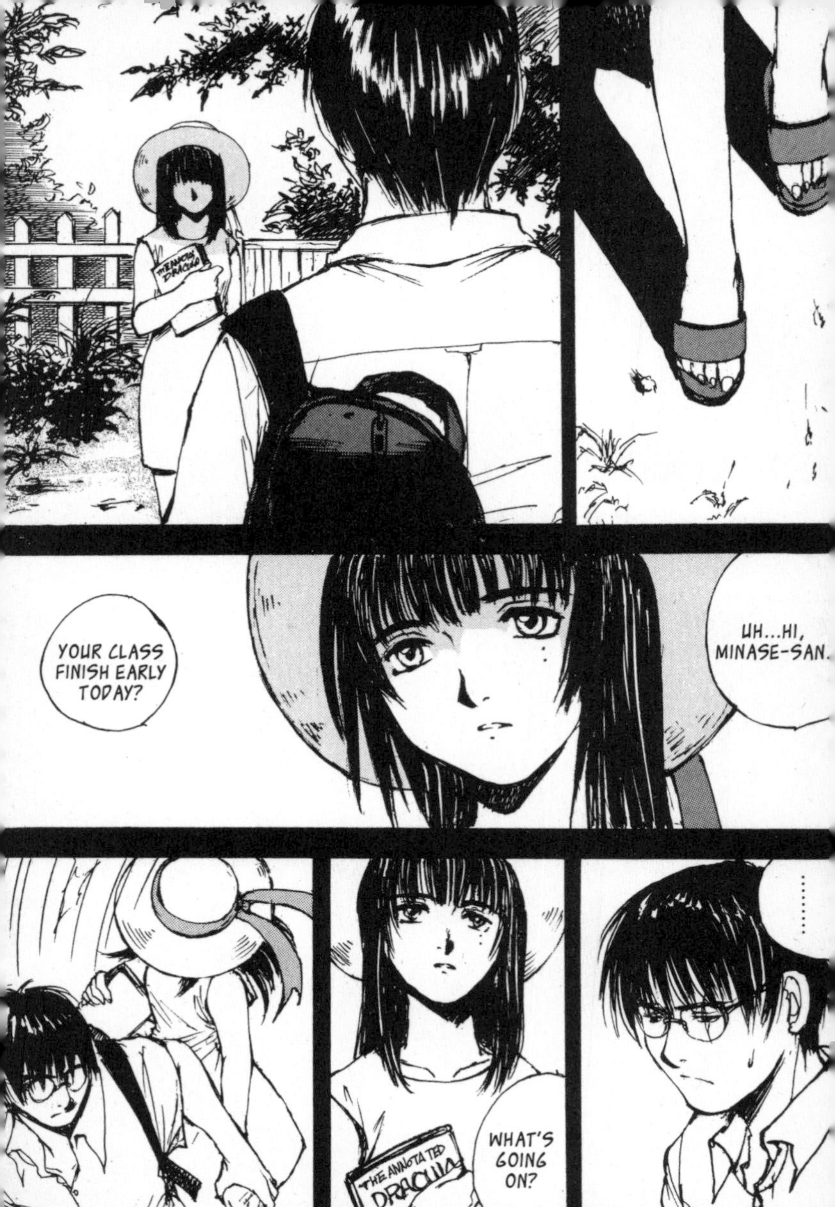
UH...HI, MINASE-SAN.
YOUR CLASS FINISH EARLY TODAY?
......
WHAT'S GOING ON?
THE ANNOTATED DRACULA

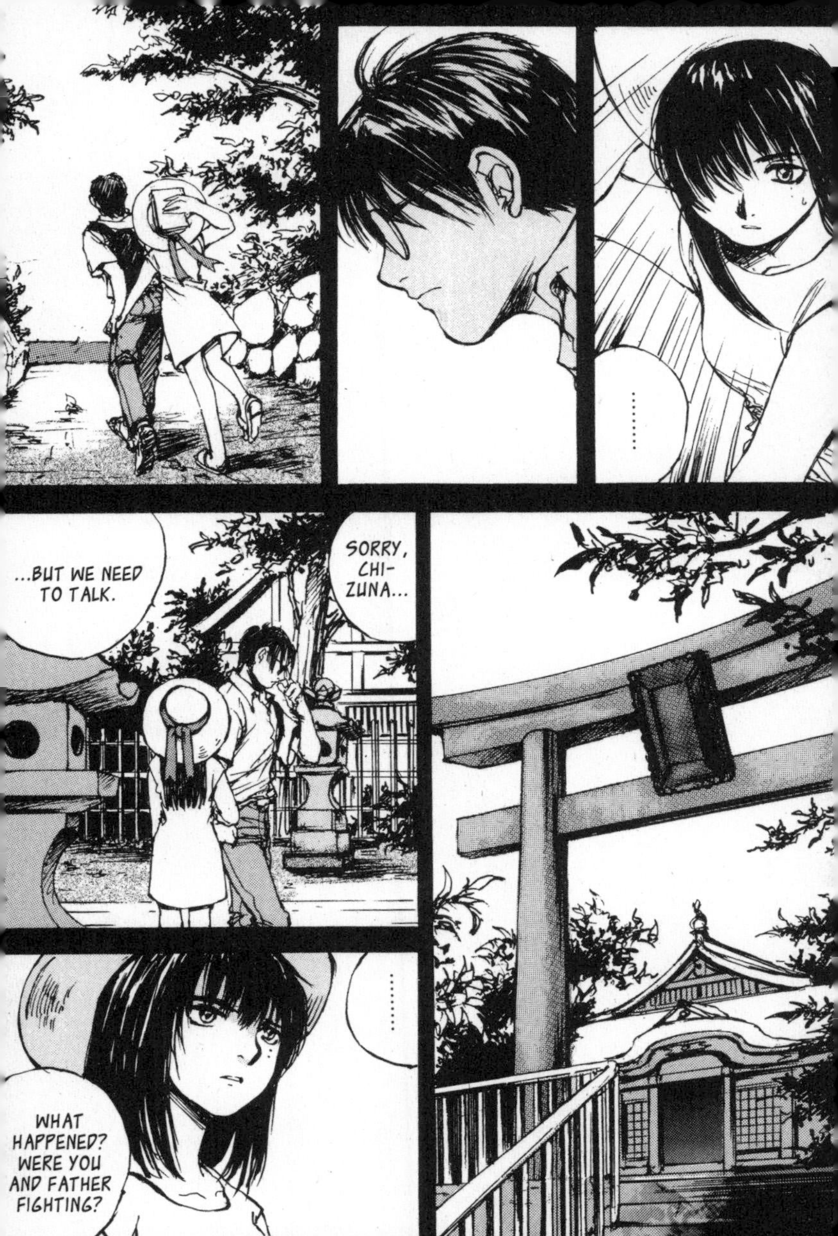
......
SORRY, CHI-ZUNA...
...BUT WE NEED TO TALK.
......
WHAT HAPPENED? WERE YOU AND FATHER FIGHTING?

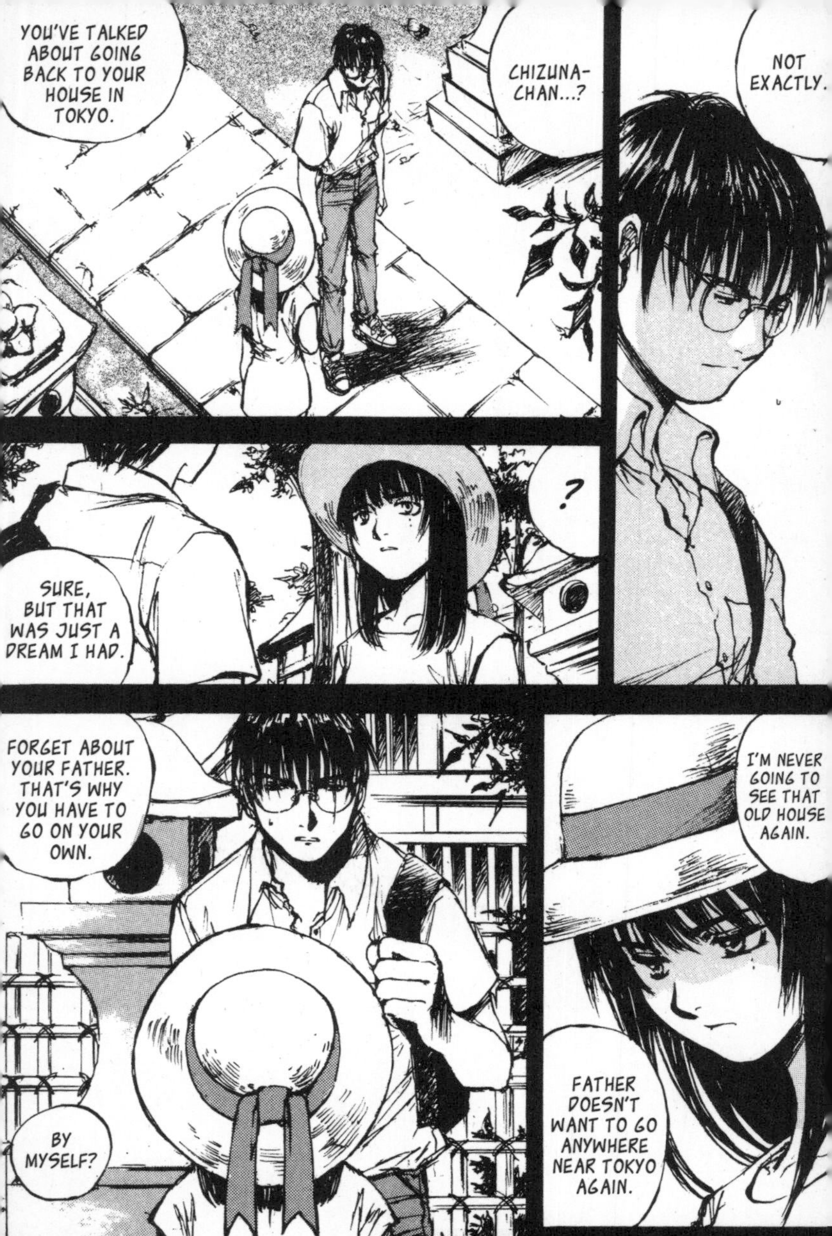
NOT EXACTLY.
CHIZUNA-CHAN...?
YOU'VE TALKED ABOUT GOING BACK TO YOUR HOUSE IN TOKYO.
?
SURE, BUT THAT WAS JUST A DREAM I HAD.
I'M NEVER GOING TO SEE THAT OLD HOUSE AGAIN.
FATHER DOESN'T WANT TO GO ANYWHERE NEAR TOKYO AGAIN.
FORGET ABOUT YOUR FATHER. THAT'S WHY YOU HAVE TO GO ON YOUR OWN.
BY MYSELF?

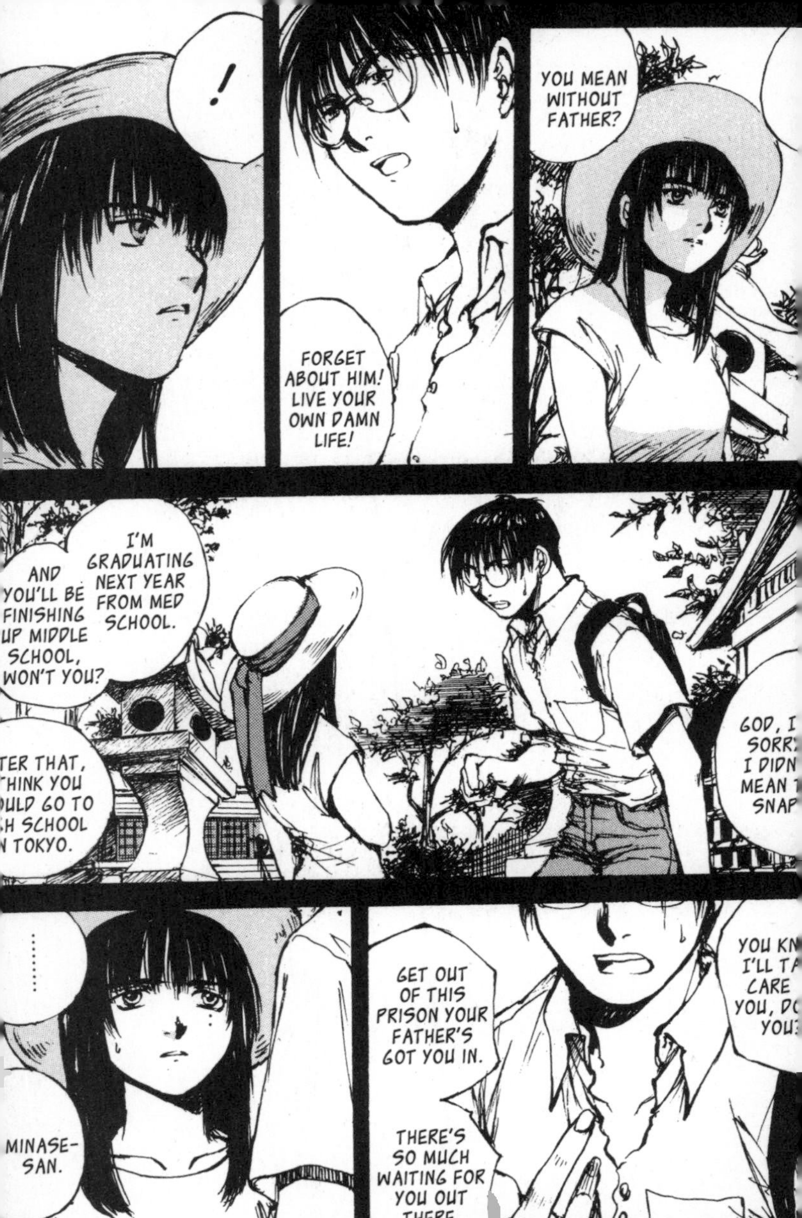
YOU MEAN WITHOUT FATHER?
FORGET ABOUT HIM! LIVE YOUR OWN DAMN LIFE!
!
GOD, I SORR I DIDN MEAN T SNAP
I'M GRADUATING NEXT YEAR FROM MED SCHOOL.
AND YOU'LL BE FINISHING UP MIDDLE SCHOOL, WON'T YOU?
TER THAT, THINK YOU ULD GO TO H SCHOOL N TOKYO.
YOU KN I'LL TA CARE YOU, DO YOU?
GET OUT OF THIS PRISON YOUR FATHER'S GOT YOU IN.
THERE'S SO MUCH WAITING FOR YOU OUT THERE.
......
MINASE-SAN.

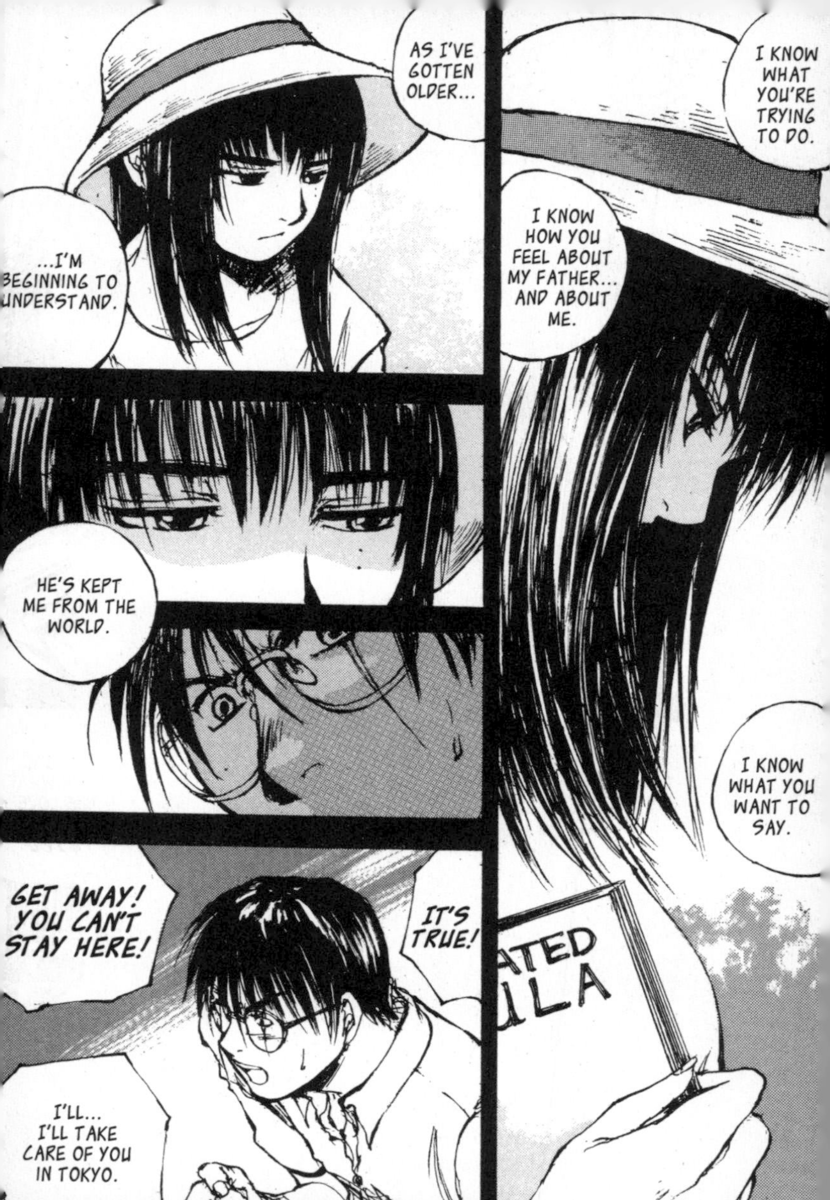
AS I'VE GOTTEN OLDER...
...I'M BEGINNING TO UNDERSTAND.
HE'S KEPT ME FROM THE WORLD.
IT'S TRUE!
GET AWAY! YOU CAN'T STAY HERE!
I'LL... I'LL TAKE CARE OF YOU IN TOKYO.
I KNOW WHAT YOU'RE TRYING TO DO.
I KNOW HOW YOU FEEL ABOUT MY FATHER... AND ABOUT ME.
I KNOW WHAT YOU WANT TO SAY.

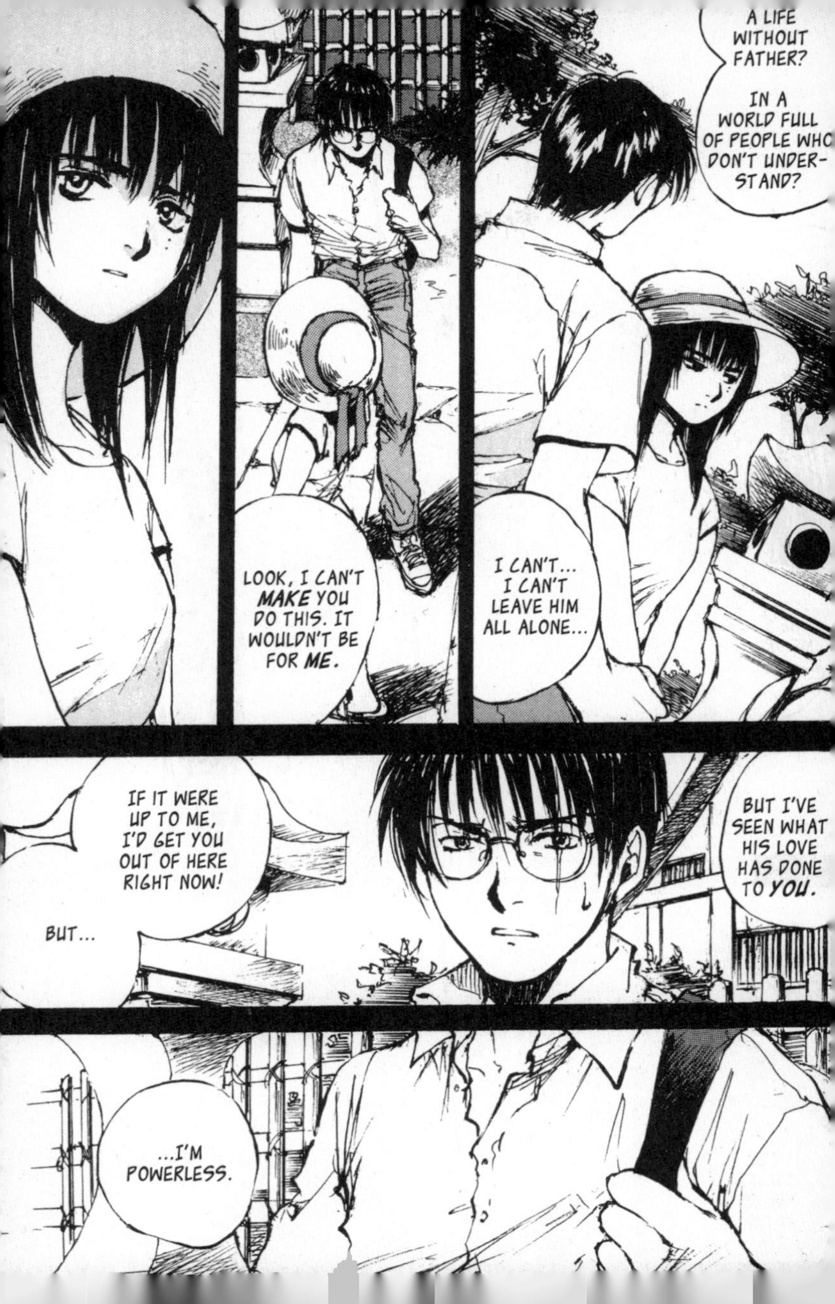
A LIFE WITHOUT FATHER?
IN A WORLD FULL OF PEOPLE WHO DON'T UNDERSTAND?
I CAN'T... I CAN'T LEAVE HIM ALL ALONE...
LOOK, I CAN'T MAKE YOU DO THIS. IT WOULDN'T BE FOR ME.
BUT I'VE SEEN WHAT HIS LOVE HAS DONE TO YOU.
IF IT WERE UP TO ME, I'D GET YOU OUT OF HERE RIGHT NOW!
BUT...
...I'M POWERLESS.

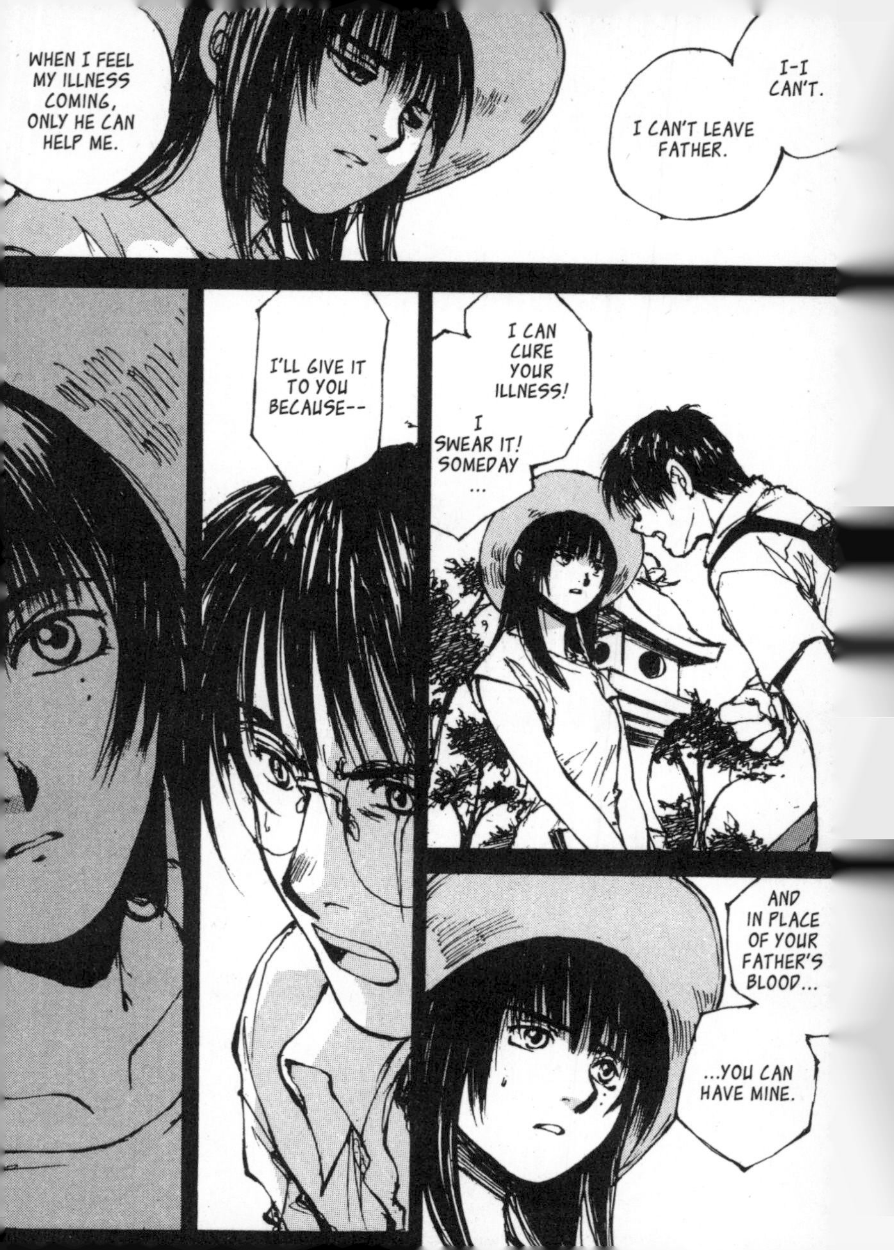
I-I CAN'T.
I CAN'T LEAVE FATHER.
WHEN I FEEL MY ILLNESS COMING, ONLY HE CAN HELP ME.
I CAN CURE YOUR ILLNESS!
I SWEAR IT! SOMEDAY ...
AND IN PLACE OF YOUR FATHER'S BLOOD...
...YOU CAN HAVE MINE.
I'LL GIVE IT TO YOU BECAUSE--

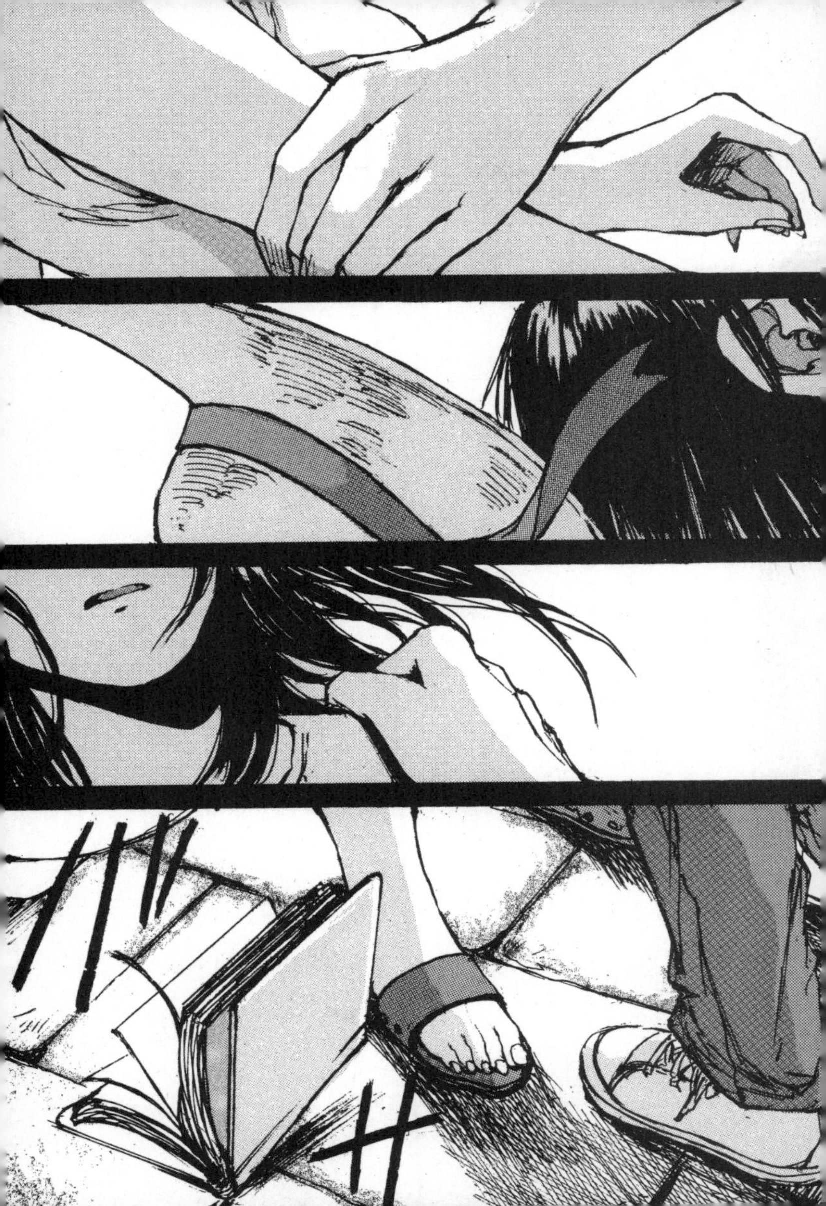

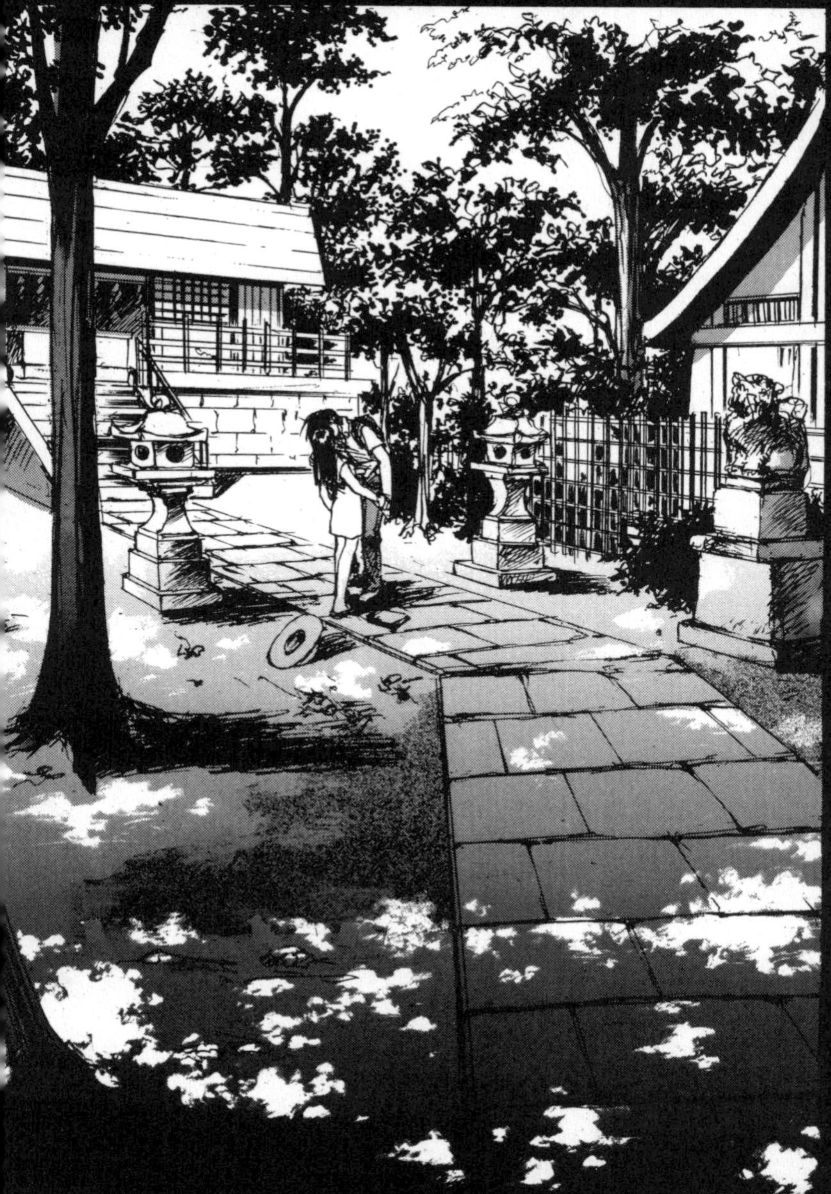

第16話

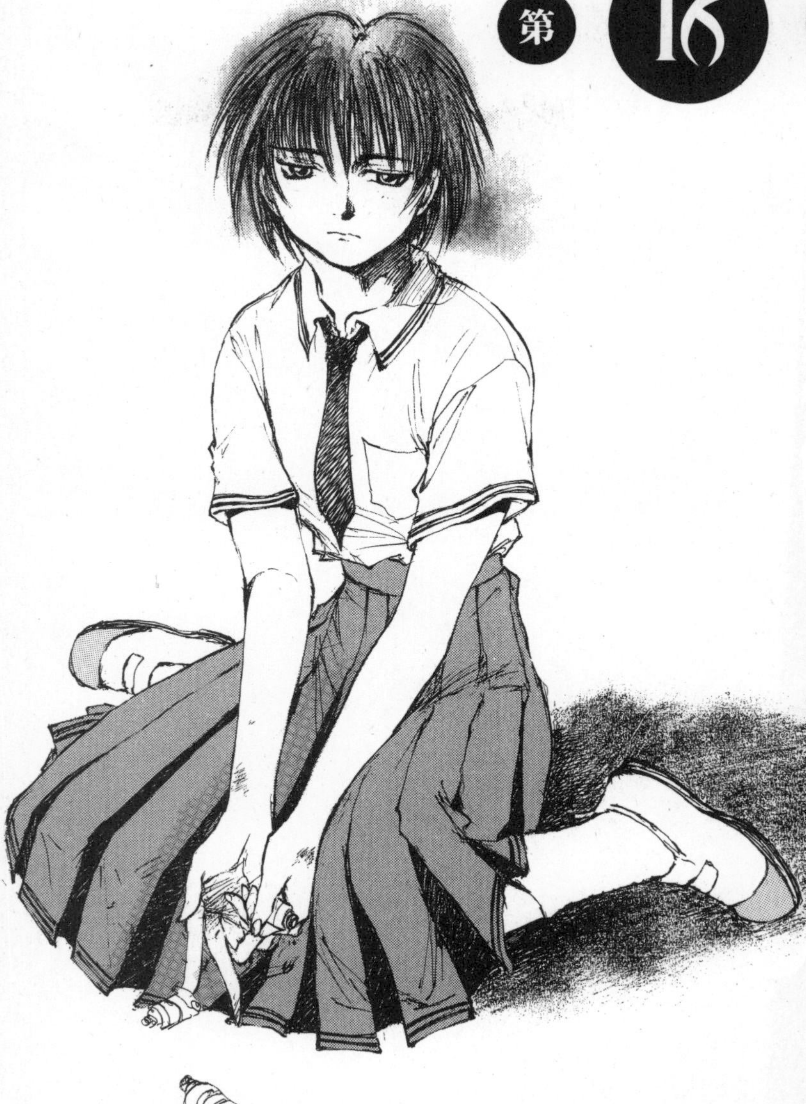

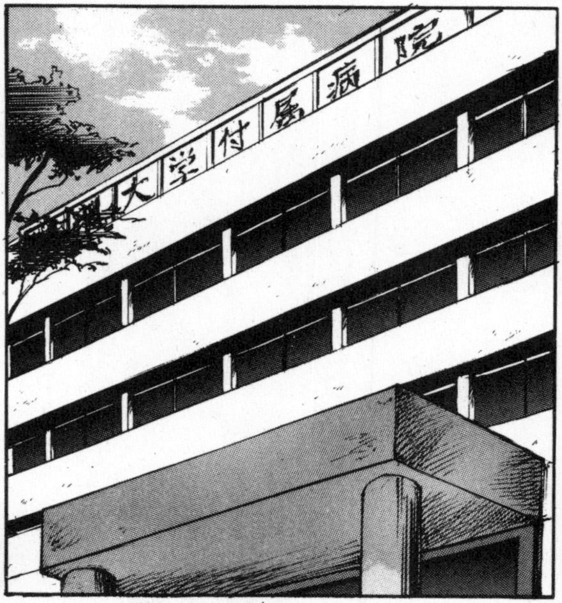
大学付属病院

*.University Hospital

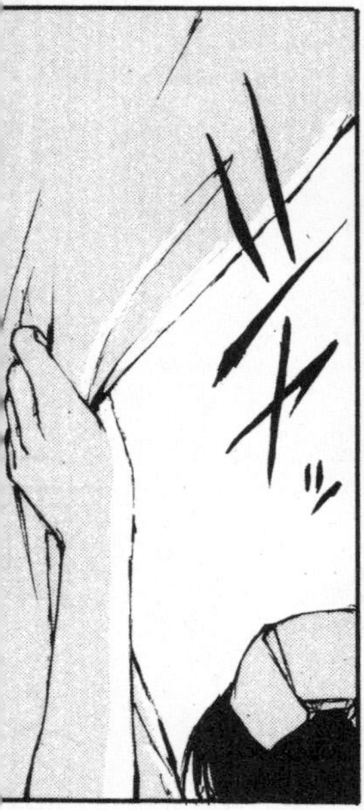

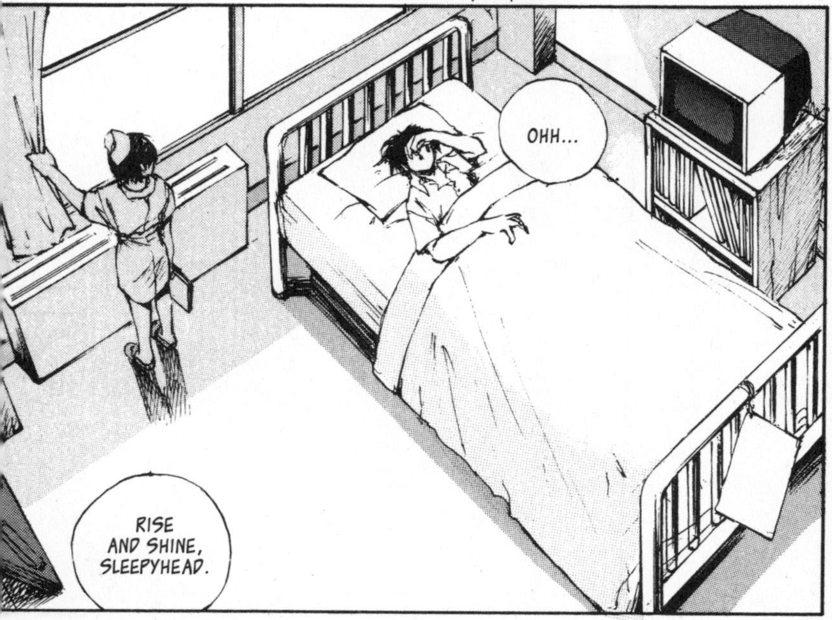
OHH...
RISE AND SHINE, SLEEPYHEAD.

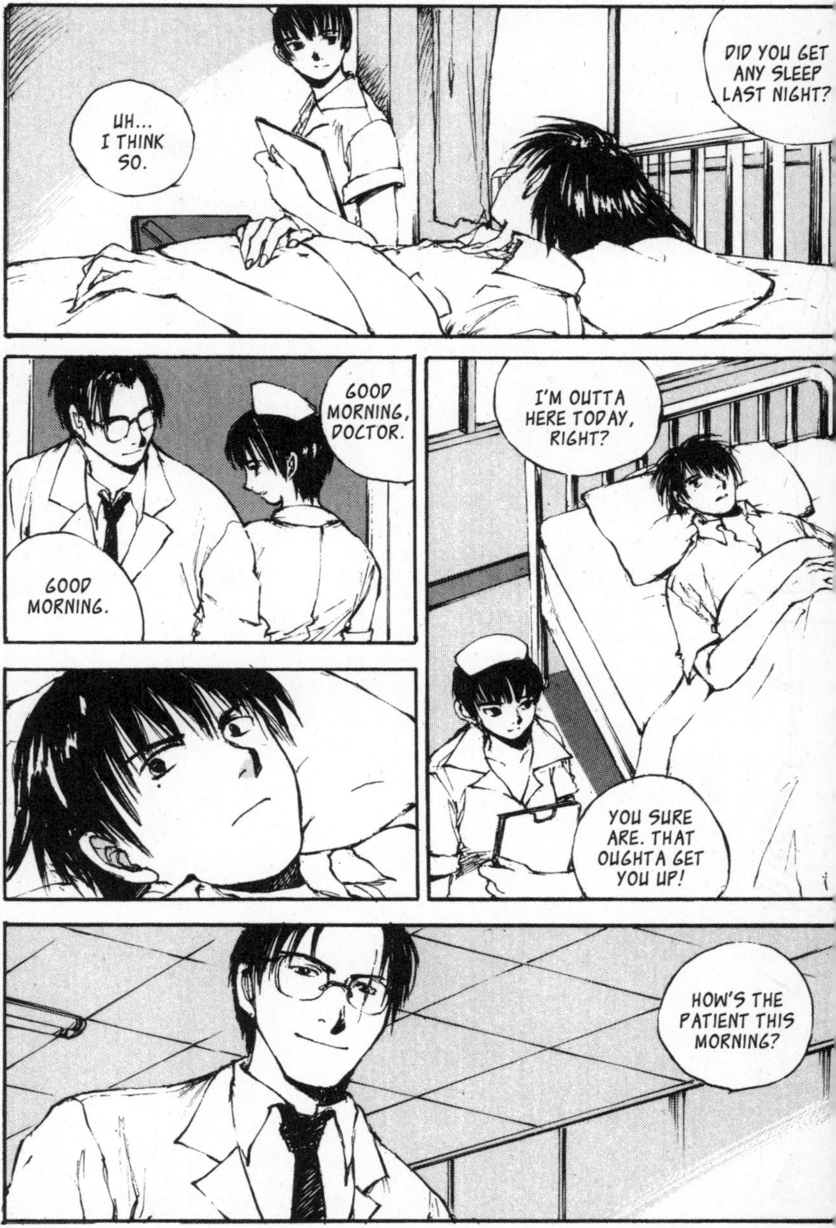
DID YOU GET ANY SLEEP LAST NIGHT?
UH... I THINK SO.
I'M OUTTA HERE TODAY, RIGHT?
YOU SURE ARE. THAT OUGHTA GET YOU UP!
GOOD MORNING, DOCTOR.
GOOD MORNING.
HOW'S THE PATIENT THIS MORNING?

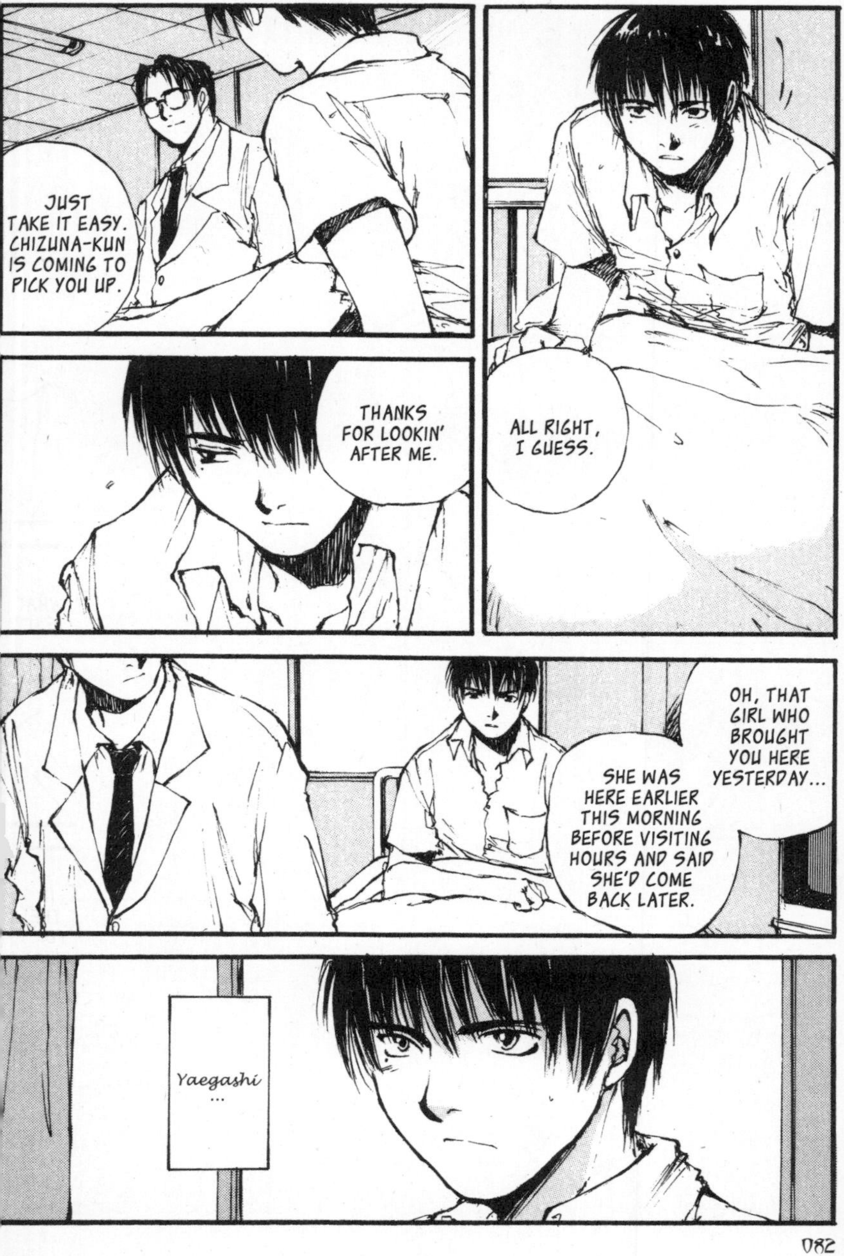
JUST TAKE IT EASY. CHIZUNA-KUN IS COMING TO PICK YOU UP.
ALL RIGHT, I GUESS.
THANKS FOR LOOKIN' AFTER ME.
OH, THAT GIRL WHO BROUGHT YOU HERE YESTERDAY...
SHE WAS HERE EARLIER THIS MORNING BEFORE VISITING HOURS AND SAID SHE'D COME BACK LATER.
Yaegashi ...

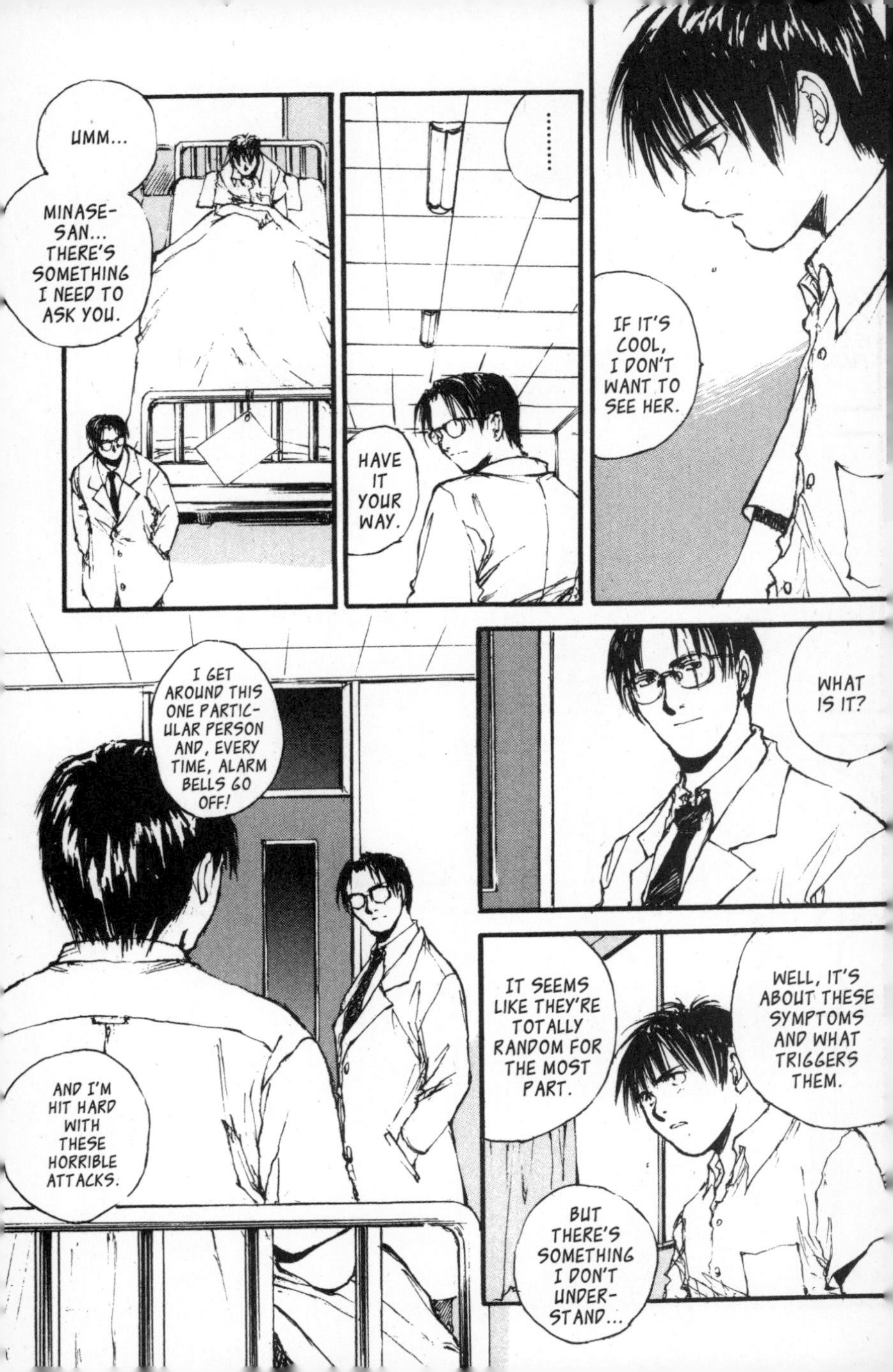
IF IT'S COOL, I DON'T WANT TO SEE HER.
......
HAVE IT YOUR WAY.
UMM...
MINASE-SAN... THERE'S SOMETHING I NEED TO ASK YOU.
WHAT IS IT?
WELL, IT'S ABOUT THESE SYMPTOMS AND WHAT TRIGGERS THEM.
IT SEEMS LIKE THEY'RE TOTALLY RANDOM FOR THE MOST PART.
BUT THERE'S SOMETHING I DON'T UNDERSTAND...
I GET AROUND THIS ONE PARTICULAR PERSON AND, EVERY TIME, ALARM BELLS GO OFF!
AND I'M HIT HARD WITH THESE HORRIBLE ATTACKS.

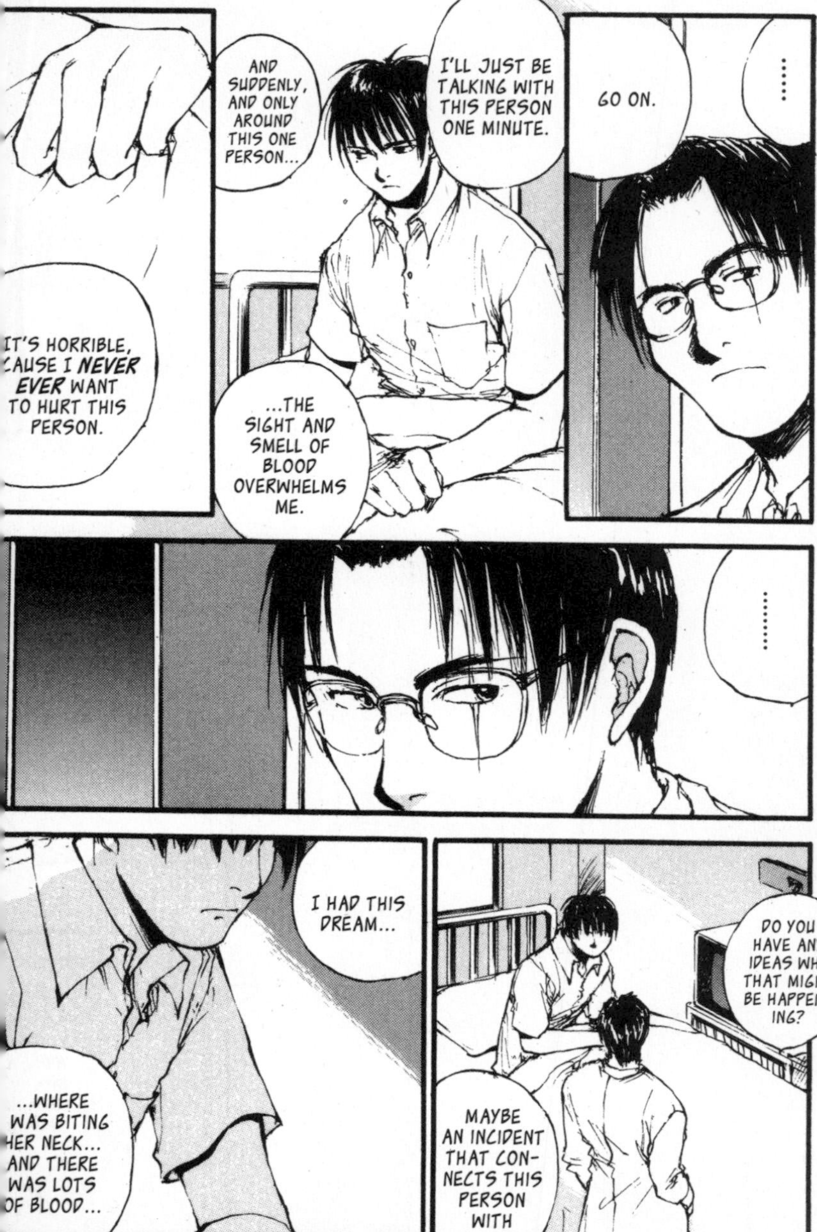
......
GO ON.
I'LL JUST BE TALKING WITH THIS PERSON ONE MINUTE.
AND SUDDENLY, AND ONLY AROUND THIS ONE PERSON...
...THE SIGHT AND SMELL OF BLOOD OVERWHELMS ME.
IT'S HORRIBLE, CAUSE I ***NEVER EVER*** WANT TO HURT THIS PERSON.
......
DO YOU HAVE ANY IDEAS WHY THAT MIGHT BE HAPPENING?
MAYBE AN INCIDENT THAT CONNECTS THIS PERSON WITH BLOOD?
I HAD THIS DREAM...
...WHERE WAS BITING HER NECK... AND THERE WAS LOTS OF BLOOD...

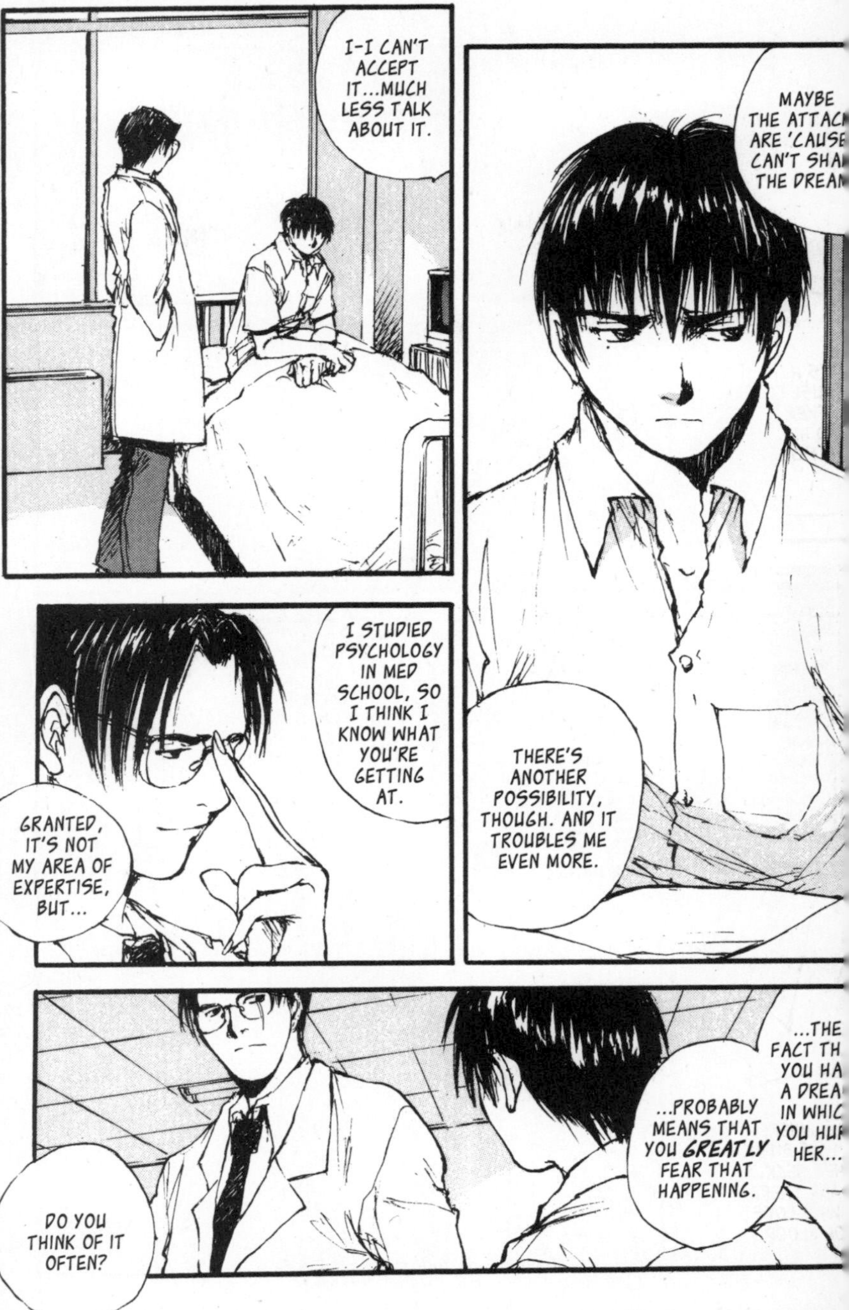
MAYBE THE ATTAC ARE 'CAUSE CAN'T SHA THE DREAM
THERE'S ANOTHER POSSIBILITY, THOUGH. AND IT TROUBLES ME EVEN MORE.
I-I CAN'T ACCEPT IT...MUCH LESS TALK ABOUT IT.
I STUDIED PSYCHOLOGY IN MED SCHOOL, SO I THINK I KNOW WHAT YOU'RE GETTING AT.
GRANTED, IT'S NOT MY AREA OF EXPERTISE, BUT...
...THE FACT TH YOU HA A DREA IN WHIC YOU HUR HER...
...PROBABLY MEANS THAT YOU **GREATLY** FEAR THAT HAPPENING.
DO YOU THINK OF IT OFTEN?

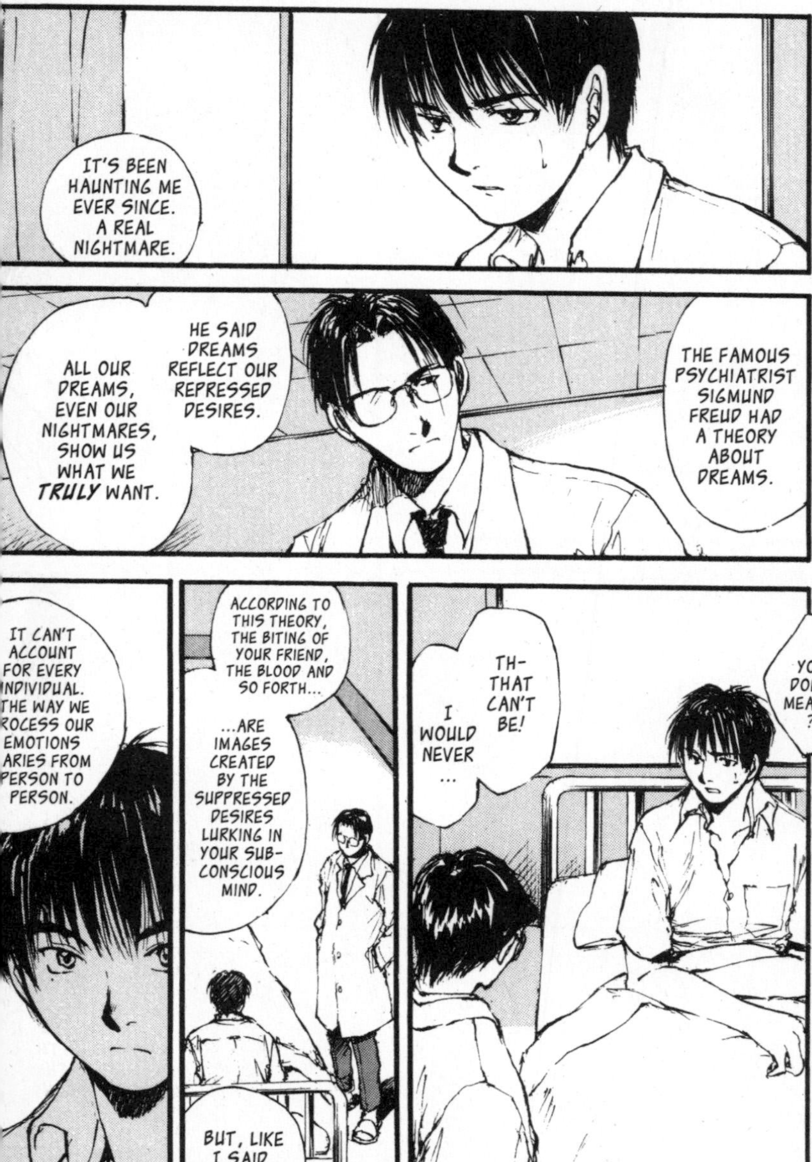
IT'S BEEN HAUNTING ME EVER SINCE. A REAL NIGHTMARE.
THE FAMOUS PSYCHIATRIST SIGMUND FREUD HAD A THEORY ABOUT DREAMS.
HE SAID DREAMS REFLECT OUR REPRESSED DESIRES.
ALL OUR DREAMS, EVEN OUR NIGHTMARES, SHOW US WHAT WE *TRULY* WANT.
YOU DON'T MEAN...?
TH- THAT CAN'T BE!
I WOULD NEVER ...
ACCORDING TO THIS THEORY, THE BITING OF YOUR FRIEND, THE BLOOD AND SO FORTH...
...ARE IMAGES CREATED BY THE SUPPRESSED DESIRES LURKING IN YOUR SUB-CONSCIOUS MIND.
BUT, LIKE I SAID, IT'S JUST A THEORY.
IT CAN'T ACCOUNT FOR EVERY INDIVIDUAL. THE WAY WE ROCESS OUR EMOTIONS ARIES FROM PERSON TO PERSON.

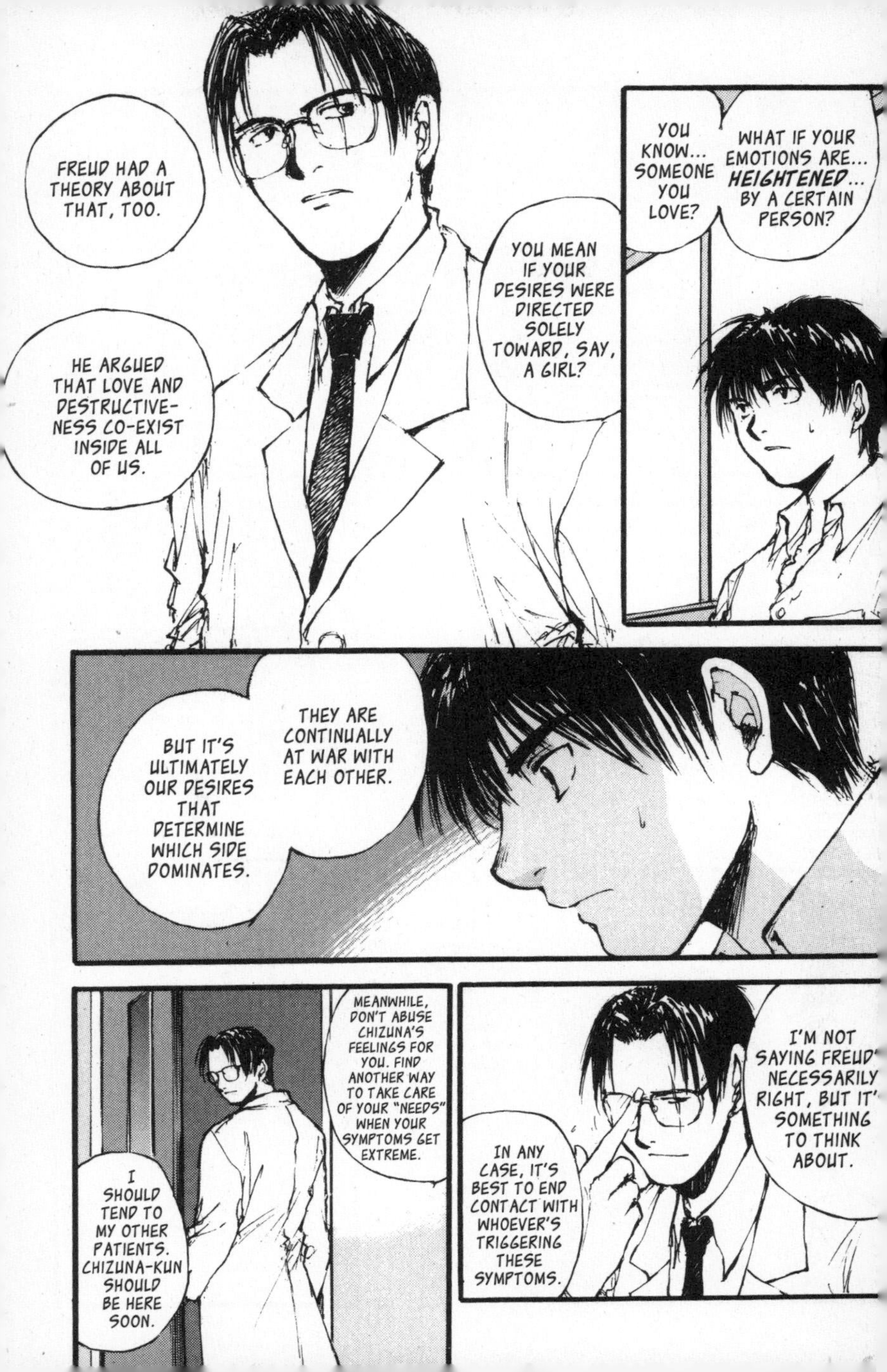
WHAT IF YOUR EMOTIONS ARE... ***HEIGHTENED***... BY A CERTAIN PERSON?
YOU KNOW... SOMEONE YOU LOVE?
YOU MEAN IF YOUR DESIRES WERE DIRECTED SOLELY TOWARD, SAY, A GIRL?
FREUD HAD A THEORY ABOUT THAT, TOO.
HE ARGUED THAT LOVE AND DESTRUCTIVE-NESS CO-EXIST INSIDE ALL OF US.
THEY ARE CONTINUALLY AT WAR WITH EACH OTHER.
BUT IT'S ULTIMATELY OUR DESIRES THAT DETERMINE WHICH SIDE DOMINATES.
I'M NOT SAYING FREUD' NECESSARILY RIGHT, BUT IT' SOMETHING TO THINK ABOUT.
IN ANY CASE, IT'S BEST TO END CONTACT WITH WHOEVER'S TRIGGERING THESE SYMPTOMS.
MEANWHILE, DON'T ABUSE CHIZUNA'S FEELINGS FOR YOU. FIND ANOTHER WAY TO TAKE CARE OF YOUR "NEEDS" WHEN YOUR SYMPTOMS GET EXTREME.
I SHOULD TEND TO MY OTHER PATIENTS. CHIZUNA-KUN SHOULD BE HERE SOON.

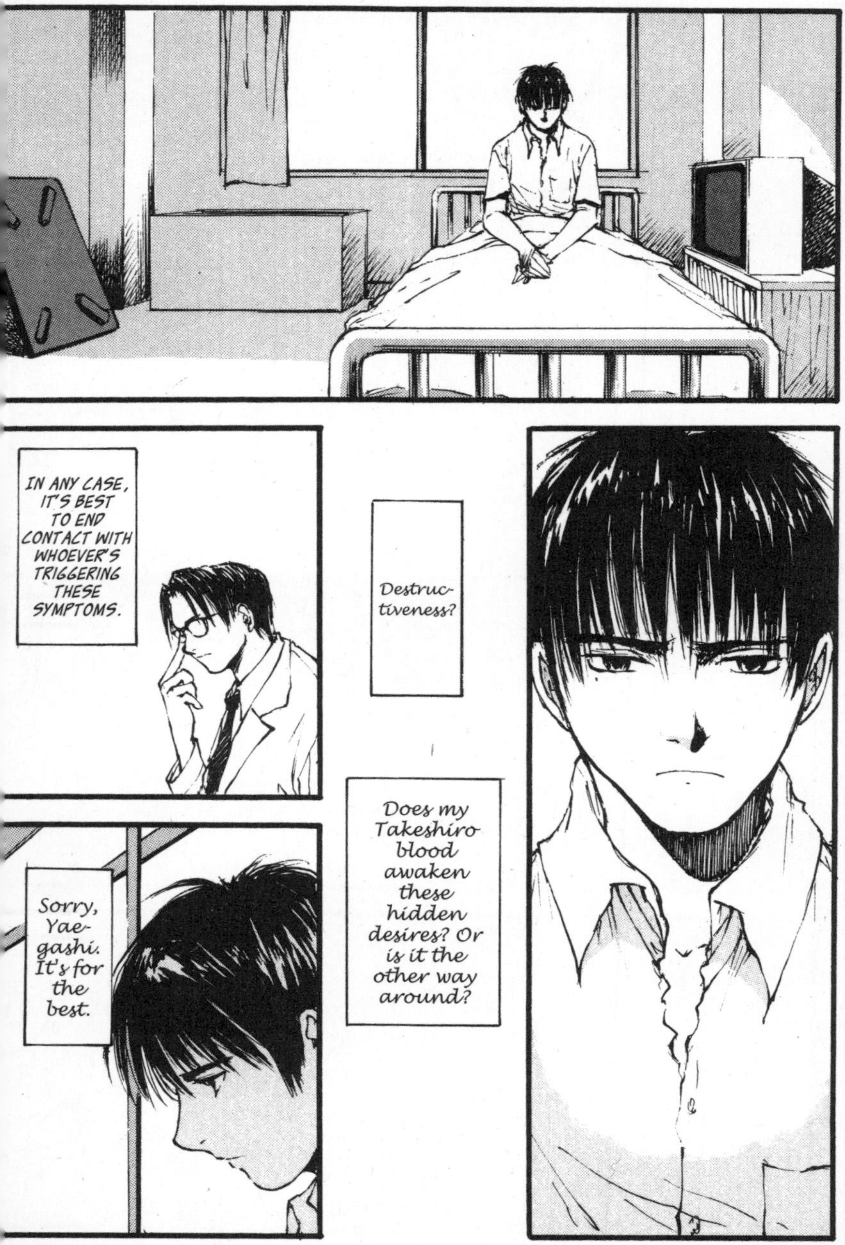
Destruc-tiveness?
IN ANY CASE, IT'S BEST TO END CONTACT WITH WHOEVER'S TRIGGERING THESE SYMPTOMS.
Does my Takeshiro blood awaken these hidden desires? Or is it the other way around?
Sorry, Yae-gashi. It's for the best.

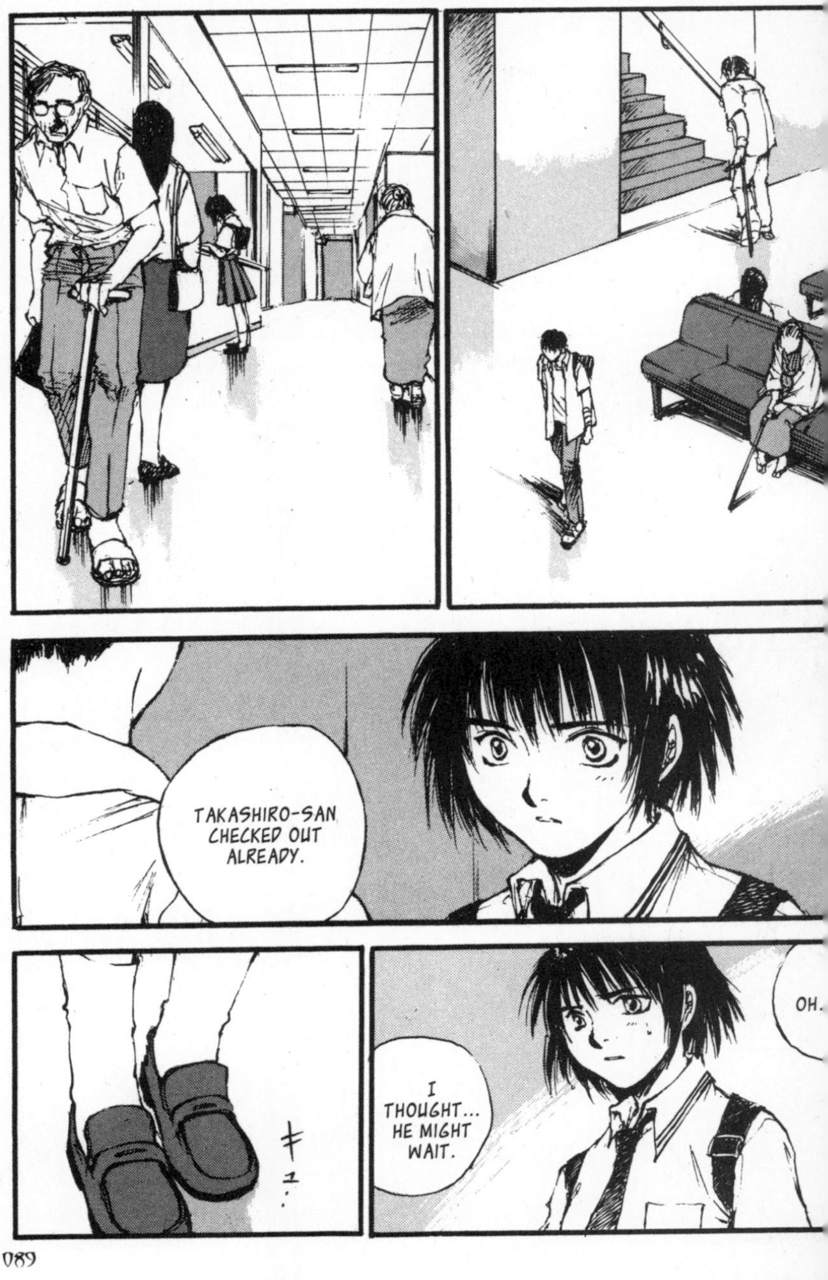
TAKASHIRO-SAN CHECKED OUT ALREADY.
OH.
I THOUGHT... HE MIGHT WAIT.
キュ.

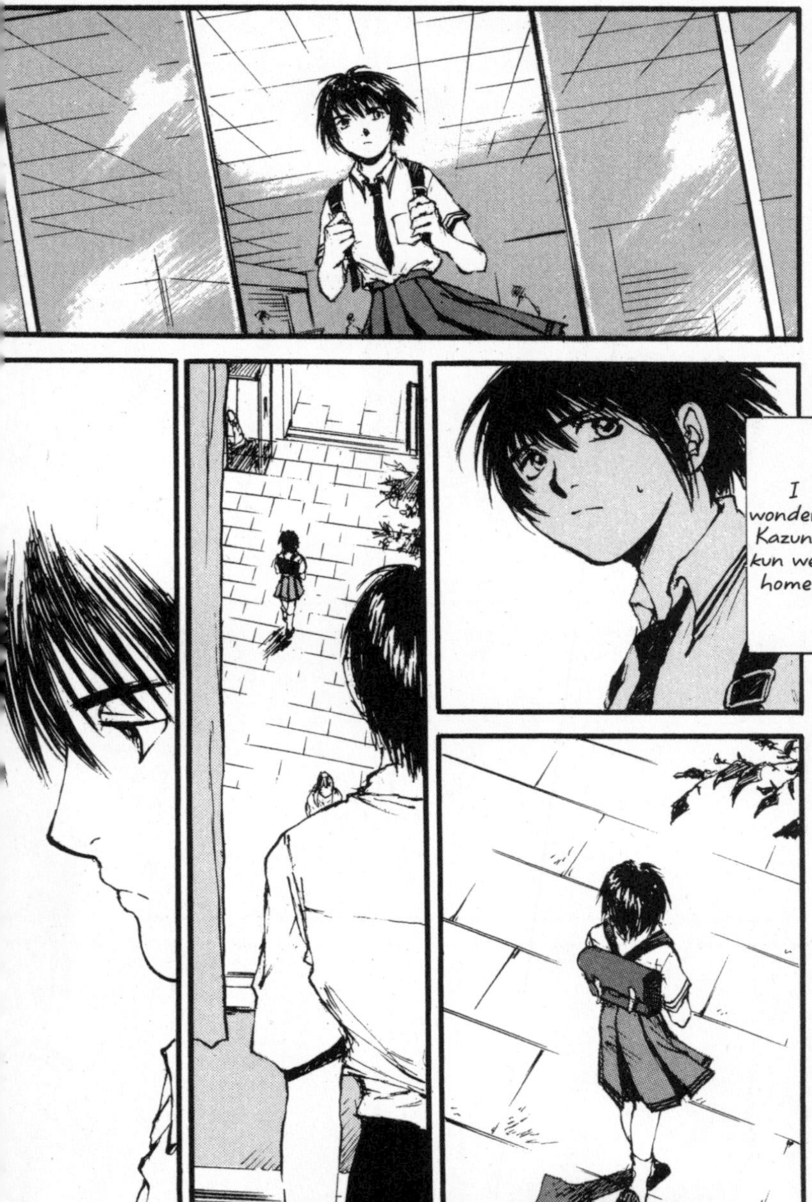
I wonder if Kazuna-kun went home...

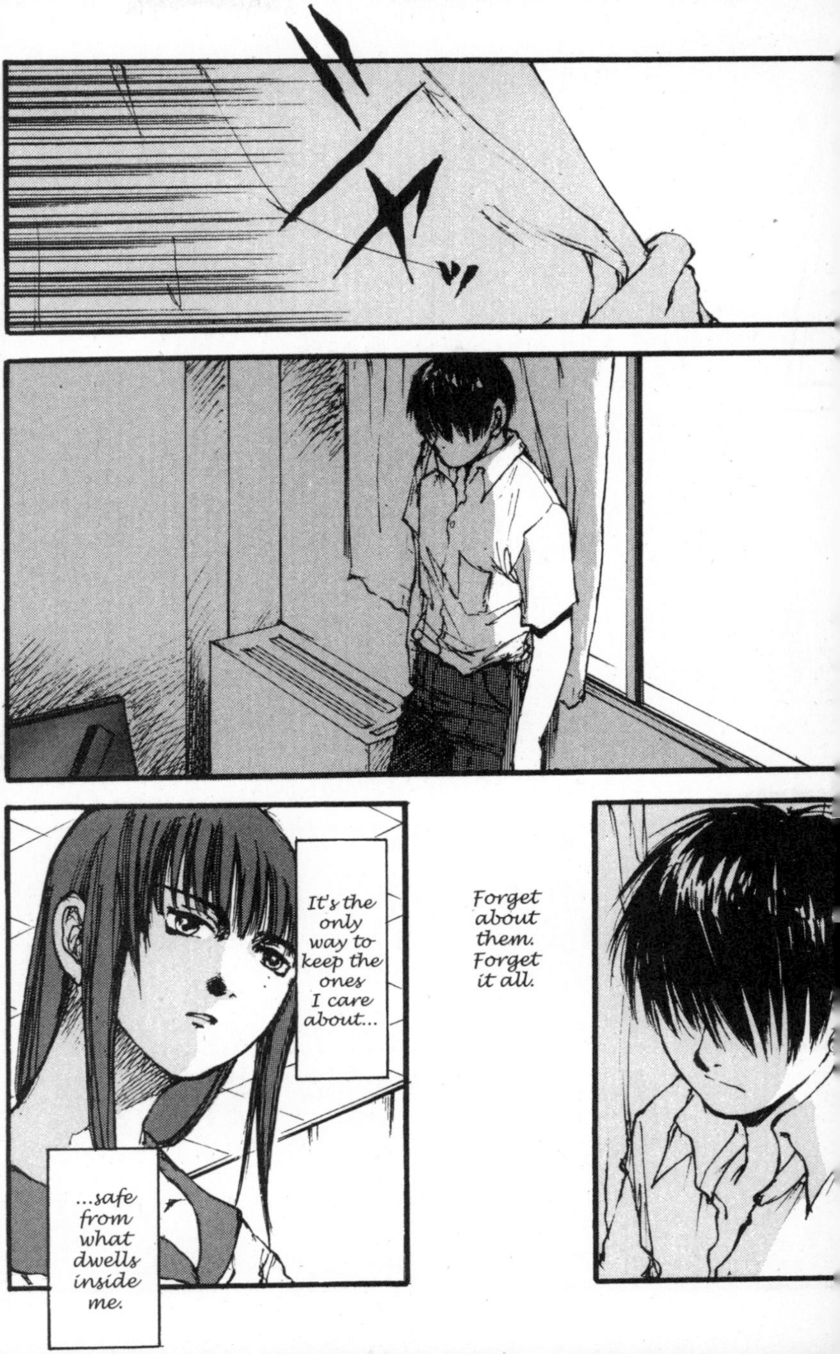
Forget about them. Forget it all.
It's the only way to keep the ones I care about...
...safe from what dwells inside me.

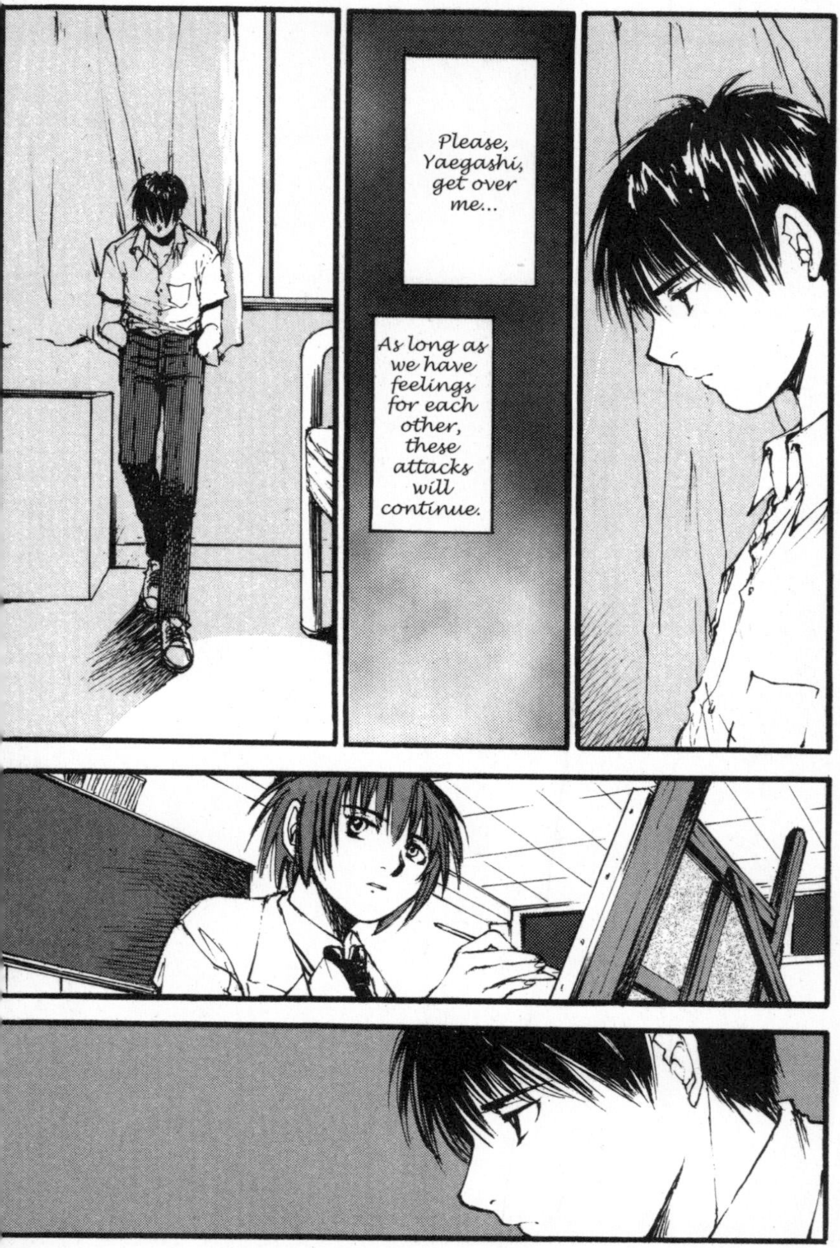
Please, Yaegashi, get over me...
As long as we have feelings for each other, these attacks will continue.

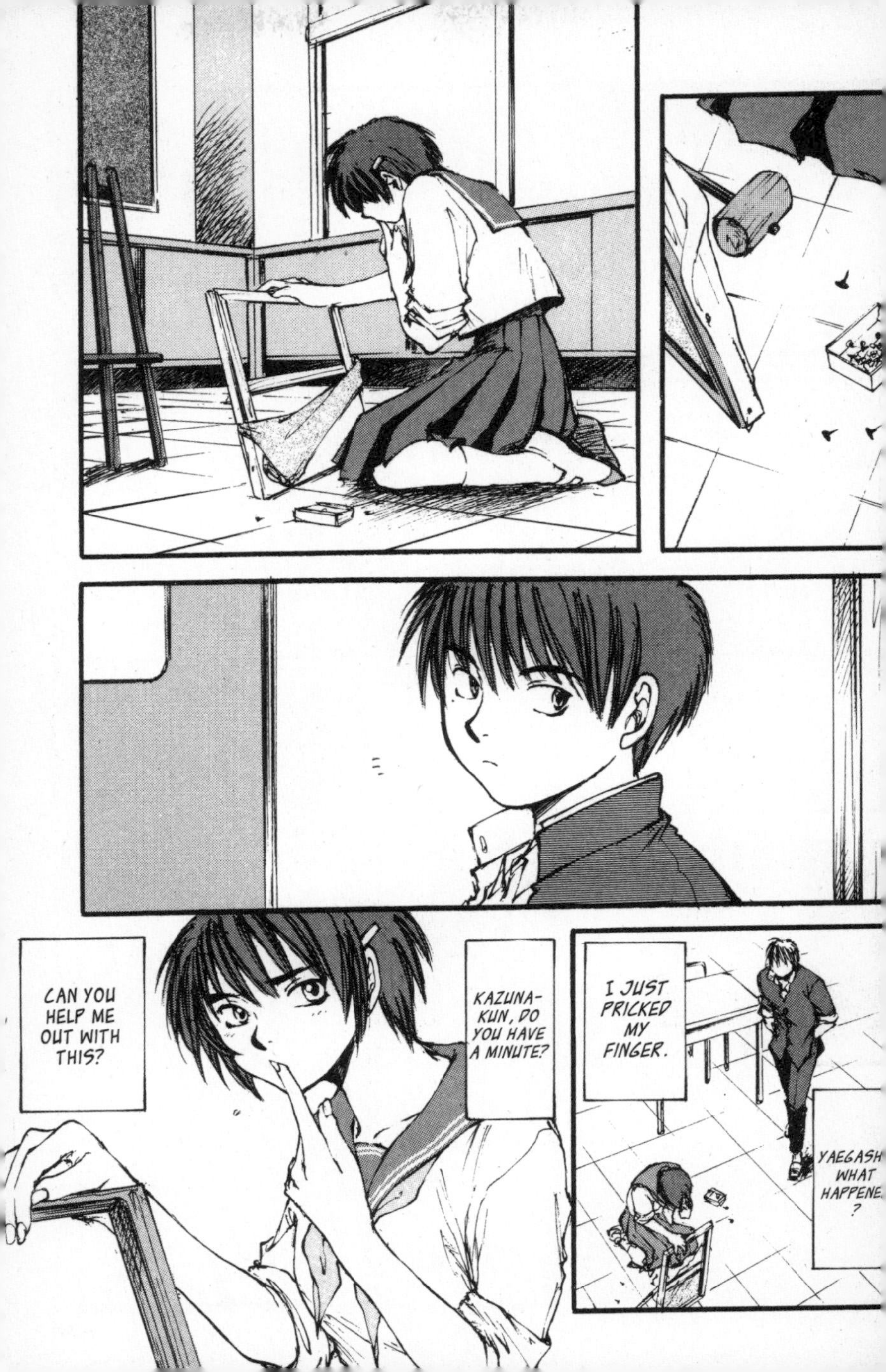
YAEGASH WHAT HAPPENE ?
I JUST PRICKED MY FINGER.
KAZUNA-KUN, DO YOU HAVE A MINUTE?
CAN YOU HELP ME OUT WITH THIS?

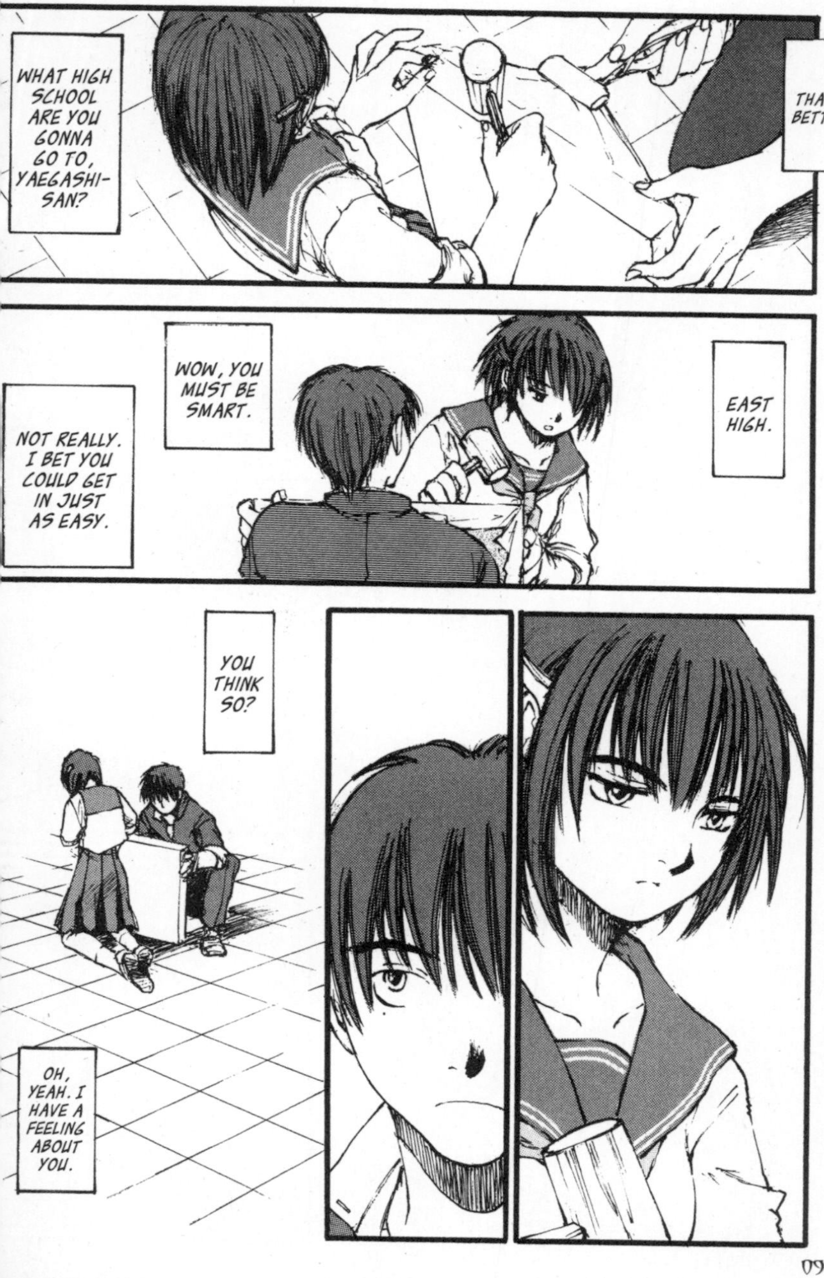
THAT'S BETTER.
WHAT HIGH SCHOOL ARE YOU GONNA GO TO, YAEGASHI-SAN?
EAST HIGH.
WOW, YOU MUST BE SMART.
NOT REALLY. I BET YOU COULD GET IN JUST AS EASY.
YOU THINK SO?
OH, YEAH. I HAVE A FEELING ABOUT YOU.

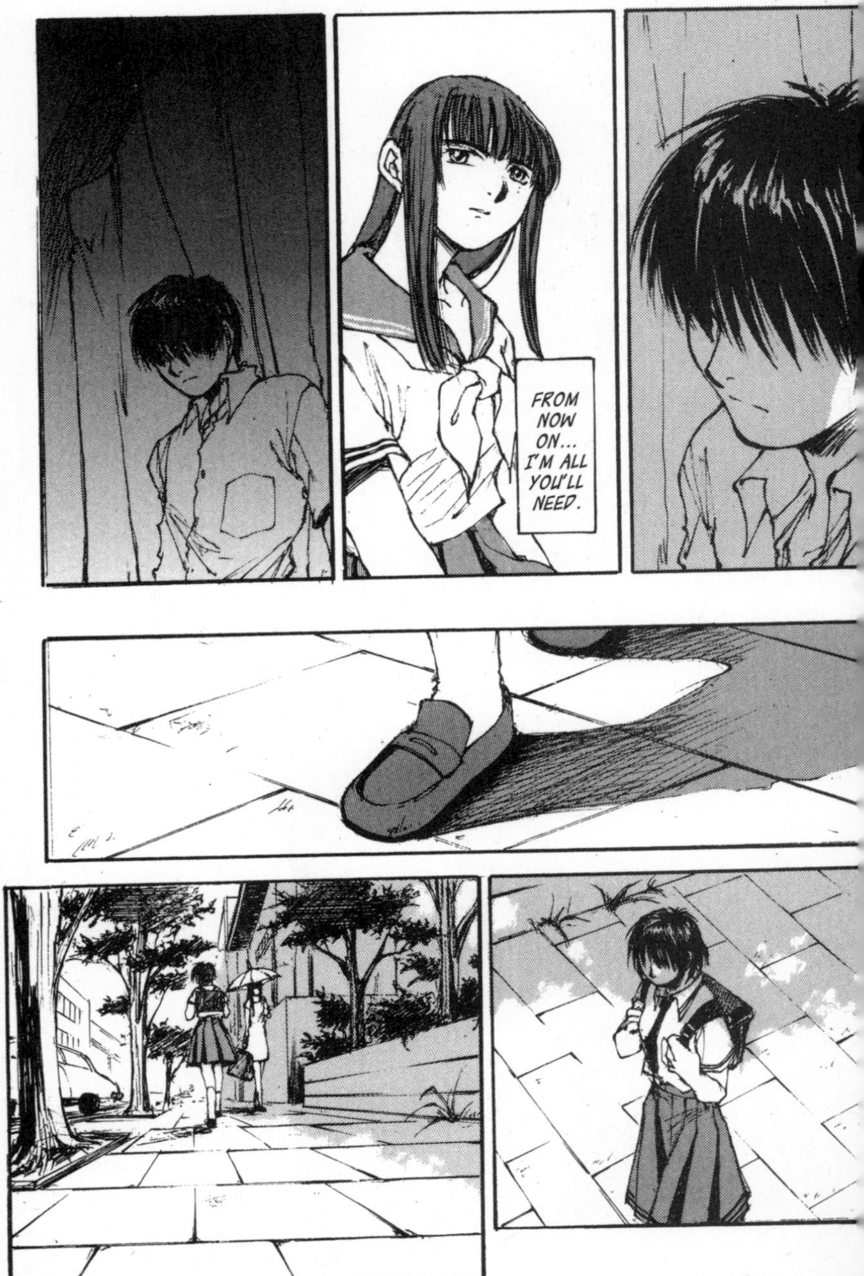
FROM NOW ON... I'M ALL YOU'LL NEED.

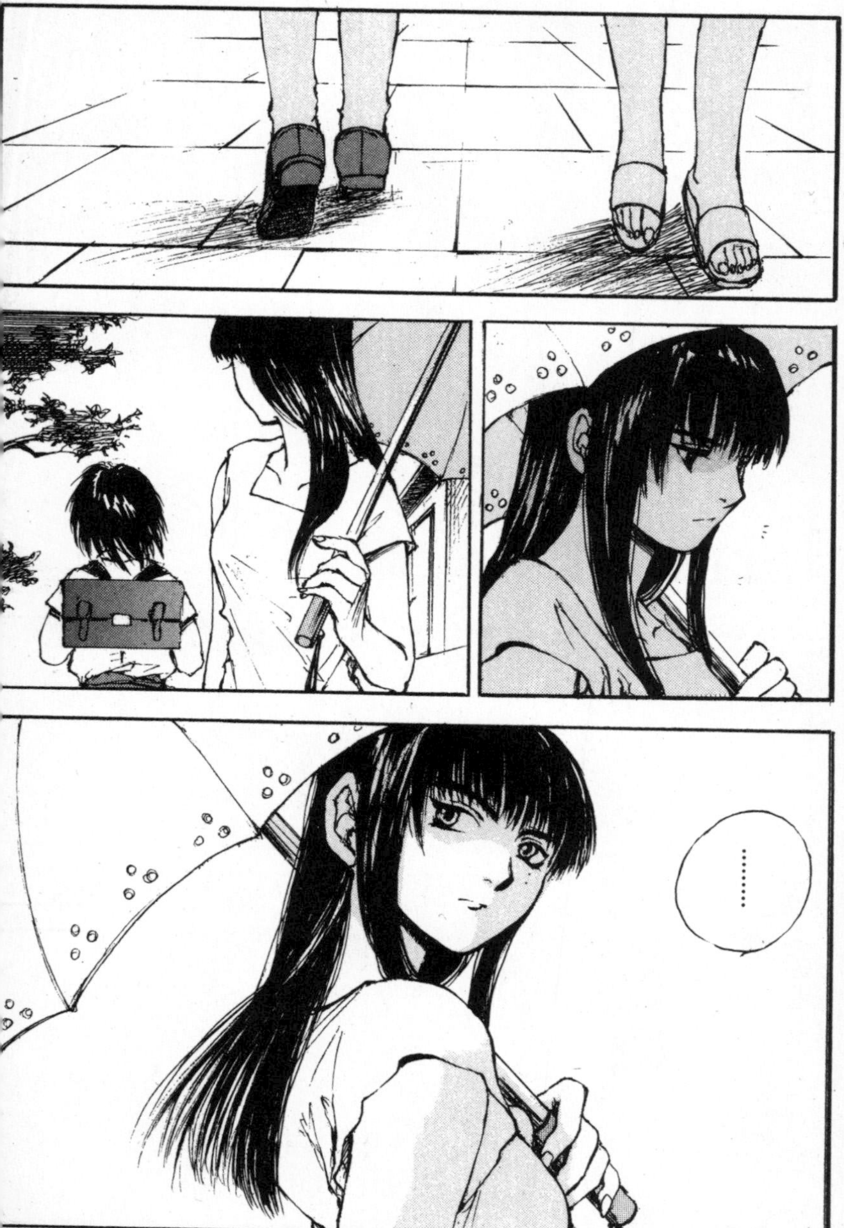
……

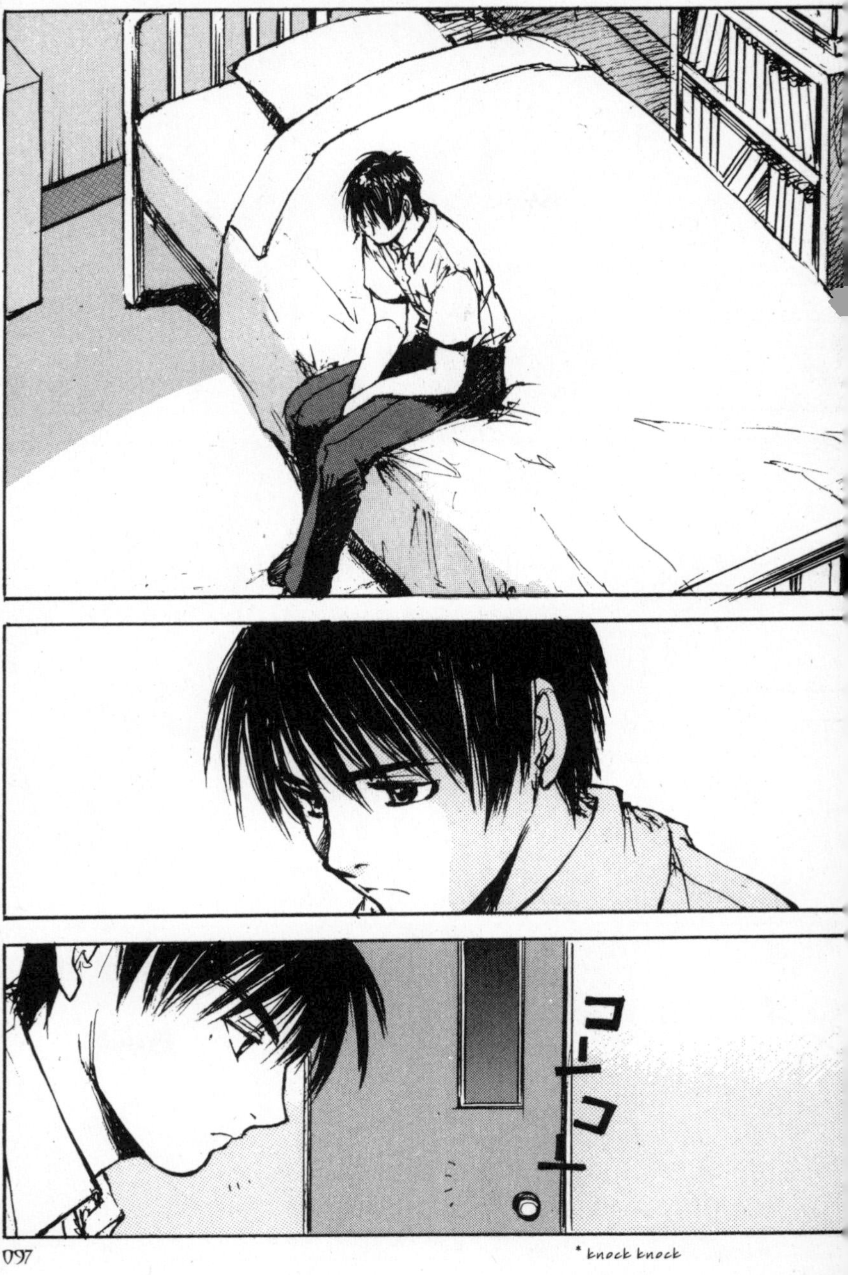
コンコン

* knock knock

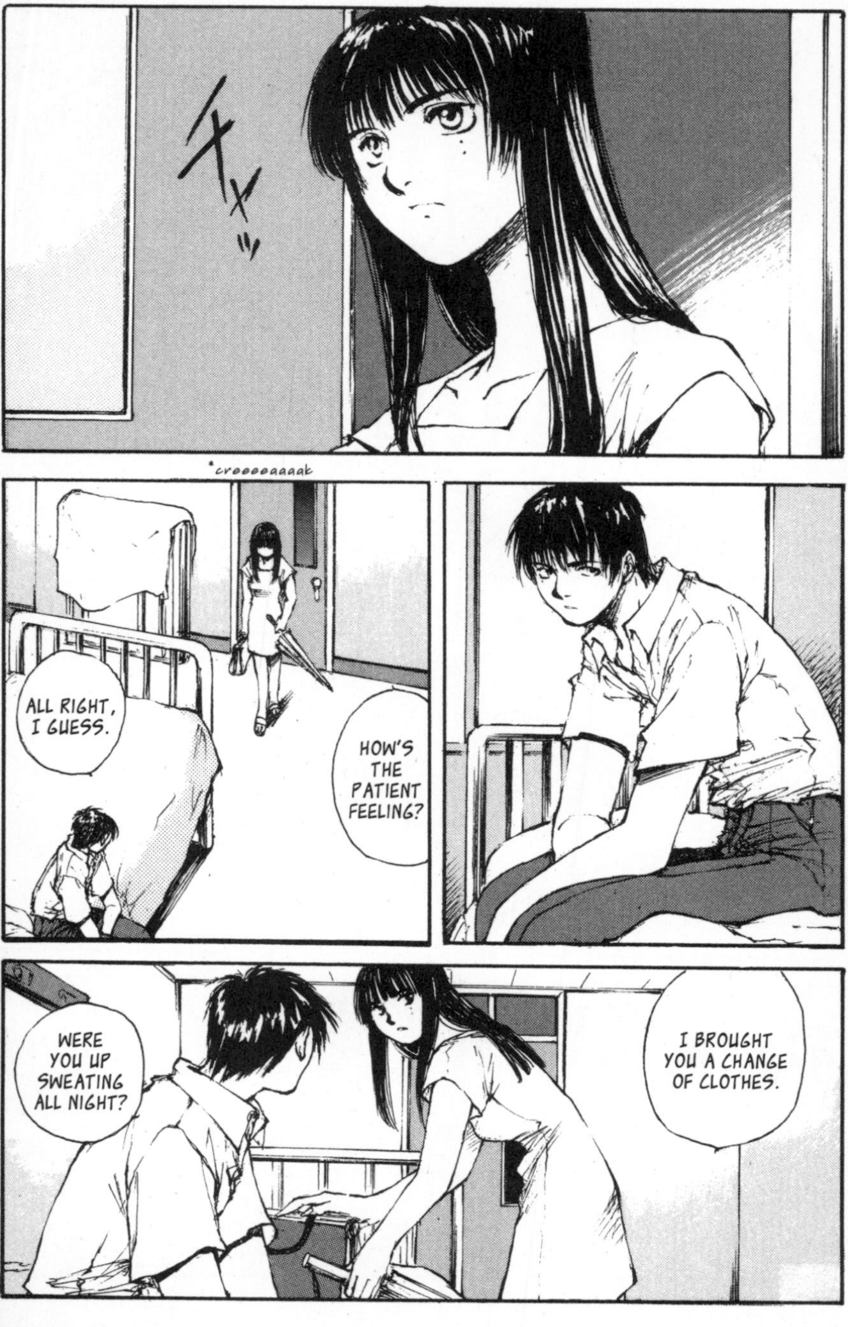
*creeeeaaaak
HOW'S THE PATIENT FEELING?
ALL RIGHT, I GUESS.
I BROUGHT YOU A CHANGE OF CLOTHES.
WERE YOU UP SWEATING ALL NIGHT?

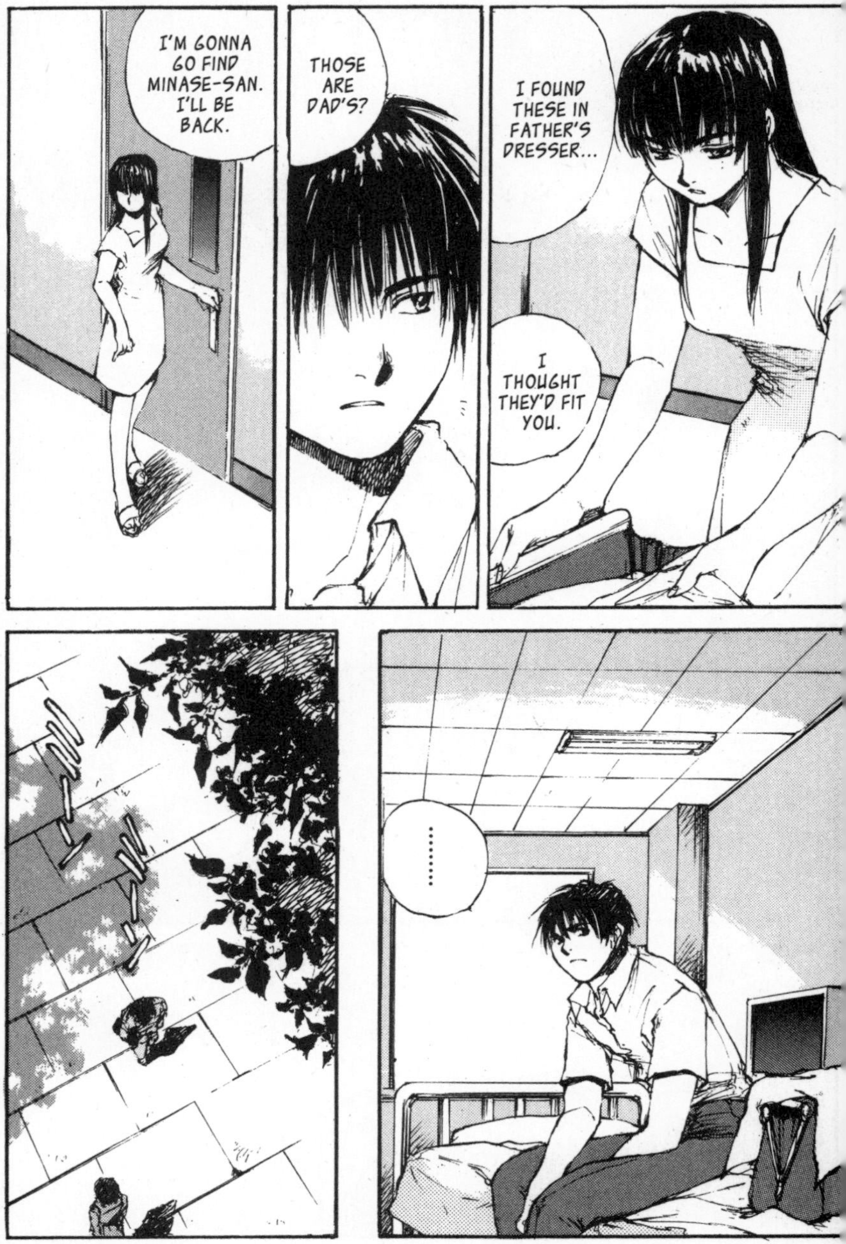
I FOUND THESE IN FATHER'S DRESSER...
I THOUGHT THEY'D FIT YOU.
THOSE ARE DAD'S?
I'M GONNA GO FIND MINASE-SAN. I'LL BE BACK.
....

*rustle rustle

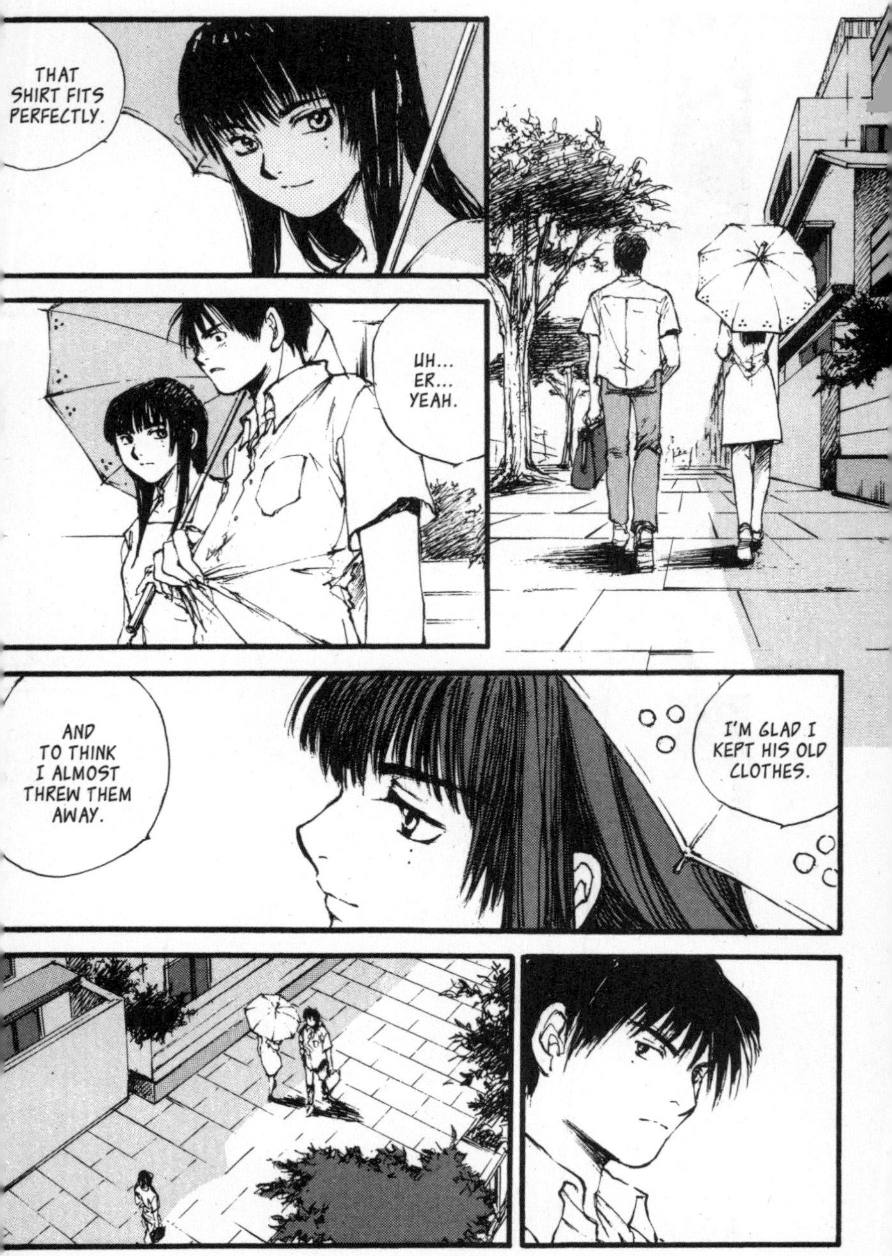
THAT SHIRT FITS PERFECTLY.
UH... ER... YEAH.
I'M GLAD I KEPT HIS OLD CLOTHES.
AND TO THINK I ALMOST THREW THEM AWAY.

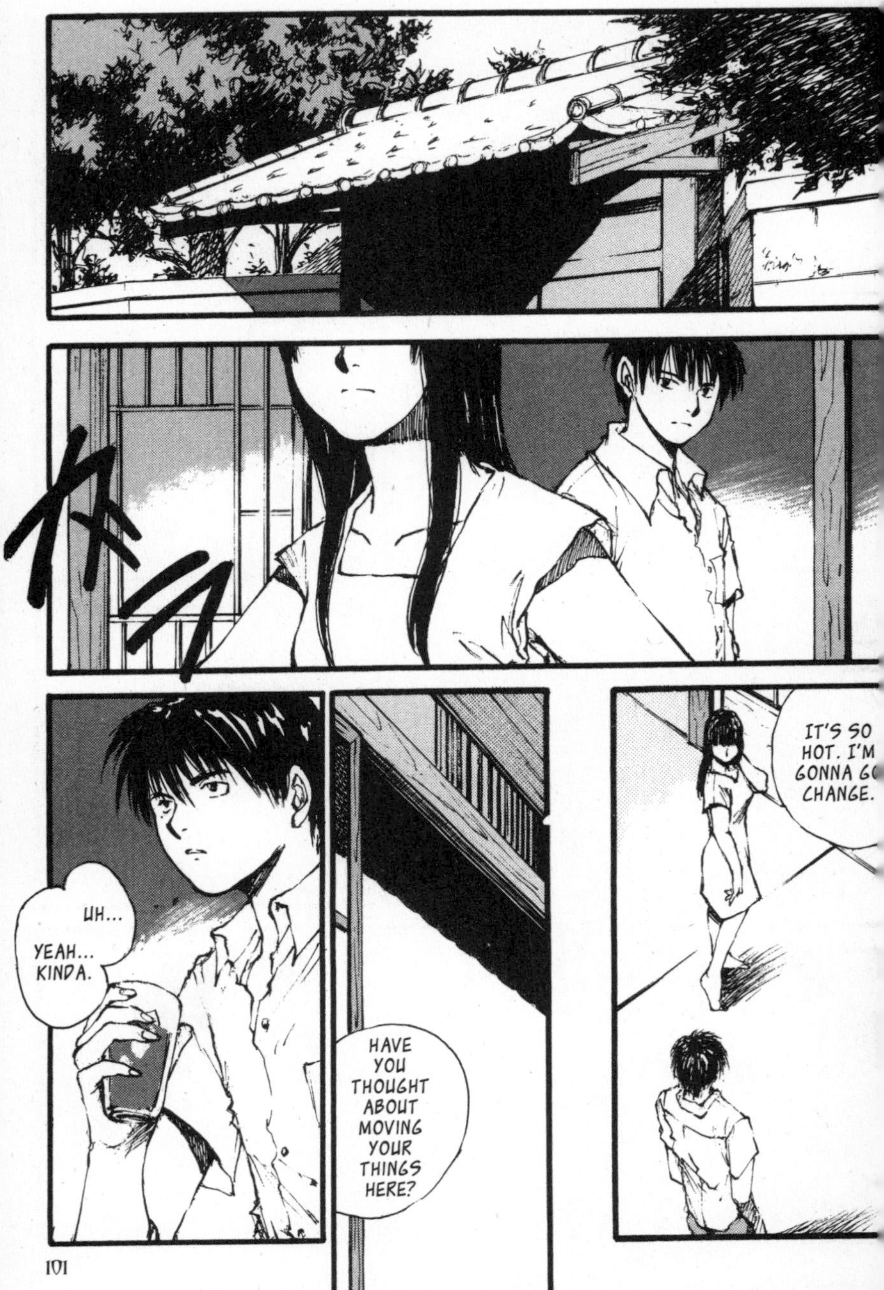
IT'S SO HOT. I'M GONNA GO CHANGE.
HAVE YOU THOUGHT ABOUT MOVING YOUR THINGS HERE?
UH... YEAH... KINDA.

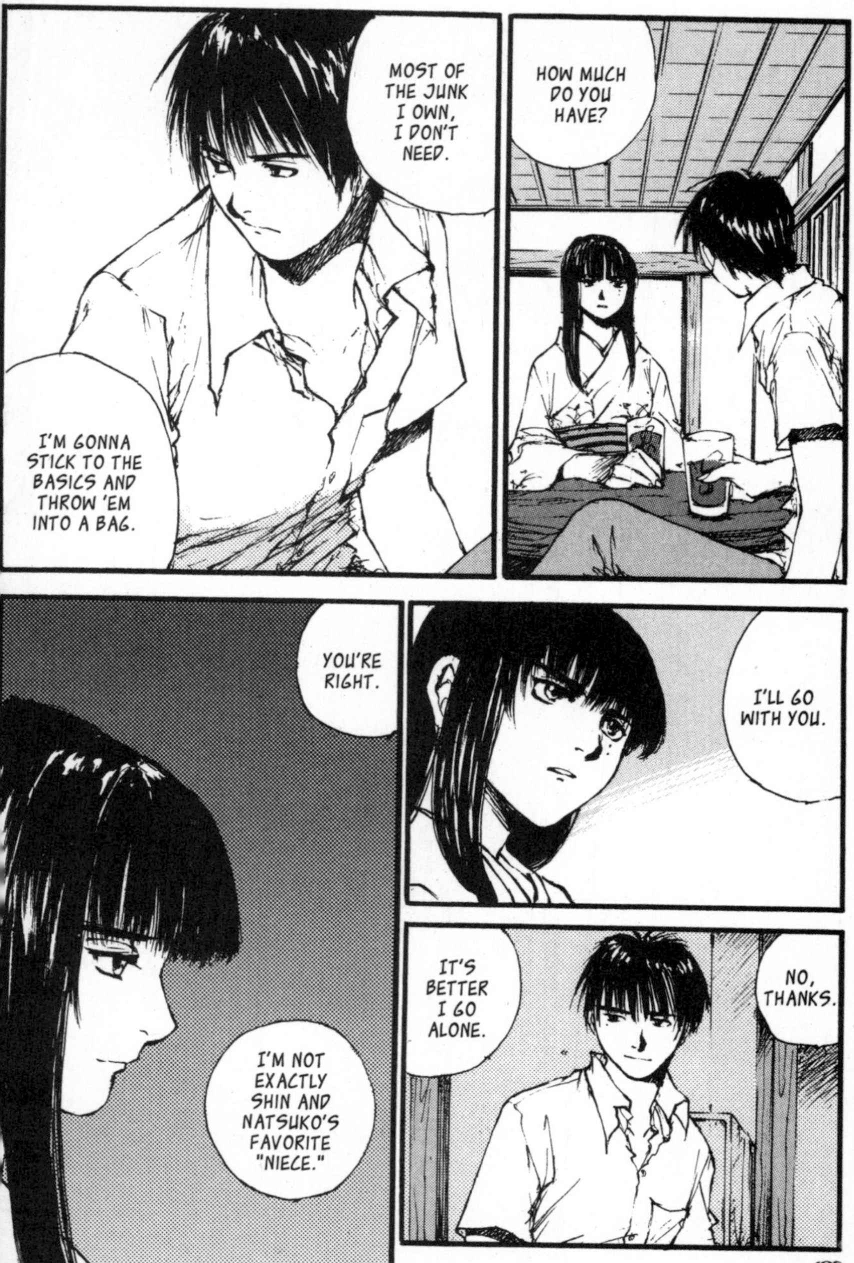
HOW MUCH DO YOU HAVE?
MOST OF THE JUNK I OWN, I DON'T NEED.
I'M GONNA STICK TO THE BASICS AND THROW 'EM INTO A BAG.
I'LL GO WITH YOU.
NO, THANKS.
IT'S BETTER I GO ALONE.
YOU'RE RIGHT.
I'M NOT EXACTLY SHIN AND NATSUKO'S FAVORITE "NIECE."

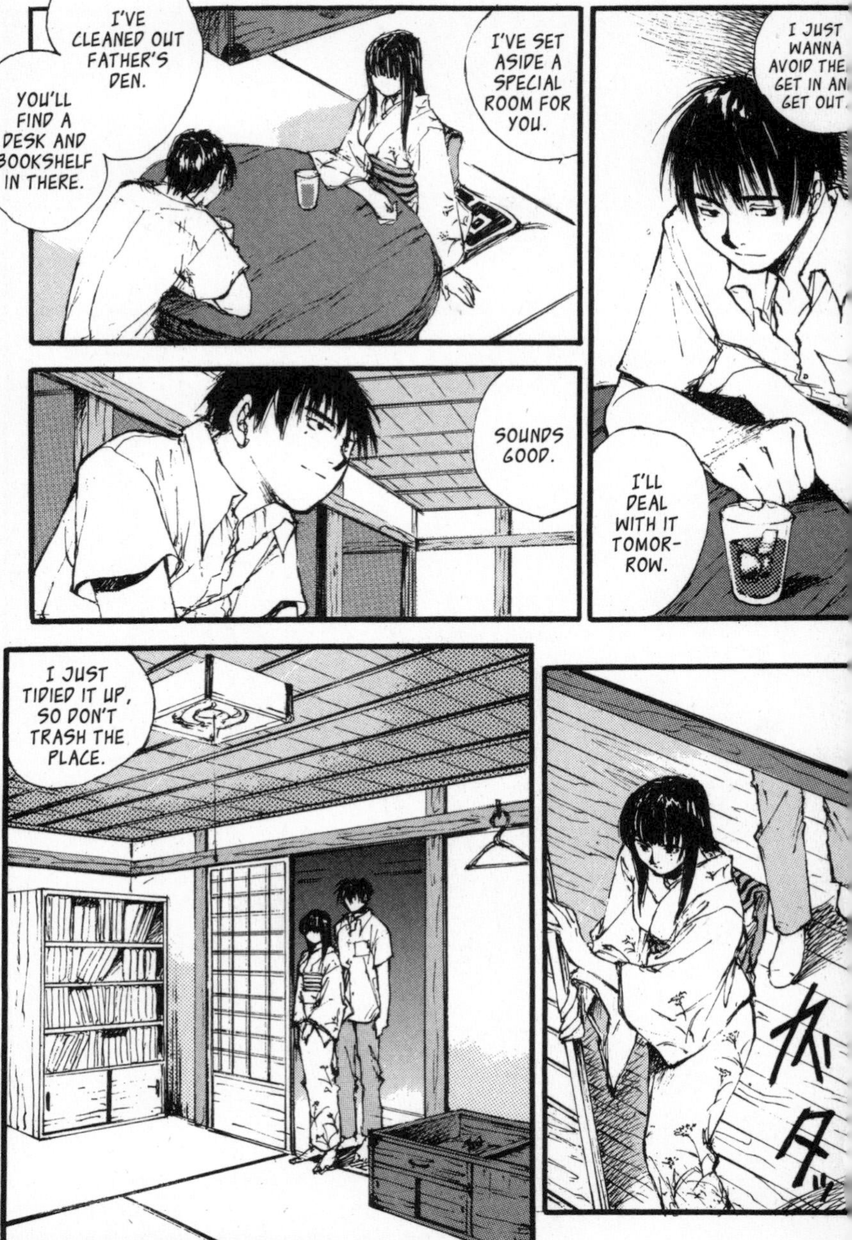
I JUST WANNA AVOID THE GET IN AN GET OUT.
I'LL DEAL WITH IT TOMOR-ROW.
I'VE SET ASIDE A SPECIAL ROOM FOR YOU.
I'VE CLEANED OUT FATHER'S DEN.
YOU'LL FIND A DESK AND BOOKSHELF IN THERE.
SOUNDS GOOD.
カタッ
I JUST TIDIED IT UP, SO DON'T TRASH THE PLACE.

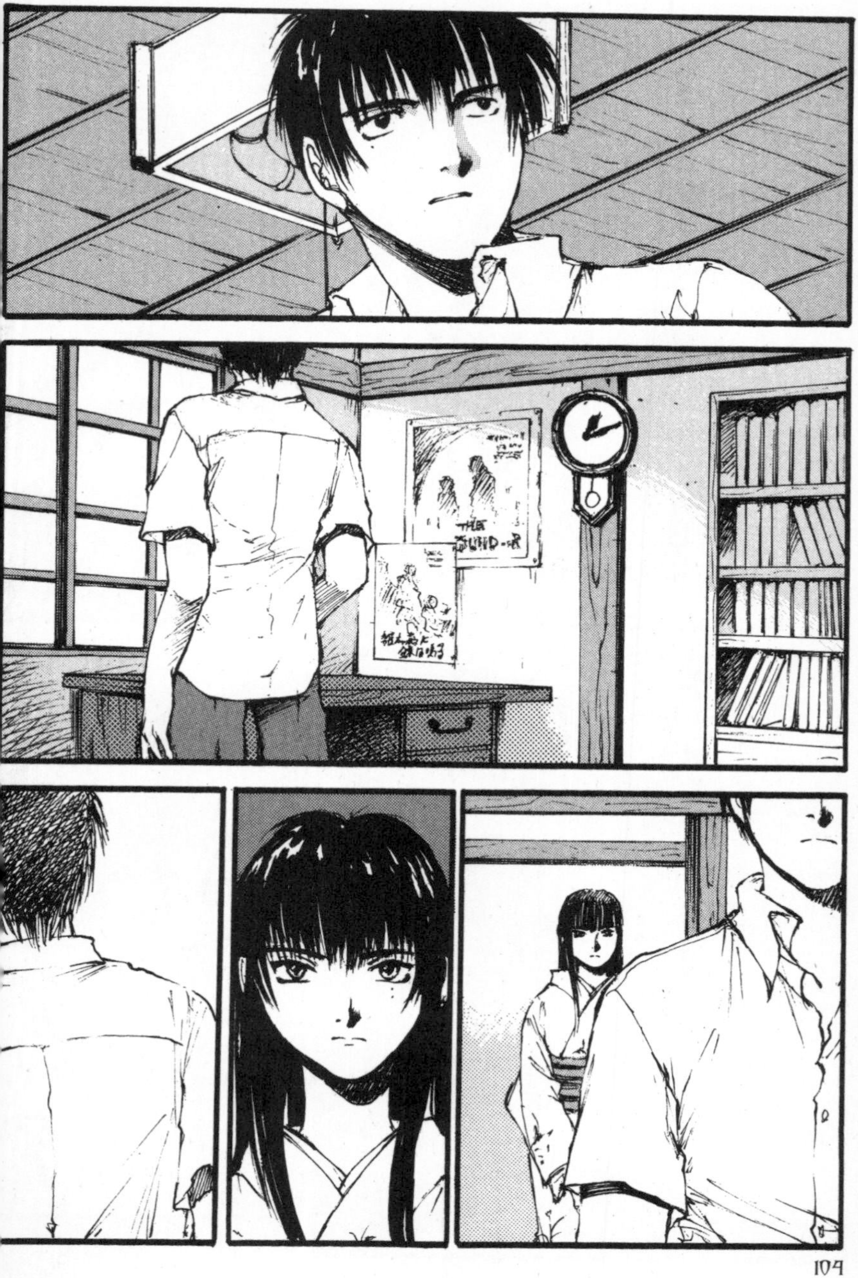

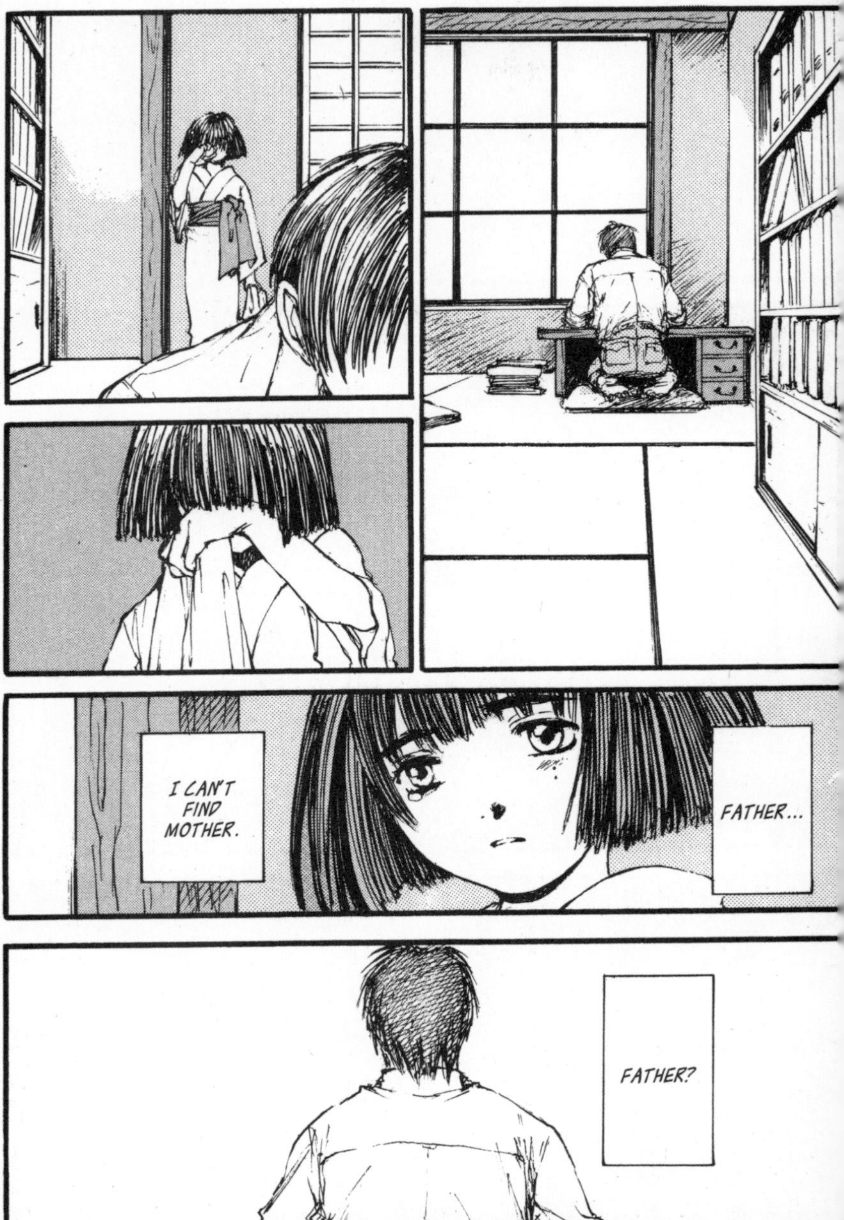
FATHER...
I CAN'T FIND MOTHER.
FATHER?

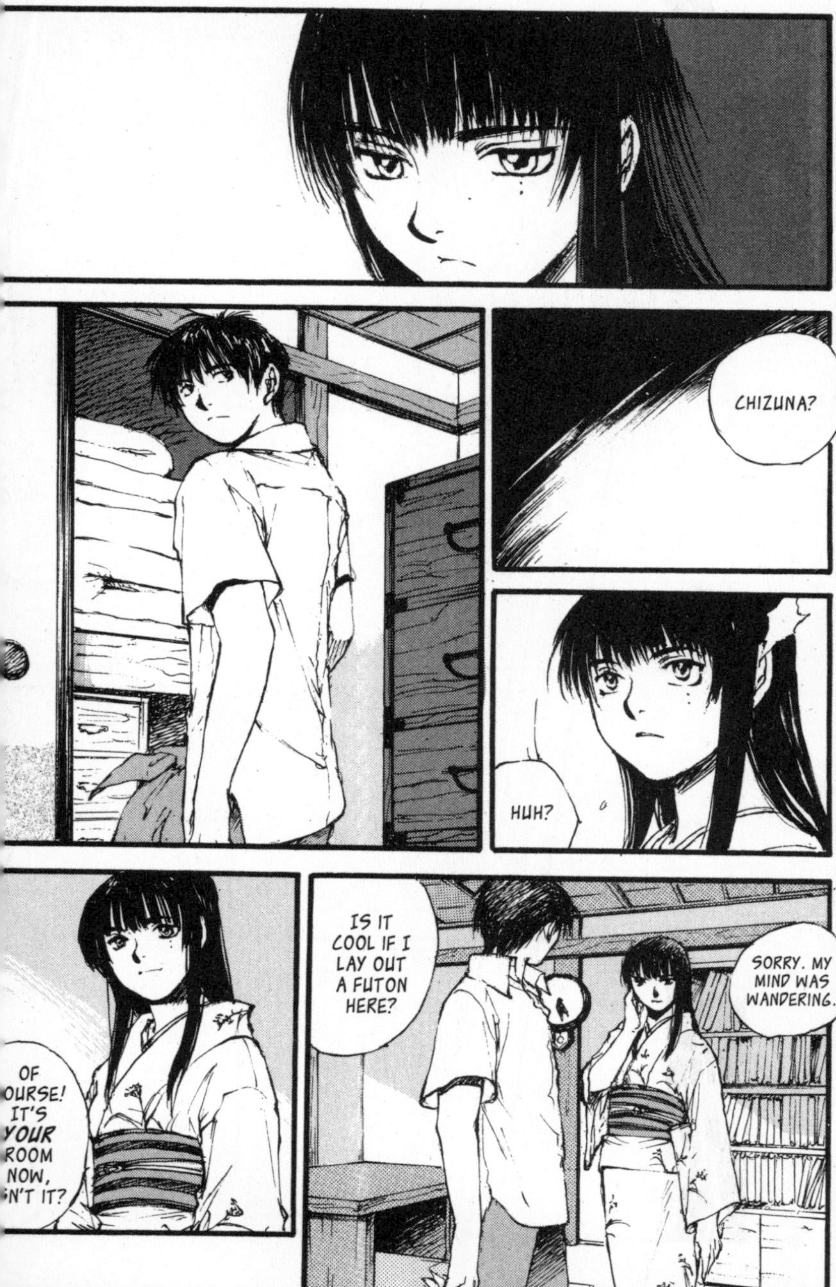
CHIZUNA?
HUH?
SORRY. MY MIND WAS WANDERING.
IS IT COOL IF I LAY OUT A FUTON HERE?
OF OURSE! IT'S YOUR ROOM NOW, N'T IT?

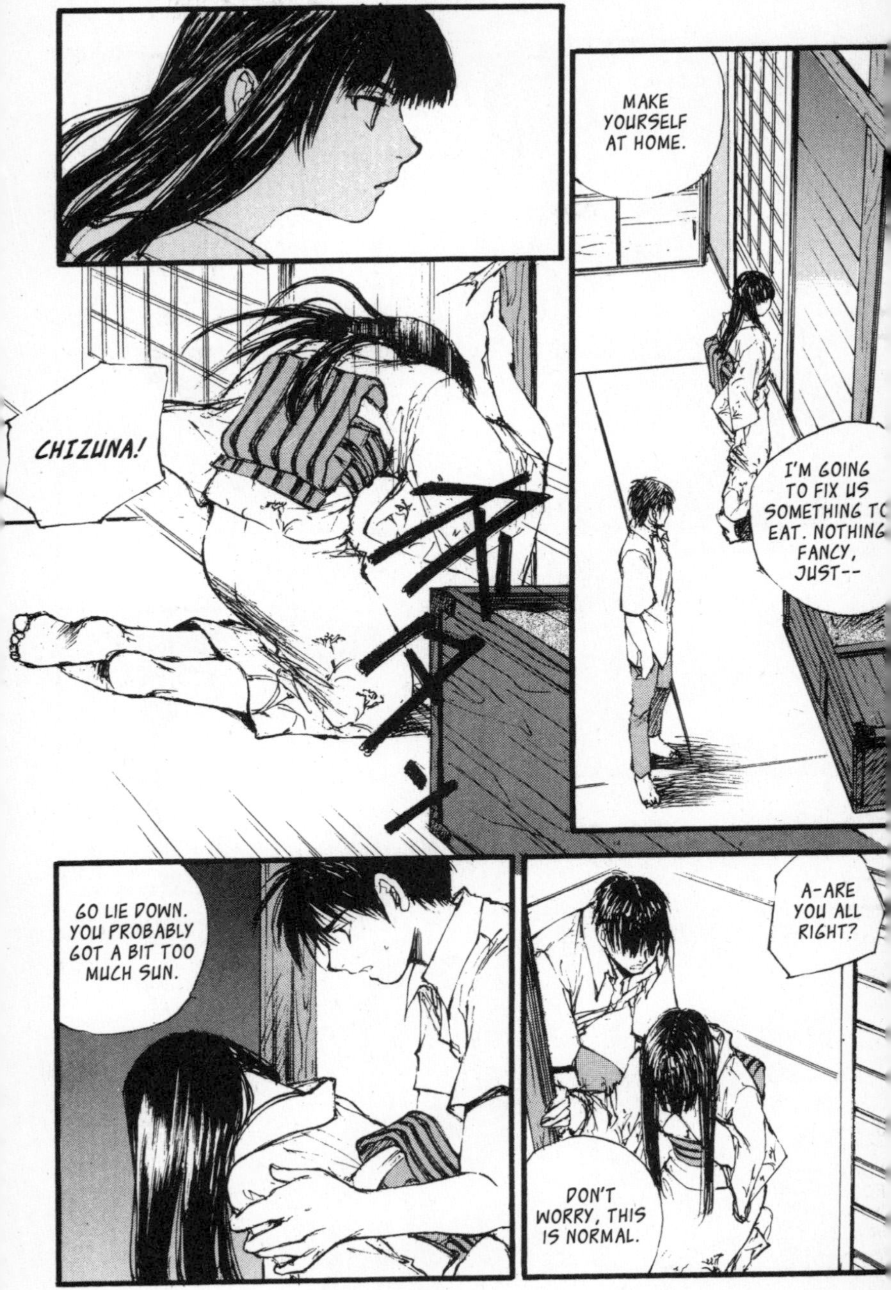
MAKE YOURSELF AT HOME.
I'M GOING TO FIX US SOMETHING TO EAT. NOTHING FANCY, JUST--
CHIZUNA!
A-ARE YOU ALL RIGHT?
DON'T WORRY, THIS IS NORMAL.
GO LIE DOWN. YOU PROBABLY GOT A BIT TOO MUCH SUN.

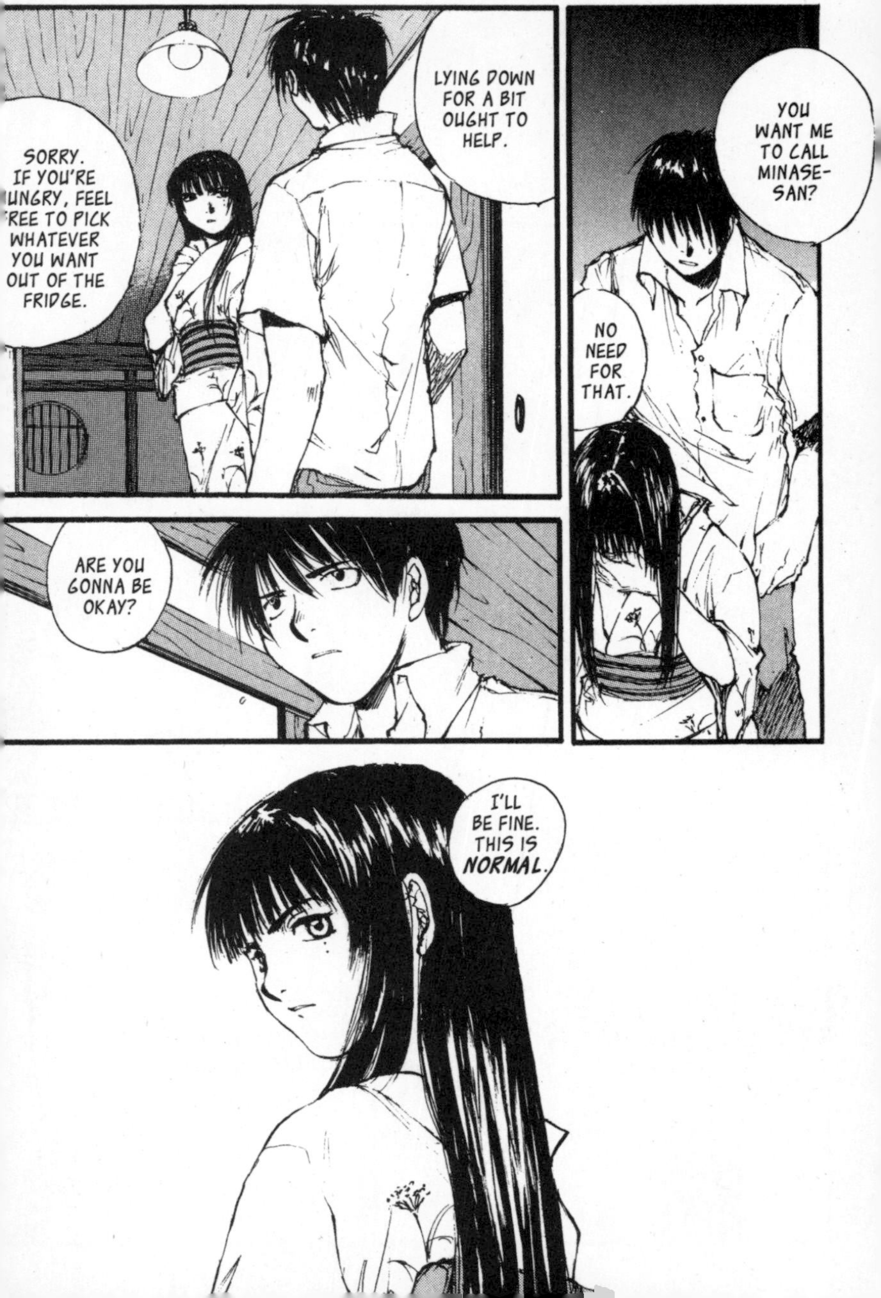
YOU WANT ME TO CALL MINASE-SAN?
NO NEED FOR THAT.
LYING DOWN FOR A BIT OUGHT TO HELP.
SORRY. IF YOU'RE UNGRY, FEEL REE TO PICK WHATEVER YOU WANT OUT OF THE FRIDGE.
ARE YOU GONNA BE OKAY?
I'LL BE FINE. THIS IS **NORMAL**.

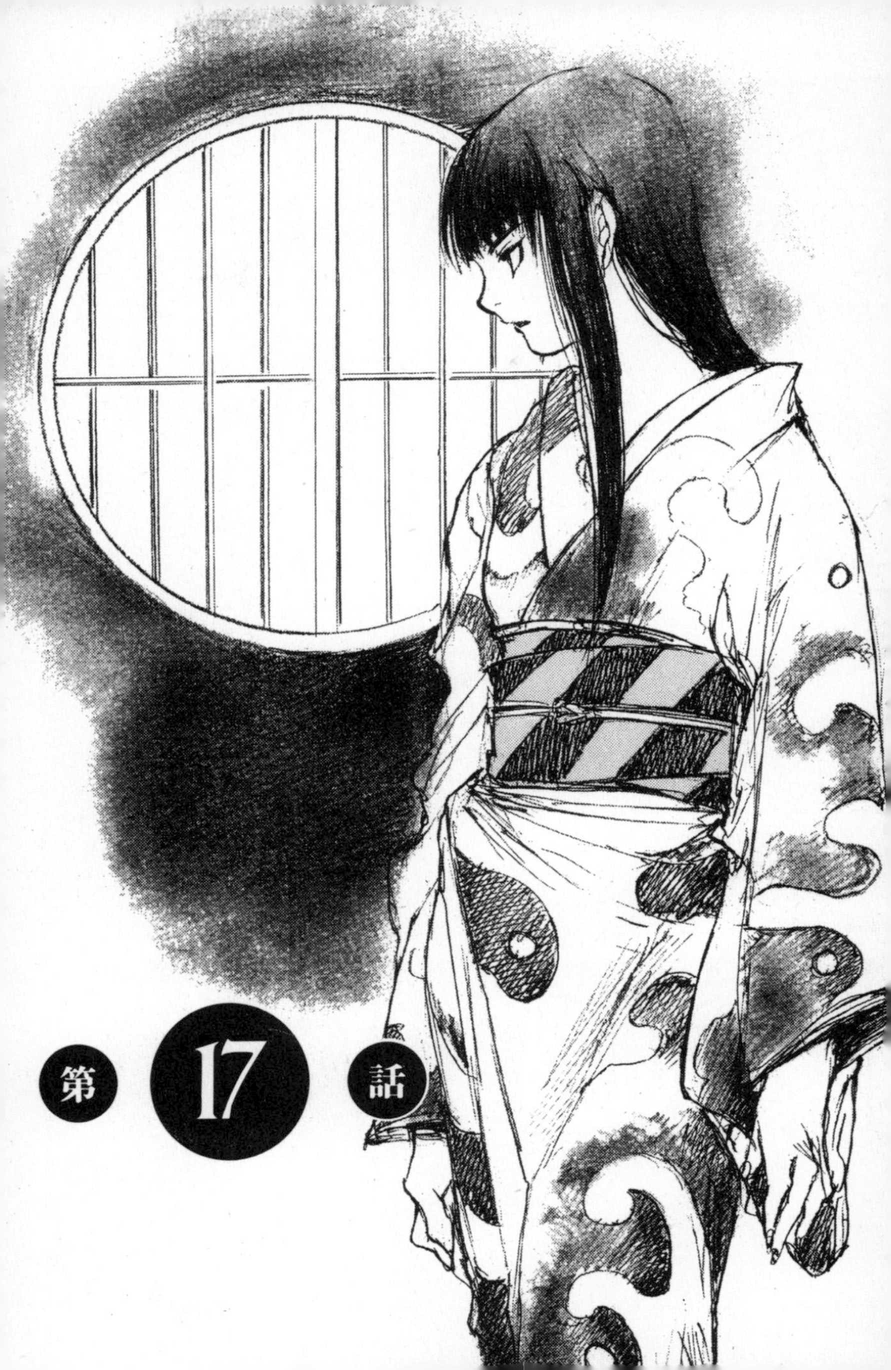
第 17 話

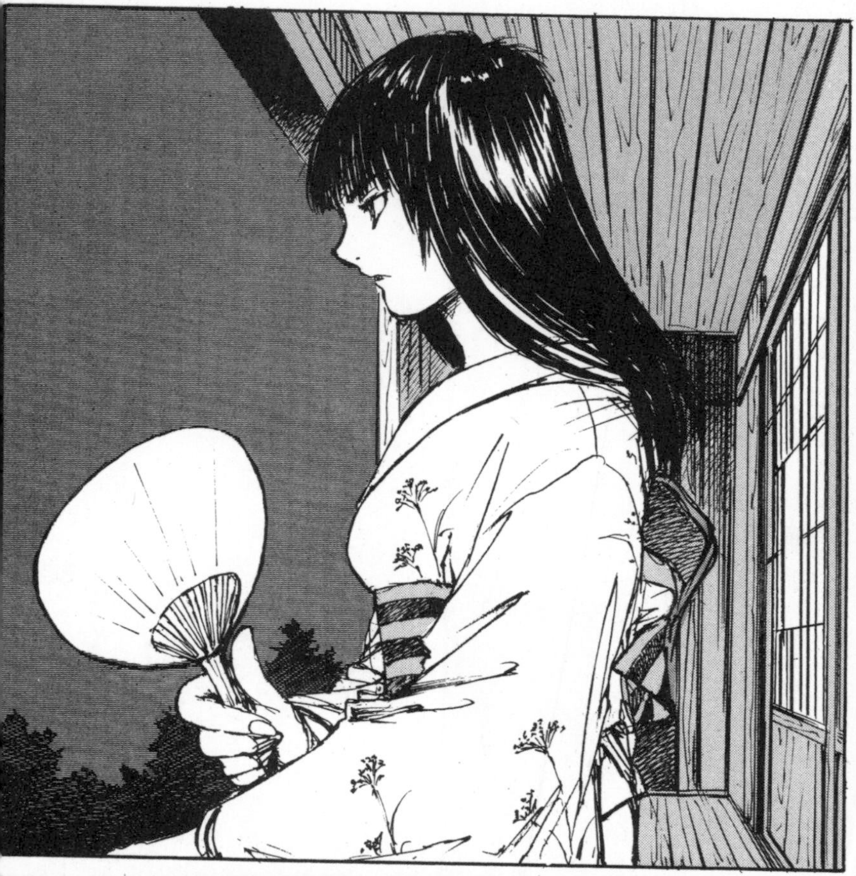

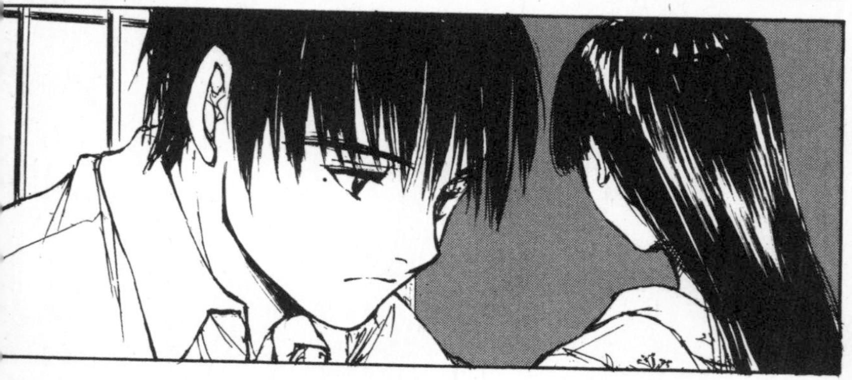

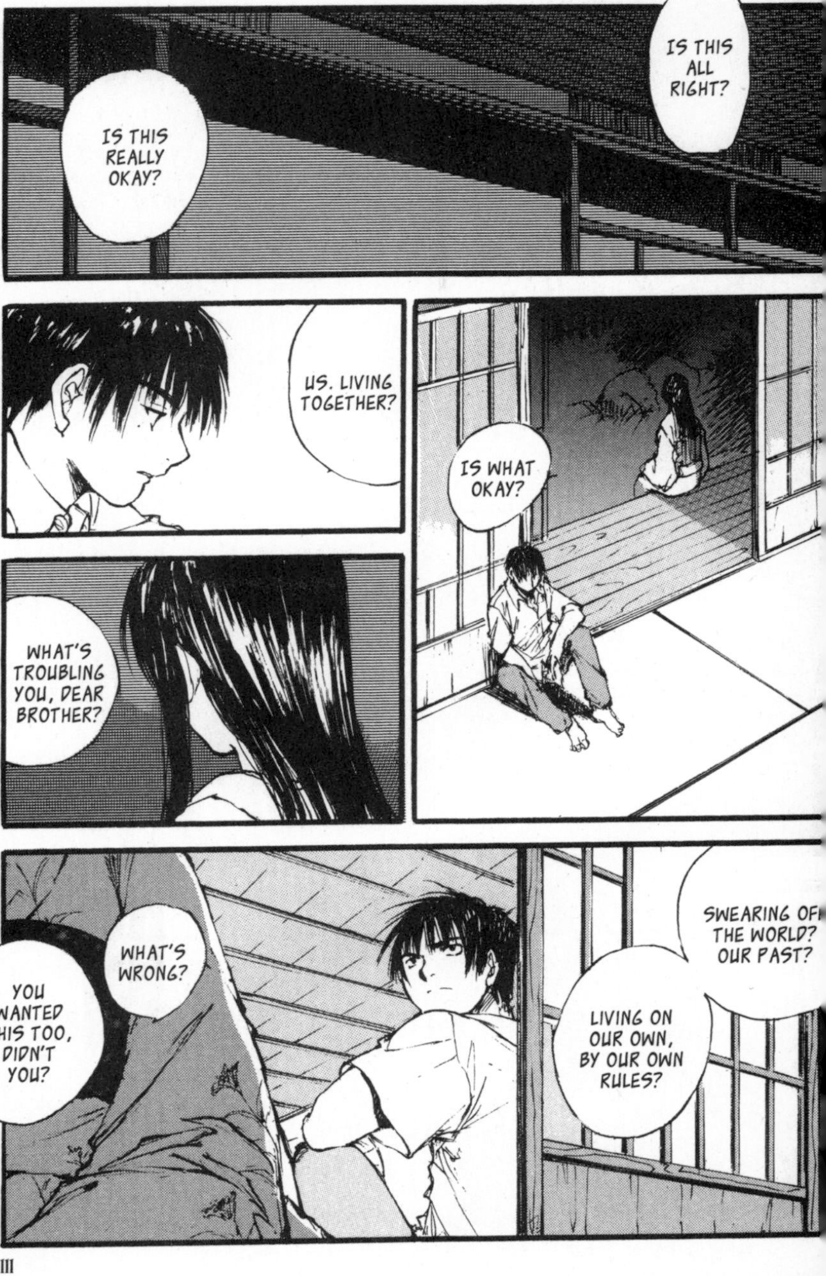
IS THIS ALL RIGHT?
IS THIS REALLY OKAY?
IS WHAT OKAY?
US. LIVING TOGETHER?
WHAT'S TROUBLING YOU, DEAR BROTHER?
SWEARING OF THE WORLD? OUR PAST?
LIVING ON OUR OWN, BY OUR OWN RULES?
WHAT'S WRONG?
YOU WANTED THIS TOO, DIDN'T YOU?

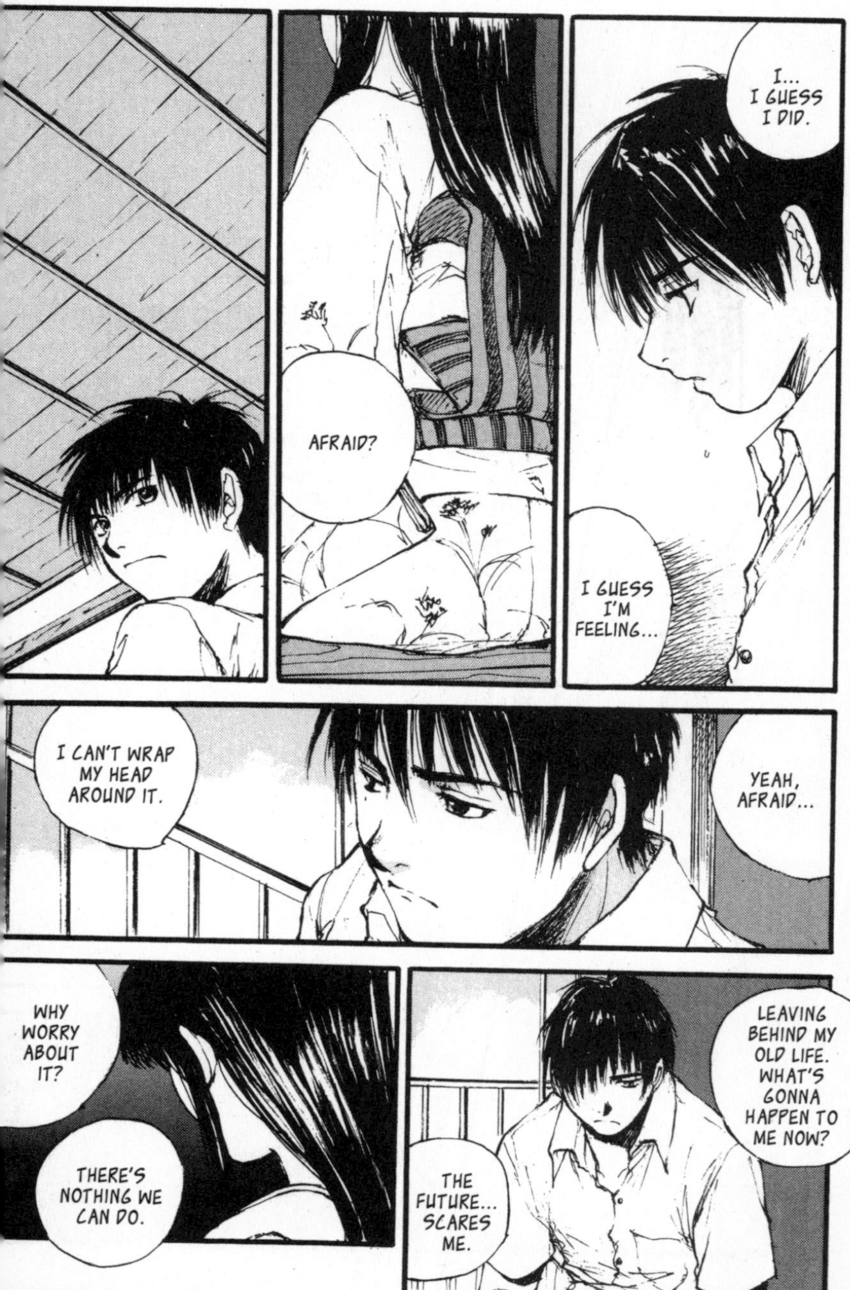
I... I GUESS I DID.
I GUESS I'M FEELING...
AFRAID?
YEAH, AFRAID...
I CAN'T WRAP MY HEAD AROUND IT.
LEAVING BEHIND MY OLD LIFE. WHAT'S GONNA HAPPEN TO ME NOW?
THE FUTURE... SCARES ME.
WHY WORRY ABOUT IT?
THERE'S NOTHING WE CAN DO.

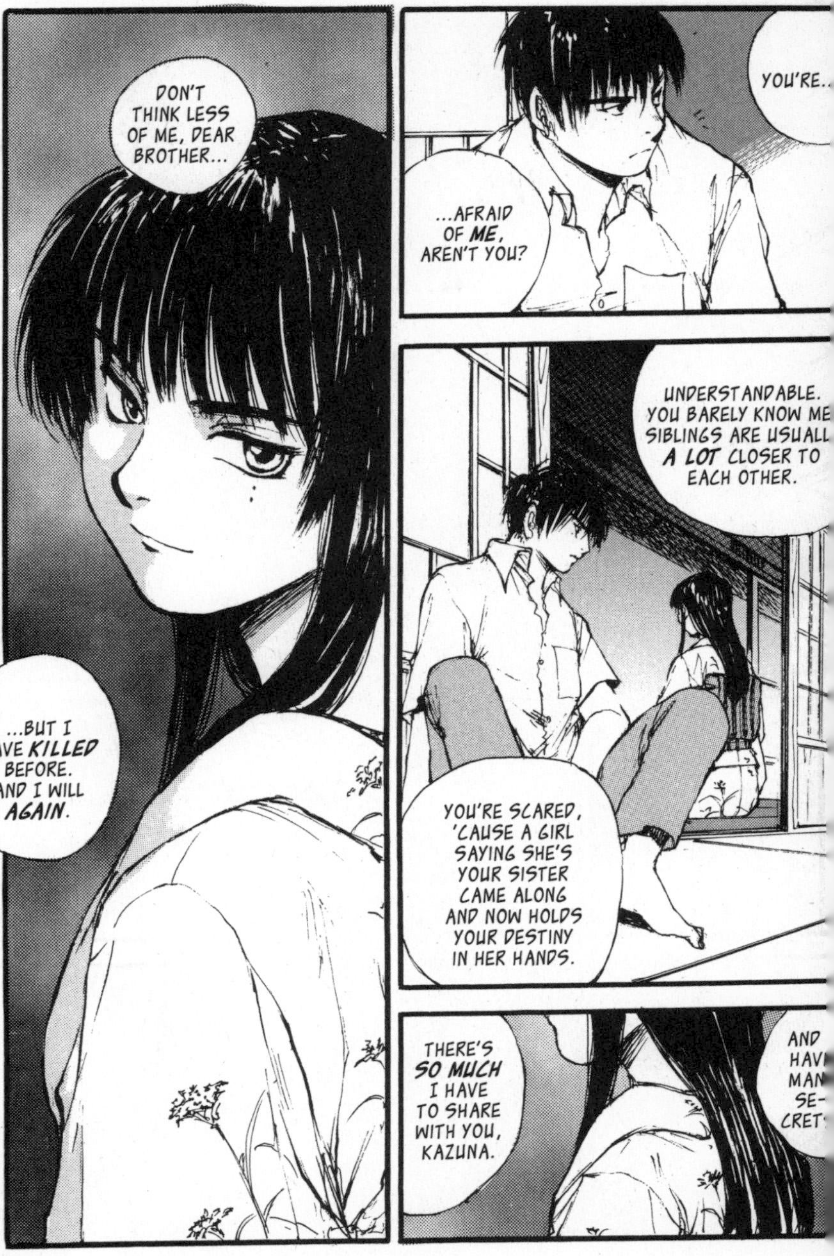
YOU'RE...
...AFRAID OF *ME*, AREN'T YOU?
UNDERSTANDABLE. YOU BARELY KNOW ME SIBLINGS ARE USUALL *A LOT* CLOSER TO EACH OTHER.
YOU'RE SCARED, 'CAUSE A GIRL SAYING SHE'S YOUR SISTER CAME ALONG AND NOW HOLDS YOUR DESTINY IN HER HANDS.
AND HAV MAN SE- CRET
THERE'S *SO MUCH* I HAVE TO SHARE WITH YOU, KAZUNA.
DON'T THINK LESS OF ME, DEAR BROTHER...
...BUT I HAVE *KILLED* BEFORE. AND I WILL *AGAIN*.

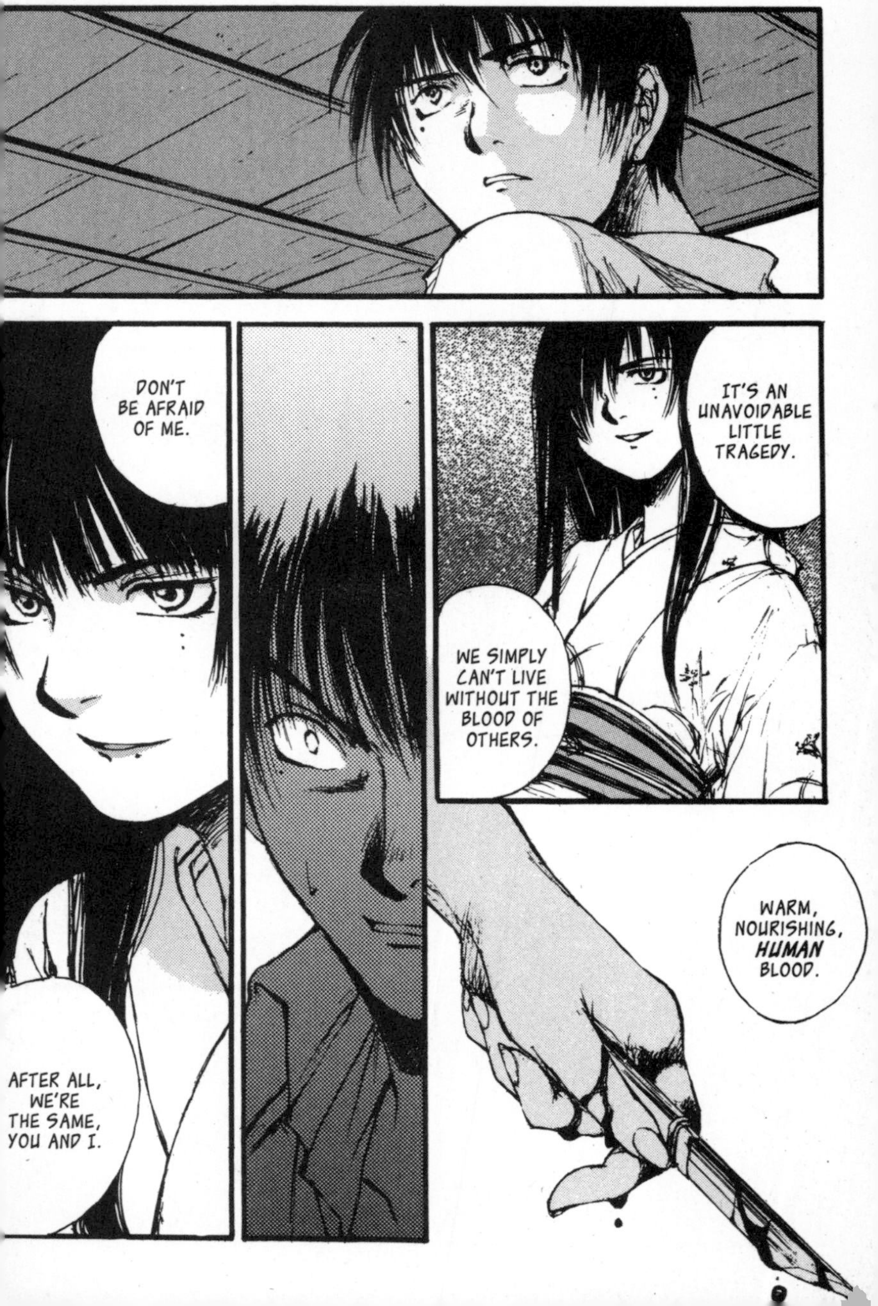
IT'S AN UNAVOIDABLE LITTLE TRAGEDY.
WE SIMPLY CAN'T LIVE WITHOUT THE BLOOD OF OTHERS.
WARM, NOURISHING, **HUMAN** BLOOD.
DON'T BE AFRAID OF ME.
AFTER ALL, WE'RE THE SAME, YOU AND I.

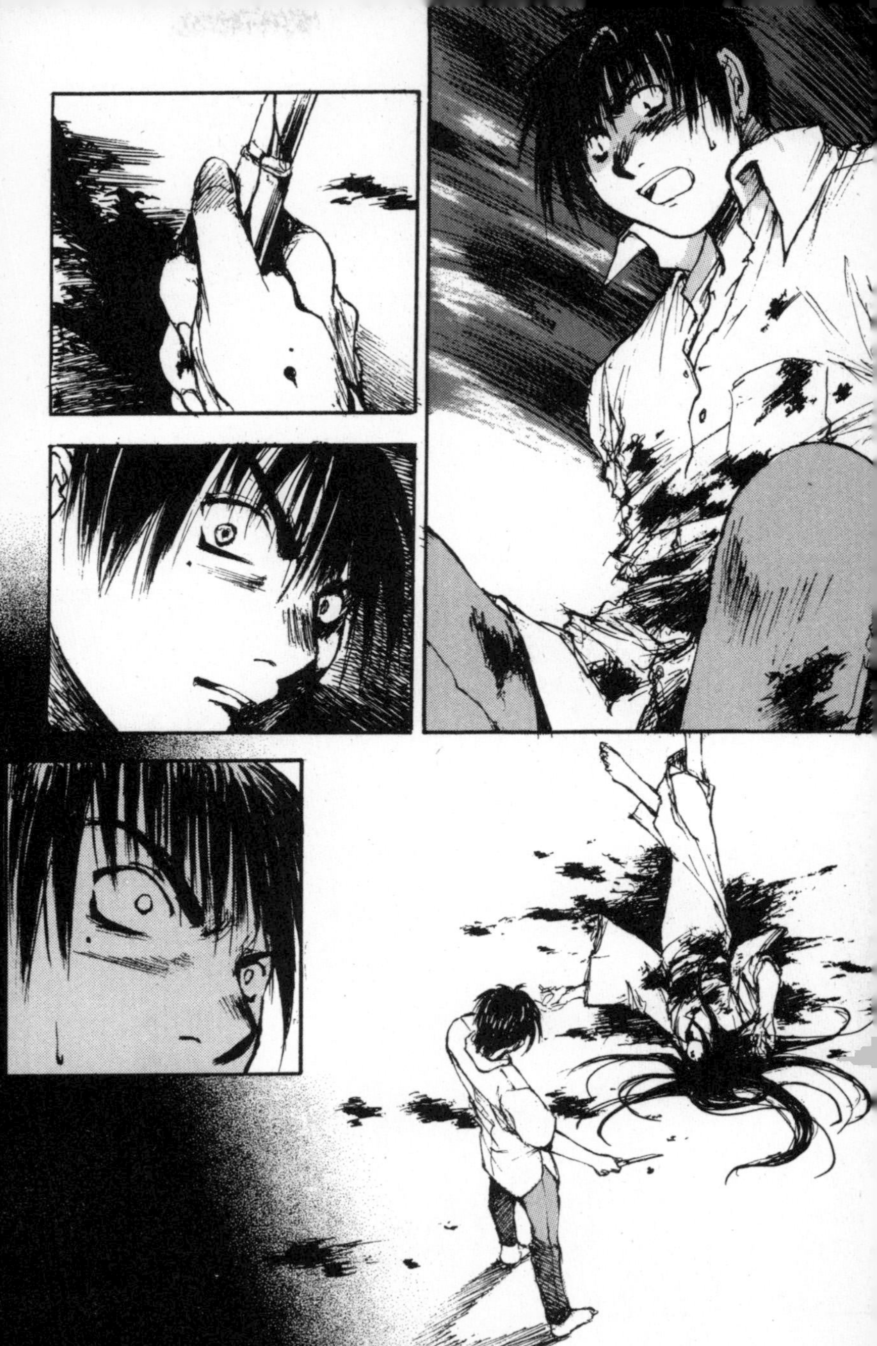

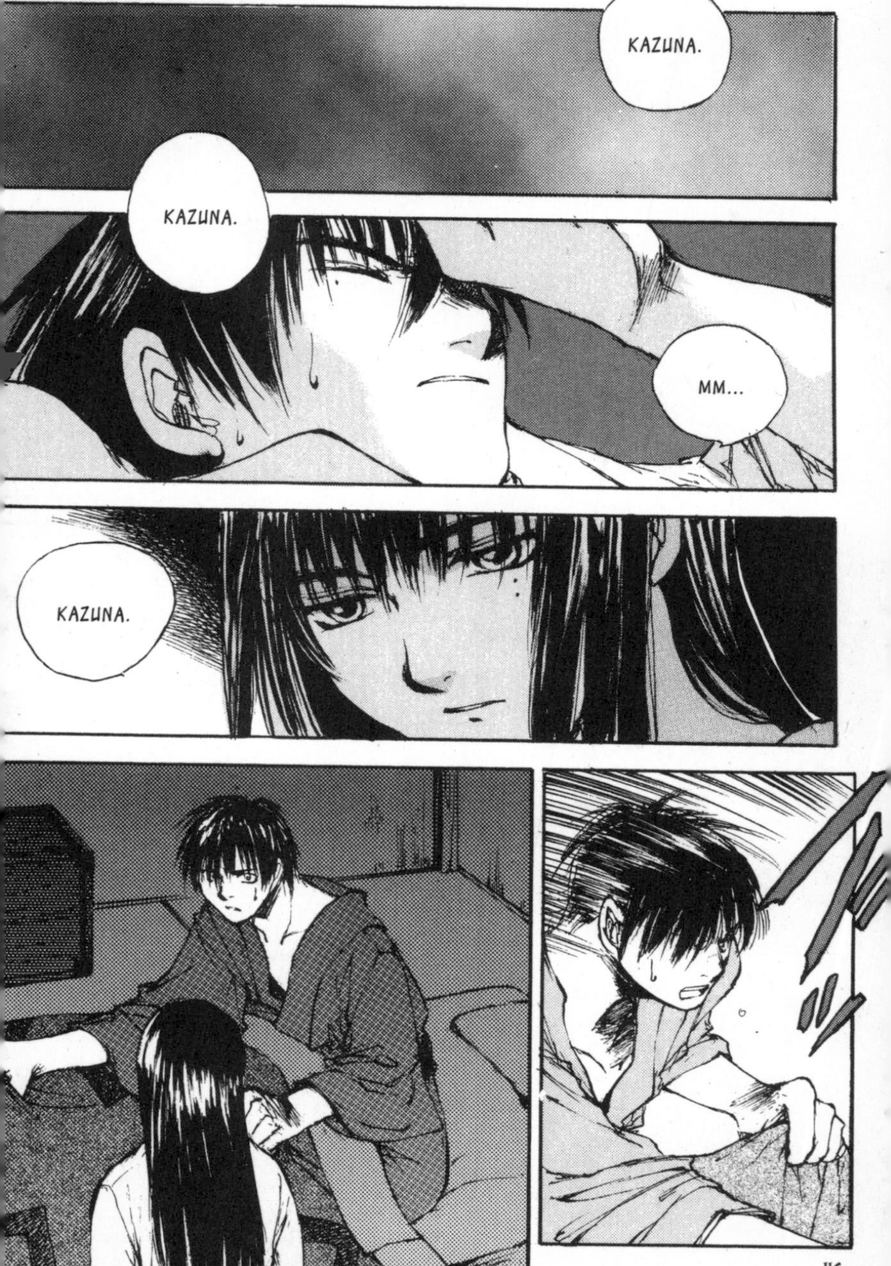
KAZUNA.
KAZUNA.
MM...
KAZUNA.

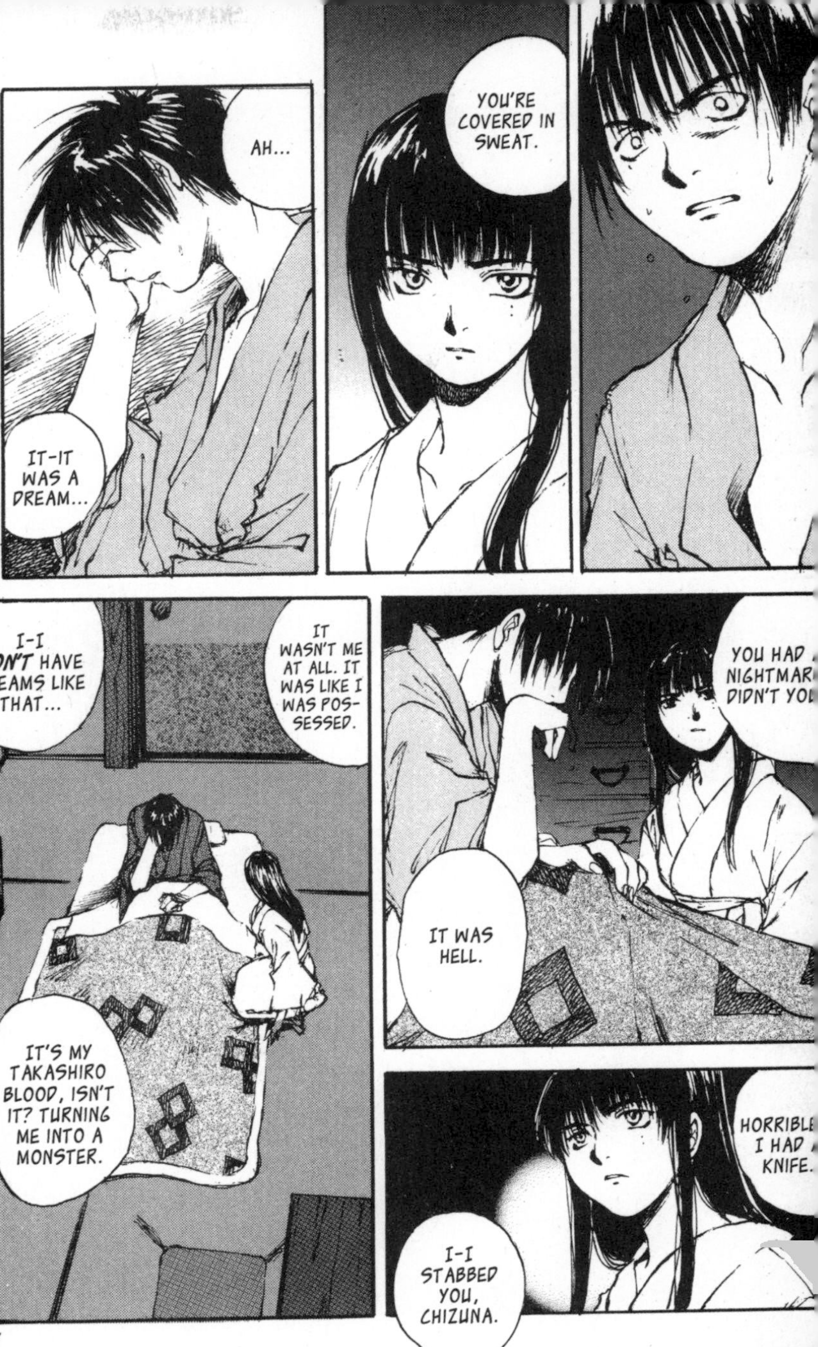
YOU'RE COVERED IN SWEAT.
AH...
IT-IT WAS A DREAM...
YOU HAD
NIGHTMAR
DIDN'T YO
IT WAS HELL.
HORRIBLE
I HAD
KNIFE.
I-I STABBED YOU, CHIZUNA.
IT WASN'T ME AT ALL. IT WAS LIKE I WAS POS-SESSED.
I-I **DON'T** HAVE DREAMS LIKE THAT...
IT'S MY TAKASHIRO BLOOD, ISN'T IT? TURNING ME INTO A MONSTER.

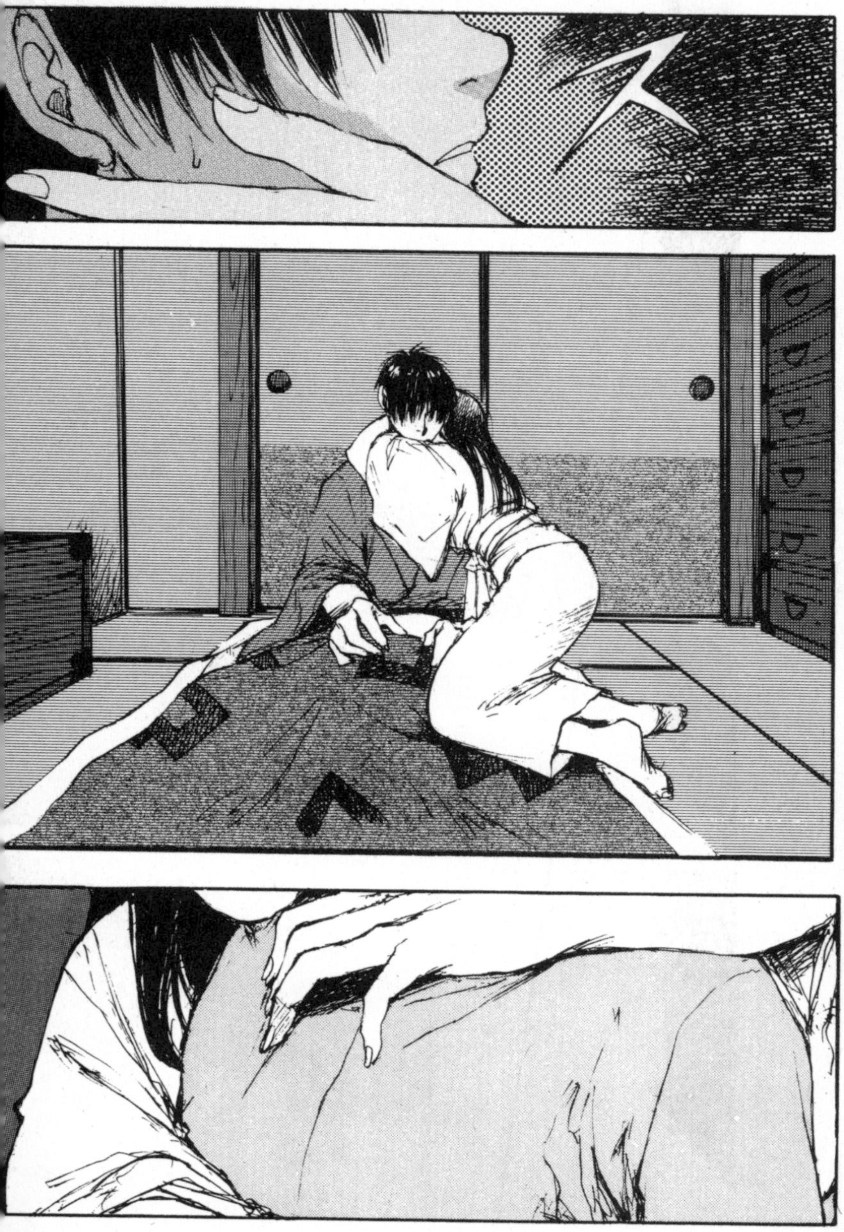
ス

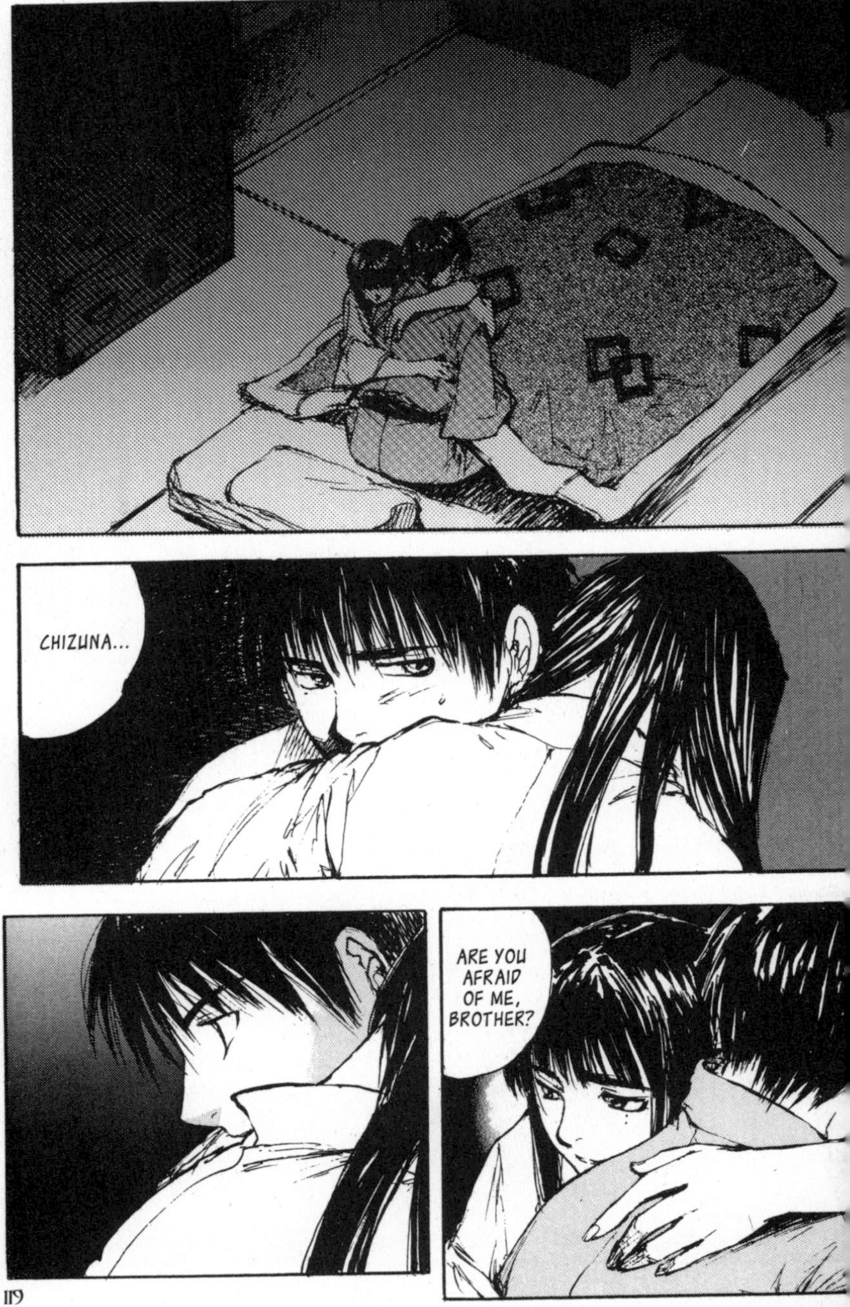
CHIZUNA...
ARE YOU AFRAID OF ME, BROTHER?

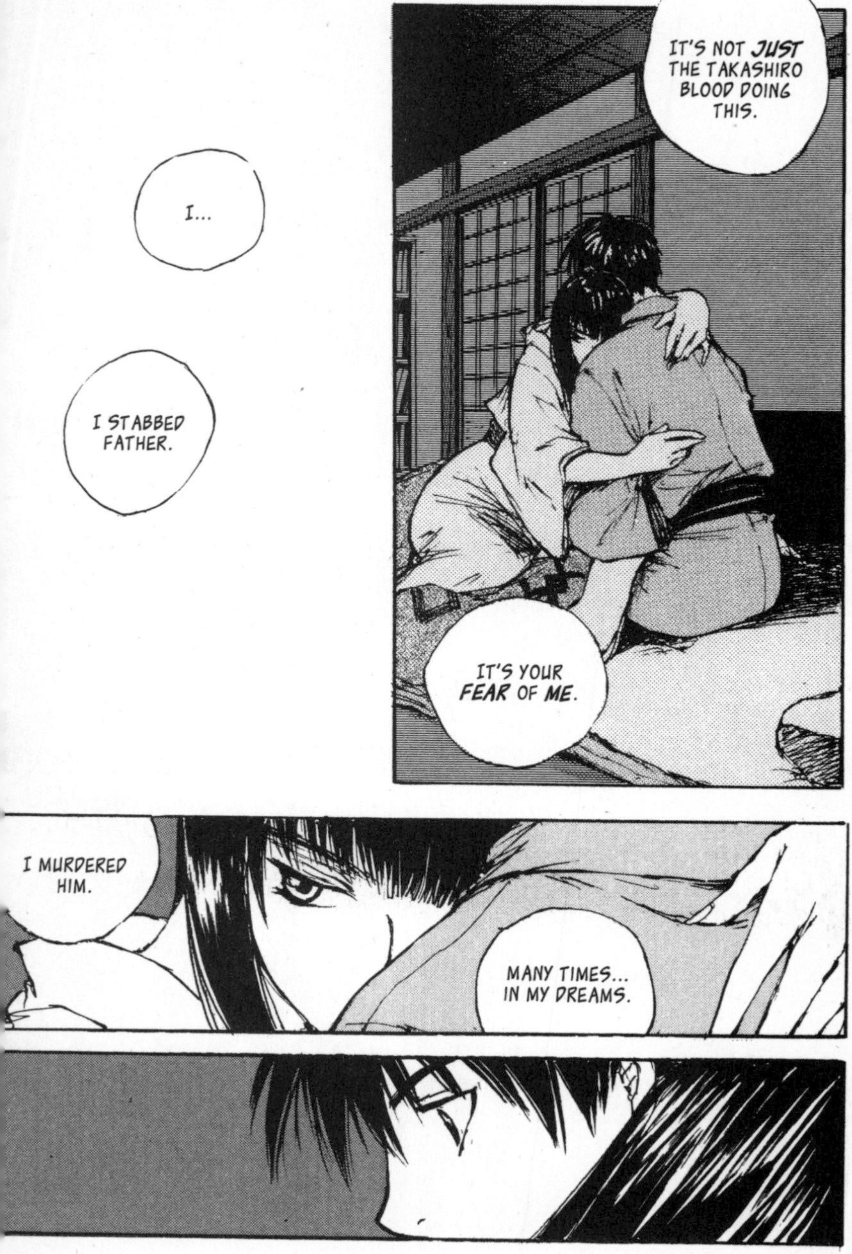
IT'S NOT JUST THE TAKASHIRO BLOOD DOING THIS.
IT'S YOUR FEAR OF ME.
I...
I STABBED FATHER.
I MURDERED HIM.
MANY TIMES... IN MY DREAMS.

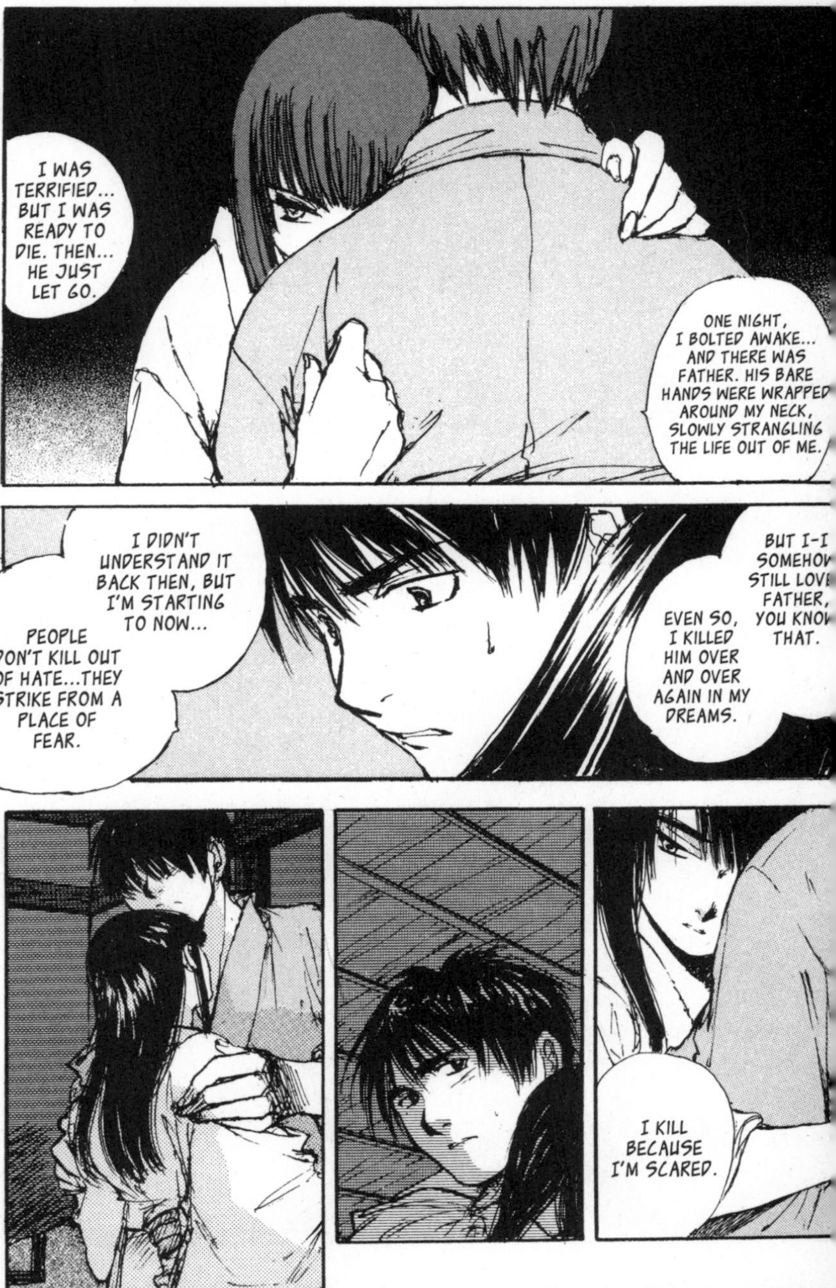
ONE NIGHT, I BOLTED AWAKE... AND THERE WAS FATHER. HIS BARE HANDS WERE WRAPPED AROUND MY NECK, SLOWLY STRANGLING THE LIFE OUT OF ME.
I WAS TERRIFIED... BUT I WAS READY TO DIE. THEN... HE JUST LET GO.
BUT I-I SOMEHOW STILL LOVE FATHER, YOU KNOW THAT.
EVEN SO, I KILLED HIM OVER AND OVER AGAIN IN MY DREAMS.
I DIDN'T UNDERSTAND IT BACK THEN, BUT I'M STARTING TO NOW...
PEOPLE DON'T KILL OUT OF HATE...THEY STRIKE FROM A PLACE OF FEAR.
I KILL BECAUSE I'M SCARED.

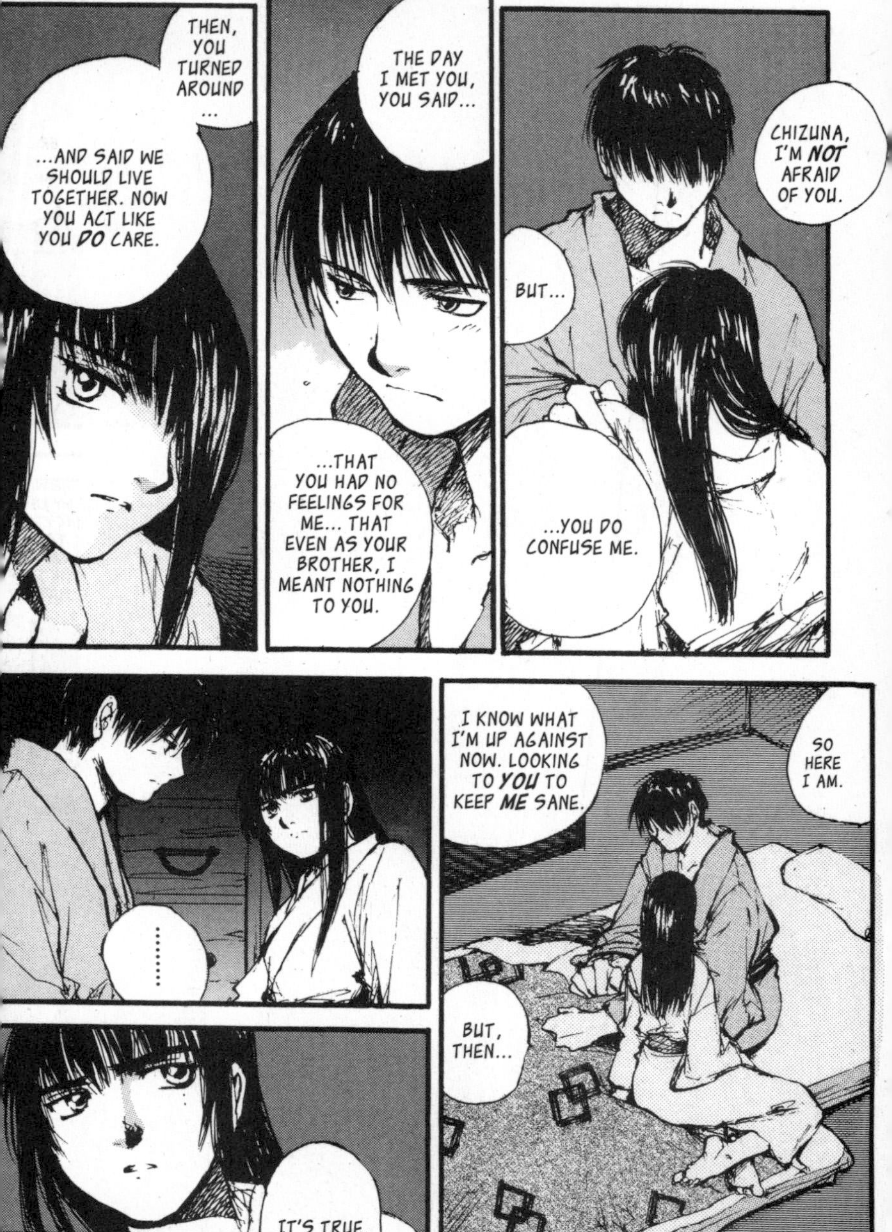
CHIZUNA, I'M **NOT** AFRAID OF YOU.
BUT...
...YOU DO CONFUSE ME.
THE DAY I MET YOU, YOU SAID...
...THAT YOU HAD NO FEELINGS FOR ME... THAT EVEN AS YOUR BROTHER, I MEANT NOTHING TO YOU.
THEN, YOU TURNED AROUND ...
...AND SAID WE SHOULD LIVE TOGETHER. NOW YOU ACT LIKE YOU **DO** CARE.
SO HERE I AM.
I KNOW WHAT I'M UP AGAINST NOW. LOOKING TO **YOU** TO KEEP **ME** SANE.
BUT, THEN...
....
IT'S TRUE.

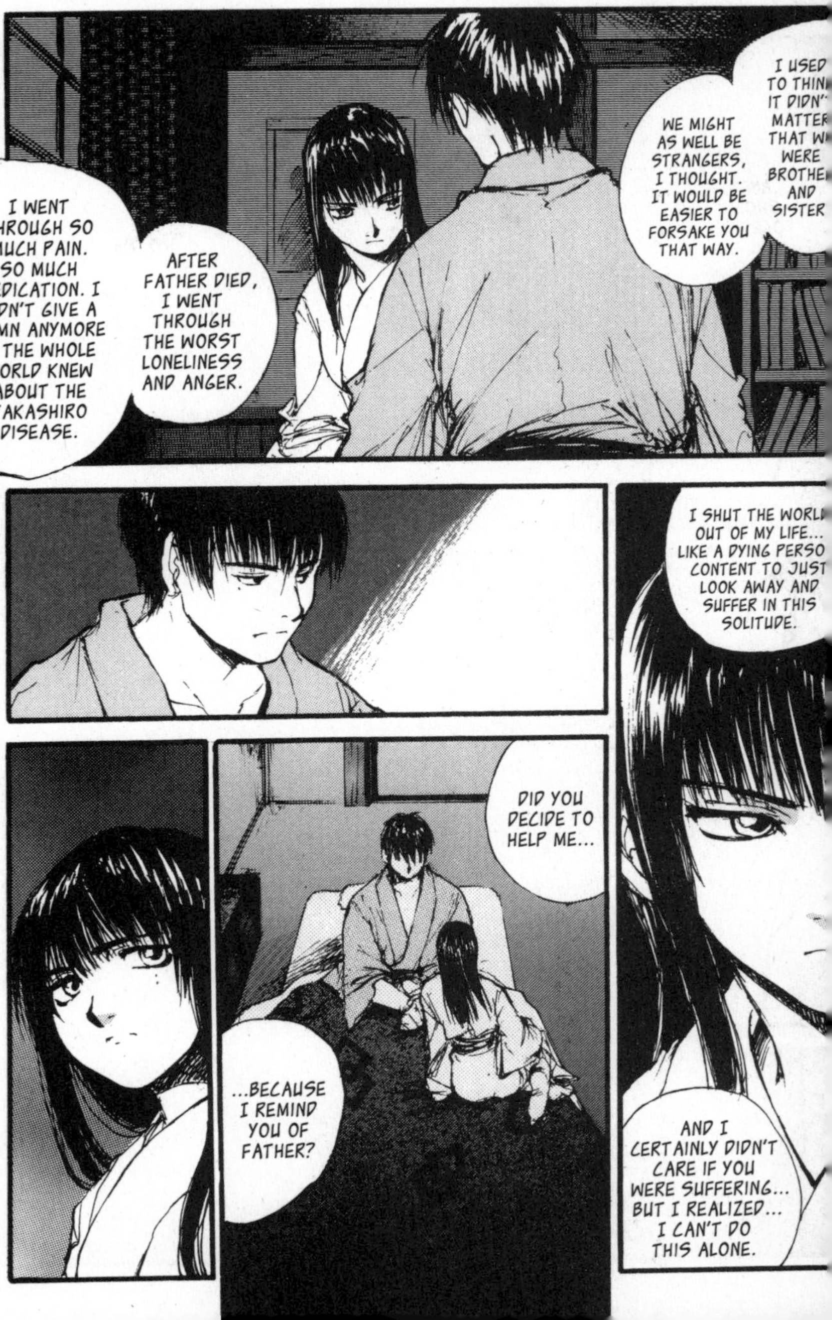

I USED TO THIN IT DIDN' MATTER THAT W WERE BROTHE AND SISTER
WE MIGHT AS WELL BE STRANGERS, I THOUGHT. IT WOULD BE EASIER TO FORSAKE YOU THAT WAY.
AFTER FATHER DIED, I WENT THROUGH THE WORST LONELINESS AND ANGER.
I WENT THROUGH SO MUCH PAIN. SO MUCH MEDICATION. I DIDN'T GIVE A DAMN ANYMORE IF THE WHOLE WORLD KNEW ABOUT THE TAKASHIRO DISEASE.
I SHUT THE WORL OUT OF MY LIFE... LIKE A DYING PERSO CONTENT TO JUST LOOK AWAY AND SUFFER IN THIS SOLITUDE.
AND I CERTAINLY DIDN'T CARE IF YOU WERE SUFFERING... BUT I REALIZED... I CAN'T DO THIS ALONE.
DID YOU DECIDE TO HELP ME...
...BECAUSE I REMIND YOU OF FATHER?

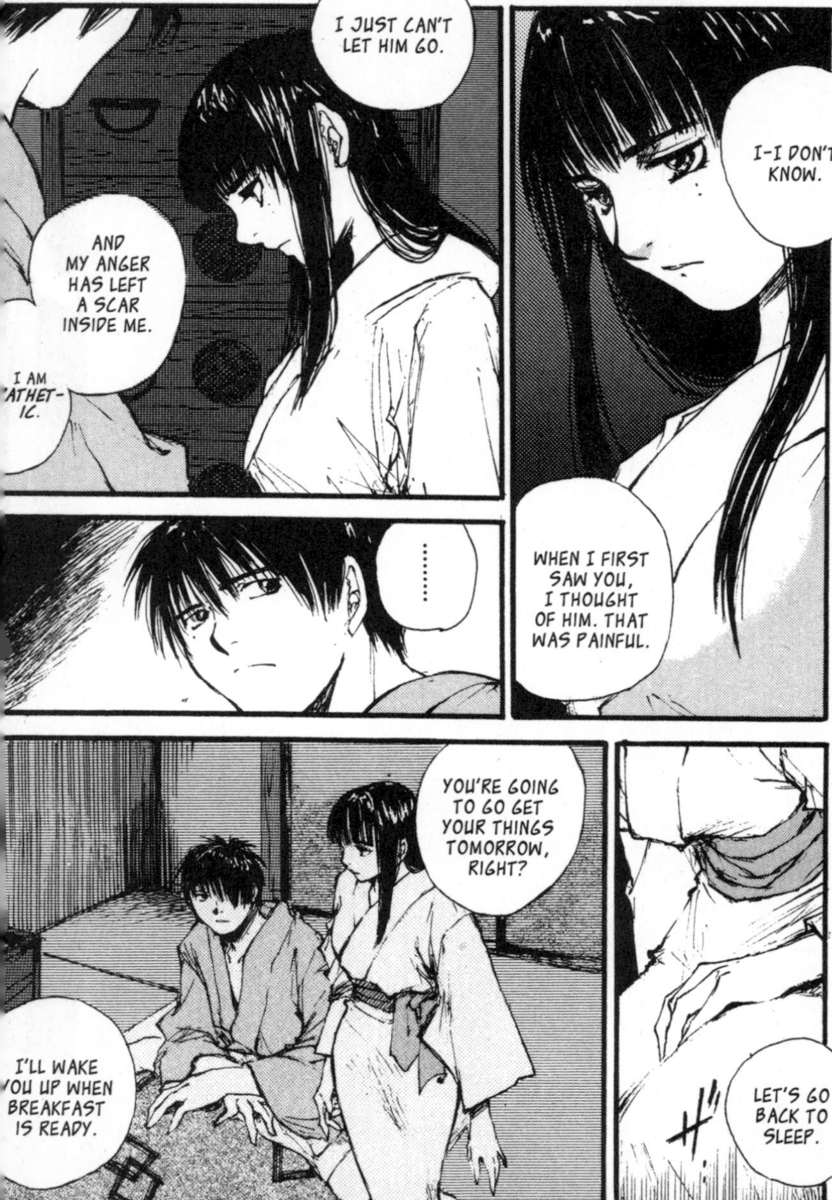
I-I DON'T KNOW.
WHEN I FIRST SAW YOU, I THOUGHT OF HIM. THAT WAS PAINFUL.
I JUST CAN'T LET HIM GO.
AND MY ANGER HAS LEFT A SCAR INSIDE ME.
I AM ATHET-IC.
......
LET'S GO BACK TO SLEEP.
YOU'RE GOING TO GO GET YOUR THINGS TOMORROW, RIGHT?
I'LL WAKE OU UP WHEN BREAKFAST IS READY.

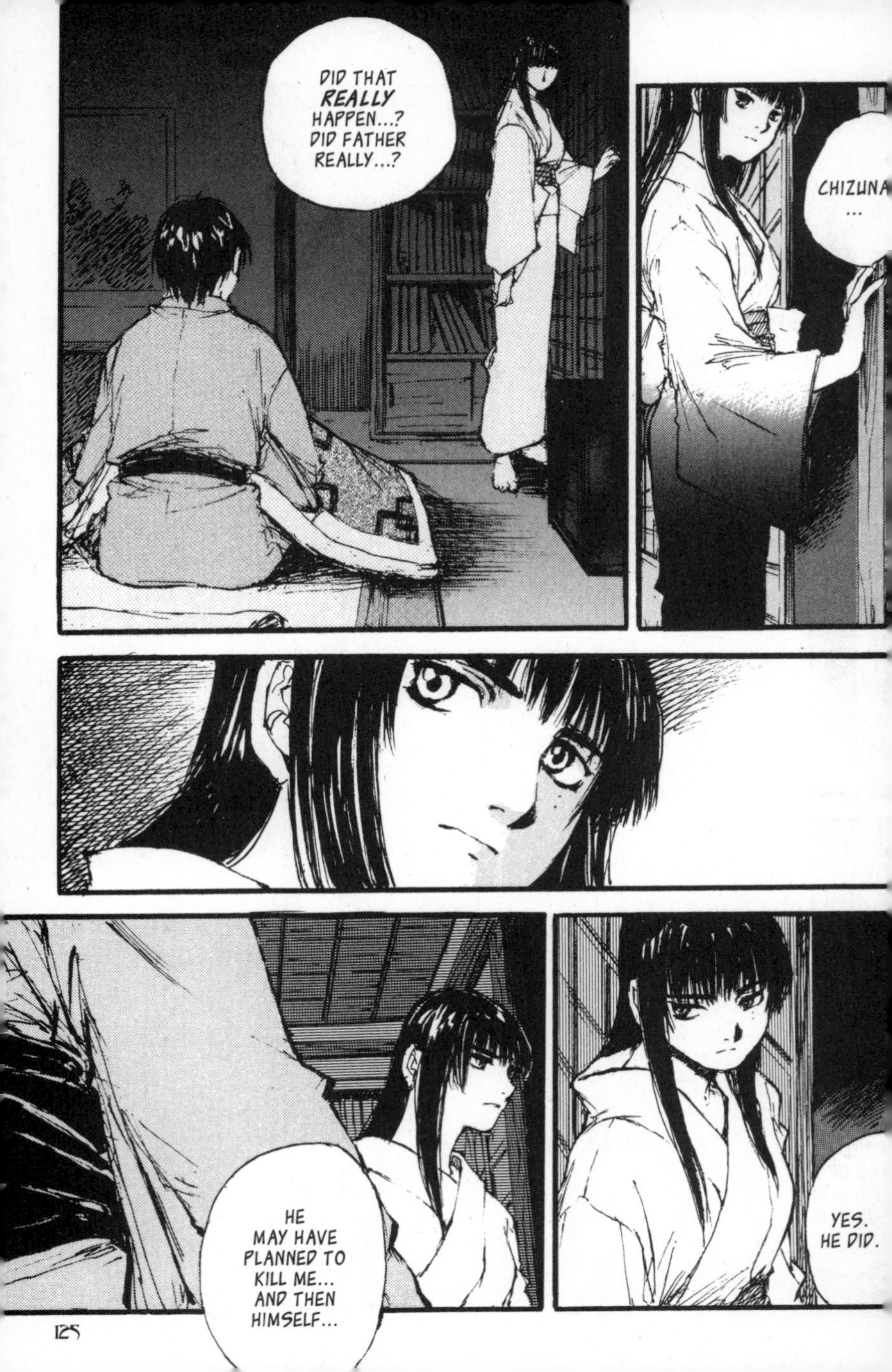
CHIZUNA...
DID THAT REALLY HAPPEN...? DID FATHER REALLY...?
YES. HE DID.
HE MAY HAVE PLANNED TO KILL ME... AND THEN HIMSELF...

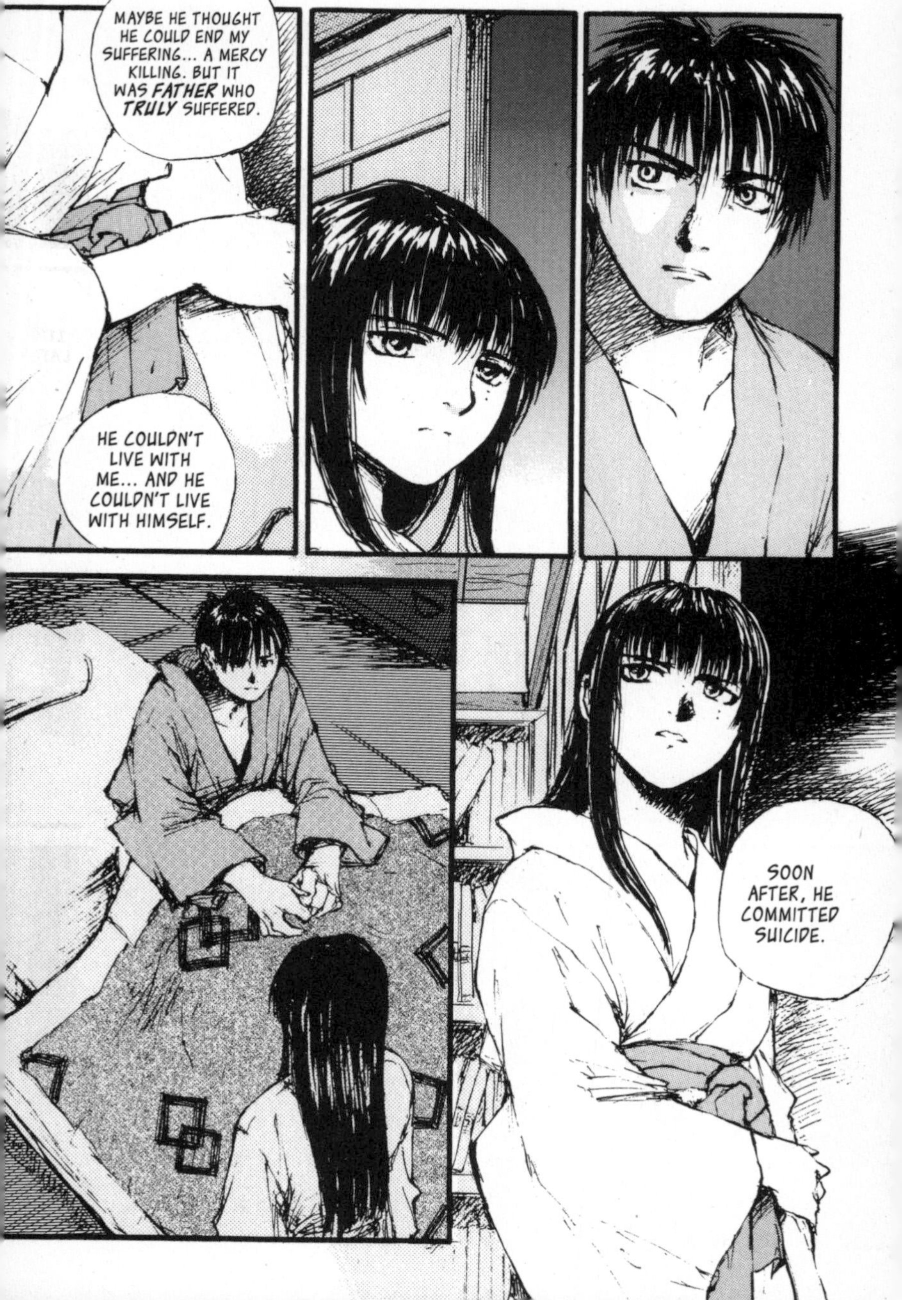
MAYBE HE THOUGHT HE COULD END MY SUFFERING... A MERCY KILLING. BUT IT WAS FATHER WHO TRULY SUFFERED.
HE COULDN'T LIVE WITH ME... AND HE COULDN'T LIVE WITH HIMSELF.
SOON AFTER, HE COMMITTED SUICIDE.

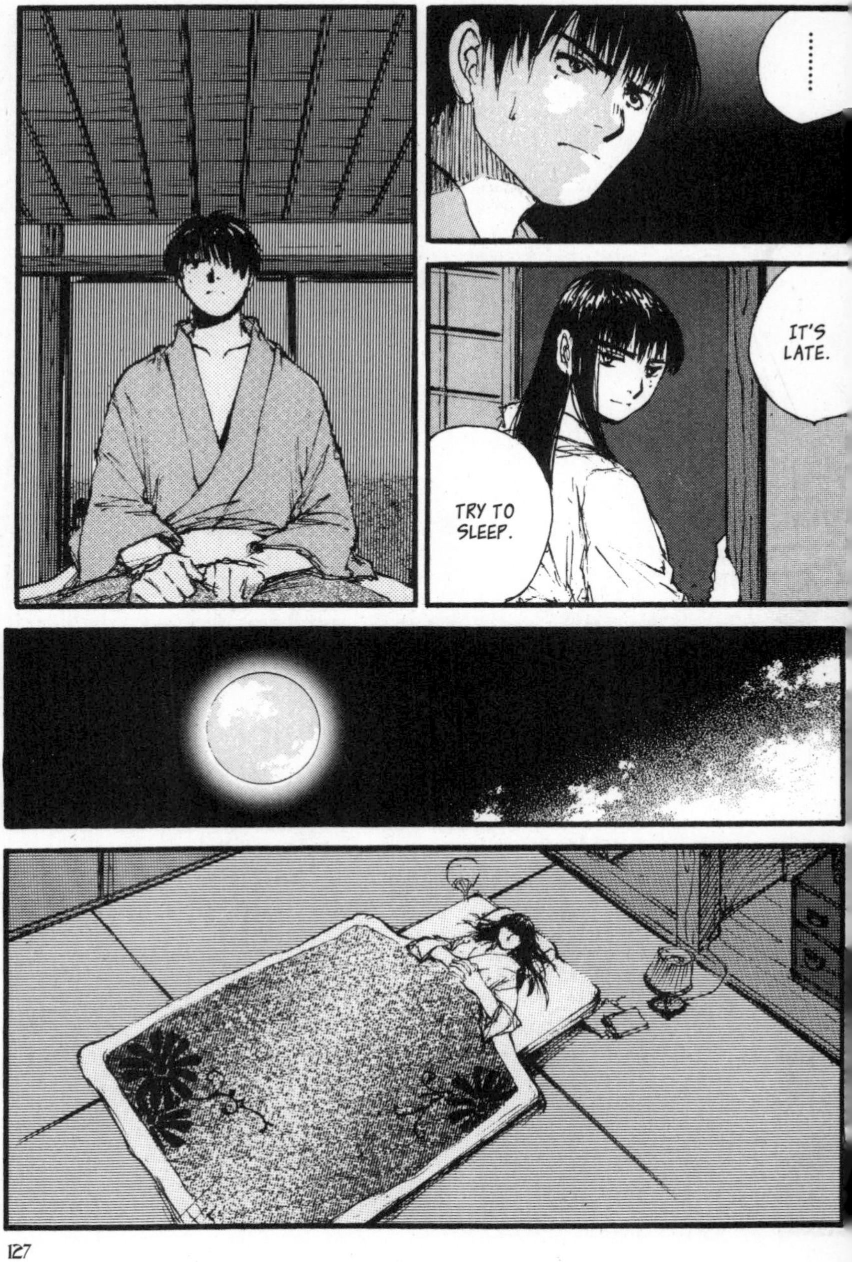
……
IT'S LATE.
TRY TO SLEEP.

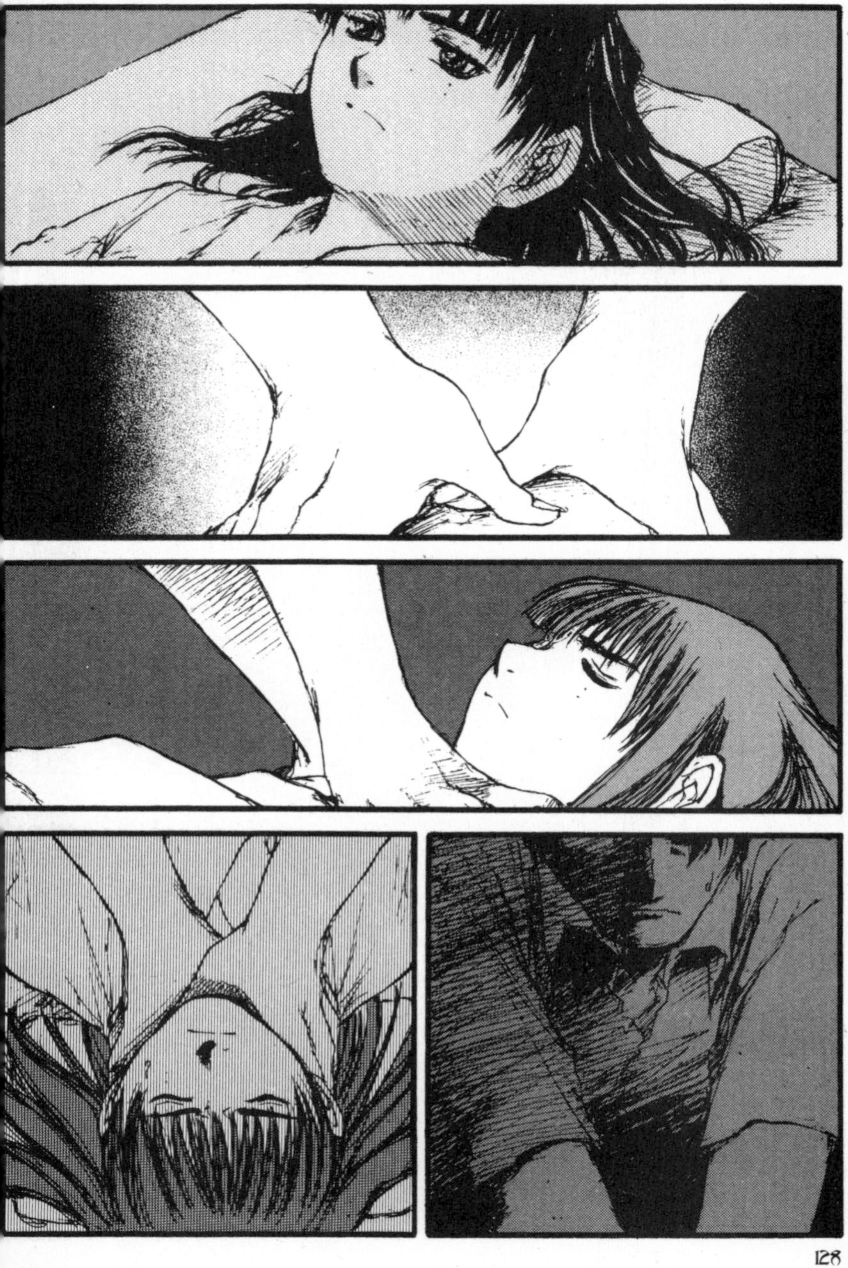

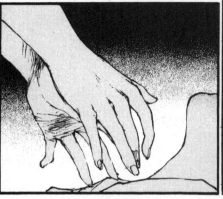

Even if Father crushed my neck with all his strength...

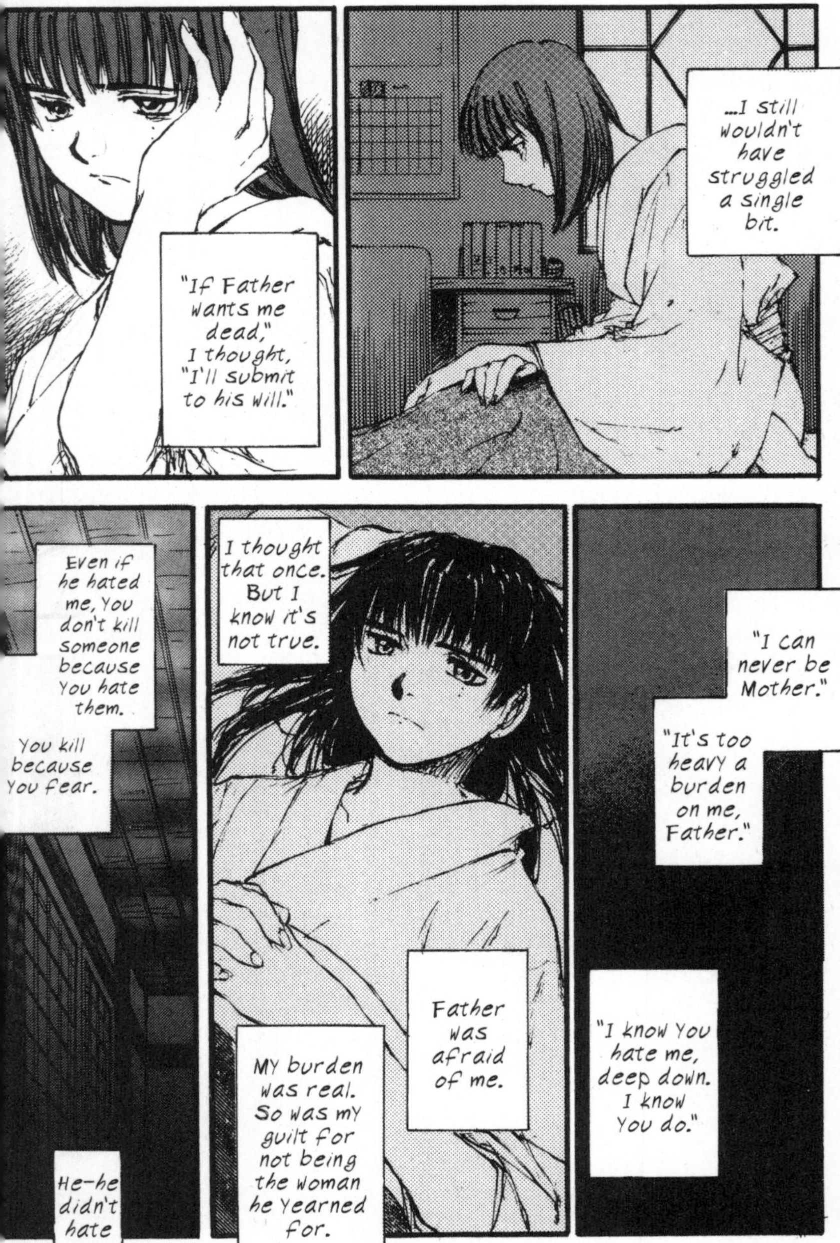
...I still wouldn't have struggled a single bit.
"If Father wants me dead," I thought, "I'll submit to his will."
"I can never be Mother."
"It's too heavy a burden on me, Father."
"I know you hate me, deep down. I know you do."
I thought that once. But I know it's not true.
Father was afraid of me.
My burden was real. So was my guilt for not being the woman he yearned for.
Even if he hated me, you don't kill someone because you hate them.
You kill because you fear.
He-he didn't hate me.

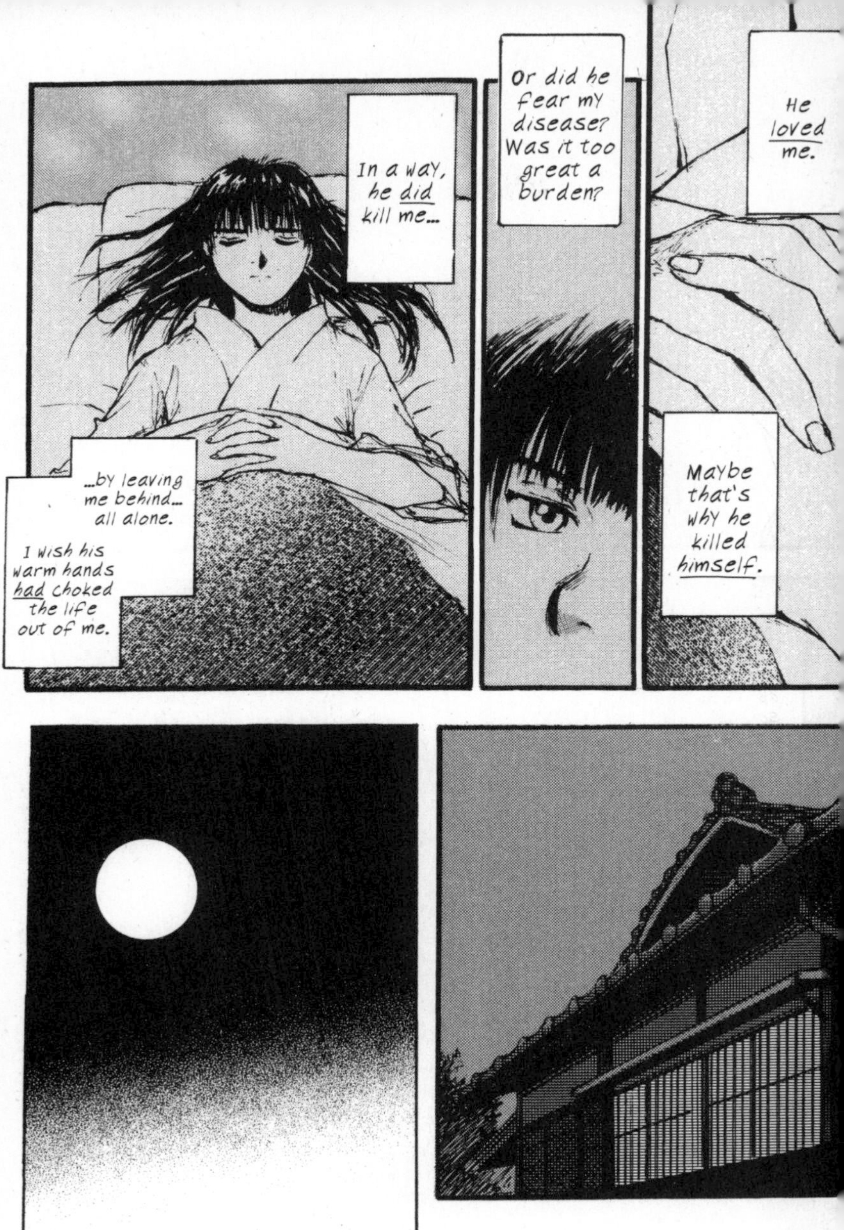
He loved me.
Maybe that's why he killed himself.
Or did he fear my disease? Was it too great a burden?
In a way, he did kill me...
...by leaving me behind... all alone.
I wish his warm hands had choked the life out of me.

WHOSO SHEDDETH MAN'S BLOOD,
BY MAN SHALL HIS BLOOD BE SHED...

--GENESIS 9:6

A CHILD WITH A MOLE IN
THE PATH OF THEIR TEARS
IS DESTINED TO HAVE A SORROWFUL
LIFE FULL OF THEM.

--JAPANESE PROVERB

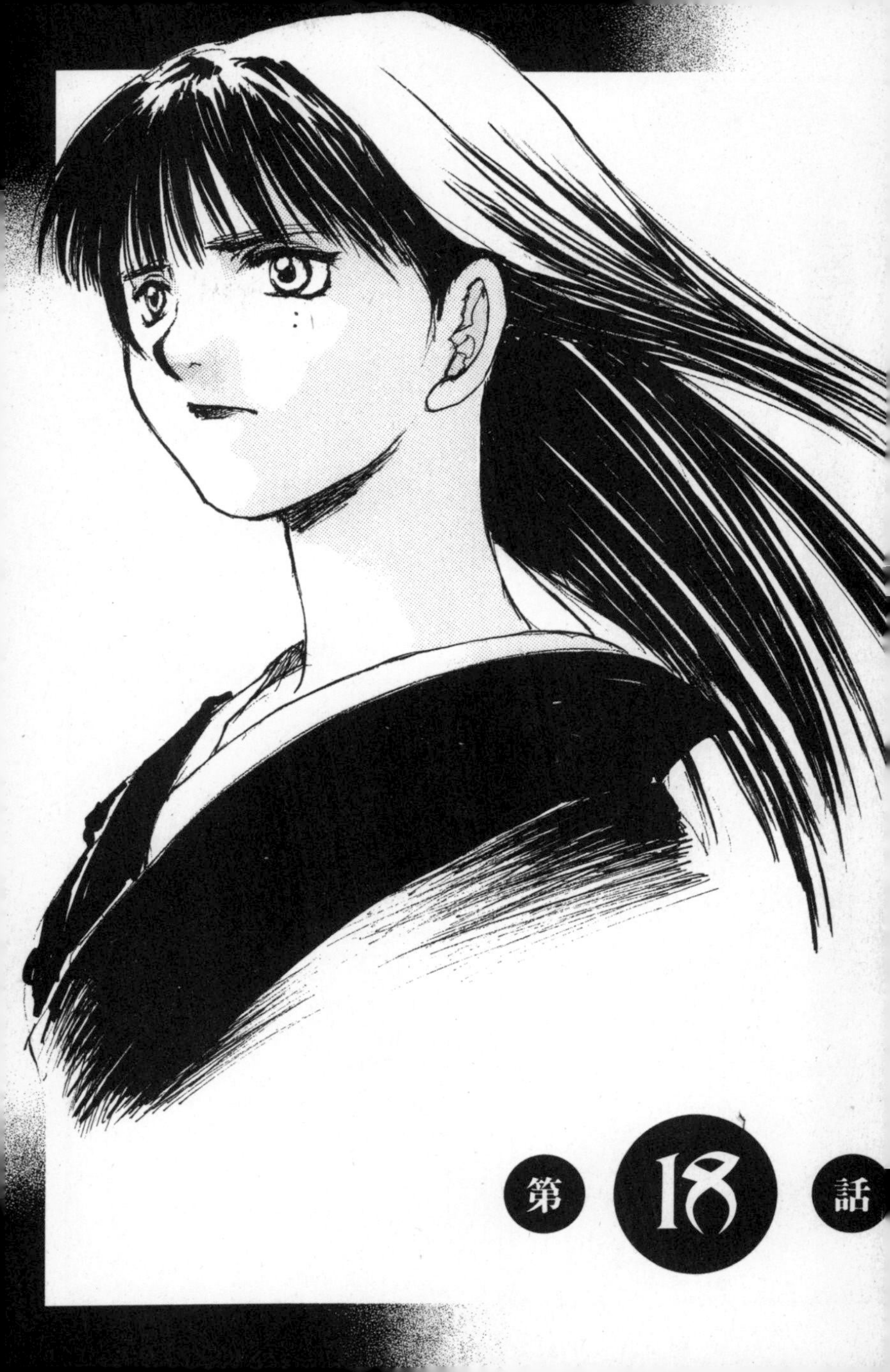
第18話

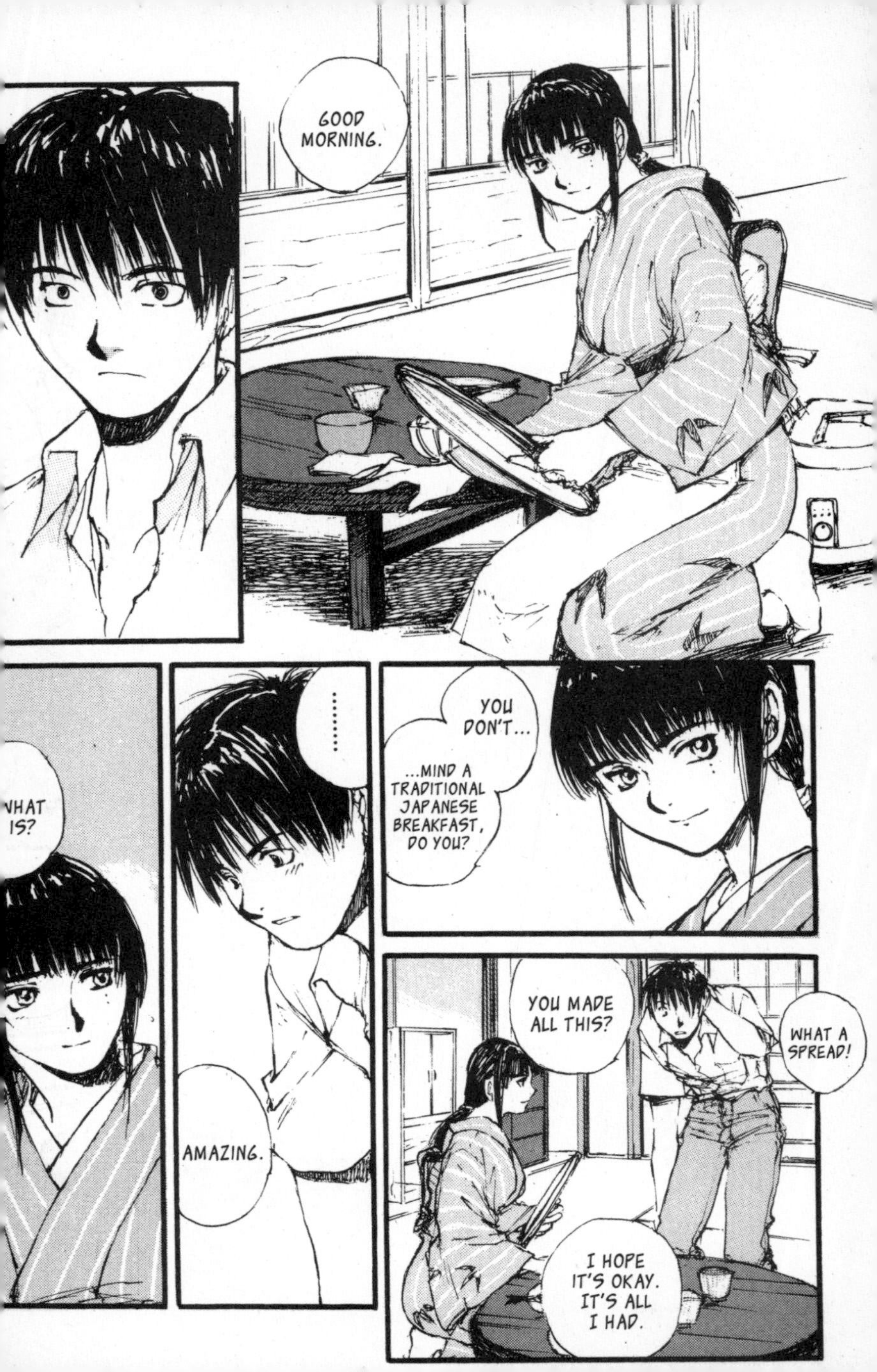
GOOD MORNING.
YOU DON'T...
...MIND A TRADITIONAL JAPANESE BREAKFAST, DO YOU?
WHAT A SPREAD!
YOU MADE ALL THIS?
I HOPE IT'S OKAY. IT'S ALL I HAD.
......
AMAZING.
WHAT IS?

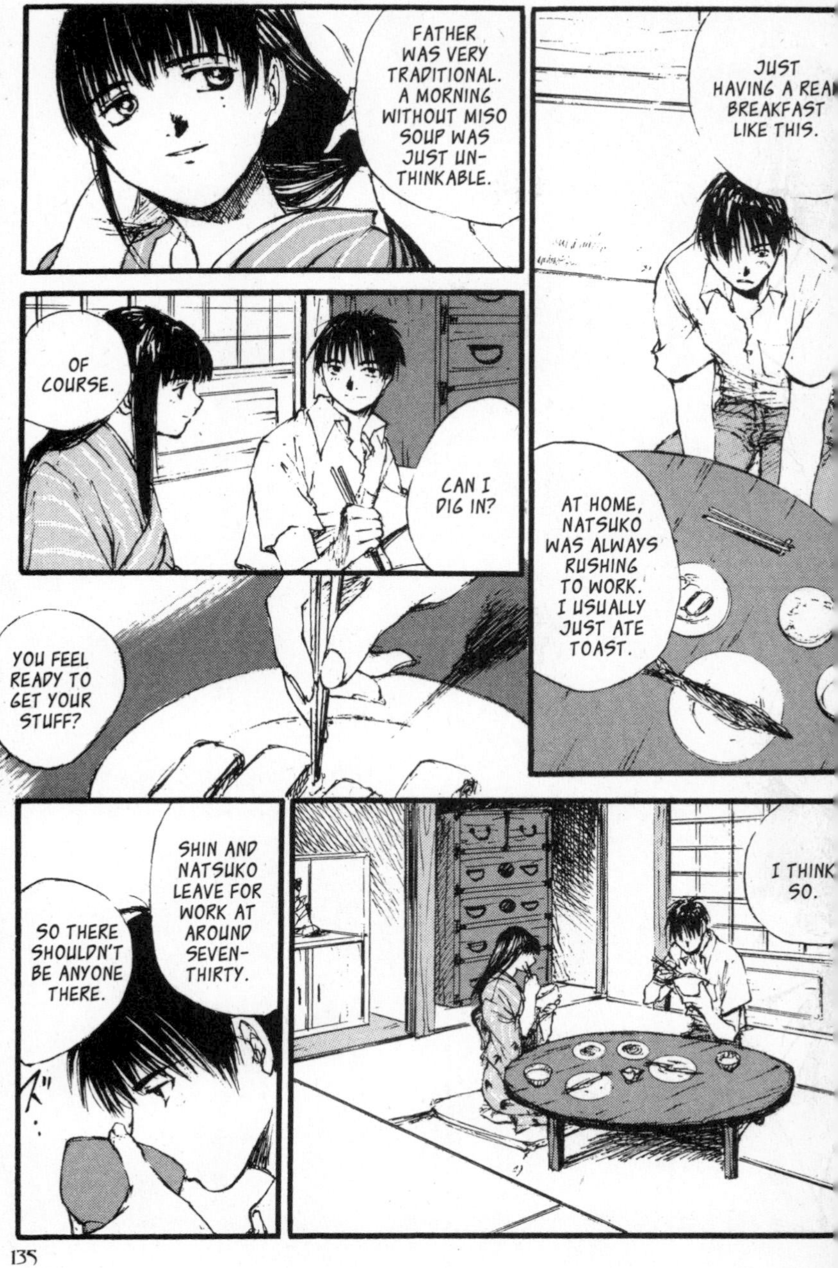
JUST HAVING A REA BREAKFAST LIKE THIS.
AT HOME, NATSUKO WAS ALWAYS RUSHING TO WORK. I USUALLY JUST ATE TOAST.
FATHER WAS VERY TRADITIONAL. A MORNING WITHOUT MISO SOUP WAS JUST UN-THINKABLE.
CAN I DIG IN?
OF COURSE.
YOU FEEL READY TO GET YOUR STUFF?
I THINK SO.
SHIN AND NATSUKO LEAVE FOR WORK AT AROUND SEVEN-THIRTY.
SO THERE SHOULDN'T BE ANYONE THERE.

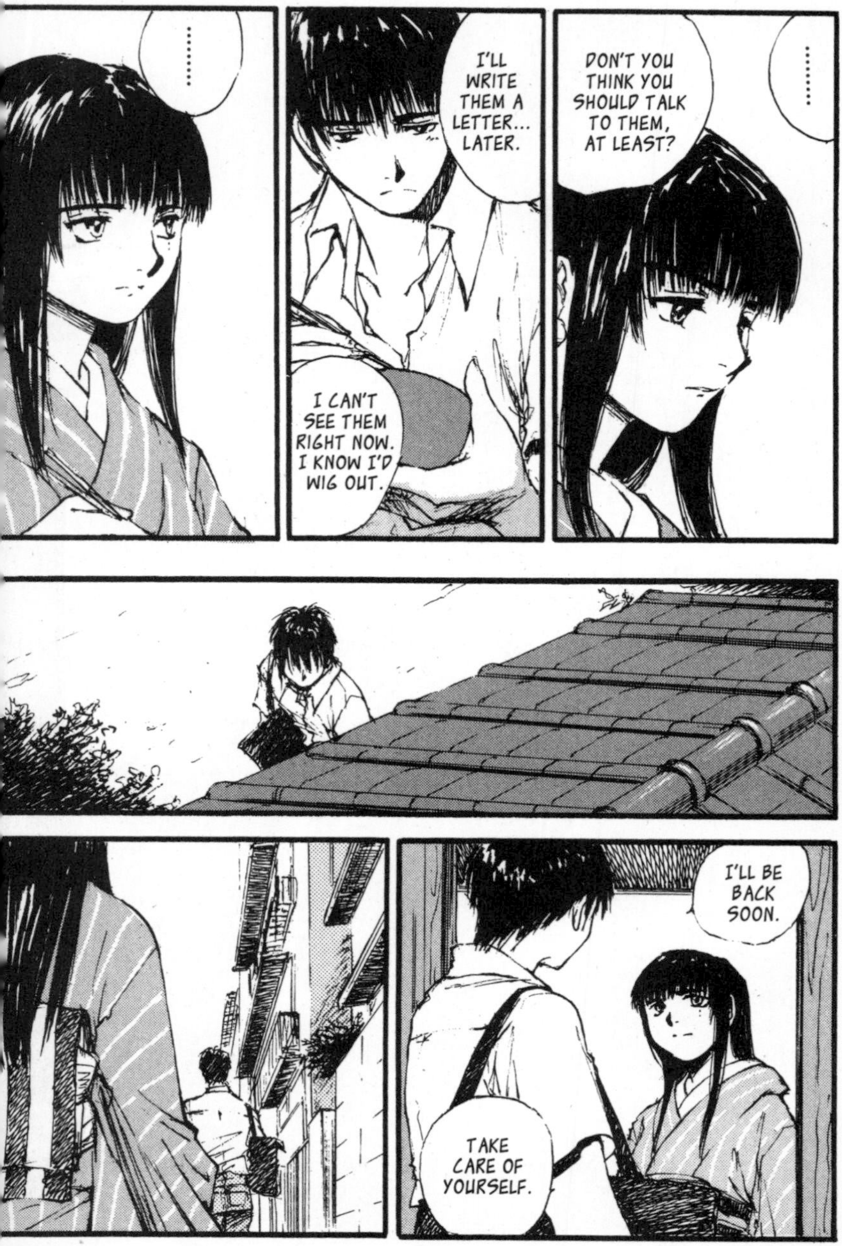
......
DON'T YOU THINK YOU SHOULD TALK TO THEM, AT LEAST?
I'LL WRITE THEM A LETTER... LATER.
I CAN'T SEE THEM RIGHT NOW. I KNOW I'D WIG OUT.
......
I'LL BE BACK SOON.
TAKE CARE OF YOURSELF.

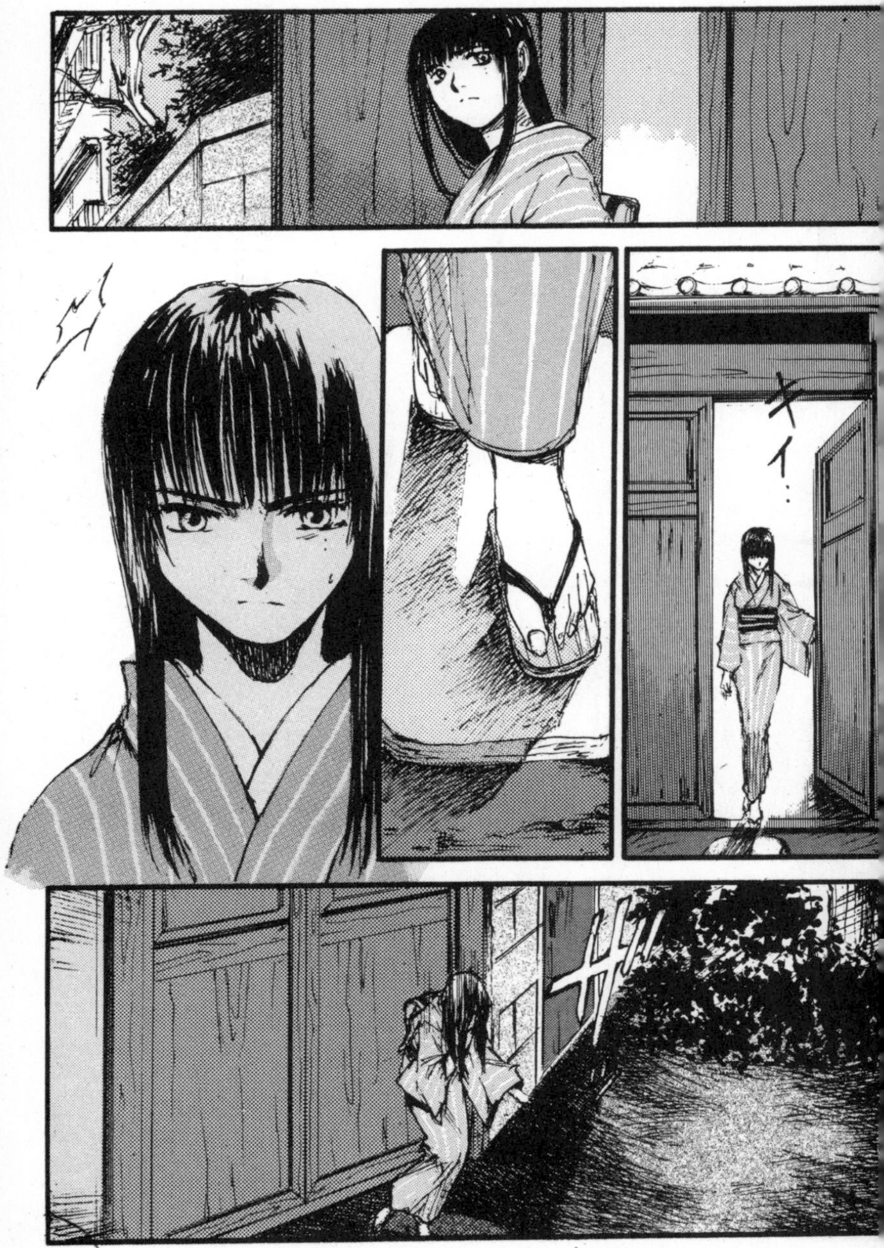
キイ…
サ!!

*stumble

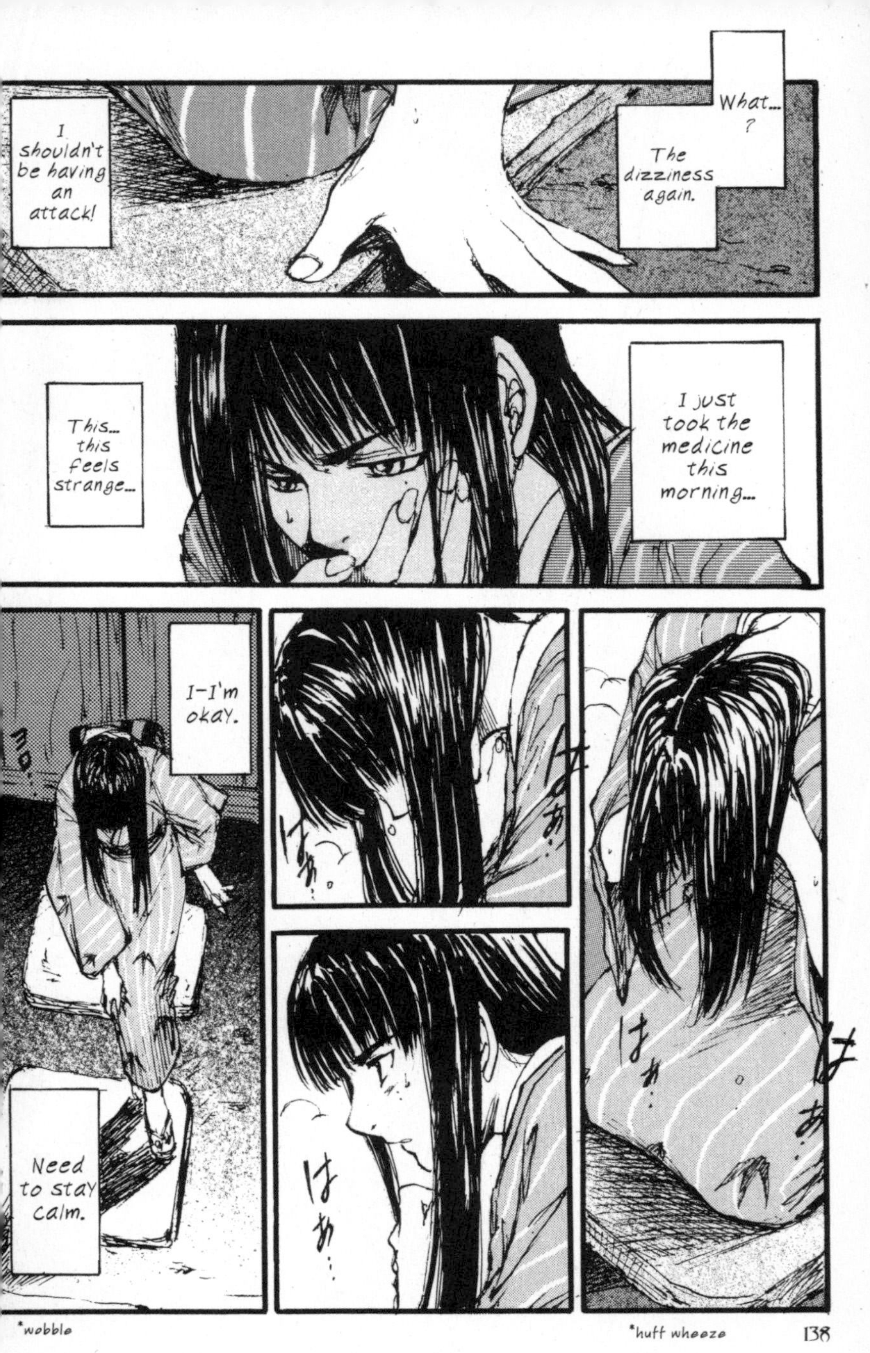

What... ?
The dizziness again.
I shouldn't be having an attack!
I just took the medicine this morning...
This... this feels strange...
はぁ
はぁ
はぁ
はぁ
はぁ...
I-I'm okay.
ヨロ
Need to stay calm.

*wobble

*huff wheeze

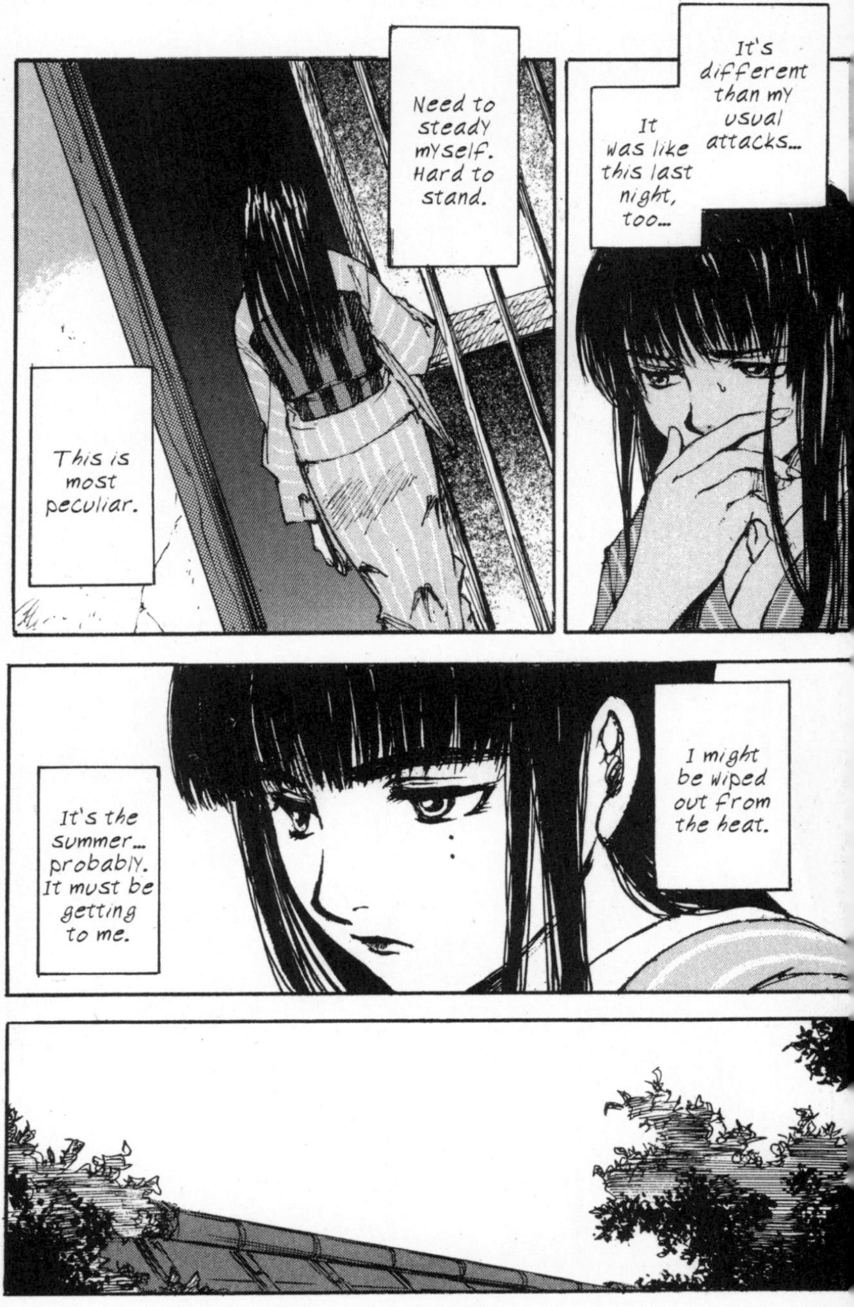
It's different than my usual attacks...
It was like this last night, too...
Need to steady myself. Hard to stand.
This is most peculiar.
I might be wiped out from the heat.
It's the summer... probably. It must be getting to me.

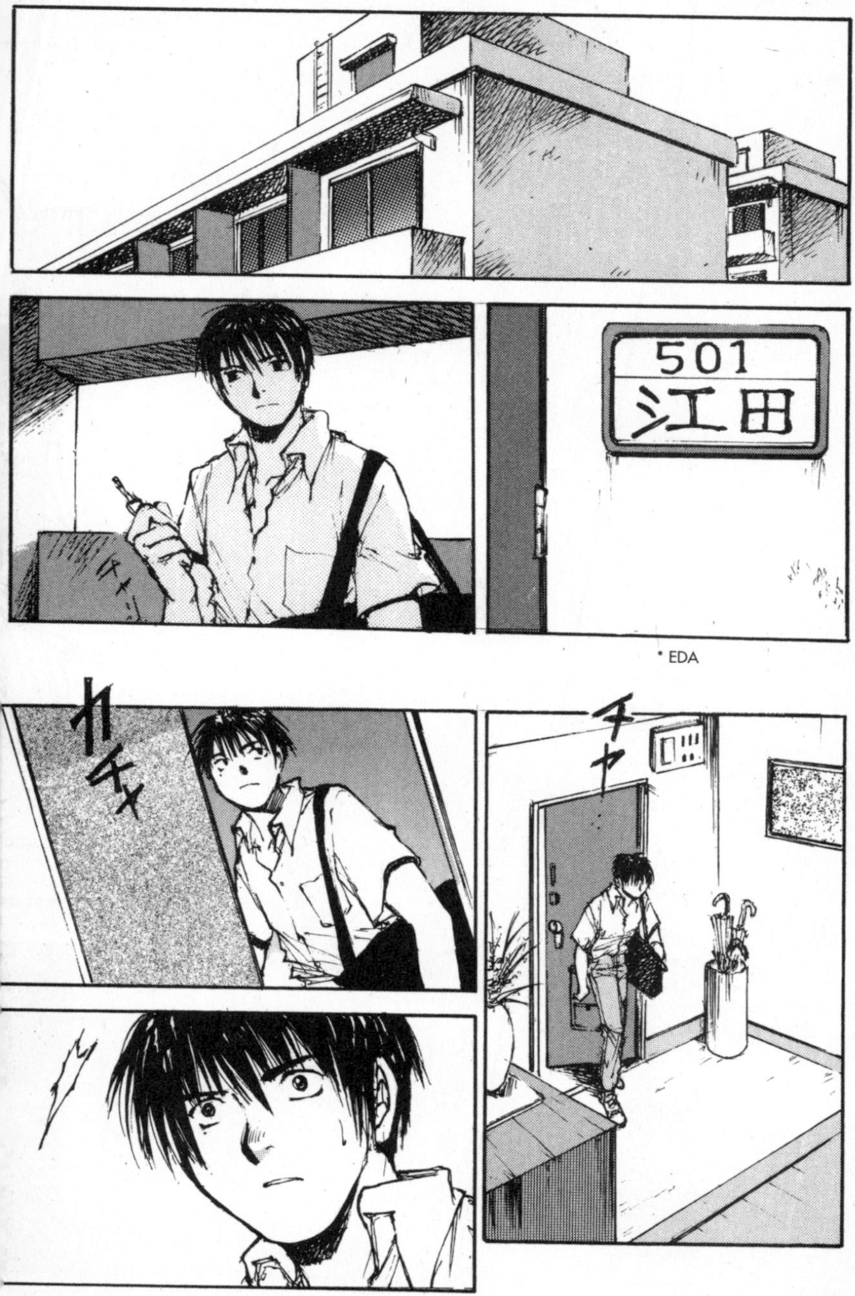
501
江田
* EDA

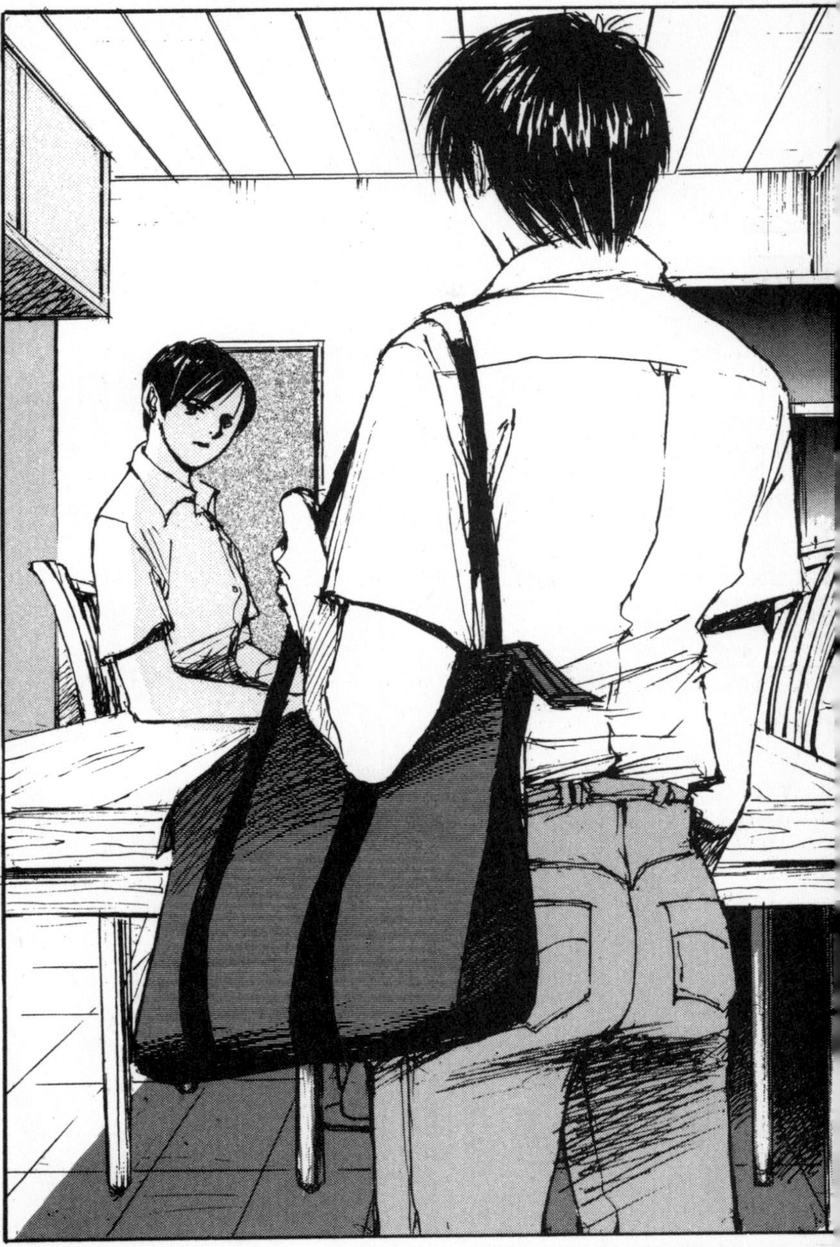

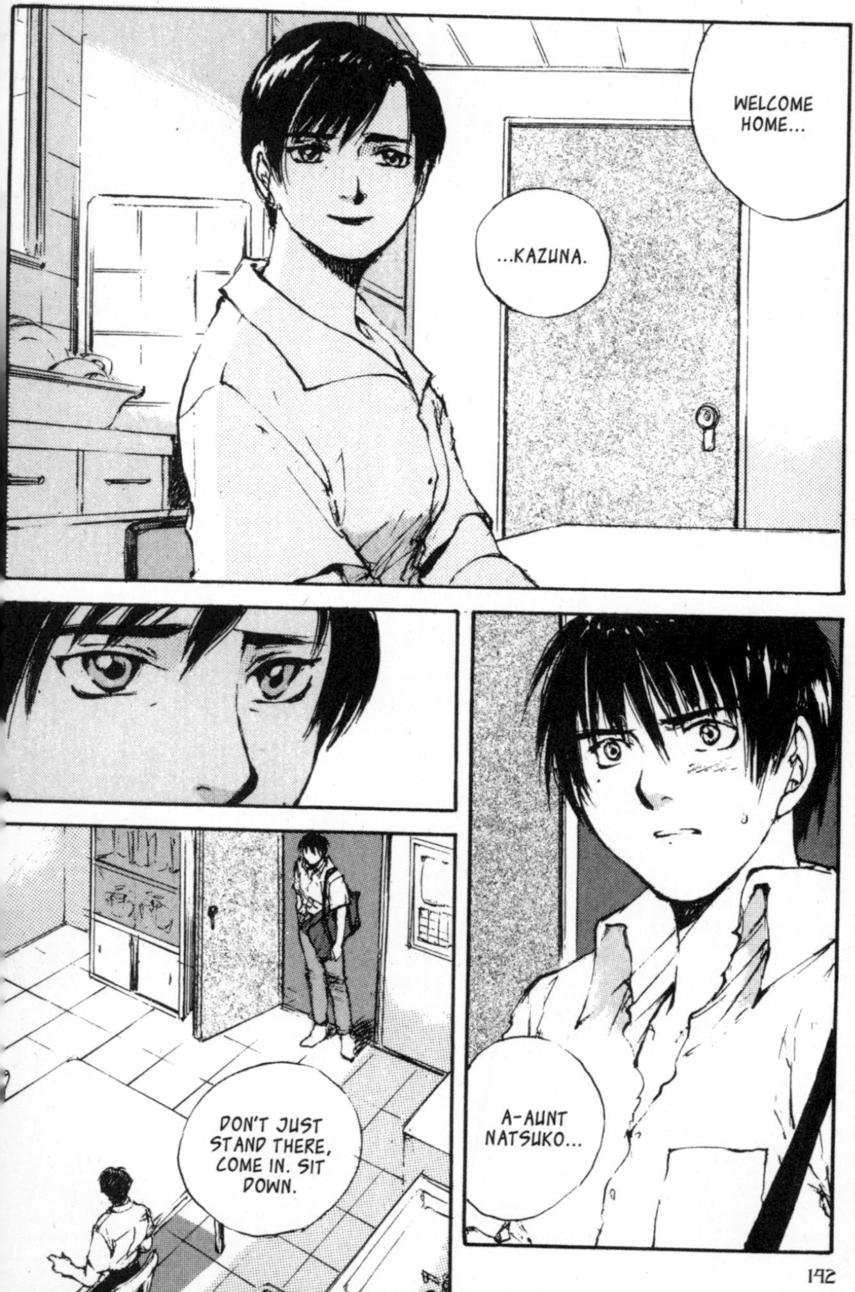
WELCOME HOME...
...KAZUNA.
A-AUNT NATSUKO...
DON'T JUST STAND THERE, COME IN. SIT DOWN.

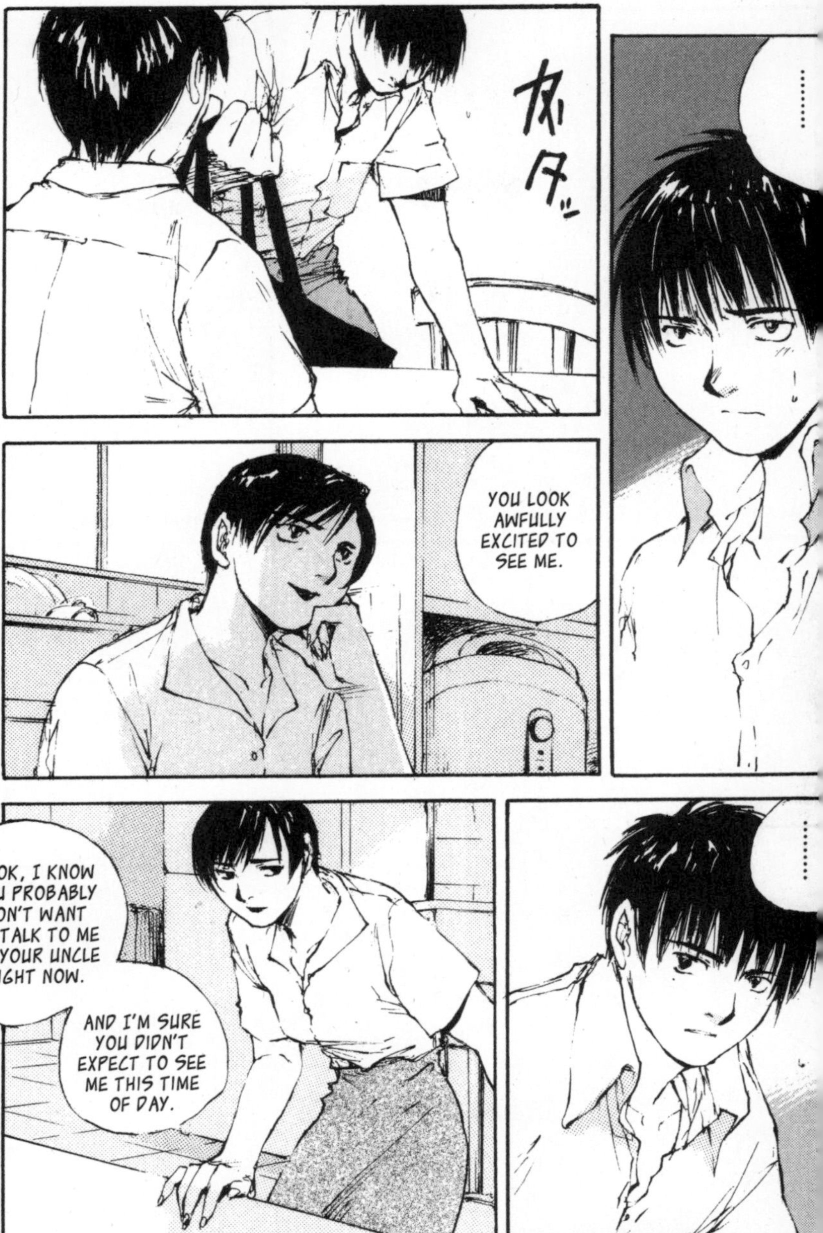
......
ガタッ
YOU LOOK AWFULLY EXCITED TO SEE ME.
......
LOOK, I KNOW YOU PROBABLY DON'T WANT TO TALK TO ME OR YOUR UNCLE RIGHT NOW.
AND I'M SURE YOU DIDN'T EXPECT TO SEE ME THIS TIME OF DAY.

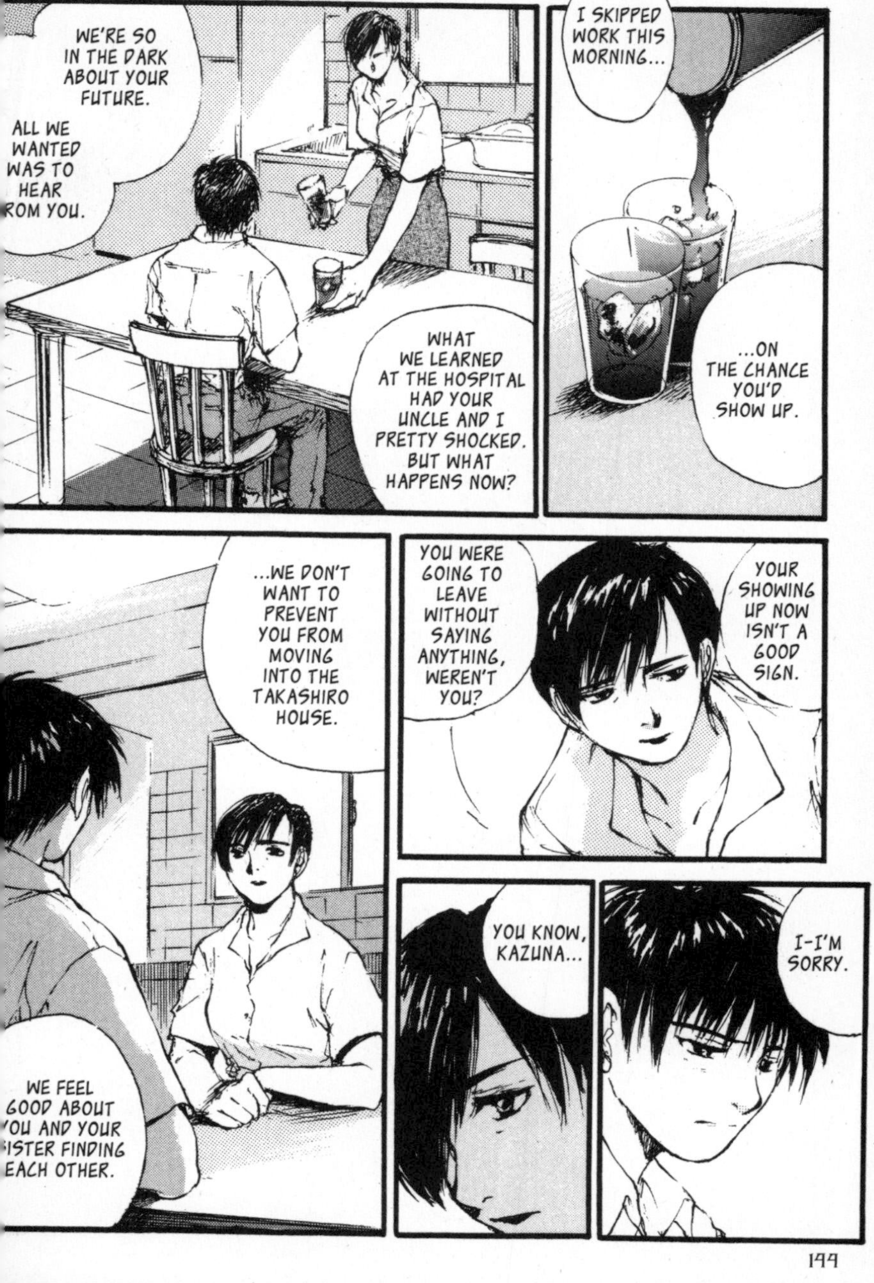
I SKIPPED WORK THIS MORNING...
...ON THE CHANCE YOU'D SHOW UP.
WE'RE SO IN THE DARK ABOUT YOUR FUTURE.
ALL WE WANTED WAS TO HEAR ROM YOU.
WHAT WE LEARNED AT THE HOSPITAL HAD YOUR UNCLE AND I PRETTY SHOCKED. BUT WHAT HAPPENS NOW?
YOUR SHOWING UP NOW ISN'T A GOOD SIGN.
YOU WERE GOING TO LEAVE WITHOUT SAYING ANYTHING, WEREN'T YOU?
I-I'M SORRY.
YOU KNOW, KAZUNA...
...WE DON'T WANT TO PREVENT YOU FROM MOVING INTO THE TAKASHIRO HOUSE.
WE FEEL GOOD ABOUT OU AND YOUR ISTER FINDING EACH OTHER.

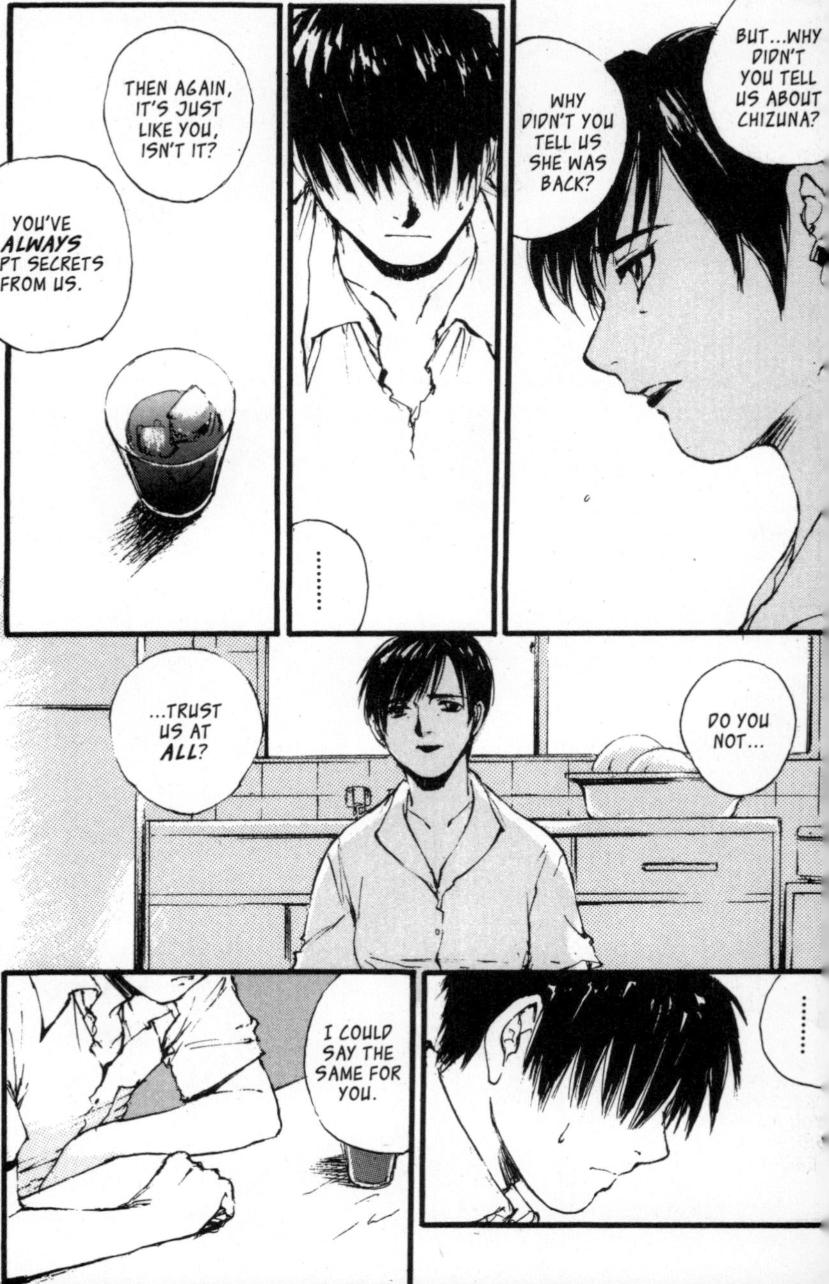
BUT...WHY DIDN'T YOU TELL US ABOUT CHIZUNA?
WHY DIDN'T YOU TELL US SHE WAS BACK?
....
THEN AGAIN, IT'S JUST LIKE YOU, ISN'T IT?
YOU'VE **ALWAYS** KEPT SECRETS FROM US.
DO YOU NOT...
...TRUST US AT **ALL**?
....
I COULD SAY THE SAME FOR YOU.

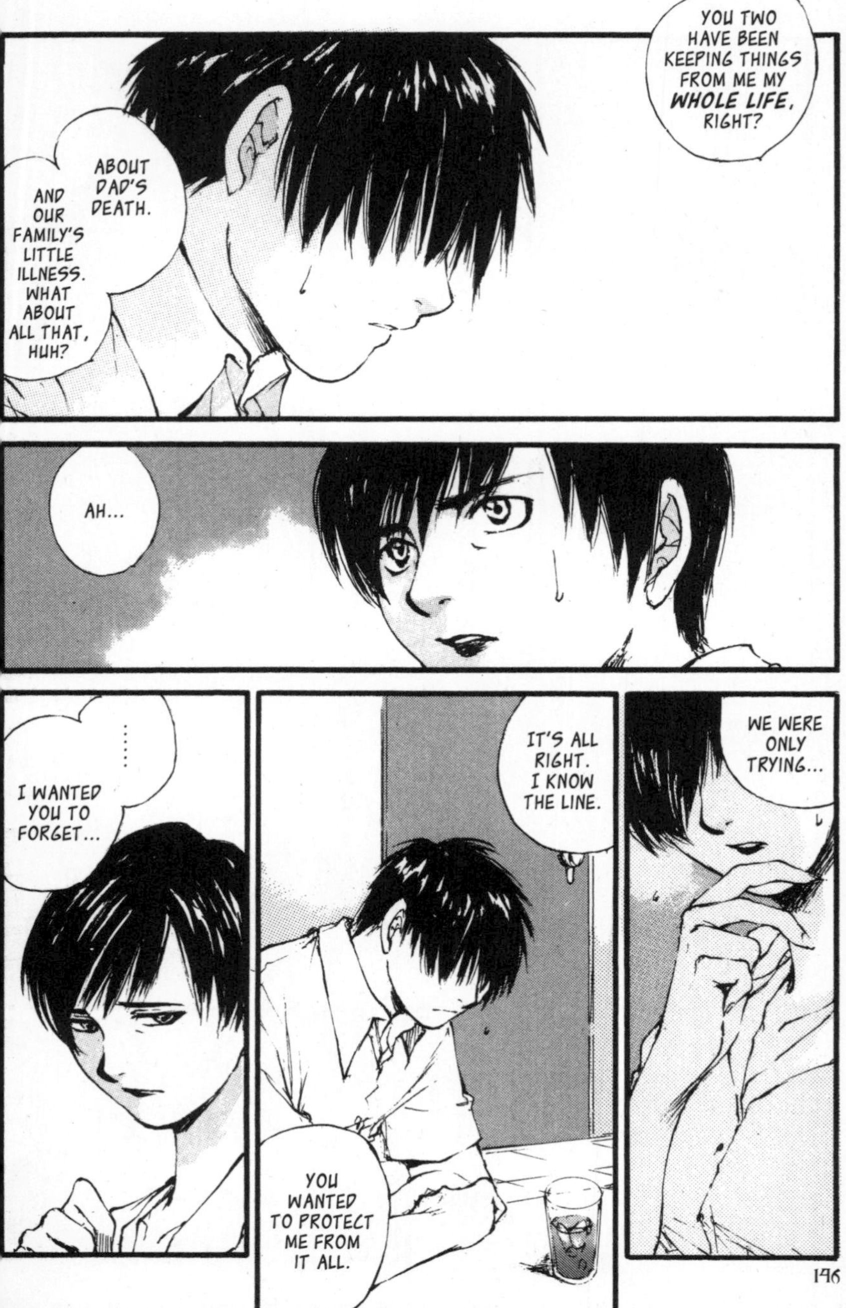
YOU TWO HAVE BEEN KEEPING THINGS FROM ME MY *WHOLE LIFE*, RIGHT?
ABOUT DAD'S DEATH.
AND OUR FAMILY'S LITTLE ILLNESS. WHAT ABOUT ALL THAT, HUH?
AH...
WE WERE ONLY TRYING...
IT'S ALL RIGHT. I KNOW THE LINE.
YOU WANTED TO PROTECT ME FROM IT ALL.
......
I WANTED YOU TO FORGET...

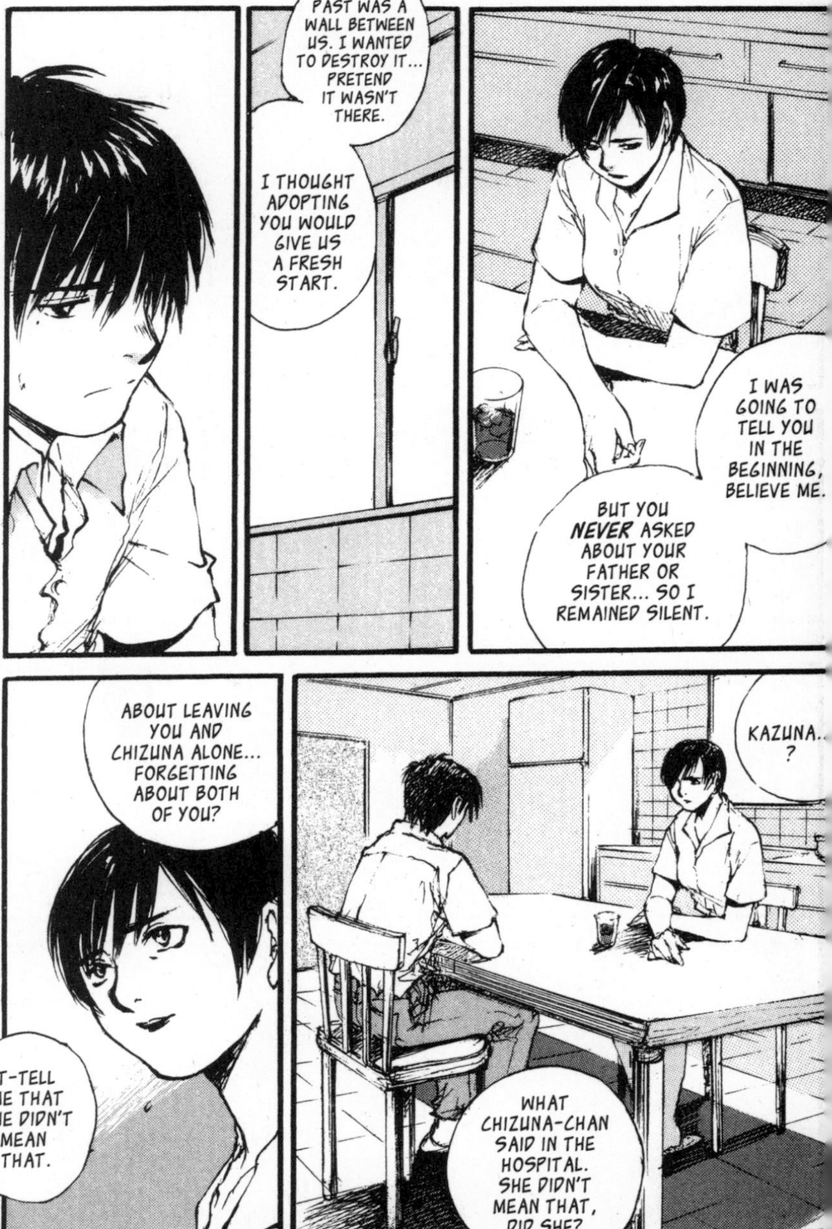
I WAS GOING TO TELL YOU IN THE BEGINNING, BELIEVE ME.
BUT YOU NEVER ASKED ABOUT YOUR FATHER OR SISTER... SO I REMAINED SILENT.
YOUR PAST WAS A WALL BETWEEN US. I WANTED TO DESTROY IT... PRETEND IT WASN'T THERE.
I THOUGHT ADOPTING YOU WOULD GIVE US A FRESH START.
KAZUNA... ?
WHAT CHIZUNA-CHAN SAID IN THE HOSPITAL. SHE DIDN'T MEAN THAT, DID SHE?
ABOUT LEAVING YOU AND CHIZUNA ALONE... FORGETTING ABOUT BOTH OF YOU?
T-TELL ME THAT SHE DIDN'T MEAN THAT.

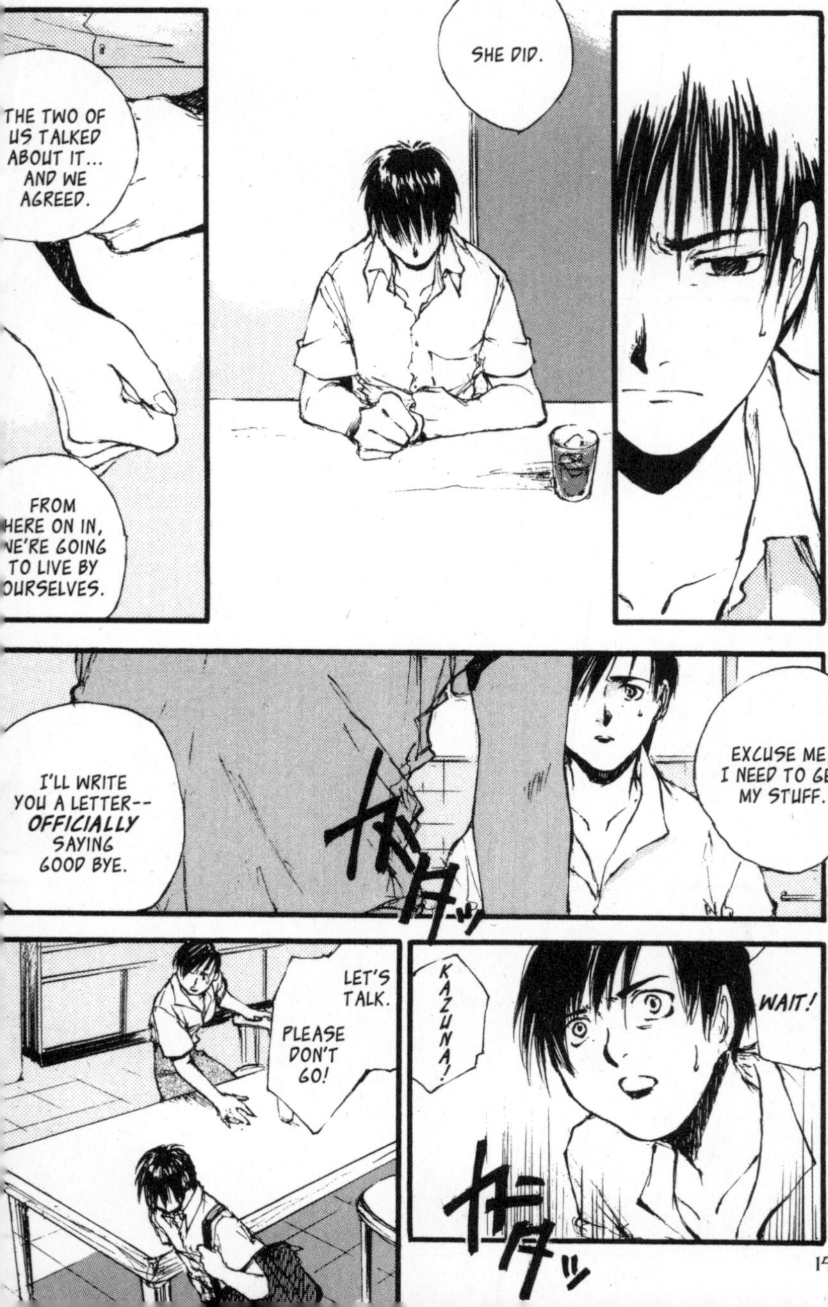
SHE DID.
THE TWO OF US TALKED ABOUT IT... AND WE AGREED.
FROM HERE ON IN, WE'RE GOING TO LIVE BY OURSELVES.
EXCUSE ME, I NEED TO GET MY STUFF.
I'LL WRITE YOU A LETTER-- ***OFFICIALLY*** SAYING GOOD BYE.
KAZUNA!
WAIT!
LET'S TALK.
PLEASE DON'T GO!

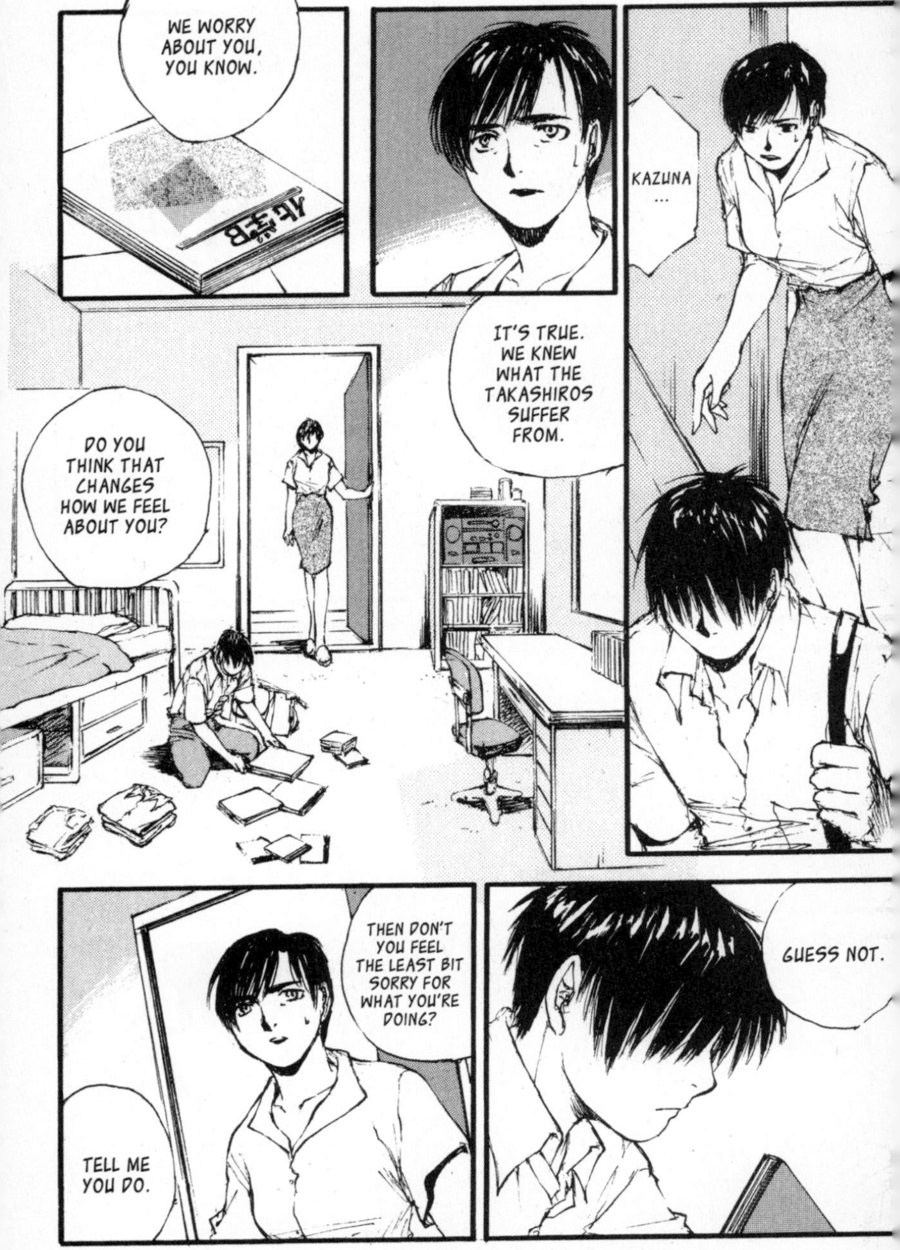
KAZUNA ...
WE WORRY ABOUT YOU, YOU KNOW.
IT'S TRUE. WE KNEW WHAT THE TAKASHIROS SUFFER FROM.
DO YOU THINK THAT CHANGES HOW WE FEEL ABOUT YOU?
GUESS NOT.
THEN DON'T YOU FEEL THE LEAST BIT SORRY FOR WHAT YOU'RE DOING?
TELL ME YOU DO.

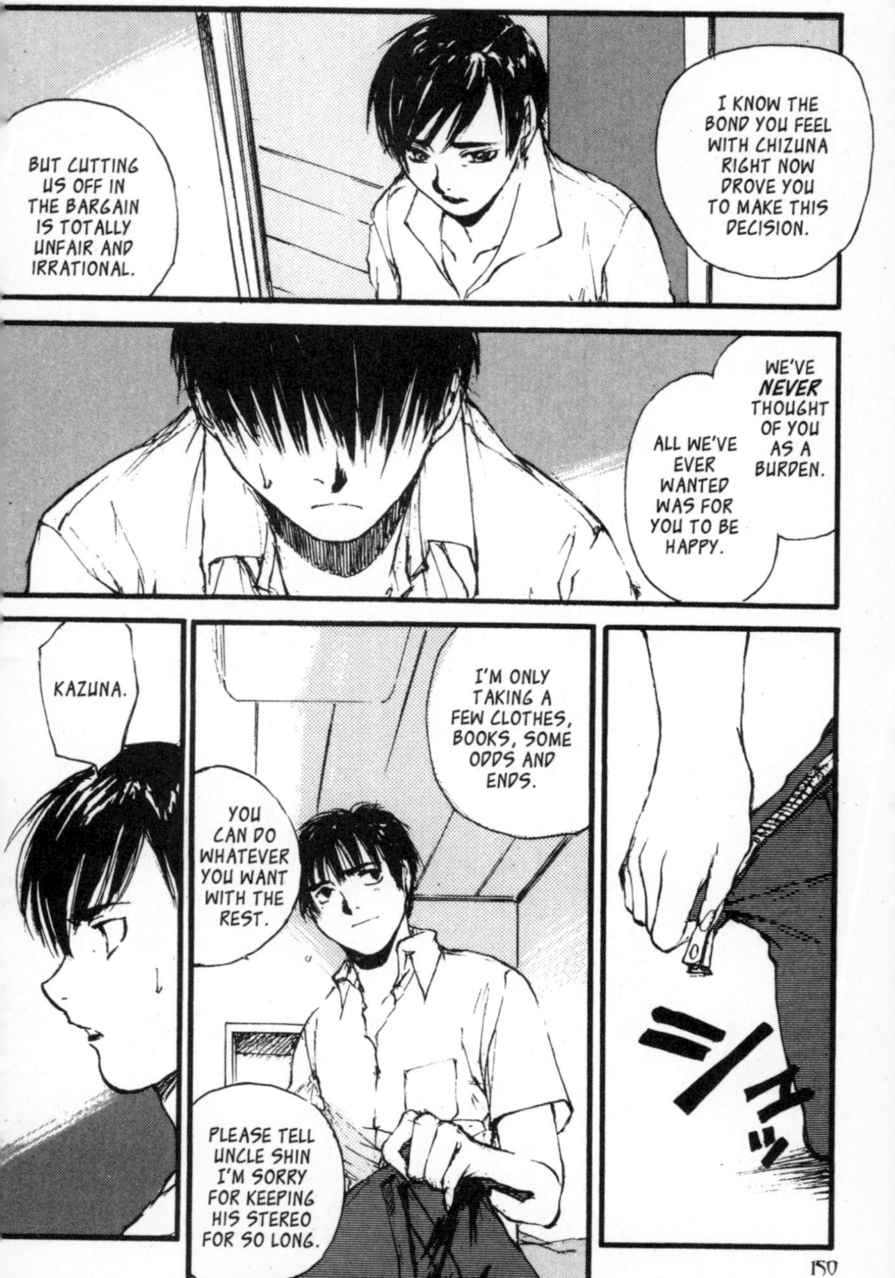
I KNOW THE BOND YOU FEEL WITH CHIZUNA RIGHT NOW DROVE YOU TO MAKE THIS DECISION.
BUT CUTTING US OFF IN THE BARGAIN IS TOTALLY UNFAIR AND IRRATIONAL.
WE'VE ***NEVER*** THOUGHT OF YOU AS A BURDEN.
ALL WE'VE EVER WANTED WAS FOR YOU TO BE HAPPY.
I'M ONLY TAKING A FEW CLOTHES, BOOKS, SOME ODDS AND ENDS.
YOU CAN DO WHATEVER YOU WANT WITH THE REST.
PLEASE TELL UNCLE SHIN I'M SORRY FOR KEEPING HIS STEREO FOR SO LONG.
KAZUNA.

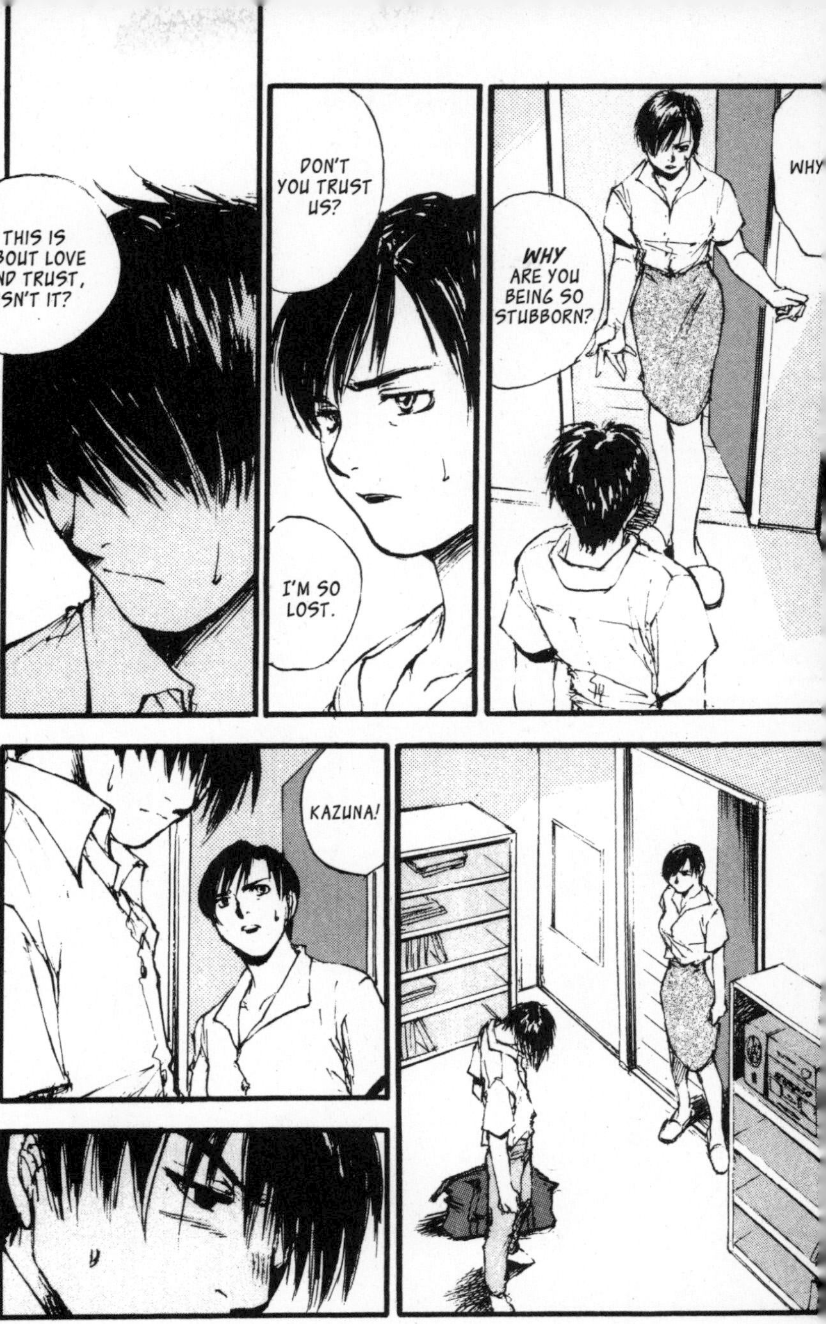
WHY
WHY ARE YOU BEING SO STUBBORN?
DON'T YOU TRUST US?
I'M SO LOST.
THIS IS ABOUT LOVE AND TRUST, ISN'T IT?
KAZUNA!

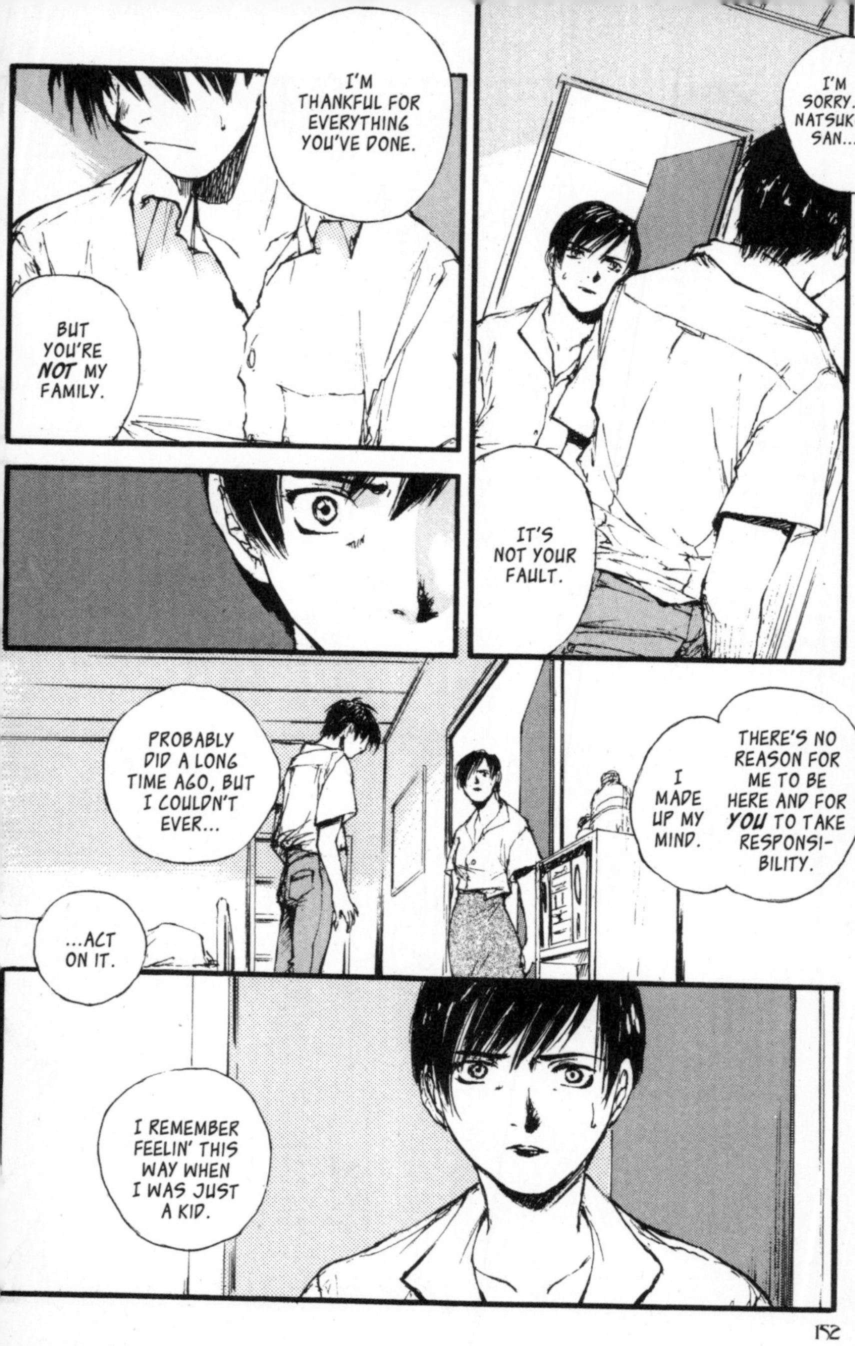
I'M SORRY... NATSUKO-SAN...
IT'S NOT YOUR FAULT.
I'M THANKFUL FOR EVERYTHING YOU'VE DONE.
BUT YOU'RE *NOT* MY FAMILY.
THERE'S NO REASON FOR ME TO BE HERE AND FOR *YOU* TO TAKE RESPONSI-BILITY.
I MADE UP MY MIND.
PROBABLY DID A LONG TIME AGO, BUT I COULDN'T EVER...
...ACT ON IT.
I REMEMBER FEELIN' THIS WAY WHEN I WAS JUST A KID.

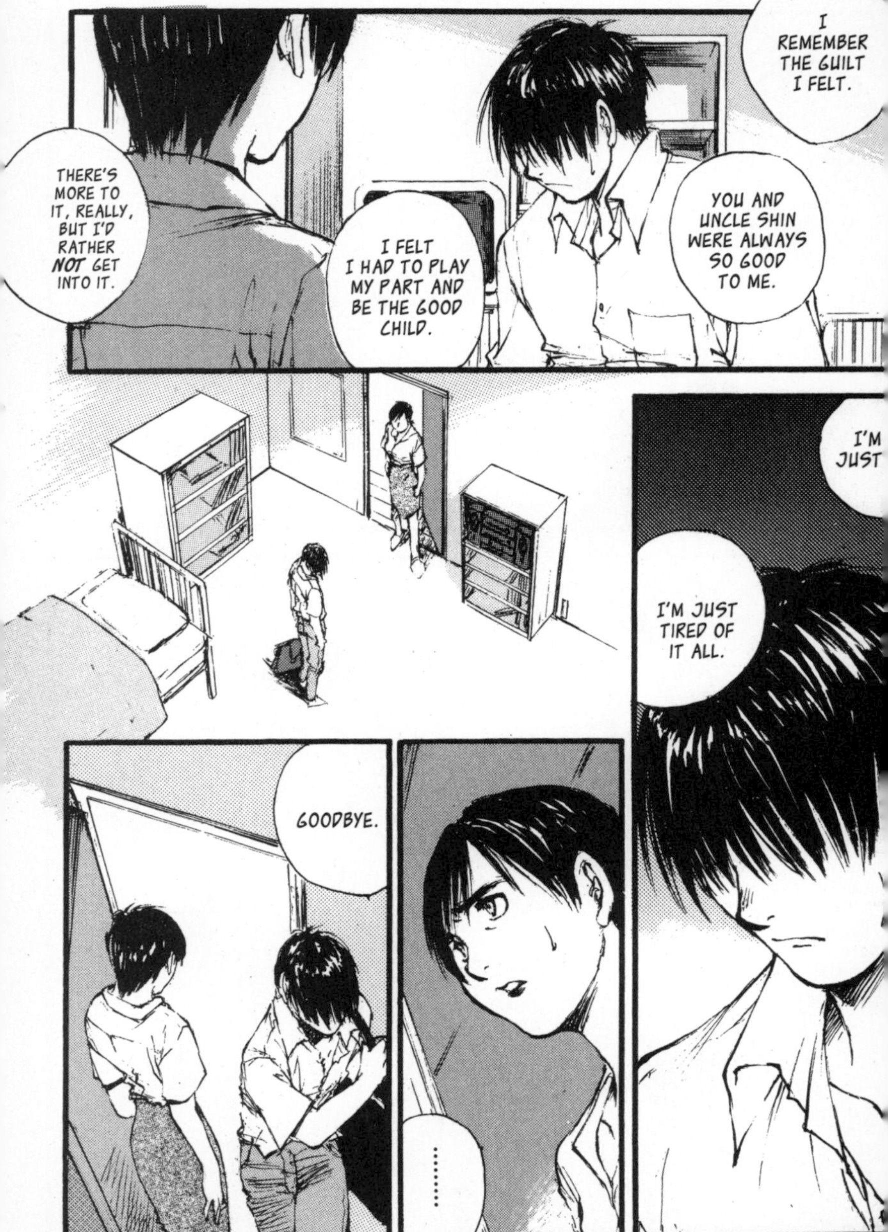
I REMEMBER THE GUILT I FELT.
YOU AND UNCLE SHIN WERE ALWAYS SO GOOD TO ME.
I FELT I HAD TO PLAY MY PART AND BE THE GOOD CHILD.
THERE'S MORE TO IT, REALLY, BUT I'D RATHER *NOT* GET INTO IT.
I'M JUST
I'M JUST TIRED OF IT ALL.
......
GOODBYE.

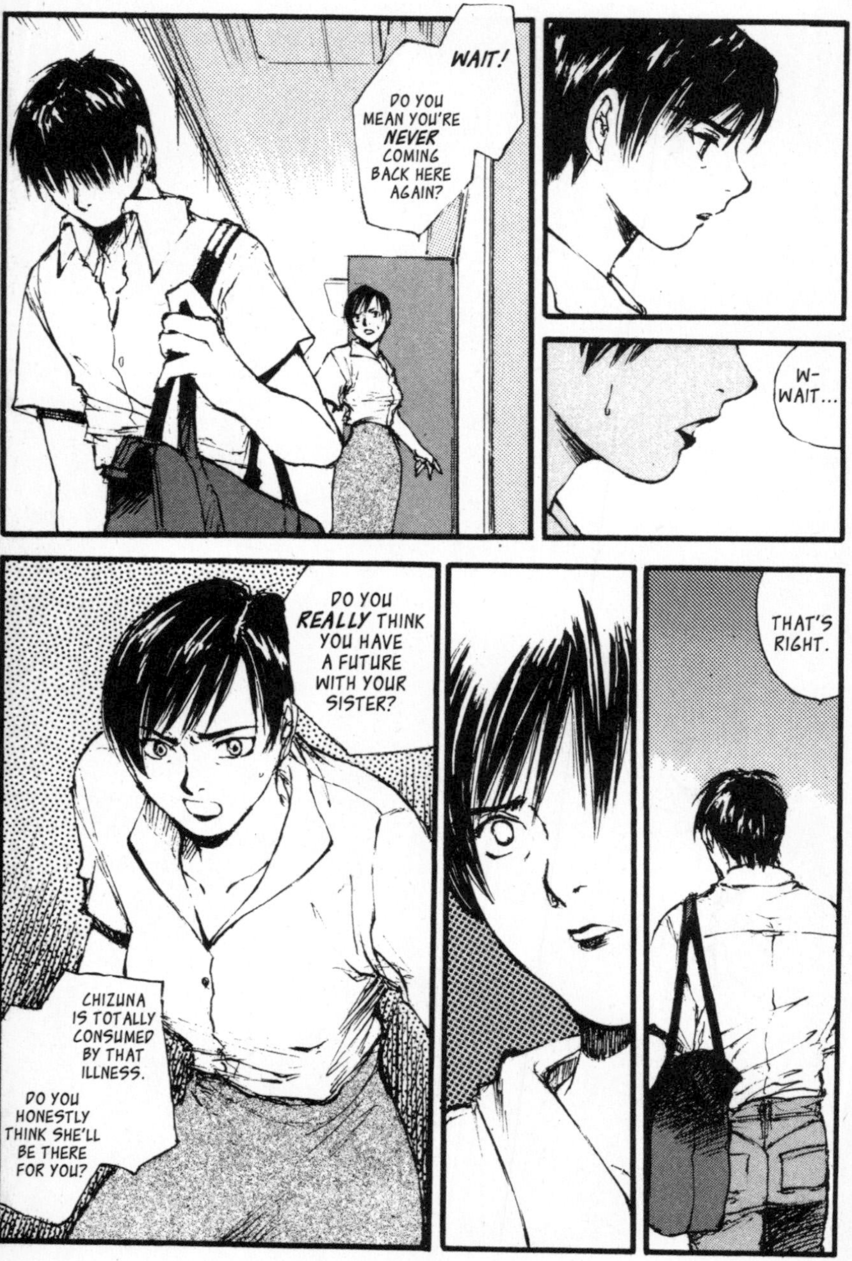
W-WAIT...
WAIT!
DO YOU MEAN YOU'RE NEVER COMING BACK HERE AGAIN?
THAT'S RIGHT.
DO YOU REALLY THINK YOU HAVE A FUTURE WITH YOUR SISTER?
CHIZUNA IS TOTALLY CONSUMED BY THAT ILLNESS.
DO YOU HONESTLY THINK SHE'LL BE THERE FOR YOU?

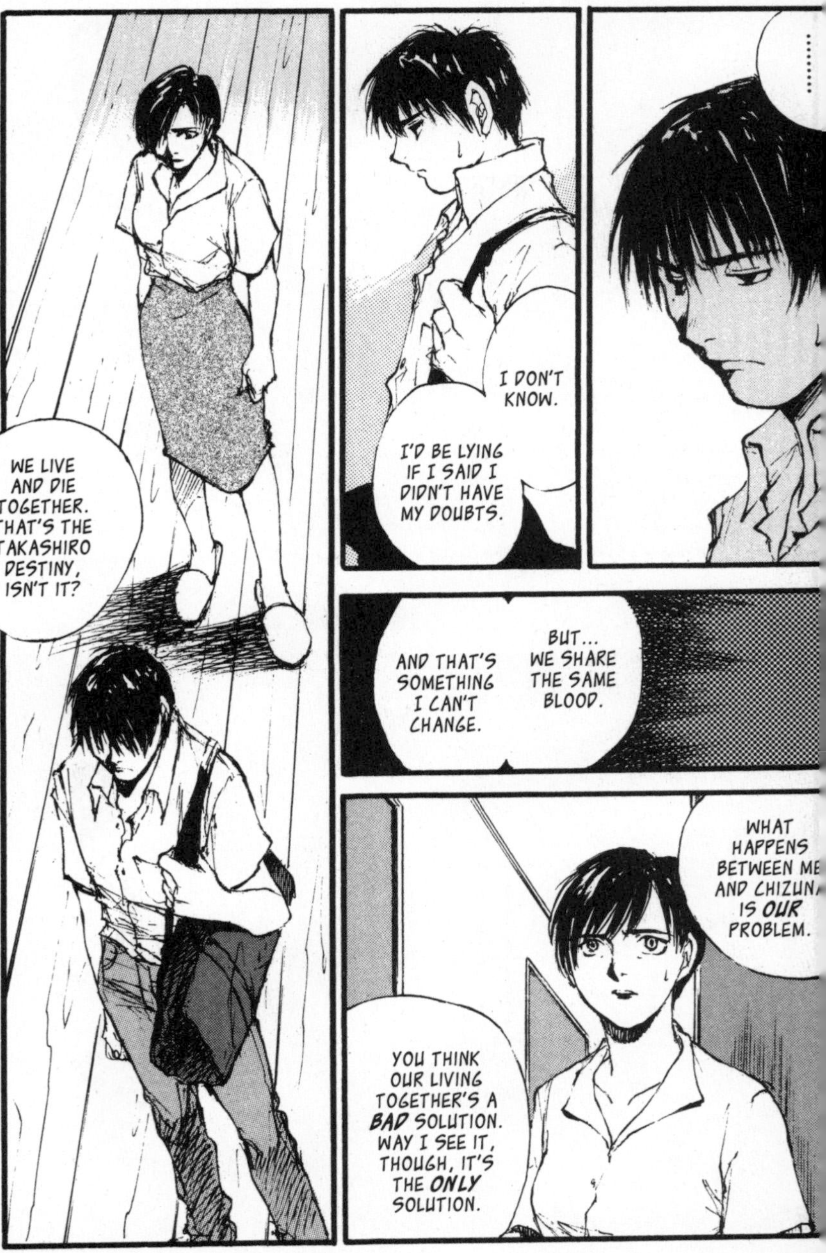
......
I DON'T KNOW.
I'D BE LYING IF I SAID I DIDN'T HAVE MY DOUBTS.
BUT... WE SHARE THE SAME BLOOD.
AND THAT'S SOMETHING I CAN'T CHANGE.
WHAT HAPPENS BETWEEN ME AND CHIZUNA IS OUR PROBLEM.
YOU THINK OUR LIVING TOGETHER'S A BAD SOLUTION. WAY I SEE IT, THOUGH, IT'S THE ONLY SOLUTION.
WE LIVE AND DIE TOGETHER. THAT'S THE TAKASHIRO DESTINY, ISN'T IT?

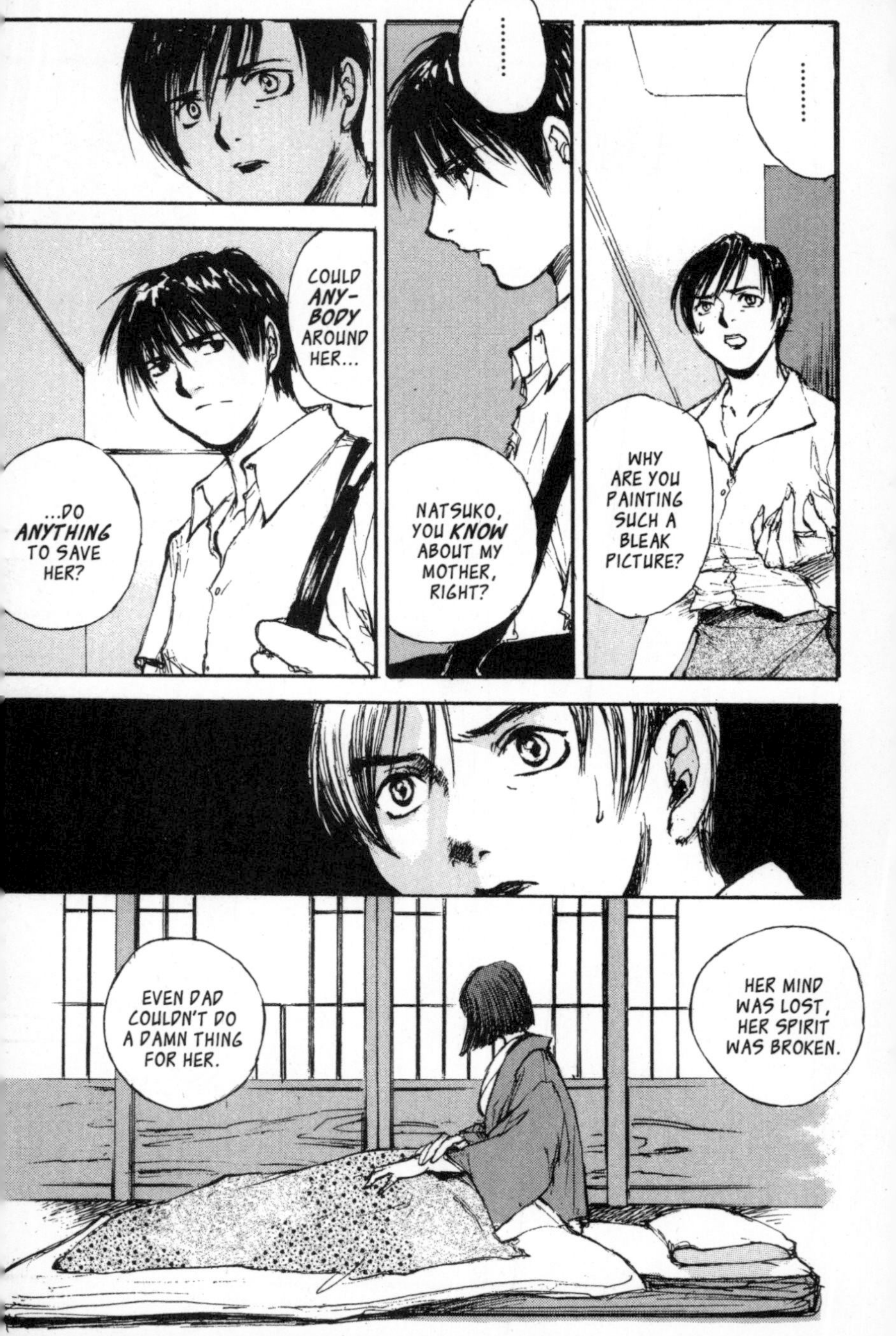
......
WHY ARE YOU PAINTING SUCH A BLEAK PICTURE?
......
NATSUKO, YOU KNOW ABOUT MY MOTHER, RIGHT?
COULD ANY-BODY AROUND HER...
...DO ANYTHING TO SAVE HER?
HER MIND WAS LOST, HER SPIRIT WAS BROKEN.
EVEN DAD COULDN'T DO A DAMN THING FOR HER.

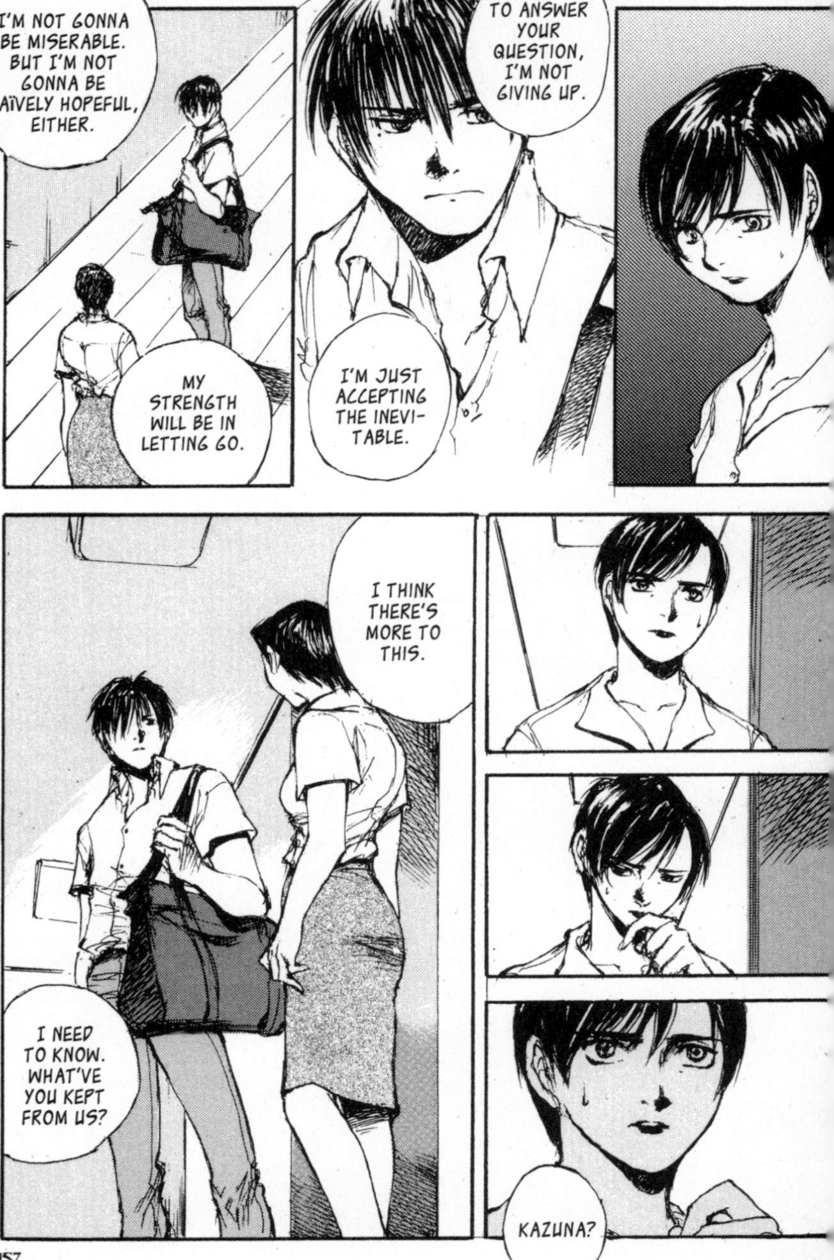
TO ANSWER YOUR QUESTION, I'M NOT GIVING UP.
I'M JUST ACCEPTING THE INEVI-TABLE.
I'M NOT GONNA BE MISERABLE. BUT I'M NOT GONNA BE NAÏVELY HOPEFUL, EITHER.
MY STRENGTH WILL BE IN LETTING GO.
KAZUNA?
I THINK THERE'S MORE TO THIS.
I NEED TO KNOW. WHAT'VE YOU KEPT FROM US?

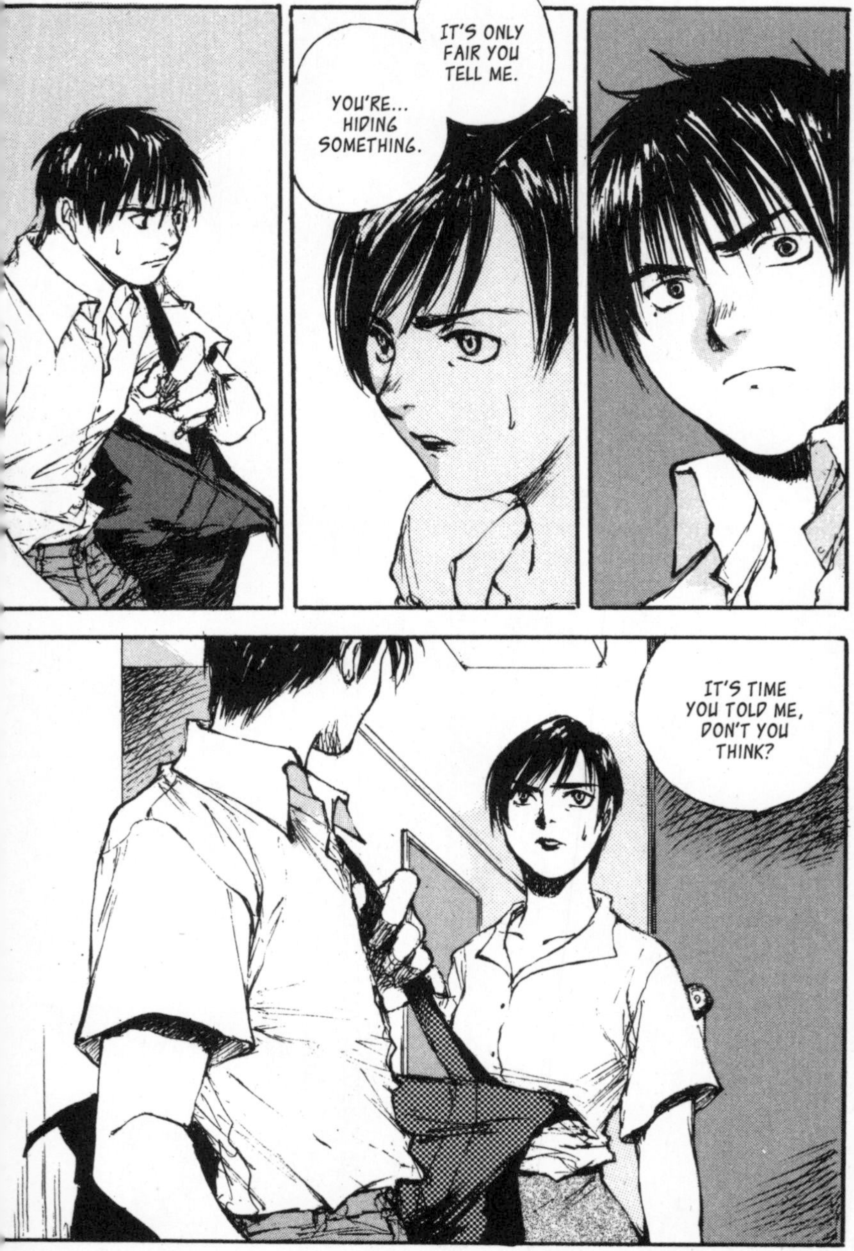
IT'S ONLY FAIR YOU TELL ME.
YOU'RE... HIDING SOMETHING.
IT'S TIME YOU TOLD ME, DON'T YOU THINK?

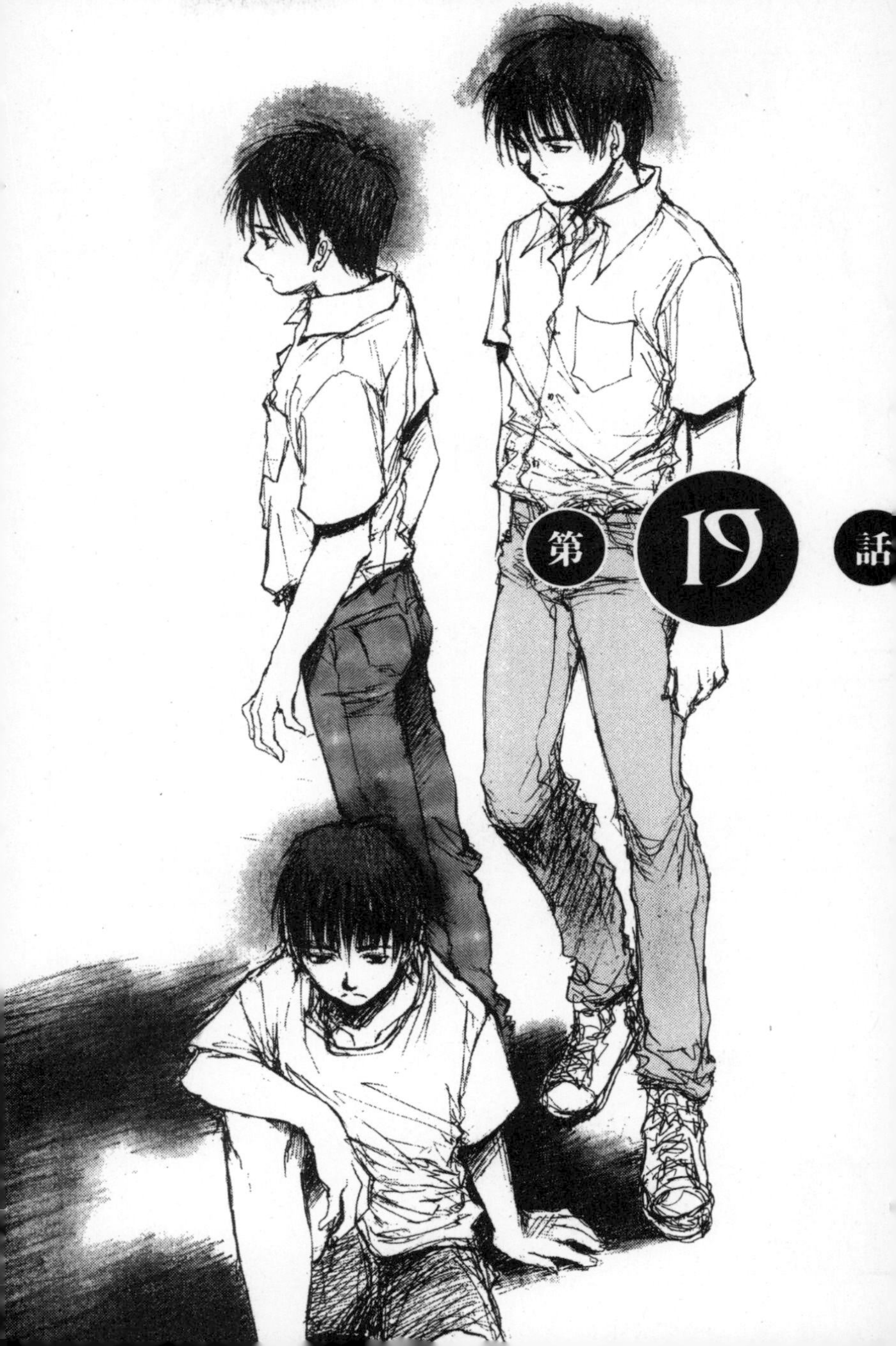
第19話

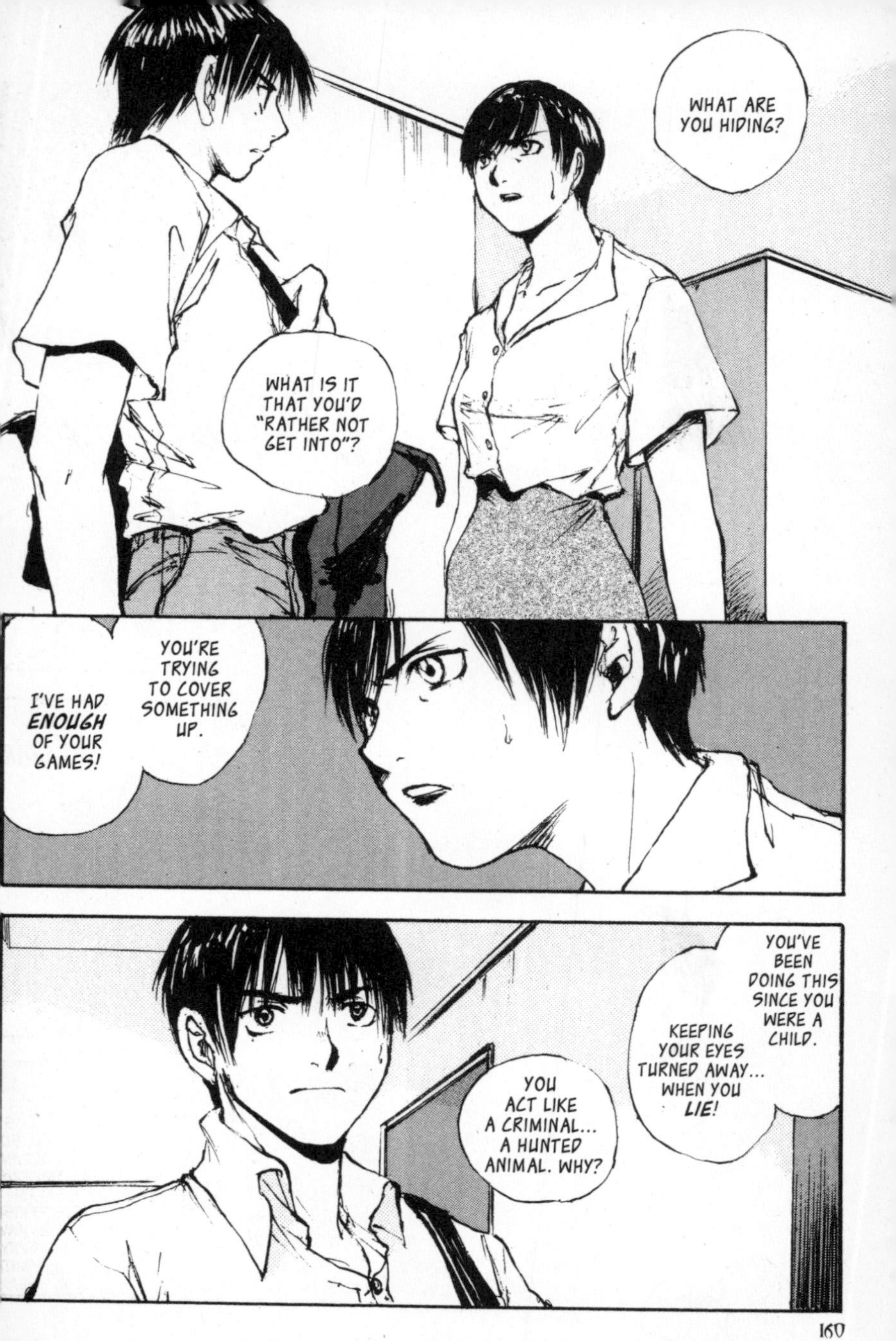
WHAT ARE YOU HIDING?
WHAT IS IT THAT YOU'D "RATHER NOT GET INTO"?
YOU'RE TRYING TO COVER SOMETHING UP.
I'VE HAD ENOUGH OF YOUR GAMES!
YOU'VE BEEN DOING THIS SINCE YOU WERE A CHILD.
KEEPING YOUR EYES TURNED AWAY... WHEN YOU LIE!
YOU ACT LIKE A CRIMINAL... A HUNTED ANIMAL. WHY?

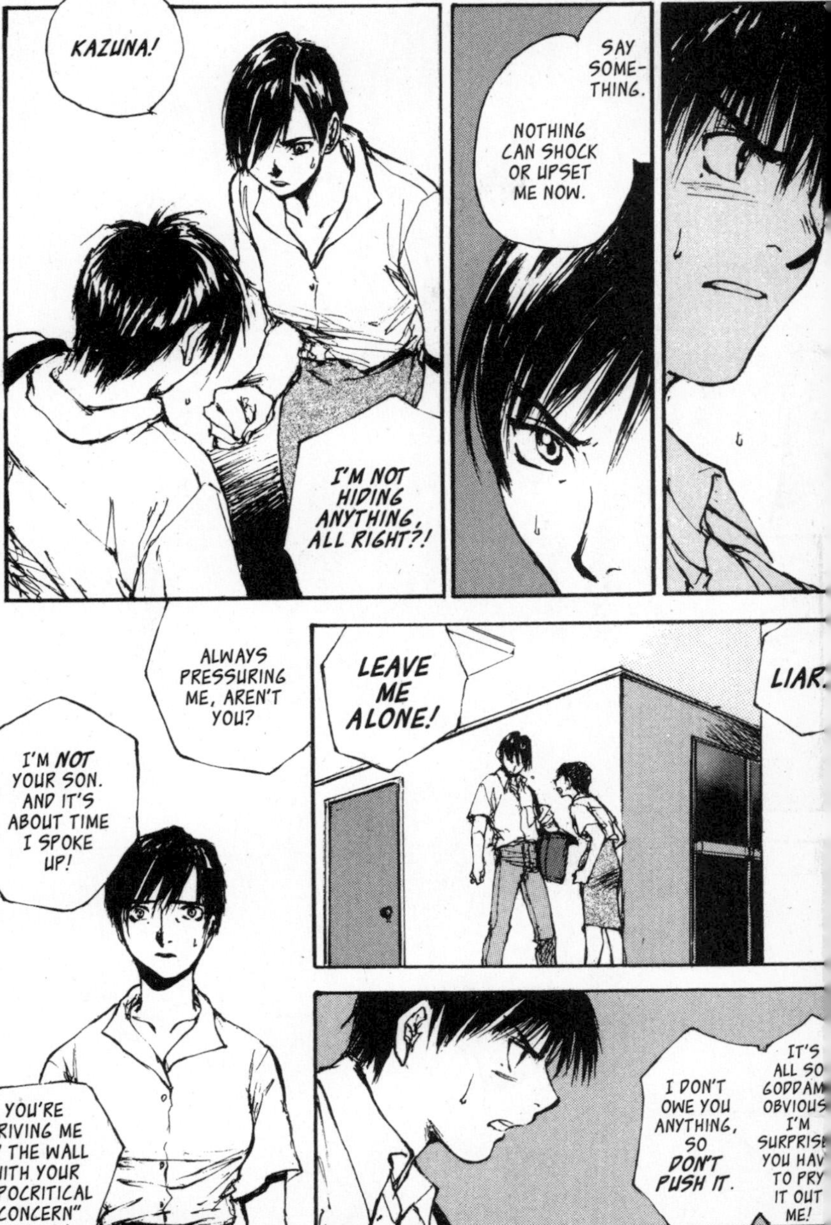
SAY SOME- THING.
NOTHING CAN SHOCK OR UPSET ME NOW.
KAZUNA!
I'M NOT HIDING ANYTHING, ALL RIGHT?!
LIAR.
LEAVE ME ALONE!
ALWAYS PRESSURING ME, AREN'T YOU?
IT'S ALL SO GODDAM OBVIOUS I'M SURPRISE YOU HAV TO PRY IT OUT ME!
I DON'T OWE YOU ANYTHING, SO DON'T PUSH IT.
I'M NOT YOUR SON. AND IT'S ABOUT TIME I SPOKE UP!
YOU'RE DRIVING ME UP THE WALL WITH YOUR HYPOCRITICAL "CONCERN" FOR ME!

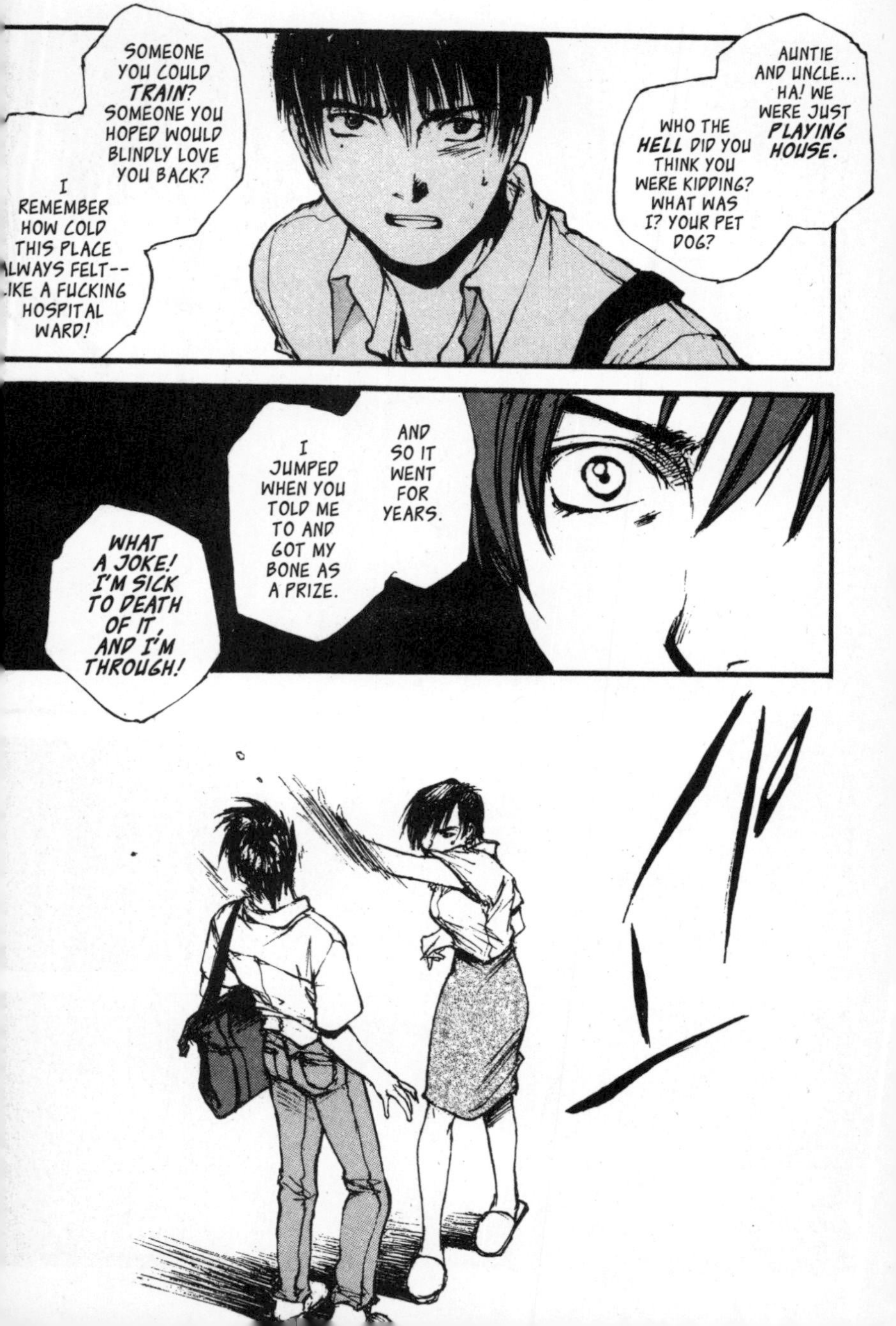
AUNTIE AND UNCLE... HA! WE WERE JUST PLAYING HOUSE.
WHO THE HELL DID YOU THINK YOU WERE KIDDING? WHAT WAS I? YOUR PET DOG?
SOMEONE YOU COULD TRAIN? SOMEONE YOU HOPED WOULD BLINDLY LOVE YOU BACK?
I REMEMBER HOW COLD THIS PLACE LWAYS FELT-- IKE A FUCKING HOSPITAL WARD!
AND SO IT WENT FOR YEARS.
I JUMPED WHEN YOU TOLD ME TO AND GOT MY BONE AS A PRIZE.
WHAT A JOKE! I'M SICK TO DEATH OF IT, AND I'M THROUGH!

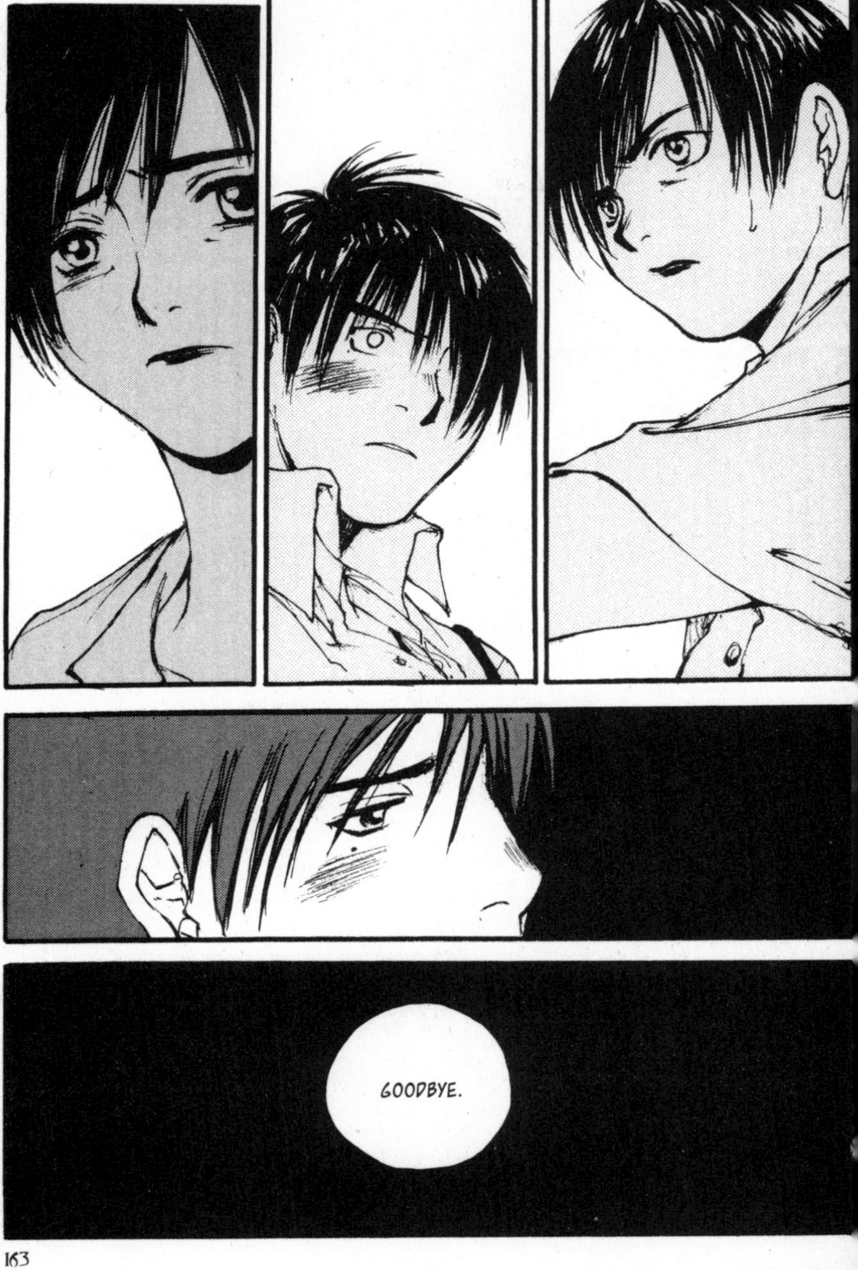
GOODBYE.

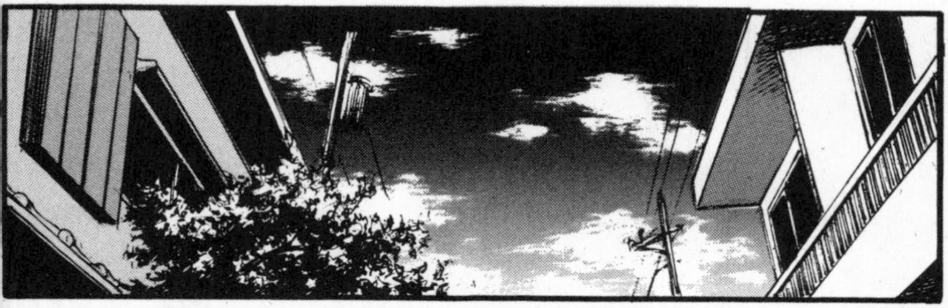

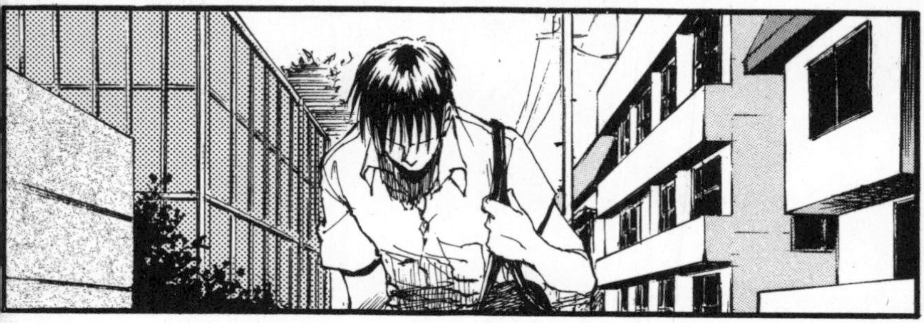

Sorry.

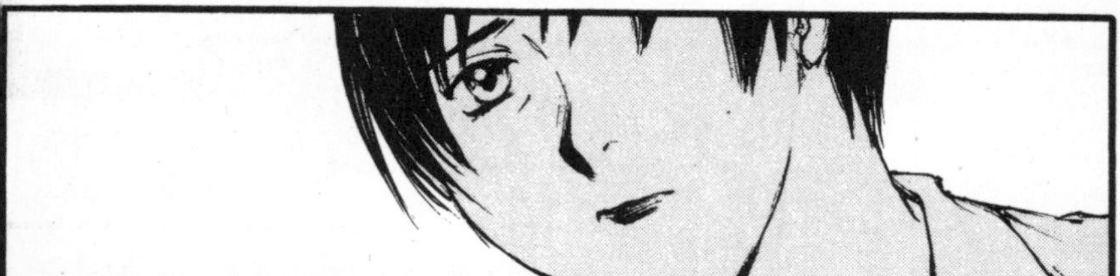

I'm sorry.

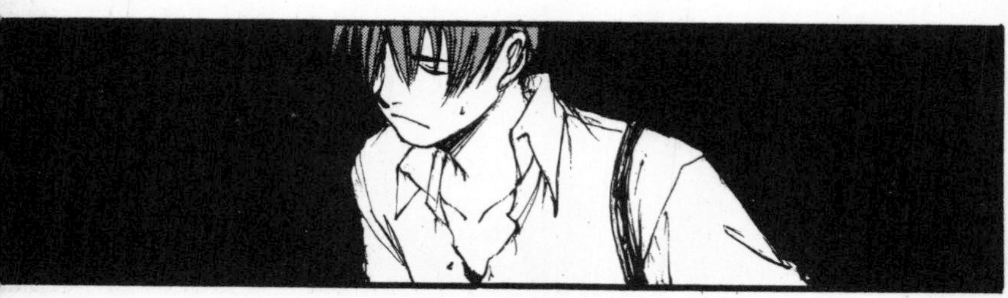

I didn't mean it.
Not <u>all</u> of it, anyway.

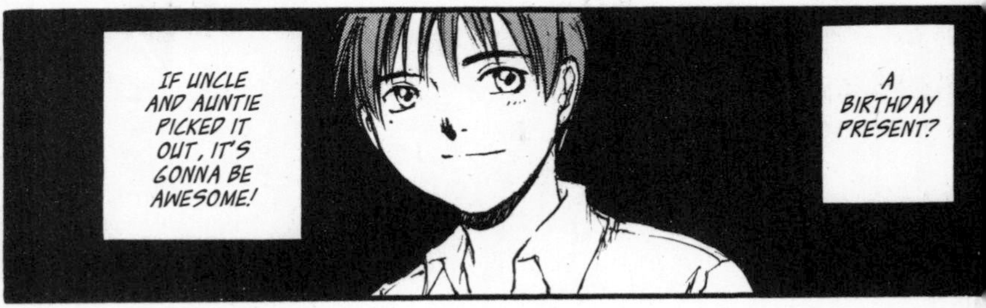
A BIRTHDAY PRESENT?
IF UNCLE AND AUNTIE PICKED IT OUT, IT'S GONNA BE AWESOME!

My past...

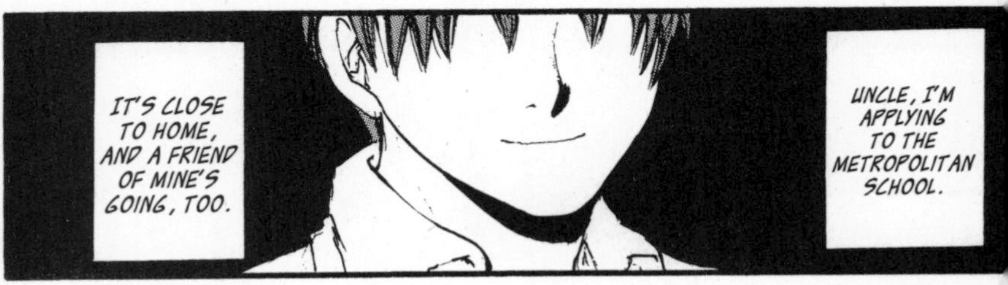
UNCLE, I'M APPLYING TO THE METROPOLITAN SCHOOL.
IT'S CLOSE TO HOME, AND A FRIEND OF MINE'S GOING, TOO.

...is now a life I must keep buried forever.

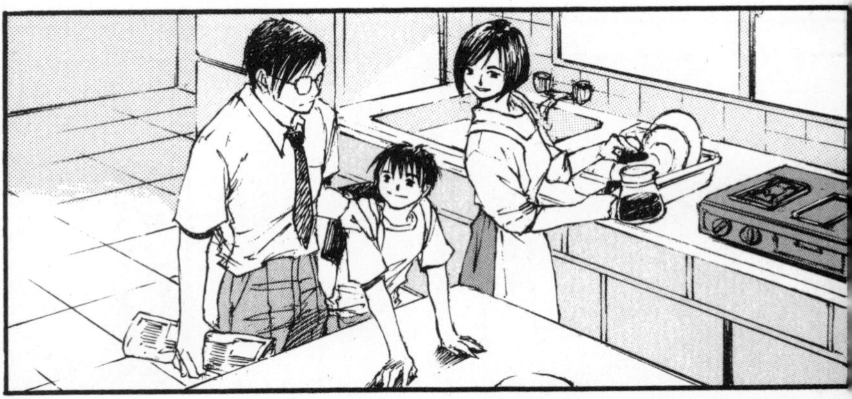

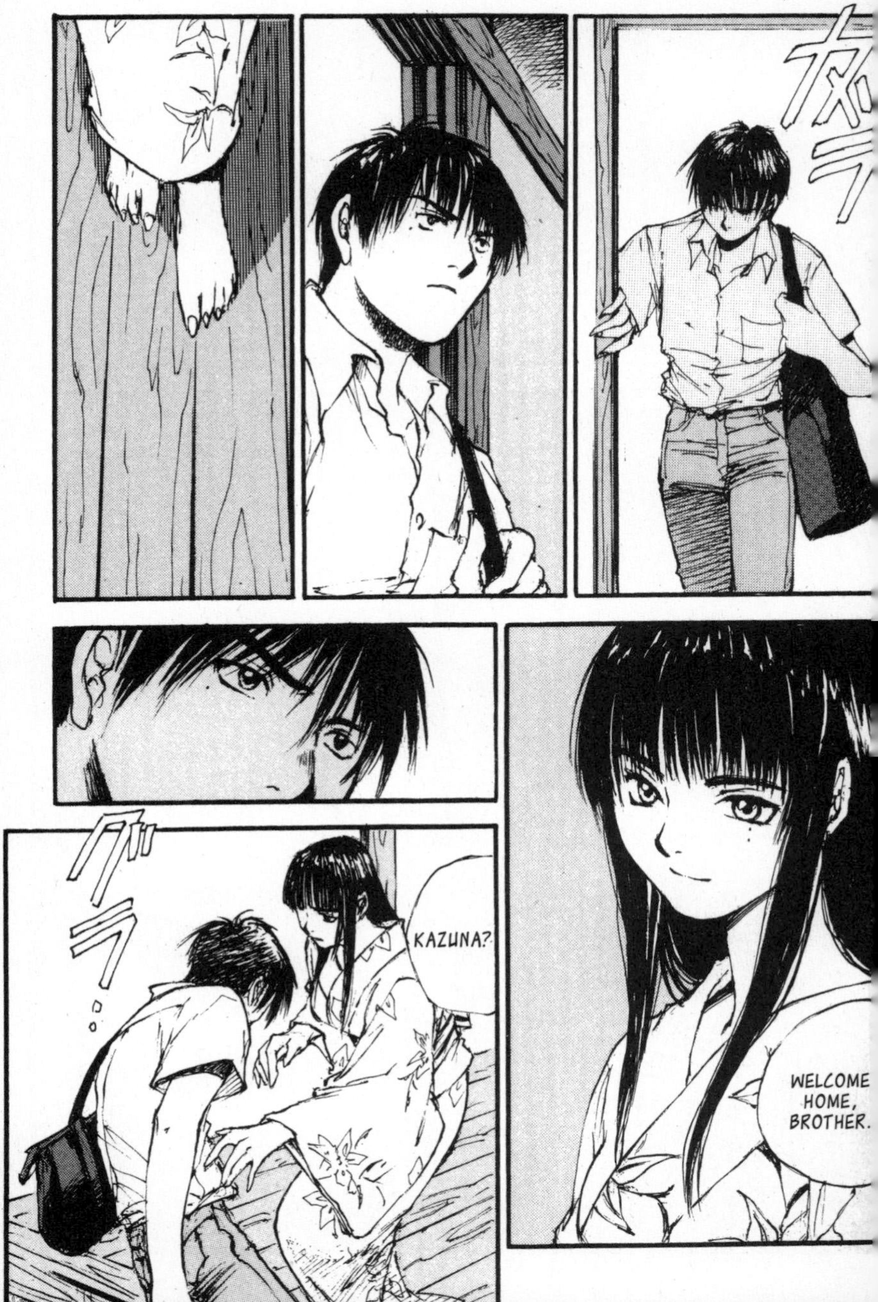
ガラ
WELCOME HOME, BROTHER.
KAZUNA?
グラ…

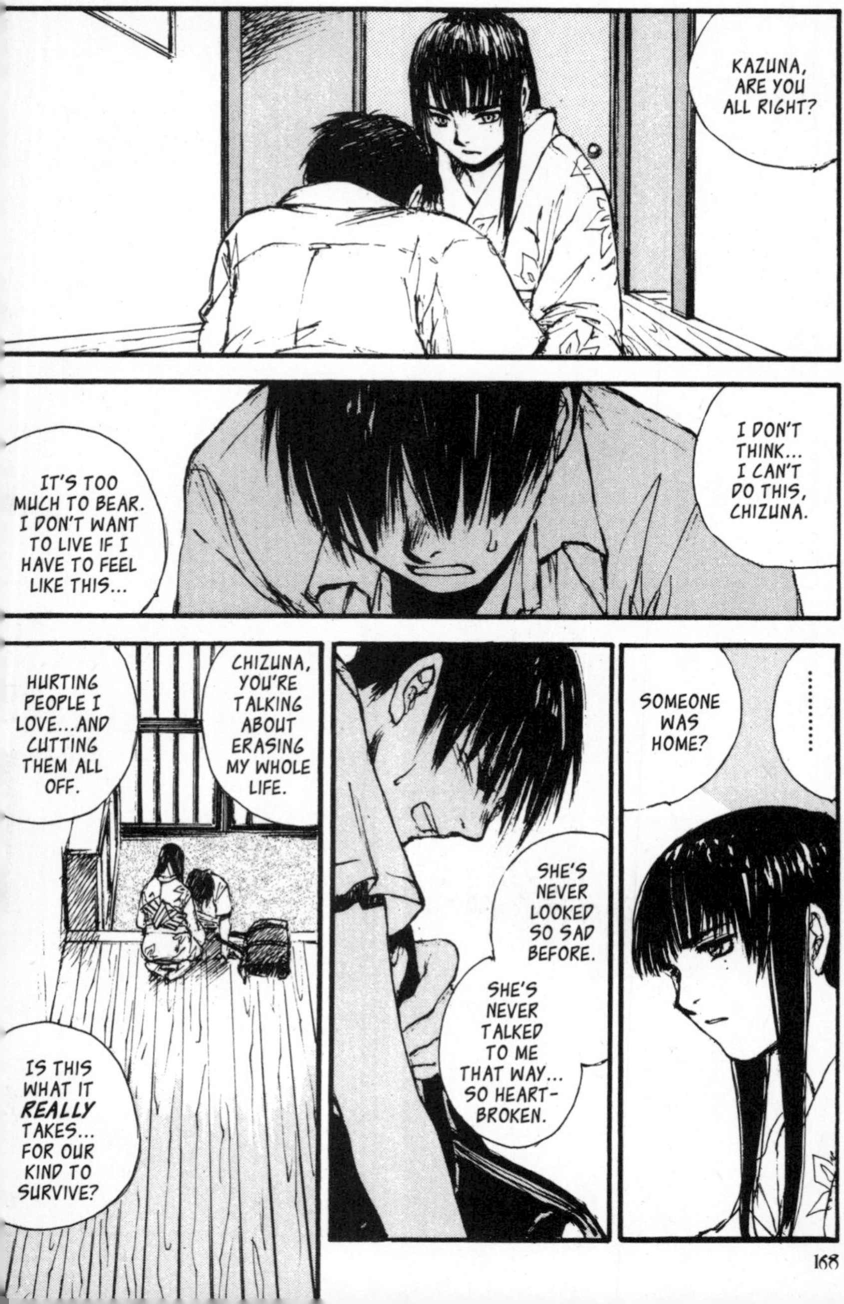
KAZUNA, ARE YOU ALL RIGHT?
I DON'T THINK... I CAN'T DO THIS, CHIZUNA.
IT'S TOO MUCH TO BEAR. I DON'T WANT TO LIVE IF I HAVE TO FEEL LIKE THIS...
....
SOMEONE WAS HOME?
SHE'S NEVER LOOKED SO SAD BEFORE.
SHE'S NEVER TALKED TO ME THAT WAY... SO HEART-BROKEN.
CHIZUNA, YOU'RE TALKING ABOUT ERASING MY WHOLE LIFE.
HURTING PEOPLE I LOVE...AND CUTTING THEM ALL OFF.
IS THIS WHAT IT *REALLY* TAKES... FOR OUR KIND TO SURVIVE?

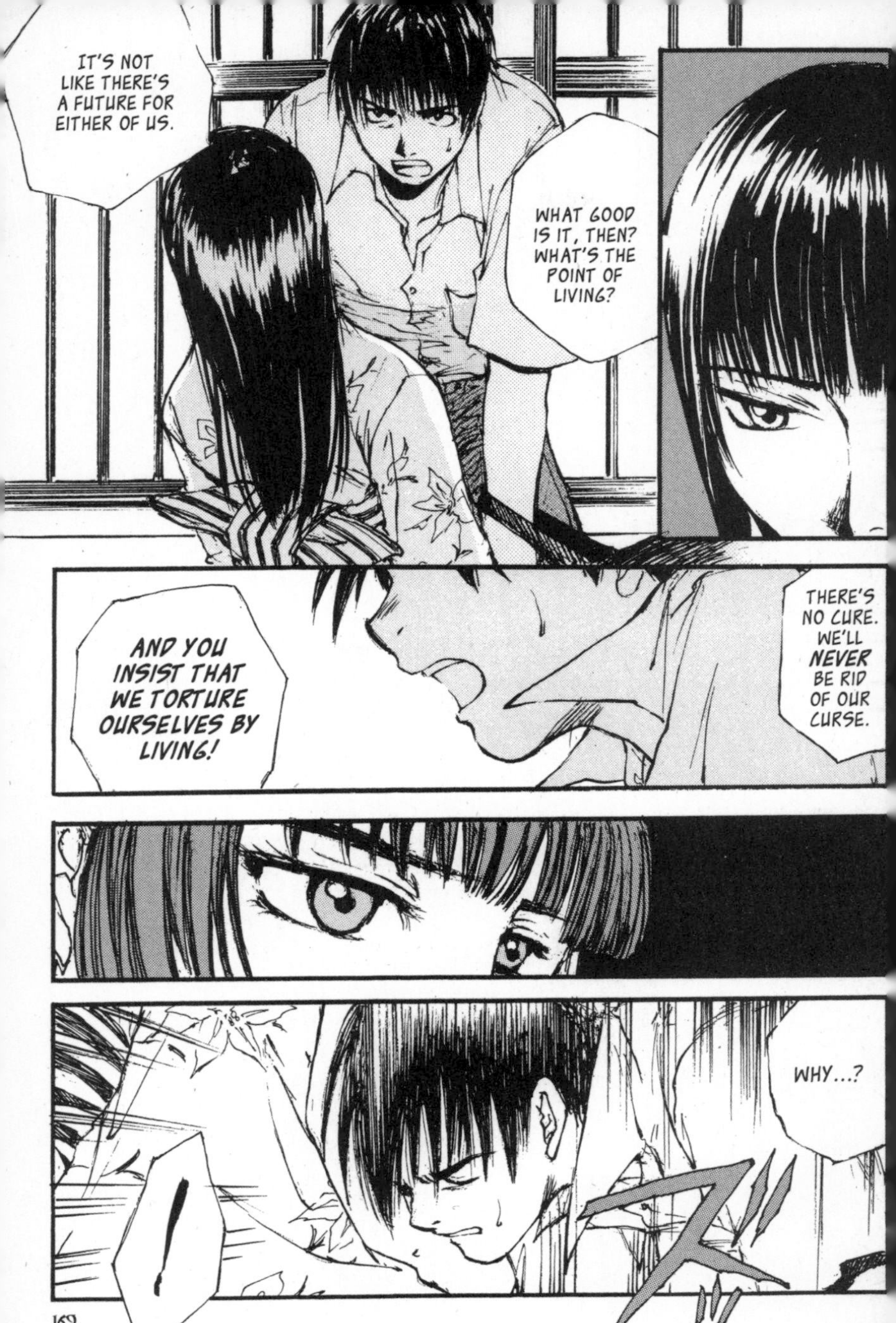
IT'S NOT LIKE THERE'S A FUTURE FOR EITHER OF US.
WHAT GOOD IS IT, THEN? WHAT'S THE POINT OF LIVING?
THERE'S NO CURE. WE'LL **NEVER** BE RID OF OUR CURSE.
AND YOU INSIST THAT WE TORTURE OURSELVES BY LIVING!
WHY...?
!

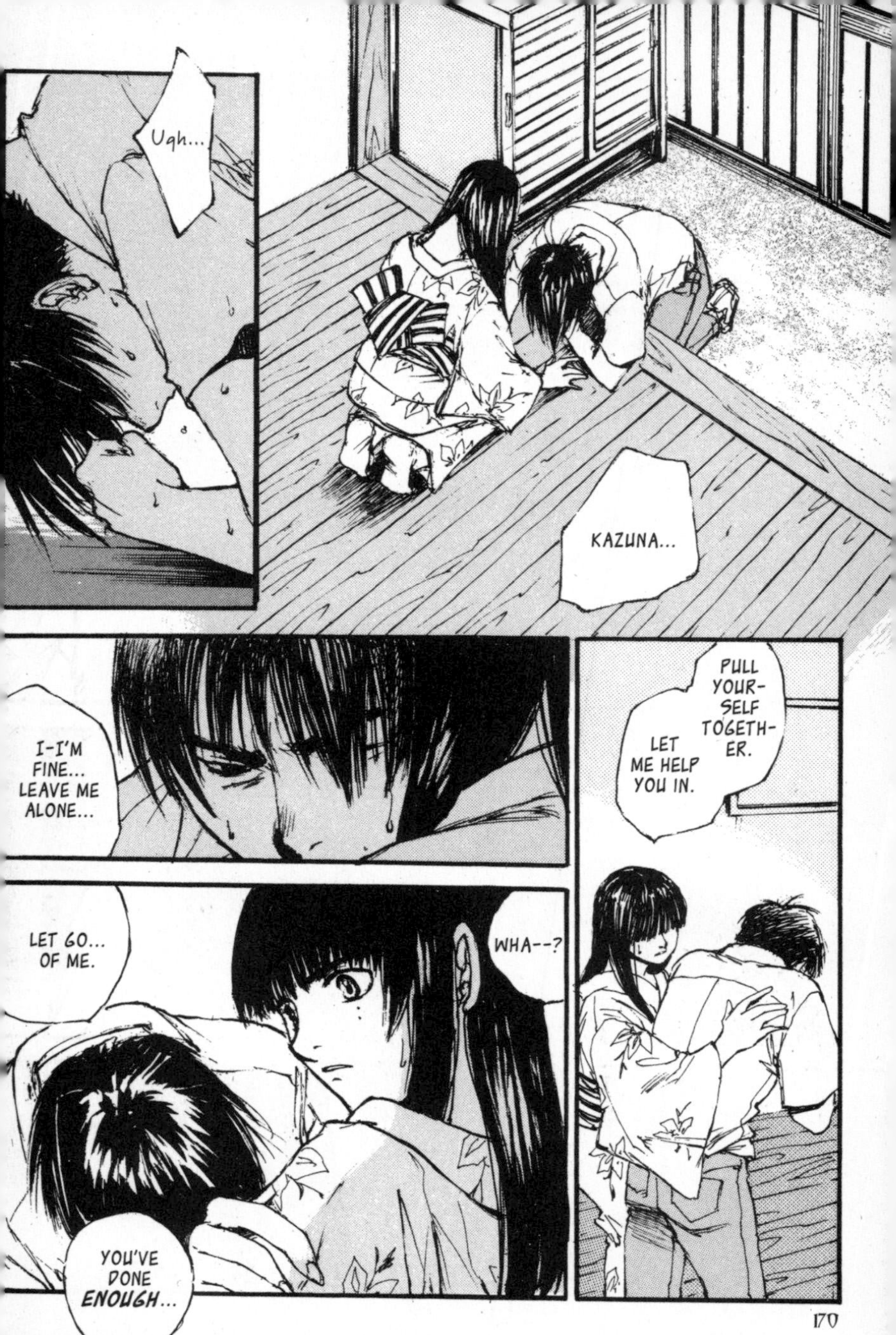
Ugh...
KAZUNA...
PULL YOURSELF TOGETHER.
LET ME HELP YOU IN.
I-I'M FINE... LEAVE ME ALONE...
WHA--?
LET GO... OF ME.
YOU'VE DONE **ENOUGH**...

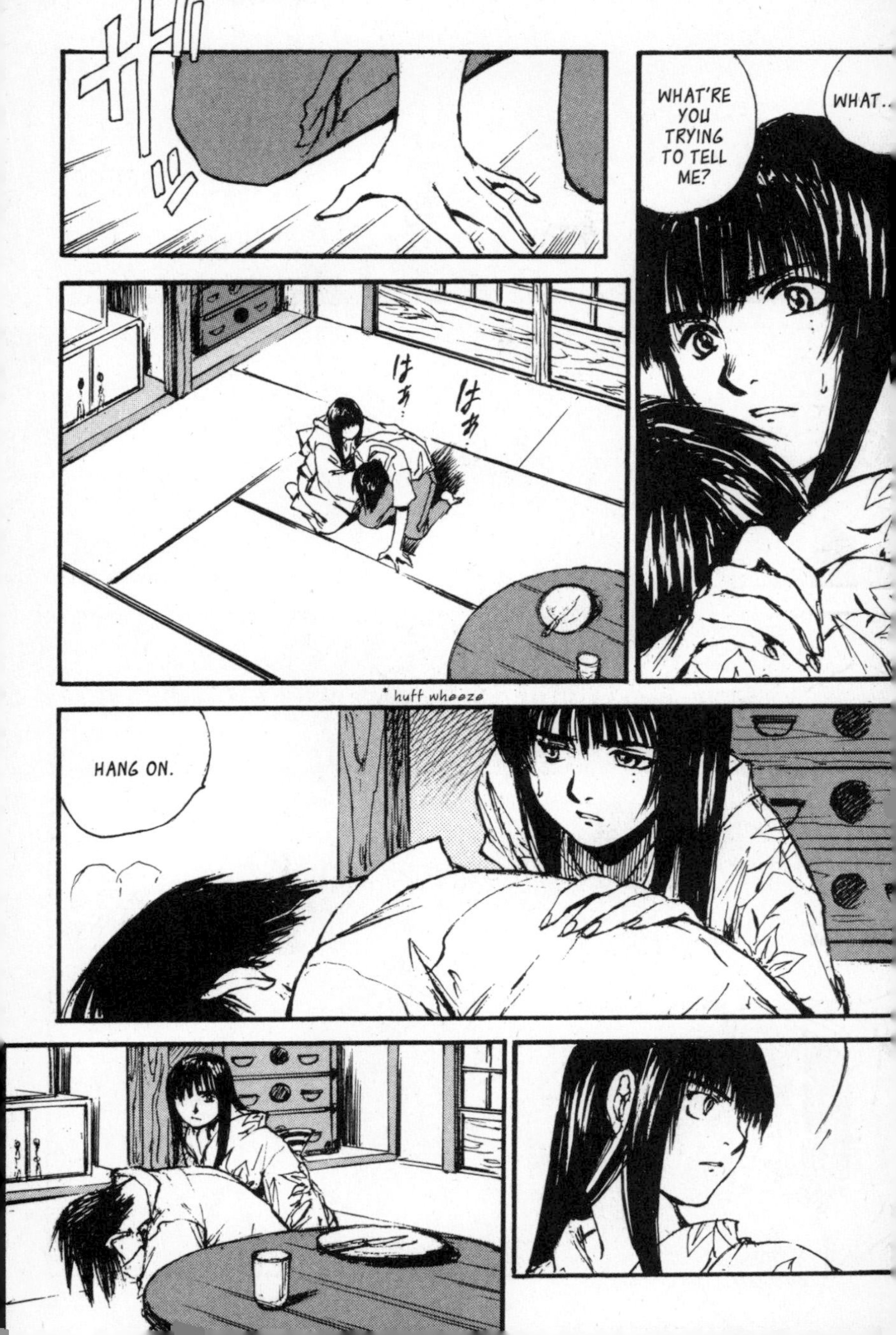
WHAT...
WHAT'RE YOU TRYING TO TELL ME?
はぁ… はぁ…
* huff wheeze
HANG ON.

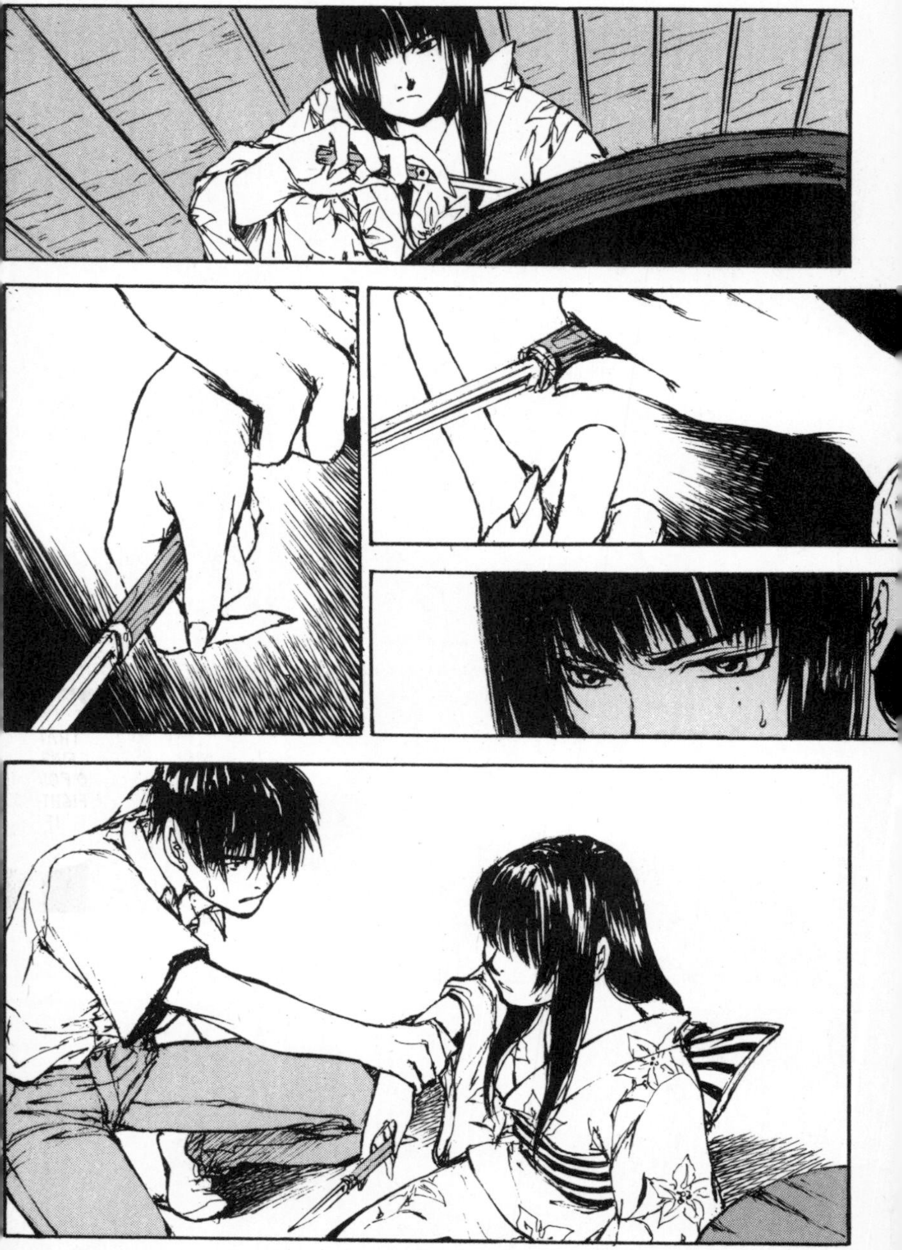

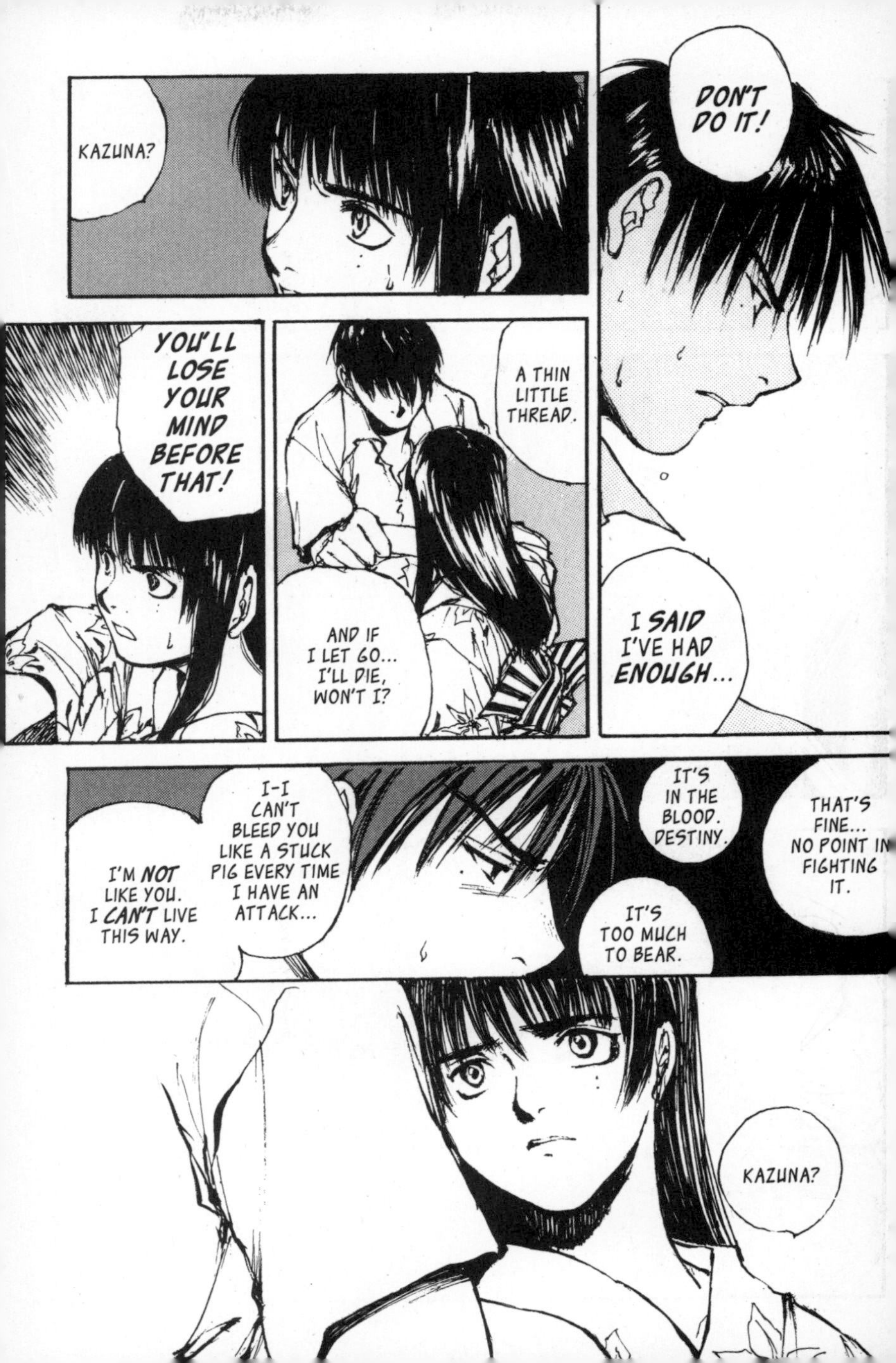
DON'T DO IT!
I SAID I'VE HAD ENOUGH...
KAZUNA?
A THIN LITTLE THREAD.
AND IF I LET GO... I'LL DIE, WON'T I?
YOU'LL LOSE YOUR MIND BEFORE THAT!
THAT'S FINE... NO POINT IN FIGHTING IT.
IT'S IN THE BLOOD. DESTINY.
IT'S TOO MUCH TO BEAR.
I-I CAN'T BLEED YOU LIKE A STUCK PIG EVERY TIME I HAVE AN ATTACK...
I'M NOT LIKE YOU. I CAN'T LIVE THIS WAY.
KAZUNA?

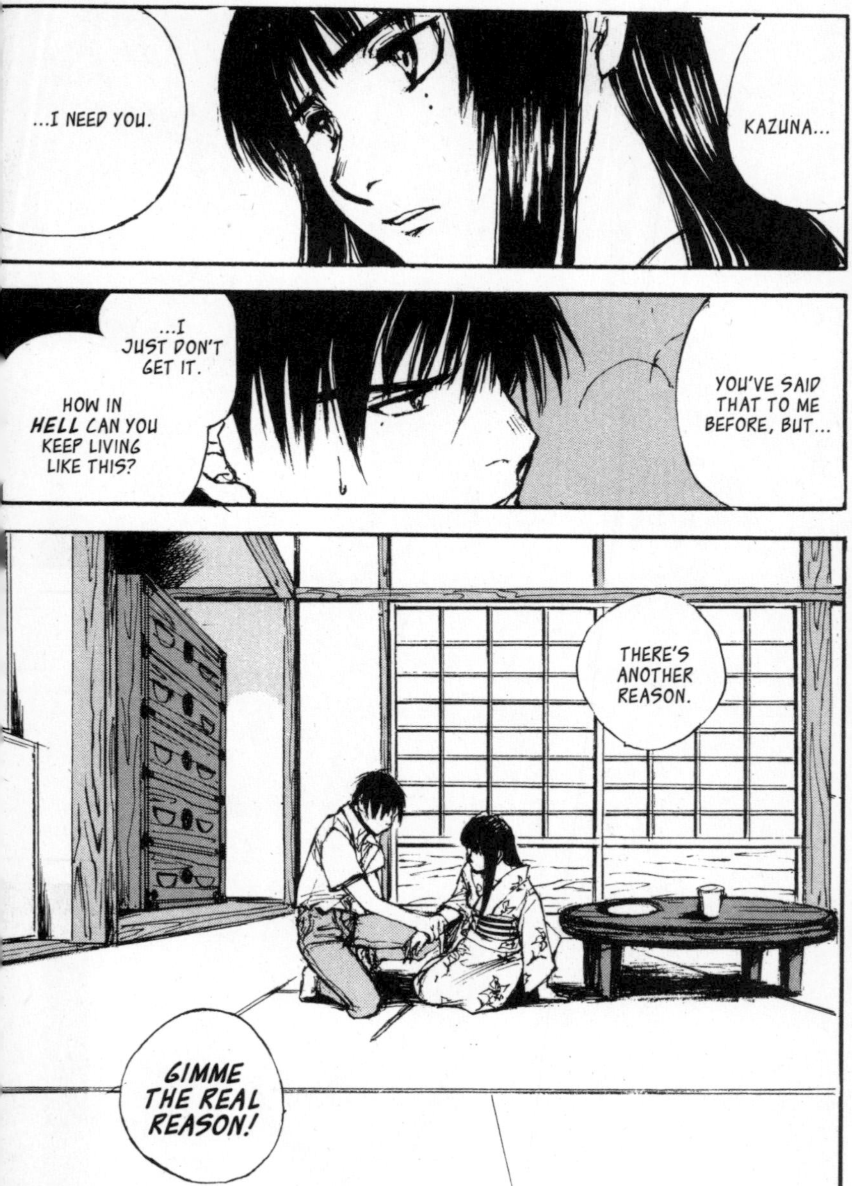
KAZUNA...
...I NEED YOU.
YOU'VE SAID THAT TO ME BEFORE, BUT...
...I JUST DON'T GET IT.
HOW IN **HELL** CAN YOU KEEP LIVING LIKE THIS?
THERE'S ANOTHER REASON.
GIMME THE REAL REASON!

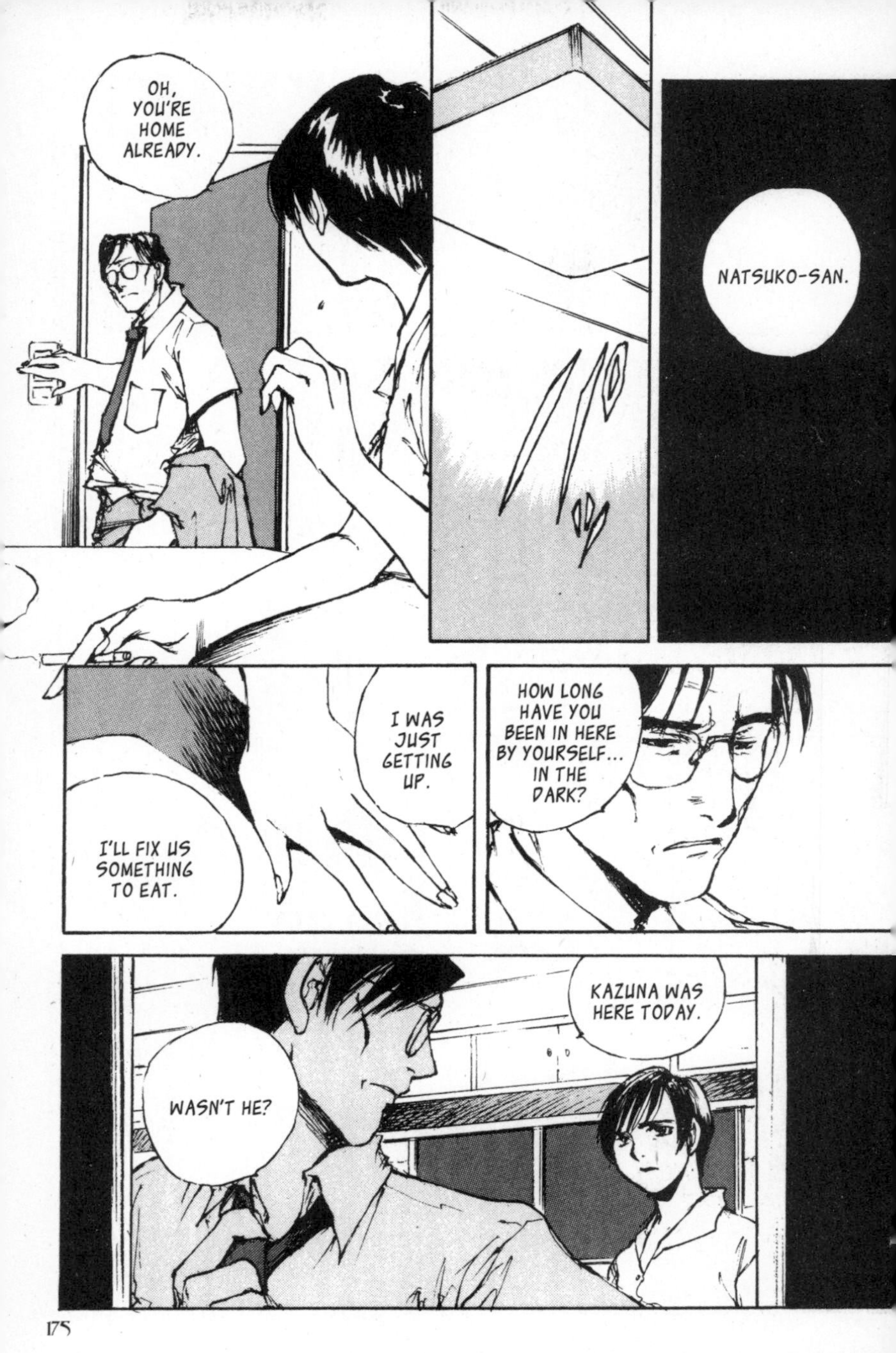
NATSUKO-SAN.
OH, YOU'RE HOME ALREADY.
HOW LONG HAVE YOU BEEN IN HERE BY YOURSELF... IN THE DARK?
I WAS JUST GETTING UP.
I'LL FIX US SOMETHING TO EAT.
KAZUNA WAS HERE TODAY.
WASN'T HE?

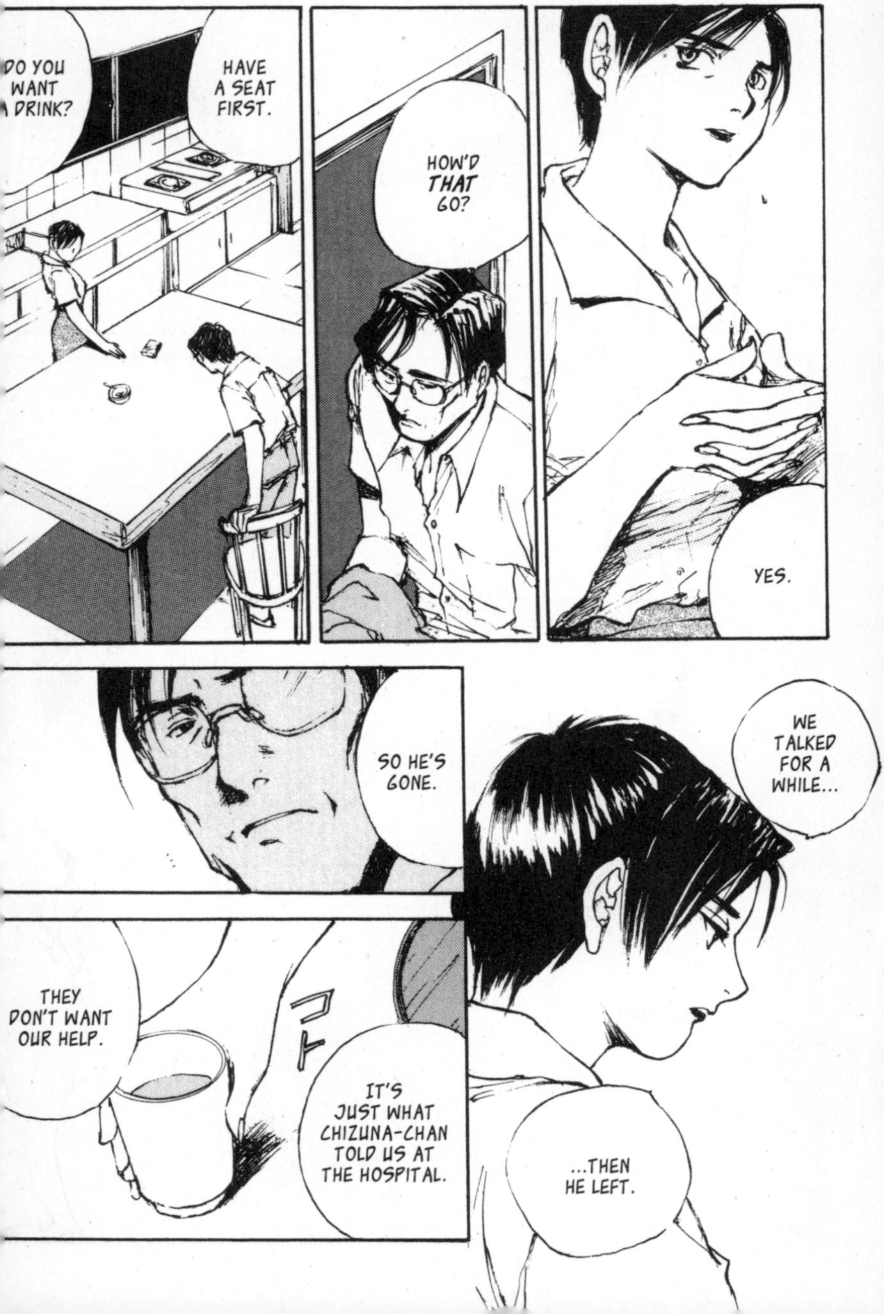
DO YOU WANT A DRINK?
HAVE A SEAT FIRST.
HOW'D *THAT* GO?
YES.
SO HE'S GONE.
WE TALKED FOR A WHILE...
...THEN HE LEFT.
THEY DON'T WANT OUR HELP.
コト
IT'S JUST WHAT CHIZUNA-CHAN TOLD US AT THE HOSPITAL.

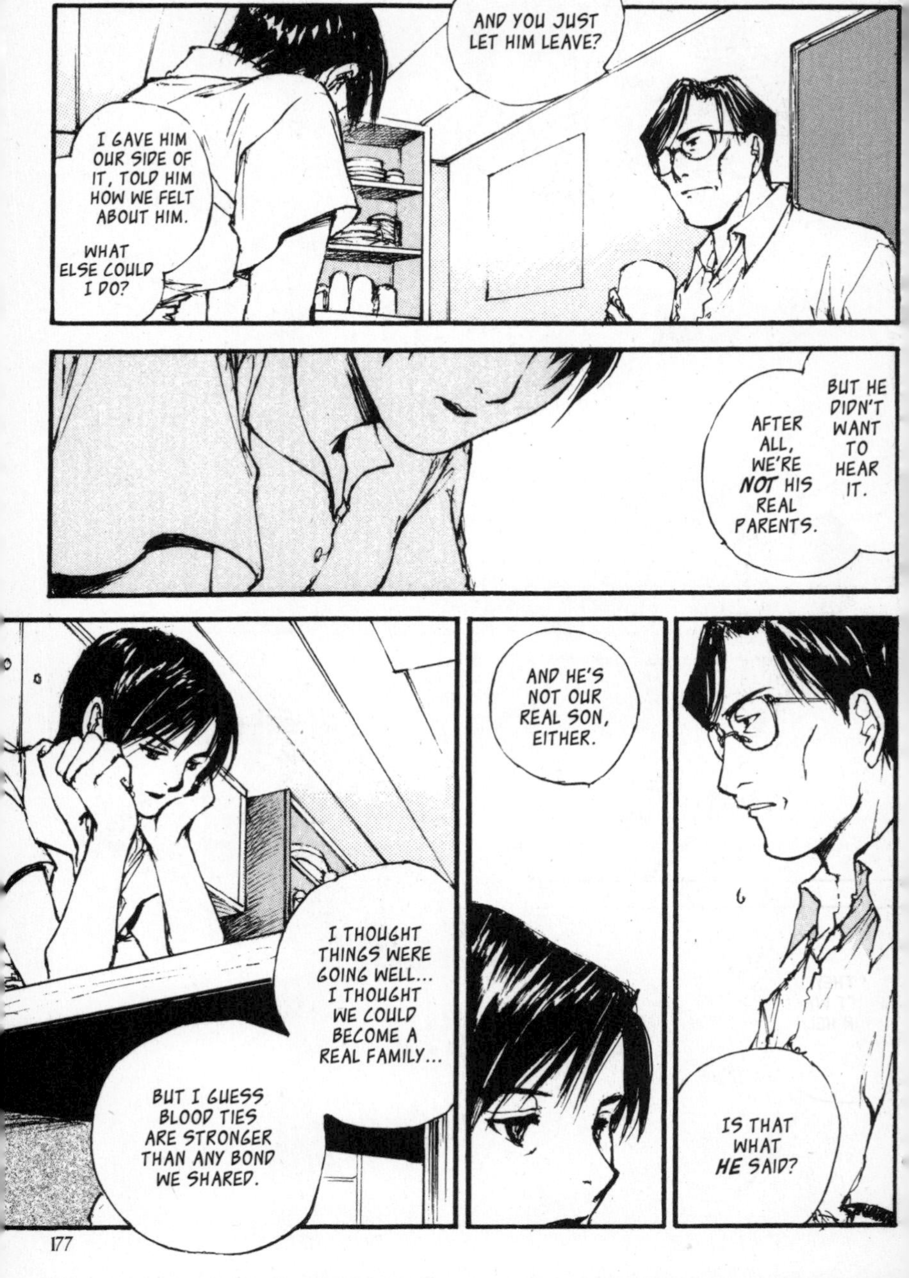
AND YOU JUST LET HIM LEAVE?
I GAVE HIM OUR SIDE OF IT, TOLD HIM HOW WE FELT ABOUT HIM.
WHAT ELSE COULD I DO?
BUT HE DIDN'T WANT TO HEAR IT.
AFTER ALL, WE'RE ***NOT*** HIS REAL PARENTS.
I THOUGHT THINGS WERE GOING WELL... I THOUGHT WE COULD BECOME A REAL FAMILY...
BUT I GUESS BLOOD TIES ARE STRONGER THAN ANY BOND WE SHARED.
AND HE'S NOT OUR REAL SON, EITHER.
IS THAT WHAT ***HE*** SAID?

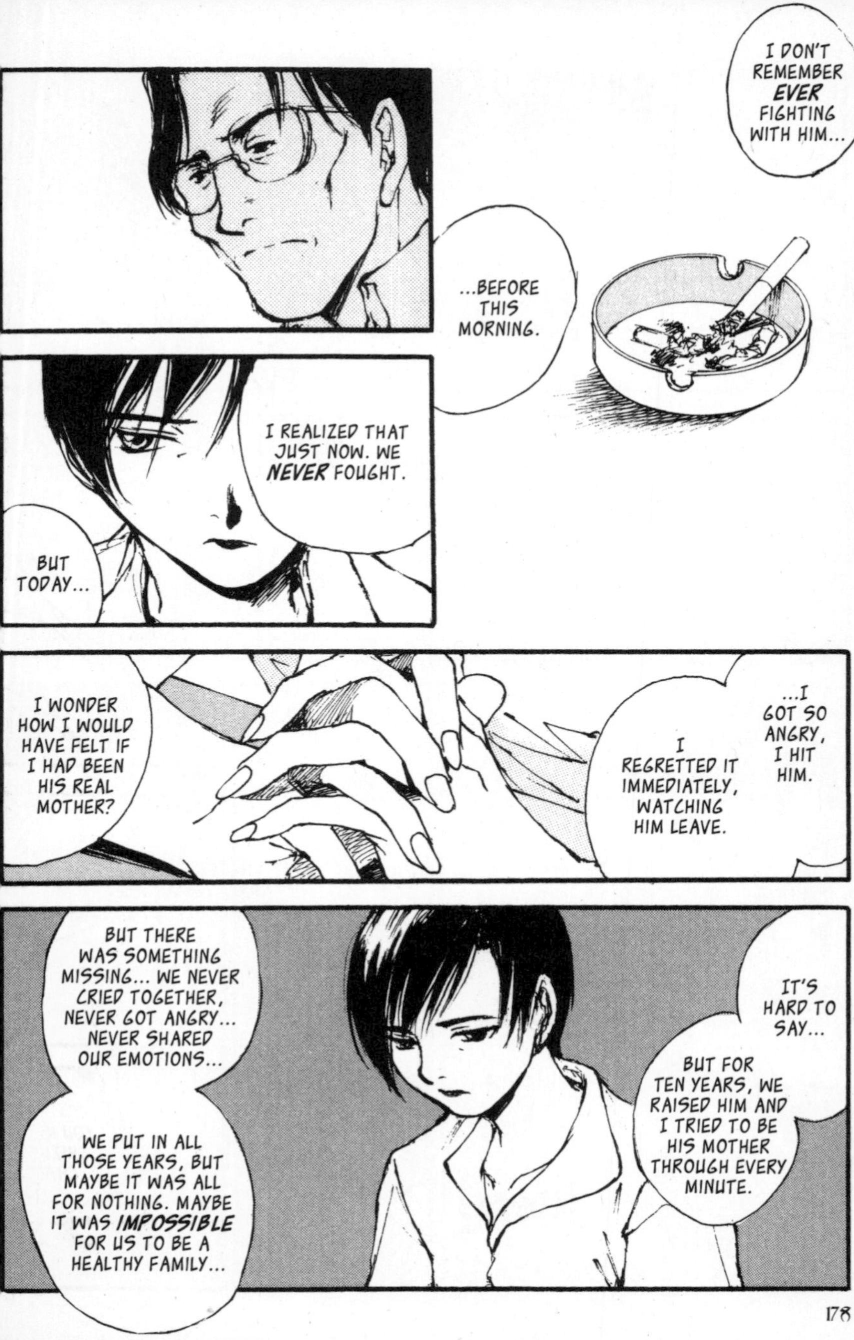
I DON'T REMEMBER ***EVER*** FIGHTING WITH HIM...
...BEFORE THIS MORNING.
I REALIZED THAT JUST NOW. WE ***NEVER*** FOUGHT.
BUT TODAY...
...I GOT SO ANGRY, I HIT HIM.
I REGRETTED IT IMMEDIATELY, WATCHING HIM LEAVE.
I WONDER HOW I WOULD HAVE FELT IF I HAD BEEN HIS REAL MOTHER?
IT'S HARD TO SAY...
BUT FOR TEN YEARS, WE RAISED HIM AND I TRIED TO BE HIS MOTHER THROUGH EVERY MINUTE.
BUT THERE WAS SOMETHING MISSING... WE NEVER CRIED TOGETHER, NEVER GOT ANGRY... NEVER SHARED OUR EMOTIONS...
WE PUT IN ALL THOSE YEARS, BUT MAYBE IT WAS ALL FOR NOTHING. MAYBE IT WAS ***IMPOSSIBLE*** FOR US TO BE A HEALTHY FAMILY...

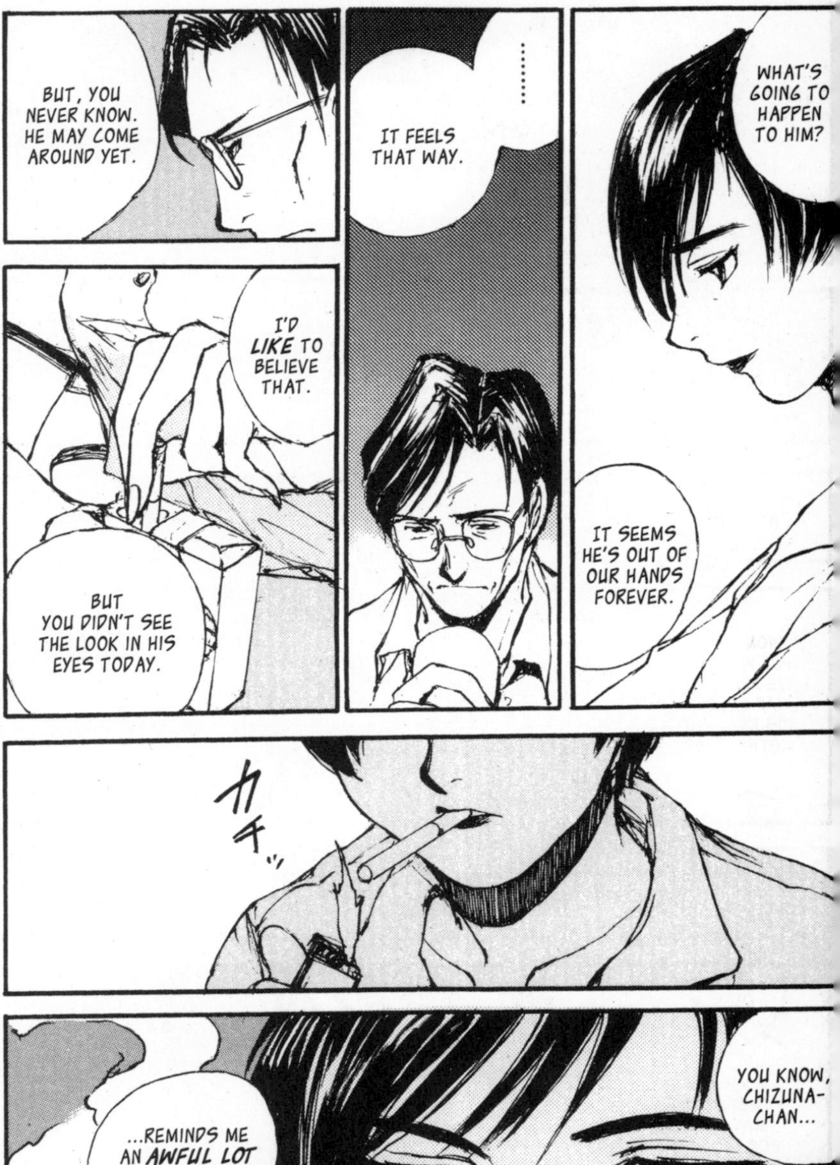
WHAT'S GOING TO HAPPEN TO HIM?
IT SEEMS HE'S OUT OF OUR HANDS FOREVER.
......
IT FEELS THAT WAY.
BUT, YOU NEVER KNOW. HE MAY COME AROUND YET.
I'D *LIKE* TO BELIEVE THAT.
BUT YOU DIDN'T SEE THE LOOK IN HIS EYES TODAY.
カチッ
YOU KNOW, CHIZUNA-CHAN...
...REMINDS ME AN *AWFUL LOT* OF MOMOKO-SAN...

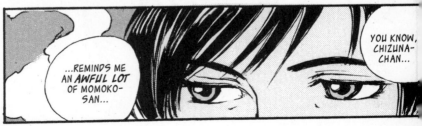

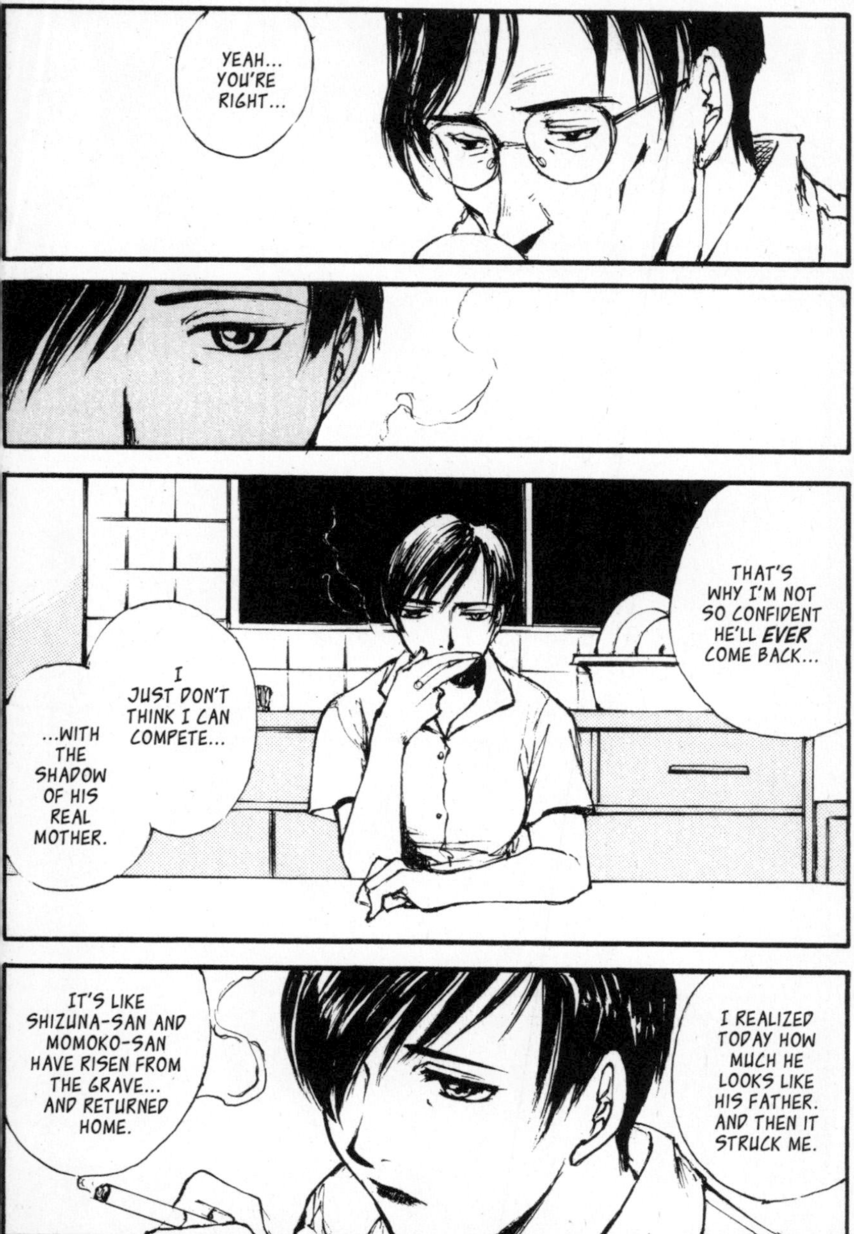
YEAH... YOU'RE RIGHT...
THAT'S WHY I'M NOT SO CONFIDENT HE'LL *EVER* COME BACK...
I JUST DON'T THINK I CAN COMPETE...
...WITH THE SHADOW OF HIS REAL MOTHER.
I REALIZED TODAY HOW MUCH HE LOOKS LIKE HIS FATHER. AND THEN IT STRUCK ME.
IT'S LIKE SHIZUNA-SAN AND MOMOKO-SAN HAVE RISEN FROM THE GRAVE... AND RETURNED HOME.

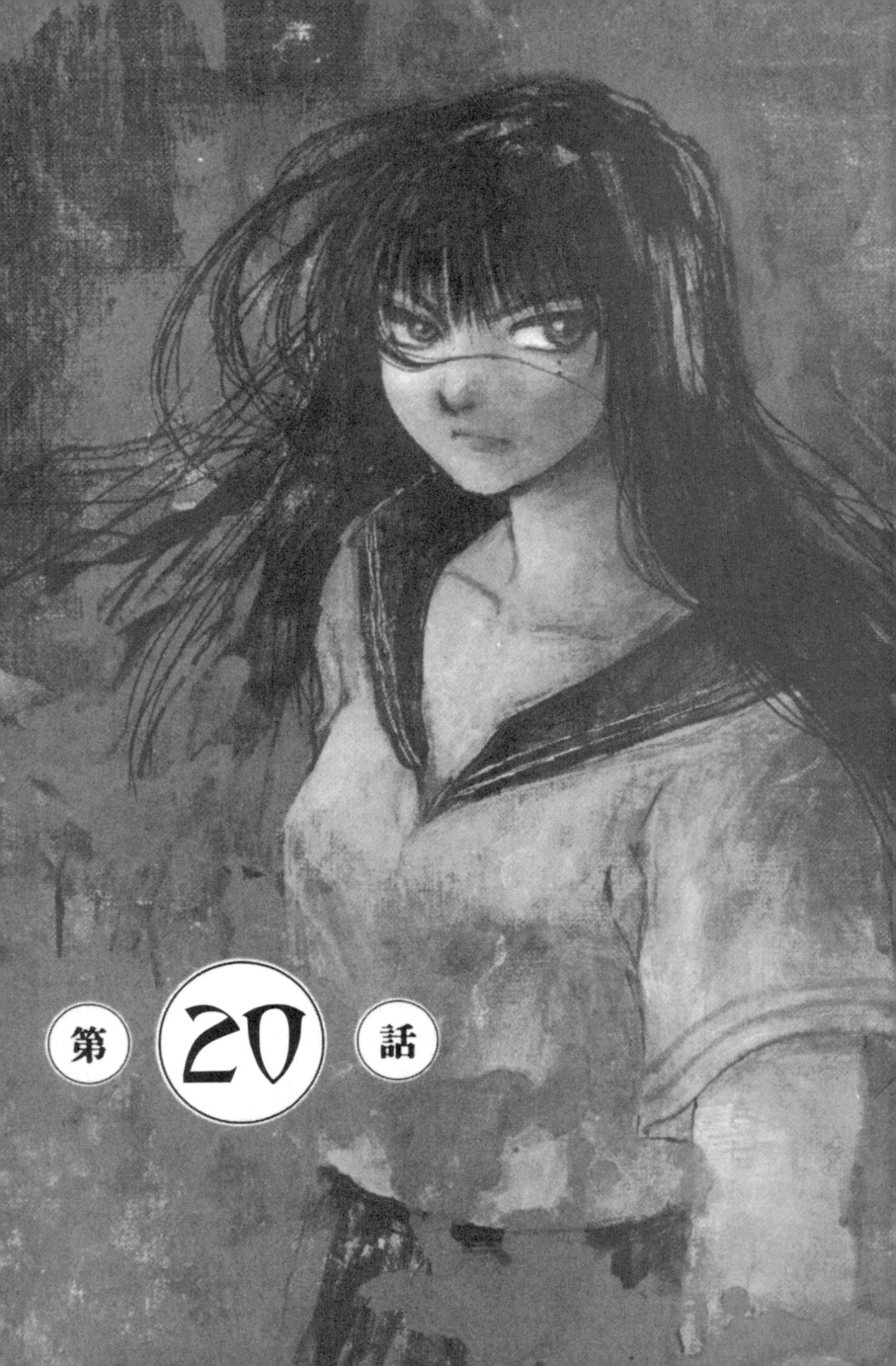
第 20 話

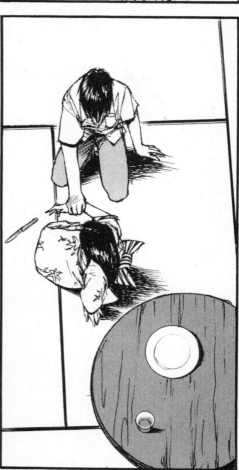

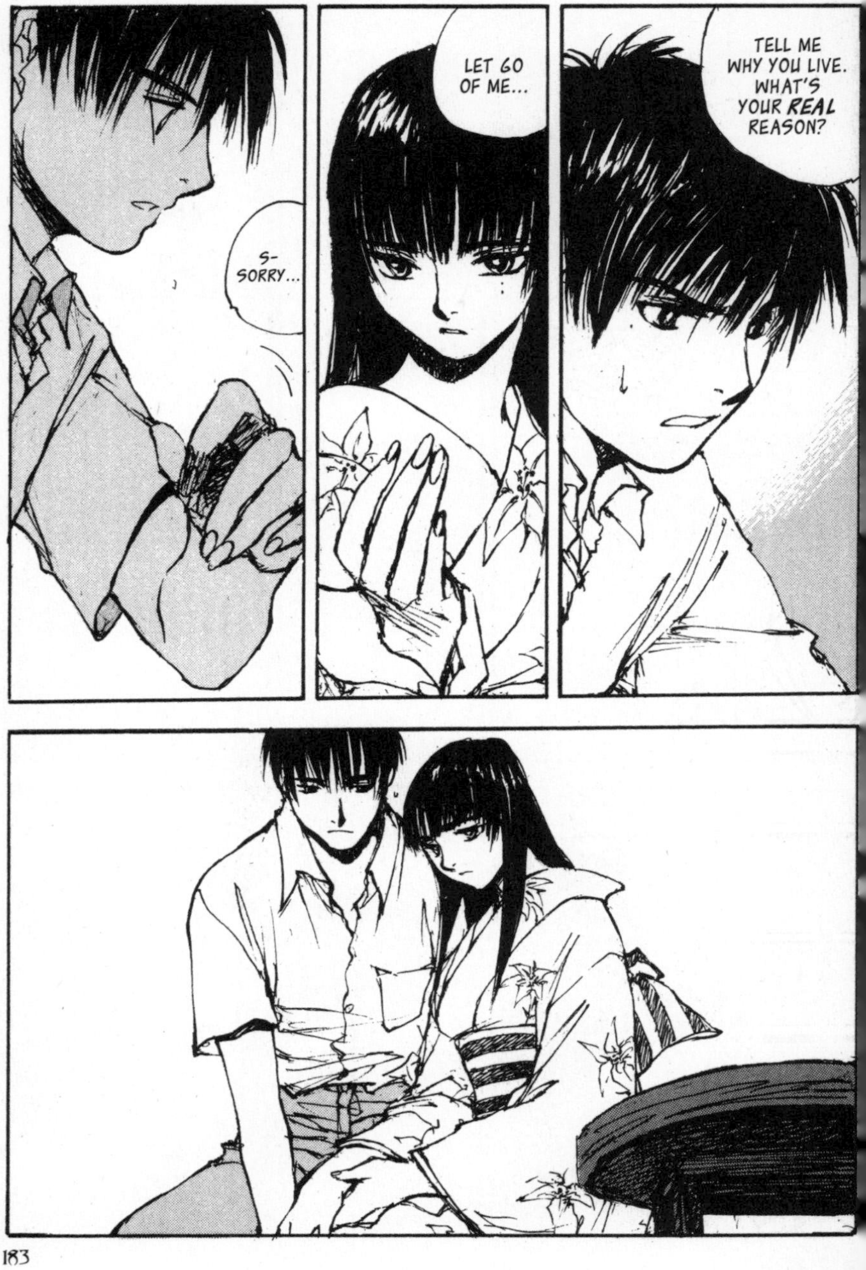
TELL ME WHY YOU LIVE. WHAT'S YOUR ***REAL*** REASON?
LET GO OF ME...
S-SORRY...

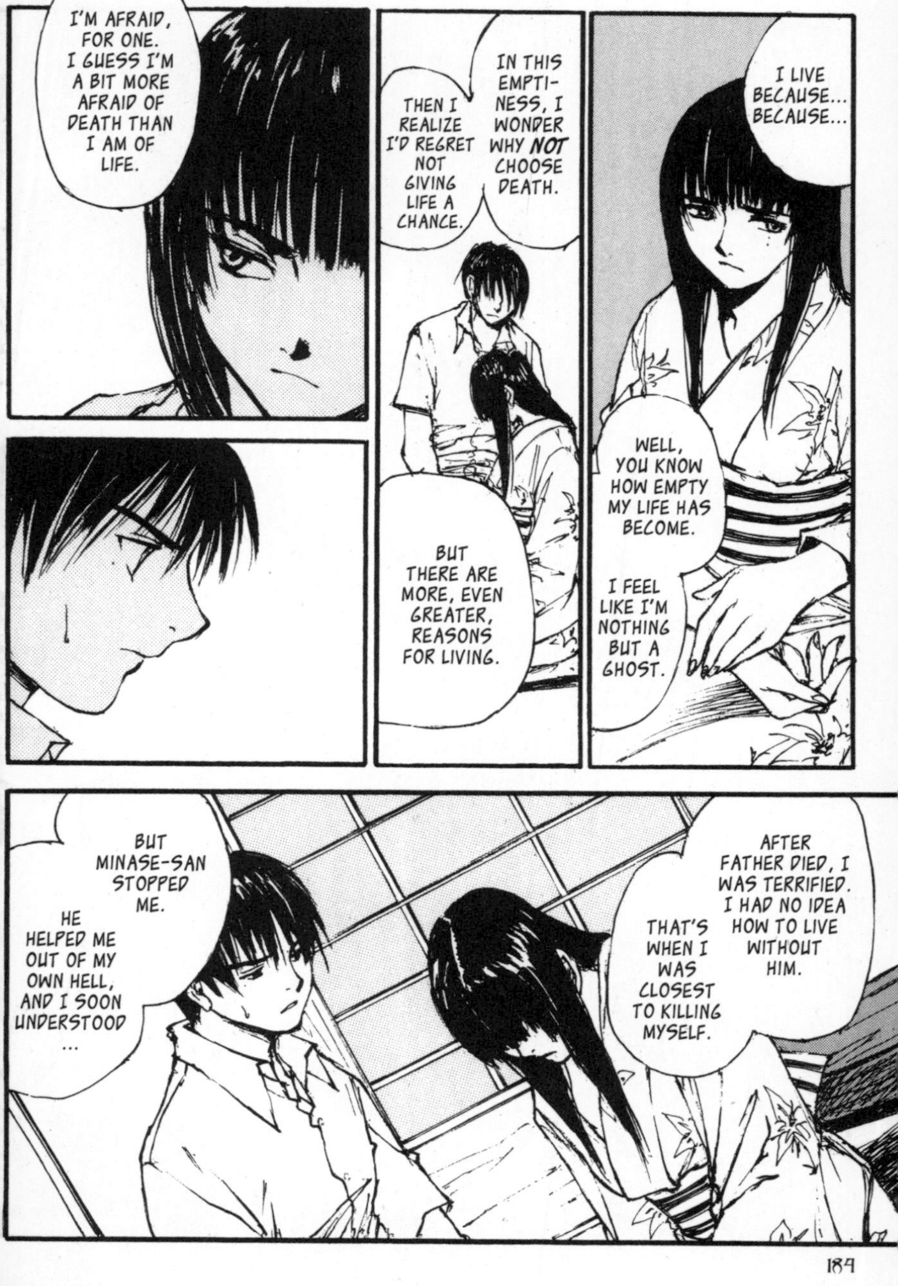
I LIVE BECAUSE... BECAUSE...
WELL, YOU KNOW HOW EMPTY MY LIFE HAS BECOME.
I FEEL LIKE I'M NOTHING BUT A GHOST.
IN THIS EMPTINESS, I WONDER WHY *NOT* CHOOSE DEATH.
THEN I REALIZE I'D REGRET NOT GIVING LIFE A CHANCE.
BUT THERE ARE MORE, EVEN GREATER, REASONS FOR LIVING.
I'M AFRAID, FOR ONE. I GUESS I'M A BIT MORE AFRAID OF DEATH THAN I AM OF LIFE.
AFTER FATHER DIED, I WAS TERRIFIED. I HAD NO IDEA HOW TO LIVE WITHOUT HIM.
THAT'S WHEN I WAS CLOSEST TO KILLING MYSELF.
BUT MINASE-SAN STOPPED ME.
HE HELPED ME OUT OF MY OWN HELL, AND I SOON UNDERSTOOD ...

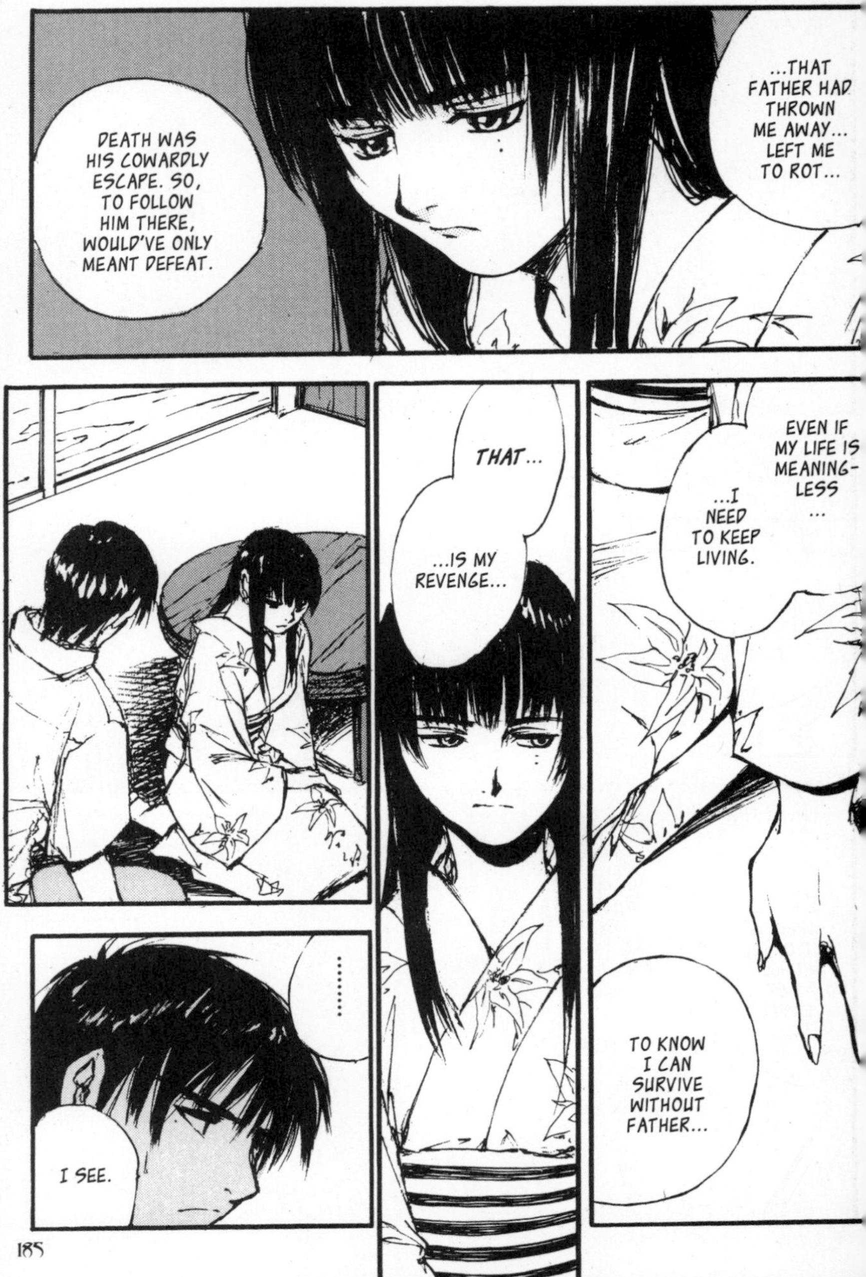
...THAT FATHER HAD THROWN ME AWAY... LEFT ME TO ROT...
DEATH WAS HIS COWARDLY ESCAPE. SO, TO FOLLOW HIM THERE, WOULD'VE ONLY MEANT DEFEAT.
EVEN IF MY LIFE IS MEANING-LESS ...
...I NEED TO KEEP LIVING.
TO KNOW I CAN SURVIVE WITHOUT FATHER...
THAT...
...IS MY REVENGE...
....
I SEE.

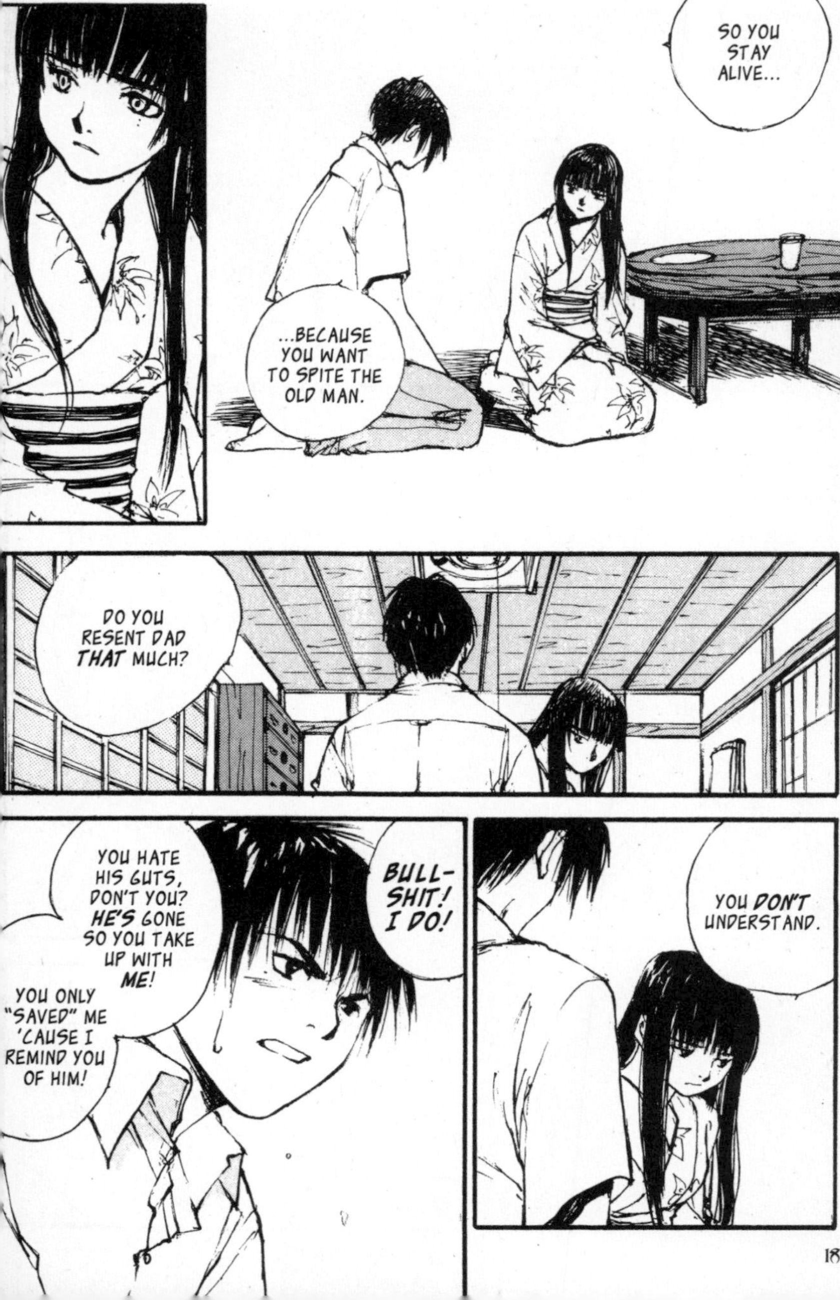
SO YOU STAY ALIVE...
...BECAUSE YOU WANT TO SPITE THE OLD MAN.
DO YOU RESENT DAD *THAT* MUCH?
YOU *DON'T* UNDERSTAND.
BULL-SHIT! I DO!
YOU HATE HIS GUTS, DON'T YOU? *HE'S* GONE SO YOU TAKE UP WITH *ME*!
YOU ONLY "SAVED" ME 'CAUSE I REMIND YOU OF HIM!

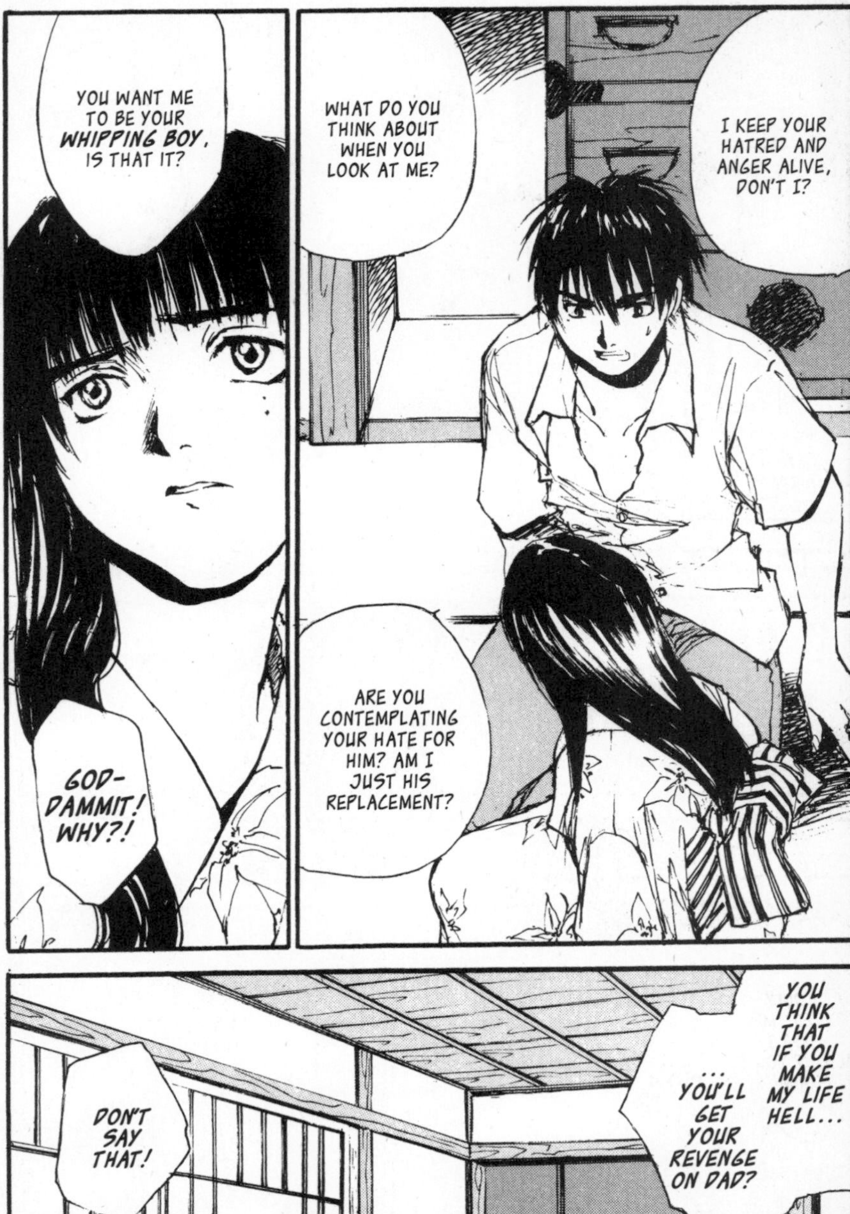
I KEEP YOUR HATRED AND ANGER ALIVE, DON'T I?
WHAT DO YOU THINK ABOUT WHEN YOU LOOK AT ME?
ARE YOU CONTEMPLATING YOUR HATE FOR HIM? AM I JUST HIS REPLACEMENT?
YOU WANT ME TO BE YOUR WHIPPING BOY, IS THAT IT?
GOD-DAMMIT! WHY?!
YOU THINK THAT IF YOU MAKE MY LIFE HELL...
...YOU'LL GET YOUR REVENGE ON DAD?
DON'T SAY THAT!

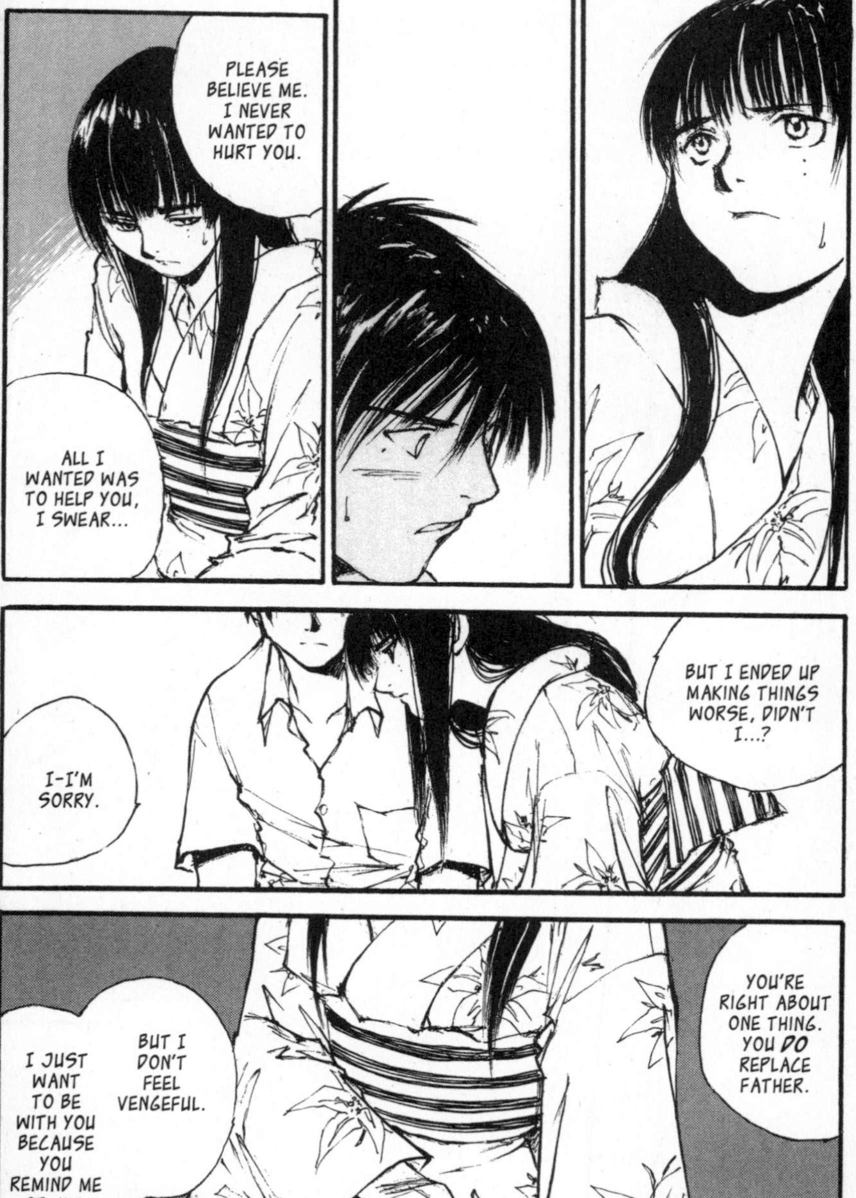
PLEASE BELIEVE ME. I NEVER WANTED TO HURT YOU.
ALL I WANTED WAS TO HELP YOU, I SWEAR...
BUT I ENDED UP MAKING THINGS WORSE, DIDN'T I...?
I-I'M SORRY.
YOU'RE RIGHT ABOUT ONE THING. YOU *DO* REPLACE FATHER.
BUT I DON'T FEEL VENGEFUL.
I JUST WANT TO BE WITH YOU BECAUSE YOU REMIND ME OF HIM.

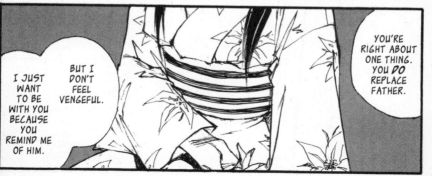

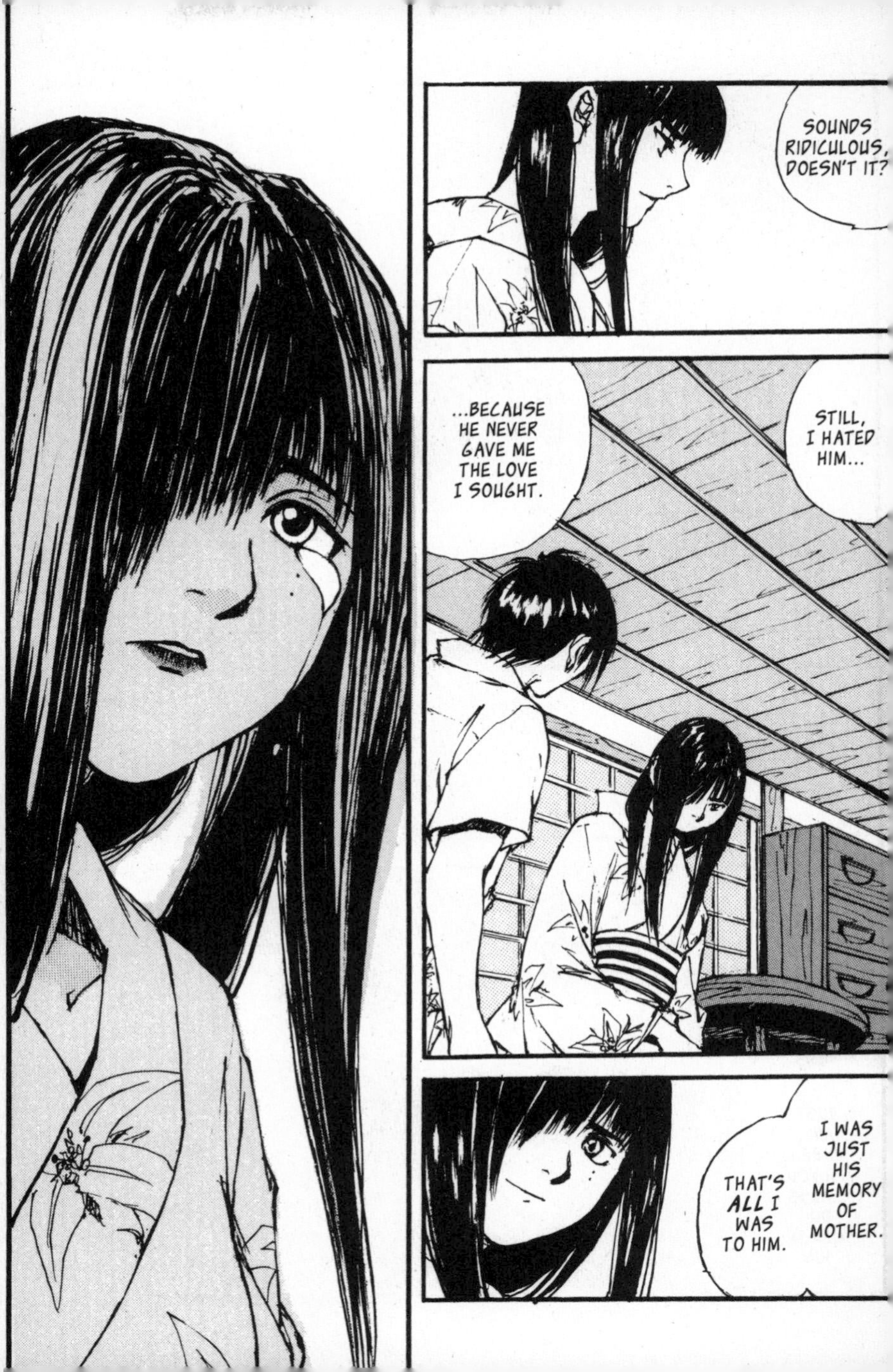
SOUNDS RIDICULOUS, DOESN'T IT?
STILL, I HATED HIM...
...BECAUSE HE NEVER GAVE ME THE LOVE I SOUGHT.
I WAS JUST HIS MEMORY OF MOTHER.
THAT'S **ALL** I WAS TO HIM.

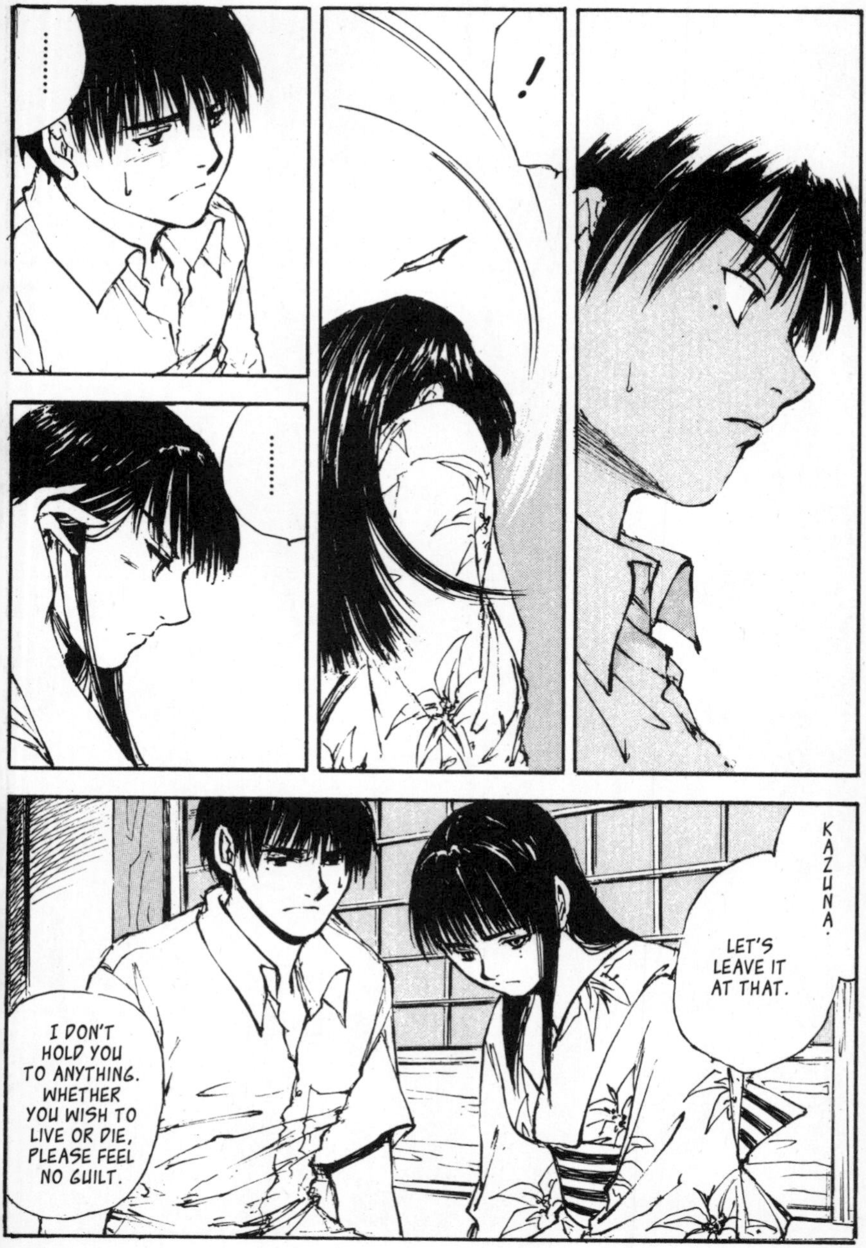
!
......
......
KAZUNA.
LET'S LEAVE IT AT THAT.
I DON'T HOLD YOU TO ANYTHING. WHETHER YOU WISH TO LIVE OR DIE, PLEASE FEEL NO GUILT.

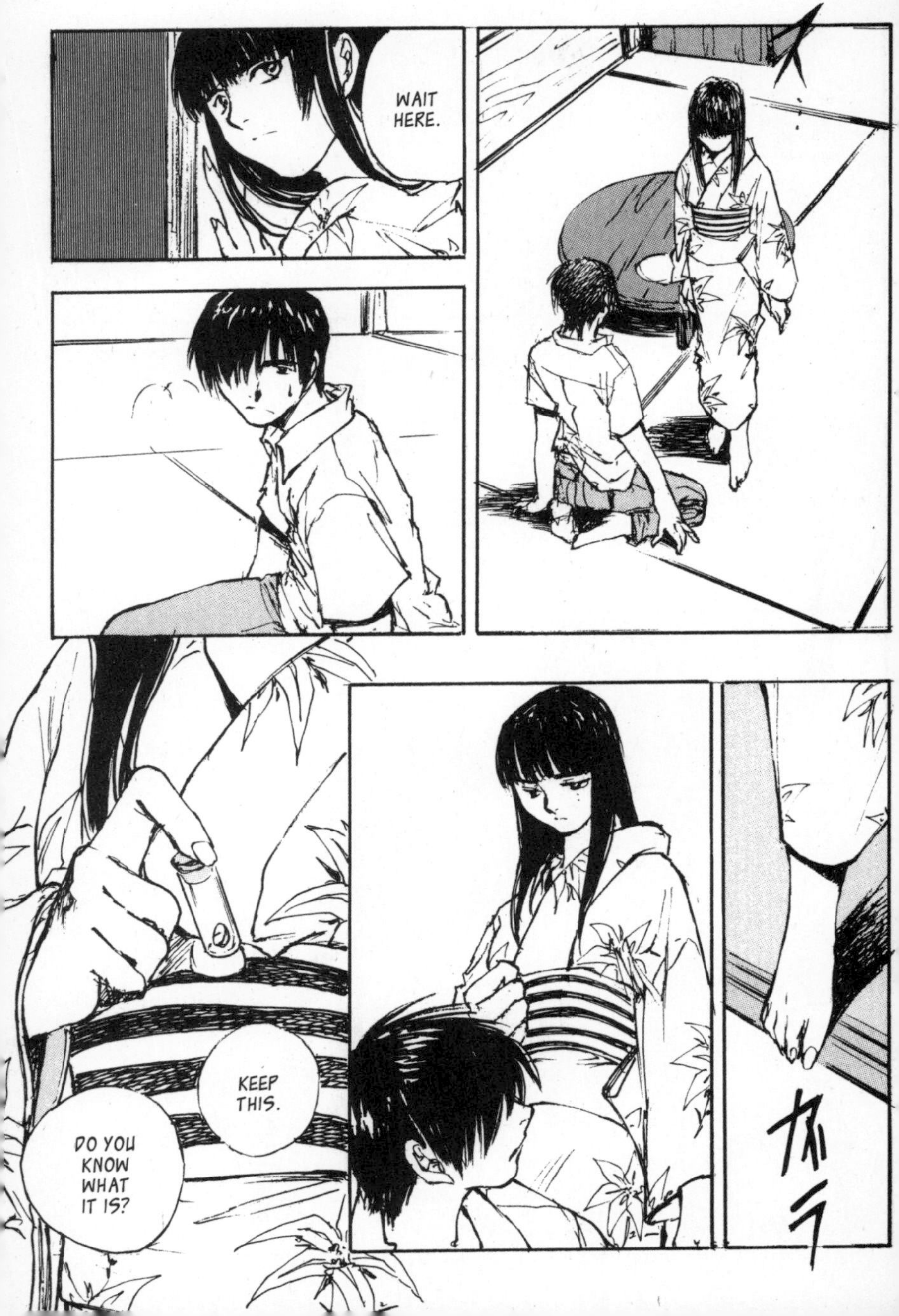
WAIT HERE.
カラ
KEEP THIS.
DO YOU KNOW WHAT IT IS?

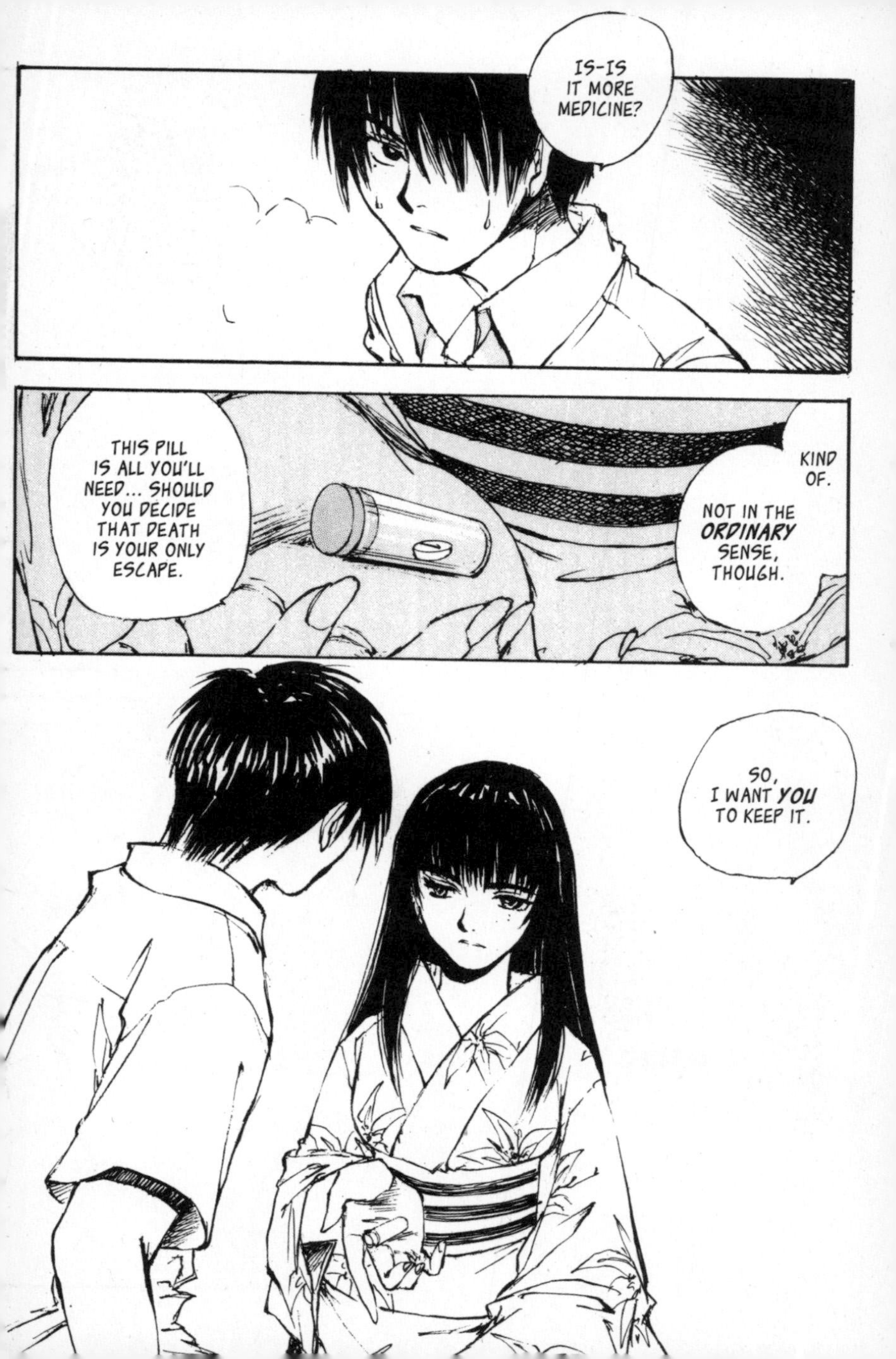
IS-IS IT MORE MEDICINE?
KIND OF.
NOT IN THE *ORDINARY* SENSE, THOUGH.
THIS PILL IS ALL YOU'LL NEED... SHOULD YOU DECIDE THAT DEATH IS YOUR ONLY ESCAPE.
SO, I WANT *YOU* TO KEEP IT.

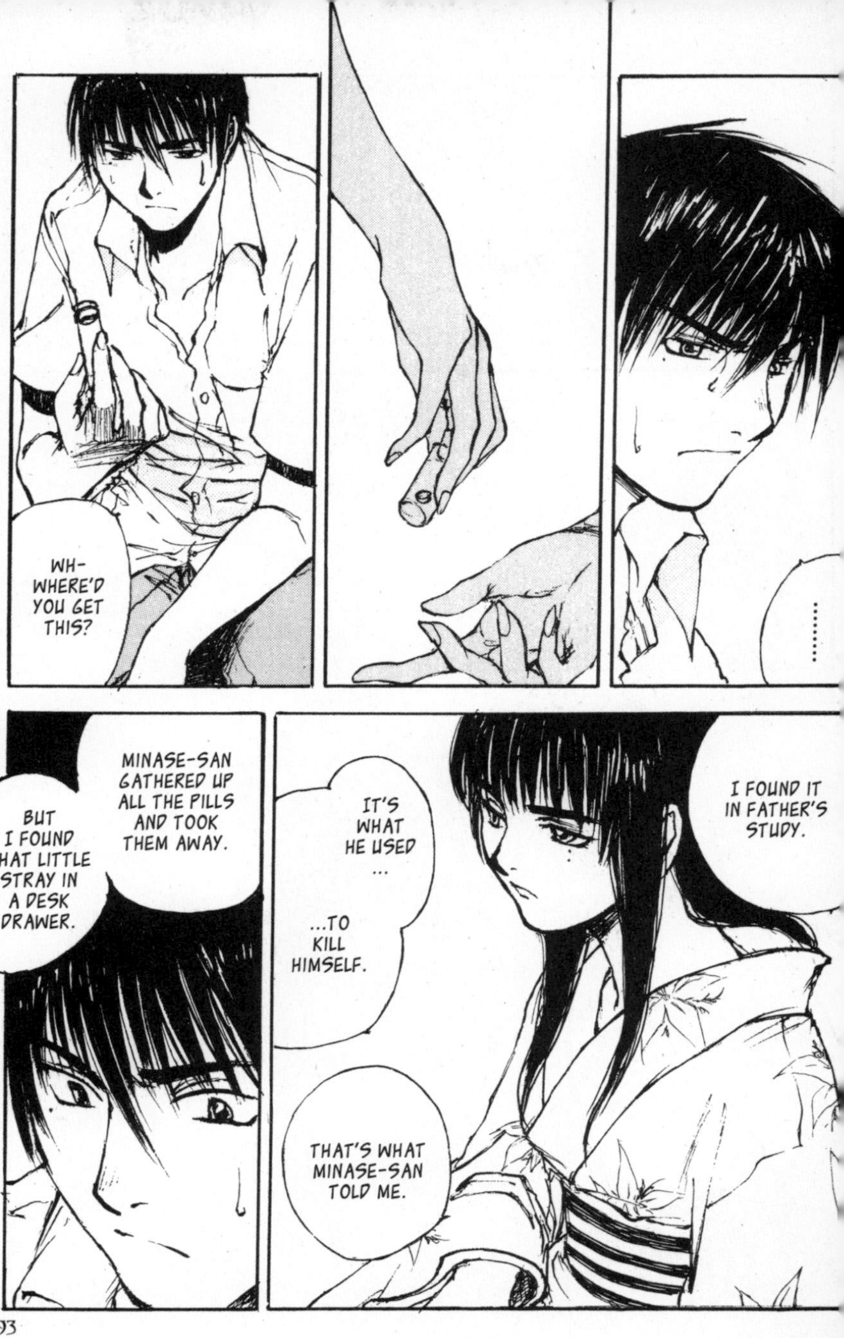
......
WH- WHERE'D YOU GET THIS?
I FOUND IT IN FATHER'S STUDY.
IT'S WHAT HE USED ...
...TO KILL HIMSELF.
THAT'S WHAT MINASE-SAN TOLD ME.
MINASE-SAN GATHERED UP ALL THE PILLS AND TOOK THEM AWAY.
BUT I FOUND THAT LITTLE STRAY IN A DESK DRAWER.

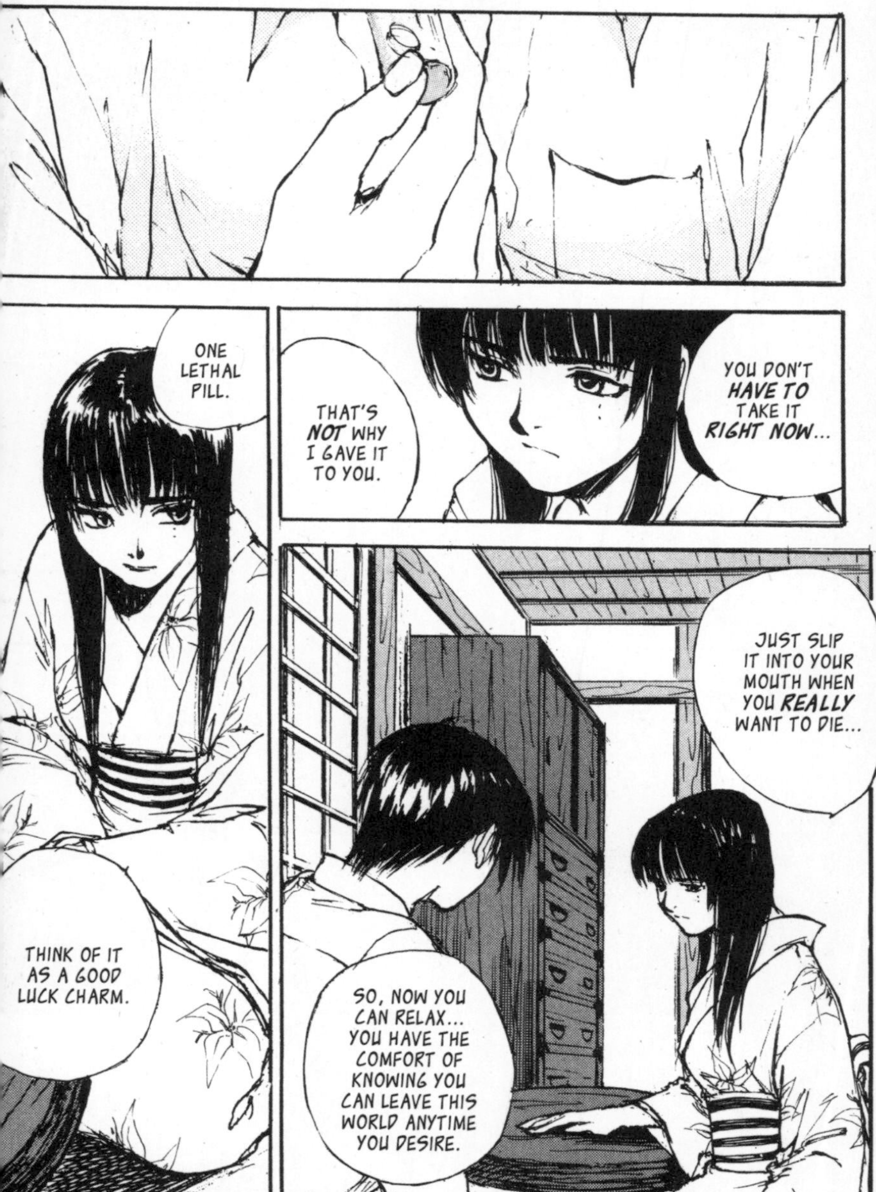
YOU DON'T *HAVE TO* TAKE IT *RIGHT NOW*...
THAT'S *NOT* WHY I GAVE IT TO YOU.
JUST SLIP IT INTO YOUR MOUTH WHEN YOU *REALLY* WANT TO DIE...
SO, NOW YOU CAN RELAX... YOU HAVE THE COMFORT OF KNOWING YOU CAN LEAVE THIS WORLD ANYTIME YOU DESIRE.
ONE LETHAL PILL.
THINK OF IT AS A GOOD LUCK CHARM.

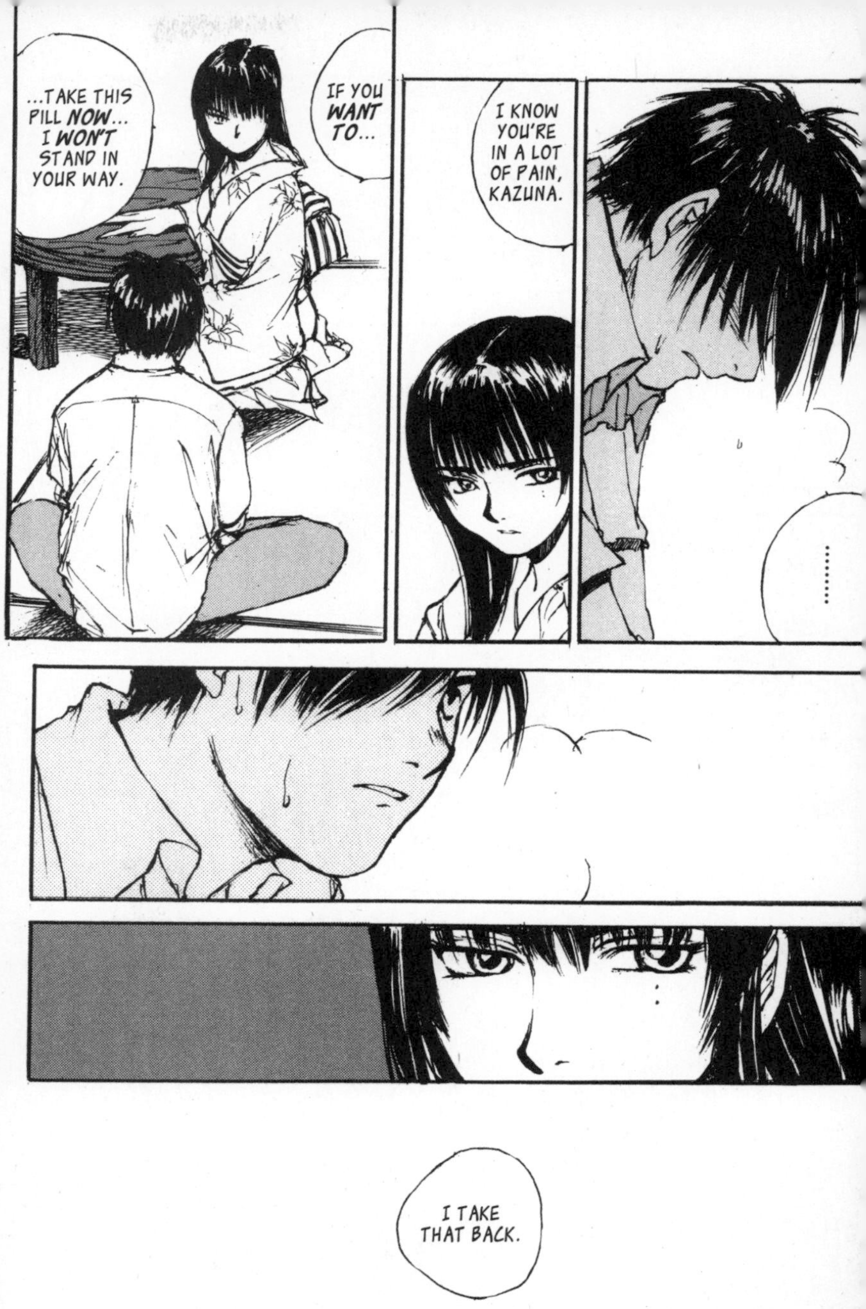

......
I KNOW YOU'RE IN A LOT OF PAIN, KAZUNA.
IF YOU WANT TO...
...TAKE THIS PILL NOW... I WON'T STAND IN YOUR WAY.
I TAKE THAT BACK.

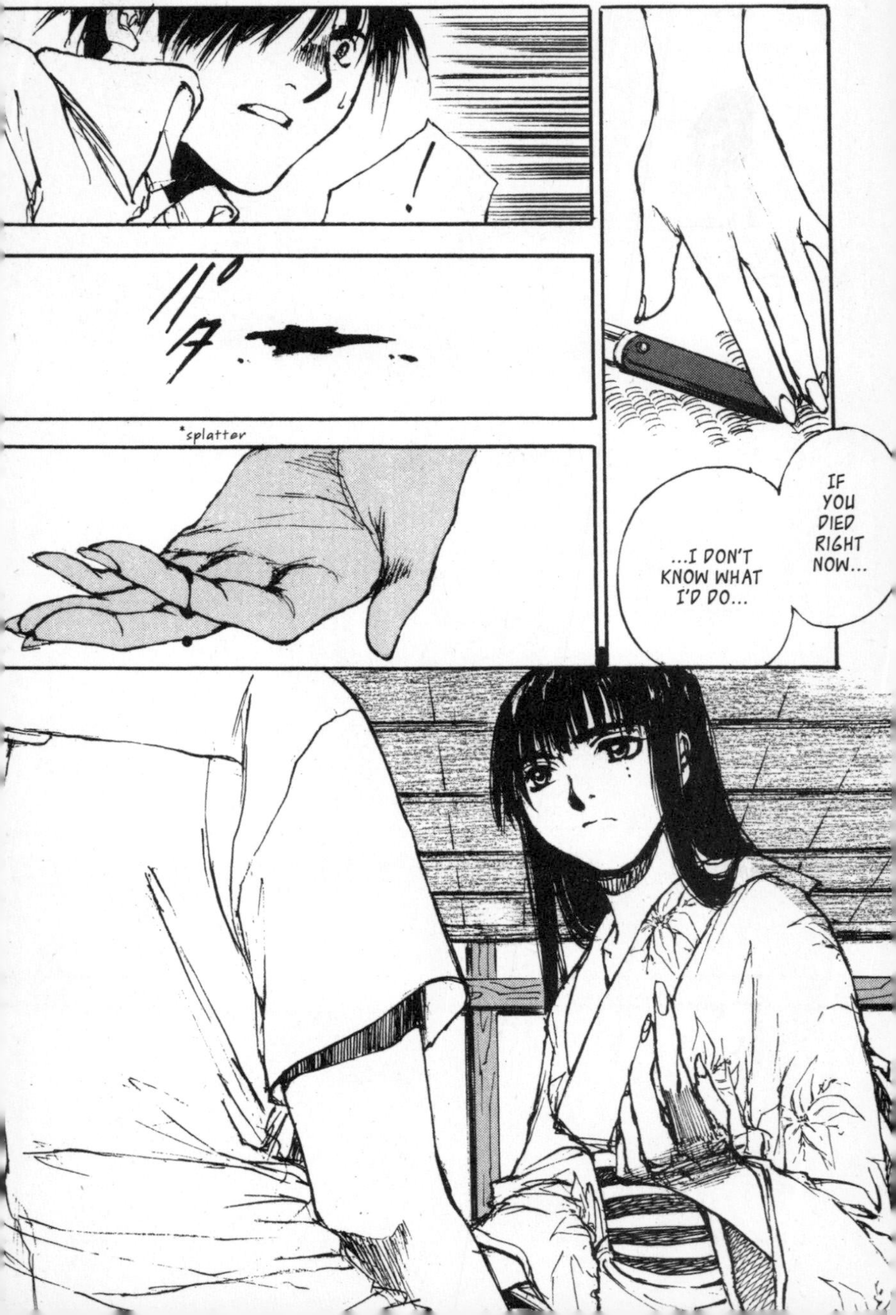
!
*splatter
IF YOU DIED RIGHT NOW...
...I DON'T KNOW WHAT I'D DO...

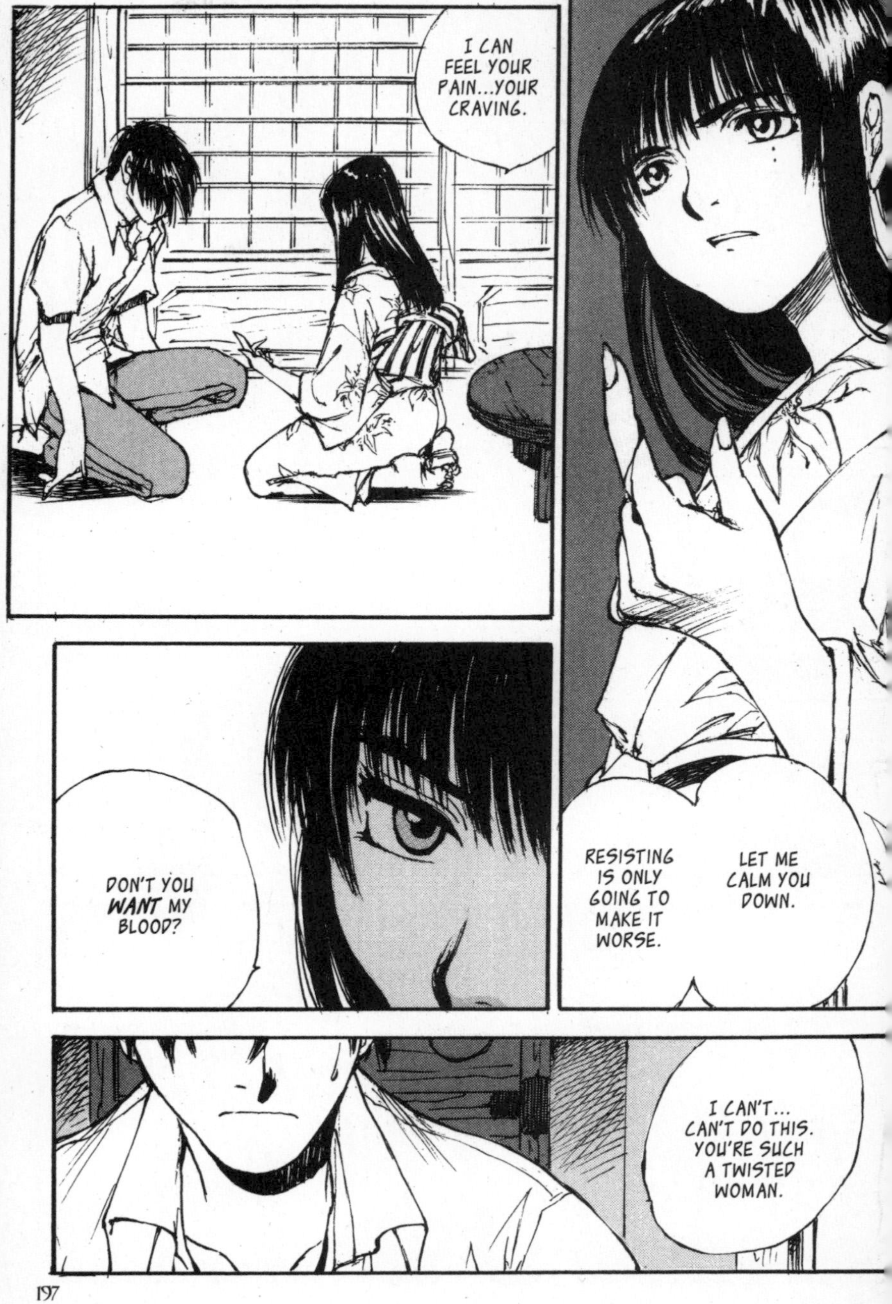
I CAN FEEL YOUR PAIN...YOUR CRAVING.
LET ME CALM YOU DOWN.
RESISTING IS ONLY GOING TO MAKE IT WORSE.
DON'T YOU *WANT* MY BLOOD?
I CAN'T... CAN'T DO THIS. YOU'RE SUCH A TWISTED WOMAN.

CAN YOU SMELL MY BLOOD?

IT'S HERE TO SLAKE YOUR THIRST.

COME CLOSER.

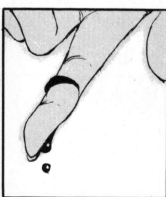

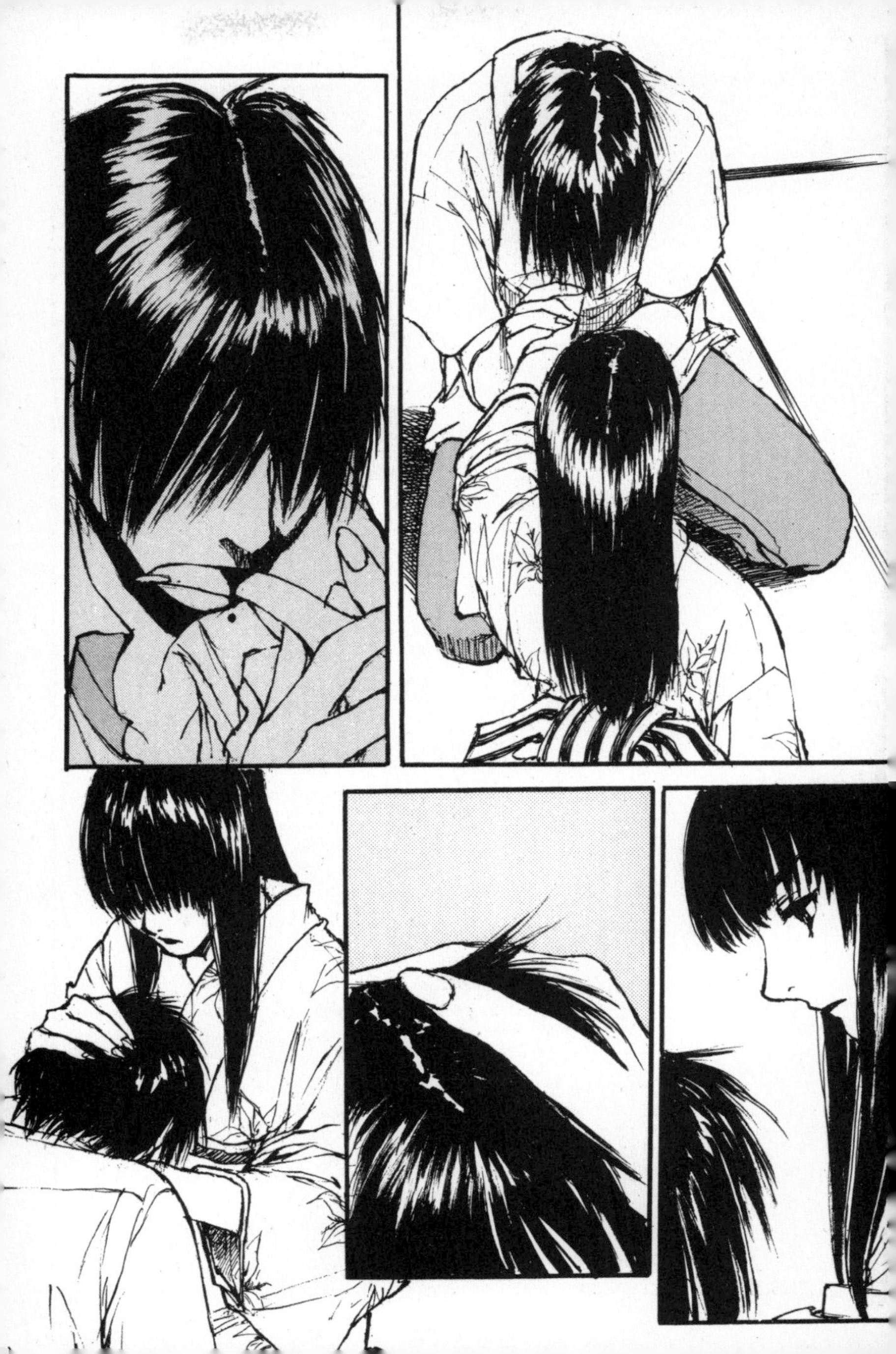

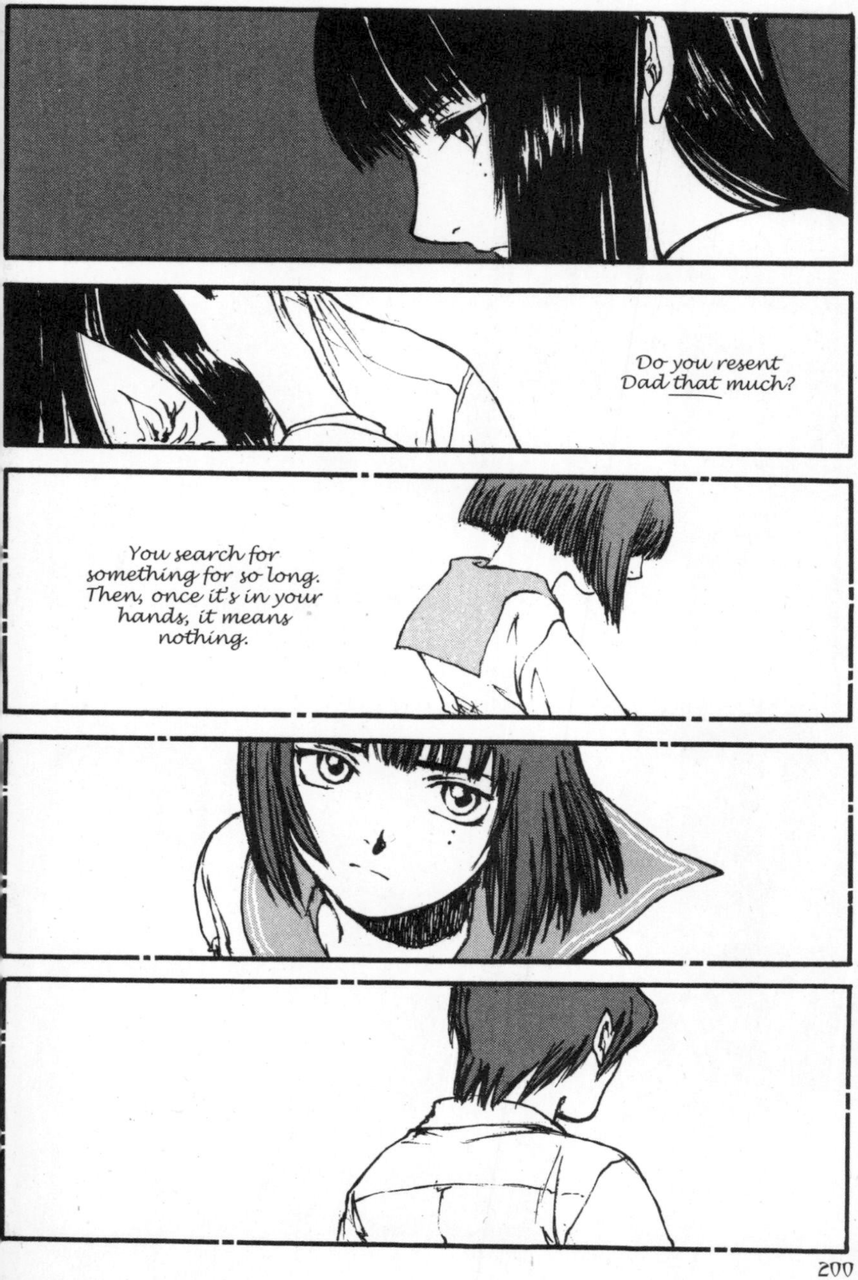
Do you resent Dad that much?
You search for something for so long. Then, once it's in your hands, it means nothing.

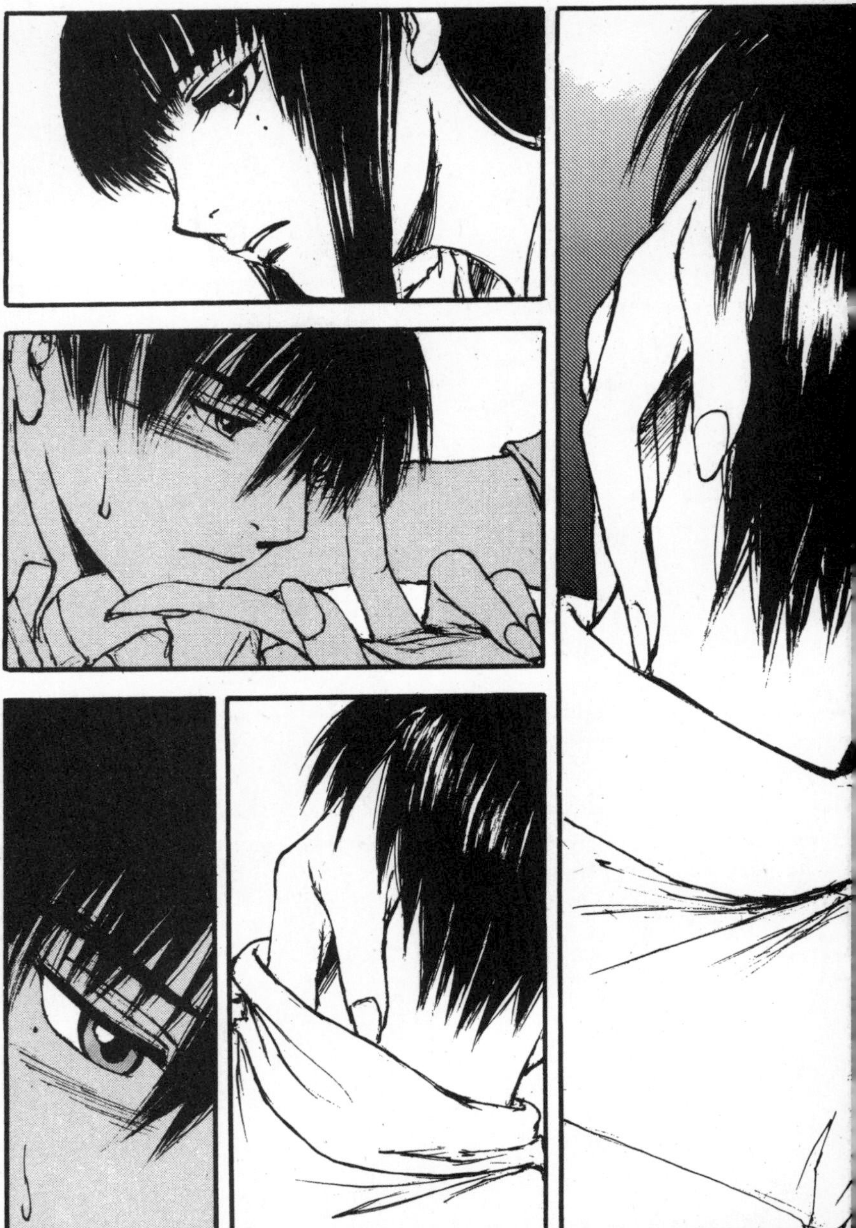

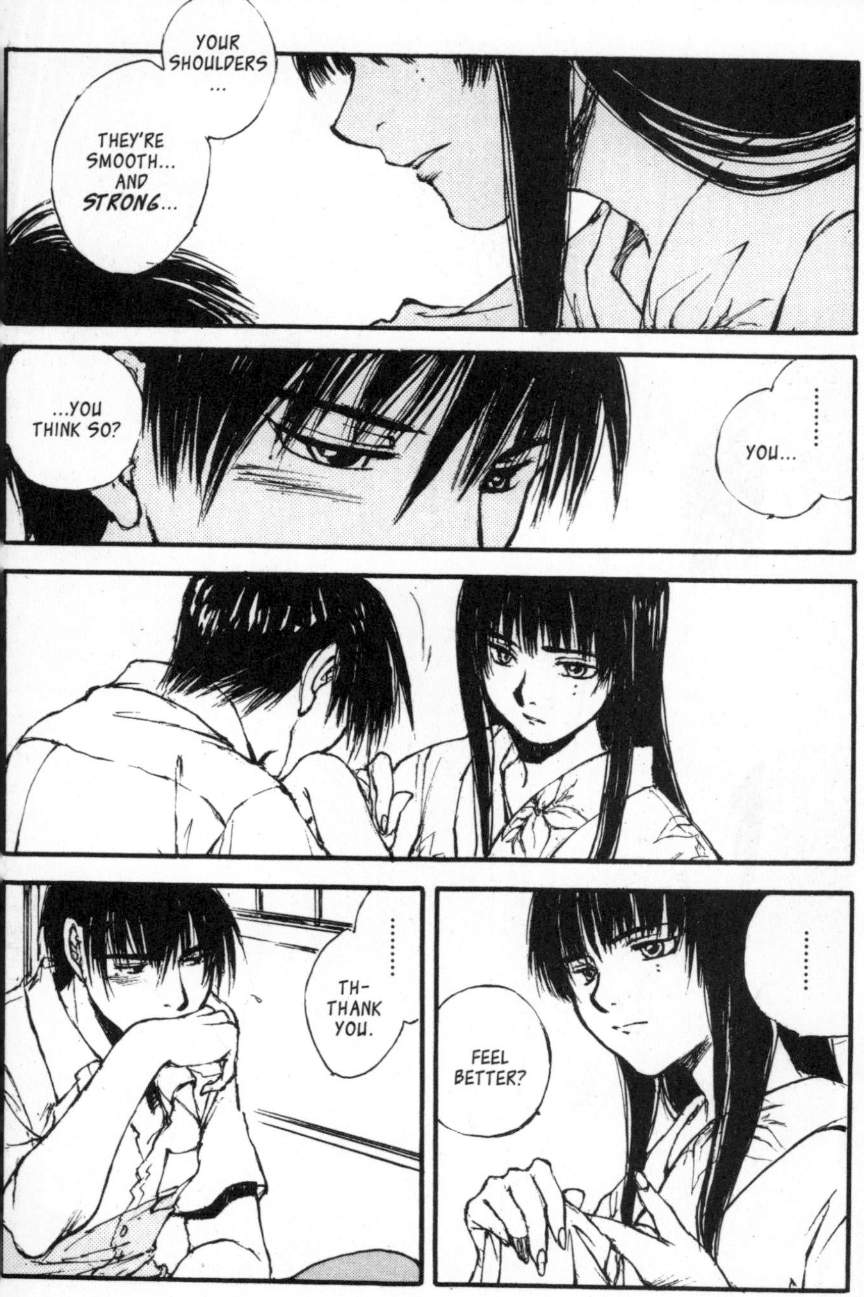
YOUR SHOULDERS ...
THEY'RE SMOOTH... AND STRONG...
...... YOU...
...YOU THINK SO?
......
FEEL BETTER?
......
TH-THANK YOU.

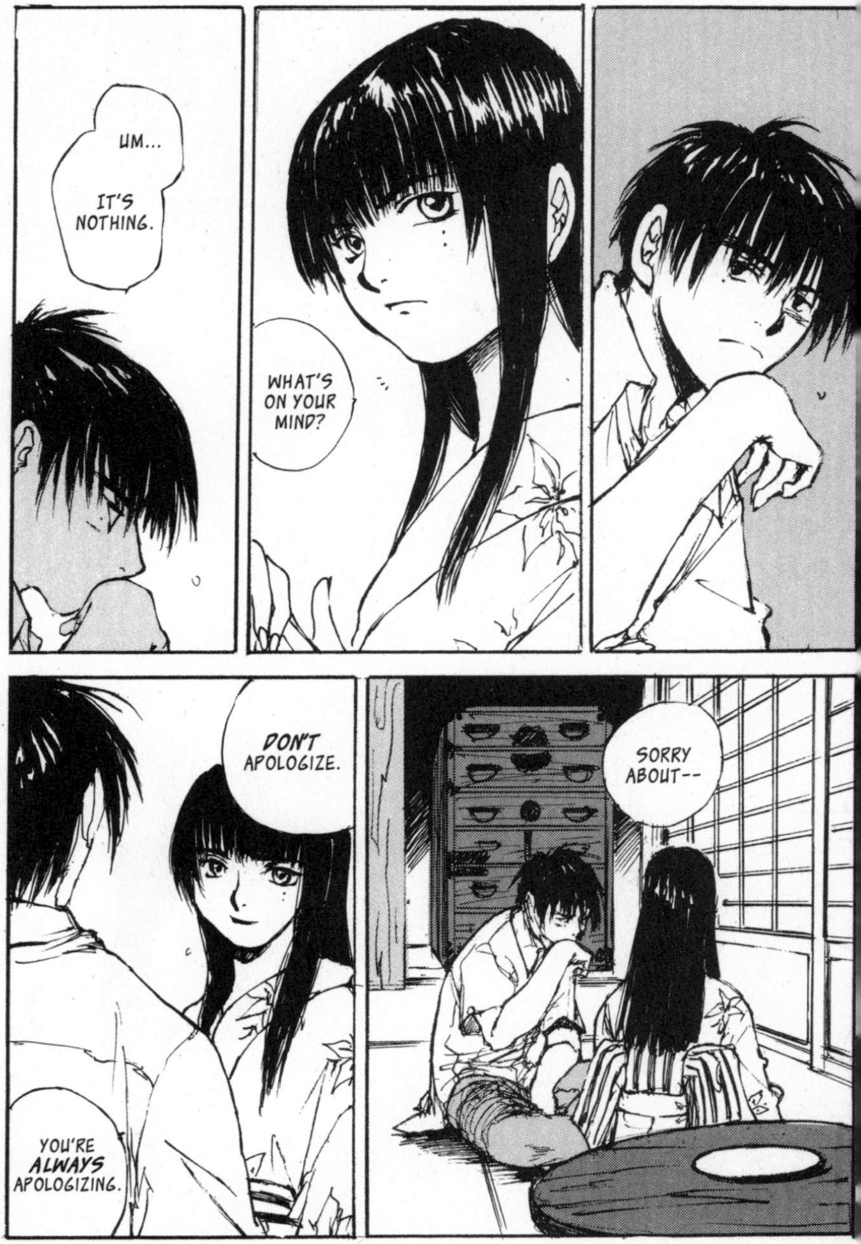
WHAT'S ON YOUR MIND?
UM... IT'S NOTHING.
SORRY ABOUT--
DON'T APOLOGIZE.
YOU'RE ALWAYS APOLOGIZING.

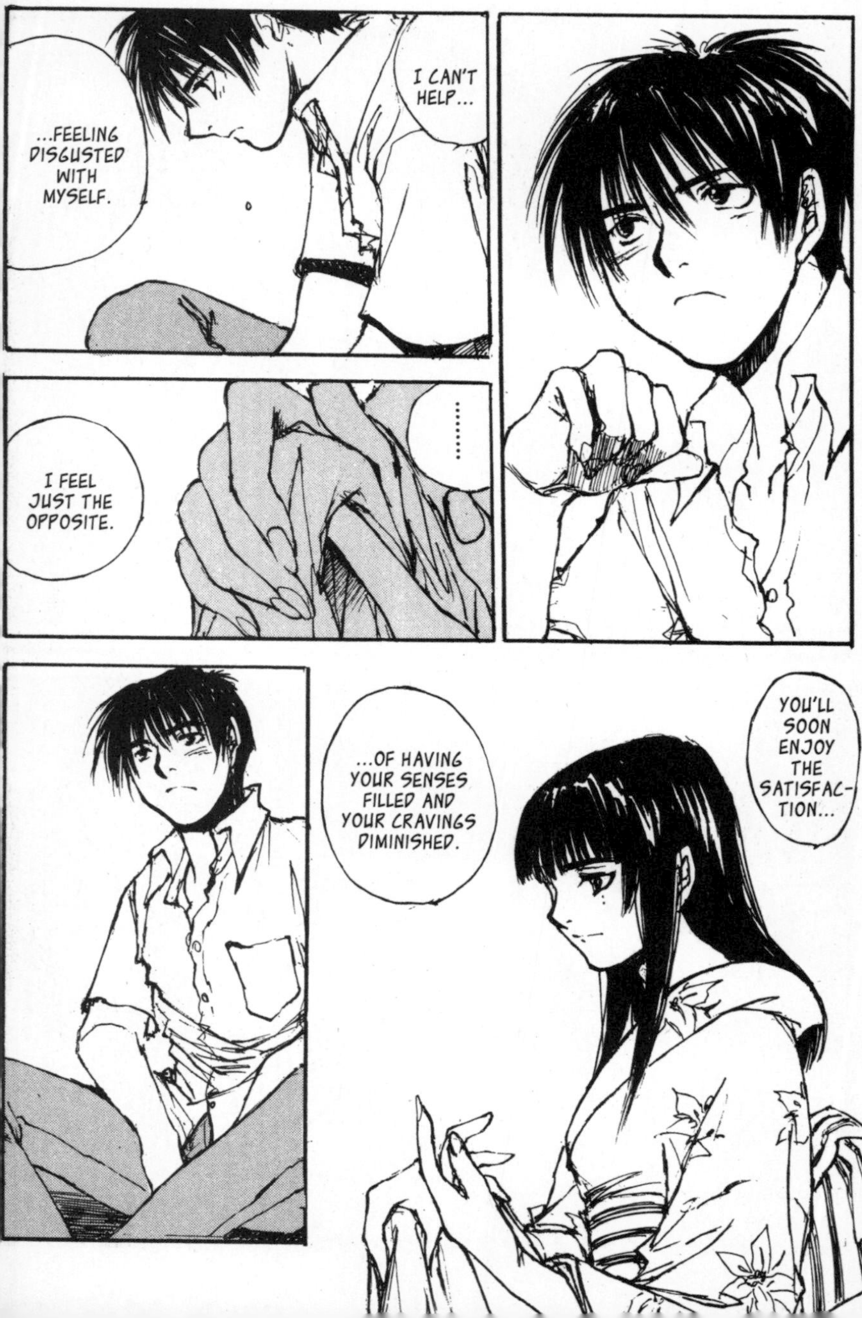
I CAN'T HELP...
...FEELING DISGUSTED WITH MYSELF.
......
I FEEL JUST THE OPPOSITE.
YOU'LL SOON ENJOY THE SATISFAC-TION...
...OF HAVING YOUR SENSES FILLED AND YOUR CRAVINGS DIMINISHED.

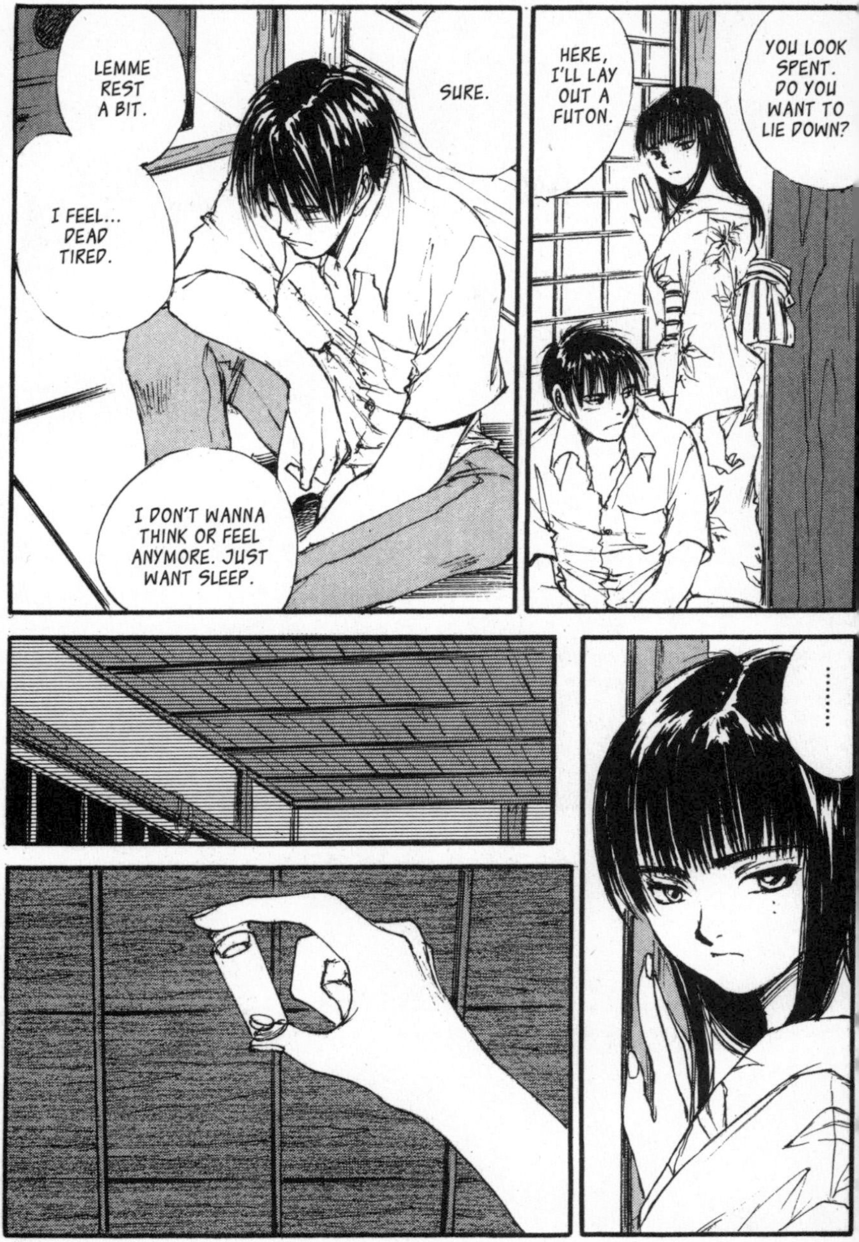
YOU LOOK SPENT. DO YOU WANT TO LIE DOWN?
HERE, I'LL LAY OUT A FUTON.
SURE.
LEMME REST A BIT.
I FEEL... DEAD TIRED.
I DON'T WANNA THINK OR FEEL ANYMORE. JUST WANT SLEEP.
......

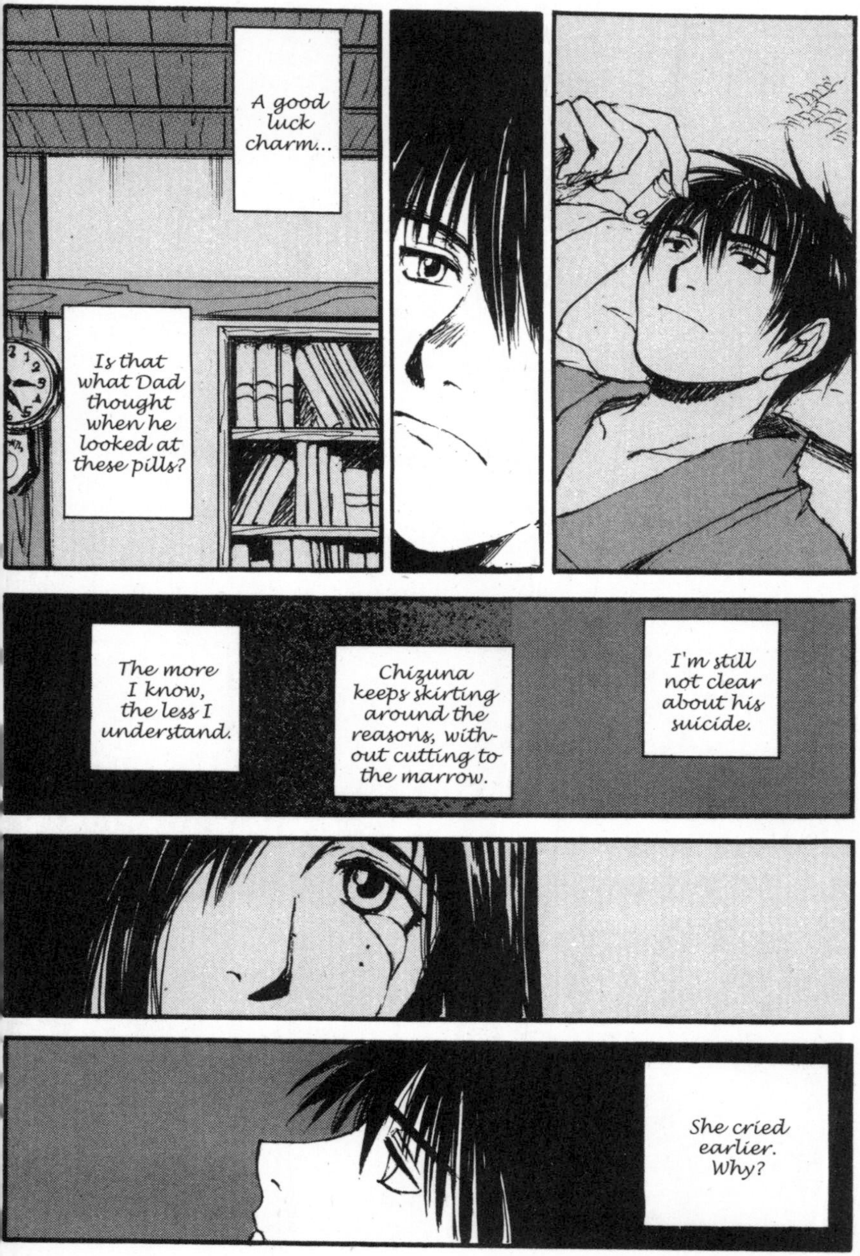
A good luck charm...
Is that what Dad thought when he looked at these pills?
I'm still not clear about his suicide.
Chizuna keeps skirting around the reasons, without cutting to the marrow.
The more I know, the less I understand.
She cried earlier. Why?

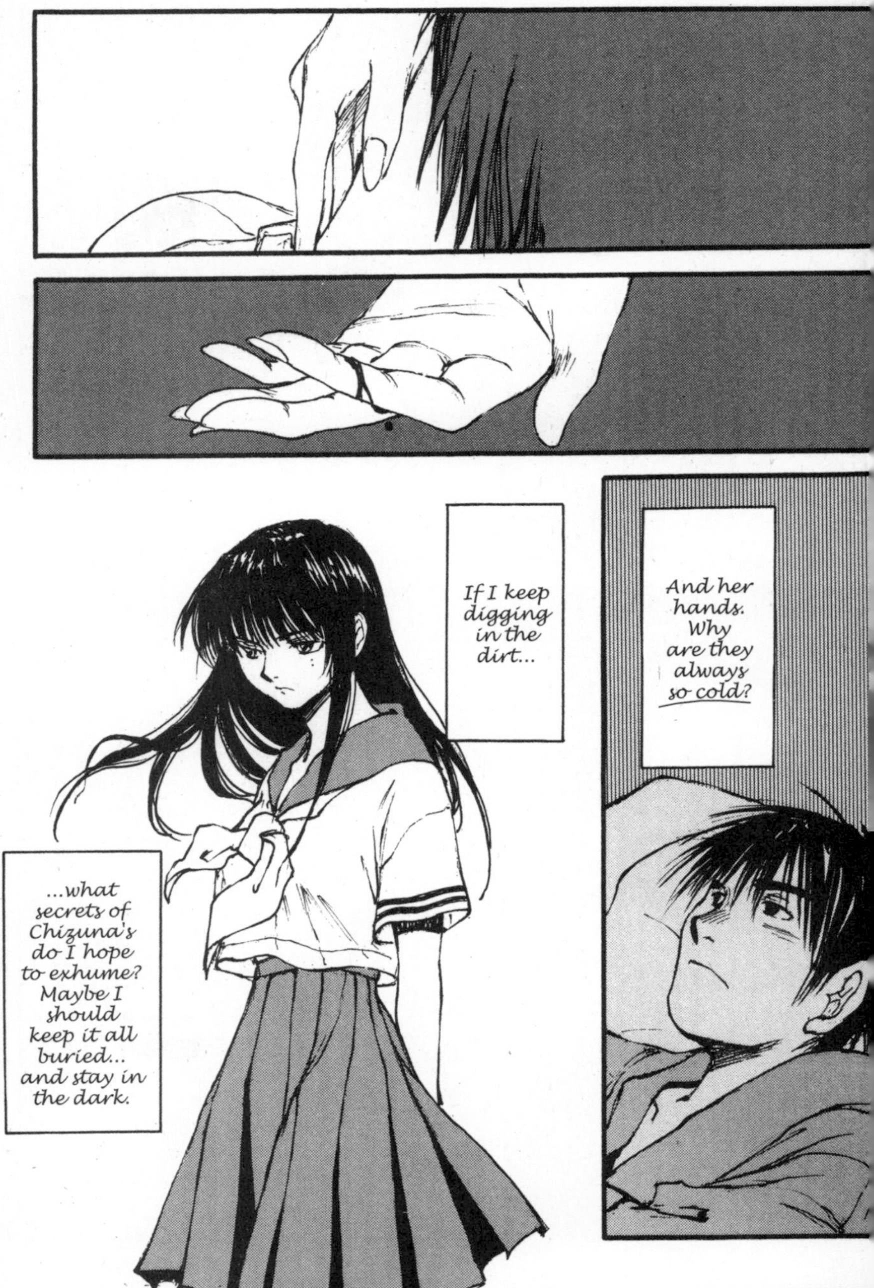
And her hands. Why are they always so cold?
If I keep digging in the dirt...
...what secrets of Chizuna's do I hope to exhume? Maybe I should keep it all buried... and stay in the dark.

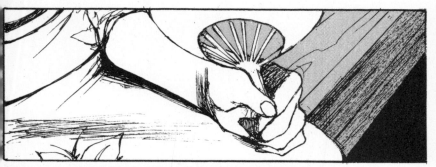

CONTINUED IN
LAMENT OF THE LAMB VOLUME 4

Lament of the Lamb Vol. 4

November 2004

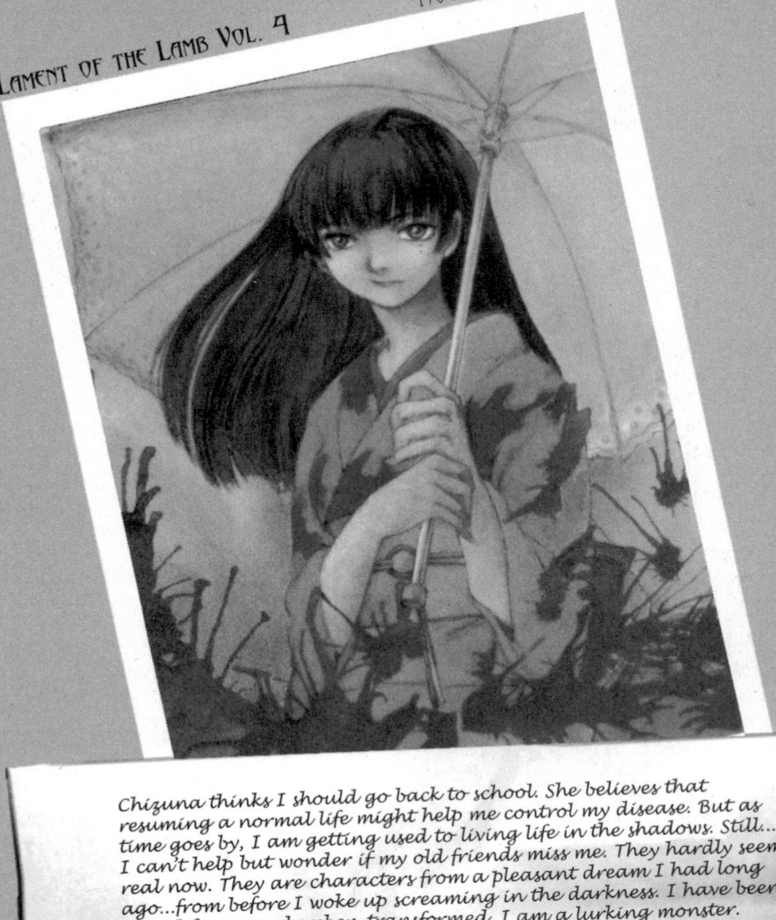

Chizuna thinks I should go back to school. She believes that resuming a normal life might help me control my disease. But as time goes by, I am getting used to living life in the shadows. Still... I can't help but wonder if my old friends miss me. They hardly seem real now. They are characters from a pleasant dream I had long ago...from before I woke up screaming in the darkness. I have been ripped from my slumber, transformed. I am a lurking monster.

That's why I will never go back to school--not while Yaegashi is there. She wouldn't be safe. I'm sorry, Yaegashi, but it has to be this way. Have you been looking for me? Have you been to the Edas? I can only hope--for your sake--that they didn't tell you where I am.

Chizuna has been restlessly dreaming of Mother and painfully longing for Father. She's on the verge of something terrible. I fear for her. Her sorrow is so strong, I'm not sure if her attacks can be kept under control. She binds herself to Father with an unbreakable tether...and it truly sickens me. But I must admit a horrible truth--it also fills me with a strange longing... And although she sees me as nothing but a pale imitation of Father, I have vowed to never abandon her.

ALSO AVAILABLE FROM TOKYOPOP®

MANGA

.HACK//LEGEND OF THE TWILIGHT
@LARGE
ABENOBASHI: MAGICAL SHOPPING ARCADE
A.I. LOVE YOU
AI YORI AOSHI
ANGELIC LAYER
ARM OF KANNON
BABY BIRTH
BATTLE ROYALE
BATTLE VIXENS
BRAIN POWERED
BRIGADOON
B'TX
CANDIDATE FOR GODDESS, THE
CARDCAPTOR SAKURA
CARDCAPTOR SAKURA - MASTER OF THE CLOW
CHOBITS
CHRONICLES OF THE CURSED SWORD
CLAMP SCHOOL DETECTIVES
CLOVER
COMIC PARTY
CONFIDENTIAL CONFESSIONS
CORRECTOR YUI
COWBOY BEBOP
COWBOY BEBOP: SHOOTING STAR
CRAZY LOVE STORY
CRESCENT MOON
CROSS
CULDCEPT
CYBORG 009
D•N•ANGEL
DEMON DIARY
DEMON ORORON, THE
DEUS VITAE
DIABOLO
DIGIMON
DIGIMON TAMERS
DIGIMON ZERO TWO
DOLL
DRAGON HUNTER
DRAGON KNIGHTS
DRAGON VOICE
DREAM SAGA
DUKLYON: CLAMP SCHOOL DEFENDERS
EERIE QUEERIE!
ERICA SAKURAZAWA: COLLECTED WORKS
ET CETERA
ETERNITY
EVIL'S RETURN
FAERIES' LANDING
FAKE
FLCL
FLOWER OF THE DEEP SLEEP
FORBIDDEN DANCE
FRUITS BASKET
G GUNDAM

GATEKEEPERS
GETBACKERS
GIRL GOT GAME
GIRLS EDUCATIONAL CHARTER
GRAVITATION
GTO
GUNDAM BLUE DESTINY
GUNDAM SEED ASTRAY
GUNDAM WING
GUNDAM WING: BATTLEFIELD OF PACIFISTS
GUNDAM WING: ENDLESS WALTZ
GUNDAM WING: THE LAST OUTPOST (G-UNIT)
GUYS' GUIDE TO GIRLS
HANDS OFF!
HAPPY MANIA
HARLEM BEAT
HYPER RUNE
I.N.V.U.
IMMORTAL RAIN
INITIAL D
INSTANT TEEN: JUST ADD NUTS
ISLAND
JING: KING OF BANDITS
JING: KING OF BANDITS - TWILIGHT TALES
JULINE
KARE KANO
KILL ME, KISS ME
KINDAICHI CASE FILES, THE
KING OF HELL
KODOCHA: SANA'S STAGE
LAMENT OF THE LAMB
LEGAL DRUG
LEGEND OF CHUN HYANG, THE
LES BIJOUX
LOVE HINA
LUPIN III
LUPIN III: WORLD'S MOST WANTED
MAGIC KNIGHT RAYEARTH I
MAGIC KNIGHT RAYEARTH II
MAHOROMATIC: AUTOMATIC MAIDEN
MAN OF MANY FACES
MARMALADE BOY
MARS
MARS: HORSE WITH NO NAME
MINK
MIRACLE GIRLS
MIYUKI-CHAN IN WONDERLAND
MODEL
MOURYOU KIDEN
MY LOVE
NECK AND NECK
ONE
ONE I LOVE, THE
PARADISE KISS
PARASYTE
PASSION FRUIT
PEACH GIRL
PEACH GIRL: CHANGE OF HEART

05.26.04T

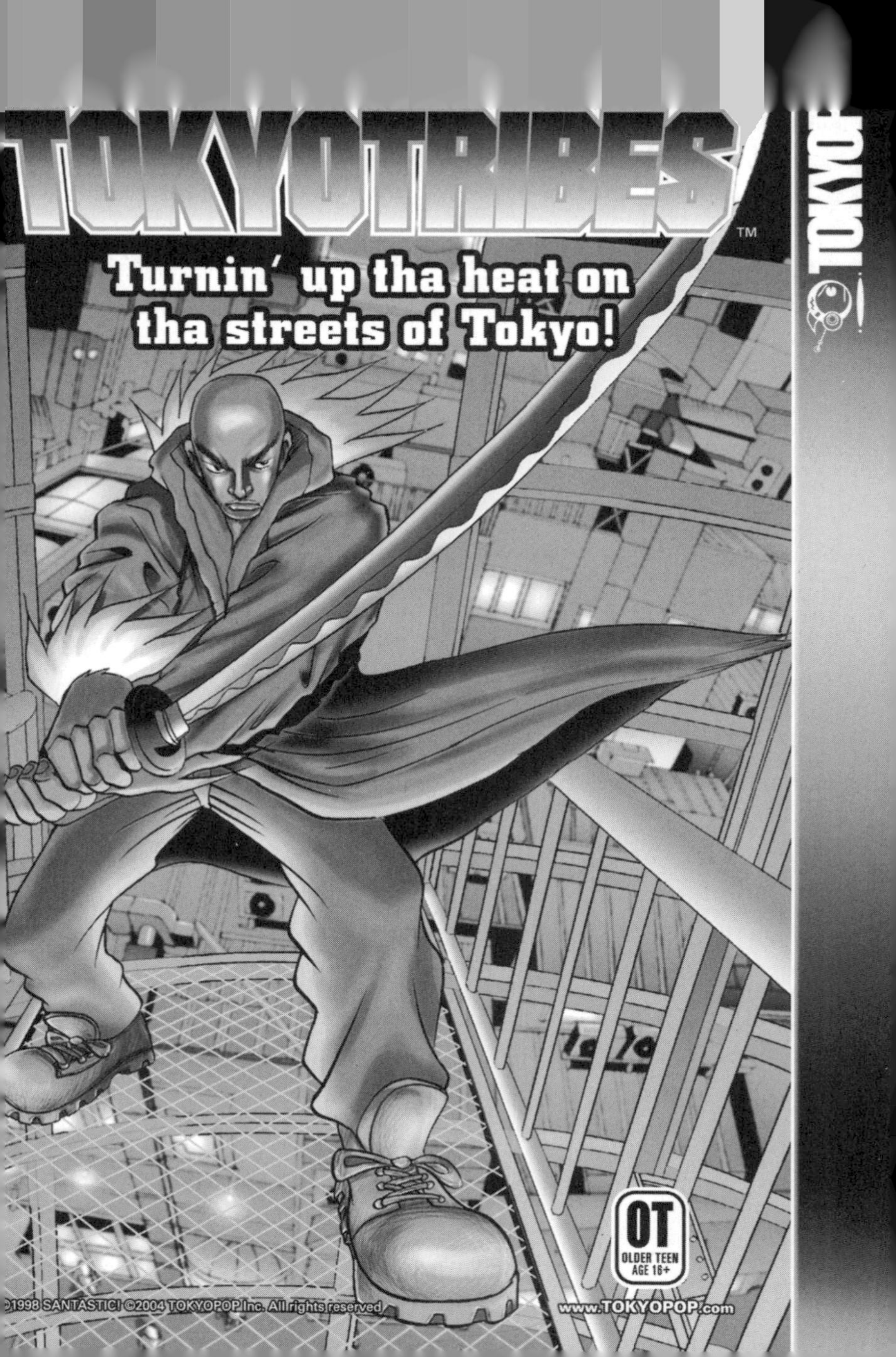
TOKYO TRIBES™
Turnin' up tha heat on tha streets of Tokyo!
TOKYOPOP
OT
OLDER TEEN AGE 16+
©1998 SANTASTIC! ©2004 TOKYOPOP Inc. All rights reserved.
www.TOKYOPOP.com

THE DEMON
ORORON

Love caught between
HEAVEN
and HELL.

www.TOKYOPOP.com

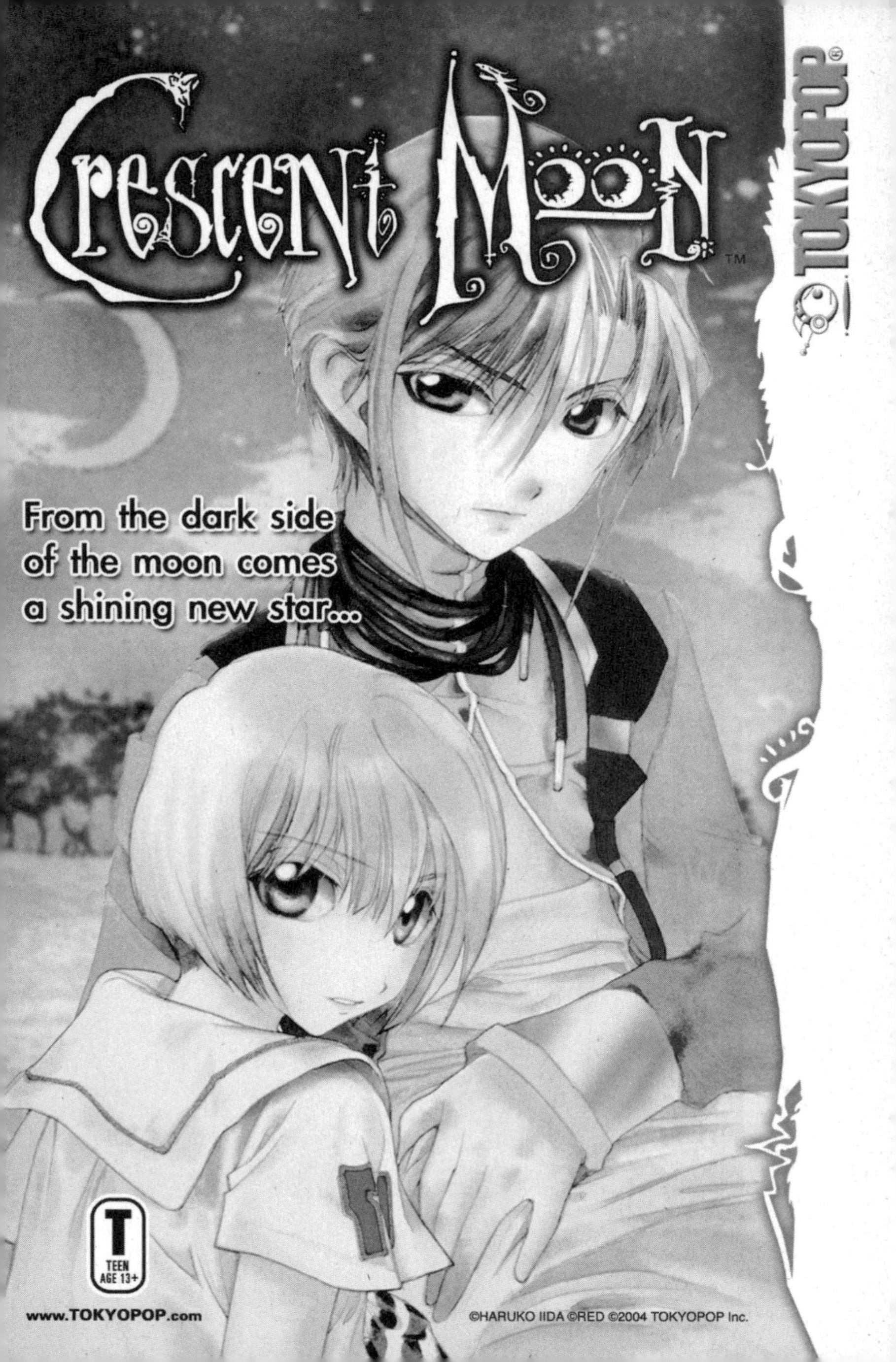
TOKYOPOP
Crescent Moon™
From the dark side
of the moon comes
a shining new star...
T
TEEN
AGE 13+
www.TOKYOPOP.com
©HARUKO IIDA ©RED ©2004 TOKYOPOP Inc.

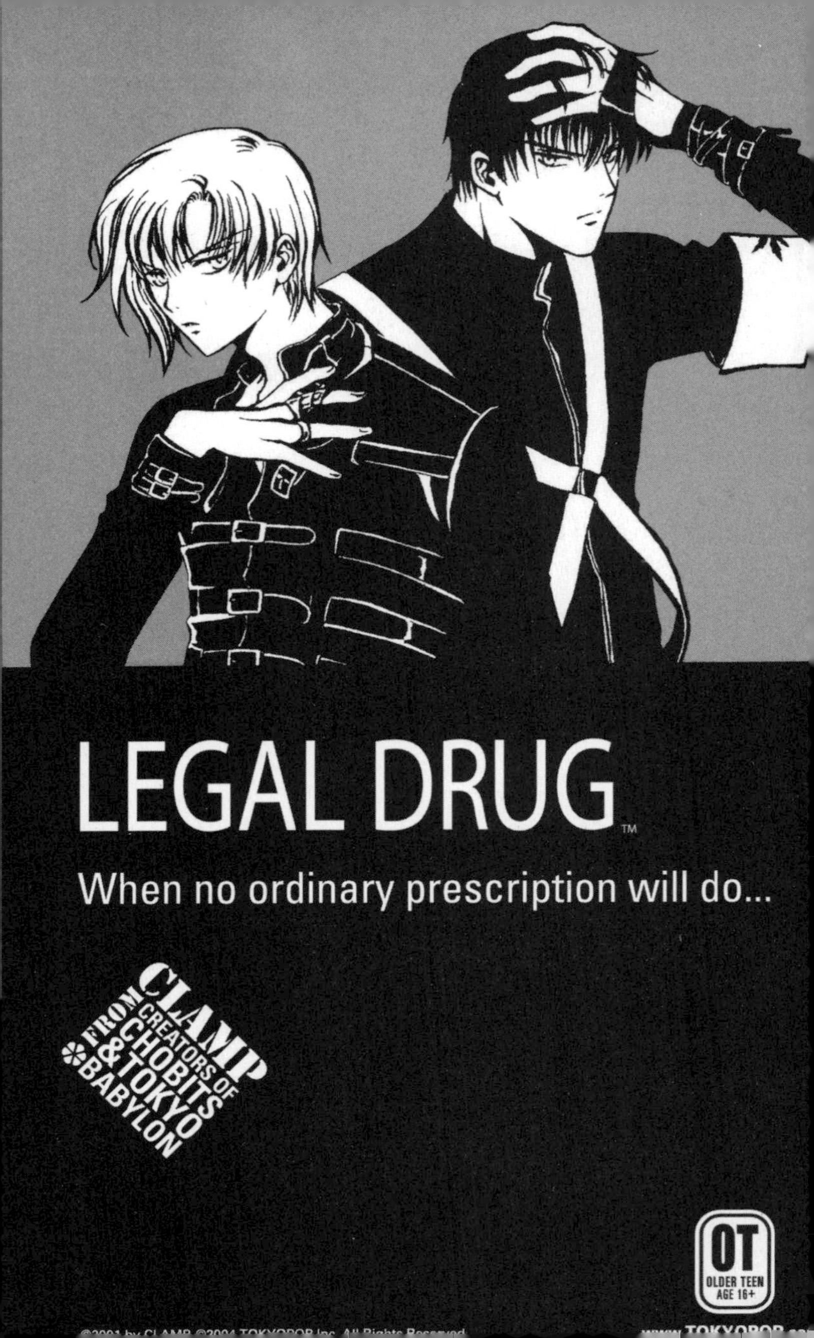
LEGAL DRUG™
When no ordinary prescription will do...
FROM CLAMP
CREATORS OF CHOBITS & TOKYO BABYLON
OT
OLDER TEEN AGE 16+
©2001 by CLAMP ©2004 TOKYOPOP Inc. All Rights Reserved.
www.TOKYOPOP.com

STOP!

This is the back of the book. You wouldn't want to spoil a great ending!

This book is printed "manga-style," in the authentic Japanese right-to-left format. Since none of the artwork has been flipped or altered, readers get to experience the story just as the creator intended. You've been asking for it, so TOKYOPOP® delivered: authentic, hot-off-the-press, and far more fun!

DIRECTIONS

1
2
3
4
5
6
7
8
9
10

If this is your first time reading manga-style, here's a quick guide to help you understand how it works.

It's easy... just start in the top right panel and follow the numbers. Have fun, and look for more 100% authentic manga from TOKYOPOP®!

100% AUTHENTIC MANGA